# Developmental Science
## and the
# Holistic Approach

# Developmental Science and the Holistic Approach

Edited by

**Lars R. Bergman**
*Stockholm University*

**Robert B. Cairns**
*University of North Carolina, Chapel Hill*

**Lars-Göran Nilsson**
**Lars Nystedt**
*Stockholm University*

2000

LAWRENCE ERLBAUM ASSOCIATES, PUBLISHERS
Mahwah, New Jersey                    London

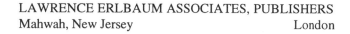

Lawrence Erlbaum Associates, Inc., Publishers
10 Industrial Avenue
Mahwah, New Jersey 07430

Cover design by Kathryn Houghtaling Lacey

**Library of Congress Cataloging-in-Publication Data**

Developmental science and the holistic approach / edited by Lars R. Bergman ... [et al.].
    p. cm.
  Includes bibliographical references and indexes.
  ISBN 0-8058-3374-9 (cloth : alk. paper)
    1. Developmental psychology--Congresses. 2. Developmental biology--Congresses. 3.
Developmental neurophysiology--Congresses. I. Bergman, Lars R.

  BF712.5 .D485 2000
  155--dc21                                           99-055359

Printed in the United States of America
10  9  8  7  6  5  4  3  2  1

# Contents

Preface                                                                          ix

PART I:  INTRODUCTION                                                              1

1.        Introduction                                                             3
          *Lars R. Bergman, Robert B. Cairns, Lars-Göran Nilsson,*
          *and Lars Nystedt*

2.        David Magnusson: The Footprints of Wisdom                               11
          *Paul B. Baltes*

PART II:  THEORETICAL CONSIDERATIONS                                             31

3.        The Individual as the Organizing Principle                              33
          in Psychological Inquiry:  A Holistic Approach
          *David Magnusson*

4.        Developmental Science:  Three Audacious                                 49
          Implications
          *Robert B. Cairns*

5.        Principles of Dynamic Pattern Formation and Change                      63
          for a Science of Human Behavior
          *J. A. Scott Kelso*

PART III:  METHODOLOGICAL CONSIDERATIONS                                          85

6.        The Modern Synthesis in Psychological Development                       87
          *Jerome Kagan*

7.        Dialectics in Development and Everyday Life                             99
          *R. A. Hinde*

8.        Beyond Static Concepts in Modeling Behavior                            121
          *John R. Nesselroade and Paolo Ghisletta*

v

9.     The Application of a Person-Oriented Approach:     137
Types and Clusters
*Lars R. Bergman*

10.    Three Tasks for Personality Psychology     155
*Jack Block*

11.    Real and Statistical Parents and Children: The     165
Varied Discoveries of Research
*Marian Radke-Yarrow*

PART IV:   A BIOLOGICAL PERSPECTIVE     177

12.    Understanding Genetic Activity Within a Holistic     179
Framework
*Gilbert Gottlieb*

13.    Lessons From the Wings of Drosophila     203
*Sarnoff A. Mednick and Matti O. Huttunen*

14.    Psychobiological Patterns at Adult Age: Relationships     209
to Personality and Early Behavior
*Britt af Klinteberg*

15.    Social Ecology and the Development of Stress     229
Regulation
*Mary Carlson and Felton Earls*

PART V:   PERSONALITY     249

16.    The Four Cs of Personality: Context, Consistency,     251
Conflict, and Coherence
*Lawrence A. Pervin*

17.    Self-Description and Personality Styles     265
*Lea Pulkkinen, Kaisa Männikkö, and Jari-Erik Nurmi*

18.    A Person-Centered Approach to Personality     281
and Social Relationships: Findings From
the Berlin Relationship Study
*Jens B. Asendorpf*

19.        Personality and Organizational Destructiveness:          299
           Fact, Fiction, and Fable
           *Sigrid B. Gustafson*


PART VI:   DEVELOPMENTAL PATHS OF ADJUSTMENT               315

20.        Studying the Etiology of Crime and Violence Among       317
           Persons With Major Mental Disorders: Challenges
           in the Definition and the Measurement of Interactions
           *Sheilagh Hodgins*

21.        Swedish Child and Adolescent Psychiatry and a           339
           Holistic Approach to the Study of Child Development
           *P.-A. Rydelius*

22.        When Do Preschool Conduct Problems Link to Future       349
           Social Adjustment Problems and When Do They Not?
           *Håkan Stattin and Kari Trost*

23.        Developmental Patterns and the Dynamics of Alcohol      377
           Problems in Adolescence and Young Adulthood
           *Tommy Andersson*

24.        Studying the Real Child Rather Than the Ideal Child:    393
           Bringing the Person Into Developmental Studies
           *Hongxin Zhao, Jeanne Brooks-Gunn, Sara McLanahan,*
           *and Burton Singer*

25.        A Holistic, Integrated Model of Risk and Protection     421
           in Adolescence: A Developmental Contextual
           Perspective About Research, Programs, and Policies
           *Richard M. Lerner and Nicole L. Simi*


PART VII:  SUMMING UP                                              445

26.        Epilogue and Prospects                                  447
           *Lars R. Bergman and Robert B. Cairns*


Author Index                                                       455
Subject Index                                                      473

# Preface

This volume is a follow-up of the Nobel symposium volume *The Lifespan Development of Individuals: Behavioral, Neurobiological, and Psychological Perspectives,* published by Cambridge University Press and Edited by David Magnusson. This book has its roots in the thinking presented at that symposium but is less general and more strongly rooted in the new developmental science, especially from the perspective of developmental psychology.

This book is the outcome of a symposium at Wik's Castle in May 1997 where leading researchers, mainly in developmental psychology, came together to discuss in depth the implications of the emerging developmental science and the holistic approach. In doing so, we also honored a distinguished colleague, David Magnusson, who has contributed so much to the field. However, the book is not a conventional festschrift because the composition of chapters is planned to provide a variety of perspectives—both theoretical and empirical—within this new paradigm and together cover the broadest possible ground. Whatever the field and perspective of the reader, it is our aim that he or she shall find something close to the heart of interest presented in a meaningful context where the new paradigm is emphasized.

The purpose of this volume is to discuss the profound implications for developmental science of the holistic paradigm, especially with regard to the study of individual development within psychology. Against the background of their own empirical, theoretical, or methodological research the contributors have tried to identify what is needed for the development of theory and methods within this paradigm and discuss possibilities and limitations in relation to conventional approaches.

## ACKNOWLEDGMENTS

This book has taken the efforts of many people and we especially want to thank Luki Hagen-Norberg for efficient secretarial help from the very beginning and Reidar Österman for help with the logistics at the symposium. Dr. Margit Wängby has carried a heavy burden, carefully going through all the manuscripts and helping out with various editorial matters. Camilla Martinsson has very efficiently assisted her in this. The symposium on which the book is based was financed by the Tercentenary Foundation of the Bank of Sweden and the Swedish Council for the Planning and Coordination of Research (main grant holder: Lars Bergman). The symposium also received support from the National Institute of Mental Health (main grant holder: Robert Cairns). The Swedish Foundation for International Cooperation in Research and Higher Education (STINT) has supported the symposium and the resulting volume through a grant to Lars Bergman. He has also received support from The Swedish Council for Research in the Humanities and the Social Sciences for research reported in this volume.

Foremost we want to thank David Magnusson, whose lifelong work has been such an inspiration to us all. It is gratifying that the ideas he vigorously has advocated for so long are now beginning to have a serious impact, and that we—together with him—with increased confidence and growing strength can take part in the formation of the new developmental science.

## Postscript

In the final stages of proofreading this volume we received the news of Robert B. Cairns' tragic death in an automobile accident. We have lost a friend and developmental Science has lost its strongest force. We now see even more clearly the great impact that Robert Cairns' thinking has had on many of the contributors' work. His spirit lives in this volume.

*Lars R. Bergman*
*Robert B. Cairns*
*Lars-Göran Nilsson*
*Lars Nystedt*

# INTRODUCTION

# 1

# Introduction

**Lars R. Bergman**
Stockholm University

**Robert B. Cairns**
University of North Carolina, Chapel Hill

**Lars-Göran Nilsson**
Stockholm University

**Lars Nystedt**
Stockholm University

During recent years a new developmental science has emerged, stressing a cross-scientific perspective and the need for taking into account a broad range of factors for explaining various forms of individual development. This view is outlined by Robert Cairns (chap. 4), who with colleagues founded the Carolina Center for Developmental Science as the first center in the world with the explicit purpose of advancing developmental science. The major research paradigm for developmental science is the holistic, interactional view in which the individual is seen as an organized whole, functioning and developing as a totality. The most forceful proponent of this view is David Magnusson, who for decades has been advocating it and carrying out research in this vein at the Stockholm Laboratory for Developmental Science. His own presentation of the holistic, interactional paradigm is given in chapter 3.

The holistically oriented material presented here is partly in contrast to the ordinary variable-oriented research that is often confined to a specific area and where one usually studies linear relations between operating factors. Taking the holistic–interactional paradigm seriously when carrying out research on individual development has implications for theory, research strategy and design, and choice of quantitative approach (both with regard to measurement and statistical method). Various facets of these implications are outlined in the chapters to follow.

This does not imply that we believe standard variable-oriented research to be misplaced or without value. It can be motivated by very common-sense and practical considerations. Often realizing that development in principle is a complex dynamic system where interactions abound it is still believed that seriously taking this into account is so difficult it is better to start with simple parts—finding out basic relationships with standard methods and then building from that. Within this paradigm, a sophisticated research methodology is also available for experimenting, testing (linear) statistical models, meta analysis, and so on.

However, as is expounded in the following chapters, the variable-oriented position just discussed has a more limited ground than is now widely thought. The three main reasons for this follow:

1. There are potential dangers in forming conclusions about individual development based on a conventional linear variable-oriented approach. Important interactions may be completely missed, even to the extent that one may not find the basic mechanisms according to which the studied system as a whole functions. These interactions may not even be captured by the accumulation of studies of specific aspects undertaken in this way. It can be like trying to understand the meaning of a picture by analyzing its small parts separately. On the other hand, if interactions are taken seriously within such a variable-oriented approach, things tend to become very complicated. Cronbach (1975) even used the metaphor of entering a hall of mirrors when pursuing it.

2. There now exists a theoretical paradigm sufficiently well worked out to serve as the basis for a new type of holistically oriented approach (see chaps. 3 and 4).

3. There is an increase in the availability of useful research methods for undertaking a holistic approach. Although, admittedly, there are still many important methodological problems unsolved, we at least now have a tool chest of research strategies and statistical and mathematical models with proven usefulness. This is exemplified in many chapters in this book and a partial overview is given in chapter 9. We also have great hopes of exciting developments coming from the mathematical study of complex systems, as pointed out in chapter 5.

There are many reasons for seriously considering pursuing developmental science from a holistic–interactional perspective. Our goal here is to introduce the theoretical perspectives and a variety of methodological approaches, as well as providing a number of empirical examples of research along these lines that hopefully will provide new ideas.

The placement of Paul Baltes' chapter in the introductory section (chap. 2) merits an explanation. It discusses the concept of wisdom. Wisdom can be viewed as a clever integration of various aspects of knowledge, and in this way the holistic perspective is introduced not only as a scientific paradigm but also as a paradigm for private thinking. It is also a nice commentary on and tribute to Magnusson's thinking and paves the way for his chapter.

The two theoretical chapters, one presenting the holistic paradigm (Magnusson) and the other presenting developmental science (Cairns) have already been mentioned. Together with chapter 5 by Scott Kelso, they constitute the theoretical part of the book. It may at first seem puzzling that Kelso's chapter appears here and not in the methodological section. The reason for this is that his fairly general presentation of complex systems hooks up so closely to key ideas of the holistic paradigm and gives them a voice through the concepts that Kelso presents. Obviously, his formulations are also of methodological relevance and the success within the natural sciences of modern mathematical models for the study of complex systems and chaos is well known. However, these methodological aspects are not elaborated here because they would demand a technical introduction and considerable space, bringing the book out of focus. Instead, Kelso offers good references for the serious reader to peruse.

The first chapter in the methodological section is by Jerome Kagan (chap. 6). It provides a nice link between theory, method, and empirical research. Starting from a theoretically sophisticated position, including giving consideration to both genes and the environment, Kagan discusses some important substantive research questions related to his own research about the roots of inhibited and uninhibited behavior in small children and the methodological issues these questions raise. For instance, Kagan's interest in extreme cases reveals the importance of the individual, not only as opposed to averages obliterating important individual differences but also in terms of extremes teaching about the constraints and possibilities of the dynamic systems under study. Kagan also points out that some individuals may follow partly different processes, being not only quantitatively but also qualitatively different. In chapter 7, Robert Hinde presents a sophisticated discussion of theory, method, and empirical research. His chapter is driven by a serious consideration of the holistic perspective and concerns the dialectics of development and social encounter. Hinde also makes a strong case for the importance of considering the dyad as a basic conceptual and analytical unit.

Chapter 8 by John Nesselroade and Paolo Ghisletta—like the remaining chapters in the methodological section—is more purely methodological than the previous ones. It goes even further than Kagans chapter in emphasizing the individual and argues for the importance of studying single individuals in their own right, often using the so-called p-technique. In doing this, these authors demonstrate that holistic, person-oriented problems can be studied using variable-oriented methods, depending on how it is done. A person-oriented standpoint is taken by Lars Bergman (chap. 9). Bergman's chapter deals with the application of methods suitable for that purpose. He also discusses different interpretations of the concept "type" and how it naturally can be seen within a holistic paradigm and translated into person-oriented research. A person-oriented approach is also discussed by Jack Block (chap. 10), who in the 1970 had already begun his pioneering research for identifying developmental types. But foremost he discusses fundamental conceptual issues in personality research, starting from the importance of recognizing the contamination of scientific thought caused by the "jingle" and "jangle" phenomena.

The last chapter in the methodological section is by Marian Radke Yarrow (chap. 11). Here she forcefully argues for the importance of attending to the growing child's total context and to bidirectional influences between parents and children. A holistic approach is taken, influenced by Lewin's and Magnusson's thinking. Attention should be paid to her discourse on the importance of measurement issues that must be studied in sufficient detail and depth to capture the child as an individual and not as an average.

It is a truism that biological factors are important to consider when explaining individual development—in their own right, in interaction with psychological factors, and as providing a necessary background for all other factors that we want to focus on in human development. In this last situation, biological aspects are like the situational frame of a phenomenon being studied, not much noted but providing constraints for what can and can not occur and in what order.

The first chapter in the section on biological factors is by Gilbert Gottlieb (chap. 12). He shows how genes and environment necessarily cooperate in the construction of organisms; specifically, how genes require environmental and behavioral inputs to function appropriately during individual development. His chapter very appropriately stresses the interaction between genes and the environment and does away with the proposition that gene activity is something totally determined by the genes. In chapter 13, Sarnoff Mednick and Matti Huttunen emphasize the critical interaction between genes and the environment with regard to the etiology of mental illness. Large epidemiological data sets show that a maternal influenza infection in the second trimester of gestation can increase the risk of adult mental illness (both schizophrenia and affective disorder). A theoretical model for explaining these results is discussed in the context of a more general hypothesis that is illustrated by data concerning the development of the fruit fly *Drosophila Melanogaster*. At the interface of biology and behavior, an exciting topic is the relations between biochemical patterns and personality. Findings along these lines are discussed by Britt af Klinteberg (chap. 14). She reports a study of the long-term relations between personality factors, as measured by the KSP personality inventory, on the one hand, and biochemical patterns including adrenaline excretion, MAO activity, and so on, on the other hand. Of course, the relations she finds do not necessarily imply that personality to a corresponding extent is genetically determined—it is fully possible and even probable that certain stable biochemical patterns are to a degree determined by the early environment.

In chapter 15, Mary Carlson and Felton Earles deal with biological factors and psychology on a more general level and argue that human behavior must be studied in the context of the complex social ecology that individuals inhabit in order to obtain both scientific validation and ethical justification. With regard to stress regulation, neuroendocrinological and psychological findings pertaining to institutionalized Romanian children are reported.

The chapters in the section on personality center around a few major themes. The first theme is self-perception in various forms. The self-concept is the focus of Larry Pervin's chapter 16 in which he discusses the stasis and flow of personality in a dynamic systems perspective. Various facets of individuals representations of "self" are introduced and the consistency, context, and coherence in personality functioning are discussed in relation to the self-concept. Lea Pulkkinen, Kaisa Männikkö, and Jari-Erik Nurmi (chap. 17) are concerned with self-description and personality style. Three different ways of studying personality are combined: an ideographic approach with free descriptions of personality, a five-factor variable-oriented model, and a holistic approach emphasizing personality as a coherent pattern of various individual and environmental features. Data are presented from a Finnish longitudinal study.

Another major theme in this section is the importance of a holistic perspective as translated into empirical research in comparison to a standard variable-oriented approach. In chapter 18, Jens Asendorpf applies both conventional variable-oriented methods and person-oriented methods to the study of university students' social relationships in a longitudinal perspective. It is shown how the methods together contribute to an understanding of how the development of social relationships is shaped in predictable, meaningful ways.

In the last chapter of this section, Sigrid Gustafson (chap. 19) discusses an important societal topic that largely has been shunned although psychology here has much to contribute. The topic is the organizational destructiveness of persons with certain psychopath-like traits. The harm caused to others by full-fledged psychopaths is becoming increasingly understood. However, there are also persons who are psychopath-like but in a less extreme form, so-called aberrant self-promoters (ASPs). Within organizations, these individuals can be very harmful, especially if given power or control of resources. This issue is discussed with emphasis on how to measure ASPs and on the relationship between ASPs and Machiavellians. From a holistic perspective, Gustafson's chapter is also methodologically interesting in its discussion of a method for producing person-oriented measurements, taking patterns into account.

The last major part of this book is devoted to another important area, namely the course and consequences of adjustment problems in a broad sense. The first two chapters apply a psychiatric perspective. In chapter 20, Sheilagh Hodgins is concerned with the etiology of crime and violence among persons with major mental disorders. Based on data from the large Swedish longitudinal Metropolitan project and a current review of the literature, the author discusses the importance of major mental disorder for the etiology of crime and violence. Possibilities and obstacles in definitions, measurement, and in studying interactions and explanatory factors of the processes are exemplified. The issue of studying interactions is of importance especially when considering this field from a holistic perspective. In chapter 21, Per-Anders Rydelius takes a bird's-eye view on the evolvement of Swedish child and adolescent psychiatry stressing its many conceptual ties to the holistic perspective. We rediscover that wise scholars in the old days had many of the ideas that now are considered "modern."

The next two chapters deal with descriptive empirical studies of the development of adjustment problems. Such studies are the nuts and bolts of a science of individual development and both of these studies are based on Swedish longitudinal data sets (the Solna program and the IDA-program, respectively). In chapter 22, Håkan Stattin and Kari Trost present an overview of the relation between early problems and later social adjustment problems. It is shown on solid longitudinal data that childhood conduct problems have limited consequences for future problems unless they are accompanied by poor parent–child relations. They also emphasize the importance of the accumulation of problems for further development. In chapter 23, Tommy Andersson reports on the significant relationship from childhood to adulthood of advanced drinking habits, but also shows that early concentration and hyperactivity problems are more strongly related to later alcohol problems than the early drinking habits. This is one of the rare instances when an earlier measurement of something other than the variable under study correlates higher with the variable than an earlier measurement of the variable itself does. The importance of social factors is also discussed.

Hongxin Zhao, Jeanne Brooks-Gunn, Sara McLanahan, and Burton Singer (chap. 24) take on a partly new perspective with regard to the resiliency–vulnerability issue. They put forth a person-centered strategy for analyzing and aggregating individual case histories, based on longitudinal data. The narrative-based methodology they present is an interesting approach for getting closer to the individual than can be done with standard variable-oriented methods and the methodology may be useful in a variety of settings.

In chapter 25 by Richard Lerner and Nicole Simi, a much broader perspective is applied than in the other chapters. They attempt nothing less than presenting a holistic integrated model of risk and protection in adolescence and they provide a developmental contextual perspective on research, programs, and policies. Starting from Magnusson's holistic model, a systemic model dealing with developmental contextualism is presented that discusses broad implications, also outside the scientific area and entering the area of policy decisions and the broad societal perspective.

In the last chapter of the book, Lars Bergman and Robert Cairns provide an epilogue and briefly discuss prospects for developmental science and the holistic paradigm, partly based on material presented in the previous chapters.

## REFERENCE

Cronbach, L. J. (1975). Beyond the two disciplines of psychology. *American Psychologist, 30,* 116–127.

# 2

# David Magnusson:
# The Footprints of Wisdom[1]

### Paul B. Baltes
Max Planck Institute for Human Development

It is a delight and a challenge to use David Magnusson as a cue for a chapter on the field of human development and the issues that make this field exciting. It is a delight because Magnusson, having produced an impressive body of methods, theoretical concepts, and empirical findings, is a world leader in the field of personality psychology and human development. It is a challenge because Magnusson's work and academic life are so rich and multifaceted that any effort to represent him adequately is bound to fall short, especially if one adds to the body of accumulated intellectual wealth his roles as a significant personage in the political world of science and as a treasured colleague and mentor to many, at home and abroad. Not surprisingly, therefore, Magnusson is more than an individual, he is the father and carrier of a school of thought that can be expected to reach far into the next generations.

## REFLECTIONS ON DAVID MAGNUSSON'S
## SCIENTIFIC OEUVRE

During the first days of this symposium on "Developmental Science and the Holistic Approach," Magnusson's scientific oeuvre was the primary source

---

[1]This chapter originated in the context of a symposium arranged to honor and reflect on the work of David L. Magnusson. At the conclusion of this symposium, Jerome Kagan and I were asked to present our more personal views on Magnusson as a person and scientist. To reflect this perspective, I try in this chapter to maintain some of the original spirit rather than editing the chapter fully in the direction of an independent scholarly piece.

of many presentations and laudatory commentaries. These presentations illustrate what it means to have an oeuvre and a legacy. A first focus was on Magnusson's contributions to the psychological metatheory of *interactionism* and *contextualism* (e.g., Magnusson, 1988, 1990, 1995; Magnusson & Endler, 1977; Magnusson & Stattin, 1997). Since the 1970s, in concert with a small number of others (e.g., Lerner, 1998), Magnusson has initiated the agenda of interactionism and contextualism, especially in work on personality and individual development. In Europe at least, there is no one who could be considered his rival in opening this new vista on developmental theory and personality psychology.

A second and equally productive focus of the symposium was on Magnusson's success in advancing *longitudinal research and theory in human development* through empirical and theory-consistent ways and means (e.g., Magnusson, 1988, 1992; Magnusson & Bergman, 1990; Magnusson, Bergman, Rudinger, & Törestad, 1991). In this work, much of which involves real-time longitudinal methods, Magnusson and his colleagues excel in linking theory with method, most notably through the application of longitudinal and multimethod paradigms, paradigms that reflect, on the level of psychological analysis, the fundamental categories of the human sciences: the role of time, space, and the holistic–transactional nature of human ontogeny (Magnusson, 1996). Indeed, time and space, so central to the natural and biological sciences, are also central to Magnusson's psychological scholarship.

With these two avenues, the theoretical and the empirical, Magnusson is in the center of a small cohort of distinguished scientists who have succeeded in moving the ontogenetic study of individuals forward. He, like few others, has succeeded in explicating the continuities and discontinuities in ontogenetic development as well as their continuous adaptations in response to biological, social, and psychological conditions. Moreover, since the inception of his longitudinal work more than 30 years ago, Magnusson has demonstrated admirable acumen in innovating his longitudinal study, using new methods and questions in response to the development of the field. Conceptually and methodologically, his longitudinal research never suffered from obsolescence. On the contrary, Magnusson and his colleagues continuously succeeded in defining the frontiers. His body of splendid longitudinal work will stand the test of time.

There is a third quality to Magnusson as a scholar, namely his ability to *link laboratory research with topics of high social relevance*. Magnusson never shied away from the complexity and ecological relevance of the human condition. His work is not artificial and elementaristic, but in its holistic–systemic approach it aims at reflecting the phenomena of the real world. While using the resources and protection of the ivory tower of science and the scientific methods of analysis and decomposition, Magnusson also ventures outside, opens his mind to the phenomena of everyday life, engages in public discourse, and returns to the laboratory with new insights and renewed vigor. By this commitment to paying heed to the phenomenological (Magnusson, 1992) and the social context of the behavioral system, Magnusson prevailed in directing the public's eye to what the field of human development can and cannot achieve; for instance, by informing society about the biological and social factors that make effective human development possible, but also by identifying factors and social conditions that prevent optimization and therefore generate dysfunction. In this way, Magnusson has made major contributions toward understanding, for instance, the origins of depression in adolescence, of aggression in youth, and of criminal development.

Magnusson's intellectual, research, and action profile, then, focuses on an integration of the whole based on well-understood parts, at several levels of analysis. For human developmental researchers to produce a comprehensive theory, Magnusson argues, like his famed American colleague Urie Bronfenbrenner (1979; see also Magnusson's [1995] contribution to the Bronfenbrenner Festschrift edited by Moen, Elder, & Lüscher), that it is necessary to intertwine micro-, meso-, and macrocontexts. And his arguments, unlike those of many others, go beyond words. In his own empirical work, he lives up to the theoretical agenda he has set forth.

This observation leads me to highlight a fourth quality of Magnusson's oeuvre, that is, the *significance of interdisciplinarity* in the study of human development. Not surprisingly perhaps, because of his commitment to wholism, interactionism, and contextualism, Magnusson also has attended to the benefits that accrue from transdisciplinary cooperation. In Magnusson's world, disciplines do not win out over each other, they work together in the true sense of collaborative and interactive minds (Baltes & Staudinger, 1996).

This same spirit of collaborative and interactive minds Magnusson also applies to his views on science as a whole. For him, individual scientists are conceived of not only as single actors but also as part of a collective system of science. Therefore, individual talent, individual motivation, commitment, and individual curiosity need to meet with the collective, with the social and professional context to make the best science possible. To this end, Magnusson has a deep commitment to institutions, such as academies or councils, whose primary agendas comprise the advancement of science as a collective enterprise and the creation of a strong voice of science in societal affairs. Perhaps this is why the concluding session of this symposium was held in the unrivaled location of international science, the Royal Swedish Academy of Sciences. This site is a fitting tribute to Magnusson's ability to link people, concepts, and institutions in novel and innovative ways.

Let me remind you, as a further illustration of his transdisciplinary and interinstitutional networking power, of his wide and effective engagement in such international organizations as the European Science Foundation, the International Society for the Study of Behavioral Development, the Academia Europaea, the American Social Science Research Council, or in my own home institution, the Max Planck Society. In each instance, Magnusson was not the seeker of these roles, but the dutiful recipient. Despite his apparent modesty, however, he rose to the occasion and treated these functions as special opportunities for delivering his gratitude to the scientific community, for improving the status and effectiveness of the science he envisioned, including the promotion of young scientists and international collaboration.

Another more recent example of Magnusson's special ability to generate new contacts and open up new territories through interdisciplinarity is the symposium on individual development across the life span that he organized with colleagues on behalf of the Nobel Foundation. Magnusson's personal standing as a scholar and the visibility of the Nobel Foundation as well as the Royal Swedish Academy formed a powerful coalition. The outcome was a remarkable and memorable transdisciplinary event and a conference publication that is a guidepost to future work on the study of ontogenesis as reflected in the orchestration of biology, psychology, and sociology (Magnusson, 1996).

## THE CONCEPT OF WISDOM

When commenting on such a respected personage and his broad systemic–holistic perspectives on the fields of psychology and human development, one is tempted to look for noted comparisons and analogies. What analogy could be adequate, however; which comparison could generate the kind of mental image that is close enough to reality, could serve as a mental guidepost? My analogy is the concept of wisdom. For millennia, wisdom and related constructs of human excellence (Ericsson, 1996) have been considered the ideal of knowledge and personal functioning (Assmann, 1994; Baltes & Smith, 1990; Baltes & Staudinger, 1993, in press; Staudinger & Baltes, 1996b; Sternberg, 1990, 1998).

There are many reasons why wisdom is a risky analogy, of course. Foremost is the fact that wisdom by definition is a utopia that cannot be reached, that can only be approximated. It gives direction without a specific point of destination. Another reason is that wisdom is an attribute that is not claimed for oneself. Wisdom is assigned by others. If one were to apply the notion of wisdom to people who have the slightest doubt about their lack of wisdom, the outcome would be a disaster. Fortunately, this risk of self-aggrandizement is completely absent in Magnusson. He would never claim to be among the wise, neither in private nor in public. On the contrary, if anything, his signature in the scientific peer community is modesty.

He, more than most, recognizes his own imperfections. This may be true in part because he knows much about the tallness of the order, about the high criteria that concepts such as excellence or wisdom entail.

Magnusson likely enjoys aphorisms that put the wise in proximity to modesty or even foolishness, as historically was true of the role of fools and jesters at the royal courts. Such aphorisms, aimed at moderation by self-criticism and by reference to folly and to the gift of silence, are plentiful (Baltes, in prep.; Baltes & Staudinger, in press). Consider, for instance, some of Shakespeare's observations on wise people: "This fellow is wise enough to play the fool," or "the fool does think he is wise, but the wise man knows himself to be a fool." Indeed, the intricate dynamics between wisdom and folly, as well as between silent reflection and ill-regulated forceful speech, are central to many social-historical analyses of the structure and function of wisdom: "Nothing resembles a wise person more than a fool who keeps quiet" (Franz von Sales); "by exhausting all folly, one gets to the bottom of wisdom" (Ludwig Börne); or "I have always observed that one should appear foolish to be wise" (Montesquieu).

In this spirit, to use another aphorism—"it is a fool who believes in wisdom"—the following report is presented on some of our efforts at the Max Planck Institute in Berlin to conceptualize and identify wisdom as a phenomenon amenable to scientific investigation (Baltes, Dittmann-Kohli, & Dixon, 1984; Baltes & Smith, 1990; Baltes & Staudinger, 1993, in press; Dittmann-Kohli & Baltes, 1990; Staudinger & Baltes, 1996b). After presenting this program of research, Magnusson is characterized using wisdom-related sentences as a frame.

## CULTURAL-HISTORICAL ANALYSIS OF WISDOM

Wisdom is a cultural and spiritual utopia, and because of this utopian characteristic, the natural and the cultural sciences need to meet for the study of wisdom, forming a mutually respectful partnership. In the context of treating wisdom as a utopia, I proceed on the premise that wisdom is truly elusive and can never be fully measured and represented by empirical methods. Parts of wisdom, then, belong to a category of human functioning that is intrinsically unexplorable by empirically grounded scientific methods. But we may be able to observe some of the consequences and manifestations of wisdom. This is what I mean when I speak of the footprints of wisdom.

To reflect the joint interests of humanists and natural scientists, our inquiries into the meaning of wisdom included an overview of cultural-historical and semantic meanings of wisdom (Baltes, 1993, in prep.; Baltes & Staudinger, in press; Sowarka, 1989). This historical and cultural-anthropological inquiry, on the one hand, suggested cultural variations in content, in the specific conditions and priorities that cultural entities attach to wisdom. Thus, in cross-cultural comparisons we observe what psychologists call domain-specificity and contextual differences in the weighting of particular aspects of what constitutes wisdom. At the same time, at a metalevel of analysis, that is, at a level that abstracts from the concrete and characterizes the general, there appeared to be much convergence (Baltes, 1993).

In summary, seven features seem to be useful in characterizing on a metalevel the concept of wisdom, in whatever culture and at whatever historical moment of time:

- Wisdom deals with important and difficult matters of the conduct and meaning of life.
- Wisdom is a truly superior level of knowledge, judgment, and advice about the human condition.
- Wisdom is knowledge with extraordinary scope, depth, and balance.
- Wisdom is developed and used for the well-being of oneself and that of others.
- Wisdom implies a perfect synergy between mind and character.
- Wisdom is knowledge from a distance and in modulation and therefore excludes extremes.
- Wisdom, although difficult to achieve, is easily recognized when manifested.

In wisdom, then (and this is not unlike Magnusson's theoretical work on the nature of human development), the focus is on systemic coordination, on the orchestration of a developmental process, and on the integration of mind and character. For a product to be wisdom-like, for a person to be close to being wise, the whole needs to be in excellent condition. For wisdom to emerge during a given lifetime, therefore, many dimensions need to come together in forming a rare coalition of qualities, in a gestalt that is expected to advance the lifetime developmental project of a particular person as well as of humankind in general (see also Figure 2 in Baltes & Staudinger, 1993).

Note that such an approach on the metatheoretical level permits the empirical scientist to approach wisdom as a testable proposition. Wisdom cannot be captured in its entirety, but it may be possible to pursue wisdom in the making, to treat it not as an end point but as a destination toward which human development attempts to move without ever reaching. As we attempt to approximate this utopia of qualities, it is not the destination that is the litmus test, but what we find along the way. The eternal quality of wisdom, so to speak, is its perpetual unfolding without ever reaching its goal.

This utopia of wisdom, as a coalition of mind and character, is also evident in writings of the Middle Ages about the nature of wisdom. In these writings of the 13th to 17th century, and in the tradition of Christianity as well as theology, personal virtues and scholastic forms of knowledge were linked together. Wisdom trees of various kinds reflective of this coalition evolved and were also part of folk art. These works of art were meant to communicate to the people that wisdom was a direction, that lifelong development could be conceived of as an approximation of the qualities inherent in these wisdom trees.

To represent one of the messages contained in the wisdom trees of the Middle Ages, Fig. 2.1 offers a schematic representation. In this instance, the tree is formed by linking branches reflecting the liberal arts, on one side of the tree, to those formed by the Christian and pagan virtues on the other side. The result is a well-ordered, holistic structure reflective of a perfect melding of mind (knowledge) and character (virtues). Other versions of these wisdom trees focus on age periods across the life span and the sequence in which wisdom putatively is acquired.

## Liberal Arts    Virtues

FIG. 2.1. A representation of the nature of wisdom in popular art during the Middle Ages: A schematic representation of the wisdom tree that joins knowledge with personal virtues.

## A PSYCHOLOGICAL CONCEPTION OF WISDOM

In our psychological work on wisdom, we have attempted to proceed within the framework generated by this cultural–historical analysis of wisdom. Keeping this framework in mind, we searched for psychological concepts and methods that could be employed to capture some of the relevant features of wisdom and to achieve a first measurement of individual differences in wisdom-related cognitions and behavior. Our psychological theory of wisdom was designed to be as consistent with these "universal" cultural–historical perspectives on wisdom as possible (Baltes et al., 1984; Baltes & Smith, 1990; Baltes & Staudinger, 1993, in press; Dittmann-Kohli & Baltes, 1990; Staudinger & Baltes, 1994, 1996b). At the same time, the approach was supposed to employ psychological concepts and methods.

### Definition of Wisdom and Framework

As a first operational definition of wisdom, we used the following: "Wisdom is a knowledge system in the fundamental pragmatics of life permitting excellent judgment and advice involving important and uncertain matters of life." At the center of wisdom are quintessential questions concerning the conduct, interpretation, and meaning of life.

Having defined the scope of wisdom, we brought to bear four psychological bodies of concepts and methods to explicate the definition and permit empirical inquiry (Table 2.1): First, we used knowledge from psychological research on expert systems and defined wisdom as an expert knowledge system similar to an expertise. In line with work on expert systems, we considered rich factual and rich procedural knowledge about important and uncertain matters of life as the first two building blocks of wisdom. Second, we employed theoretical elements from life-span psychology and characterized wisdom-related knowledge as involving life-span contextualism, value relativism, and uncertainty. Third, we considered dimensions of positive aging and thereby specified a constellation of ontogenetic factors, which we postulated as facilitators of wisdom. And finally, we focused, in the tradition of cognitive psychology, on problem solving and thinking aloud about problem solving as empirical means of gathering information about wisdom-related knowledge.

Recently (Baltes & Staudinger, in press), we have added to the notion of wisdom as an expert system the idea that it represents a metaheuristic aimed at orchestrating the mind and virtues toward excellence. This exposition highlights the fact that wisdom is aimed at the integration of cognitive, emotional and motivational qualities. As shown in Table 2.1, these considerations led to an ensemble of five criteria. In our approach, we apply this set of five criteria when evaluating a given wisdom-related performance such as a verbal or written text in response to a wisdom task.

TABLE 2.1
A Family of Five Criteria Characterizing Wisdom and Wisdom-Related Performance

*Basic Expertise Criteria*

| | |
|---|---|
| Factual knowledge | To what extent does this performance show general *(conditio humana)* and specific (e.g., life events, variation, institutions) knowledge about life knowledge matters as well as demonstrate scope and depth in the coverage of issues? |
| Procedural knowledge | To what extent does this performance consider strategies of decision making (e.g., cost–benefit analysis), self-regulation, life interpretation, life planning (e.g., means–ends analysis), and advice-giving (e.g., timing, withholding)? |

*Specific Wisdom Metacriteria*

| | |
|---|---|
| Life-span contextualism | To what extent does this performance consider possible contexts of life and the many circumstances (e.g., culturally graded, age-graded, idiosyncratic) in which a life is embedded, and how they relate to each other? |
| Value relativism/tolerance | To what extent does this performance consider variations in values and life priorities and the importance of viewing each person within his or her own framework of values and life goals, despite a small set of universal values such as an orientation toward the well-being of oneself and others? |
| Recognition and management of uncertainty | To what extent does this performance consider the inherent uncertainty of life (in interpreting the past, predicting the future, managing the present) and effective strategies for dealing with uncertainty (e.g., back-up solutions, optimizing gain–loss ratios)? |

## Measurement of Wisdom

The footprints of wisdom, its empirical measurement, can proceed along several lines. Our central approach has been to present people with life dilemmas, to have them think aloud about these life dilemmas (Ericsson & Simon, 1984), and subsequently to score their responses using the set of five criteria we have developed. Table 2.2 provides an example. The five criteria outlined in Table 2.1 can be applied to the two text protocols presented. Suffice it here to state that we have developed a reliable procedure to score such protocols on the five criteria outlined.

Other wisdom tasks include vignettes such as: "Somebody gets a phone call from a good friend who says that he or she cannot go on anymore, that he or she has decided to commit suicide. What should one do and consider?" Or: "In reflecting over their lives, people sometimes realize that they

TABLE 2.2
Illustration of Two Extreme Responses to Wisdom Tasks
(Baltes, Staudinger, Maercker, & Smith, 1995)

---

*Task: A 15-year-old girl wants to get married right away. What should she consider and do?*

---

Low Wisdom Score

A 15-year-old girl wants to get married? No, no way; marrying at age 15 would be utterly wrong. One has to tell the girl that marriage is not possible. (After further probing) It would be irresponsible to support such an idea. No, this is just a crazy idea.

High Wisdom Score

Well, on the surface, this seems like an easy problem. On average, marriage for 15-year-old girls is not a good thing. I guess many girls might think about it, however, when they fall in love for the first time. And then there are situations where the average case does not fit. Perhaps in this instance, special life circumstances are involved—perhaps the girl has a terminal illness. Or the girl has just lost her parents. And also, this girl may not be from this country. Perhaps she lives in another culture and historical period where age has a different meaning.

---

have not achieved what they once had planned to achieve. What should one/they do and consider?" Note that these tasks were selected to reflect the notion of life planning, life management, and life review. They also varied by other characteristics such as content domain and age salience. The procedure of engaging the subjects in these tasks and having them think aloud was standardized.

## WHAT PREDICTS INDIVIDUAL DIFFERENCES IN WISDOM-RELATED PERFORMANCE?

Initially, because of the original intellectual motivation for this work, much of our research effort was concentrated on the role of chronological age and on age comparisons (Smith & Baltes, 1990). Subsequently, as we attempted to place this research on wisdom into the larger context of psychology, we focused increasingly on other factors such as professional expertise (Smith, Staudinger, & Baltes, 1994), personality processes (Staudinger, Lopez, & Baltes, 1997), and the nature of the social foundation of wisdom (Baltes & Staudinger, 1996; Staudinger, 1996; Staudinger & Baltes, 1996a). In the present context, four findings are of particular interest: the role of age, the role of lifetime experience, the role of personality, and the role of social discourse.

First, as to the role of chronological age, and when one compares young adults with older adults from about 25 up to age 75, the dominant finding is one of no age differences, that is, age stability. On the one hand, because wisdom is expected to be a characteristic of positive aging (Heckhausen, Dixon, & Baltes, 1989), this outcome may come as a surprise. On the other hand, a lack of negative age differences is a rarity in research on cognitive aging (Baltes, Lindenberger, & Staudinger, 1997; Blanchard-Fields & Hess, 1996; Craik & Salthouse, 1992; Lindenberger & Baltes, 1994; Salthouse, 1994). Thus, the finding of age stability from about age 25 to age 75 stands in sharp contrast to other research, especially work involving the so-called mechanics of cognition. Wisdom-related knowledge and judgment is part of those domains of functioning where aging permits maintenance or even further refinement.

Second, *Lebenserfahrungen*, or lifetime experiences, are important, especially experiences related to difficult life situations (Staudinger & Dittmann-Kohli, 1994). Such a view is also consonant with the general view in developmental theory that critical life events represent an opportunity, not only for demonstrating available resources, but also for new engagements and progress (Datan & Ginsberg, 1975; Hultsch & Plemons, 1979; Montada, Filipp, & Lerner, 1992). In our work on wisdom, we have two findings to support this claim. One is the fact that biographies of people nominated as candidates for wisdom and demonstrating high levels of performance in wisdom tasks (Baltes, Staudinger, Maercker, & Smith, 1995) identified lifetime experiences as important ingredients. The second finding is that, when compared with people of equal educational and professional standing, clinical psychologists, who are expected to have much experience and training in dealing with difficult problems of life, when participating in a wisdom study indeed showed a higher level of functioning in wisdom tasks (Smith et al., 1994; Staudinger, Smith, & Baltes, 1992).

Third, regarding associations with measures of personality, intelligence, and cognitive style and creativity, the pattern of correlational associations between performances in wisdom tasks supports the view that wisdom-related knowledge and judgment encompasses mind and character. Figure 2.2 summarizes the main findings. Note especially the multidimensional nexus of the predictors and the fact that the largest uniqueness of prediction was associated, aside from life experience, with measures located in the interface between personality and intelligence.

A central study (Staudinger et al., 1997), aimed at examining the correlational nexus of wisdom measures, involved a heterogeneous sample of adults and considered correlations of 33 psychometric measures with performance in wisdom tasks. The outcome showed the firm grounding of wisdom-related knowledge and judgment in the interface between mind and personality. For instance, none of the 33 measures (which included many

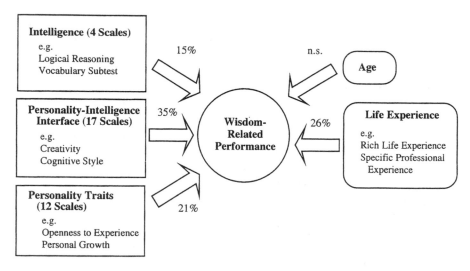

FIG. 2.2. Predictors of wisdom-related performance: summary of three studies involving adults (Age is relevant as predictor when adolescents are studied). The percentages refer to the proportions of variance that all scales indicated on the left predicted jointly when used as multiple predictors of wisdom-related performance in think-aloud protocols (Baltes et al., 1995; Staudinger et al., 1997; Staudinger, Maciel, Smith, & Baltes, in press). Not shown are results of communality analyses aimed at examining uniqueness of predictors. Uniqueness in descending order of magnitude was Personality–intelligence interface, life experience, personality, intelligence.

of the well-known measures of personality, such as the NEO; as well as measures of fluid and crystallized intelligence; and of cognitive style, such as creativity and psychological mindedness), predicted more than 15% of the variance in wisdom tasks. Second, all correlations were in the expected direction, supporting the view that it is a coalition or a family of positive attributes from diverse domains that generates a move toward wisdom. Furthermore, the measures located in the interface between personality and intelligence, such as cognitive flexibility and creativity, showed the strongest association. Finally, even after controlling for all 33 variables as predictors, we found a sizable amount of variance that could be accounted for by parallel tests of wisdom. This pattern of outcomes is solid evidence for the multidimensional nature of wisdom-related knowledge, its embeddedness in both mind and character, the relative uniqueness of wisdom, and its close association with individual lifetime experiences.

Fourth, our research supports the theoretical argument that wisdom has a strong social-interactive or interactive-minds component (Staudinger, 1996; Staudinger & Baltes, 1996a). The very definition of wisdom suggests that advice-giving and consultation is part of the ensemble of footprints-of-wisdom-related behavior. Similarly, in the wisdom literature the role of mentorship and continuous engagement in dialogue with mentors are emphasized. Thus, in many accounts of wisdom, wisdom is not so much a characteristic of single individuals but of collective ensembles and intersubjective consensus. This view is in line with recent developments in the study of cognition and the self that emphasize the social foundation of action and thought.

This interactive-minds or collaborative facet of wisdom received strong support in a study that exposed subjects in wisdom experiments to various conditions of social interaction, internal as well as external (Staudinger & Baltes, 1996a). An internal condition of interactive minds consisted of having subjects imagine "inner conversations (voices)" with significant others of their own choice before responding to wisdom tasks. External conditions of interactive minds involved direct conversations with a significant other whom the subjects had brought to the laboratory. This research showed that such conditions of interactive minds had significant and facilitative effects on wisdom-related performance. For instance, having a conversation with a significant other and having five minutes to digest the information raised the performance level in wisdom tasks by close to one standard deviation. Such findings highlight the role of the social and collaborative in the development and manifestation of wisdom.

## SUBJECTIVE CONCEPTIONS OF WISDOM

Another stream of psychological research on wisdom concerns the attributes that people, when asked about wisdom, identify as the core of wisdom and wise people. Table 2.3 summarizes some of the main findings. The table also includes information about specific items that index the dimensions involved. Furthermore, the right side of the table notes the characteristics we identified in our own work when examining the match between our performance-based model of wisdom and subjective theories of wisdom.

This research into subjective theories of wisdom highlights the systemic property of wisdom, the interconnectivity and interpenetration of psychological qualities, their coordination into a gestalt. In Sternberg's (1985) work on subjective conceptions of wisdom, for instance, people gave responses that when analyzed suggested that sagacity, perspicacity, judgment, learning from ideas and the environment, reasoning ability, and expeditious use of information needed to converge to generate wisdom. Table 2.1 can be examined to determine whether these criteria exhibit sufficient similarity with the metatheoretical dimensions extracted from the cultural and historical literature on wisdom.

In research and scholarship on a psychology of wisdom we pursue a concept of mind and behavior that has utopian qualities. The utopian qual-

TABLE 2.3
Theories of Wisdom and Wise People: (Staudinger & Baltes, 1996b)
Some Characteristics (Based on Naive Folk Theories [Sternberg, 1985; Holliday & Chandler, 1986]
and a Psychological Theory of Wisdom [Baltes, Smith, & Staudinger, 1992)]

| Sternberg (1985) | Holliday and Chandler (1986) | Berlin Model: Baltes, Smith, and Staudinger (1992) |
| --- | --- | --- |
| Sagacity<br>—concern for others<br>—considers advice | Interpersonal Skills<br>—sensitive<br>—sociable | Factual Knowledge<br>—comprehends the nature of human existence |
| Perspicacity<br>—intuition<br>—offers right and true solution | Judgment and Communication Skills<br>—is a good source of advice<br>—understands life | Procedural Knowledge<br>—thinks independently and is able to form his or her own opinion |
| Judgment<br>—acts within own limitations | Social Unobstrusiveness<br>—discreet<br>—nonjudgmental | Life-Span Contextualism<br>—recognizes and considers the life domains that are particularly important for a specific life problem |
| Learning from Ideas and Environment<br>—perceptive<br>—learns from mistakes | Exceptional Understanding as Based on Ordinary Experience<br>—has learned from experience<br>—sees things in a larger context | Value Relativism<br>—knows that the importance of different life domains changes during the life span |
| Reasoning Ability<br>—good problem-solving ability<br>—logical mind | General Competence<br>—intelligent<br>—educated | Awareness and Management of Uncertainty<br>—recognized the limits of his or her own knowledge |
| Expeditious Use of Information<br>—experienced<br>—seeks out information | | |

ity of wisdom makes explicit that its manifestation is never perfect. And indeed, in our work, the level of performance achieved by individual subjects, even those who were selected as exceptional, suggests modesty about what individuals *by themselves* can accomplish in brief testing situations. The typical responses are located below the average of the scale we constructed for the assessment of wisdom-related knowledge, and none of the subjects has come close to touching the ceiling of the scale. This is not surprising considering the triangulation of character, knowledge, and life contexts that must be present in concert for a high level of wisdom-related standing to emerge. And finally, this outcome is also not surprising considering the brevity of the contexts of assessment and the fact that wisdom in real life, often involving collective and sequential multiperson transactions, benefits from a richer context and longer time span than our testing paradigm entailed.

## DAVID MAGNUSSON IN THE CONTEXT OF RESEARCH ON WISDOM

Let me now return to David Magnusson. His intellectual legacy includes interactionism and wholism as guiding principles. The view of wisdom presented here involves a high level of developmental orchestration, the kind of holistic–structural conception that is at the core of Magnusson's oeuvre. Yet it would be an exaggeration to suggest that this line of research fulfills Magnusson's mandates. Much is missing in our own research on wisdom, including the long-term longitudinal data that are a hallmark of Magnusson's research program on human development (Magnusson, 1998; Magnusson & Bergman, 1990).

This research on wisdom, however, although selected for its similarity with Magnusson's holistic and developmental contextualism, is supposed to carry primarily another message. Today, my research on wisdom reaches out to touch one special person, and as I continue, please keep in mind that the concept of wisdom in psychological research is not a perfect utopia, it is a direction, a goal toward which humankind and individuals aspire. Some have travelled further toward that goal than others. Therefore, Magnusson will have to grant me pardon if I now use some principles from the wisdom literature to characterize him: as a person, as a scientist, as a colleague, as an international herald of the ontogenetic–developmental enterprise.

To project research on wisdom onto Magnusson, I cannot rely on objective performance assessments. Unfortunately, he was not one of our research participants. What I can do, however, is draw from research on everyday conceptions of wisdom (Holliday & Chandler, 1986; Sternberg, 1985). In our own work on subjective theories of wise people (Staudinger, Sowarka, Maciel, & Baltes, 1997), we have identified the following four factors as the core dimensions:

1. Exceptional knowledge about the use of wisdom.
2. Exceptional knowledge about contexts of life.

3. Exceptional personality and high social intelligence.
4. Exceptional knowledge about the acquisition of wisdom.

Table 2.4 also identifies the salient items that define the four factors and the reader can judge how well, as I claim, these statements characterize Magnusson.

According to this work, a wise person is someone who knows when to give and withhold advice, a person whose advice one would solicit for difficult life problems, a person who knows that goals and priorities may change during the life course. The wise person is one who knows about possible conflicts between different life domains, who is a good listener and a very humane person, one who comprehends the nature of human existence and tries to learn from personal mistakes. For many international scholars in the field of human development, this describes Magnusson exactly.

Science lives from replications. Therefore, I have added another set of statements, statements that do not come from psychological research on the beliefs which people hold about the core characteristics of wise people, but from the humanist literature, the so-called historical wisdom literature. I begin with the characterization of the ideal citizen and scientist, a characterization that we owe to the British philosopher Thomas Hobbes: "The welfare of mankind is the goal, betterment of science is the way, reason and persistence are the methods." No less fitting are the following characterizations, each of which highlights a different facet of David Magnusson as a person and scientist: "Everyone must have the courage of his convictions" (Alexander von Humboldt), "Don't forget, one needs little to lead a

TABLE 2.4
Subjective/Everyday Theories About Wise People: Four Dimensions
(Based on Staudinger, Sowarka, Maciel, & Baltes, 1997)

| | |
|---|---|
| Factor 1: | Exceptional knowledge about use of wisdom<br>—Knows when to give/withhold advice<br>—Is a person whose advice one would solicit for difficult life problems |
| Factor 2: | Exceptional knowledge about context of life<br>—Knows that life priorities may change during the life course<br>—Knows about possible conflicts between different life domains |
| Factor 3: | Exceptional personality and social functioning<br>—Is a good listener<br>—Is a very humane person |
| Factor 4: | Exceptional knowledge about wisdom acquisition<br>—Comprehends the nature of human existence<br>—Tries to learn from his or her own mistakes |

happy life" (Aurel). Or reflect on another saying by the same Aurelius: It's better to limp along the right path slowly than to walk steadily in the wrong direction." Equally prototypical of Magnusson seems to me the sentence attributed to Confucius: "Wisdom is modulation, like the golden mean."

In conclusion, I offer one of my favorite aphorisms, Pablo Picasso's words about uniqueness and successful originators. I like these words because being an artist—being flamboyant, showy, or ostentatious—is not a necessary condition for being original. Other virtues besides artistic flamboyance and ostentation can do the trick of originality. Said Picasso: "There are few originals, but many copies." Magnusson certainly is not a copy, he is an original. Yet, in the interest of the future of the academic world of human development, copyists are more than welcome! In this spirit, I encourage us to consider in our work the scientific and personal wisdom of Magnusson, a herald and visionary in the creation of a new holistic, interactional, and longitudinal vista on the study of human functioning, someone whose footprints are unmistakable and worthwhile to follow because they give us direction and lead us to a better science of human development.

# REFERENCES

Assmann, A. (1994). Wholesome knowledge: Concepts of wisdom in a historical and cross-cultural perspective. In D. L. Featherman, R. M. Lerner, & M. Perlmutter (Eds.), *Life-span development and behavior* (Vol. 12, pp. 187–224). Hillsdale, NJ: Lawrence Erlbaum Associates.

Baltes, P. B. (1993). The aging mind: Potential and limits. *The Gerontologist, 33*, 580–594.

Baltes, P. B. (in preparation). *Wisdom: The orchestration of mind and virtue.* Boston: Blackwell.

Baltes, P. B., Dittmann-Kohli, F., & Dixon, R. A. (1984). New perspectives on the development of intelligence in adulthood: Toward a dual-process conception and a model of selective optimization with compensation. In P. B. Baltes & O. G. Brim, Jr. (Eds.), *Life-span development and behavior* (Vol. 6, pp. 33–76). New York: Academic Press.

Baltes, P. B., Lindenberger, U., & Staudinger, U. M. (1997). Life-span theory in developmental psychology. In R. M. Lerner (Ed.), *Handbook of child psychology: Vol. 1. Theoretical models of human development* (5th ed., pp. 1029–1143). New York: Wiley.

Baltes, P. B., & Smith, J. (1990). The psychology of wisdom and its ontogenesis. In R. J. Sternberg (Ed.), *Wisdom: Its nature, origins, and development* (pp. 87–120). New York: Cambridge University Press.

Baltes, P. B., Smith, J., & Staudinger, U. M. (1992). Wisdom and successful aging. In T. Sonderegger (Ed.), *Nebraska symposium on motivation* (Vol. 39, pp. 123–167). Lincoln: University of Nebraska Press.

Baltes, P. B., & Staudinger, U. M. (1993). The search for a psychology of wisdom. *Current Directions in Psychological Science, 2*, 75–80.

Baltes, P. B., & Staudinger, U. M. (Eds.). (1996). *Interactive minds: Life-span perspectives on the social foundation of cognition.* New York: Cambridge University Press.

Baltes, P. B., & Staudinger, U. M. (in press). Wisdom: A metaheuristic to orchestrate mind and virtues toward excellence. *American Psychologist.*

Baltes, P. B., Staudinger, U. M., Maercker, A., & Smith, J. (1995). People nominated as wise: A comparative study of wisdom-related knowledge. *Psychology and Aging, 10*, 155–166.

Blanchard-Fields, F., & Hess, T. M. (Eds.). (1996). *Perspectives on cognitive change in adulthood and aging.* New York: McGraw-Hill.

Bronfenbrenner, U. (1979). *The ecology of human development.* Cambridge, MA: Harvard University Press.

Craik, F. I. M., & Salthouse, T. A. (Eds.). (1992). *The handbook of aging and cognition.* Hillsdale, NJ: Lawrence Erlbaum Associates.

Datan, N., & Ginsberg, L. H. (Eds.). (1975). *Life-span developmental psychology: Normative life crises.* New York: Academic Press.

Dittmann-Kohli, F., & Baltes, P. B. (1990). Toward a neofunctionalist conception of adult intellectual development: Wisdom as a prototypical case of intellectual growth. In C. Alexander & E. Langer (Eds.), *Higher stages of human development: Perspectives on adult growth* (pp. 54–78). New York: Oxford University Press.

Ericsson, K. A. (1996). *The road to excellence: The acquisition of expert performance in the arts and sciences, sports and games.* Mahwah, NJ: Lawrence Erlbaum Associates.

Ericsson, K. A., & Simon, H. A. (1984). *Protocol analysis: Verbal reports as data.* Cambridge, MA: MIT Press.

Heckhausen, J., Dixon, R. A., & Baltes, P. B. (1989). Gains and losses in development throughout adulthood as perceived by different adult age groups. *Developmental Psychology, 25,* 109–121.

Holliday, S. G., & Chandler, M. J. (1986). Wisdom: Explorations in adult competence. In J. A. Meacham (Ed.), *Contributions to human development* (Vol. 17, pp. 1–96). Basel, Switzerland: Karger.

Hultsch, D. F., & Plemons, J. K. (1979). Life events and life-span development. In P. B. Baltes & J. O. G. Brim (Eds.), *Life-span development and behavior* (Vol. 2, pp. 1–37). New York: Academic Press.

Lerner, R. M. (1997). Theories of human development: Contemporary perspectives. In R. M. Lerner (Ed.), *Handbook of child psychology: Vol. 1. Theoretical models of human development* (5th ed., pp. 1–24). New York: Wiley.

Lindenberger, U., & Baltes, P. B. (1994). Aging and intelligence. In R. J. Sternberg (Ed.), *Encyclopedia of human intelligence* (Vol. 1, pp. 52–66). New York: Macmillan.

Magnusson, D. (1988). *Individual development from an interactional perspective: A longitudinal study.* Hilldsdale, NJ: Lawrence Erlbaum Associates.

Magnusson, D. (1990). Personality development from an interactional perspective. In L. A. Pervin (Ed.), *Handbook of personality: Theory and research* (pp. 193–222). New York: Guilford.

Magnusson, D. (1992). Individual development: A longitudinal perspective. *European Journal of Personality, 6,* 119–138.

Magnusson, D. (1995). Individual development: A holistic, integrated model. In P. Moen, G. H. Elder Jr., & K. Lüscher (Eds.), *Examining lives in context* (pp. 19–60). Washington, DC: American Psychological Association.

Magnusson, D. (Ed.). (1996). *The life-span development of individuals: Behavioural, neurobiological and psychosocial perspectives.* Cambridge, UK: Cambridge University Press.

Magnusson, D. (1998). The logic and implications of a person approach. In R. B. Cairns, L. R. Bergman, & J. Kagan (Eds.), *Methods and models for studying the individual* (pp. 33–63). New York: Sage.

Magnusson, D., & Bergman, L. R. (1990). *Data quality in longitudinal research.* New York: Cambridge University Press.

Magnusson, D., Bergman, L. R., Rudinger, G., & Törestad, B. (Eds.). (1991). *Problems and methods in longitudinal research: Stability and change.* Cambridge, UK: Cambridge University Press.

Magnusson, D., & Endler, N. S. (1977). *Personality at the crossroads: Current issues in interactional psychology.* Hillsdale, NJ: Lawrence Erlbaum Associates.

Magnusson, D., & Stattin, H. (1997). Person-context interaction theories. In R. M. Lerner (Ed.), *Handbook of child psychology: Vol. 1. Theoretical models of human development* (pp. 685–760). New York: Wiley.

Moen, P., Elder Jr., G. H., & Lüscher, K. (Eds.). (1995). *Examining lives in context: Perspectives on the ecology of human development.* Washington, DC: American Psychological Association.

Montada, L., Filipp, S.-H., & Lerner, M.-J. (Eds.). (1992). *Life crises and experiences of loss in adulthood.* Hillsdale, NJ: Lawrence Erlbaum Associates.

Salthouse, T. A. (1994). Age-related differences in basic cognitive processes: Implications for work. *Experimental Aging Research, 20,* 249–255.

Smith, J., & Baltes, P. B. (1990). A study of wisdom-related knowledge: Age/cohort differences in responses to life planning problems. *Developmental Psychology, 26,* 494–505.

Smith, J., Staudinger, U. M., & Baltes, P. B. (1994). Occupational settings facilitating wisdom-related knowledge: The sample case of clinical psychologists. *Journal of Consulting and Clinical Psychology, 62,* 989–999.

Sowarka, D. (1989). Weisheit und weise Personen: Common-Sense-Konzepte älterer Menschen [Wisdom and wise persons: Common-sense views from elderly people]. *Zeitschrift für Entwicklungspsychologie und Pädagogische Psychologie, 21,* 87–109.

Staudinger, U. M. (1996). Wisdom and the social-interactive foundation of the mind. In P. B. Baltes & U. M. Staudinger (Eds.), *Interactive minds: Life-span perspectives on the social foundation of cognition* (pp. 276–318). New York: Cambridge University Press.

Staudinger, U. M., & Baltes, P. B. (1994). Psychology of wisdom. In R. J. Sternberg (Ed.), *Encyclopedia of human intelligence* (Vol. 2, pp. 143–152). New York: Macmillan.

Staudinger, U. M., & Baltes, P. B. (1996a). Interactive minds: A facilitative setting for wisdom-related performance? *Journal of Personality and Social Psychology, 71,* 746–762.

Staudinger, U. M., & Baltes, P. B. (1996b). Weisheit als Gegenstand psychologischer Forschung. *Psychologische Rundschau, 47,* 57–77.

Staudinger, U. M., & Dittmann-Kohli, F. (1994). Lebenserfahrung und Lebenssinn [Life experience and meaning of life]. In P. B. Baltes, J. Mittlestraß, & U. M. Staudinger (Eds.), *Alter und Altern: Ein interdisziplinärer Studientext zur Gerontologie* (pp. 408–436). Berlin: de Gruyter.

Staudinger, U. M., Lopez, D., & Baltes, P. B. (1997). The psychometric location of wisdom-related performance: Intelligence, personality, and more? *Personality and Social Psychology Bulletin, 23,* 1200–1214.

Staudinger, U. M., Maciel, A. G., Smith, J., & Baltes, P. B. (1998). What predicts wisdom-related performance? A first look at personality, intelligence, and facilitative experiential contexts. *European Journal of Personality.*

Staudinger, U. M., Smith, J., & Baltes, P. B. (1992). Wisdom-related knowledge in a life review task: Age differences and the role of professional specialization. *Psychology and Aging, 7,* 271–281.

Staudinger, U. M., Sowarka, D., Maciel, A. G., & Baltes, P. B. (1997). *Subjective theories of wisdom and the Berlin Wisdom Theory.* Unpublished manuscript, Max Planck Institute for Human Development, Berlin, Germany.

Sternberg, R. J. (1985). Implicit theories of intelligence, creativity, and wisdom. *Journal of Personality and Social Psychology, 49,* 607–627.

Sternberg, R. J. (Ed.). (1990). *Wisdom: Its nature, origins, and development.* New York: Cambridge University Press.

Sternberg, R. J. (1998). A balance theory of wisdom. *Review of General Psychology, 2,* 347–365.

# THEORETICAL CONSIDERATIONS

# 3

# The Individual as the Organizing Principle in Psychological Inquiry: A Holistic Approach

David Magnusson
Stockholm University

Making the individual the organizing principle for individual functioning and development is basically a holistic view, rooted in the history of scientific psychology. In the early part of this century, a holistic position was strongly advocated, from different perspectives, by some of the most distinguished psychologists, among them Gordon Allport, Alfred Binet, Wilhelm Stern, Egon Brunswik, and Kurt Lewin. The Kraepelin approach to psychiatric diagnoses from the turn of the last century, which still influences psychiatric thinking and practice, and the typologies, for example, Jung's categorical typology and its transformation into a dimensional typology by Sheldon, likewise reflect an early holistic approach in psychological practice and research.

But dominant trends change. During the 1950s and 1960s the holistic view was out of fashion. In an article in 1965 in which he used the term *holism* and formulated some of the main elements of a holistic view and its implications, Nevitt Sanford gave his interpretation of the state of affairs:

> We have produced a whole generation of research psychologists who never had occasion to look closely at any person, let alone themselves, who have never imagined what it might be like to be a subject in one of their experiments, who, indeed, have long since lost sight of the fact that their experimental subjects are, after all, people. They can define variables, state hypotheses, design experiments, manipulate data statistically, get publishable results—and miss the whole point of the thing. (p. 192)

Rae Carlson, in a much-cited article from 1971, asked "Where is the person in personality research?"

The situation Nevitt Sanford described had multiple causes. Two interrelated, overriding perspectives that dominated the postwar research paradigm in psychology contributed: one has to do with structural characteristics and the other with the content of the dominant paradigm.

The most conspicuous structural characteristics of the scientific scene were the dominance of S-R models with reference to behavioristic theory; the use of the experiment as the ultimate criterion of the discipline's scientific status, regardless of the character of the phenomena; the misuse of theoretical models due to misunderstanding of the role of theory in natural sciences; and the strong emphasis on theoretical models at the microlevel of individual functioning, in perception, learning, cognition, and memory. These micromodels lacked a foundation in careful, systematic analyses of the character of the phenomena under investigation, and were not formulated within a common, integrated theoretical framework for individual functioning and development. The end result was compartmentalization and fragmentation of psychological theorizing and empirical research.

A main circumstance behind this fragmentation was the absence of a holistic integrated model for individual functioning and development, which could serve as the common theoretical framework for theorizing and empirical research on psychological phenomena. The traditional holistic view was empty; it lacked specific content about the functioning and interplay of basic psychological and biological elements operating in the processes of the integrated organism. What went on between the stimulus and the response was regarded as unknown and inaccessible to scientific inquiry. The reason for this state of affairs was formulated in 1943 by Clark Hull, who drew a distinction between molar behavior and specific properties of living organisms and argued that:

> Any theory of behavior is at present, and must be for some time to come, a molar theory. This is because neuroanatomy and physiology have not yet developed to a point such that they yield principles which may be employed as postulates in a system of behavior theory. (p. 275)

In recent decades, however, an increasing number of voices have been raised in support of the neglected perspective. An early proponent in this movement for a holistic view in developmental research was Jack Block in *Lives Through Time* (1971); others have followed. In his 1979 volume, Robert Cairns formulated a view of developmental processes in a way that is still up to date and summarized it thus: "Behavior, whether social or nonsocial, is appropriately viewed in terms of an organized system, and its explanation requires a 'holistic analysis' " (p. 325).

The development of this issue in recent decades has two characteristics. First, it is restricted almost exclusively to research on social development and personality. Only slowly, and in rare cases, has the holistic view influenced theorizing and empirical research on central psychological functions, such as perception, cognition, and memory. The limited impact of a holistic view in these fields is surprising, considering the impact such a view has had in many disciplines in life sciences and natural sciences.

Second, the application of a holistic view has been and, to some extent, still is dominated by theoretical discussions, with fewer examples of empirical studies where a holistic view is the explicit frame of reference.

## ENRICHMENT OF THE HOLISTIC MODEL

The more general scientific scenery in which psychological research operates has been changing dramatically in respects that, besides emphasizing the old claim for the necessity of a holistic approach to psychological inquiry, help to turn such an approach into a solid theoretical foundation for planning, implementing, and interpreting empirical research on specific problems. Four main sources have contributed to this by enriching the empty holistic view with substantive content and providing methodological tools and research strategies which are compatible with the nature of the phenomena with which we are concerned.

### Research on Mental Processes

One consequence of the postwar dominance of S-R models was the neglect of mental processes. My first textbook in psychology was David Katz' *Handbook of Psychology* published in 1950. Considering what psychology is about, it is noteworthy that the only chapter we were not expected to read was Richard Meili's on thinking. Since the 1960s, research on cognitive processes has been the most rapidly developing field in psychological theorizing and research. Research on information processing, memory, and decision making has made dramatic progress and contributed essential knowledge necessary for the understanding and explanation of individual development and functioning. I am convinced that these areas extended to include emotions and values, would gain much from a serious assessment of what a holistic theoretical framework would imply for future research.

### Research on Biological Aspects of Individual Development and Functioning

By 1970, Roger Russell, referring, in an APA address, to the formulation by Hull that I quoted earlier, concluded:

The situation is now different and is changing so rapidly that the psychologist is hard pressed to keep abreast of even those major developments in other biological sciences that are most relevant to his area of primary competences. Thus, the stage is already set for the play in which the actors are properties of living biological systems and in which the plot unfolds within the concept of the "integrated organism." (p. 211)

Since then, research in biological and medical sciences has advanced at an increasing pace. The progress in these fields has helped to enrich the empty holistic model with new content from three main, interrelated directions, which are of interest for understanding and explaining psychological processes.

First, research in these areas has contributed detailed knowledge about the brain, how it develops from conception onwards over the life-span in a process of interaction between constitutional factors and context factors; and how it functions at each stage of development, as an active organ, selecting, interpreting, and integrating information from the environment. This research has yielded new insights about brain development at all levels, from the role of the continuous interaction process among cells, which is fundamental for cell growth and cell death, to the role of external environmental factors in this process.

Access to advanced techniques for brain-imaging has made it possible to investigate the brain's ongoing functioning while an individual performs a mental task. This introduces the time perspective, which is fundamental for understanding and explaining processes and contributes to an understanding of the interplay of mental and biological aspects of individual functioning. This research has shown how multiple brain regions, operating in synchronic interaction, are involved in complex perceptual–cognitive processes. The rapid development of research on brain functioning and its role in understanding mental processes has helped bridge the gap between biological and psychological models that hampered a deeper understanding and explanation of mental and behavioral processes. An issue of *Science* (March 1997) summarizes and discusses the far-reaching implications of the new scenery, both for theoretical models and for application, in such central areas for psychological inquiry as learning, memory, reasoning, intelligence, perception, language, and mental illnesses.

Research in medicine and biology has also provided new insights into the role of internal biological structures and processes in the total functioning and development of individuals. The following is a simplified (but essentially correct) description of what happens psychologically and biologically in a situation that an individual interprets as threatening or demanding, for example, a stressful work situation or an important examination: When the individual interprets the situation as threatening or demanding, the cognitive act stimulates—via amygdala and the hypothalamus—the excretion of adrenaline from the adrenal glands, which in turn triggers a series of other physiological processes. The cognitive–physiological interplay is accompanied by emotional states and feelings of fear and/or anxiety and/or generally experienced arousal. These emotions play an important role in the further process of cognitive, physiological, and behavioral adaptation to the situation.

What happens in this situation illustrates how perceptual, cognitive–emotional, biological, and behavioral aspects of an individual's functioning, and the perceived and interpreted aspects of the environment, are involved in a continuous loop of interaction in a current situation. In the dynamic interaction process, psychological factors may operate as initiating factors, and biological factors can influence psychological phenomena. What initiates a specific process and what maintains it over time may vary. A psychological factor may start a biological process which is then maintained by physiological factors. Similarly, psychological factors can maintain a process that was triggered by biological factors. Environmental factors influence an individual's physical and mental well-being and, at the same time, an individual affects his or her own environment in many different ways, directly and indirectly.

Research into the role of biochemicals in the processes involved in the individual's way of dealing with situational–environmental conditions and in the developmental processes of individuals is expanding at an increasing pace. Developmental research in this area has been summarized by Elizabeth Susman (1993). In our longitudinal research program this has been an issue since the 1960s. The first results of a study demonstrating low physiological activity–reactivity in antisocial behavior in boys in real-life situations were presented in 1973 (Johansson, Frankenhaeuser, & Magnusson). Since then, a series of studies have been performed in this area in the longitudinal program, investigating the role of biochemicals and different kinds of problem behaviors in the developmental background of adult functioning. One basic study was concerned with the role of aggressiveness, hyperactivity, and autonomic activity in the development of social adjustment (Magnusson, 1988). (Another example is offered by af Klinteberg in chap. 14, this volume.)

For us as psychologists, the overriding goal is to understand and explain individuals' thoughts, feelings, actions, and reactions. The conclusion from what I have summarized above is that any general model which seeks to contribute to this goal must incorporate mental, biological, behavioral, and social factors into a single integrated model. These factors function simultaneously and need to be placed in a coherent theoretical framework, in which the total individual is the organizing principle. That is, any general framework for psychological research must be holistic (Magnusson, 1995, 1996).

The third enriching source from biology is recent development in research on the role of genes in individual development processes. Traditionally, research in human genetics was dominated by investigations where the role of genes was estimated from the relative degree to which the distribution of measures for a certain variable could be attributed to such factors. The value of this research has been considerably increased by the introduction of theoretical models that emphasize the interaction between genetic factors and environmental factors in the developmental processes of individuals. An important step forward in understanding the role of genes was the discovery of DNA and the genetic code in the 1960s. This discovery opened up new windows for mapping the individual genome structure and for research on the mechanisms by which genetic factors operate in individuals.

## The Development of Modern Models for Dynamic Complex Processes

The way mental, biological, behavioral, and social factors operate together in individual development and individual functioning can be likened to a series of complex dynamic and adaptive processes. The third important source for the application of a holistic perspective in psychological research lies in the general modern models that have been developed in the natural sciences for the study of such processes: chaos theory, general systems theory, and catastrophe theory. These theoretical models, particularly chaos theory, have had an almost revolutionary impact on both theory building and empirical research in scientific disciplines that focus on multidetermined stochastic processes such as meteorology, biology, chemistry, and ecology.

In psychology, the general systems view has been applied in theoretical analyses more than chaos theory and catastrophe theory. A growing number of researchers have discussed developmental issues in the framework of systems theory and some of the authors in this volume have made substantial contributions. Research using a general systems theory was recently summarized by Thelen and Smith (1998).

The modern models for dynamic complex processes are important for psychological research in a number of interrelated respects that have implications for planning, implementation, and interpretation of empirical studies.

Most empirical psychological research is concerned with the relation between causal factors and results. Among other things, this characteristic is reflected in the most frequent designs, which focus on the relation between predictor and criteria, and between independent and dependent variables. The new models draw attention to the process character of the life course rather than to the outcomes of developmental processes. The importance of studying the "stasis and flow" of processes in individual functioning is emphasized by Pervin (chap. 16, this volume).

These modern models all emphasize the holistic, integrated nature of dynamic, complex processes. The holistic principle holds for all systems of interest in research on human ontogeny, regardless of the level at which the system is operating; they are "undivided" in structure and function. This proposition holds at the cellular level, at the level of subsystems such as the coronary system, the immune system, the cardiovascular system, the cognitive system, and the behavioral system, as well as at the level of the individual as a total system. It also holds for the environment and its subsystems, such as the peer system among youngsters or the family system.

The models also provide a theoretical framework for understanding the dynamic processes of interaction of operating factors within the individual, and the continuous bidirectional interaction between the individual and his or her environment in the person–environment system, within a single integrated perspective. Interaction among operating factors is a fundamental characteristic of the processes at all levels of the dynamic, integrated person–environment system. Interaction with other cells is a prerequisite both for a cell's functioning and for cell growth and cell death. Interaction among cells is also a necessary condition for the lawful organization of cells into systems to fulfill their developmental role in the total organism. At all levels of the total organism, subsystems interact in order to maintain the functioning of the organism and adapt to changing conditions, due to maturation and experience. So, for example, continuous dynamic interaction with other biological systems is a necessary condition for the immune system to play its proper role in the functioning of the totality. Interaction is also a fundamental characteristic of the individual's process of adaptation to environmental conditions.

Emphasizing the interactive, often nonlinear character of the processes which are our concern, these models now provide a theoretical basis for investigating, with effective methodological tools, the interactive, dynamic processes underlying individual functioning and development. In natural sciences, the formulation of the new models has initiated a strong methodological development, for example, in a revival of nonlinear mathematics. For further real progress in psychological research it is important that, without slavishly copying these methods, we adopt this approach and create methodological tools appropriate to the nature of the psychological phenomena that are our main concern.

With reference to the interactive character of the processes, the models confirm and provide a theoretical basis for the old proposition that a particular variable's psychological significance for the functioning of an individual cannot be understood by studying it in isolation, outside the context of other, simultaneously operating variables in the individual. The total process can never be understood by summing results from studies of single variables.

Recognition of the interactive character of dynamic processes means that the models highlight the concept of context. The role of context is important for understanding individual development and functioning at all levels of the total system—from the cellular level to the individual's interaction with the environment. The development and functioning of cells and their synapses are dependent on the context of surrounding cells and how they function. Each biological, mental, and behavioral subsystem is dependent upon the context of other subsystems. The behavior of an individual cannot be understood without reference to the environment with which he or she has to deal, and systems at different levels function and develop in an interdependent way.

With respect to the application of the concept of context in developmental psychology and personality, three phases can be distinguished. In the first phase, a unidirectional view of the relationship between the individual and the external environment dominated—the environment was the cause of individual functioning and development. For example, the child was the target of the parents' influence. The second phase was dominated by what is now being called the classical interactionistic view, which emphasized the reciprocal interaction between the individual and his or her environment; the child and the parents are involved in a continuous process of interaction in which each part influences the other's behavior. This view was central in models that were presented under different headings in the 1960s, 1970s, and 1980s. The third phase, that of holistic interactionism, underlines the importance of incorporating mental, behavioral, and biological processes bound to the individual as involved in the individual's reciprocal interaction with the environment (Magnusson, 1988, 1995). At the same time, an individual's development and ongoing functioning cannot be understood in isolation from the proximal and distal properties of the environment in which he or she lives. The individual is an active, purposeful part of an integrated, complex, and dynamic person—environment system. Thus, the specific way in which mental, biological, behavioral, and social factors operate may not be the same in cultures with differing social norms, rules, and role expectations.

## Longitudinal Research

The fourth main source of enrichment for the holistic perspective lies in the revival of longitudinal research. Inadequacies of the piecemeal or variable-oriented approach to the study of developmental issues become obvious in well-planned longitudinal studies that track individuals over time and contexts. This longitudinal design for understanding developmental processes is necessary for a number of reasons. One is that operating factors shift over time, both with respect to which factors operate (their distinct character per se) and to their significance and role in the total integrated interactive processes of the individual. It is only the organism that remains distinct and identifiable. A critical mass of longitudinal methods, data, and solid empirical information has rendered previous versions of the interaction model unacceptable.

An empirical study in our longitudinal research program in Stockholm illustrates what I have just said (Magnusson, 1988; Stattin & Magnusson, 1990). A cohort of all the boys and girls in one community in Sweden was followed from the age of 10 to adulthood. At the age of 14.5, girls who matured early reported a much higher alcohol consumption than girls who matured later. However, in the follow-up of the same girls at the age of 26–27, no systematic relation was found between age of menarche and frequency of drinking. Thus, high alcohol consumption at the age of 14 among the girls who matured early was not a precursor of alcohol abuse at adult age.

Nonetheless, very early biological maturation did have long-term consequences in other respects. As adults, the early maturing girls married sooner, had more children, completed less education, and acquired a lower job status than average- or late-maturing girls. These effects could not be attributed to early maturation per se; rather they were the net result of many interrelated factors, linked to biological maturation during adolescence: self-perception, self-evaluation, and above all, the social characteristics of close friends in puberty. The short-term deviances in norm-breaking behavior and the long-term consequences for family life, education, and job status were observed only among early maturing girls who perceived themselves as more mature than their agemates and who affiliated in early adolescence with older males or with peers who were out of school and working.

This implies that the biological age for onset of sexual maturity plays a role in, but does not alone account for, the short- and long-term consequences observed. Early biological maturation provides predisposing conditions for a process in which mental, biological, behavioral, and social factors are involved. In order to understand the developmental process of girls and individual differences in this respect, all these factors must be integrated in a holistic framework and empirically investigated in a longitudinal design. Cross-cultural studies on teenage girls by the Cairns in the United States, by Caspi and Moffit in New Zealand, by Pulkkinen in Finland, and by Silbereisen and Kracke in Germany, replicating our study, illustrate the role of social and cultural factors.

## Conclusion

Thus, the contributions from cognitive research, from neurosciences, from modern models for dynamic complex processes, and from longitudinal research have enriched the old holistic view of individual functioning and development in a way that makes it a fruitful theoretical framework for planning, implementing, and interpreting empirical research. The modern holistic–interactionistic view offers a stable platform for further scientific progress in psychology, enabling us to fall into step with recent developments in other disciplines in the life sciences.

## THE EMERGENCE OF A NEW SCIENTIFIC DISCIPLINE—DEVELOPMENTAL SCIENCE

The total space of phenomena involved in the process of lifelong individual development forms a clearly defined and delimited domain for scientific discovery, which constitutes a scientific discipline of its own: Developmental science. The content of this domain goes beyond developmental psychology; it is located at the interface of developmental psychology, developmental biology, molecular biology, physiology, neuropsychology, social psychology, sociology, anthropology, and neighboring disciplines (Cairns, Elder, & Costello, 1996; Magnusson & Cairns, 1996). The relevance of this proposition is indicated by the recent establishment of the Center for Developmental Science at the University of North Carolina in Chapel Hill, and the publication of new scientific journals.

The establishment of developmental science as a specific field for psychological inquiry implies a need for real cross-disciplinary collaboration. By participating in that collaboration, we as psychologists can contribute unique knowledge to the understanding and explanation of why individuals think, feel, act, and react as they do; and we can do this more effectively than if we proceed in isolation from the mainstream of research in life sciences.

## HOLISTIC INTERACTIONISM

A modern holistic view emphasizes an approach to the individual and the person–environment system as organized wholes functioning as integrated totalities. At each level, the totality derives its characteristic features and properties from the interaction among the elements involved, not from the effect of each isolated part on the totality. Each aspect of the structures and processes that are operating (perceptions, plans, values, goals, motives, biological factors, conduct, etc.), as well as each aspect of the environment, takes on meaning from the role it plays in the total functioning of the individual (Magnusson, 1990). This view is consistent with progress in related scientific disciplines.

A holistic model does not offer a specific hypothesis or an explanation for all problems. The Newtonian model did not answer all questions in natural sciences about the structure and functioning of the physical world. But it did serve two fundamental purposes: It provided a common theoretical framework for planning and implementation of empirical research on specific problems, and it offered a common conceptual space for effective communication among researchers concerned with problems at very different levels of the total universe. The same role can be played by a holistic model of individual functioning and development. Furthermore, the holistic, integrated model for individual functioning and individual development does not imply that the entire system of an individual must be studied in every research endeavor. Acceptance of a common model of nature for research in natural sciences has never implied that the whole universe should be investigated in every study.

The formulation of a modern holistic–interactionist view of individual development and functioning has prompted some colleagues to make sceptical comments about the scientific status and value of the approach as a theoretical framework for empirical research. However, this approach has now provided a solid theoretical foundation for the planning, implementation, and interpretation of empirical studies on specific issues at all levels of individual functioning within a common theoretical framework.

The basis for the claim that the processes of individual functioning and development are accessible to systematic, scientific inquiry is that these processes are not random; they occur in a specific way within organized structures and are guided by lawful principles.

Lawful organization is a characteristic of individual structures and processes at all levels; it is a characteristic of mental structures and processes, of behavior, of biological structures and processes, as well as of the environment. The lawfulness of the processes is reflected in the development and functioning of all organized subsystems as well as in the functioning of the organized totality. An interesting question at the individual level is whether the differences between early development and aging are essentially a discontinuity in organizational directionality toward more organization as opposed to less organization (Baltes & Graf, 1996).

A basic principle in the development of biological systems is the ability to self-organize. Self-organization is a characteristic of open systems and refers to a process by which new structures and patterns emerge. From the beginning of fetal development, self-organization is a guiding principle in developmental processes. To quote the Nobel laureate Jacob (1989): "Final-ity in the living world thus originates from the idea of organism, because the parts have to produce each other, because they have to associate to form the whole, because, as Kant said, living beings must be self-organized" (p. 112).

Within subsystems the operating components organize themselves to maximize the functioning of each subsystem with respect to its purpose in the total system. At a higher level subsystems organize themselves in order to fulfill their role in the functioning of the totality. We find this principle in the development and functioning of the brain, the coronary system, and the immune system. The principle can also be applied to the development and functioning of the sensory and cognitive systems and to manifest behavior (Carlson, Earls, & Todd, 1988). Its role in developmental psychology has been discussed by Thelen (1989).

Two aspects of this self-organization are important for the discussion here. First, individuals differ to some extent in the way operational factors are organized and function within subsystems. Individuals also differ in subsystem organization and function. These organizations are manifested in *patterns* of operating factors within subsystems, and *patterns* of functioning subsystems. Organization in terms of patterns is also a fundamental characteristic of the integrated social environment of which the individual forms an active part. Environmental organization is a prerequisite for the individual to deal with the external world purposefully and effectively.

Second, the number of ways in which operating factors in a certain subsystem can be organized in patterns, in order to allow the subsystem to play its functional role in the totality, and the number of ways in which subsystems can be organized to form the total pattern for the total organism, is restricted. Only a limited number of states are functional for each subsystem and for the totality.

The organization of structures and processes involved in the functioning and development of the individual has implications for research design and models for data treatment. The application of the theoretical framework advocated here requires that the traditional variable approach is complemented with what has been designated the person approach (Block, 1971). These are theoretical concepts. The essential difference between the two approaches was summarized by Magnusson and Allen (1983): "The person-centered approach to research (in contrast to the variable-centered approach) takes a holistic and dynamic view; the person is conceptualized as an integrated totality rather than as a summation of variables" (p. 172). Using the person approach as the theoretical framework, individuals are studied empirically in terms of their characteristic patterns of data for the variables which are relevant for the problem under investigation.

The application of pattern analysis has played an important part in our research group's work in recent decades. In the first pattern analysis, published in 1975, we studied norm-breaking behaviors among boys and girls in early adolescence by grouping the individuals on the basis of their behaviors across specific, well-defined situations, using latent profile analysis (Magnusson, Dunér, & Zetterblom). In another study during the 1970s, P-technique was applied in the study of the stability of cross-situational patterns of behavior (Magnusson & Stattin, 1981). During the 1980s and 1990s pattern analyses have been applied to adult functioning of individuals using various clustering techniques in a number of studies on developmental background. The merits and limitations of the variable and person approaches, respectively, were analyzed and discussed by Bergman (1993, 1998), Bergman and Magnusson (1991), and Magnusson (1988, 1998). (The methodological implications of a person approach is dealt with by Bergman, in chap. 9, this volume. Lars Bergman has been responsible for the methodological section of our program for a long period of time. His work has been of substantial value for the progress of the total research program.)

A holistic perspective directs the interest to processes rather than to outcomes. With reference to this analysis, a prerequisite for further progress in empirical research is access to methodological tools that are compatible with the nature of structures and processes involved in individual functioning and development. The development and application of such tools is an urgent challenge.

## A HOLISTIC VIEW TIMELY

The adoption of a holistic view is now a characteristic of recent developments in all scientific fields concerned with dynamic complex processes. Those who are represented in this volume have made important contributions to emphasizing this perspective in psychological research. Let me mention one among many indications that a holistic–interactionistic view is in the mainstream of current developments in life sciences. This perspective formed the theoretical framework for the organization of a Nobel symposium in Stockholm in 1994 under the auspices of the Royal Swedish Academy of Sciences, which is responsible for the selection of most of the Nobel prize winners. Leading specialists in medical, biological, and psychological fields, concerned with different aspects of individual development, presented state-of-the-art reviews of their specialities and discussed how knowledge from these fields can contribute to the understanding and explanation of developmental processes in a holistic, interactionistic perspective (Magnusson, 1996). The holistic view of psychological phenomena not only has deep roots in scientific psychology but also belongs to the scientific zeitgeist today. It is a strong challenge for the future of scientific psychology to analyze carefully the theoretical, methodological, and research strategy consequences of this conclusion and take these consequences seriously.

# REFERENCES

Baltes, P. B., & Graf, P. (1996). Psychological aspects of aging: Facts and frontiers. In D. Magnusson (Ed.), *The life-span development of individuals: Behavioral, neurobiological, and psychosocial perspectives* (pp. 427–460). Cambridge, UK: Cambridge University Press.

Bergman, L. R. (1993). Some methodological issues in longitudinal research: Looking forward. In D. Magnusson & P. Casaer (Eds.), *Longitudinal research on individual development: Present status and future perspectives* (pp. 217–241). Cambridge, UK: Cambridge University Press.

Bergman, L. R. (1998). A pattern-oriented approach to studying individual development: Snapshots and processes. In R. B. Cairns, L. R. Bergman, & J. Kagan (Eds.), *Methods and models for studying the individual* (pp. 83–121). Thousand Oaks, CA: Sage.

Bergman, L. R., & Magnusson, D. (1991). Stability and change in patterns of extrinsic adjustment problems. In D. Magnusson, L. R. Bergman, G. Rudinger, & B. Törestad (Eds.), *Problems and methods in longitudinal research: Stability and change* (pp. 323–346). Cambridge, UK: Cambridge University Press.

Block, J. (1971). *Lives through time*. Berkeley, CA: Bancroft Books.

Cairns, R. B. (1979). *Social development: The origins and plasticity of interchanges*. San Francisco, CA: W. H. Freeman & Company.

Cairns, R. B., Elder, G. H., Jr., & Costello, E. J. (1996). *Developmental Science*. Cambridge, UK: Cambridge University Press.

Carlson, M., Earls, F., & Todd, R. D. (1988). The importance of regressive changes in the development of the nervous system: Towards a neurobiological theory of child development. *Psychiatric Developments, 1*, 1–22.

Carlson, R. (1971). Where is the person in personality research? *Psychological Bulletin, 75*, 203–219.

Hull, C. L. (1943). The problem of intervening variables in molar behavior theory. *Psychological Review, 50*, 273–291.

Jacob, F. (1989). *The logic of life. A history of heredity and the possible and the actual*. London: Penguin.

Johansson, G., Frankenhaeuser, M., & Magnusson, D. (1973). Catecholamine output in school children as related to performance and adjustment. *Scandinavian Journal of Psychology, 14*, 20–28.

Katz, D. (1950). *Handbok i psykologi* [Handbook of Psychology]. Stockholm: Svenska Bokförlaget.

Magnusson, D. (1988). Individual development from an interactional perspective. In D. Magnusson (Ed.), *Paths through life* (Vol. 1). Hillsdale, NJ: Lawrence Erlbaum Associates.

Magnusson, D. (1990). Personality development from an interactional perspective. In L. Pervin (Ed.), *Handbook of Personality* (pp. 193–222). New York: Guilford.

Magnusson, D. (1995). Individual development: A holistic integrated model. In P. Moen, G. H. Elder, Jr., & K. Luscher (Eds.), *Linking lives and contexts: Perspectives on the ecology of human development* (pp. 19–60). Washington, DC: American Psychological Association.

Magnusson, D. (Ed.). (1996). *The lifespan development of individuals: Behavioral, neurobiological, and psychosocial perspectives. A synthesis*. Cambridge, UK: Cambridge University Press.

Magnusson, D. (1998). The logic and implications of a person-oriented approach. In R. B. Cairns, L. R. Bergman, & J. Kagan (Eds.), *Methods and models for studying the individual* (pp. 33–63). Thousand Oaks, CA: Sage.

Magnusson, D., & Allen, V. L. (1983). Implications and applications of an interactional perspective for human development. In D. Magnusson & V. L. Allen (Eds.), *Human development: An interactional perspective* (pp. 369–387). New York: Academic Press.

Magnusson, D., & Cairns, R. B. (1996). Developmental science: Principles and illustrations. In R. B. Cairns, G. H. Elder Jr., & E. J. Costello (Eds.), *Developmental science* (pp. 7–30). New York: Cambridge University Press.

Magnusson, D., Dunér, A., & Zetterblom, G. (1975). *Adjustment—a longitudinal study.* Stockholm: Almqvist & Wiksell.

Magnusson, D., & Stattin, H. (1981). Stability of cross-situational patterns of behavior. *Journal of Research in Personality, 15,* 488–496.

Meili, R. (1950). Tankepsykologi [The psychology of thinking]. In D. Katz (Ed.), *Handbok i psykologi* [Handbook of psychology] (pp. 124–145). Stockholm: Bonniers.

Russell, R. W. (1970). "Psychology": Noun or adjective? *American Psychologist, 25,* 211–218.

Sanford, N. (1965). Will psychologists study human problems? *American Psychologist, 20,* 192–202.

Stattin, H., & Magnusson, D. (1990). *Pubertal maturation in female development.* Hillsdale, NJ: Lawrence Erlbaum Associates.

Susman, E. J. (1993). Psychological, contextual, and psychobiological interactions: A developmental perspective on conduct disorder. *Development and Psychopathology, 5,* 181–189.

Thelen, E. (1989). Self-organization in developmental processes: Can systems approaches work? In M. R. Gunnar & E. Thelen (Eds.), *Systems theory and development* (pp. 77–117). Hillsdale, NJ: Lawrence Erlbaum Associates.

Thelen, E., & Smith, L. B. (1998). Dynamic systems theory. In R. M. Lerner (Ed.), *Handbook of child psychology: Vol. 1. Theoretical models of human development* (5th ed., pp. 563–634). New York: Wiley.

# 4

# Developmental Science: Three Audacious Implications

Robert B. Cairns

University of North Carolina, Chapel Hill

This chapter addresses three audacious implications of the holistic-developmental framework. The descriptor "audacious" applies for a couple of reasons. In some contexts, the definition is "extremely bold, original, and inventive." In others, it means "brazen and insolent." Depending on one's perspective, either meaning may apply to the primary implications of developmental science.

I also hope to draw attention to the less revolutionary properties of the framework. To the extent the proposals outlined in this volume are adopted, they involve more than assigning a new name to old ideas or continuing business as usual in the study of social behaviors and psychological functioning.

## IMPLICATION #1: THE SCOPE OF DEVELOPMENTAL SCIENCE

Developmental science refers to nothing less than a new interdisciplinary framework for the investigation of behavioral and psychological phenomena—a metatheory rooted in developmental principles to guide work and thinking on biology and social behavior and their interactions over ontogeny (Magnusson & Cairns, 1996).

## What Is Developmental Science?

The first audacious implication is drawn directly from the definitions of developmental science that have been recently offered. Magnusson and Cairns (1996) proposed:

> the total space of phenomena involved in the development of individual functioning forms a domain that, for effective investigation, must involve interdisciplinary integration. We propose that this domain constitutes a scientific discipline of its own, *developmental science*. (p. 7, italics in the original)

This definition is consistent with a more lengthy statement provided by the Carolina Consortium on Human Development (1996). In forming an advanced studies institute in developmental science, a group of faculty collaborators prepared a definition of what they meant by developmental science. The collaborative statement reads:

> Developmental science refers to a fresh synthesis that has been generated to guide research in the social, psychological, and biobehavioral disciplines. It describes a general orientation for linking concepts and findings of hitherto disparate areas of developmental inquiry, and it emphasizes the dynamic interplay of processes across time frames, levels of analysis, and contexts. Time and timing are central to this perspective. The time frames employed are relative to the lifetime of the phenomena to be understood. Units of focus may be as short as milliseconds, seconds, and minutes, or as long as years, decades, and millennia. In this perspective, the phenomena of individual functioning are viewed at multiple levels—from the subsystems of genetics, neurobiology, and hormones to those of families, social networks, communities, and cultures. (p. 1)

The members of the Carolina Consortium on Human Development who formulated the definition represented multiple scientific disciplines, from sociology to epidemiology and psychobiology. The formulation was written to ensure that the term would not be confused with the methodologies and concepts of psychology or its subdisciplines.

To underscore the scope and potential of the proposal, the Consortium faculty followed their definition with these two clarifying paragraphs:

> Developmental science has roots in both the biological and social disciplines. The need for a systematic developmental perspective has long been recognized in comparative psychology and behavioral biology. Fresh statements of this kernel assumption have recently evolved in developmental psychobiology, dynamic systems approaches, and models of neurobehavioral development. Simultaneously, the need for a developmental approach to social and cognitive phenomena was expressed in the work of Baldwin (1897), Piaget (1950), Lewin (1933), and Vygotsky (1978). Over the past two decades, these ideas, too, have been extended and elaborated in social ecology, social development, cognitive development, and life course analysis.

The modern developmental orientation—including the term "developmental science" itself—has won reasonably broad acceptance over the last decade. Nonetheless, shortcomings remain in attempts to translate it into an effective program of research, training, and application. Part of the problem appears to be the inertia of traditional disciplines and the rigidity of existing research boundaries. To the extent that ideas remain at an abstract level, they do not demand a reorientation of existing academic disciplines and separate domains of knowledge. On this score, advances in scholarship typically precede changes in institutional structure. The study of development is no exception. Discipline and institutional barriers are deeply rooted, and the gap between biological-health training and behavioral-social training has proved difficult to bridge. (pp. 1–2)

In accord with the consortium faculty's proposition, laboratories have been organized, training institutes established, seminars conducted, international/interdisciplinary conferences held, and recognition won by academic institutions and scientific foundations. Specifically:

- The Carolina Consortium on Human Development was established in 1988 across four universities as a new advanced research training program by the National Institute of Human Health and Child Development. Since its establishment, the Consortium has been an advanced studies institute for graduate students, postdoctoral fellows, and faculty researchers in developmental science. In 1993, the Consortium faculty created the Center for Developmental Science to support collaborative research, with funding by the National Institute of Mental Health.

- Scientific presentations were given at successive Biennial Meetings of the Society for Child Development Research from 1989 to the present, along with presentations at other meetings that described the programs and the concepts.

- A collaborative volume entitled *Developmental Science* (Cairns, Elder, & Costello, 1996) was published by the original Consortium faculty, along with complementary volumes in specific areas (e.g., Tudge, Shanahan, & Valsiner, 1996).

- A Nobel Foundation Symposium recognized the framework as an emergent interdisciplinary discipline (Magnusson, 1996).

- International workshops have been offered on developmental science in Europe and North America that examine the substantive and methodological issues raised by the framework.

The idea that "developmental science refers to a fresh synthesis" has won broad currency, but its success has inevitably invited uses that threaten to diminish the distinctiveness of the proposal and the considerations that gave rise to it. Hence a few comments are necessary to indicate what developmental science is not.

## What's in a Name?

Not much, as it turns out. Developmental science was first used three decades ago to refer to the need for a new interdisciplinary framework beyond psychology (Cairns, 1970) and was not challenged through the early 1990s (e.g., Cairns, 1990, 1992). It has been only in the past couple of years that "developmental science" has been used as a synonym for "developmental psychology." Ultimately, the redefinition may be of modest consequence, much as the label "child psychology" was displaced by "developmental psychology" in the second half of the 20th century. But if the framework of ideas and premises underlying developmental science are obfuscated or otherwise compromised, there may be a hazard in permitting one label to refer to quite different scientific frameworks.

The term developmental science has been recently employed as if it were synonymous with developmental psychology or one of its subdisciplines. For example, "developmental science" has been used as the title for a new journal in Great Britain that seems primarily concerned with cognitive development in childhood. In addition, "developmental science" was used in March 1997 as the title of a special issue of *American Psychologist,* along with a set of articles that described recent research trends in child and developmental psychology. In both instances, the term was borrowed but not the cross-disciplinary, comparative focus on developmental change.

A fresh and distinctive name seemed to be required three decades ago to define a set of proposals rooted in developmental principles but which extended beyond psychology. Developmental science—as the framework was labeled—transcended not only the constructs, methods, and subject matter of developmental psychology, it transcended many of the traditions in psychology. The introduction of this term was an effort to achieve clarity of concepts in an otherwise open discipline. Only time will tell whether a new term will be required to ensure the integrity of the framework that has been called developmental science.

## IMPLICATION #2: METHODS AND MODELS

The proposal by Magnusson (1998; chap. 3, this volume) that there should be a closer fit between methods and models appears on the surface to be a benign idea, one to which few reasonable scientists would object. However, the proposal qualifies as audacious because it contradicts a traditional idea in psychology. It has been broadly accepted in psychology that methods should transcend theories and hypotheses, and thereby gain independence from them. Otherwise, the argument goes, methods could be biased toward, or against, models to be investigated. That courses in statistics and research design constitute one of the few area requirements common for graduate students in psychology demonstrates the institutionalization of this assumption. As a byproduct, it provides a common ground for researchers in an otherwise fractured and fractious discipline.

Given the breadth of commitment in psychology to the "methodology transcends domain" proposition, any proposal that it should be reexamined or revised may seem audacious. Nonetheless, developmental researchers from Alfred Binet to David Magnusson, have joined in calling for such a reexamination. For instance, Radke-Yarrow, Campbell, and Burton argued in 1968 for the need to ensure that there is a fit between methods and models. They wrote:

> The findings from the preceding analyses of data [on child rearing research] make it difficult to continue to be complacent about methodology, and difficult to continue to regard replication as a luxury. The child's day-to-day experiences contribute significantly to his behavior and development and are in many respects the essence of developmental theory. An exact understanding is important to science and society. In attempting to build on this knowledge, each researcher is a methodologist and as such has a responsibility for excellence. (p. 152)

In effect, Radke-Yarrow and her colleagues argued that the field must reach a better fit between developmental theory, developmental methods, and the concrete events of lives in context.

More recently, Bronfenbrenner (1996, p. ix) observed that "the defining properties of the emergent model [developmental science] contradict, almost point for point, the now prevailing conceptual and operational strategies of choice in each specialized field of inquiry."

What are the point for point contradictions in methodology? Some of the more prominent ones discussed in Cairns and Cairns (1994) are:

• Aggregation versus disaggregation. Prevailing methods frequently begin with a research design that involves sampling persons and aggregating across individuals and contexts. Aggregation across persons into the sample typically occurs at the first stage of the study in order to obtain estimates of population parameters and to identify the distinctive residual that reflects individual differences. By contrast, a primary goal of developmental methods is to understand the individual processes that contribute to the ontogeny of the child's adaptations in the particular settings of life (Bergman, 1998; Bergman & Magnusson, 1990; Magnusson & Bergman, 1990). Hence, developmental research ultimately seeks description of the person-in-context in terms of a configuration of influences.

• Disentangling variables versus integrating variables. A goal of prevailing research methods is to identify the unique contribution of a variable in predicting a particular outcome independent of other sources of variance. The statistical dilemma is that higher order interactions among variables constitute some of the findings for theory, yet they present formidable problems for analysis. By contrast, a major goal of developmental research is to understand how characteristics (i.e., variables) function together to guide, regulate, and constrain actions. This aim leads, in turn, to a focus on the relations among characteristics and how the resultant configurations are associated with later adaptive behaviors. Developmental analyses over time require a holistic approach, but not all holistic models or dynamic systems are developmental.

• Eliminating time versus understanding the processes that occur in time. Many of the conventional research and statistical procedures eliminate, control, or mute the effects of time and age. These include the standard use of correlations, $z$-scores, and the transformations that control for age by attempts to rule out age effects. Once eliminated methodologically, the effects of age tend to be forgotten theoretically. For developmental analyses, however, variations in age and timing are central to understanding effective change and continuity processes. Rather than getting rid of the effects associated with time and timing, this information can be exploited in developmental designs to clarify how integration occurs. Time becomes a friend in analysis, not an enemy. How longitudinal information is employed can identify whether investigators are operating within a developmental framework. Conventional analyses tend to focus on the latent structures of individual functioning. Once these structures of personality, cognition, or temperament are identified, longitudinal observations can be employed as successive panel observations to plot changes in individual status or structure. The implicit aim is to identify continuities, because changes over time present increasingly complex problems of analysis and interpretation. In contrast, the developmental orientation is as concerned with the dynamics of what happens in-between longitudinal observations as with antecedent–consequent relationships.

• The primacy of social interactions. Developmental science presupposes integration of influences within and without the individual. On this score, social interactions occur at the interface between individuals and their contexts, hence the analysis cannot be reduced to one without information from the other. This methodological assumption leads inevitably to the implication that social interactions require a level of mutual analysis that is radically different from the one traditionally endorsed in psychology. Rather than focus exclusively on individual states or individual variables, the organizing units over time become the dynamic interactions in which persons are involved in particular contexts. A new set of theoretical and design considerations—for example, the bidirectionality of feedback between internal states and external stimulation, the need to consider levels of analysis that describe interactional units rather than persons—must come into play.

• Controlling contexts versus measuring contexts. Conventional research procedures also tend to hold constant, isolate, or otherwise eliminate variations in context. This is a research goal for experimental laboratory and medical procedures that try to control for potentially confounding effects (e.g., circadian variations, environmental distractions, and other confounds). Such controls are necessary to bring into focus the effects of the variables of interest. Developmental analyses, by contrast, view social contexts and the everyday events of life as critical agents of developmental stability and change. Attention must be given to identifying units of social context beyond the individual, including the social network in which the person is embedded. Hence social-contextual influences must be assessed and integrated into any analysis of individual prediction, and units of analysis beyond the person become key. The characteristics of the person and the properties of the environment tend to correlate. These "correlated constraints" are key to understanding continuity and change over time.

• One method fits all? The multilevel emphasis of the developmental framework demands that methods, measures, and analyses fit the problem. In the words of Radke-Yarrow et al. (1968), "each researcher is a methodologist and as such has a responsibility for excellence" (p. 152). The selection of method—whether observations, surveys, interviews, tests, or experiments—depends upon the phenomenon to be clarified. Methodological monism is not acceptable. To illustrate, Xie (1998) used verbatim accounts of conflicts by teenagers to infer whether they employed hidden or nonconfrontational aggressive strategies involving gossip and social alienation. Given the nature of the construct (i.e., the occurrence of hidden or undisclosed social aggression), more direct observational, survey, or rating procedures were unsuccessful, or yielded conflicting outcomes (e.g., Crick & Grotpeter, 1995). The definition of the construct disqualified most direct measures, whether obtained from the self, peers, teachers, or parents (Cairns & Green, 1979).

• Convergence across levels. It has been traditionally assumed that methods and measures should converge across levels and, thereby, identify latent variables or latent structures. By contrast, a developmental framework does not presuppose convergence since systems may be organized in a semiautonomous fashion. By way of example, reports of behavior obtained from the self often differ from reports from sources outside the self (e.g., peers, teachers, parents). Presumably the information sources have distinct functions, and distinct biases. The problem for developmental researchers is to identify rules by which alignment occurs and fails to occur. On this score, observations over time can help clarify the distinctive functions served by self-concepts relative to concepts of the individual formed by others. For instance, teacher perceptions provide robust predictions of long-term academic success. Self-perceptions do not (Xie, Mahoney, & Cairns, 1999).

Are these points really contradictions, or are they extensions of methodology to a broader, more inclusive level? It should not be forgotten that the methods of developmental science rely upon advances that have been made in psychology and sister sciences, without some of the superfluous baggage that has accumulated. These points may be viewed as proposals to extend—rather than displace—the hard-won advances in methodology that have been achieved over the past century.

## The Pitfalls of New Procedures

"If it ain't broke, don't fix it." This colloquial expression supports conservatism and suggests a guard against changes that have unintended negative consequences. Because the developmental framework presupposes that fresh ways are required to organize information about individuals in context over time, it may appear immune to the hazards of change. That is an illusion. Calls for change may be, for some, an invitation to revisit procedures and data collection methods that have intuitive appeal yet which are inherently misleading. This includes, for example, exclusive reliance upon the "case study" method to study individuals, subject self-reports, or undisciplined use of either "quantitative" or "qualitative" methods (Cairns, Bergman, & Kagan, 1998).

What are the protections against the hazards inherent in shifting to new methodology? One safeguard would be to require rigorous and public criteria for the acceptance or rejection of any new research strategy, measure, or analysis. This rule applies with special force when unconventional designs are proposed, new and unproved measurement methods are adopted, or fresh statistical approaches are suggested. As a minimum, direct linkages and comparisons between the traditional, conventional procedures and the new ones proposed should be offered in published reports. Unless the gains and conventions of traditional models are respected, researchers run the risk of substituting one inadequate set of procedures for another. In practice, this means that (a) the criteria for the acceptance of findings should be made explicit in any scientific report, (b) the data should, when feasible, be described and analyzed by both conventional and newly proposed procedures, with points of similarity and difference explicitly noted, and (c) the relative advantages and pitfalls of the new procedures should be outlined and summarized in the conclusion, along with any fresh implications. Accordingly, this means a large methodological assignment confronts researchers who subscribe to the integrative developmental framework.

## IMPLICATION #3: EARLY EXPERIENCE, NOVELTY, AND CHANGE

One of the principles of developmental science is that change and adaptation are fundamental to development, along with the corollary that novelty can arise throughout the life course (Magnusson & Cairns, 1996). Depending upon one's perspective, this proposition on change and novelty could be viewed as pedestrian, revolutionary, or imprudent. What muddies the conceptual waters is that virtually every modern model of behavior and biology accepts developmental propositions on the inevitability of change. The corollary assumption about when developmental plasticity ends, however, has rarely been emphasized.

### Beyond Freud and Developmental Neurobiology

One of the most audacious implications of developmental science is that behavioral and interactional change are possible throughout the life course. It is a bold, even revolutionary implication because diverse traditional models—from developmental neurobiology to personality development—hold just the opposite. They tend to agree on what might be called a two-stage theory of development. Accordingly, the dynamic processes of developmental organization are restricted to the formative stages of neurobiological development or personality organization in the earliest years of life. Once essential dispositions become established—for example, neurobiological, social attachment—they become fixed as structures and other nondevelopmental system processes come into play. Formative developmental processes for attachment—reciprocal interaction, bidirectionality, behavioral plasticity, biobehavioral organization—are assumed to be active only during a critical period in infancy and early childhood. According to this view, the end point of development occurs in infancy or early childhood. It is a two-factor model of development because the processes become stabilized rather early, and the attachment structures and neurobiological processes then remain relatively stable.

How can these structures be changed once they are established? This was originally a large problem for psychoanalysis, since it was as much a theory of therapy and change as it was a theory of development. Sigmund Freud (1933) offered a characteristically innovative solution by proposing that, under the special conditions of psychoanalysis, the very early experiences of life and fixations produced could be "relived" and thereby modified. Change required the creation, under therapeutic conditions, of a transference neurosis where the relationship between therapist and patient was transformed to the earlier parent–child relationship and the earlier problems were "worked through." Even under these special conditions, the reconstruction process was lengthy and rarely complete.

Importantly, this mystical and mysterious proposition of psychoanalysis gained a strong ally in a newly evolving discipline, experimental embryology. Early research on embryos provided strong confirmation of the two-stage model of development. The significant breakthrough in embryological research occurred when Nobel laureate, Hans Spemann, found that living tissue, early in its development, is highly susceptible to the influence of the context in which it is placed. In an elegant series of experiments, Spemann found that presumptive skin tissue of the embryonic newt could be excised and transplanted to areas where the nervous system was to develop (Spemann, 1938). The transplanted cells developed as nerve tissues, not skin. For the induction to be successful, the transplantation must be performed within a narrow span of time, early in the organization of the structure and the tissue. There is a "critical period" of high plasticity, and once this period has ended, the character of the structure and tissue becomes fixed. Attempts to produce plasticity thereafter are rejected. Spemann proposed that the surroundings organize the character and functions of the tissues in early development.

What has been overlooked in current discussions is that Spemann's critical periods refer to stages in organization, not to chronological age. Earlier is not necessarily more critical than later in social development, since the organization of new patterns and systems of relationships continues over a lifetime. Moreover, Atz (1970) has observed that the history of the study of animal behavior shows that to think of behavior as structure has led to the most pernicious kind of oversimplification. A similar case has been made for the study of social interactions by Magnusson (1988).

Are the first three years critical for the establishment of attachment and personality and, if so, why worry about childhood, youth, and early maturity? This question concerns the developmental timing for the organization of human nature. The role of early experience in establishing personality and social behavior patterns has been debated in one form or another since 1897 when J. M. Baldwin wrote that "personality is, after all, a continuously changing thing." Sigmund Freud made the opposite point, and he won the battle of the century. He argued for the primacy of early experience, along with the concepts of fixation, regression, and irreversibility. Recent empirical evaluations of the concept of "critical period" have led to a refinement of the idea. It has been discovered that there is considerably more malleability in behavior than was originally recognized.

The matter speaks to a core proposition of developmental science—the events that trigger the establishment of a behavior pattern are usually different from the events that maintain it. This proposition has been employed to explain diverse phenomena, from the distinctive effects of early maturation versus late maturation in girls (Magnusson, 1988) to the role of infantile social attachment in the formation of friendships in childhood and adolescence (Cairns, 1979). The developmental synthesis holds that both early experiences and later ones may be critical, yet for different reasons. The scientific task is to determine how the effects work in any given behavioral domain, and why they have different impacts at different ages. The first three years are important, but so are the next three, and so are the transition years of youth. At each developmental stage, new behaviors and functions emerge.

The social actions of an individual typically occur within a social organization; as such, they are under the control of other individuals within that organization. Social acts are often inappropriately viewed as structures of the individual rather than as part of an interaction organization. An interactive view of social development requires that equal attention be given to the activities of the other individuals. New relationships can be formed, and old ones changed, throughout the lifetime of the individual.

What is audacious about the theoretical stance of developmental framework on change and the effects of early experience? It holds that the development of social and behavioral processes does not end in early ontogeny, else the distinctive adaptive functions of interactions are lost. In support of this proposition, longitudinal research conducted over the past half century indicates that the formative dynamic functions of development are not limited to the early years. Basic developmental modifications in social patterns, including close relationships and attachment bonds, continue throughout life.

## CONCLUDING COMMENTS

In 1988, in a description of Magnusson's classic longitudinal project, I observed that:

> the wisdom and insights of the investigator are as important as the procedures adopted. It is commonly assumed that data speak for themselves—especially if they are prompted by multivariate statistics. That is an illusion. The story told by any longitudinal data set is necessarily filtered through several layers of method, statistical manipulation, and inference, then narrated and amplified by the researcher. So readers must trust that investigators are in tune with the meaning of their findings, not with the glitter of probability values. (p. vi)

In his career, David Magnusson has provided a model for the science. In his emphasis on the need for a holistic approach to understanding development (Magnusson, 1995), he has joined forces with many of the most thoughtful contributors of the century, from J. M. Baldwin, J. W. Mills, and A. Binet to Z.-Y. Kuo and T. C. Schneirla. But there is a danger in this history. If the voices of Baldwin, Binet, Kuo, and Schneirla failed to change the direction of psychology as a science, must we repeat the cycles of the past? Radke-Yarrow (chap. 11, this volume) raised the problem of construct confusion, and Block (chap. 10, this volume) gave it a name. J. W. Mills (1899) was one of the first—with Binet and Baldwin—to advocate the establishment of a developmental science. He was appalled by the direction the new psychology was taking—nondevelopmental and noncontextual. The way was being led by Thorndike's studies of elements of animal learning and Freud's two-stage theory of development wherein early behavior became as fixed as other biological structures.

Will a century of benign neglect of the developmental framework continue? There are some happy signs that it will not, including new techniques, appropriate institutions, a critical mass of longitudinal data, and a fresh generation of researchers. David Magnusson deserves credit for much of the progress. He has provided a model for developmental theory and longitudinal study, and he has directly influenced the foundation of institutions devoted to developmental study worldwide. Moreover, there is an element in his approach to individual functioning that seems essential for the success of the scientific enterprise. Without a commitment to parsimony in understanding and explanation, the principles could be compounded by layers of complexity that render the system unmanageable.

Magnusson has been driven by a need to achieve elegant simplicity in formulation as well as in measurement and analysis. He strives to formulate the simple structure that underlies the complexity. His first line of defense against becoming overwhelmed by data was to understand the structure of the phenomena in the first place.

Magnusson's version of holism begins with the assumption that the individual is functional, adaptive, and generally competent. What has distinguished Magnusson's scientific life and his work has been the way he has proceeded in implementing these ideas—in method, in analysis, and in theory. In a simple and direct way, he reversed the usual way of doing things. At the outset, he saw the need to enlist the whole community rather than simply one segment. Rather than hide the purposes of the work, he made them as public as possible and enrolled all segments of the community. He recognized that this was a new way of doing business, and provided a model for all of us.

In summary, a challenge for the future is to take seriously "audacious" developmental propositions, enjoying their novelty rather than redefining them as traditional formulations. An additional element is a concern with indeterminacy and development. The system should not become so rigid that it is not open to modification, if the appropriate rules were spelled out. It is not a capitulation to fate so much as it is a challenge to understand the principles of modification and change.

Throughout his career, David Magnusson has been concerned with values and how they are generated in development and activated in life. A deep concern with values and how they become established and guide individuals is rarely emphasized in contemporary models. Indeed, the holistic-developmental framework would be deficient without explicit consideration of individual values.

## REFERENCES

Atz, J. W. (1970). The application of the idea of homology to behavior. In L. R. Aronson, E. Tobach, D. S. Lehrman, & J. S. Rosenblatt (Eds.), *Development and evolution of behavior: Essays in memory of T. C. Schneirla.* San Francisco: Freeman.

Baldwin, J. M. (1897). *Social and ethical interpretations in mental development: A study in social psychology.* New York: Macmillan.

Bergman, L. R. (1998). A person-oriented approach to studying individual development: Snapshots and processes. In R. B. Cairns, L. R. Bergman, & J. Kagan (Eds.), *Methods and models for studying the individual: Essays in honor of Marian Radke-Yarrow* (pp. 83–121). Thousand Oaks, CA: Sage.

Bergman, L. R., & Magnusson, D. (1990). General issues about data quality in longitudinal research. In D. Magnusson & L. R. Bergman (Eds.), *Data quality in longitudinal research* (pp. 1–31). Cambridge, UK: Cambridge University Press.

Bronfenbrenner, U. (1996). Foreword. In R. B. Cairns, G. H. Elder, Jr., & E. J. Costello (Eds.), *Developmental science* (pp. iv–xvii). New York: Cambridge University Press.

Cairns, R. B. (1970). Towards a unified science of development. *Contemporary Psychology, 15,* 214–215.

Cairns, R. B. (1979). *Social development: The origins and plasticity of social interchanges.* San Francisco: Freeman.

Cairns, R. B. (1988). Foreword. In D. Magnusson, *Individual development from an interactional perspective* (p. vi). Hillsdale, NJ: Lawrence Erlbaum Associates.

Cairns, R. B. (1990). Toward a developmental science. *Psychological Science, 1,* 42–44.

Cairns, R. B. (1992). The making of a developmental science: The contributions and intellectual heritage of James Mark Baldwin. *Developmental Psychology, 28,* 17–24.

Cairns, R. B., Bergman, L. R., & Kagan, J. (Eds.). (1998). *Methods and models for studying the individual: Essays in honor of Marian Radke-Yarrow.* Thousand Oaks, CA: Sage.

Cairns, R. B., & Cairns, B. D. (1994). *Lifelines and risks: Pathways of youth in our time.* New York: Cambridge University Press.

Cairns, R. B., Elder, G. H., Jr., & Costello, E. J. (Eds.). (1996). *Developmental science.* New York: Cambridge University Press.

Cairns, R. B., & Green, J. A. (1979). How to assess personality and social patterns: Ratings or observations? In R. B. Cairns (Ed.), *The analysis of social interaction: Methods, issues, and illustrations* (pp. 214–232). Hillsdale, NJ: Lawrence Erlbaum Associates.

Carolina Consortium on Human Development. (1996). An integrated statement. In R. B. Cairns, G. H. Elder, Jr., & J. Costello (Eds.), *Developmental science* (pp. 1–6). New York: Cambridge University Press.

Crick, N. R., & Grotpeter, J. K. (1995). Relational aggression, gender, and social-psychological adjustment. *Child Development, 66,* 710–722.

Freud, S. (1933). *New introductory lectures on psycho-analysis.* New York: Norton.

Lewin, K. (1933). Environmental forces in child behavior and development. In C. Murchison (Ed.), *A handbook of child psychology* (2nd ed., pp. 590–625). Worcester, MA: Clark University Press.

Magnusson, D. (1988). *Individual development from an interactional perspective.* Hillsdale, NJ: Lawrence Erlbaum Associates.

Magnusson, D. (1995). Individual development: A holistic integrated model. In P. Moen, G. H. Elder, Jr., & K. Luscher (Eds.), *Examining lives in context: Perspectives on the ecology of human development* (pp. 19–60). Washington, DC: American Psychological Association.

Magnusson, D. (Ed.). (1996). *The life-span development of individuals: Behavioral, neurobiological, and psychosocial perspectives: A synthesis.* New York: Cambridge University Press.

Magnusson, D. (1998). The logic and implications of a person-oriented approach. In R. B. Cairns, L. R. Bergman, & J. Kagan (Eds.), *Methods and models for studying the individual: Essays in honor of Marian Radke-Yarrow* (pp. 33–62). Thousand Oaks, CA: Sage.

Magnusson, D., & Bergman, L. R. (1990). A pattern approach to the study of pathways from childhood to adulthood. In L. N. Robins & M. Rutter (Eds.), *Straight and devious pathways from childhood to adulthood* (pp. 101–115). Cambridge, UK: Cambridge University Press.

Magnusson, D., & Cairns, R. B. (1996). Developmental science: Principles and illustrations. In R. B. Cairns, G. H. Elder, Jr., & J. Costello (Eds.), *Developmental science* (pp. 7–30). New York: Cambridge University Press.

Mills, J. W. (1899). The nature of animal intelligence and the methods of investigating it. *Psychological Review, 6,* 262–274.

Piaget, J. (1950). *The psychology of intelligence.* London: Routledge and Kegan Paul.

Radke-Yarrow, M., Campbell, J. D., & Burton, R. V. (1968). *Child rearing: An inquiry in research and methods.* San Francisco: Jossey-Bass.

Spemann, H. (1938). *Embryonic development and induction.* New Haven: Yale University Press.

Tudge, J., Shanahan, M., & Valsiner, J. (Eds.). (1996). *Comparisons in human development: Understanding time and context.* New York: Cambridge University Press.

Vygotsky, L. S. (1978). *Mind in society.* Cambridge, MA: Harvard University Press.

Xie, H. (1998). *Social manipulation and the development of aggressive behaviors.* Unpublished doctoral dissertation, University of North Carolina at Chapel Hill.

Xie, H., Mahoney, J. L., Cairns, R. B. (1999). Through a looking glass or a hall of mirrors? Self ratings and teacher ratings of academic competence. *International Journal for the Study of Behavioral Development, 23,* 163–183.

# 5

# Principles of Dynamic Pattern Formation and Change for a Science of Human Behavior

J. A. Scott Kelso
Center for Complex Systems and Brain Sciences
Florida Atlantic University

## INTRODUCTION

In person-oriented research (Magnusson, 1995) the goal is to understand individual function and development as a complex, dynamic, holistic, interacting system. This chapter seeks to affirm, and perhaps supplement, the person approach both conceptually and methodologically. Because pattern analysis figures prominently in person-oriented research, and because my charge here is to discuss some key concepts in the study of complex systems, I begin with a brief review of how patterns form and change in nature. Before proceeding, a caveat is in order: the intent here is not to broker physics or to try to "physicalize" human behavior. Instead, it is to elaborate pattern-formation principles as a foundation for understanding the patterns of behavior produced by brains and people, and how these patterns may be modified both by internal factors (intentions, values, memories, emotions, etc.) and interactions with the environment (Kelso, 1995). Clearly this builds upon, but also goes beyond, theories of self-organized pattern formation in physical and chemical systems (e.g., Haken, 1983; Nicolis & Prigogine, 1989).

I also address the question of how to identify relevant pattern variables— or "regularities" as Murray Gel-Mann (1994) might say—and their time-dependent dynamics (equations of motion) in complex living systems. This is an empirical issue that has to be guided by theoretically motivated strategies. I advance one particular strategy—seeking qualitative change—as a means of identifying relevant pattern variables and the pattern-forming dynamics (stability, change, etc.) at both behavioral and brain levels. I show how qualitative change complements, and is complemented by, more standard correlational approaches. Then, I address a number of implications that arise from this "complex systems" view using the example of an elementary law of coordinated behavior that describes how different, individual components of a complex system are coupled together. These implications include how we are to understand the whole–part relation, the connection between levels, and perhaps even dichotomies in general. Like Magnusson (1995; chap. 3, this volume), I view such dichotomies and either-or propositions in science as shackles impeding progress and insight. In my view, a synthesis is needed that embraces contradictions.

In addition, I briefly describe how two essential aspects of individual functioning—intention and learning—may be incorporated into the present law-based approach to understanding human behavior. Such an approach attempts to reconcile individual diversity with features of behavior (albeit limited) that are common to us all. Finally, I sketch several main themes or core principles that stem from the laws of human coordinated behavior—so-called coordination dynamics—that have been identified through empirical and theoretical research over the last two decades or so. These principles represent a first attempt to explore the meaning of coordination dynamics in the broader context of human experience and activity.

One overall goal I have is to put clothes (in the sense of spelling out the theory–experiment relation) on sometimes vague, even mystical new ideas from so-called "complexity theory," such as self-organization, emergence, and symmetry-breaking. This, and related terminology, is frequently invoked in a metaphorical fashion. But science demands that we go beyond metaphor by checking the validity of concepts, usually by observation and experiment. As we reach the end of a century in which remarkable achievements have been made by reductionist science, I believe it is time to eliminate the tension between reductionistic and holistic thinking. Understanding ourselves depends on it.

## SOME ELEMENTARY CONCEPTS OF PATTERN FORMATION IN NATURE

*Self-Organization.* In a wide variety of systems that exchange matter, energy, and information with their surroundings, spatiotemporal patterns arise spontaneously as a result of a large number of nonlinearly interacting components. Although the word "self-organization" is used (abused, possibly) in a wide variety of scientific contexts, it is restricted here to the spontaneous formation of pattern and pattern change in so-called open systems that are far from equilibrium. How far from equilibrium, no one really knows. Self-organization means there is no "self" inside the system responsible for emergent pattern. Rather, under certain conditions, the system organizes itself. There is no ghost in the machine, instructing the parts how to behave.

That the organism is an open system is one of the two essential criteria for life postulated by Francis Crick in *Of Molecules and Men* (1966), yet it has received much less attention in biology than Crick's other criterion, the need for organisms to reproduce and pass on "copies" of themselves to their descendants. Here we see a dichotomy between a complex system's natural ordering tendencies and the need (certainly in living systems) to guide that order in specific ways. The computer—an organized system constructed by human beings—and the computer metaphor with its attendant constructs (programmed instructions, encoding, decoding, central processing unit, etc.), have amplified this dichotomy in fields ranging from psychology to molecular genetics. To some, the dichotomy doesn't exist because self-organization is irrelevant. The molecule is the message. The organism is an information-processing device. I will say more about this later on.

**Collective Variables.**     Emerging patterns are characterized by collective variables or what physicists call an order parameter (e.g., Haken, 1983). Collective variables are relational quantities that are created by the cooperation among the individual parts of a system. Yet they, in turn, govern the behavior of the individual parts. This is sometimes referred to as *circular causality*, the consequences of which have yet to be fully appreciated in a number of scientific fields (e.g., materialist views of mind). In self-organizing systems the stranglehold of linear causality is broken. At best, simple cause–effect relations are the exception, not the rule. One can intuit why the concept of collective variable is central to a science of complex living systems. The reason is that interactions in such systems are so complicated that understanding may be possible only in terms of system-specific collective variables. I hesitate to call these "macroscopic quantities" because the identification of collective variables depends on the level of description. What is "macro" at one level (or for a given scientific discipline) may be "meso" or "micro" at another.

**Control Parameters.**     These are analogous to what a social or behavioral scientist might call an independent variable. But the concept is entirely different, and the implications for experimental design in the social, behavioral, and cognitive sciences far reaching (Kelso, 1990). In physical systems, control parameters refer to naturally occurring environmental variations or specific experimental manipulations that move the system through patterned states and cause them to change. In fact, you only know for certain you have identified a control parameter if, when varied, it causes the system's behavior to change qualitatively or discontinuously. Qualitative change does not mean that quantification is impossible. To the contrary, qualitative change is at the heart of self-organized pattern formation and, provided care is taken to evaluate system timescales (e.g., how quickly a control parameter changes relative to the typical time of the system to react to perturbations; see Kelso & Schöner, 1987), quantitative predictions ensue that may be, and have been, tested experimentally. I discuss some of these later in the chapter.

*(Nonequilibrium) Phase Transitions.* When a continuous change in a control parameter crosses a critical value, the system's behavior may change qualitatively or discontinously. Such qualitative changes always arise due to *instability.* Instability is the dynamical mechanism underlying spontaneous, self-organized formation of patterns and pattern change in nature's open systems. In such systems that are open to material and communicational exchanges with their environment, these are called *nonequilibrium* phase transitions (the term preferred by physicists) or bifurcations (the mathematical term used in dynamical systems theory). Because all living systems are dissipative, and dissipative systems always contain fluctuations (Einstein's famous fluctuation–dissipation theorem) I have followed the physicists' terminology (Haken, 1983; Kelso, 1984; Kelso & Haken, 1995). Moreover, this way of trying to understand the functional behavior of living things goes beyond mere metaphor or mathematical curiosity. In biological self-organization, fluctuations are always present, constantly probing the stability of existing states and allowing the system—through the mechanism of fluctuation enhancement—to discover new collective states whether of behavior (Kelso, 1984; Kelso, Scholz, & Schöner, 1986; Schöner, Haken, & Kelso., 1986) or the brain (Fuchs, Kelso, & Haken, 1992; Kelso et al., 1991, 1992; Wallenstein, Kelso, & Bressler, 1995).

*Collective Variable Dynamics.* The patterns that emerge at such nonequilibrium phase transitions are defined as attractors (stable fixed points) of the collective variable dynamics. That is, the collective variable may converge in time to a certain limit set or attractor solution, a so-called nonequilibrium steady state. Stable fixed point, limit cycle, and chaotic solutions—as well as a variety of other transient and irregular behaviors (see following comments) are thus possible in the same system, depending on the values of control parameters (and their dynamics).

## Comments on Complexity

*Definitions of Complexity.* According to a May 6, 1997, article in *The New York Times* by George Johnson (see also Horgan, 1996) researchers on complexity are still trying to struggle with the definition of complexity, as if defining it were a precondition for studying it. Science still cannot define life, but that has not prevented major discoveries in the biological sciences. The same, I expect, will be true of "consciousness" and other tantalizing subjects of interest to contemporary science. Definition is not a necessary precondition for discovery. Johnson and others wonder how the essence of complexity can be captured and quantified in a precise and objective way. Yet one of the most fascinating results from complex systems research in the last 20 years is that the key quantities that characterize the behavior of complex living systems (collective variables or order parameters) are *function* or *context-dependent*. This does not mean that every possible context a system finds itself in requires a new collective variable or order parameter. Rather, the same order parameter and the same order parameter dynamics have been shown to apply over a range of contexts. For example, many studies have shown that a phase-like quantity captures the complex, time-varying coupling between different kinds of things (e.g., fireflies, heart cells, neurons, limb movements, brains, lovers, etc.; see Kelso, 1995). One of the most profound impacts of the "new sciences of complexity" (to some of us in the trenches they are not so new) is that the key to understanding ourselves lies in the complementary nature of objective physical description and the no-less-fundamental, apparently subjective context-dependence of living systems. The sciences of life and mind rest on this complementarity (Kelso, 1997).

***Types of Complexity.*** These elementary concepts of pattern formation represent one of nature's main themes for handling complexity and are at the core of what some call "emergent properties." One can intuit that enormous *material complexity* (very many microscopic subsystems) is compressed near instabilities giving rise to lower dimensional behavior that is described by the dynamics of collective variables. The collective variable dynamics are essentially nonlinear, a consequence of which is rich *behavioral complexity,* including phase transitions, chaos, and stochastic features (Kelso,1988). Complicated transient phenomena typical of "messy systems" are also possible, though a great deal of care needs to be taken to distinguish them as real (not artifactual) phenomena.

***Order–Disorder/Stability–Instability/Integration–Segregation.*** To be both viable and flexible, complex living systems must be neither too rigid nor too plastic. Experiments, analysis, and theory suggest that they are *metastable* (Friston, 1997; Kelso, 1995). This means that biological systems tend to lie in between order and disorder, stability and instability. For the brain, this means a balance between integration (areas of the brain acting together in time) and segregation (areas of the brain acting independently). Complexity measures are highest between these regimes of dynamical behavior (Tononi, Sporns & Edelman, 1994). Of course, from the present perspective it behooves science to identify the collective or pattern variables in order to characterize the nature of functional integration, its stability, and so forth. Nevertheless, a recurring theme in complex systems expressed by the "duals" in the heading is that one should not assume living things are stable, in any asymptotic sense. As a consequence there is a need to appreciate the limitations of conventional experimental designs and statistical tools such as analysis of variance. Long-range correlations, for example, are of both practical and conceptual importance in complex systems: they arise precisely because complex systems live near critical points where competition between ordering and disordering influences is finely balanced (Bak, 1996; Iberall & Soodak, 1978; Stanley, 1971). Recent studies have demonstrated the existence of long-range correlations in human perception (Tuller, Ding, & Kelso, 1997) and timing behavior (Chen, Ding, & Kelso, 1997; Treffner & Kelso, 1997, 1999), and a case can be made that long-term correlations capture the adaptive behavior of many complex organizations, from physiologic to socioeconomic. The essential idea is that continuous adjustive changes at lower levels (such as the replacement of cells in the body or the coming and going of employees in a large company) help maintain the functional stability of the system as a whole. Long-range, power-law correlations mean that change is occurring on all scales simultaneously. It is the relation between the magnitude of change and the rate of occurrence that follows a power law (many small amplitude changes, fewer medium ones and very few large ones). The origins and mechanisms of such phenomena are as yet unknown and pose a challenge to the sciences of complexity. For living systems to "live" near critical points suggests that control parameters are tuned to just the right values. Self-organized systems may even tune themselves to stay near critical points, a notion that Bak, Tang, and Wiesenfeld (1987) call *self-organized criticality* ( SOC). To me, the basic idea behind SOC is a natural extension of nonequilibrium phase transition theory in physics (cf. Haken, 1983). It suggests that in complex systems one should always be looking to identify the opposing forces or tendencies that underlie metastability. Self-organized criticality is another way of saying that complex systems have access to and thereby can change their own control parameters.

**Selection and Instability.** It has been suggested that many features of the development and functioning of the brain are governed by selectionist mechanisms (Edelman, 1987; Edelman & Tononi, 1996). Darwinian (natural) selection results in the differential reproduction of "fitter" individuals, that is, those whose variations better adapt to the environment or successfully compete with others. Edelman and his colleagues have emphasized like processes of selection upon variation in his theory of neuronal group selection (TNGS). Thus, instead of ignoring observed fluctuations and variance in neuroanatomy and neural dynamics, TNGS brings them on center stage, as essential to biological function. This is entirely consistent with some of the principles of self-organization described above. Selection, however, is not unique to biology. Instability and transitions in all nonequilibrium systems (alive or not) arise because of competitive forces that result in the amplification and selection of a given pattern or mode of organization (and the elimination of others). Empirical evidence for selection qua pattern forming instabilities has accumulated over the last 20 years at several levels of brain and behavioral function (see Kelso, 1995, for a review). In a number of specific cases the pattern selection equations have been identified (see Haken, 1996, for a review). Such generic mechanisms of pattern selection and change appear to complement Darwinian selection and its various extensions to the development and functioning of the brain by Edelman and colleagues. Here again, theories of selection and self-organization—merely because they arise in different disciplines, biology and physics respectively—should not be viewed as either-or propositions. In fact, Darwinian selection is assumed to act on already organized entities (e.g., genes, cells, organisms). The theory of self-organization addresses the origins of such integrated entities.

**"Agent" Dynamics.** A popular notion among complexologists is that every system—from economies to brains—has "agents," whose interaction on the basis of simple rules can lead to complex behavior. Anthills and bird flocking are favorite examples. Analogies to business organizations are rampant. A powerful theme emerging from such intuitions is that surface complexity arises from deep simplicity (Gel-Mann, 1994; Holland, 1995). In a sense this is no more than a restatement of physics that the diversity of the world around us is due to a small number of fundamental forces and their interactions, supplemented by historical contingency. When we deal with complex systems, however, it is a mistake (or at least a convenient fiction) to assume that our agents are simple (a typical strategy is to take a complicated entity such as a gene or a neuron, and code it as a sequence of 1's and 0's in a computer simulation). Rather, the "agents" or individual components are complex entities in their own right, whose individual dynamics have to be understood in detail. Moreover, the interactions between these agents may be complicated, web-like, and continuously modulated by many factors, both internal and external. Thus, at least one other major theme needs be struck, namely that deep (material) complexity (consider, for instance, the manifold connections among diverse neuron types in the nervous system, the large number of neurotransmitters, hormonal influences, etc.) may give rise in a self-organized fashion to surface (behavioral) simplicity and/or surface complexity (Kelso, 1988, 1995). Think of what is going on in the nervous system at multiple levels when we walk or talk, emote, think, and remember.

# FINDING DYNAMICAL LAWS IN COMPLEX LIVING SYSTEMS

*The Problem of Identifying Relevant Variables.* A cogent remark in Magnusson (1995) is that many, if not most of the variables studied in empirical studies of development are hypothetical variables (e.g. intelligence, aggression, hyperactivity, etc) that run the risk of reification. Collinearity among variables is typical. In open, many-particle physical systems, from which the elementary concepts mentioned earlier stem, the identification of key collective variables or order parameters is less of a problem, mostly because these systems are familiar and the parts of which they are composed are homogeneous. This enhances the ability to uniquely define and objectively describe relevant quantities. Living systems, however, are hierarchically organized; the component elements and connections among them are heterogeneous; and the relevant variables are always context-, task-, or function-dependent.

How does one find relevant variables in such complex, living systems? And which can one reasonably discard as not relevant? This is precisely the problem that confronted me over 20 years ago in my efforts to understand the control and coordination of systems containing very many degrees of freedom. Put bluntly, given ~$10^3$ muscles, ~$10^2$ articulating joints, and a nervous system with ~$10^{14}$ neurons and neural connections, how can coordinated behavior like walking or talking emerge from a system of such complexity? The conventional approach of unraveling the material substrate component by component in such a complex system is clearly untenable. An alternative strategy was required that should specify what empirical steps need to be taken. These steps, if fully carried out at both collective and component levels, should allow different levels of description to be connected. A possible limitation here is the restriction to a laboratory frame of reference. However, some of the same steps may be adopted in other contexts such as observational or epidemiological studies. For example, qualitative change may be used to infer relevant quantities in more naturalistic settings. Where many variables may be changing collinearly, the ones that change abruptly are likely to be the most informationally meaningful, both for the phenomena of interest and our understanding of them (Kelso, 1994).

*Experimental Windows.* The first, perhaps hardest, step is to find or invent experimental model systems that prune away the details but retain the essence of the real-world problem. I call this the Galilean strategy. By studying balls rolling down an inclined plane and abstracting away friction Galileo was able to understand a great deal about planetary motion. To be honest, there is no formula or recipe that may be applied to this step. Moreover, the choice of a level of description is the scientist's and can only be made with informed insight. Nor, I believe, is this an issue of "top-down" versus "bottom-up". The first step at any level of description, whether one is studying biomolecular processes or social behavior, requires the identification of relevant variables and their dynamics (equations of motion).

***Focus on Qualitative Change.*** Science always needs special entry points that enable understanding as well as appropriate abstractions. It is necessary to prune away irrelevant details while retaining the essentials. Newton did not give us the equations of motion for a leaf falling from a tree. Somewhat counterintuitively, but entirely consistent with theories of pattern formation, the focus here is on nonlinear qualitative change. Why qualitative change? The reason is that qualitative change allows us to clearly distinguish the (collective, pattern) variables that define the states of a system. If a complex system is changing smoothly and linearly it is hard to distinguish the variables that matter, so-called state variables, from those that don't. As state variables, they matter to the system itself, as well as to the scientist trying to understand or theoretically model the system. Moreover, near critical points various theoretically motivated measures are available to test predicted features of self-organization (this is discussed later). The underlying processes governing a state's stability, flexibility, and selection may thus be uncovered near critical points. Remember, in complex living systems one typically does not know the relevant (i.e., collective) state variables a priori, or the dynamical laws governing them. Within the present framework, this is one of the main scientific goals and the basis of understanding.

***The Modeling Step.*** Finding collective state variables or order parameters is the "yin" of the complex systems strategy. The "yang" is identifying the control parameters that move the system through these collective states and cause them to change. Knowing the collective variables and control parameters enables one to obtain the lawful dynamics—the equations of motion that describe the stability and change of the system's states on a given level of description.

***Next Level Down: The Individual Components.*** The steps alluded to here may all be repeated at the level of the individual components. Ideally, their state variables and dynamics have also to be identified empirically. In general, in complex systems it is difficult to isolate the components and study their dynamics. The reason is that the individual components seldom exist outside the context of the functioning whole, and have to be studied as such.

*Derivation and Emergence.* A final but nontrivial step is to derive collective states and their dynamics from the, in general, nonlinear coupling between the individual components. This is what some people call "emergence," and it allows us to see how different levels are connected. But there is no mystery here, just a lot of hard work usually involving a close collaboration between people with very different skills (e.g., in theoretical physics, applied mathematics, biology and psychology) that stresses as intimate a connection between theory and experiment as possible.

## Comments on Dynamics

*The Tripartite Scheme.* From the preceding discussion, it should be clear that no level is any more or less "fundamental" than any other. A complete description at the collective variable level requires three adjacent tiers: The boundary conditions and control parameters that establish the context for a particular phenomenon; the collective level and its dynamics; and the component level and its dynamics. I call this the "tripartite scheme." The physicist Atlee Jackson calls it "one level down," but the basic idea is the same.

*Macro–Micro.* Relatedly, the intuition is that in complex systems the best one can do is derive a given phenomenon from the level below. There are no absolute "macro" or "micro" levels. The component level may be "macro" for one scientist and "micro" for another. For example, a group of neurons in one area of the brain with a characteristic frequency response may couple with another like group under a particular set of conditions. In the present terminology, the coherent integrated activity between the groups constitutes a collective level of description. The individual activity of each group constitutes the component level. But it is easy to see that the group or ensemble may constitute a collective activity with respect to levels of description below, for example, individual neuronal properties. Dynamics is the language of understanding and transcends levels. In every case, however, dynamics must be filled with content, that is, dynamics of collective variables, control parameters, and so forth, that have to be identified one way or another in order to learn how things work.

*Linkage Across Levels.* Notice that the descriptors at each level are always different from each other. To use a most extreme case, the typical description of the nervous system differs greatly from the typical description of behavior. One is in the language of "internal" variables, the other is in the "external" language of overt behavior. But without commensurability of description, how is it possible to see the connection between the two? The language of dynamics serves to bridge different domains. Recent work shows that once the laws are known at the behavioral level, it is possible to derive them from the dynamics of neural populations and their excitatory and inhibitory interactions (Jirsa, Fuchs, & Kelso, 1998). Linkage across levels of description or observation is thus by virtue of shared dynamics (see Kelso, 1995).

*Examples of Empirically Identified Collective Variables.* I restrict discussion to a few examples that have been identified via the strategy spelled out here. By doing so, speculation is limited to a minimum. But there is reason to believe that there are many candidates for collective variables in complex, living systems. The task is to find them. Murray Gel-Mann is often quoted as saying that the "first step" in complexity research is to identify a system's regularities. But what is the research program? I have already offered a specific strategy aimed at systematically identifying the key variables characterizing behavioral patterns or regularities on a given level of description. This strategy has been found to work especially well near points of qualitative change.

For the behavior of complex, multidegree-of-freedom systems that evolve in time, the relative phase between interacting components has been identified as a key collective variable or order parameter (Kelso, 1995). The reason is that the relative phase characterizes stable functional relationships among component parts. The individual "components" may be fireflies, heart cells, neurons in vertebrate and invertebrate central pattern generators, finger and limb movements, neurons in the mammalian cortex giving rise to synchronization, even people engaged in a common task. Such coordinative coupling realized through a phase relation is ubiquitous in biology in many activities and at different levels.

In tasks that require adjustments in space such as trajectory formation, amplitude adjustments in the components are also crucial, the ratio of which may act as an order parameter (Buchanan, Kelso, & DeGuzman, 1997; DeGuzman, Kelso, & Buchanan, 1997). When events in the brain are monitored in space using a number of different recording techniques (optical dyes, high density electrode and SQuID [Superconducting Quantum Interference Device] arrays, etc.) they may be decomposed into a set of spatial patterns and time-varying amplitudes. The spatial modes then act as order parameters (Fuchs, Kelso, & Haken, 1992; Jirsa, Friedrich, Haken, & Kelso, 1994; Kelso & Fuchs, 1995; Kelso et al., 1991, 1992, 1998). The "microscopic" basis of these order parameters and their time-dependent dynamics can be derived from basic properties of neurons and their connectivity which give rise to neural ensemble dynamics (Jirsa, Fuchs, & Kelso, 1998). In all cases but the last, the actual equations of collective variables are phenomenological, a situation not unlike where physics was 70 years ago. After it was discovered that matter consisted of atoms, it might have seemed straightforward to derive the macroscopic properties of matter directly from the individual atoms. Only much later, however, did it become possible (and then only in a few cases such as ferromagnets and lasers) to derive the equations governing macroscopic behavior from a more microscopic theory.

Developmental (Thelen, Kelso, & Fogel, 1987; Thelen & Smith, 1994), cognitive (Port & van Gelder, 1995), and social psychologists (Vallacher & Novak, 1997) have been attracted to the present approach. In the former, the developing system is viewed as a dynamic system in which patterns of behavior act as collectives—attractor states—of the component parts within different environmental and task contexts. Development has been depicted as a landscape of collective variables against time (Thelen, 1995). Thus far, this is metaphorical and the difficult task of actually identifying collective variables, the control parameters that act on them, and the collective variable dynamics (not to speak of the component level) has yet to be accomplished in the developing organism for even a single task or functional context. The same can be said for work that posits an existing "movement repertoire" on which selection acts (Sporns & Edelman, 1993). So far, only in the cases of acquiring perceptual-motor coordination (Zanone & Kelso, 1992, 1997) and learning new speech sounds (Case, Tuller, & Kelso, in press) has it been possible to identify an individual's initial "attractor landscape" ( so-called intrinsic dynamics) prior to learning, and to track how it changes during the learning process. Importantly, the intrinsic dynamics turn out to be unique to each learner. How new information (the task to be learned) does or does not match (cooperates or competes) each person's preexisting dynamics determines the nature and form of the learning process (Kelso, 1995).

## LAWS FOR REGULARITIES:
## AN ELEMENTARY EXAMPLE

In general terms some of the key level-independent attributes of living things are:

> *Synergy:* on most levels, the individual parts of a system are coupled together as functional units, thereby making it possible to coordinate a system with many heterogeneous components using only a few controls.
>
> *Multifunctionality:* in a given context, multiple forms of behavior can be generated by the same set of anatomical or functional components and for the same parameter value(s). The property of multifunctionality is seen at many scales, from pleiotropic genes and peptides to neural pattern generators.
>
> *Stability:* the ability to produce the same behavior despite perturbations from the (internal or external) environment (see comments on allostasis by Carlson and Earls, chap. 15, this volume).

*Invariance of function:* the ability to realize the same goal using materially different components and a multitude of pathways.

*Flexibility:* the ability to switch from one mode of behavioral organization to another according to circumstances and/or the ability to recruit new components (and suppress others) to meet internal or external demands. Switching is based on stability considerations and may be viewed as a selection mechanism, that is, as a means of favoring one mode of organization over another.

These, and several other features (such as primitive memory) were identified in specific experiments and later captured in an elementary nonlinear law of coordinated behavior, the predictions of which were checked experimentally (for review, see Schöner & Kelso, 1988). This dynamical law, progressively established in a series of detailed experiments and theoretical steps, contains three essential kinds of parameters (see equation in Fig. 5.1): one that reflects whether the individual components are the same or different ($\delta\omega$); one that reflects external or internal factors (control parameters, $\lambda_1, \lambda_2$) that govern the strength of coupling between the components, and one that reflects the fact that all real systems contain noise or fluctuations ($\zeta_t$) of a given strength $Q$. Experiments showed that the relevant collective variable describing the synergy or spatiotemporal ordering between individual components was the relative phase, $\varphi$. For high values of the coupling ratio, $\lambda_1/\lambda_2$ both modes of behavioral organization coexist, the essentially nonlinear property known as bistability (Fig. 5.1, left). Bistability (or, in general, multistability) confers *multifunctionality* on the system. That is, at least two forms of behavior are possible for exactly the same conditions. Notice that each is stable over a range of coupling, though the degree of stability may change. In the stable region of its dynamics, for example, near the stable fixed points (solid circles) on the left side of Fig. 5.1, the system's behavior will be restored despite any slight perturbation. As the coupling ratio is decreased, however, the system switches from one mode of behavior to another (Fig. 5.1, middle). Near the critical point, the slightest fluctuation will kick the system into a new form of stable organization.

We may refer to this spontaneous transition as a form of pattern selection or decision making that underlies the flexibility of the system's behavior (the acronyms CEVA, SVI, and ASA will be discussed later). Switching is due to instability: under certain conditions (i.e., for certain values of control parameters) one mode of behavioral organization is less stable than another. The less stable mode dies out, only to be replaced with another more stable behavioral organization that is able to persist under the new conditions. Notice in Fig. 5.1, that if the direction of control parameter values changes after this transition, the system stays in this more stable mode. Thus the system exhibits *hysteresis*, a primitive form of memory.

$$\dot{\phi} = \delta\omega - \lambda_1 \sin\phi - \lambda_2 \sin 2\phi + \sqrt{Q}\xi_t$$

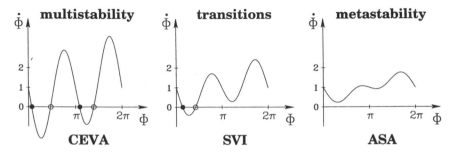

FIG. 5.1.   An empirically validated elementary law of behavioral coordination.

## Comments on Dynamical Laws

*Predictors of Change.*   The stability of a given behavioral organization is portrayed in Fig. 5.1 by the slope of the function where it crosses the *x*-axis. The negative slopes near $\varphi = 0$ and $\varphi = \pi$ indicate these are stable and attracting states (solid circles). Points at which the slope is positive through the *x*-axis are unstable, repelling states (open circles). Thus, the left part of the figure shows that two different behavioral organizations are stable under the same set of conditions, one near $\varphi = 0$ and one near $\varphi = \pi$. Notice the following predicted features of change: In the middle part of the figure the stable behavioral organization near $\varphi = 0$ has shifted to a higher value. Change occurs, but the shifted behavioral organization is still stable. The slope around this shifted state, however, is less than before, meaning that the shifted state is less stable than before. Quantities like the mean and variance of the collective variable, $\varphi$ have allowed this prediction to be quantitatively checked (Schöner & Kelso, 1988). In Fig. 5.1 the stable behavioral organization near $\varphi = \pi$ has totally disappeared. Mathematically, the function has lifted off the *x*-axis—called a saddle-node or tangent bifurcation—meaning that there is no longer any stable state near $\varphi = \pi$. The flattening of the function and the disappearance of the antiphase state is due to loss of stability. Predicted features of loss of stability are critical slowing down and critical fluctuations. These predictions are easy to intuit. As the slope flattens, the system will take increasingly longer to recover from a small perturbation. Thus the local relaxation time is predicted to take longer and longer as the instability is approached (critical slowing down). Similarly, the variability is expected to increase owing to the flattening of the function near the transition point (critical fluctuations). All of these predicted effects have been confirmed in a wide variety of different experiments and are open to investigation in many other systems. The take-home message is: Whether you see smooth change or abrupt, nonlinear change depends on where the system lives in the space of its parameters. Thus, on the left part of Fig. 5.1, for a large range of control parameter values, the behavior of the system changes very little. But then, as shown in the middle part of the figure, even a small change in the control parameter causes a bifurcation or phase transition which produces a large qualitative change in behavioral organization.

On the right side of Fig. 5.1, there are no longer any stable states in the system, where the term "stable" is used in the usual mathematical sense of asymptotic stability. Due to changes in control parameters or coupling ratio, the entire function has lifted off the $x$-axis. Note, however, that the function retains its curvature; there is still attraction to, or remnants of, previously stable states (so-called *metastability*). This effect is entirely due to broken symmetry in the dynamics, which is a result of the fact that the individual parts of the system or their properties are not the same (given by the $\delta\omega$ parameter in the equation). Due to broken symmetry, the system produces a far more flexible form of behavioral organization in which the individual components are free to express themselves yet still work together in a looser kind of harmony.

## SOME SPECIAL FEATURES OF REGULARITIES IN LIVING SYSTEMS

*Informational Coupling.* Although collective variables may characterize the behavioral organization among physical entities in complex living systems, they themselves are not usually physical quantities defined in physical dimensions such as mass, length, and time. Collective variables reflect the coupling relation between different kinds of things. The medium through which the parts are coupled does not have to be the same for the same regularity to arise or, significantly, for the same dynamical law to govern the system's behavior. Crucial experiments show that the same collective variables and the same collective variable dynamics describe and predict the coordination activity of a system (and lack of it) whether it be the central nervous system, an organism interacting with its environment, or even shared actions between organisms (Kelso, 1994; Turvey, 1994 for reviews). Such meaningful informational coupling (what could be more meaningful to a system than information that communicates the relation between its parts), constitutes an essential difference between self-organization in the living and the nonliving.

**Special Boundary Conditions.** In physical experiments, physicists set the initial and boundary conditions and study how behavior evolves in space and time. Then they check their observations against known laws. The boundary conditions on living things are quite special: they nearly always include the system's intentions or goals. One of the remarkable consequences of discovering that the regularities in living systems are informational in nature is that in order to modify or change the system's behavior, its boundary conditions must be expressed in terms of system-relevant (read, informationally meaningful) variables. Thus, if a system is to learn, any new information (say a task to be learned, an intention to change) must be expressed in terms of the system's existing/current dynamics. Remember, these dynamics are at least metastable and possess memory. They correspond to the system's set of predispositions or preexisting responses prior to learning. The positive benefit of identifying relevant collective variables is that one now knows which variable is modifiable and therefore what to modify. Information is not lying out there as mere data. Rather, information is meaningful only in terms of the individual's existing capabilities. The foregoing statements are not mere intuitions. They are grounded in empirical studies and theoretical modeling of learning and intentional change (for review, see Kelso, 1995, chaps. 5 & 6).

**Implications.** A number of interesting implications for learning and development follow from this research. One is that change may take the form of highly abrupt transitions depending on how new information cooperates or competes with the existing (so-called intrinsic) dynamics of the learner. Another is that the learner's existing capabilities and predispositions place real constraints both on what can be learned and how it is learned. Conversely, the best learning environment is one that is structured in terms of those constraints (which, as stressed here, must be identified). The teacher must tune in to the child's preexisting capabilities and modify them. The implications for education policy (and learning theory) are apparent: the individual learner is the primary unit, not the group (although in line with the notion of level-independent dynamics, if the group is collectively organized around exactly the same information, then it may constitute a significant unit, but now at the group level of analysis).

For so-called "learning organizations," the notion of intrinsic dynamics says that you had better know the metrics of the "fitness landscape" if you want to climb up it. For foreign policy, you had better know the variables that matter and the internal dynamics of the system you are trying to change before you intervene. Said internal dynamics are a product of historical and cultural factors. They are ignored at the policymaker's peril.

## GENERAL THEMES FROM THE LAW-BASED APPROACH

What lasting and durable themes, if any, emerge from these tentative efforts to identify laws of behavioral pattern formation and change in complex living systems? Laws, of course, do not have to possess any meaning at all for either the individual or society. The fundamental laws of physics presumably do not, although the philosophical foundations of quantum mechanics may be an exception. In contrast, the laws that characterize regularities in human behavior seem full of meaning. Whereas classical physics defines its variables in terms of a mechanical system, that is, $n$ mass points possessing position and momentum in a space of $3n$ dimensions, the coordination law shown in Fig. 5.1 is defined in the space of meaningful, function-specific collective variables.

Obviously, if one is trying to understand something as complicated as the coordinated behavior of human beings, or the lack of it, one must be prepared to make a fool of oneself. I believe several core themes arise from the law-based approach that may provoke new (or different) patterns of thought. The first, which might be called the *principle of Coexisting Equally Valid Alternatives (CEVA)* stems from the multistability property of the elementary dynamical law shown in Fig. 5.1. Notice again on the left side of the figure that there are two stable fixed points (solid circles) for exactly the same conditions, a simple form of multistability which, as already noted, is called bistability. If we accept that bistability is a fundamental and essentially nonlinear feature of the behavioral dynamics, what might it mean? Surely it means what it says: For any specific situation or context, several alternative solutions coexist. This, I suspect is actually the general case in living systems, and may be one of the hallmarks of their complexity. One-to-one relations between cause and effect may thus be the exception, not the rule. The CEVA principle embraces simple dualisms and dichotomies. Indeed, a failure to appreciate this essentially nonlinear principle may be a potential source of human conflict, as, for instance, in the inability to recognize ideological alternatives. Though the essence of wisdom and tolerance, the CEVA principle is not taught in our schools. Marriages fail because of it. Typical either-or, hypothesis testing approaches in science are the very antithesis of the CEVA principle, which seems to embody Bohr's complementarity interpretation of quantum mechanics (but now, notice, at the "macroscopic" scale of living things). Whether you see a wave or a particle depends on what you choose to measure. Both views are equally valid, complementary representations of reality.

A second principle stems from the (apparently universal) fact that the (essentially nonlinear) dynamics contain both attractive (stable) and repelling (unstable) fixed points (open and closed circles in Fig. 5.1) which mutually coexist. I call this the *principle of Coexisting Opponent Tendencies (COT)*. For a system to be maximally flexible, adaptive, and creative, processes normally in competition with each other must coexist. The stable must coexist with the unstable. Life, as the poets have always told us, is suspended between contradictions. Depending on circumstances, opposing tendencies can sometimes collide and give rise to new ways of thinking and acting. Notice in the empirically validated law shown in Fig. 5.1, the disappearance of the stable organization near $\varphi = \pi$ is because a stable fixed point (an attractor) and an unstable fixed point (a repeller) collide, causing a so-called saddle-node bifurcation. It is the tension between opposites, stability and instability, that produces a new behavioral organization. More generally, it is this tension that, when pushed to the extreme, may lead to a new outlook.

To survive and prosper, living systems must be neither too rigid nor too plastic. I call this the *Attraction Sans Attractors principle (ASA)*. A better name might be the Principle of the In-Between (PIB). In the metastable regime of the behavioral dynamics (right side of Fig. 5.1) there are no longer any attractors (stable fixed points), though there is still attraction to where the attractors used to be. The reason is that the functioning parts of the system now have a tendency to do their own thing while still retaining a tendency to cooperate. This is likely the way large organizations work best: By allowing a certain degree of individual expression and autonomy they are able to function as a looser, more effective form of global organization. This tendency for the parts to do their own thing (individual variation) must coexist with the tendency for the system to harmonize as a whole. Likewise, in the world of politics, any trends toward global integration and homogenization must acknowledge, and live with, the parochialism of individual states. Metastable dynamics (and more generally the ASA or PIB principle) provides insight into a longstanding either-or conflict in brain theory, namely, how global integration, in which parts of the brain are locked together, is reconciled with localized, independent action of individual brain areas. Metastable dynamics says that the brain, like other complex living systems, uses a subtle blend of both. Otherwise it would be trapped in a stable collective state from which it is difficult to escape. Or, it would be too disordered, with the parts acting independently of each other. The ASA principle asserts that the greatest complexity lies between regular and irregular behavior. Interestingly, theoretical measures of brain complexity (Tononi, Sporns, & Edelman, 1994) bear this idea out. ASA arises as a natural consequence of empirically observed metastable dynamics. It is, literally, a principle of the "in between."

A fourth principle deals with the essential nature of "stability–change" in living things. I tentatively call it the *principle of Selection Via Instability (SVI)*. The SVI principle is manifest in the form of bifurcations in the observed dynamics (Fig. 5.1, middle). In SVI, variability plays a central role and pattern selection is a self-organized process, occurring without homunculus-like agents. Although instability is a universal mechanism for self-organized pattern formation and change in complex systems in nature, it has yet to be incorporated in evolutionary theory, even by advocates of punctuated equilibrium (Eldredge & Gould, 1972); and it is ignored as a mechanism by currently popular selectionist theories of brain function (Edelman, 1987). Selectionist theories often use the term self-organization but do not exploit instability for selection purposes, even though much evidence suggests that organisms do. Such theories have been criticized precisely because they lack a physical/mathematical foundation (Eigen, 1994). Many believe that selection is the *sine qua non* of biology. Still others wonder whether there is a new principle of order formation in life beyond Darwin (Kauffman, 1995). I offer SVI in the interest of resolving such conflicting visions and because it is a unifying principle of selection that applies to all self-organized systems whether living or not. And it may lie at the heart of human behavior.

## ACKNOWLEDGMENTS

Much of the work described herein was supported by NIMH, NSF, and The Human Frontier Science Program.

## REFERENCES

Bak, P. (1996). *How nature works*. New York: Springer-Verlag.

Bak, P., Tang, C., & Wiesenfeld, K. (1987). Self-organized criticality: An explanation of 1/f noise. *Physical Review Letters, 59,* 381.

Buchanan, J. J., Kelso, J. A. S., & DeGuzman, G. C. (1997). The self-organization of trajectory formation: I. Experimental evidence. *Biological Cybernetics, 76,* 257–273.

Case, P., Tuller, B., & Kelso, J. A. S. (in press). Learning to hear new speech sounds: A dynamical approach. *Journal of the Acoustical Society of America.*

Chen, Y., Ding, M., & Kelso, J. A. S. (1997). Long-term memory processes (1/f$\alpha$ type) in human coordination. *Physical Review Letters, 79,* 4501–4504.

Crick, F. (1966). *Of molecules and men.* Seattle: University of Washington Press.

DeGuzman, G. C., Kelso, J. A. S., & Buchanan, J. J. (1997). The self-organization of trajectory formation: II. Theoretical model. *Biological Cybernetics, 76,* 275–284.

Edelman, G. M. (1987). *Neural Darwinism: The theory of neuronal group selection.* New York: Basic Books.

Edelman, G. M., & Tononi, G. (1996). Selection and development: The brain as a complex system. In D. Magnusson (Ed.), *The life-span development of individuals: Behavioral, neurobiological, and psychosocial perspectives.* New York: Cambridge University Press.

Eigen, M. (1994). Selection and the origin of information. *International Review of Neurobiology, 37,* 35–46.

Eldredge, N., & Gould, S. J. (1972). Punctuated equilibria: An alternative to phyletic gradualism. In T. J. M. Schopf (Ed.), *Models in paleobiology.* San Francisco: Freeman.

Friston, K. (1997). Transients, metastability and neuronal dynamics. *Neuroimage, 5,* 164–171.

Fuchs, A., Kelso, J. A. S., & Haken, H. (1992). Phase transitions in the human brain: Spatial mode dynamics. *International Journal of Bifurcation and Chaos, 2,* 917–939.

Gel-Mann, M. (1994). *The quark and the jaguar.* New York: W. H. Freeman.

Haken, H. (1983). *Synergetics, an introduction: Non-equilibrium phase transitions and self-organization in physics, chemistry and biology.* Berlin: Springer.

Haken, H. (1996). *Principles of brain functioning.* Berlin: Springer.

Holland, J. H. (1995). *Hidden order.* Reading, MA: Addison-Wesley.

Horgan, J. (1996). *The end of science.* Reading, MA: Addison-Wesley.

Iberall, A., & Soodak, H. (1978). Physical basis for complex systems: Some propositions relating levels of organization. *Collective Phenomena, 3,* 9–24.

Jirsa, V. K., Friedrich, R., Haken, H., & Kelso, J. A. S. (1994). A theoretical model of phase transitions in the human brain. *Biological Cybernetics, 71,* 27–35.

Jirsa, V. K., Fuchs, A., & Kelso, J. A. S. (1998). Connecting cortical and behavioral dynamics: Bimanual coordination. *Neural Computation, 10,* 2019–2045.

Kauffman, S. A. (1995). *At home in the universe.* New York: Oxford University Press.

Kelso, J. A. S. (1984). Phase transitions and critical behavior in human bimanual coordination. *American Journal of Physiology: Regulatory, Integrative and Comparative, 15,* R1000–R1004.

Kelso, J. A. S. (1988). Dynamic patterns. In Kelso, J. A. S., Mandell, A. J., & Shlesinger, M. F. (Eds.), *Dynamic patterns in complex systems.* Singapore: World Scientific.

Kelso, J. A. S. (1990). Phase transitions: Foundations of behavior. In H. Haken & M. Stadler (Eds.), *Synergetics of cognition* (pp. 249–268). New York: Springer-Verlag.

Kelso, J. A. S. (1994). The informational character of self-organized coordination dynamics. *Human Movement Science, 13,* 393–413.

Kelso, J. A. S. (1995). *Dynamic patterns: The self-organization of brain and behavior.* Cambridge, MA: MIT Press.

Kelso, J. A. S. (1997). The "other" sciences of complexity. *Complexity, 3,* 7–8.

Kelso, J. A. S., Bressler, S. L., Buchanan, S., DeGuzman, G. C., Ding, M., Fuchs, A., & Holroyd, T. (1991). Cooperative and critical phenomena in the human brain revealed by multiple SQUIDS. In D. Duke & W. Pritchard, (Eds.), *Measuring chaos in the human brain* (pp. 97–112). Singapore: World Scientific.

Kelso, J. A. S., Bressler, S. L., Buchanan, S., DeGuzman, G. C., Ding, M., Fuchs, A., & Holroyd, T. (1992). A phase transition in human brain and behavior. *Physics Letters A, 169,* 134–144.

Kelso, J. A. S., & Fuchs, A. (1995). Self-organizing dynamics of the human brain: Critical instabilities and Sil'nikov chaos. *Chaos, 5,* 64–69.

Kelso, J. A. S., Fuchs, A., Holroyd, T., Lancaster, R., Cheyne, D., & Weinberg, H. (1998). Dynamic cortical activity in the human brain reveals motor equivalence. *Nature, 392,* 814–818.

Kelso, J. A. S. & Haken, H. (1995). New laws to be expected in the organism. In M. Murphy & L. O'Neill (Eds.), *What is life? The next 50 years.* Cambridge, England: Cambridge University Press.

Kelso, J. A. S., Scholz, J. P., & Schöner, G. (1986). Nonequilibrium phase transitions in coordinated biological motion: Critical fluctuations. *Physics Letters A, 118,* 279–284.

Kelso, J. A. S., & Schöner, G. (1987). Toward a physical (synergetic) theory of biological coordination. *Springer Proceedings in Physics, 19,* 224–237.

Magnusson, D. (1995). Individual development: A holistic, integrated model. In P. Moen, G. H. Elder Jr., and K. Lüscher (Eds.), *Examining lives in context.* Washington, DC: American Psychological Association.

Nicolis, G., & Prigogine, I. (1989). *Exploring complexity.* New York: W. H. Freeman.

Port, R. F., & van Gelder, T. (1995). *Mind as motion: Explorations in the dynamics of cognition.* Cambridge, MA: MIT Press.

Schöner, G., Haken, H., & Kelso, J. A. S. (1986). A stochastic theory of phase transitions in human hand movements. *Biological Cybernetics, 53,* 442–452.

Schöner, G., & Kelso, J. A. S. (1988). Dynamic pattern generation in behavioral and neural systems. *Science, 239,* 1513–1520.

Sporns, O., & Edelman, G. M. (1993). Solving Bernstein's problem: A proposal for the development of coordinated movement by selection. *Child Development, 64,* 960–981.

Stanley, H. E. (1971). *Introduction to phase transitions and critical phenomena.* New York: Oxford University Press.

Thelen, E. (1995). Motor development. *American Psychologist, 50,* 79–95.

Thelen, E., Kelso, J. A. S., & Fogel, A. (1987). Self-organizing systems and infant motor development. *Developmental Review, 7,* 39–65.

Thelen, E., & Smith, L. B. (1994). *A dynamic systems approach to the development of cognition and action.* Cambridge, MA: MIT Press.

Tononi, G., Sporns, O., & Edelman, G. M. (1994). A measure for brain complexity: Relating functional segregation and integration in the nervous system. *Proceedings of the National Academy of Sciences, USA, Vol. 91,* 5033–5037.

Treffner, P. J., & Kelso, J. A. S. (1997). Scale invariant memory during functional stabilization. In M. Schmuckler (Ed.), *Studies in perception and action IV.* Mahwah, NJ: Lawrence Erlbaum Associates.

Treffner, P. J., & Kelso, J. A. S. (1999). Dynamic encounters: Long-memory during functional stabilization. *Ecological Psychology, 11,* 103–137.

Tuller, B., Ding, M., & Kelso, J. A. S. (1997). Fractal timing of phonemic transforms. *Perception, 26,* 913–928.

Turvey, M. T. (1994). From Borrelli (1680) and Bell (1826) to the dynamics of action and perception. *Journal of Sport and Exercise Psychology, 16,* S128–S157.

Vallacher, R. R., & Novak, A. (1997). The emergence of dynamical social psychology. *Psychological Inquiry, 8,* 73–99.

Wallenstein, G. V., Kelso, J. A. S., & Bressler, S. L. (1995). Phase transitions in spatiotemporal patterns of brain activity and behavior. *Physica D, 84,* 626–634.

Zanone, P. G. & Kelso, J. A. S. (1992). The evolution of behavioral attractors with learning: Nonequilibrium phase transitions. *Journal of Experimental Psychology: Human Perception and Performance, 18,* 403–421.

Zanone, P. G. & Kelso, J. A. S. (1997). Coordination dynamics of learning and transfer: Collective and component levels. *Journal of Experimental Psychology: Human Perception and Performance, 23,* 1454–1480.

# METHODOLOGICAL
# CONSIDERATIONS

# 6

# The Modern Synthesis in Psychological Development

Jerome Kagan
Harvard University

The deep premises of every scientific discipline determine, in a major way, the specific experiments and formal analyses that investigators implement. Hence, when one or more of these premises is not faithful to nature, progress is blocked and scientists must wait for wise scholars to detect the flaw in the web of ideas, describe it with clarity, and prescribe a constructive solution.

David Magnusson is acknowledged to be the titular head of a small group of psychologists who are performing this intellectual service for those who study the complex problem of variation in human development. In lucid, gracefully written papers, chapters, and books, Magnusson has articulated some of the imperfect assumptions that guide much research in personality development. One of these flawed ideas is the belief that individuals should be compared on a single, continuous dimension and that persons differ from each other only quantitatively, not qualitatively. A corollary of this traditional assumption is that the relations among a set of psychological variables should be similar across individuals of different gender, class, and temperament and the magnitude of a correlation between two variables, for example, social anxiety and school achievement, is a sound basis for inferring how those variables function within every individual. This is rarely the case.

· Magnusson and colleagues Lars Bergman (Bergman & Magnusson, 1990, 1991) and Robert Cairns (Magnusson & Cairns, 1996) have documented the fact that these assumptions do not fit nature. Their critique is reminiscent of Wittgenstein's (1984) comment that the language of philosophers can be likened to a tight shoe that deforms the foot on which it is placed.

Magnusson has suggested several fruitful ideas that are in closer accord with the facts. First, the proper unit in theoretical and empirical work in development is not a variable but a person or a class of persons with a history acting at a particular time and in a particular context. One cannot generalize about classes of people without specifying the situation in which an agent behaves (Magnusson, 1992a, 1992b; 1995).

No scientist should make broad generalizations about psychological processes, like fear or aggression, without specifying the class of agent— whether a boy or a girl, a child or an adult, a lower- or an upper-middle-class individual—as well as the context in which the agent is acting. This principle holds for strains of rats as well as humans. The popularity of abstract human psychological qualities in which class of agent and context are unspecified derives part of its power from a historically popular premise in Western philosophy, which Bertrand Russell favored but Alfred North Whitehead did not, that every object and, by inference, each person can be viewed in isolation as an entity with properties that are not altered by the circumstances in which it is observed. In this frame, a person is treated as if he or she were a stone that retained shape, color, and hardness, whether on a path or at the bottom of a lake.

Although the shape, color, and hardness of a stone do not change, the stone is also a member of a functional category that might be called "potentially dangerous objects." However, membership in that category requires an agent and a situation and it is not obvious in the stone lying on a path. Almost all current theoretical terms for cognitive, emotional, and behavioral processes in humans are functional categories, like potentially dangerous stones. Thus, it is an error to write about processes, whether they be introversion, emotionality, or fear, as if they were inherent qualities of a person that were preserved unaltered across all situations and during an indefinitely long epoch. This is the seminal insight that Magnusson brings to the social sciences.

Research from my laboratory on a large longitudinal sample of children illustrates the validity of some of these new premises. The first example affirms the influence of temperament and the importance of positing categories of children. We studied more than 450 children who were first observed at 4 months of age. The episodes in the 4-month battery included: the mother looking down at the child, a recording of voices speaking short sentences, brightly colored mobiles containing one, three, or seven moving objects, a cotton swab dipped in dilute butyl alcohol applied to the nostrils, recording of a female voice speaking syllables at three levels of loudness, and last of all, the mother returning to look down at her child for a final minute of observation (Kagan, 1994).

About 20% of the infants showed a combination of vigorous motor activity combined with frequent fretting and crying. These infants were classified as possessing a temperamental disposition we call *high reactive*. About 40% showed the opposite profile of low motor arousal and no fretting; they were classified as *low reactive*. These differences in motor activity and distress could be mediated by inherited differences in the excitability of the amygdala and its projections to the ventral striatum, cingulate, and central gray (Kagan, 1994). If this hypothesis were true, the two groups should be very different in the display of fearful or avoidant reactions to unfamiliar incentives in the second year. These infants were observed again at 14 and 21 months as they encountered unfamiliar people, rooms, and procedures. The combination of vigorous motor activity and distress, which defines the high-reactive infant, was a better predictor of fearful, subdued behavior in the second year than either motor behavior or distress considered alone. Thirty-five percent of the high reactives showed high levels of fear ($\geq 4$ fears) at both 14 and 21 months, compared with 4% of low reactives. In contrast, 36% of low reactives were minimally fearful at these two ages (less than two fears) compared with 3% of high reactives (Kagan, 1994).

These facts support the importance of positing categories of individuals. When we treated the motor arousal and distress scores as separate continuous variables, the prediction of fear at 14 and 21 months was less effective than when we treated the children who were high or low on both responses as belonging to two different categories. It is of interest that, in an independent study, 10-month-old infants who showed frequent irritability combined with infrequent smiling and laughter became inhibited and fearful at 3 years of age. However, the prediction of inhibited behavior was less powerful when irritability or smiling was considered alone (Parke, Belsky, Putnam, & Crnic, 1997).

When samples of 74 high-reactive and 119 low-reactive infants were observed at 4½ years of age as they interacted with an unfamiliar woman, the former were more subdued and less spontaneous than the latter (see Table 6.1). The high reactives made significantly fewer comments and smiles than the low reactives ($F(1,189) = 13.35$, $p < .001$ for smiles; $F(1,189) = 4.03$, $p = .07$ for spontaneous comments). But the correlation between the 4-month motor and irritability scores, considered separately, and spontaneous comments and smiling at 4½ years were nonsignificant (see Schmidt, Fox, Rubin, Sternberg, Gold, Smith, & Schulkin, 1997, for a partial replication).

A month later these children were observed as they played in trios of unfamiliar children of the same sex and age in a large playroom with all three mothers present. After the initial 25 minutes of free play, the parents

TABLE 6.1
Mean Scores on Comments, Smiles, and Social Behavior for High- and Low-Reactive Children

| Variable | Low-Reactive Girls | High-Reactive Girls | Low-Reactive Boys | High-Reactive Boys |
|---|---|---|---|---|
| Spontaneous comments | 47.0 | 37.5 | 60.8 | 44.1 |
| | (46.7) | (35.7) | (47.7) | (42.1) |
| Smiles | 28.5 | 19.6 | 26.9 | 16.5 |
| | (21.1) | (17.7) | (17.5) | (12.6) |
| *Behavior with peers* | | | | |
| Uninhibited | 53% | 26% | 81% | 27% |
| Intermediate | 30% | 27% | 15% | 27% |
| Inhibited | 17% | 48% | 4% | 46% |

left the room for 5 minutes. A small number of children (12%) protested the parental departure. After the parents returned, the examiner reentered the room and placed an attractive toy on the rug. Low-reactive children took first possession of the toy more often than high-reactive children (43 vs. 16%); 46% of the high reactives never played with the toy, usually because they were unable to compete successfully with one or both of the other children who retained possession during the 3 minutes it was in the room. By contrast, only 27% of the low reactives failed to gain access to the toy ($\chi^2$ $2df = 13.7$, $p < .001$).

In addition to the continuous scores representing total time in proximity to the parent and total time staring at one or both of the unfamiliar children while isolated, the reactions to parental departure and behavior with the novel toy also reflect signs of uncertainty. A coder studied the videotapes of these sessions and placed each child into one of three categories based on all of their behaviors over the entire session. One category reflected a bold, sociable, uninhibited style (51% of the group). A second category reflected a shy, timid, inhibited style (26% of the group), and a third category applied to children who were not clearly inhibited or uninhibited (the remaining 23% of the children). An independent coder studied the videotapes of 24 subjects and made the same three category classifications. The two coders agreed exactly on 75% of the classifications and no child classified as inhibited by one coder was classified as uninhibited by the other.

Table 6.1 reveals that 67% of the children who had been low reactive infants, but only 27% of high reactives, were uninhibited in the play session with peers. By contrast, only 10% of low reactives but 46% of high reactives were inhibited ($\chi^2 = 35.5$, $p < .001$). Thus, social behavior with unfamiliar children clearly differentiated the two temperamental groups.

It is important to appreciate that the high and low reactive temperamental categories predict avoidant, fearful, or subdued behavior in specific contexts; namely, unfamiliar situations that contain strangers, discrepant objects, or unusual procedures. High-reactive infants are not fearful in all environments nor do they develop conditioned fears more easily than low-reactive infants.

A small group of 10 children who were high reactive at 4 months, very fearful in the second year, subdued with the examiner at 4½ years, and inhibited with the unfamiliar peers, appeared to be a qualitatively distinctive group. Six of these 10 had seven or more fears when they were evaluated at 14 months of age (only 8% of the remaining high reactives had fear scores that high), and five or more fears at 21 months (compared with only 21% of the remaining high reactives).

Examination of the stability of inhibited and uninhibited behavior displayed by the two temperamental types revealed that only 13% of the high reactives (10 children) were highly fearful at 14 and 21 months and, in addition, extremely subdued with the examiner and shy/inhibited with peers at 4½ years of age. However, not one high-reactive infant actualized the opposite profile of minimal fear in the second year and affective spontaneity and uninhibited social behavior with peers at 4½ years. Among low reactives, 10% (12 children) were fearless in the second year and spontaneous and uninhibited at 4½ years, while only one low reactive infant developed a profile of consistently high fear and a subdued inhibited style at 4½ years. I infer from these facts that environmental events can shape high- or low-reactive infants into phenotypes that begin to resemble the average child. But the original temperamental bias constrains the likelihood that a high- or low-reactive infant will develop, and maintain over 4 years, the seminal characteristics of the other temperamental type.

The fact that only a small proportion of high- and low-reactive children preserved their theoretically expected profile motivates an interest in children with extreme scores. The importance of extreme scores is seen in many settings. For example, 4 phobic adults (of a group of 28) who experienced the return of symptoms, after showing improvement with treatment, had significantly higher baseline heart rates than the remaining 24 patients (Grey, Rachman, & Sartory, 1981).

One child from our large longitudinal sample showed a unique developmental profile. This boy frowned spontaneously many times during the 4-month infant battery. Spontaneous frowns are rare among infants, especially when there is no stimulus in the perceptual field. This boy also retained a sad facial expression for periods as long as 30 seconds. He emitted a sharp scream when presented with the moving mobiles—no other infant behaved that way. When he was 14 months, he maintained his earlier

sad facial expression throughout the 90-minute battery, had several tan-
trums, and refused many episodes by screaming. When he was 3½ years
old, he seemed calmer, but in a play situation with one other unfamiliar boy
of the same age, he showed a single act of impulsive aggression not observed in any other child. After 10 minutes in the room with the other boy
and the two mothers, he picked up a wooden pole, went to the plastic tunnel
in which the other boy was sitting, and began to strike the tunnel with force
in the place where the other boy was sitting. This unprovoked act of
aggression to an unfamiliar child is a rare event in this context, especially
when both mothers were in the room. However, most psychologists observ-
ing this child for the first time would probably dismiss the single act of
aggression as reflecting greater-than-normal frustration on that day. In light
of his history, however, I suspect that the impulsive act of aggression
reflects a deep psychological quality and that this boy is a member of a rare
temperamental category.

There is a statistical procedure that permits one to detect the presence
of very deviant subjects. This procedure examines simultaneously the $t$
distributions and the intercorrelations among the variables of interest. The
procedure assigns each subject a value that represents a sum of that
subject's squared deviations from each of the weighted means. That sum is
called delta. A probability value can be assigned to each delta and, therefore, to each subject that represents how deviant each subject is from the
rest of the sample on the variables of interest. We applied that analysis to
a sample of 171 high- and low-reactive children. The six variables were:
continuous scores of motor activity, crying, vocalization, and smiling (gathered during the 4-month battery) and the number of fears the child displayed at 14 months and again at 21 months. The distribution of delta (for
these 6 variables) is illustrated in Fig. 6.1. The distribution is skewed to the
right and delta values greater than 32 are statistically significant at $p < .05$;
values greater than 81 are significant at $p < .01$. Although high-reactive
infants comprised only 40% of the sample, they made up 90% of the extreme
outliers; 10 high reactives but only 1 low-reactive child had a delta score
greater than 32.

We then asked whether the 10 high reactives with delta scores greater
than 32 were different at 4½ years from the remaining 55 high reactives, as
well as from the 106 low reactives, on spontaneous comments and smiles.
These 10 deviant children were either very quiet or very talkative when they
were 4½ years old. Six children made fewer than 7 comments or more than
99 comments; only 16% of the remaining high reactives had such extreme
scores ($\chi^2 = 7.9$, $p < .01$). Two of the 10 did not smile at all.

These 10 deviant children also had higher sitting heart rates and larger
average differences in temperature between the fingertips of the right and
left index finger. The temperature differences are due to differential con-

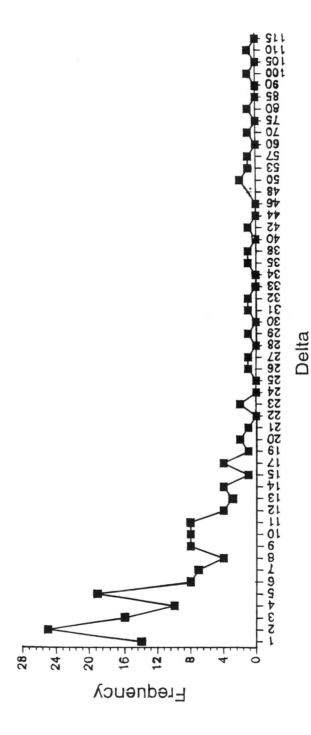

FIG. 6.1. The distribution of delta scores for high- and low-reactive infants.

striction or dilation of the arteriovenous anastomoses on the fingertips. Thus, large asymmetry values imply greater sympathetic lability. Other differences between these 10 and the other children are more clinical in nature. Seven of the 10 cried in fear when they were 4 months old while listening to the recording of the voices speaking sentences (compared with only 32% of the remaining high reactives) ($\chi^2 = 3.9$, $p < .05$).

One girl was extremely aggressive to the examiner during the 4½ year battery. A second deviant child was surly and extremely resistant as an accompaniment to her initially shy behavior. A third child was one of the most fearful 4½-year-olds we observed. He did not look at the examiner and showed an odd pronation of his hands when he was anxious. This boy refused to draw a picture of himself and placed a few dots on the blank piece of paper. No other child refused this simple request. These data suggest, but do not prove, that these 10 children should be regarded as qualitatively different from the remaining high reactives and certainly different from all of the low reactives.

Our data continually point to the potentially fruitful discoveries that follow a search for individuals who have special profiles. Measurement of the temperature of the fingertips of the index and ring fingers of both hands were made on high- and low-reactive children at 4½ years while they were watching films (Kagan, Arcus, Snidman, Peterson, Steinberg, & Rimm-Kaufman, 1995). When we examined the mean asymmetry on the ring finger for all 83 children with adequate data, there were no significant differences between high and low reactives nor any relation to earlier fearfulness. However, when we restricted the analysis to those children whose temperature asymmetries were in the top and bottom quartile, that is, a very cool right ring finger ($< -.48$ C) versus a minimally cool right ring finger ($> -.10$ C), more high reactives were in the former group. And among the high reactives who showed distress fears at 21 months, 35% had very cool right ring fingers, while 50% of the low reactives who showed no distress fears had minimally cool right ring fingers.

Gender provides another illustration of the importance of categories. The sexes differ biologically as well as in socialization experiences; therefore, some dependent variables might have different psychological meanings in the two sexes. This expectation is affirmed in the results of a potentiated startle procedure administered to 6 to 8 year olds. After electrodes were placed on the orbicularis oculi of the left eye, each child was told that he or she would experience a brief, but strong, blast of air directed at the larynx. This stimulus is not painful but all children find it aversive. Each child sat facing a green light bulb, and was told that when the green light was on, there might be a brief blast of air. However, when the green light was off, there would not be an air blast. No child ever experienced a second blast of air. The children were then administered a series of six acoustic probes (50 msec of white noise at 92 dB); the probe usually causes a reflex eye blink. Our purpose was to determine if the magnitude of the blink was larger when the acoustic probe was delivered while the green light was on, as the children were anticipating the aversive blast of air. The results point to the importance of gender.

The girls who showed larger magnitude blinks when the green light was on than when it was off—that is, they showed a potentiated startle reflex— were among our most inhibited girls (see column "Pot" in Table 6.2). Fifty percent were subdued with the examiner and 75% were reported by their mothers to be fearful in many situations. However, the boys who showed potentiation of the eye blink when the green light was on were among our most uninhibited, minimally fearful boys. This surprising fact suggests that the magnitude of potentiation of the eye blink may have different signifi-cance for boys and girls, and potentiation of startle to a stimulus that warns of an aversive event may not be a useful index of fear, anxiety, or uncer-tainty in all children.

TABLE 6.2
Behavioral Differences Among Three Startle Groups (by Gender; Percent of Each Group)

| Variable | Notblink | Girls NotPot | Pot |
|---|---|---|---|
| Age 7 | | | |
| Percent inhibited with examiner | 0 | 17 | 50 |
| Percent not inhibittedwith examiner | 28 | 41 | 12 |
| Mother Report | | | |
| Percent shy | 27 | 50 | 50 |
| Percent fears | 45 | 33 | 75 |

| Variable | Notblink | Boys NotPot | Pot |
|---|---|---|---|
| Age 7 | | | |
| Percent inhibitedwith examiner | 10 | 11 | 9 |
| Percent not inhibited with examiner | 40 | 33 | 64 |
| Mother Report | | | |
| Percent shy | 30 | 11 | 18 |
| Percent fears | 10 | 22 | 18 |

A final example of the differential meaning of well-defined responses for the two sexes is seen in the fact that high sympathetic tone in girls was associated with being quiet in an unfamiliar social situation (infrequent spontaneous comments), but among boys there was no relation between sympathetic tone and amount of talking with the examiner. We computed a mean standard score that averaged the standard scores for sitting and standing heart rate, sitting and standing heart rate variability, and sitting and standing systolic and diastolic blood pressure (8 variables in all). A high score implied that a child had a high and stable heart rate combined with high sitting and standing systolic and diastolic blood pressure values. Among girls, there was a negative correlation between this index of sympathetic tone and number of spontaneous comments ($r = -0.3$, $p < .05$). The higher the sympathetic tone, the quieter the girl was with the examiner. However, among boys there was no relation at all ($r = .09$). This same result was replicated on an independent sample of inhibited and uninhibited boys and girls who were assessed at 13 years of age. Thus, these data provide examples of the fact that the same variable—in this case sympathetic tone— can have different behavioral implications for the two sexes.

I have presented illustrations of the influence of temperament, the importance of specifying the class of agent and the context, the utility of categories, a willingness to award significance to extreme cases and, therefore, an appreciation of nonlinear psychological functions. It remains to provide an illustration of the influence of cultural context.

The social class in which children are reared exerts a profound effect on their development. It is difficult to find a cognitive or behavioral variable in children older than 5 years that is not correlated, to some degree, with the education and income of the parents. It is likely that low-reactive children who grow up in upper-middle-class families become very different adolescents from low reactives who are reared in lower-class homes. Most middle-class parents impose socialization demands on their free-spirited, uninhibited children and, as a result, these children are not likely to become conduct disordered or delinquent. However, low-reactive boys who grow up in a climate that is permissive of aggression and stealing are probably at greater risk for developing asocial syndromes.

There will never be a determinant relation between an underlying temperament and an adult psychological profile because historical and cultural contexts influence the details of the profile. The journals of the writer John Cheever (1993), who died in the second half of this century, and the biography of William James' sister Alice James (Strouse, 1980) who died 100 years earlier, imply that both writers inherited a very similar, if not identical, diathesis that favored a chronically dysphoric, melancholic mood. But Cheever, whose premises about human nature were formed when Freudian theories were ascendant, assumed that his melancholy was due to childhood experiences and tried, with the help of drugs and psychotherapy, to overcome the conflicts he imagined his family had created. By contrast, Alice James believed, with most of her contemporaries, that she had inherited her dour mood. And she concluded, after trying baths and galvanic stimulation, that because she could not change her heredity she wished to die. The historical context in which each of these creative writers lived exerted a profound influence on the coping strategies each selected and, by inference, on the quality of their emotional lives.

## CONCLUSIONS

The history of biology contains lessons for the younger behavioral sciences. First, one should specify the class of agent and the context in which a process or behavior is actualized. When biologists use the word "bleach," colleagues understand that the term refers to a pigment change in the cells of the retina produced by photic stimulation. Second, categories of children, not single variables, are the preferred concepts in theory. The concept of species, one of the most important ideas in evolutionary biology, is defined by a profile of characteristics, not by any single continuous dimension. Third, investigators should expect that relations among most psychological phenomena will be nonlinear. Rhythmic activity emerges in an ant colony only after the density of insects reaches a critical value (Goodwin, 1994).

Finally, the child's biology and environmental encounters interact continually. The industrialization of England produced darker tree trunks and the gradual replacement of light-colored moths with darker ones that were less salient targets to bird predators. In a similar vein, the environment acts on high- and low-reactive infants in different ways.

Doreen Arcus observed 50 high- and 50 low-reactive infants in their homes on five different occasions between 5 and 13 months of age. The analyses of the videotapes from these visits revealed that high-reactive children who had mothers who set limits and did not overprotect them were less fearful in the second year than high reactives whose mothers did not set consistent limits and overprotected them. The variation in these maternal behaviors had a minimal effect on the behavior of low-reactive infants.

However, the child's biology does set constraints. The data discussed earlier reveal that it is easy for a high-reactive infant to develop a phenotype that resembles that of the average child, but it is much more difficult to create environments that will make a high-reactive infant a consistently fearless, exuberant youngster. It is unlikely that T. S. Eliot's parents could have sculpted a personality that resembled that of Churchill, nor is it likely that Lyndon Johnson's family could have created an adult with the personality of Alfred North Whitehead. Such transformations recall the alchemy that 16th-century naturalists sought without success.

These data and conclusions are in accord with Magnusson's assumptions and his own rich corpus of empirical data. Most of Magnusson's colleagues recognize that he shares many qualities with Alfred North Whitehead. Whitehead believed that the entities that are participants in a functional relation form a unitary whole and the understanding of that unity changes as one learns more about it. Whitehead regarded the phenomena to which our symbolic concepts apply as more like a "pot of treacle" than steel balls—Bertrand Russell's cynical comparison of Whitehead's image of nature with his own. Finally, Whitehead never forgot the difference between a symbol and its referent. Ideas inferred from valid observations are the absolute bedrock of the empirical work that lasts. Words are simply dark shapes on paper.

## REFERENCES

Bergman, L. R., & Magnusson, D. (1990). General issues about data quality in longitudinal research. In D. Magnusson & L. R. Bergman (Eds.), *Data quality in longitudinal research* (pp. 1–31). Cambridge, UK: Cambridge University Press.

Bergman, L. R., & Magnusson, D. (1991). Stability and change in patterns of extrinsic adjustment problems. In D. Magnusson, L. R. Bergman, G. Rudinger, & B. Törestad (Eds.), *Problems and methods in longitudinal research: Stability and change* (pp. 323–346). Cambridge, UK: Cambridge University Press.

Cheever, J. (1993). *The journals of John Cheever.* New York: Ballantine.

Goodwin, B. (1994). *How the leopard changed its spots.* New York: Scribner's.

Grey, S. J., Rachman, S., & Sartory, G. (1981). Return of fear. *Behavioral Research and Therapy, 19,* 133–144.

Kagan, J. (1994). *Galen's prophecy.* New York: Basic Books.

Kagan, J., Arcus, D., Snidman, N., Peterson, E., Steinberg, D., & Rimm-Kaufman, S. (1995). Asymmetry of finger temperature in early behavior. *Developmental Psychobiology, 28,* 443–451.

Magnusson, D. (1992a). Back to the phenomena: Theory, methods and statistics in psychological research. *European Journal of Personality, 6,* 1–14.

Magnusson, D. (1992b). Individual development: A longitudinal perspective. *European Journal of Personality, 6,* 119–138.

Magnusson, D. (1995). Individual development: A holistic integrated model. In P. Moen, G. H. Elder Jr., & K. Lüscher (Eds.), *Examing lives in context: Perspective on the ecology of human development* (pp. 19–60). Washington, DC: American Psychological Association.

Magnusson, D., & Cairns, R. B. (1996). Developmental science: Toward a unified framework. In R. B. Cairns, G. H. Elder Jr., E. J. Costello, & A. McGuire (Eds.), *Developmental science* (pp. 7–30). Cambridge, UK: Cambridge University Press.

Parke, S. Y., Belsky, J., Putnam, S., & Crnic, K. (1997). Infant emotionality, parenting, and three year inhibition. *Developmental Psychology, 33,* 218–227.

Schmidt, L. A., Fox, N. A., Rubin, K. H., Sternberg, E. M., Gold, D. W., Smith, C. C., & Schulkin, J. (1997). Behavioral and neuroendocrine responses in shy children. *Developmental Psychobiology, 30,* 127–140.

Strouse, J. (1980). *Alice James.* Boston: Houghton-Mifflin.

Wittgenstein, L. (1984). *Culture and value.* Chicago: University of Chicago Press.

# 7

# Dialectics in Development and Everyday Life

R. A. Hinde

St. John's College, Cambridge
and Behaviour Research Group, Madingley, Cambridge, U.K.

The close interrelations between brain, mind, and body are increasingly recognised in psychopathology (e.g., Damasio, 1994), but in developmental and social psychology a holistic approach, although having a long history, has been slower to gain respectability. There are a number of reasons for this, among the most important being the success achieved by the analysis of variables across individuals, and the difficulty of generalizing across individuals from studies of the relations between variables within an individual. Yet the facts that people both function as, and see themselves as, integrated wholes, and that each physiological-psychological process is related to others, albeit in an idiosyncratic way, suggest a person-centred, holistic approach (Magnusson & Törestad, 1993; Rogers, 1980). "Each aspect of the structures and processes (perceptions, cognitions, plans, values . . .) takes on meaning from the role it plays in the functioning of the individual" (Magnusson & Törestad, 1993, p. 436). Relations among variables and their way of functioning in the totality cannot be assumed to be the same in all individuals.

Holistic research is not to be seen as in opposition to more traditional variable-centred studies, for the two approaches are complementary (Magnusson & Törestad, 1993; Mekos & Clubb, 1997). However, as described by Magnusson and Törestad, in addition to its person-centred approach holistic research brings together many desiderata at present characteristic of diverse other disciplines: the need to see individuals as active, functionally integrated wholes, the undesirability of using physics as a model, and the

need for accurate description of individual behavior in the real world, by
ethologists (Hinde, 1966; Lorenz, 1935; Tinbergen, 1951); the potential pitfalls
of generalizing across individuals by ecologists (Clutton-Brock, 1988; Krebs
& Davies, 1991); the necessity of recognizing the interactions between biological and psychological systems (insofar as they are seen as distinct) by
clinicians (Damasio, 1994); and the potentially misleading nature of linear
models and the need for categorization by developmental psychologists
(Kagan, 1994). In the work we have been doing in Cambridge on the social
behavior of preschool children, with sample sizes small enough to permit
detailed inspection of the data, we found that a categorization approach,
followed where possible by replication, is the most profitable procedure.
The categorization used was based on theoretical assumptions about the
relevance of the variables, and did not necessarily involve separate treatment of extreme groups. In other circumstances cluster analysis may provide the best route (Cairns, Bergman, & Kagan, 1998; Hinde & Dennis, 1986;
Hinde, Tamplin, & Barrett, 1993, 1995).

As characteristic of a holistic approach, Magnusson (1990, 1993) lays
special emphasis on interaction in development. Interactions take place at
many levels, "from the interaction between a cell and its environment in the
early stage of the development of the fetus, up to the interaction between
generations and their environments" (pp. 203–204). It is thus not surprising
that the term "interaction" is used to cover a broad spectrum of complexity.
Considering for the moment person–environment relations, note first that
the environment may have been actively selected or passively encountered.
One can immediately distinguish four types of interaction:

1. The environment is passive. Here the environment merely sets the
   scene or elicits the behavior.
2. The behavior results in a change in the perception of the environment,
   without change in the enviroment's physical nature. Accommodation
   to a bright light would be a simple example.
3. The behavior results in a change in perception of the environment
   because its physical nature has changed—for instance, when one
   switches on a light when entering a dark room.
4. The environment is constituted by another active agent or agents.

This brings one to a new level of complexity. Social behavior involves not
only processes within individuals, but also interactions between individuals,
and behavior within groups and societies. In such cases one must not only
treat the individual as a totality, but see the dyad and group in similar
terms. The totality of processes within each individual cannot be understood independently of those within the other, for the other is not simply
a passive part of the first's environment: both are active agents. Processes

within individuals, interactions between individuals, relationships, and groups together form a total system. Feedback and feed-forward effects ensure that similar principles apply to many interactions between intraindividual processes (Magnusson, 1996).

A variety of terms have been used to describe this complexity—for instance "transaction" (Pervin, 1968; Sameroff, 1975), or "reciprocal determination" (Bandura, 1978). Such terms were intended to indicate that interactions between individuals were not merely stimulus–response sequences. Yet traditional notions make it easy to lapse into stimulus–response ways of thinking. Even Magnusson (1990), who elsewhere clearly emphasized the complexity of the issues, wrote: "The best illustration of the reciprocity in person–environment interaction can be drawn from person–person interaction. . . . To a certain extent, the behavior of one individual influences the behavior of others, whose behavior in turn will affect the reactions and actions taken by the first, and so on" (p. 199). But an interaction between two individuals is much more than a chain reaction, and cannot be fully understood if the changes in expectancies, mood, and motivation that are intrinsic to its course, and the manner in which each interaction can create a new situation, are ignored. Each participant is continually influencing the other, so that the dynamic relations between them are *dialectical* in nature, leading to a new state or "truth" (see Shorter Oxford Dictionary).

Furthermore, development affects and is affected by the conditions of life (Kohn, 1977), and involves continuing dialectical processes within interactions, relationships, and groups. It also involves a continuing dialectic with the sociocultural structure of norms, values, beliefs, and so on; for culture is not a given, something static and "out there," but is being continually remoulded by the activities of people going about their lives. Individuals must be seen as purposeful and active agents, and groups, relationships, interactions, and even individuals must be seen in continuous creation, maintenance, or degradation through these dialectical relations (Hinde, 1979, 1997; Shanahan, Valsiner, & Gottlieb, 1997).

Thus the holistic approach will prove inadequate if it treats individuals and environment (or social companion) merely as stimuli for each other. Researchers must both look at the processes within each individual, and treat as totalities not only the individual but also the dyad, group, or society according to the task in hand. A similar approach, focusing specifically on developmental problems, has recently been advocated by Rogoff (1996), who emphasized that the development of an individual is inseparable from his or her involvement in sociocultural activity. "The usual unit of analysis has been the isolated individual, with research attempting to extract the individual from the milieu in order to determine what happens within the individual and then to consider which influences on the outside must be added" (p. 278), whereas "transitions in development can fruitfully be studied as transitions in people's participation in sociocultural activities" (p. 291).

The following discussion is intended to illustrate the dialectical nature of interaction, starting with interactions between whole organisms but leading to a consideration of intraorganismic psychological processes. Although the orientation is in part synchronic, the understanding of development demands an understanding of the nature of interaction at any one stage and over time.

## RHESUS MONKEY MOTHER–INFANT INTERACTION

I will start with a purely behavioral, mainly nomothetic approach, illustrated by some early data on rhesus monkeys.

The rhesus monkey mother carries her infant continuously for a week or two after birth, but the infant then spends progressively more time off her, and more of that time at a small distance from her. To understand the processes involved, it is necessary to be very precise about the questions being asked. It must be considered (a) whether mother or infant is primarily responsible for contact or proximity over successive age-periods, (b) whether changes in mother or changes in infant are primarily responsible for changes in contact or proximity, and (c) whether differences between mothers or differences between infants are primarily responsible for interdyad differences. In disentangling these issues, it is essential to take into account the relations between variables as well as the changes in the variables themselves, and to remember that the observational variables reflect the behavior of the dyad, not of each individual independently. The data are shown in Fig. 7.1 (Hinde, 1969; Hinde & Spencer-Booth, 1967; Hinde & White, 1974).

### Responsibility Within Periods

During the first week or two the mother is responsible for nearly all the nipple contacts and seldom rejects the infant's attempts to gain the nipple. The mother is thus initially primarily responsible for contact. As the weeks go by, the responsibility becomes progressively more the infant's: the mother initiates a smaller and smaller proportion of contacts and rejects the infant more often.

Responsibility for proximity can be assessed from the frequencies with which mother and infant approach and leave each other. (Approaches and leavings were recorded when the distance between infant and mother changed from less than to more than 60 cm—approximately the mother's arm's reach—by movement of one or the other animal). The difference between the percentage of approaches due to movement by the infant and the percentage of leavings due to movement by the infant gives an indica-

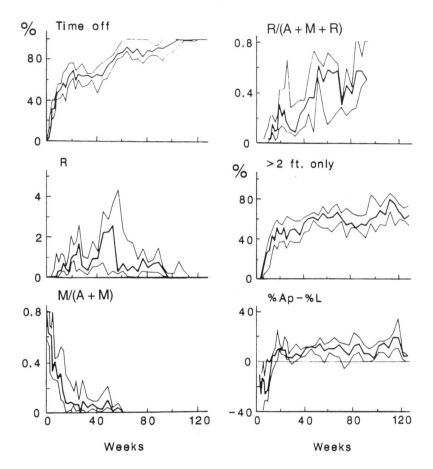

FIG. 7.1. Age changes in rhesus mother–infant interaction. Time off mother: number of half minutes in which infant was off mother as percentage of those observed. R: number of times infants were rejected by their mothers per unit time observed. M/(A + M): ratio of number of times infants were picked up by mothers on the mothers' initiative to total number of times they were picked up or accepted by them. R/(A + M + R): ratio of number of times infants were rejected to total number of times infants attempted to gain the nipple or were picked up by their mothers. >2 ft. only: Number of half minutes that infants spent more than 2 ft (approx 60 cm.) from their mothers as a percentage of the number of hlaf minutes in which they were off their mothers at all. % Ap - % L: Proximity Index, as explained in text. In each case the thick line represents the median and the thinner lines the interquartile range.

tion of the role of the infant in maintaining proximity. This is referred to here as the proximity index (Hinde & Atkinson, 1970). This index is negative during the infant's early weeks, indicating that the mother is primarily responsible for maintaining proximity, and then becomes positive, indicating that the infant is primarily responsible.

However, that is not all. After reaching a peak, the absolute frequency of rejections falls while the relative frequency rises. This indicates that one or both partners change behavior in accordance with that of the other: for instance, the infant may reduce its attempts to gain the nipple when it is rejected, each response leading to a different state.

Further evidence along these lines is provided by a more detailed examination of the course of bouts of contact and proximity between infant and mother. In the early weeks, the infant is more likely to terminate bouts of contact initiated by the mother than those initiated by the infant, while the mother is more likely to terminate bouts initiated by the infant. Similar relations apply in bouts off the mother. At about week 20 these relations disappear or are even reversed. This strongly suggests that the motivational states of infant and mother become adjusted to each other, or that each becomes better able to adjust its behavior according to the state of the other. At first each sometimes initiates a bout to which the other is not disposed, and so terminates it; later each is more attuned to the other's state.

## Responsibility for Age-Changes

A change over time in the amount of contact or proximity could be due to a change in mother, infant, or both. As shown in Table 7.1, if mother or infant responds more positively to the other, time off and time out of arm's reach will decrease. However, if the change is due to a change in the mother, the relative frequency of rejections and the proximity index would change in the same direction as time off or time at a distance, and maternal initiations would change in the opposite direction: the reverse would be the case if the change were due to the infant. Thus the correlations between time off and the relative frequencies of maternal rejections or initiations, and between proximity and the proximity index, indicate the relative importance of changes in mother or infant. The data (Table 7.2) indicate that the age changes are primarily due to changes in the mother. This might seem surprising, in that it is the infant who is changing physically, becoming more capable of looking after itself. But these data show that, even in the early weeks, although the mother is primarily responsible for the maintenance of contact and proximity, it is changes in the mother that are primarily responsible for the decrease of contact and proximity.

Of course, this does not mean that the changes in the mother arise endogenously. They may be initiated by changes in the infant's behavior

TABLE 7.1
Predicted Effects of Each of Four Types of Change in Mothers or in Infants on Direction of
Changes in Measures of Mother–Infant Interaction

| | Time off | M/(A + M) | R/(A + M + R) | > 60 cm. | %Ap–%L |
|---|---|---|---|---|---|
| Infant Mother ← | + | + | − | + | − |
| Infant Mother → | − | − | + | − | + |
| Infant Mother → | + | − | + | + | + |
| Infant Mother ← | − | + | − | − | − |

*Note.* The arrows indicate a change in the individual with which they are associated, such that the individual seeks proximity with its partner more or less. M/A + M refers to the proportion of contacts initialed by the mother, R/A + M + R to the proportion of contacts or attempted contacts that were rejected by the mother; > 60 cm. to the proportion of half-minute intervals in which the infant was out of the mother's arm's reach; and % Ap–% L to the difference between the proportion of approaches due to movement by the infant and the proportion of leavings.

TABLE 7.2
Rank Order Correltion Coefficients Between Median Values for all Individuals in Each Age Span

| | M/(A + M) | R/(A + M + R) | > 60 cm. | %Ap–%L |
|---|---|---|---|---|
| Time off | -.95** | — | +.98** | +.96** |
| | -.85* | +.54 | +.96** | +.94** |
| | -.53* | +.69** | +.74** | +.38 |
| M/(A + M) | | — | -.88* | -.73 |
| | | -.40 | -.74* | -.86* |
| | | -.42 | -.07 | +.07 |
| R/(A + M + R) | | | — | — |
| | | | +.50 | +.36 |
| | | | +.57* | +.63** |
| > 60 cm. | | | | +.79 |
| | | | | +.93** |
| | | | | +.57* |

*Note.* From upper left to lower right figures refer to weeks 1–6 ($N = 6$), 7–20 ($N = 7$), and weeks 21 on ($N = 16$). In some time intervals insufficient data were available for the coefficient to be calculated. Symbols as in Table 7.1.
\* - $p < .05$; \*\* - $p < .01$.

consequential on its development, which in turn depends on the mother. And, as we have seen, the infant may learn not to seek the nipple so often if it is rejected often. An effort must be made to understand the complicated dialectical relationship between mother and infant.

## Interdyad Differences

The same type of analysis can be applied to individual differences within any one period. The correlations in this case, shown in Table 7.3 are smaller than those seen in Table 7.2, and many are not significant. This indicates that differences between mothers and differences between infants are more equally important in contributing to the interdyad differences. However, the signs of the correlation coefficients change with age in a manner which suggests that differences were primarily due to differences between the mothers in the early weeks and to differences between both mothers and infants later.

While these data were obtained from captive groups, essentially similar relations have been found in a more natural situation (Berman, 1980). Of

TABLE 7.3
Correlation Coefficients Between Individual Mean Scores for the Weeks 1–6, 7–12, 13–18, and Weeks 20 and later (upper left to bottom right)

|  | M/(A + M) | R/(A + M + R) | > 60 cm. | %Ap–%L |
|---|---|---|---|---|
| Time off | -.56* | — | +.62** | +.04 |
|  | -.30 | +.41 | +.59** | +.50* |
|  | -.30 | +.13 | +.79** | -.14 |
|  | -.28 | -.44 | +.35 | +.01 |
| M/(A + M) |  | — | -.74** | -.90** |
|  |  | -.42 | -.53* | -.53** |
|  |  | -.36 | -.58* | -.06 |
|  |  | -.07 | -.05 | +.05 |
| R/(A + M + R) |  |  | — | — |
|  |  |  | +.72** | +.84** |
|  |  |  | +.26 | +.37 |
|  |  |  | +.20 | +.49 |
| > 60 cm. |  |  |  | +.26 |
|  |  |  |  | +.69** |
|  |  |  |  | -.11 |
|  |  |  |  | -.0 |

Note. In the first three cases the coefficient is based on 14-22 individuals. In the last case the figure is the median coefficient for eight individuals for all 6 or 8 week periods up to week 132. (For further explanation see Hinde, 1969.) Symbols as in Tables 7.1 and 7.2.

course the precise nature of the mother–infant relationship is known to depend on many factors including the parity, age, rank, and individual characteristics of the mother.

This same method can be applied to assess the bases of differences between groups of monkeys, or whether the effects of treatment are due more to effects on mothers or on infants, and even to the nature of the differences between a mother's relationships with twins. In the latter case, it is then essentially idiographic, though the totality examined involves the two dyads (Hinde, 1969).

Thus a nomothetic approach indicates that simplistic questions like "Who is responsible for the nature of the parent–child relationship?" need further analysis to be meaningful, and that the relationship is not simply a chain reaction, but dialectical. The developing relationship involves mutually determined changes in both partners, so that each provides a continuously changing environment for the other. The "central unit of analysis" must be the dyad, not the individual (Magnusson & Törestad, 1993), and it is the relations between variables that provide clues to development dynamics.

However, this sort of analysis still provides only a superficial view of the changes, and is limited to the behavioral level. Although further insights could be obtained by the application of single-subject longitudinal methods (Mekos & Clubb, 1997), the methods' success must depend on the variables chosen for study. In any case, it may be necessary to go beyond the behavioral level; and, although the data cited so far concern interactions within one relationship, in the real world each individual is involved in many relationships.

## PERSON AND SITUATION

Individuals may change their behavior according to the situation, or according to whom they are with. To cite an example from studies of 4-year-old children, behavior was recorded with mother and siblings at home, and with peers and teachers in preschool. Few of the rank order correlations between behavioral items comparable between home and school (e.g., friendly to mother, friendly to teacher, friendly to peer) were significant (13% for girls and 4% for boys; $p < 0.05$, one-tailed). In other words, children who were friendly in one situation were not necessarily so in another, or even with another partner in the same situation (Hinde et al., 1995).

Even more interesting, and indicating the need for an idiographic approach, is the fact that individuals differ in their cross-situational consistency (Block & Kremen, 1996). For example, 4-year-olds were selected (on the basis of maternal ratings backed up by observational data) as "shy" or "not shy" on meeting strangers in naturally occurring contexts. After screening, each child visited the laboratory where responses (verbal and nonverbal) to another female stranger were rated on a 9-point "social anxiety" scale (1–3, low; 4–6, medium; 7–9, high). Forty-three percent of the children were consistent—either "low" or "high" shy in both situations. By contrast, only 7% were high shy in one context but low shy in the other. A dimensional approach, in which either maternal or paternal ratings were correlated with laboratory ratings, yielded only modest correlations (.54 and .50 respectively). These correlations were almost identical for boys and girls, but the use of a categorisation approach revealed a sex difference. Of those girls who were initially categorised as shy in natural contexts, 58% were in the high shy category in the laboratory, while only 24% of boys shy in natural contexts were high shy in the laboratory ($\chi^2$, $p < .01$). Six of the nine inconsistent children were boys. All had been categorized as shy at home but low shy in the laboratory. As a group they differed significantly over a variety of measures from the low and medium shy boys, and all had presented problems in infancy. Three were Caesarean births, surrounded with anxiety (e.g. previous miscarriage, slow to breathe, etc.); one was a traumatic delivery (facially presented) with subsequent speech problems; and two had early appearing neurological problems, including suspected cerebral palsy not subsequently apparent (Stevenson-Hinde, 1998; Stevenson-Hinde & Glover, 1996). Thus, a categorization approach can lead one toward an idiographic analysis not only if it is based on individual characteristics in one situation (Hinde et al., 1993), but also if it is based on the cross-situational stability of such characteristics (Stevenson-Hinde, 1998; Stevenson-Hinde & Glover, 1996).

From a nomothetical perspective, a shortcoming in consistency in behavior across situations can be accounted for in terms of person by situation interaction (Endler & Magnusson, 1976): the situation elicits different facets of the personality. But that tells little about the processes involved. More should be known about the emotional–cognitive mechanisms that make such flexibility possible, as well as "the configuration and systematic connection of personality variables as these dynamically operate within a particular person" (Block, 1971, p. 13).

One important route to this end is to categorize individuals in terms of patterns of covariation across time with respect to a specified set of variables. Comparison of two such categories, or examination of exceptional individuals who fail to follow the development course of their peers, can give important information about the factors acting in, and the processes of, development (Block, 1971; Cairns, Bergman, & Kagan, 1998; Hinde & Dennis, 1986; Kagan, 1994; Shanahan & Elder, 1997). Magnusson & Cairns (1996) have rightly stressed that, in pursuing a holistic approach, psychology's hard-won gains in statistical rigour and empirical objectivity must not be compromised. But if an understanding of process is to be achieved, statistical rigour must be applied to variables whose relevance has been established by observation in real-life situations; and the pursuit of empirical objectivity must take account of the fact that the course of an interaction or relationship is determined at least as much by the perceptions of what happens by those involved as by what actually does happen. The next section indicates some of the complexity inherent even in a brief two-person interaction. This suggests another route that must be followed if such interactions are to be understood.

## THE DRAMATURGICAL PERSPECTIVE

A metaphorical approach useful for the understanding of interactions involves the dramaturgical perspective of Goffman (1959, 1967) and the symbolic interactionists (e.g. McCall, 1970, 1974). I offer no apology for resurrecting work published a few decades ago, as its insights are easily neglected in the pursuit of statistical purity. Goffman emphasized that, in an interaction, each individual not only conveys information in the conventional way, but also "gives off" messages that convey what sort of person he or she is and his or her expectations. Each uses the information provided by the other to surmise what to expect of him or her and what the other expects, and thereby each attempts to "define the situation." If the interaction or relationship is to proceed smoothly, both must define the situation similarly, with agreement about what they should do and not do together, cultural norms, values, and so on. The definition is usually worked out actively, progressively, and in part unconsciously.

Symbolic interactionists define a "character" as a person with a distinctive organization of personal characteristics in a particular context, and a "role" as a plausible line of action truly expressive of a "character." Each person may generate different characters in different contexts, and a number of "role identities," that is, a number of ways in which one likes to see oneself in that context or as occupant of a particular social position. These role identities are to be seen as hierarchically organized, with some more prominent than others. When two individuals meet, each displays a selection of role identities; each gives differential support to the role identities displayed, thereby influencing their relative prominence. Each tries to perceive the character underlying the role identities that the other displays, and devises a role for him- or herself that can best make use of what the other offers. To the extent that each gives the other "role support"—that is, confirms the other's role identity—the interaction or relationship is likely to continue.

This symbolic interactionist approach rings true, but lacks the support of hard data. However, it is important as a way of describing interactions so as to bring out their dialectical nature, and in calling attention to internal psychological processes that must be taken into account if the dynamics of interaction are to be fully understood. It shows that even a two-person interaction may involve both seeking for a goal (What sort of interaction is this going to be?), adjusting the goal (In this context I must behave in a subordinate manner), and pursuing a goal (How can I make this interaction go the way that seems best for me?). It thus provides some insight into the complexity involved, and also indicates that, within the dyad, the interaction must be seen as a totality with intrinsic feed-forward and feed-back processes. However, although it takes account of the influence of an active other on the course of an interaction, it does not go far enough in that respect—when two individuals come together in a close relationship, they change. There is more to a relationship, and even to an interaction, than the selection of roles; it is a process of creation. Furthermore, the emphasis in this metaphor is primarily (though not exclusively) on cognitive processes.

## TACKLING THE SELF

If the essential element in the holistic approach is to treat the individual as a totality, a first task must surely be to describe the nature of that totality. "An individual's view of himself or herself plays a central role in the process of interaction with the environment" (Magnusson, 1990, p. 201). That brings one directly to one of the most difficult issues in psychology—the nature of the "self." Because, as emphasized above, what matters in an interaction or relationship is not so much what the participants do as what they feel about it and what they perceive each other to be doing and feeling, subjective aspects cannot be disregarded. The challenge is to come to grips with them in a hard-headed way. An essential preliminary to that is a consideration of the nature of the self.

It is convenient first to distinguish between the "subjective self," which is outside conscious awareness, and the "objective self"—though the distinction may be of only heuristic value. It is the latter that will be focused on here (Lewis, 1992).

Because we perceive a certain continuity in our lives, and to the extent that we see the several aspects of our behavior as integrated, we find it convenient to postulate a "self" which continues across situations even though aspects of behavior, emotion, and cognition change. There is no need to ask what it means to say that someone "has" a self: the self is merely a convenient abstraction which represents an organized set of perceptions and helps tie together aspects of our relations with the social and nonsocial world (Rogers, 1980). Clearly, we could hardly have a concept of self without self-consciousness, and it may be that possessing self-consciousness carries with it a tendency to elaborate a concept of self—a propensity that may be realized in different ways in different cultures.

The only access to the self is through self-descriptions. A can know about B's behaviour, and to a certain extent about B's emotions, by watching B. But A can find out about B's self only by asking B. Indeed, "self" usually means a person's view of herself or himself. (Of course problems can arise. We say "She is not herself today" when no doubt she would say that she was. And that individuals like to be seen in a good light is an issue that need not detain us here. The operation of defence mechanisms arises later.) What an individual knows about himself or herself is mostly acquired from self-observation, or from perceptions of how others perceive her or him—that is, from how he or she interprets others' responses to him or her (Cooley, 1902; Mead, 1934; Sullivan, 1953). Most important are the perceptions of the views of others with whom he or she has close relationships, and especially members of the family of origin.

One's view of oneself in a particular situation is drawn primarily from narratives that represent sequences of events in that situation. Its construction is undoubtedly a complex process—the narratives may be characterized by adjectives, which may in their turn affect the narrative; and the goals, emotions, self-image, and so on relevant to that situation must be integrated, defensive processes often being involved.

How an individual sees himself or herself has considerable consistency. One sees oneself as the same person (the same "self") as one moves from context to context and through life. One can do this only because one's views of oneself at one time or in one situation are related to those views in other situations. A variety of processes contribute to this continuity. People tend to associate with similar others over the years, and thus maintain similar orientations. Within socially recognized partnerships, social norms and values provide constraints on behavior, so that couples may continually seek after an ideal relationship, or avoid situations in which disruption becomes a real possibility. And in everyday life there are powerful psychological mechanisms that help to maintain the self-concept. We tend to choose friends and situations that will confirm our self-concept; we attend selectively to evidence that confirms our current self-image, and discredit evidence that appears to contradict it (Backman, 1988). We even behave in ways that will channel the behavior of others in such a way that they will confirm our expectancies about ourselves (Snyder, 1984; Swann, 1987). The self thus develops and is maintained by a series of dialectical exchanges involving the individual's behavior, affect, cognitions, and relationships with others.

But although how an individual sees herself or himself has considerable consistency, there may be changes with age, with social status ("success has gone to his head"), and with the current situation at any one age.

McGuire and McGuire (1988) wrote: "A woman psychologist in the company of a dozen women who work at other occupations thinks of herself as a psychologist: when with a dozen male psychologists, she thinks of herself as a woman" (p. 102). In describing themselves, children and adolescents tended to emphasize passivity in relation to the home and activity in relation to the school. There are now reliable methods for assessing such changes (Acitelli & Young, 1996; McGuire & McGuire, 1988).

These changes could be described in several ways. It could be said that we have a number of selves for different occasions. This would be equivalent to saying that we have a number of "characters," in the language of the symbolic interactionists. However, for the most part individuals see their behavior as changing only within limits as they go about their lives. Thus one could describe the self as persisting across situations, and therefore think not of static and multiple selves, but rather of a unitary self which, while having great resilience, is somewhat modifiable by experience, relationships, and current context. Or one could postulate a core self, with somewhat discrepant selves brought out by different situations but overlapping in the central core area; though the core would not correspond with the symbolic interactionists' "character," which McCall (1974) stated is "not an attribute of its possessor, but rather a product of the whole scene of his action" (p. 220). But if a person appears not to have a sense of his or her own continuity across the changes, we may speak of him or her as having something approaching "Multiple Personality Disorder" (Humphrey & Dennett, 1989). There are important cultural differences here. In some the self may extend farther into relationships with other selves, and in some cultures the self may seem more differentiated into situation-specific elements than is the case in Europe and North America.

Thus, people may appear to change their behavioral and psychological characteristics with the situation, and they may see themselves somewhat differently in different situations. It is reasonable to suppose both that experience in a situation affects one's self-concept in that situation, and that how one sees oneself affects how one behaves. And there is evidence that how one sees oneself both influences and is influenced by the way in which one sees (or has seen) the world. For example, Murray and Holmes (1996) found that individuals perceived their partners with a mixture of illusion and reality. Individuals' standards for an ideal partner were higher, the more positively they felt about themselves. Their ideals bore little relation to their partner's actual qualities, but their views of their partners were related to their own ideals: the higher their ideals, the more idealized their impression of their partners. Their perceptions of their partners were also related to how their partners saw themselves. And other studies show that a person's self-perception may be influenced by perception of the partner. For instance, bathing in "reflected glory" from the partner's accomplishments (Tesser, 1988).

But although one may think of oneself somewhat differently in different situations, at the same time one sees oneself as the same person (the same "self"). To some extent, then, the self can be seen as a store of self-knowledge. But insofar as the self is different in different contexts, it must also store knowledge of those contexts and relationships (Bowlby, 1982; Stern, 1995). And we have views about what we might like to be, ought to be, or could be (Markus & Nurius, 1986): The discrepancy between how we see ourselves and what we feel we ought to or could be like, our self-esteem, is an important aspect of the self and can be a determinant of behavior (Higgins, 1989). Also stored is knowledge about how to behave in specific physical and social situations (Honeycutt, Cantrill, & Allen, 1992), including norms, values, conventions, and so on, against which we evaluate ourselves, forming a further datum for self-esteem. In addition, we have knowledge about the course of specific emotions: affect is involved in both the organization and representation of knowledge and in the processing of new information. Knowledge about emotion is, at least in part, socially constructed and held in common with others, and in part idiosyncratic (Fitness, 1996). Damasio (1994) has reviewed evidence that decision making involves assessing the relative emotional appeal of cognitively (but not necessarily consciously) reviewed possibilities—a suggestion compatible with the dramaturgical perspective mentioned earlier.

One might well ask which of this stored information is part of the self and which is what the self uses, but that would be a logical mistake, for the self is an abstraction, loosely framed at the moment, useful in particular ways and not in others: it is not a hypothetical construct (in the sense of MacCorquodale & Meehl, 1954), and certainly not a physical entity.

A variety of models of the self-system have been proposed. Bowlby (1982) postulated "internal working models" of the self, others, and relationships (see also Bretherton, 1995); Stern (1995) wrote of "schemata-of-being-with" subordinated to "representations of being with"; and Schank's script theory involves four levels of schemata. The precise nature of these models need not be pursued here, their commonalities are more important than their differences (Hinde, 1997). But it is important to note that the knowledge structures involved must be seen as organized in part in a historical form involving a fairly coherent narrative—a narrative which has some consistency over time but may also be modified or reconstructed to suit new circumstances or in interaction with others (Fletcher & Fitness, 1996; Fletcher & Thomas, 1996; Harvey, Agostinelli, & Weber, 1989; Winterhoff, 1997). To cite but one example of narrative flexibility, the descriptions of wedding and honeymoon made a few days after the events were similar in couples who experienced a large fall in well-being over the next two years and in more stable couples, but memories of the wedding after the two-year period were much more negative in the distressed couples than in the nondistressed (Holmberg & Veroff, 1996). Such narratives not only integrate past and present experience, they influence the future.

The important point here is that it is necessary to postulate a series of dialectical relations between how individuals perceive others to perceive them, the range of ways in which they perceive themselves, how they behave, and how they induce others to behave toward them, in order to account for both the perceived continuity of the self and its flexibility. Dialectical relations between individuals depend on dialectical relations within individuals. To account for behavior and for the development of personality, subjective and objective data must be synthesized, and to understand behavior in interaction with another it is necessary to see not just the individual as a totality but to see the dyad.

## THE SELF AND THE GROUP

We have seen that one's view of oneself is influenced by, and influences, one's relations with others. In fact, individuals see themselves not only as autonomous individuals but also as partners in relationships and as members of groups—and often feel conflict between a desire for autonomy and a desire for connectedness (Baxter, 1990). Tajfel and Turner (1986) distinguished between an individual's personal identity, based on perceptions of comparisons with others, and social identity, derived from membership of emotionally significant groups or categories. The greater the salience of one's social identity, the less that of one's personal identity: if you see yourself as an interchangeable unit in a social group, you are less prone to see yourself as unique and special. Partial depersonalisation is basic to the methods used to instill discipline and group loyalty into military recruits, and basic to many group phenomena (Turner, Hogg, Oakes, Reicher, & Wethrell, 1987; Turner, Oakes, Haslam, & McGarty, 1994).

Members of a psychological group not only label themselves as a group, but also see themselves as more similar to each other in group-relevant dimensions than they are to outsiders, and may see themselves as interdependent. They tend to treat members of their own group as heterogeneous differentiated individuals, and members of the out-group as undifferentiated individuals. They tend both to elaborate and to adhere to group norms and values (Rabbie, 1991; Tajfel & Turner, 1986; Turner, 1981).

Important in the present context is the extent to which group membership contributes to the knowledge structures of the self-system and to self-esteem. Individuals need to find support for their beliefs (Festinger,

1957), and such support can be found in those who share the same beliefs. One is more inclined to be attracted to those who share one's beliefs, especially if those beliefs are otherwise unverifiable (Byrne, Nelson, &, Reeves, 1966). Reciprocally common group membership authenticates the potential of others to provide verification (Gorenflo & Crano, 1989).

All these issues involve dialectical relations between the individual and the group. Again, individuals like to think of themselves positively. They therefore tend to associate with groups that they evaluate favourably, and to evaluate favourably groups with which they identify, even if objective evidence for their high regard is lacking. The more they identify with the group, the more likely are they to contribute to it, because thereby they contribute to their own self-image. They may receive "reflected glory" from the achievements of fellow group members, even though they did not contribute themselves (Cialdini, Borden, Thorne, Freeman, & Sloan, 1976) (for review see Brewer & Brown, 1997). Thus the holistic approach must embrace not only a view of the individual as a totality, and not only the dyad, but also see the group as a greater totality, understanding of which is essential for the understanding of the individual.

There are also dialectical relations between the sociocultural structure of the group—its norms, values, beliefs, institutions, and so forth, and the behavior of individuals within it. For example, the greater the frequency of divorce, the less the belief in the sanctity of marriage; and the less the belief in the sanctity of marriage, the greater the frequency of divorce. From the holistic perspective we can see the sociocultural structure as internalized in the individual (Hinde, 1979), together with the individual's perceptions of cultural artifacts and the meanings (idiosyncratic or societal) ascribed to them (Rawson, 1992). This internal structure is in dialectical relation with the individual's perceptions of his or her own and others' behavior.

## CONCLUSION

As Magnusson and Törestad clearly show, a holistic approach, used together with more traditional nomothetic methods, can bring important new insights to psychology. The variable-centered approach has proved its value, but a focus on the relations between variables within the individual is also necessary. Choice of the variables examined must be based on the best description to be made of the processes involved.

This contribution is limited to that descriptive phase—a phase that, in the present state of research, is facilitated by the use of metaphor. It focuses on interactions between individuals, arguing for the necessity of going beyond a simple stimulus–response model in two ways. First, social behavior involves two active participants each attempting to create a situation in which his or her ends can best be achieved, and becoming to some extent a different individual in the process. Any understanding of the genesis of personality must involve a multilevel, dialectical approach that integrates subjective experience and objective behavior. The dialectical processes between the two individuals also involve dialectics of many types within each individual. It must be added that, although the interactions between the physiological-psychological processes within each individual may be harmonious, so that the subsystems organize themselves in order to fulfill their role in the functioning of the totality (Magnusson & Törestad, 1993), and indeed one must expect natural selection to have operated toward producing such a result, this is not always the case. Tension and conflict may occur both within and between individuals—tension and conflict which is not necessarily developmentally disadvantageous (Shantz & Hartup, 1992).

Second, individual development is a consequence, in part, of interactions and relationships in a sociocultural context. Whereas Magnusson (1990) points to the individual as stable and developing across time, it is also necessary to see the changes in individuals as inseparable from their involvements in social activity. Therefore, either the individual, the dyad, the individual in the group, or the individual in society, according to the problem, must be seen as a totality.

Of course, one must ask how far that is just playing with words. For instance, because what matters in an interaction is the perception that each participant has of the other, can one regard each individual as internalising the other, and thus see each individual (including the internalized other) as the unit of analysis, that is, as a totality? I suggest that one cannot. The perception that each has of the other does not embrace the whole other, who may behave unexpectedly. The dyad must be treated as a whole. The same is true of the individual in the group. And societal norms and values are only partly shared with others, and change with the current situation, so that a short-term dialectic is always involved as well as the longer term one that may lead to cultural change.

Perhaps the bottom line lies in the issue of the sort of goal we see for psychology. The success of ethology was based in part on the fact that it did not try to emulate physics by seeking for overall generalizations, but looked rather for limited generalizations coupled with statements of the limitations of their validity. The same principle must apply to psychology. It may be useful to think of the goal as a dichotomously branching tree, with the trunk representing characteristics more or less common to all humans, and the ends of the twigs as individuals constituted by the branches that lead to them. If we were to achieve our goal, we could pursue a particular individual through successive bifurcations—female, 28, married, secure childhood, sensitive, pregnant, and so on until we reached full understanding of that individual. At present, in striving for that goal, we can either start at one of the bifurcations, looking for differences between its two branches—the variable approach—or start at the tips of the outermost twigs and work inwards—the individual-oriented, holistic approach.

# REFERENCES

Acitelli, L. K., & Young, A. M. (1996). Gender and thought in relationships. In G. J. O. Fletcher & J. Fitness (Eds.), *Knowledge structures and interaction in close relationships* (pp. 147–168). Mahwah, NJ: Lawrence Erlbaum Associates.

Backman, C. W. (1988). The self: A dialectical approach. *Advances in Experimental Social Psychology, 21,* 229–260.

Bandura, A. (1978). The self system in reciprocal determinism. *American Psychologist, 33,* 344–358.

Baxter, L. (1990). Dialectical contradictions in relationship development. *Journal of Social & Personal Relationships, 7,* 69–88.

Berman, C. M. (1980). Mother–infant relationships among free-ranging rhesus monkeys on Cayo Santiago: A comparison with captive pairs. *Animal Behaviour, 28,* 860–873.

Block, J. (1971). *Lives through time.* Berkeley, CA: Bancroft.

Block, J. & Kremen, A. (1996). IQ and ego-resiliency: Conceptual and empirical connections and separateness. *Journal of Personality and Social Psychology, 70,* 349–361.

Bowlby, J. (1969/1982). *Attachment and Loss. 1. Attachment.* London: Hogarth.

Bretherton, I. (1995). Attachment theory and developmental psychopathology. In D. Cicchetti & S. L. Toth (Eds.), *Emotion, cognition, and representation* (pp. 231–260). Rochester: University of Rochester Press.

Brewer, M. B., & Brown, R. J. (1997). Intergroup relations. In D. Gilbert, S. T. Fiske, & G. Lindzey (Eds.), *Handbook of social psychology* (4th ed.). New York: McGraw-Hill.

Byrne, D., Nelson, D., & Reeves, K. (1966). Effects of consensual validation and invalidation on attractiveness as a function of verifiability. *Journal of Experimental Social Psychology, 2,* 98–107.

Cairns, R. B., Bergman, L. R., & Kagan, J. (Eds.). (1998). *Methods and models for studying the individual: Essays in honor of Marian Radke-Yarrow.* Thousand Oaks, CA: Sage.

Cialdini, R. B., Borden, R. J., Thorne, A., Freeman, S., & Sloan, L. R. (1976). Basking in reflected glory: three (football) field studies. *Journal of Personality & Social Psychology, 34,* 366–374.

Clutton-Brock, T. H. (Ed.). (1988). *Reproductive success.* Chicago: University of Chicago Press.

Cooley, C. H. (1902). *Human nature and the social order.* Glencoe, IL: The Free Press.

Damasio, A. R. (1994). *Descartes' error: emotion, reason, and the human brain.* New York: Grosset & Dunlap.

Endler, N. S., & Magnusson, D. (1976). Toward an interactional theory of personality. *Psychological Bulletin, 83,* 956–979.

Festinger, L. (1957). *A theory of cognitive dissonance.* Evanston, IL: Row, Peterson.

Fitness, J. (1996). Emotion knowledge structures in close relationships. In G. J. O. Fletcher & J. Fitness (Eds.), *Knowledge structures and interaction in close relationships* (pp. 195–218). Mahwah, NJ: Lawrence Erlbaum Associates.

Fletcher, G. J. O., & Fitness, J. (Eds.). (1996). *Knowledge structures and interaction in close relationships.* Mahwah, NJ: Lawrence Erlbaum Associates.

Fletcher, G. J. O., & Thomas, G. (1996). Close relationship lay theories. In G. J. O. Fletcher & J. Fitness (Eds.), *Knowledge structures and interaction in close relationships* (pp. 3–24). Mahwah, NJ: Lawrence Erlbaum Associates.

Goffman, E. (1959). *The presentation of self in everyday life.* New York: Anchor.

Goffman, E. (1967). *Interaction ritual.* New York: Anchor.

Gorenflo, D. W., & Crano, W. D. (1989). Judgemental subjectivity/objectivity and locus of choice in social comparison. *Journal of Personality and Social Psychology, 57*, 605–614.

Harvey, J. H., Agostinelli, G., & Weber, A. L. (1989). Account-making and the formation of expectations about close relationships. In C. Hendrick (Ed.), *Close relationships* (pp. 39–62). Newbury Park, CA: Sage.

Higgins, E. T. (1989). Continuities and discontinuities in self-regulatory self-evaluative processes: A developmental theory relating self and affect. *Journal of Personality, 57*, 404–444.

Hinde, R. A. (1966/1970). *Animal Behaviour.* New York: McGraw-Hill.

Hinde, R. A. (1969). Analyzing the roles of the partners in a behavioral interaction—mother–infant relations in rhesus macaques. *Annals of the New York Academy of Sciences, 159*, 651–667.

Hinde, R. A. (1979). *Towards understanding relationships.* London: Academic Press.

Hinde, R. A. (1997). *Relationships: A dialectical perspective.* Hove, UK: Psychology Press.

Hinde, R. A., & Atkinson, S. (1970). Assessing the roles of social partners in maintaining mutual proximity, as exemplified by mother–infant relations in rhesus monkeys. *Animal Behaviour, 18*, 169–176.

Hinde, R. A., & Dennis, A. (1986). Categorizing individuals: An alternative to linear analysis. *International Journal of Behavioural Development, 9*, 105–119.

Hinde, R. A., & Spencer-Booth, Y. (1967). The behaviour of socially-living rhesus monkeys in their first two and a half years. *Animal Behaviour, 15*, 169–96.

Hinde, R. A., Tamplin, A., & Barrett, J. (1993). Home correlates of aggression in preschool. *Aggressive Behaviour, 19*, 85–95.

Hinde, R. A., Tamplin, A., & Barrett, J. (1995). Consistency within and between relationships. *Czowiek i Spoleczenstwo, 12*, 7–18.

Hinde, R. A., & White, L. E. (1974). The dynamics of a relationship: Rhesus mother–infant ventro-ventral contact. *Journal of Comparative and Physiological Psychology, 86*, 8–23.

Holmberg, D., & Veroff, J. (1996). Rewriting relationship memories. In G. J. O. Fletcher & J. Fitness (Eds.), *Knowledge structures and interaction in close relationships* (pp. 345–368). Mahwah, NJ: Lawrence Erlbaum Associates.

Honeycutt, J. M., Cantrill, J. G., & Allen, T. (1992). Memory structures for relationship decay. *Human Communication Research, 18*, 528–562.

Humphrey, N., & Dennett, D. C. (1989). Speaking for ourselves: An assessment of multiple personality disorder. *Raritan, 9*, 68–98.

Kagan, J. (1994). *Galen's prophecy.* New York: Basic Books.

Kohn, M. L. (1977). *Class and conformity.* Chicago: Chicago University Press.

Krebs, J., & Davies, N. (Eds.). (1991). *Behavioural Ecology.* Oxford, UK: Blackwell.

Lewis, M. (1992). *Shame: The exposed self.* New York: The Free Press.

Lorenz, K. (1935). Der Kumpan in der Umwelt des Vogels [The companion in the bird's world]. *Journal für Ornithologie, 83*, 137–213, 289–413.

MacCorquodale, K., & Meehl, P. (1954). Edward C. Tolman. In W. K. Estes, S. Koch, K. MacCorquodale, P. E. Meehl, C. G. Mueller, W. N. Schoenfeld, & W. S. Verplanck, (Eds.), *Modern learning theory* (pp. 177–266). New York: Appleton-Century-Crofts.

Magnusson, D. (1990). Personality development from an interactional perspective. In L. A. Pervin (Ed.), *Handbook of personality* (pp. 193–222). New York: Guilford.

Magnusson, D. (1993). Human ontogeny: An interactional perspective. In D. Magnusson & P. Casaer (Eds.), *Longitudinal research on individual development* (pp. 1–25). Cambridge: Cambridge University Press.

Magnusson, D. (Ed.). (1996). *The life-span development of individuals. Behavioral, neurobiological and psychosocial perspectives.* Cambridge, UK: Cambridge University Press.

Magnusson, D., & Cairns, R. B. (1996). Developmental science: Toward a unified framework. In R. B. Cairns, G. H. Elder, & E. J. Costello (Eds.), *Developmental science* (pp. 7–30). Cambridge, UK: Cambridge University Press.

Magnusson, D., & Törestad, B. (1993). A holistic view of personality: A model revisited. *Annual Review of Psychology, 44*, 427–452.

Markus, H., & Nurius, P. (1986). Possible selves. *American Psychologist, 41*, 951–964.

McCall, G. J. (1970). The social organisation of relationships. In McCall, G. J., McCall, M., Denzin, N. K., Suttles, G. D., & Kurth, B. (Eds.), *Social relationships*. Chicago: Aldine-Atherton.

McCall, G. J. (1974). A symbolic interactionist approach to interaction. In T. L. Huston (Ed.), *Foundations of interpersonal attraction*. New York: Academic Press.

McGuire, W. J., & McGuire, C. V. (1988). Content and process in the experience of self. *Advances in Experimental Social Psychology, 21*, 97–144.

Mead, G. H. (1934). *Mind, self, and society*. Chicago: Chicago University Press.

Mekos, D., & Clubb, P. A. (1997). The value of comparisons in developmental psychology. In J. Tudge, M. J. Shanahan, & J. Valsiner (Eds.), *Comparisons in human development* (pp. 137–162). Cambridge, UK: Cambridge University Press.

Murray, S. L. & Holmes, J. G. (1996). The construction of relationship realities. In G. J. O. Fletcher & J. Fitness (Eds.), *Knowledge structures and interaction in close relationships* (pp. 91–120). Mahwah, NJ: Lawrence Erlbaum Associates.

Pervin, L. A. (1968). *Personality*. New York: Wiley.

Rabbie, J. (1991). Determinants of instrumental intra-group cooperation. In R. A. Hinde & J. Groebel (Eds.), *Cooperation and prosocial behaviour* (pp. 238–262). Cambridge, UK: Cambridge University Press.

Rawson, J. (1992). *Chinese art*. London: British Museum.

Rogers, C. R. (1980). *A way of being*. Boston: Houghton Mifflin.

Rogoff, B. (1996). Developmental transitions in children's participation in sociocultural activities. In A. J. Sameroff & M. H. Haith (Eds.), *The five to seven year shift* (pp. 273–294). Chicago: Chicago University Press.

Sameroff, A. J. (1975). Transactional models in early social relations. *Human Development, 18*, 65–79.

Schank, R. C. (1982). *Dynamic Memory*. Cambridge, UK: Cambridge University Press.

Shanahan, M. J., & Elder, G. (1997). Nested comparisons in the study of historical change and individual adaptation. In J. Tudge, M. J. Shanahan, & J. Valsiner (Eds.), *Comparisons in human development* (pp. 109–136). Cambridge, UK: Cambridge University Press.

Shanahan, M. J., Valsiner, J., & Gottlieb, G. (1997). Developmental concepts across disciplines. In J. Tudge, M. J. Shanahan, & J. Valsiner (Eds.), *Comparisons in human development* (pp. 34–72). Cambridge, UK: Cambridge University Press.

Shantz, C. U., & Hartup, W. W. (Eds.). (1992). *Conflict in child and adolescent development*. Cambridge, UK: Cambridge University Press.

Snyder, M. (1984). When belief creates reality. *Advances in Experimental Social Psychology, 18*, 248–305.

Stern, D. (1995). *The motherhood constellation*. New York: Basic Books.

Stevenson-Hinde, J. (1998). The individual in context. In R. B. Cairns, L. R. Bergman, & J. Kagan (Eds.), *Methods and models for studying the individual: Essays in honor of Marian Radke Yarrow* (pp. 123–132). Thousand Oaks, CA: Sage.

Stevenson-Hinde, J. & Glover, A. (1996). Shy boys and girls: A new look. *Journal of Child Psychology & Psychology, 37*, 181–187.

Sullivan, H. S. (1953). *Conceptions of modern psychiatry*. New York: Norton.

Swann, W. B. (1987). Identity negotiation: Where two roads meet. *Journal of Personality & Social Psychology, 66*, 857–869.

Tajfel, H., & Turner, J. (1986). The social identity theory of inter-group behaviour. In S. Worchel & W. G. Austin (Eds.), *Psychology of intergroup relations* (pp. 7–24). Chicago: Nelson.

Tesser, A. (1988). Toward a self-evaluation maintenance model of social behavior. *Advances in Experimental Social Psychology, 21*, 181–228.

Tinbergen, N. (1951). *The study of instinct*. Oxford, UK: Clarendon.

Turner, J . (1981). The experimental social psychology of intergroup behaviour. In J. Turner & H. Giles (Eds.), *Intergroup behaviour*. Oxford, UK: Blackwell.

Turner, J . C., Hogg, M. A., Oakes, P. J., Reicher, S. D., & Wethrell, M. S. (1987). *Rediscovering the social group: A self-categorisation theory*. Oxford, UK: Blackwell.

Turner, J. C., Oakes, P. J., Haslam, S. A., & McGarty, C. (1994). Self and collective cognition and social context. *Personality & Social Psychology Bulletin, 20*, 454–463.

Winterhoff, P. A. (1997). Sociocultural promotions constraining children's social activity. In J. Tudge, M. J. Shanahan, & J. Valsiner (Eds.), *Comparisons in human development* (pp. 222–251). Cambridge, UK: Cambridge University Press.

# 8

# Beyond Static Concepts in Modeling Behavior

John R. Nesselroade
Paolo Ghisletta
The University of Virginia

The arguments presented herein are in the spirit of the other chapters in the volume in that they are motivated by a belief that the time is ripe for more vigorous consideration of alternatives to some of the dominant emphases in the way we study behavior and behavior change. *Stability* is a metatheoretical concept that in one guise or another (e.g., stasis, equilibrium, balance) has dominated both methodological and theoretical aspects of the study of behavior (Nesselroade & Featherman, 1997), in some ways to their detriment.

Calls for more holistic and integrated views in planning and conducting developmental research (e.g., Baltes, 1997; Magnusson, 1995, 1998), a perspective with which we are generally sympathetic, signal a longing for more satisfying ways to portray the behaving, developing human organism in its various contexts. However, we believe that a potentially costly limitation of much research being conducted within this orientation involves too much reliance on static measurements as the basis for identifying key patterns of behavioral attributes that will, in turn, lead to the articulation of more potent statements of lawful relationships. Alternatives such as using patterns of intraindividual variability and change defined across time, situation, or both (Shoda, Mischel, & Wright, 1994) as the basis for identifying those relatively homogeneous subsets of individuals whose behavior may be more subject to lawful description need to be more fully explored (Lamiell, 1988). The pervasive nature of the stability orientation is illustrated well, for example, by some forms of growth curve analysis—what should produce exemplary statements of change—that reduce growth and change to a series of individual differences parameters (and thus putative stability). We develop these few themes in the remainder of this chapter and conclude with some suggestions for strengthening the research emphasis on individuals as an important path to furthering our understanding of behavior and its development and change.

## Stability- Versus Intraindividual Variability-Based View of the Organism

Fundamental scientific perspectives, world views, basic paradigms, whatever one might choose to call them, affect how researchers gather, analyze, and interpret data, including developmental data (Cairns, 1986; Overton & Reese, 1973; Reese & Overton, 1973). The influence of our fundamental perspectives is subtle in some cases and obvious in others. Either way, it is a powerful force which helps shape the evolution of a scientific discipline for generations, if not centuries. Valsiner (1984), for example, examined the broad influence of the stability and intraindividual variability orientations in his discussion of typological versus variational modes of thinking. The study of personality and behavior in general has been dominated by an orientation toward stability that has had a pervasive effect on the way psychologists approach the study of behavior and behavior development (Helson, 1993; Nesselroade & Featherman, 1997). Even in the context of studying developmental change, a stability orientation has held sway for decades (Gergen, 1977).

The pervasiveness of the stability orientation can be seen in many of psychology's most critical arenas. Consider two examples from psychological measurement, an activity without which psychology's scientific aspirations would be quite hopeless and thus a highly visible influence on empirical research. A key concept is *reliability of measurement*, which is defined in classical test theory as the correlation between two parallel forms of a test (Gulliksen, 1950). Under the assumptions of classical test theory (which still drives much of our measurement activity), this is also the proportion of the total variance in a set of measurements that is true score variance. Reliability of measurement is thus an instantaneous concept, yet it is often assessed by test—retest correlations. A measure is administered twice to the same sample of individuals and the correlation between the two sets of scores is taken as an estimate of reliability. In other words, what is in principle an instantaneous value is estimated by means of a time interval between two separate measurements! Why do psychologist estimate reliability this way? Because of a strong underlying emphasis on stability! That attribute, deemed well-enough measured to be worthy of further study, is presumed to inhere in the individual as a stable entity, and thus a test—retest correlation will reflect the part that really matters—the stable attribute. The test—retest coefficient does not tell us how reliably we have measured at Time 1 and Time 2. Rather, it tells us a complex story of how well we measured and how much differential change is manifested among persons over the interval between measurements. Although there are some arguments why test—retest estimates of reliability need to be reconsidered (Cronbach, Gleser, Nanda, & Rajaratnam, 1972; Nunnally & Bernstein, 1994), how often does one actually see the test—retest correlation questioned for its capacity to reflect reliability of measurement?

A second example of the dominance of the stability orientation drawn from the measurement literature concerns the apparent difficulties in meaningfully measuring change (Cronbach & Furby, 1970). The psychology literature manifests nearly one hundred years of disagreement about how to represent psychological change or whether it can be done at all! What kind of a science can one have if its precepts and fundamental tools don't afford opportunities and powerful methodologies for studying change? The obvious answer is: One that relies heavily on stability and its derivative concepts.

Why this jam with regard to conceptualizing and measuring changes? We believe that the primary culprit is the fundamental perspective of stability that dominates the ways behavioral phenomena are conceptualized and studied. Among its manifestations is an often uncritical assumption of a fundamentally stable organism and all that it implies. Admittedly, stability in some form is a seemingly necessary feature of phenomena if one is to make valid predictions regarding behavior, but the search for stability needs to take into account the inherent intraindividual variability in a living, breathing, behaving organism, rather than to assume an ambulatory reticule of essentially fixed, true scores.

Human beings are "wired" to detect and respond to variability, rather than stability. Survival depends on it. Psychologists, just as any other scientists, study variability. It may be variability that exists "naturally" or it may be variability created in the laboratory (Cronbach, 1957). On the one hand, with the essential stability of the organism as a dominant precept, many psychologists have focused their attention on the only kind of meaningful variability that remains—differences among individuals. On the other hand, if interindividual differences are the sources of variation one is committed to studying, there has to be a presumption of stability for some features in order to implement prediction schemes. In a very basic sense, concepts of stability and the study of individual differences have reinforced each other and, in the process, the former have utterly dominated how psychologists think about measurement, data analysis, and interpretation. As a consequence of these limitations, both empirical research and theory development have suffered. We extend this concern to attempts to implement more holistic approaches to studying behavior and its development.

An alternative emphasis to stability is that of intraindividual variability (Valsiner, 1984), wherein the fundamental state of the organism is taken to be one of dynamics and change, rather than statics and stability. We believe that several thrusts are acting to bring this point of view into direct conflict with the dominant stability orientation. Included are a wider acceptance of living systems thinking and modeling procedures (Ford, 1987), both linear and nonlinear, and emergent lines of research and promising findings regarding the pervasiveness and nature of short-term, intraindividual variability. This theme, as we will try to show, is quite compatible with the holistic, integrated approach favored by Magnusson and his colleagues. We will illustrate some of the methodological work that we believe demonstrates promise for further substantive research from the intraindividual variability perspective. First, however, we will take a brief look at some of the current research unfolding within the stability tradition.

## Personality Research and the Resurgence of the Big Five Personality Factors

Presently, there is a resurgence of interest in identifying certain structural features of personality. The enthusiasm for this activity manifested by some (Goldberg, 1993) has been countered to some extent by others (Block, 1995). Both sets of protagonists have done much to foster personality structure research in the past (Block, 1981; Goldberg, 1993a), but, in our view, what is going on at present is not a "turf war." Rather, what does seem to be at stake is whether personality research will cycle or spiral through the current revisiting of former issues. What, one may ask, have personality researchers "learned" from their relatively fallow period from the late 1960s to the present? Other than some "fine tuning" of labels and item-analytic work on the measurement devices, the present day versions of most personality trait systems do not seem to differ a great deal from their counterparts of 30 years ago (Digman, 1989; Norman, 1963).

Advocates of the "Big Five" personality factors, for example, have promoted the notion of stability as one of two important features (Costa & McCrae, 1994). The other is factorial invariance (Meredith, 1964, 1993). As prominent and important as both of these two concepts are in the scientific arena, we believe that information about stability qua stability needs to be buttressed more compellingly with information concerning predictive validities and other shortcomings identified 30 years ago (Mischel, 1968). Some of this needed buttressing, we believe, can come from capitalizing on a more liberal definition of stable attributes of the organism.

Indeed, it is more than a little ironic that some of the keenest critics of the status of personality trait research in the 1960s (Mischel, 1968) are now helping to build the case for consistency of personality (Shoda et al., 1994).

However, the consistency is being defined in terms of patterns of intraindividual variability—a notion featuring the careful identification of patterns at the level of the individual before attempting any aggregation into subgroups. This orientation is fully consistent with the holistic, integrated approach pursued by Magnusson and his colleagues.

## Evidence of Alternative Views About the Fundamental Nature of the Organism

West (1985) identified a progression in the development of scientific disciplines that includes moving from static descriptions to dynamic concepts and lawful relations. The evidence is mounting that behavioral scientists are exploring more dynamic conceptions, despite the limitations imposed by the dominant stability orientation. This work is by no means new, as witnessed by the study of "quotidian variability" (Woodrow, 1932) and other aspects of intraindividual variability (Flugel, 1928; Thouless, 1936). Here we will briefly indicate some of the range of empirical work that is characterized by an emphasis on intraindividual variation instead of stability.

## KEY LINES OF INTRAINDIVIDUAL VARIABILITY RESEARCH

Several promising research directions are found in the literature that, despite "flying in the face" of the stability orientation, we believe are beginning to have an impact on the study of behavior and its development. We will identify and discuss each briefly. More to the point, examples of the work will be identified in the existing literature. The labels and examples are somewhat idiosyncratically chosen and equally apt alternatives are no doubt possible. Our objective here is to demonstrate that there are important supplements and refinements, if not alternatives, to the stability orientation. We believe that sufficient evidence is accruing for the validity of focusing on intraindividual variability that it can be argued to constitute an overdue challenge to the dominance of the stability orientation; one that has the potential to lead to a more enlightened view of behavior and behavior change. These lines of research will be characterized as: (a) the state-trait distinction; (b) intraindividual variability as predictor of later attributes; (c) intraindividual variability as diagnostic tool; (d) patterning of intraindividual variability; (e) parameters of intraindividual variability; and (f) idiographic and idiothetic orientation. Each of these labels represents an extant line of theoretical and empirical research that pushes at the boundaries demarcated by the stability perspective. The lines of research are by no means unrelated. But discussing each separately will help to illustrate the main point that a large number of findings support the promotion of alternatives to the stability-based orientation to studying the organism. Our purpose here is not to review each of these systematically but, rather, to highlight significant research on intraindividual variability as a promising complement, if not an alternative, to the stability perspective at a time when serious attempts are being made to strengthen the study of developmental phenomena by means of implementing perspectives such as the holistic one.

## The State–Trait Distinction

Eysenck (1983) credited Cicero with early contributions (45 B.C.) to the state-trait distinction. Although the term state-trait, per se, did not catch on until the 1960s (Cattell, 1961, 1963; Singer & Singer, 1972; Spielberger, Gorsuch, & Lushene, 1969), more than a century of scientific work on emotions and other kinds of intraindividual variability such as performance oscillation and movement helped to pave the way for its acceptance. Both methodological innovation and measurement instrument development helped to nurture interest in the relatively transient individual differences represented by state dimensions and to render them operational in measurement devices (Spielberger et al., 1969).

Instrumental in the instantiating of the state-trait distinction were a number of factor analyses of frequently repeated measurements on the single case, dubbed P-technique factor analysis by Cattell, Cattell, and Rhymer (1947). These studies were reviewed by Luborsky and Mintz (1972) and Jones and Nesselroade (1990). Recent P-technique work reflects additional developments in factor analytic sophistication and computational power (Shifrin, Hooker, Wood, & Nesselroade, 1997). Applications of P-technique have further aided the understanding of psychoanalytic counseling (Patton, Kivilighan, & Multon, 1997); child therapy sessions (Russell, Bryant, & Estrada, 1996); adult psychotherapy (Czogalik & Russell, 1994, 1995); mood changes associated with depression (Garfein & Smyer, 1991) and Parkinson's disease (Shifrin et al., 1997); and individual transitions due to retirement (Hooker, 1991). These instances provide up-to-date empirical evidence of the validity and utility of P-technique factor analysis in a wide range of research domains.

Spurred on in many respects by the trait-state distinction, innovations in the use of statistical modeling for intensive, intraindividual variability data are becoming more prominent (Molenaar, 1985; Nesselroade & Molenaar, 1999; Wood & Brown, 1994). Research in this tradition is yielding evidence for the value of intraindividual variability as a predictor of later attributes (e.g., Eizenman, Nesselroade, Featherman, & Rowe, 1997), a topic to which we next turn.

## Intraindividual Variability as Predictor of Later Attributes

Deeply embedded in behavioral science's notions of validity of concepts and their measurement is the capacity to predict scores on other concepts. From this perspective comes additional evidence for the promise of research and theory reflecting the intraindividual variability perspective. Consider, for example, the subdiscipline of developmental psychology. Researchers such as Fox and Porges (1985) and Kagan (1994) have examined the ability of intraindividual variability in variables such as heart rate to predict later developmental outcomes, including aspects of temperament. In the arena of temperament research, investigators have explicitly recognized such dimensions as *rhythmicity* which, by their very definition, highlight the manifestation of intraindividual variability (Windle & Lerner, 1986). Even in popular discourse, we characterize individuals with labels such as "volatile," "erratic," and "fickle," all of which imply the prediction of future behavior based on currently noted intraindividual variability. A study by Butler, Hokanson, and Flynn (1994) illustrates the point. They compared the relationship between self-esteem lability (SEL) and depression proneness with the relationship between trait self-esteem (TSE) and depression proneness and concluded, "Consistent with psychodynamic and cognitive theories, SEL was found to be a better index of depression proneness than TSE" (p. 166).

## Intraindividual Variability as Diagnostic Tool

Classification and selection are important components of prediction. The ability to diagnose certain outcomes such as particular clinical disorders is of major significance for psychologists. In this context, too, intraindividual variability indices have been shown effectively to supplement more traditional kinds of information regarding stable aspects of a person's behavior. Siegler (1994) identified increased intraindividual variability in performance as a forerunner of cognitive developmental transition. Rubin, Schachter, and Ragins (1984) analyzed the variability of children's drawings, and suggested that intraindividual variability indices might be indicative of creativity, or perhaps even of emotional disturbances. Aikens, Wallander, Bell, and Cole (1992) noticed that variability in stress accounted for more of the variation in diabetic functioning than did mean stress. They proposed that the concept of intraindividual variability be considered when studying òther illnesses. Jensen (1992) concluded that the reaction time median (used instead of the mean because of highly positively skewed distributions) and the reaction time standard deviation (representative of intraindividual variability in reaction time) are two independent sources of variance in mental abilities. This finding was further substantiated by Bruhn and Parsons (1977) who remarked that reaction time means conceal important information about the central nervous system. On the basis of comparing reaction time variability parameters of a control group with those of either epileptic or brain-damaged patients, Bruhn and Parsons (1977) concluded that the usual way of assessing these disorders (i.e., EEG) is not sufficient. They stressed the diagnostic relevance of the parameters investigated in the diagnostic process. Collins and Long (1996) analyzed median visual reaction time scores and intraindividual variability of visual reaction time scores in three groups: impaired traumatic brain injury; nonimpaired traumatic brain injury; and normal controls. It was found that the median reaction time scores were better able to discriminate between impaired traumatic brain injury patients and normal controls, while intraindividual variability reaction time scores were better able to discern nonimpaired traumatic brain injury patients from the normal controls. Collins and Long concluded that the addition of two short visual reaction time tests to neuropsychological test batteries would provide more accurate diagnosis of patients' level of cognitive functioning. Finally, Hertzog, Dixon, and Hultsch (1992) encouraged the use of intraindividual variability designs in the study of cognitive aging, in part because intraindividual performance provides a much more sensitive base line against which to detect pathological and nonnormative cognitive change.

## Patterning of Intraindividual Variability

Another highly germane line of research has established the patterning of intraindividual variability as an important class of features characterizing the human organism. Shoda et al. (1994), for example, argued that the kinds of consistency for which personality researchers have been seeking lies in the organization and patterning of intraindividual variability as it is manifested across differing psychological situations.

Hampson (1990) demonstrated temporal patterns in ability measure fluctuations that appeared to be hormonally driven. Horn (1972) reported patterns of short-term, intraindividual variation in ability test performance that reflected the fluid-crystallized intelligence distinction. May, Hasher, and Stoltzfus (1993) showed how within-day intraindividual variability in intellectual performance could confound age comparisons. These last three studies illustrate that even such thought-to-be-rock-stable attributes as human abilities manifest systematic patterns of intraindividual variability over short time intervals.

## Parameters of Intraindividual Variability

A research focus that further highlights the potential value of intraindividual variability manifestations concerns attempts to conceptualize and measure interindividual differences in the parameters of intraindividual variability. Defining trait measurements as average state scores is one such example. Larsen (1987) has summarized much of this work in explicating what he called second-order differences among individuals. Virtually any parameter of distributions of scores on variables that change intraindividually could potentially be useful as a predictor of differences in behavior.

Among the indices used to capture magnitude of intraindividual variability are the standard deviation (Eizenman et al., 1997; Kim, Nesselroade, & Featherman, 1996), the mean square of successive differences (Leiderman & Shapiro, 1962), and the index of quotidian variability (Woodrow, 1932). Larsen (1987) argued for the use of spectral analysis for the study of intraindividual variability. None of the indices proposed to capture individual differences in the nature of intraindividual variability is universally preferable to the others. Each has properties that should be matched to the nature of the data being analyzed. The more salient point is that a potential linking of intraindividual variability to the individual differences tradition resides in the identification of key parameters of the former that carry the kind of information that has been used in the latter to predict important outcomes. Via this avenue, stability becomes an important aspect of intraindividual variability and change. The person who is highly volatile all the time has a different prognosis than the person who is highly volatile only rarely.

### Idiographic and Idiothetic Orientation

Running through much of the research that has been identified in the preceding discussion is a concern with better understanding behavior at the individual level before performing steps to aggregate information in the service of evolving general lawfulness. Lamiell (1981, 1988) has argued forcefully for this point of view. Resurrection of the term idiographic serves the valuable purpose of emphasizing that there are alternatives to the prevalent, one-shot assessment of differences among large groups of individuals as the prime source of data on which to model behavior. Zevon and Tellegen (1982) argued for using an idiographic approach to bolster the search for nomothetic laws and illustrated the ideas with a large number of concurrent intraindividual variability studies.

### Which Perspective Incorporates the Other?

We see the intraindividual variability perspective primarily as an alternative rather than an adjunct to the stability perspective. The primary reason for taking this stance is that from a logical point of view, stability is a special case of the intraindividual variability perspective. The converse is not true. Thus, in empirical research grounded in an intraindividual variability perspective and using measurement procedures that are sensitively attuned to the possibilities of change and fluctuation, it may still be that an attribute is identified to be relatively stable. If so, that is an interesting phenomenon and ascertaining the mechanism responsible for the stability is a worthy research objective.

## SOME METHODOLOGICAL ISSUES AND CONCERNS

The aforementioned various lines of research involve concepts and relationships that we believe are compatible with the general aims and goals of the holistic, integrated modeling of behavior supported by Magnusson and colleagues. From a methodological perspective, the bulk of research on developmental issues rests on the study of individual differences and thus relies heavily on correlational methods. Magnusson (1995) identified three central characteristics of individual differences research in the study of development, the understanding of which is critical to interpreting empirical results. The three characteristics are: an emphasis on variables rather than whole persons in searching for lawfulness; a search for lawfulness that relies heavily on linear regression analysis which, in turn, rests on assumptions that may not be compatible with understanding how the person functions; and a heavy reliance on hypothetical variables. The person-centered approach, which Magnusson argues is needed to complement the variable-centered approach that drives the bulk of individual differences work, features the identification of patterns of variables defining subsets of individuals. Tools such as cluster analysis are mainstays for this purpose. We illustrate briefly a few of the ways that methods generally thought of as working tools of the variable-centered approach are being used to study behavior and behavior change while respecting the basic integrity of the person.

### Dynamic Factor Analysis Modeling

More than 50 years ago, Cattell et al. (1947) presented a factor analysis of one person's changes on a variety of variables over several weeks. The approach, which has been popularized as "P-Technique Factor Analysis," was characterized as "the logical way" to study the interdependencies of measures over changing conditions (Bereiter, 1963). Because P-technique is based on one individual, any relationships found among variables are, by definition, patterns of intraindividual variability of that individual. After three decades of somewhat controversial application (Anderson, 1963; Cattell, 1963; Holtzman, 1963; Molenaar, 1985), the appearance of substantial improvements in the way the basic model is specified and fitted to allow for serial correlations in the repeated measurements (McArdle, 1982; Molenaar, 1985) and newer applications that make the data collection tasks more manageable (Nesselroade & Molenaar, 1999), the approach promises to flourish.

### Clustering Individuals on Change Dynamics

The second illustration involves some work on implementing the dynamic factor modeling procedures mentioned previously in situations where one has multivariate time-series data on multiple persons but the individual time series are too short for separate analysis. Nesselroade and Molenaar (1999) proposed a method for identifying subsets of individuals whose "change dynamics" do not differ from each other in a statistically significant way. The lagged covariance structures of these homogeneous subsets can be pooled to provide one lagged covariance matrix for analysis by the dynamic factor modeling procedures described previously. This procedure, which amounts to a pattern analysis of change patterns with subsequent "clustering" of those individuals who manifest similar dynamics, is closely aligned to the person-centered approach of Magnusson and his colleagues that has recently been made operational in the statistical analysis package SLEIPNER (Bergman & El-Kouri, 1998).

### CONCLUSION

Our major aim for this chapter has been to heighten awareness concerning some of the difficulties that we believe concepts deeply rooted in a perspective of stability, stasis, and equilibrium have wrought in studying behavior and its development. We believe that the promise of alternative approaches such as the person-centered approach will not be realized unless more emphasis is given to intraindividual variability and change when behavioral relationships are analyzed to detect patterns that are relatively homogeneous across subsets of persons. Many lines of empirical research are converging on the view that intraindividual variability is not "noise" to be swept aside but, rather, valuable information about individual functioning. Procedures for pooling individuals based on their patterns of change, for example, and for fitting dynamic factor models representing enhancements of P-technique factor analysis are, we believe, very compatible with the goals of the holistic, integrated, person-centered approach. Variations on approaches such as P-technique accommodate the measurement of individuals on many variables, some of which may be environmental (Cattell & Scheier, 1961), and the modeling of data to establish patterns that describe the way a person changes over time. Generality across persons is also examined, but at the level of similarity and differences in patterns. This, perhaps, is the critical feature and is one that blends well with the goals of a person-centered approach. Rather than immediately aggregating across individuals and seeing which variables "go together," one first ascertains how variables "go together" in the individual over time, and then attempts to establish the generality and significance of such patterns across individuals.

## ACKNOWLEDGMENT

Supported by the Institute for Developmental and Health Research Methodology.

## REFERENCES

Aikens, J. E., Wallander, J. L., Bell, D. S. H., & Cole, J. A. (1992). Daily stress variability, learned resourcefulness, regimen adherence, and metabolic control in Type I Diabetes Mellitus: Evaluation of a path model. *Journal of Consulting and Clinical Psychology, 60*(3), 113–118.

Anderson, T. W. (1963). The use of factor analysis in the statistical analysis of multiple time series. *Psychometrika, 28*(1), 1–24.

Baltes, P. B. (1997). On the incomplete architecture of human ontogeny: Selection, optimization, and compensation as foundation of developmental theory. *The American Psychologist, 52*, 366–380.

Bereiter, C. (1963). Some persisting dilemmas in the measurement of change. In C. W. Harris (Ed.), *Problems in measuring change* (pp. 3–20). Madison: University of Wisconsin Press.

Bergman, L. R., & El-Kouri, B. M. (1998). *SLEIPNER: A statistical package for pattern-oriented analyses, vs. 2.0.* Stockholm: Department of Psychology, Stockholm University.

Block, J. (1981). Some enduring and consequential structures of personality. In A. Rabin, J. Aronoff, A. Barclay, & R. Zucker (Eds.), *Further explorations in personality* (pp. 27–43). New York: Wiley.

Block, J. (1995). A contrarian view of the five-factor approach to personality description. *Psychological Bulletin, 117*, 187–215.

Bruhn, P., & Parsons, O. A. (1977). Reaction time variability in epileptic and brain-damaged patients. *Cortex, 13*, 373–384.

Butler, A. C., Hokanson, J. E., & Flynn, H. A. (1994). A comparison of self-esteem lability and low trait self-esteem as vulnerability factors for depression. *Journal of Personality and Social Psychology, 66*, 166–177.

Cairns, R. B. (1986). Phenomena lost: Issues in the study of development. In J. Valsiner (Ed.), *The individual subject and scientific psychology* (pp. 97–112). New York: Plenum.

Cattell, R. B. (1961). Theory of situational, instrument, second order, and refraction factors in personality structure research. *Psychological Bulletin, 58*(2), 160–174.

Cattell, R. B. (1963). The interaction of hereditary and environmental influences. *The British Journal of Statistical Psychology, 16*, 191–210.

Cattell, R. B., Cattell, A. K. S., & Rhymer, R. M. (1947). P-technique demonstrated in determining psychophysical source traits in a normal individual. *Psychometrika, 12*(4), 267–288.

Cattell, R. B., & Scheier, I. H. (1961). *The meaning and measurement of neuroticism and anxiety.* New York: Ronald.

Collins, L. F., & Long, C. J. (1996). Visual reaction time and its relationship to neuropsychological test performance. *Archives of Clinical Neuropsychology, 11*, 613–623.

Costa, P. T., & McCrae, R. R. (1994). Set like plaster? Evidence for the stability of adult personality. In T. F. Heatherton & J. L. Weinberger (Eds.), *Can personality change?* (pp. 21–40). Washington, DC: American Psychological Association.

Cronbach, L. J. (1957). The two disciplines of scientific psychology. *American Psychologist, 12*, 71–84.

Cronbach, L. J., & Furby, L. (1970). How we should measure "change"—or should we? *Psychological Bulletin, 74*(1), 68–80.

Cronbach, L. J., Gleser, G. C., Nanda, H., & Rajaratnam, N. (1972). *The dependability of behavioral measurement: Theory of generalizability for scores and profiles.* New York: Wiley.

Czogalik, D., & Russell, R. L. (1994). Therapist structure of participation: An application of P-technique and chronographic analysis. *Psychotherapy Research, 4*, 75–94.

Czogalik, D., & Russell, R. L. (1995). Interactional structures of therapist and client participation in adult psychotherapy: P-technique and chronography. [Special Section: Multivariate process research]. *Journal of Counseling Psychology, 63*, 28–36.

Digman, J. M. (1989). Five robust trait dimensions: Development, stability, and utility. *Journal of Personality, 57*, 195–214.

Eizenman, D. R., Nesselroade, J. R., Featherman, D. L., & Rowe, J. W. (1997). Intra-individual variability in perceived control in an elderly sample: The MacArthur Successful Aging Studies. *Psychology and Aging, 12*, 489–502.

Eysenck, H. J. (1983). Cicero and the state–trait theory of anxiety: Another case of delayed recognition. *The American Psychologist, 38*, 114.

Flugel, J. C. (1928). Practice, fatigue, and oscillation. *British Journal of Psychology, Monograph Supplement, 4*(13), 1–92.

Ford, D. H. (1987). *Humans as self-constructing living systems: A developmental perspective on behavior and personality.* Hillsdale, NJ: Lawrence Erlbaum Associates.

Fox, N. A., & Porges, S. W. (1985). The relationship between neonatal heart period patterns and developmental outcome. *Child Development, 56*, 28–37.

Garfein, A. J., & Smyer, M. A. (1991). P-technique factor analyses of the Multiple Affect Adjective Checklist MAACL. *Journal of Psychopathology and Behavioral Assessment, 13*, 155–171.

Gergen, K. J. (1977). Stability, change, and chance in understanding human development. In N. Datan & H. W. Reese (Eds.), *Life-span developmental psychology* (pp. 135–158). New York: Academic Press.

Goldberg, L. R. (1993a). The structure of personality traits: Vertical and horizontal aspects. In D. C. Funder, R. D. Parke, C. Tomlinson-Keasey, & K. Widaman (Eds.), *Studying lives through time: Personality and development* (pp. 169–188). Washington, DC: American Psychological Association.

Goldberg, L. R. (1993b). The structure of phenotypic personality traits. *American Psychologist, 48*, 26–34.

Gulliksen, H. (1950). *Theory of mental tests.* New York: Wiley.

Hampson, E. (1990). Variations in sex-related cognitive abilities across the menstrual cycle. *Brain and Cognition, 14*, 26–43.

Helson, R. (1993). Comparing longitudinal studies of adult development: Toward a paradigm of tension between stability and change. In D. C. Funder, R. D. Parke, C. Tomlinson-Keasey, & K. Widaman (Eds.), *Studying lives through time: Personality and development* (pp. 93–119). Washington, DC: American Psychological Association.

Hertzog, C., Dixon, R. A., & Hultsch, D. F. (1992). Intraindividual change in text recall of the elderly. *Brain and Language, 42*, 248–269.

Holtzman, W. H. (1963). Statistical models for the study of change in the single case. In C. W. Harris (Ed.), *Problems in measuring change* (pp. 199–211). Madison: University of Wisconsin Press.

Hooker, K. A. (1991). Change and stability in self during the transition to retirement: An intraindividual study using P-technique factor analysis. *International Journal of Behavioral Development, 14,* 209–233.

Horn, J. L. (1972). State, trait, and change dimensions of intelligence. *The British Journal of Educational Psychology, 42*(2), 159–185.

Jensen, A. R. (1992). The importance of intraindividual variation in reaction time. *Personality and Individual Difference, 3*(8), 869–881.

Jones, C. J., & Nesselroade, J. R. (1990). Multivariate, replicated, single-subject designs and P-technique factor analysis: A selective review of the literature. *Experimental Aging Research, 16,* 171–183.

Kagan, J. (1994). *Galen's prophecy.* New York: Basic Books.

Kim, J. E., Nesselroade, J. R., & Featherman, D. L. (1996). The state component in self-reported world views and religious beliefs in older adults: The MacArthur Successful Aging Studies. *Psychology and Aging, 11,* 396–407.

Lamiell, J. T. (1981). Toward an idiothetic psychology of personality. *American Psychologist, 36,* 276–289.

Lamiell, J. T. (1988, August). *Once more into the breach: Why individual differences research cannot advance personality theory.* Paper presented at the annual meeting of the American Psychological Association, Atlanta, GA.

Larsen, R. J. (1987). The stability of mood variability: A spectral analytic approach to daily mood assessments. *Journal of Personality and Social Psychology, 52,* 1195–1204.

Leiderman, P. H., & Shapiro, D. (1962). Application of a time series statistic to physiology and psychology. *Science, 138,* 141–142.

Luborsky, L., & Mintz, J. (1972). The contribution of P-technique to personality, psychotherapy, and psychosomatic research. In R. M. Dreger (Ed.), *Multivariate personality research: Contributions to the understanding of personality in honor of Raymond B. Cattell* (pp. 387–410). Baton Rouge, LA: Claitor's Publishing Division.

Magnusson, D. (1995). Individual development: A holistic, integrated model. In P. Moen, G. H. Elder, Jr., & K. Lüscher (Eds.), *Examining lives in context: Perspective on the ecology of human development* (pp. 19–60). Washington, DC: American Psychological Association.

Magnusson, D. (1998). The logic and implications of a person approach. In R. B. Cairns, L. R. Bergman, & J. Kagan (Eds.), *Methods and models for studying the individual* (pp. 33–63). New York: Sage.

May, C. P., Hasher, L., & Stoltzfus, E. R. (1993). Optimal time of day and the magnitude of age differences in memory. *Psychological Science, 4,* 326–330.

McArdle, J. J. (1982). *Structural equation modeling of an individual system: Preliminary results from "A case study in episodic alcoholism".* Unpublished manuscript, University of Denver.

Meredith, W. (1964). Notes on factorial invariance. *Psychometrika, 29*(2), 177–185.

Meredith, W. (1993). Measurement invariance, factor analysis and factor invariance. *Psychometrika, 58,* 525–543.

Mischel, W. (1968). *Personality and assessment.* New York: Wiley.

Molenaar, P. C. M. (1985). A dynamic factor model for the analysis of multivariate time series. *Psychometrika, 50*(2), 181–202.

Nesselroade, J. R., & Featherman, D. L. (1997). Establishing a reference frame against which to chart age-related change. In M. Hardy (Ed.), *Studying aging and social change: Conceptual and methodological issues* (pp. 191–205). Thousand Oaks, CA: Sage.

Nesselroade, J. R., & Molenaar, P. C. M. (1999). Pooling lagged covariance structures based on short, multivariate time-series for dynamic factor analysis. In R. H. Hoyle (Ed.), *Statistical strategies for small sample research* (pp. 223–250). Newbury Park, CA: Sage.

Norman, W. T. (1963). Toward an adequate taxonomy of personality attributes: Replicated factor structure in peer nomination personality ratings. *Journal of Abnormal and Social Psychology, 66,* 574–583.

Nunnally, J. C., & Bernstein, I. H. (1994). *Psychometric theory* (3rd ed.). New York: McGraw-Hill.

Overton, W. F., & Reese, H. W. (1973). Models of development: Methodological implications. In J. R. Nesselroade & H. W. Reese (Eds.), *Life-span developmental psychology: Methodological issues* (pp. 65–86). New York: Academic Press.

Patton, M. J., Kivlighan, D. M., & Multon, K. D. (1997). The Missouri Psychoanalytic Counseling Research Project: Relation of changes in counseling process to client outcomes. *Journal of Counseling Psychology, 44*, 189–208.

Reese, H. W., & Overton, W. F. (1973). Models of development and theories of development. In L. R. Goulet & P. B. Baltes (Eds.), *Life-span developmental psychology: Research and theory* (pp. 116–145). New York: Academic Press.

Rubin, J. A., Schachter, J., & Ragins, N. (1983). Intraindividual variability in human figure drawings: A developmental study. *American Journal of Orthopsychiatry, 53*, 654–657.

Russell, R. L., Bryant, F. B., & Estrada, A. U. (1996). Confirmatory P-technique analyses of therapist discourse: High-test versus low-test quality child therapy sessions. *Journal of Consulting and Clinical Psychology, 64*, 1366–1376.

Shifrin, K., Hooker, K. A., Wood, P. K., & Nesselroade, J. R. (1997). The structure and variation in mood in individuals with Parkinson's disease: A dynamic factor analysis. *Psychology and Aging, 12*, 328–339.

Shoda, Y., Mischel, W., & Wright, J. C. (1994). Intraindividual stability in the organization and patterning of behavior: Incorporating psychological situations into the idiographic analysis of behavior. *Journal of Personality and Social Psychology, 67*, 674–687.

Siegler, R. S. (1994). Cognitive variability: A key to understanding cognitive development. *Current Directions in Psychological Science, 3*(1), 1–5.

Singer, J. L., & Singer, D. G. (1972). Personality. *Annual Review of Psychology, 23*, 375–412.

Spielberger, C. D., Gorsuch, R. L., & Lushene, R. (1969). *The State-Trait Anxiety Inventory (STAI) test manual, form x.* Palo Alto, CA: Consulting Psychologists Press.

Thouless, R. H. (1936). Test unreliability and function fluctuation. *British Journal of Psychology, 26*, 325–343.

Valsiner, J. (1984). Two alternative epistemological frameworks in psychology: The typological and variational modes of thinking. *The Journal of Mind and Behavior, 5*(4), 449–470.

West, B. (1985). *An essay on the importance of being nonlinear.* Berlin: Springer.

Windle, M., & Lerner, R. M. (1986). Reassessing the dimensions of temperamental individuality across the life span: The Revised Dimensions of Temperament Survey (DOTS). *Journal of Adolescent Research, 1*, 213–229.

Wood, P., & Brown, D. (1994). The study of intraindividual differences by means of dynamic factor models: Rationale, implementation, and interpretation. *Psychological Bulletin, 116*(1), 166–186.

Woodrow, H. (1932). Quotidian variability. *Psychological Review, 39*, 245–256.

Zevon, M., & Tellegen, A. (1982). The structure of mood change: Idiographic/nomothetic analysis. *Journal of Personality and Social Psychology, 43*(1), 111–122.

# 9

# The Application of a Person-Oriented Approach: Types and Clusters

Lars R. Bergman
Stockholm University

As pointed out elsewhere in this volume, a holistic, interactional view is receiving increased attention. According to this view, the individual is seen in terms of a complex system, functioning and developing as a totality. The totality is formed by the ongoing interactions among the elements involved with each aspect achieving its meaning from the role it plays in the individual's total functioning. An overview of the holistic interactional paradigm is given by Magnusson (chap. 3, this volume; see also Magnusson, 1985, 1996, 1998).The new developmental science takes this paradigm seriously as indicated by Cairns (chap. 4, this volume; see also Cairns, Elder, & Costello, 1996).

When carrying out research on individual development, the variable is usually the main conceptual and analytical unit (Thomae, 1988; Wohlwill, 1973): Most research has been *variable-oriented*. Not only the statistical analyses have been undertaken using variables as the main units, but the theory has often been formulated using variables and hypothetical constructs. Interpreting the results has been done in terms of establishing a correspondence between the observed relations among the variables on one hand and the relations among hypothetical constructs indicated by the theory on the other.

A *person-oriented* approach originates within an interactional paradigm. The focus is then on understanding and explaining the processes characterizing the developmental system under study, taking into account that the system functions as a whole. Methodologically speaking, this can sometimes be done by using various types of variable-oriented methods. However, often it is a more natural approach to use methods that directly aim at capturing wholes or structures believed to reflect the system; for instance, studying profiles of variable values believed to reflect the states of the system under study.

## Some Implications for Research Methodology
## of a Holistic–Interactional View of Human Development

Within a holistic–interactional view of human development, a natural way of viewing development is through the framework provided by the study of complex dynamic models. From this perspective, the usefulness of a standard variable-oriented approach based on a linear model can be more limited than is usually believed. Such an approach can be difficult to reconcile with an acceptance of the following properties assumed by the holistic–interactional paradigm and the person-oriented framework:

1. The model for the relations between different factors need not apply to every studied individual.
2. Linear relations are frequently not very useful approximations of relations that hold in reality.
3. Interactions between factors are the standard rather than the exception. It may even be that the variable values characterizing an individual have their most salient meaning as parts in configurations and patterns and not by themselves, as advocated within the person-oriented approach.

An acceptance of these three propositions is natural from the perspective of the paradigm presented in this volume and has implications for the choice of research strategy and method. If these propositions are taken seriously, theoretical formulations in terms of theoretical constructs as separate units influencing each other (often symbolized by a diagram with boxes and arrows) can be misleading, and it can imply a denial of the three propositions at least in the methodological translations. This is exemplified by the frequent use of structural equation modeling (SEM) where often the variance–covariance or correlation matrix provides the data for the modeling. Thus, all interactions not captured by this matrix are disregarded, which can lead to serious errors. A major problem is that the procedure is not self-correcting, because the fit of the model is tested against, for instance, the correlation matrix. Hence, a perfect fit of the model can be obtained but the model may still not represent the essential features of the "real" data, as represented by the Persons x Variables data matrix (see Bergman, 1988 for a demonstration of this). In addition, in SEM often the same linear model is assumed to hold for everyone—a violation of propositions 1 and 2.

From the perspective presented above, one would like to see increased research efforts using other approaches. Here different avenues are open, for instance:

1. The study of latent growth curve models allowing for individual differences in the model followed through development (McArdle & Epstein, 1987). In this way, individual development can be modeled as a continuous phenomenon. It also offers ways of achieving a rapprochement of results pertaining to the study of intra- and interindividual differences.

2. The use of mathematical models taken from the study of dynamic systems (see Kelso, chap. 5, in this volume). Such models open up the possibility of getting closer to the motor of change than one usually can with the ordinary statistical models. In contrast to the later category of models which tend to have a static focus on modeling status at different points in time, the study of dynamic systems emphasizes the modeling of change using differential or difference equations.

3. Theoretical work on the "science of science" aspects of theory, mathematical or statistical modeling, and estimation methods, as exemplified by the work of Casti (1989). For instance, what are the requirements for a model of a phenomenon if the model is to be compatible with certain propositions made within the holistic–interactional framework?

4. The use of a pattern-oriented approach, focusing on information about individuals as gestalts (see Magnusson, chap. 3, this volume). From this perspective, the study of typical configurations of values is relevant. The assumption of emerging types is suggested by analogies to system theoretic thinking—normally only a small number of states are in some sense optimal and lead to a stable behavior of the system. For instance, in biological systems often distinct types are found (e.g., of species, ecotypes, see Colinvaux, 1980). Within psychology a similar point has been made by Block (1971, p. 110) talking about ". . . "system designs" with more enduring properties" and by Gangestad and Snyder (1985) who argued for the existence of distinct types, each sharing a common source of influence. It is this fourth approach— the pattern-oriented approach—that will be expounded in a later section of this chapter.

Of course, none of these four approaches offers a panacea for adjusting to the demands of the new paradigm. The application of the approaches can pose many difficult problems, both theoretically and methodologically. However, they may more often be aligned to the new theoretical view and therefore may hold promise for carrying out an interactional approach.

To summarize the contrast between the person-oriented approach and the variable-oriented approach: Sometimes reality may not be continuous and may operate to produce more or less discrete types. It may be that specific configurations of system states are in some way optimal and therefore become stable and often observed. Using pattern-based methods can be a more direct way of finding these important types of states than is using variable-based methods.

## The Concepts of Typology and Type

Few concept have caused so much confusion and even resentment within psychology as the concepts of *type* and *typology*. For instance, Cattell (1957) discusses 45 meanings of the concept type in psychology. The concepts are also used with varying meanings within other sciences such as sociology and biology (Bailey, 1994; Blashfield, 1980). Waller and Meehl (1998) make a number of thoughtful distinctions with regard to type and typology, preferring the use of the terms *taxon* for, roughly speaking, a meaningful type and *taxometrics* as a generic name for (their) procedures for finding taxa. The following brief discussion of the typology and type concepts is given to clarify how these concepts are used here.

What is common for typologies, almost irrespective of how they are defined, is that they contain a number of classes. A typology means a set of class descriptions that is of some general or theoretical use. If an empirical classification, for instance the clusters resulting from a cluster analysis of a sample of individuals, fulfils this condition, the clusters indicate a typology. Then it is not the clusters and their members per se that consitute the typology but rather the generic properties of these clusters. A type here means the properties of one such class in a typology. A type is sometimes referred to as a *natural cluster*. Often, the properties of a type are stated in terms of a profile of values in the studied variables. For instance, the cluster centroids ( = profiles of means for the variables in the clusters) for a set of natural clusters would be one way of presenting the types in a typology.

Two perspectives on an empirical classification are (a) the identification of the properties of the clusters emerging in terms of their typical characteristics (usually the cluster centroids), and (b) the allocation of individual members to the different clusters. It is the first aspect that most directly relates to the issue of typology and type. From this viewpoint, it is heartening that an empirical classification analysis may be better at identifying "true" centroids through the mist of sampling error and errors of measurement than the analysis is at allocating the sample members to the "right" cluster.

It is, of course, of the greatest importance to carefully devise procedures for investigating the validity and generalizability of a purported typology,

whether it is based on theoretical considerations, an empirical classification, or both. The starting point should be an examination of the internal
consistency of the purported typology referring to the information it is
based on. With regard to an empirical classification this could mean a study
of the degree to which the classification reflects the similarities between the
objects (Milligan, 1981). As usual, replication is of paramount importance.
This issue is discussed in Waller and Meehl (1998), and various empirical
approaches are presented by Breckenridge (1989).

It is important to point out that a typology, in the sense the term is used
here, does not represent anything fixed or unchangeable; a connotation
sometimes given to the term. Although a certain degree of stability and
generality is implied, the changing typologies during development and
changing type membership of the individual during his or her development
are also of primary interest. Researchers are interested in both stability and
change and there is nothing fixed or innate in a typology as defined here.
The preceding discussion brings the issue of a longitudinal typology into
focus. A longitudinal typology could be (a) a typology containing developmental types arrived at theoretically, (b) empirically based on a genuinely
longitudinal analysis, or (c) a set of cross-sectional typologies for which the
developmental connections are indicated.

Typologies of types (a) or (b) may be more attractive than a typology of
type (c), theoretically speaking, but may be more difficult to accomplish in
practice. The issue will be discussed in a later section.

Robins, John, and Caspi (1998) provide further perspectives and empirical examples concering typopologies. See also chapters 17 to 19 in this
volume.

## PATTERN-ORIENTED METHODS FOR STUDYING
## INDIVIDUAL DEVELOPMENT

### Overview

It could be argued that at the heart of understanding individual development is the detailed study of the single individual's development (intraindividual change), followed by a careful generalization on the basis of an
integration of studies of many such single cases. This line of inquiry is
forcefully advocated by John Nesselroade and Paolo Ghisletta (chap. 8, this
volume). Here I will instead concentrate on the nomothetic issue of studying
interindividual differences in the development of patterns in relevant characteristics, a task that also is important from a person-oriented perspective.

A basic distinction can be made between model-based and descriptive
methods for pattern analysis, although the borderline is not always that

clear. An example of a model-based method with latent variables is Latent Transition Analysis which was developed within the framework of latent class analysis (Collins & Wugalter, 1992). An example of a model-based method without latent variables is loglinear modeling (Bishop, Feinberg, & Holland, 1975); examples of tailoring this method to the study of change are given by, for instance, Clogg, Eliason, and Grego (1990). Although model-based methods are highly useful in certain situations they will not be further pursued in this chapter. I will instead concentrate on robust descriptive methods. (For a more extensive review, see Bergman, 1998.) Hypothesis testing is to a certain extent also possible within the methodological framework presented here, as will be indicated later.

In the descriptive analysis of pattern development, the focus need not be on classification based on the patterns of values. Other aspects of the patterns could be examined, such as profile scatter or profile maximum–minimum values, but such aspects are not further elaborated here. (Graphical representations of similarities between profiles can sometimes be highly useful in developmental research of small samples, for instance based on multidimensional scaling [Wood, 1990], but are not discussed here either.) I will instead concentrate on classification procedures where profiles of variable values are analyzed and that also can be used for large samples. Before discussing developmental classification it is necessary to briefly discuss measurement issues and some methods for cross-sectional classification.

## Measurement of Patterns

An individual value pattern consists of the values in the variables constituting the pattern. This pattern is the basic unit of analysis and interpretation in a person-oriented analysis. It is also used for calculating the degree of dissimilarity or similarity between the individuals. Some implications of the properties of the measurements constituting the pattern are pointed out in the following discussion.

*Multivariate Scaling and the Effect of Linear Transformations.* It is well known that for many standard variable-based methods the results do not depend on whether one or another type of scaling of an involved variable is used—as long as the scales are linearly related. In other words: The results are invariant under linear transformations of the involved variables. In such situations it is of no importance whether the different variables have the same or different means or variances at a given age or whether the same variable has the same or different means or variances at different ages—it does not change the results. However, in classification analysis the situation is different. Usually, the classification analysis uses as input a similarity or dissimilarity matrix. Such measures are normally not invariant under linear transformations, so a decision to standardize the variables affects the results obtained. Normally, when variables are used that have different types of "natural" scales and ranges of variation, a standardization should be undertaken. However, sometimes when studying patterns in a developmental setting an essential function of the patterns may be to capture differences in scatter and level for the different variables at a given point in time and for the same variable measured at different points in time (Bergman & Magnusson, 1997). In such situations a standardization should not be undertaken. Instead some procedure for multivariate scaling should be used, creating the desired comparability. Bergman and Magnusson (1991) discussed one such procedure, called *quasi-absolute scaling*.

*Measuring Profile Dissimilarity Between Individuals.* In most classification analyses the profiles of scores of the variables under study are compared for each pair of individuals and some (dis)similarity coefficient is computed. Discussions of different ways of measuring (dis)similarities between profiles are given by Cronbach and Gleser (1953) and Budescu (1980). Two common coefficients are (a) the average squared Euclidean distance, taking both profile form and scatter and level into account; and (b) the correlation coefficient with the pair of persons as the two variables, taking only profile form into account. Just which coefficient is appropriate depends on the specific situation, but the Euclidean distance has probably the largest applicability.

## The Residue Concept

Multivariate outliers may considerably affect the results of a classification analysis, a phenomenon especially noted within cluster analysis. For instance, the results from Ward's method appear to be sensitive to the effects of outliers (Milligan, 1980). It has been suggested that in some situations, it might be useful to have less than 100% coverage, that is, to not classify everybody (Edelbrock, 1979). Often there exist also theoretical reasons for not classifying everybody (Bergman, 1988). The possibility was pointed out of the existence of a small number of "unique" subjects due to various types of extreme conditions, and it was argued that such subjects should not be forced into a cluster. Indicated was a semi-objective procedure, RESIDAN, for a priori identifying and analyzing separately a *residue* of unclassified cases. Often, the residue will contain 1 to 3% of the original sample. The classification analysis is then undertaken on the sample minus the residue.

## Cross-Sectional Classification Analysis

The typologies within early abnormal psychology are one example of our basic tendency to impose structure on the phenomena we encounter (Misiak & Sexton, 1966; Skinner & Blashfield, 1982). The most widespread set of methods for obtaining a classification is the cluster analysis family of methods. Objects are sorted into clusters according to their (dis)similarity to other objects so that those in the same cluster tend to be alike. Although a large number of methods are available, we focus here on methods based on comparisons of individuals' value profiles. (Of course, other ways of obtaining (dis)similarities are possible, for instance by using raters.)

Major types of cluster analysis are hierarchical methods (agglomerate or divisive), partitioning methods, and methods that allow overlap between clusters. Within each major category of methods a variety of different specific methods and algorithms exist. For general overviews of cluster analysis and related methods, see Blashfield (1980), Bock (1988), and Gordon (1981). This presentation will concentrate on Ward's (1963) hierarchical minimum variance method and RELOCATE, a method for relocating already classified objects to improve the homogeneity of the clusters (Wishart, 1987). Evaluations of the sensitivity of different clustering algorithms to error perturbation and of their ability to recover a known structure suggest that, as expected, no method is generally superior to the others. However, Ward's method, and k-means relocation based on a sound start classification are reported to be often well-functioning methods (Milligan, 1980, 1981; Morey, Blashfield, & Skinner, 1983). More recently, promising methods based on so called Beta-Flexible clustering have been proposed (Belbin, Faith, & Milligan, 1992) but these procedures will not be further discussed here. Ward's method and RELOCATE are included in the cluster analysis procedure LICUR presented later.

A different approach to classification analysis is taken in configural frequency analysis (CFA). It is a set of methods for analyzing all possible value patterns. Instead of relying on a method for sorting patterns into groups according to their similarity, all patterns are studied directly. Each theoretically possible pattern is called a *configuration*. To carry out a CFA, the involved variables have to be discrete, often dichotomized or trichotomized, to make manageable the number of configurations for which the observed frequencies are to be examined. Lienert and his coworkers have developed CFA in a number of ways, and an introduction to the approach is given by Krauth and Lienert (1982). A more recent overview is given by von Eye (1990a). In CFA, an observed frequency that is significantly more frequent than expected under a null hypothesis of independence between the variables is called a *type*, and an observed frequency that is significantly smaller than the expected one is called an *antitype*. The definition of a type within CFA is thus different from the definition used here for the type concept. Within the CFA paradigm, many families of methods have been developed for handling a large variety of situations, including repeated measurement designs and longitudinal analysis (von Eye, 1990b; von Eye, Spiel, & Wood, 1996). The CFA rationale is fairly simple and robust. Note the obvious relation to residual analysis within the framework of log-linear modeling.

An interesting set of methods for cross-sectional classification has been developed and refined during more than three decades by Meehl (1995; Waller and Meehl, 1998). The procedures have been labeled multivariate taxometrics, and their foundation is the general covariance mixture theorem expressing the covariance of a mixture as a function of the covariances of its subpopulations (classes, called taxa by Meehl) and other parameters of the classes. Using the "coherent cut kinetics method," taxa are identified and attention is given to testing whether the taxa indeed represent natural clusters.

## Direct Longitudinal Pattern Analysis

Perhaps the most natural way of studying developmental types is to directly form longitudinal patterns and in the same classification analysis to identify longitudinal groupings believed to reflect developmental types. Ideally, this means that full account is taken of each individual's specific pattern of change. To accomplish this, the complete longitudinal patterns could be subjected to cluster analysis or, if the number of possible value combinations is not too large, to CFA. Sometimes an ordination strategy is used in which the number of dimensions are first reduced by means of principal components analysis and then the factor scores are cluster analyzed (e.g., Mumford & Owens, 1984).

A direct longitudinal classification has, in comparison with a cross-sectional procedure followed by linking (discussed in the next section), the advantage of being closer to the individuals' processes of change. However, in practice the direct longitudinal approach can be problematic. For instance, applying longitudinal cluster analysis where data from all measurement occasions are included in a comprehensive profile of scores, the clustering can result in very heterogeneous clusters that are difficult to interpret. If only profile form is the focus of interest, a direct longitudinal classification might work better because less information has to be summarized by the cluster membership variable. An example of the potential of a longitudinal classification strategy in this situation is offered by Block's (1971) study of longitudinal personality types. For a further discussion of this issue, see Bergman (1998).

Sometimes it makes sense to categorize change for each variable as either positive or negative. The dichotomous variables could then be subjected to a CFA. However, one has to be careful with disturbances caused by errors of measurement because change scores tend to be much less reliable than ordinary scores (Bergman, 1972; Harris, 1963). The CFA rationale has also been applied in longitudinal analyses by, for instance, Lienert and zur Oeveste (1985) and von Eye (1990b).

## Cross-Sectional Pattern Analysis Followed
## by Linking Over Time

Many methods are possible for undertaking cross-sectional pattern analysis followed by linking over time and the choice of method should be tailored to the specific case. However, it is useful to have a standard method that is applicable in a variety of situations and can serve as a reference or comparison method. When profiles of scores based on interval scaled data are to be analyzed and cluster analysis is judged appropriate as the method for obtaining the classifications, there is a procedure LICUR for cross-sectional classification after removal of a residue followed by linking of results between measurement occasions (Bergman, 1998). LICUR is suitable when both the form and the level of the profile are of relevance and when it is considered as important to obtain homogeneous clusters. A brief outline of LICUR follows:

1. First the RESIDAN approach is used at each measurement occasion separately to remove a residue that is analyzed separately. This can be important since it may not be reasonable to expect that everybody belong to one of a small number of types, and those who do not should not be classified with the others (Bergman, 1988; Edelbrock, 1979).

2. A cluster analysis is then undertaken at each measurement occasion separately using Ward's hierarchical cluster analysis method, and an optimal number of clusters is decided on. Four different criteria are used in this decision.

3. When the hierarchical property of the cluster solution is important, each cross-sectional analysis stops here, but when there is a strong focus on obtaining clusters as homogenous as possible, the Ward cluster solutions are used as start solutions in k-means relocation cluster analyses where objects are relocated to maximize the explained error sum of squares and, hence, minimize cluster heterogeneity.

4. Finally, the results of the cluster analyses are linked across time by cross-tabulating adjoining classifications and testing for significant types and antitypes of cluster membership combinations, preferably by using exact cell-wise tests (Bergman & El-Khouri, 1987). Often the linking of the results from adjoining ages is sufficient.

LICUR appears to be a robust and basic method, applicable in a number of settings, as when different variables are measured at the different measurement occasions and during periods of developmental change (it is not necessary to assume that the same constructs or even the same variables are measured at the different points in time).

The CFA rationale has also been applied for linking cross-sectional results by Lienert and Bergman (1985). By a special cross-tabulation procedure, configurations at one age can be related to configurations at another age.

## I-States as Objects Analysis (ISOA)

Within the framework of studying individuals as dynamic systems in an interactional paradigm, I have stressed the usefulness of the concept of *i-state*, defined as a specific subject's profile of scores at a specific point in time (Bergman, 1995a; Bergman & El-Khouri, in press). From a dynamic system perspective it could be argued that it is basic first to identify the typical i-states that exist irrespective of the time-points they refer to. This is done in ISOA by considering each i-state as a "subindividual" and then subjecting all i-states to a classification analysis. After that, each individual's sequence of i-states is translated into the sequence of class memberships defined by the classification analysis and the sequence is further analyzed. In this way both structural and individual stability and change can be studied. In certain situations, ISOA can extract more information from the data than conventional methods, especially when there are many measurement occasions.

## Hypothesis Testing in Developmental Classification Analysis

Even if a mainly descriptive method is used for classification analysis, various ways of testing hypotheses exist. One basic issue in classification is whether the reported classification "means anything" or whether it is just the product of chance. It is well known that in a random data set a certain degree of structure is found by the analysis. A simple procedure is then to start from the data set on which the initial classification analysis was based and convert the data into a random data set with the same marginal distributions in all variables. This simulation is repeated a number of times. It is preferable that the classification structures found on these random data sets, using the original classification procedure, be less clear than the structure found for the real data set in, say, at least 95% of the cases. A program doing this simulation is included in the SLEIPNER package described in the next section.

When undertaking a LICUR analysis, perhaps the most crucial result tables are the cross-tabulations linking the clusters at two different ages. The observed frequency of each combination of cluster memberships can be related to the expected frequency under some baseline model, most often an independence model. Using prediction analysis, hypotheses about multiple cells can also be tested (Hildebrand, Laing, & Rosenthal, 1977; von Eye, 1990b). Of course, other types of cross-tabulations of classifications than those resulting from the cluster analysis based LICUR approach can be treated in the same way.

Possibilities exist for carrying out confirmatory analyses in cluster analysis, for instance, based on the nonparametric testing strategy "quadratic assignment" (Eckes, 1986).

## Computer Programs for Undertaking Pattern-Oriented Analyses with Linking

Many of the analyses discussed previously can be accomplished within the major statistical packages with some juggling. The most extensive package for cluster analysis is the CLUSTAN package (Wishart, 1987). Both the residue analysis and cluster analyses suggested above can be conveniently accomplished by SLEIPNER, a new package developed especially for pattern-oriented analyses (Bergman & El-Khouri, 1998). It also contains modules for the exact analysis of single cells in contingency tables and for CFA. A package for CFA analysis has been developed by Krauth (1993). Waller and Meehl (1998) list programs for performing taxometric analyses.

## DISCUSSION

When studying individual development it is important that a person-oriented theoretical approach is not confused with a person-oriented methodological approach using pattern analysis. It is in most cases natural to use pattern-based methods when person-oriented research is carried out within a holistic orientation, but standard variable-based methods also can be appropriate, depending on the specific purpose. Results from a pattern analysis can also be used for constructing new variables. For instance, the presence or absence of a specific typical pattern is transformed into a dichotomous variable. However, there has been an overemphasis on using standard variable-based methods for conducting "person-oriented" research. Normally it is more straightforward to take care of complex interactions by concentrating on profiles of values rather than by introducing interaction terms within a variable-oriented framework. Cronbach (1975) even made the metaphor of entering a hall of mirrors when pursuing such a goal.

Models for complex dynamic systems within the natural sciences have resulted in the development of powerful new tools for their analysis. These tools include nonlinear mathematics, data simulation methods, the study of patterns, chaos theory, and catastrophe theory. NOLIDS is an acronym for such models together with their associated tools. It is important that the behavioral sciences make full use of the opportunities opened up by NOLIDS; appropriately applied, they also have implications for theory and empirical research in the developmental field (Barton, 1994; Wallacher & Nowak, 1994). The interest is also increasing for applying NOLIDS in the study of individual development (e.g., Smith & Thelen, 1993). The differences must be recognized between the systems where NOLIDS so far have been successfully applied and the systems regulating individual development, which are examined here. Nevertheless, many of the ideas and concepts of NOLIDS are of key interest for everyone pursuing research within a holistic–interactional paradigm.

An important aspect of NOLIDS is the Janus-faced emphasis on typical attractor states on the one hand, and the emergence of chaos on the other hand. It could be argued that if similar attractor states apply to different individuals, these might show up as frequently occurring typical value profiles—provided the studied variables cover the essential aspects of the system under study. In other words, certain states of the system are in some way optimal and therefore become stable attractor states, leading to their frequent observation. From this perspective, person-oriented methods like the ones presented here may be more natural than variable-oriented methods in certain settings. This line of thinking also provides a fresh perspective to the classic criticism against a typological approach, launched by Ekman (1951, 1952). He argued that a typological representation of data is an oversimplification of the available information compared with the representation given by what he called a dimensional system of reference. This criticism must be taken seriously if the typological information is created directly, for instance by ratings by a clinical observer as in the old typologies. However, it does not constitute a serious problem in modern typological analysis based on dimensional data. In this latter case the truthfulness of a representation of the multivariate data by a classification can be measured and other methods applied for comparative purposes. The lesson from NOLIDS is that, not infrequently, we can hope for a typological representation to catch essential attractor states.

In the context just discussed, it is of interest to note that classification methods are now being developed that to some extent incorporate ideas and concepts taken from NOLIDS. ISOA was briefly presented in an earlier section. Another method is I-State Sequence Analysis (ISSA) in which an a priori taxonomy of theoretically expected common types of individuals' developmental i-state sequences is used to structure the data set into subsets and then, within each subset, typical developmental sequences are looked for (Bergman, 1995b). ISOA and ISSA can in certain situations be considerably more powerful and extract more information than conventional methods especially when small samples and many measurement occasions are involved. However, the methods share one important limitation: It must be assumed possible to measure the (dis)similarity between i-states pertaining to different measurement occasions. Studies covering time periods with dramatic developmental changes and where the measured variables cannot be assumed to measure "the same thing" at different measurement occasions are thus not suited for this type of analysis. ISSA and ISOA are just evolving and it is still too early to judge the possibilities they hold.

The concepts of type and typology were discussed in a previous section, where it was argued that a careful validation procedure is necessary before a classification can be assumed to be of more general use and deserves to be called a typology. An interesting view of a type was put forward by Krauth (1985) who emphasized the importance of identifying combinations of variable values that emerge above chance level. His line of reasoning started from the CFA framework in which each observed frequency was compared to the expected frequency computed from the marginal frequencies of the variable values that made up the pattern. He saw this as an objective method for identifying types when data containing discrete variables were analyzed. Without denying the usefulness of this approach to type identification, a limitation of it should be pointed out. In essence, Krauth says that if a frequently observed value pattern is not a type in the sense of a significantly over-frequented cell in a CFA analysis, it is "uninteresting" because its occurrence is only what could be expected by the marginal frequencies. To say that, one has to assume that the marginal frequencies are given entities not to be explained or questioned. But from a person-oriented perspective it could be argued that the same process that creates the cell frequencies also creates the marginal frequencies and that their size is of importance for interpreting types if a "type" is given our broader definition. (Of course, this presupposes that the variables are scaled so that the values have some meaning above a purely relative one.)

It often is of interest to complement the search for typical patterns with a search for what have been called "white spots" (Bergman and Magnusson, 1997); the patterns that occur seldom or not at all. This could be done cross-sectionally or developmentally, looking for pathways of pattern development that for some reason are not tread on. A number of approaches are possible to accomplish this, such as searching for antitypes within CFA and the identification of a residue within a cluster analytic framework. Within the confinement of phase-space (i.e., what theoretically can be observed), the patterns that occur often and those that occur very rarely or not at all describe a large part of the empirical world. A mapping of the boundaries of areas containing nonoccurring developmental patterns is seldom made despite the obvious relevancy for theory testing. Research along these lines has been discussed by Lewin (1933), who analyzed boundary conditions in terms of "region of freedom of movement" (p. 598). Valsiner (1984) pointed out that the observed behavioral variability of a person constitutes only a fraction of the possible range of variability. Cairns and Rodkin (1998) presented a "prodigal analysis" for highlighting pathways for persons who do not follow the normative developmental pathways of the configural subgroup they belong to. Kagan, Snidman, and Arous (1998) discussed the value of studying extreme cases. To sum up: The concept of white spots offers additional ways of testing theories in terms of predictions of what should not happen in development according to the theory.

The types in a typology can be ordered in a hierarchy or they can be nonhierarchic. Hierarchic typology permits both an overview, by allowing the researcher to move up the classification tree, and increased detail, by moving down the classification tree. A class at a higher level usually includes several classes at a lower level. This means the interpretation of the classes at a specific level can derive increased meaning by comparing the results with those obtained at a more detailed level and at a less detailed level. Compare this to factor analysis where no such property holds for comparing factor solutions with more or fewer factors extracted. The deeper meaning of a hierarchic classification and how it is to be secured and validated deserves further attention from those within developmental science who are interested in a person-oriented approach. This is an issue that has been extensively studied within biology.

The choice of an appropriate method is, of course, always the question of matching the problem and the method (Bergman & Magnusson, 1991). In this chapter, heavy reliance on conventional variable-oriented methods has been criticized within the field of individual development. Possible kinks in the correspondence between theories within the person-oriented paradigm and commonly used variable-oriented methods have been pointed out and a case has been presented for the more extensive use of person-oriented methods. Comparatively speaking, these methods are less developed than many variable-oriented methods. It is highly desirable that the person-oriented methods receive the same intense attention from mathematical statisticians and other methodologists that, for instance, SEM has been given. Researchers may then hope for a breakthrough in the use of truly person-oriented methods for studying truly person-oriented theories. To bring theory and methods into alignment in this regard would be a major step forward.

## REFERENCES

Bailey, K. D. (1994). *Typologies and taxonomies*. New York: Sage.
Barton, S. (1994). Chaos, self-organization, and psychology. *American Psychologist, 49*, 5–15.
Belbin, L., Faith, D. P., & Milligan, G. W. (1992). A comparison of two approaches to Beta-Flexible clustering. *Multivariate Behavioral Research, 27*, 417–433.

Bergman, L. R. (1972). Change as the dependent variable. *Reports from the Psychological Laboratories* (Suppl. 14). Stockholm: University of Stockholm.

Bergman, L. R. (1988). You can't classify all of the people all of the time. *Multivariate Behavioral Research, 23,* 425–441.

Bergman, L. R. (1995a). Describing individual development using i-states as objects analysis (ISOA). *Reports from the Department of Psychology* (No. 806). Stockholm University.

Bergman, L. R. (1995b). *Describing individual development using i-state sequence analysis (ISSA).* Reports from the Department of Psychology (No. 805). Stockholm University.

Bergman, L. R. (1998). A pattern-oriented approach to studying individual development: Snapshots and processes. In R. B. Cairns, L. R. Bergman, & J. Kagan (Eds.), *Methods and models for studying the individual* (pp. 83–121). Thousand Oaks, CA: Sage.

Bergman, L. R., & El-Khouri, B. M. (1987). EXACON—a Fortran 77 program for the exact analysis of single cells in a contingency table. *Educational and Psychological Measurement, 47,* 155–161.

Bergman, L. R., & El-Khouri, B. M. (1998). *SLEIPNER: A statistical package for pattern-oriented analyses. Version II:* (Manual). Stockholm: Stockholm University, Department of Psychology.

Bergman, L. R., & El-Khouri, B. M. (in press). Studying individual patterns of development using i-states as objects analysis (ISOA). *Biometrical Journal.*

Bergman, L. R., & Magnusson, D. (1991). Stability and change in patterns of extrinsic adjustment problems. In D. Magnusson, L. R. Bergman, G. Rudinger & B. Törestad (Eds.), *Problems and methods in longitudinal research: Stability and change* (pp. 323–346). Cambridge, UK: Cambridge University Press.

Bergman, L. R., & Magnusson, D. (1997). A person-oriented approach in research on developmental psychopathology. *Development and Psychopathology, 9,* 291–319.

Bishop, Y. M. M., Feinberg, S. E., & Holland, P. W. (1975). *Discrete multivariate analysis: Theory and practice.* Cambridge, MA: MIT Press.

Blashfield, R. K. (1980). The growth of cluster analysis: Tryon, Ward and Johnson. *Multivariate Behavioral Research, 15,* 439–458.

Block, J. (1971). *Lives through time.* Berkeley, CA: Bancroft.

Bock, H. H. (1988). *Classification and related methods of data analysis.* New York: North-Holland.

Breckenridge, J. N. (1989). Replicating cluster analysis: Method, consistency and validity. *Multivariate Behavioral Research, 24,* 147–161.

Budescu, D. V. (1980). Some new measures of profile dissimilarity. *Applied Psychological Measurement, 4,* 261–272.

Cairns, R. B., Elder, G. H., Jr., & Costello, E. J. (Eds.). (1996). *Developmental science.* Cambridge, UK: Cambridge University Press.

Cairns, R. B., & Rodkin, P. C. (1998). Phenomena regained: From configurations to pathways. In R. B. Cairns, L. R. Bergman, & J. Kagan (Eds.), *Methods and models for studying the individual* (pp. 245–264). Newbury Park, CA: Sage.

Casti, J. L. (1989). *Alternate realities. Mathematical models of nature and man.* New York: Wiley.

Cattell, R. B. (1957). *Personality and motivation structure and measurement.* Yonkers, NY: World Book.

Clogg, C. C., Eliason, S. R., & Grego, J. M. (1990). Models for the analysis of change in discrete variables. In A. von Eye (Ed.), *Statistical methods in longitudinal research, Vol. II: Time series and categorical longitudinal data* (pp. 409–441). New York: Academic Press.

Colinvaux, P. (1980). *Why big fierce animals are rare.* London: Pelican Books.

Collins, L. M., & Wugalter, S. E. (1992). Latent class models for stage-sequential dynamic latent variables. *Multivariate Behavioral Research, 27,* 131–157.

Cronbach, L. J. (1975). Beyond the two disciplines of scientific psychology. *American Psychologist, 30,* 116–127.

Cronbach, L. J., & Gleser, G. C. (1953). Assessing similarity between profiles. *Psychological Bulletin, 50,* 456–473.

Eckes, T. (1986). Confirmatory methods in cluster analysis. In W. Gaul & M. Schader (Eds.), *Proceedings of the 9th Annual Meeting of the Classification Society. Classification as a tool of research* (pp. 105–112). Karlsruhe, Germany: University of Karlsruhe.

Edelbrock, C. (1979). Mixture model tests of hierarchical clustering algorithms. The problem of classifying everybody. *Multivariate Behavioral Research, 14*, 367–384.

Ekman, G. (1951). On typological and dimensional systems of reference in describing personality. *Acta Psychologica, 8*, 1–24.

Ekman, G. (1952). *Differentiell psykologi [Differential psychology]*. Uppsala, Sweden: Almqvist & Wiksell.

Gangestad, S., & Snyder, M. (1985). To carve nature at its joints: On the existence of discrete classes in personality. *Psychological Review, 92*, 317–349.

Gordon, A. D. (1981). *Classification: Methods for the exploratory analysis of multivariate data*. London: Chapman and Hall.

Harris, C. W. (1963). *Problems in measuring change*. Madison: University of Wisconsin Press.

Hildebrand, D. K., Laing, J. D., & Rosenthal, H. (1977). *Prediction analysis of cross-classifications*. New York: Wiley.

Kagan, J., Snidman, N., & Arcus, D. (1998). The value of extreme groups. In R. B. Cairns, L. R. Bergman, & J. Kagan (Eds.), *Methods and models for studying the individual* (pp. 65–80). Newbury Park, CA: Sage.

Krauth, J. (1985). Typological personality research by configural frequency analysis. *Personality and Individual Differences, 6*, 161–168.

Krauth, J. (1993). *Einführung in die Konfigurationsfrequenzanalyse (KFA)* [Introduction to configural frequency analysis (CFA)]. Weinheim, Basel: Beltz, Psychologie-Verl.-Union.

Krauth, J., & Lienert, G. A. (1982). Fundamentals and modifications of configural frequency analysis (CFA). *Interdisciplinaria, 3*, Issue 1, pp. 1–14.

Lewin, K. (1933). Environmental forces. In C. Murchison (Ed.), *A handbook of child psychology* (2nd ed., pp. 590–625). Worcester, MA: Clark University Press.

Lienert, G. A., & Bergman, L. R. (1985). Longisectional interaction structure analysis (LISA) in psychopharmacology and developmental psychopathology. *Neuropsychobiology, 14*, 27–34.

Lienert, G. A., & zur Oeveste, H. (1985). CFA as a statistical tool for developmental research. *Educational & Psychological Measurement, 45*, 301–307.

Magnusson, D. (1985). Implications of an interactional paradigm for research on human development. *International Journal of Behavioral Development, 8*, 115–137.

Magnusson, D. (Ed.). (1996). *The life-span development of individuals: Behavioral, neurobiological and psychosocial perspectives. A synthesis*. Cambridge, UK: Cambridge University Press.

Magnusson, D. (1998). The logic and implications of a person approach. In R. B. Cairns, L. R. Bergman, & J. Kagan (Eds.), *Methods and models for studying the individual* (pp. 33–62). Newbury Park, CA: Sage.

McArdle, J. J., & Epstein, D. B. (1987). Latent growth curves within developmental structural equation models. *Child Development, 58*, 110–133.

Meehl, P. E. (1995). Bootstraps taxometrics: Solving the classification problem in psychopathology. *American Psychologist, 50*, 266–275.

Milligan, G. W. (1980). An examination of the effect of six types of error perturbation on fifteen clustering algorithms. *Psychometrika, 45*, 325–342.

Milligan, G. W. (1981). A review of Monte Carlo tests of cluster analysis. *Multivariate Behavioral Research, 16*, 379–407.

Misiak, H., & Sexton, V. (1966). *History of psychology*. New York: Grune & Stratton.

Morey, L. C., Blashfield, R. K., & Skinner, H. A. (1983). A comparison of cluster analysis techniques within a sequential validation framework. *Multivariate Behavioral Research, 18*, 309–329.

Mumford, M. D., & Owens, W. A. (1984). Individuality in a developmental context: Some empirical and theoretical considerations. *Human Development, 27*, 84–108.

Robins, R. W., John, O. P., & Caspi, A. (1998). The typological approach to studying personality. In R. B. Cairns, L. R. Bergman, & J. Kagan (Eds.), *Methods and models for studying the individual* (pp. 135–157). Newbury Park, CA: Sage.

Skinner, H. A., & Blashfield, R. K. (1982). Increasing the impact of cluster analysis research: The case of psychiatric classification. *Journal of Consulting and Clinical Psychology, 50,* 727–735.

Smith, L. B., & Thelen, E. (1993). *A dynamic systems approach to development. Applications.* Cambridge, MA: MIT Press.

Thomae, H. (1988). *Das Individuum und seine Welt: Eine Persönlichkeitstheorie* [The individual and his world: A theory of personality]. Göttingen, Germany: Hogrefe.

Valsiner, J. (1984). Two alternative epistemological frameworks in psychology: The typological and variational modes of thinking. *The Journal of Mind and Behavior, 5,* 449–470.

von Eye, A. (1990a). Configural frequency analysis of longitudinal multivariate responses. In A. von Eye (Ed.), *Statistical methods in longitudinal research* (Vol. 2, pp. 545–570). New York: Academic Press.

von Eye, A. (1990b). *Introduction to configural frequency analysis. The search for types and antitypes in cross-classifications.* Cambridge, UK: Cambridge University Press.

von Eye, A., Spiel, C., & Wood, P. (1996). Configural Frequency Analysis in applied psychological research. *Journal of Applied Psychology.*

Wallacher, R. B., & Nowak, A. (1994). *Dynamical systems in social psychology.* New York: Academic Press.

Waller, N. G., & Meehl, P. E. (1998). *Multivariate taxometric procedures. Distinguishing types from continua.* Thousand Oaks, CA: Sage.

Ward, J. H. (1963). Hierarchical grouping to optimize an objective function. *Journal of the American Statistical Association, 58,* 236–244.

Wishart, D. (1987). *CLUSTAN. User Manual. Cluster analysis software.* Computing Laboratory, University of St. Andrews.

Wohlwill, J. F. (1973). *The study of behavioral development.* London: Academic Press.

Wood, P. (1990). Applications of scaling to developmental research. In A. von Eye (Ed.), *Statistical methods in longitudinal research* (Vol. 1, pp. 225–256). New York: Academic Press.

# 10

# Three Tasks for Personality Psychology[1]

Jack Block

University of California, Berkeley

In a volume that celebrates the long career of David Magnusson, it is not inappropriate to talk of some scientific tasks confronting personality psychology. Magnusson's work has been substantively most influential. In my belief, however, his deeper contribution has been to provide a consolidating, holistic perspective on the field that, besides identifying important accomplishments to date, also points the path that must be taken if we are to advance our common science (Magnusson, 1990, 1995, 1996; Magnusson & Törestad, 1993).

As the millennium rushes toward us, it has seemed to me presumptuous but perhaps useful to attempt some suggestions for bettering personality psychology. Personologists, however, must make sure "the future is not only the past again entered by another gate" (Pinero, 1893 as cited in Bartlett's Familiar Quotations). I would hope that the imminent century motivates personologists to go beyond reflexive continuation of extant thinking and practice. The aspirations of personality psychology require renewed and restructuring scrutiny of its concepts; methodological approaches that have become conventional need evaluation of their incisive-

[1]Preparation of this chapter was supported in part by National Institute of Mental Health Grant MH 16080 to Jack and Jeanne H. Block. Address correspondence regarding this chapter to Jack Block, Department of Psychology, University of California, Berkeley, CA 94720-1650 or via Internet: jblock@socrates.berkeley.edu.

ness; empirical accomplishments to date warrant critical evaluation of both their salutary and their unhelpful contributions.

It has long seemed to me that the study of personality lies at the apex of the field of psychology. Personality psychology is concerned with the biosocial adaptations of the individual in a world not entirely clear and logical that is also both threatening and appealing (see, e.g., Block, 1982; Block & Kremen, 1996). It subsumes the fields of learning and cognition which are concerned with adaptations of a certain kind, when affective considerations are not especially regnant or are present in unrecognized or unacknowledged ways; it subsumes developmental psychology which is concerned with how individuals with different temperamental inclinations construct adaptations and evolve life paths; it subsumes social psychology which attempts to specify the interpersonal context and received influences within which adaptational efforts must so often take place; and it subsumes clinical psychology which is concerned with adaptational efforts that subjectively (intrapersonally) or objectively (societally) are judged as having failed.

Given this personal, admittedly somewhat partisan, intellectual framework, what at this juncture might be some immediate aspirations of personality psychology? I offer three suggestions:

1. Achieve or at least approximate a lingua franca for the field.
2. Seek to integrate the study of general laws characterizing behaviors with study of between-individual differences.
3. Seek to integrate the study of general laws characterizing behavior of all individuals with study of general laws characterizing the behavior of different "types" of individuals.

**The Need for a Lingua Franca.** I have long, and repetitiously, voiced my concern regarding the confusing, casual, conflated, ahistoric, compartmentalized, even ego-driven way in which crucial terms or concepts are employed in personality psychology. I am not unique in this concern. This general problem has been well recognized since early in this century when a Professor Aitken coined the phrase, "the jingle fallacy," to characterize the situation in psychology wherein the same term with very different meanings refers to quite different psychological happenings (see Thorndike, 1904, p. 11). Operation of the jingle fallacy can cause the scientifically uncareful to believe they are talking of the same phenomenon when indeed they are not.

Sometime later, Kelley (1927) complemented the jingle fallacy with "the jangle fallacy," the situation in psychology wherein different terms are used for the same or almost the same underlying construct. Operation of the jangle fallacy confuses and may defeat efforts at understanding, it limits discernment of important empirical and conceptual convergences. Instances abound in the field of personality of both jingle and jangle confusions; many examples might be cited. In this limited space, I mention only a couple that especially trouble me.

A jingle instance: The term "extraversion" has achieved widespread, even colloquial usage. But, operationally, it is not employed equivalently by different psychologists or even by the same psychologist at different times. Consequently, the conceptual implications of "extraversion" differ as a function of the particular operational measure used.[2] Given materially different operational emphases, the term extraversion has been interpreted as reflecting the psychological qualities of sociability, impulsivity, energy level, and dominance, in various combinations and weightings. I submit that these four characteristics are conceptually and behaviorally distinguishable and that it is important theoretically for the science of personality psychology to make the distinction.

A jangle instance: Inventory scales have been developed to index the nominally different constructs of "sensation-seeking" (Zuckerman, Kuhlman, Joireman, Teta, & Kraft, 1994), "disinhibition" (Watson & Clark, 1993), "novelty seeking" (Cloninger, 1987), "constraint" (Tellegen, 1985), and "ego-control" (J. Block, 1950, 1965; J. H. Block, 1951; Block & Block, 1980). These scales (and a number of others) all prove to correlate very highly, often at close to the limit set by their respective reliabilities; their common denominator is that they all relate to the way impulse is monitored. To the extent that a strong common core is indeed present in these differently named constructs and operationalizations, many separate lines of inquiry can and should be brought into the same conceptual tent.[3]

Thus, there is need to conceptually and empirically refine and calibrate the meaning of crucial psychological terms about which there currently is not consensual agreement. The wish for a lingua franca has long gnawed at psychologists and doubtless has contributed to the recent ardent push for and popular acceptance of what is called the five-factor approach to personality description. But however noble the intentions of its protagonists to resolve the Tower of Babel problem, in my view the five-factor approach relies too heavily and unwarily on an assumption-ridden statistical method as a mechanical truth generator (Meehl, 1992). I have expressed my many concerns with the five-factor approach elsewhere (Block, 1995).

---

[2]Thus, in a stimulating exchange, Guilford (1975, 1977) and Eysenck (1977) debate whether the extraversion concept should be defined as meaning impulsivity or sociability or both. Guilford opts for impulsivity; Eysenck has been variable over the years in the meaning he has imbedded in his several extraversion sclaes (see the MPI, the EPI, and the EPQ extraversion scales).

[3]And to the extent that these similar constructs and measures are considered to be not sufficiently equivalent, conceptual argument and refining empiricism should seek to specifically identify the differences claimed.

In working toward achieving a careful, consensual language, it will also be important to remember to be historically grounded as well as *au courant* in evaluating the frequently ahistoric field of personality. Past recognitions should be acknowledged but of course not necessarily deferred to; what is most recent should be evaluated for what is new and what is significant. What is new is not necessarily significant and what is significant is not necessarily new.

***Integrating Study of General Laws Characterizing Behaviors With Study of Between-Individual Differences.*** It seems to me that, for some and for too long, the field of personality has been construed as primarily, even solely, the study of interindividual differences. The study of intraindividual differences (i. e., changes over time or circumstance) has been neglected. However, of between-individual differences there can be no end. Another basis for studying between-individual differences can always be found or created and so the literature bulges with findings regarding a host of usually disparate (or seemingly so) constructs or variables. Although this emphasis has produced many intriguing and consequential findings, I believe the approach has been overused. It is formulaic and, as frequently implemented by means of questionnaires and scales, more seductively convenient than it should be. A consequence of this emphasis on individual differences in response to questionnaires is that psychologists have failed to attend sufficiently to the circumstances in which these individual differences emerge or are influenced.

Needed as well, in the effort at understanding personality, is study of intraindividual psychodynamics as a function of the situation enveloping the person. Such study is extraordinarily difficult to implement in research-sufficient ways, for ethical, logistical, and institutional reasons. Human subjects committees tend to frown on administering mind-altering substances (e.g., mescaline, amphetamine, reserpine, bourbon) to experimentally manipulate latent personality structure while also manipulating the anxiety-inducing properties of various environmental conditions. What psychologists are allowed—understandably—to do in research settings is affectively pallid by comparison with what happens unpredictably but inevitably in real life.

Into this breach of personality inquiry have come, for the most part, experimental social psychologists. Experimental social psychologists have emphasized the creation of situation-units intended to elicit lawful normative response to commonly held motivations or introduced influences active in commonly understood contexts. Much useful knowledge has been generated by this approach, some supporting intuitive anticipations and some being counterintuitive. In my view, however, this research too often has been constrained to involve eco-invalid circumstances, the collection of opportune but conceptually impoverished or ephemeral operational indicia, and a consequent misreading of the human motivations involved. And, in a parallel overemphasis, the study of situational influences has failed to attend sufficiently to the individual differences ("nuisance variance") moderating the behaviors being studied.

The continued parochialisms of workers in both fields thus have slowed an integration of the study of normative behaviors with the study of between-individual personality variations as these relate to and reinforce normative understandings (Underwood, 1975). Lewin (1946) expressed well (and very early) the relation between these two approaches: The "problems of individual differences, of age levels, of personality, of specific situations, and of general laws are closely interwoven. A law is expressed in an equation which relates certain variables. Individual differences have to be conceived of as various specific values which these variables have in a particular case. In other words, general laws and individual differences are merely two aspects of one problem; they are mutually dependent on each other and the study of one cannot proceed without the study of the other" (p. 794). Thus the antinomy between the two approaches does not truly exist; it is really quite impossible intellectually to insist on but one of these orientations toward inquiry; they have to be seriously conjoined.

*Integrating Study of General Laws Characterizing Behavior of All Individuals With Study of General Laws Characterizing the Behavior of Different "Types" of Individuals.* The aspiration to establish general laws while viewing individual differences as representing only different values of the parameters for these general laws rests on a fundamental, usually unevaluated assumption—the existence of a common human nature. Certainly, there is "human nature," evolutionarily ingrained laws and rules of behavior that are universally operative. Thus, everyone viscerally reacts with panic when, suddenly, there looms the danger of a head-on collision with another car. Some individuals may react more than others, albeit all are reacting with some degree of panic. Or, as another illustration, all individuals more or less adapt to "strangeness," with some only slowly dropping their wariness while others rather quickly accommodate and may even go on to relish new "strangenesses" (that are not, however, too "strange"). These are instances of universals of human nature and, as such, should certainly be preoccupations of motivational psychologists.

However, within limits, there also may be different kinds of "human nature," different kinds of lawfulnesses for different "types" of individuals. By the notion of "type," I mean "a subset of individuals characterized by a reliably unique or discontinuously different pattern of covariation . . . with respect to a specifiable (and nontrivial) set of variables" (Block, 1971, pp.

109–110).[4] This definition is not especially new nor is it outdated; equivalent or related formulations have been offered by Block (1955), Cattell (1952), Cronbach (1953), Hinde and Dennis (1986), Meehl (1992), Tellegen and Lubinski (1983), Stephenson (1953), and Waller and Meehl (1998), among others. A wide variety of methodologies may be invoked in the effort to discern or impose types.

Too often, it seems to me, psychologists assume unthinkingly a grand universality of the lawfulness of behavior. They do not inquire whether the covariance pattern of a set of variables within one group of individuals is reliably different from the covariance pattern characterizing another group of individuals. If there is such a reliable difference, the possibility comes into play that we psychologists are dealing with importantly different kinds of individuals, differently motivated and differently responsive. If there indeed is, in the sample or population being studied, a mixture of two or more kinds or latent classes of individuals, it would advance conceptual understanding and predictability if we identify and keep analytically separate these commingled categories of persons.

It is convenient here to use my own research over the years studying the behavioral relevance of gender—that great and unquestionable "moderator" variable—to exemplify the cruciality of respecting the idea of typology or taxons. Very frequently, I have found that the relations among psychological variables are remarkably different in men and in women.

Thus, IQ correlates positively with depressive tendencies in young women but negatively with depressive tendencies in young men (Block, Gjerde, & Block, 1991); relatively intelligent young women in their dysphoria tend to blame their unhappiness on themselves while the relatively less intelligent young men in their dysphoria tend to blame their unhappiness on the world in which they must live.

A frequently used index of information processing capacity is the Stroop color-word task (Stroop, 1935). In this procedure, subjects are presented with words naming colors but these color words are themselves printed in colors different from the color named. That is, the word, "red," might be printed in green; the word, "blue," might be printed in yellow, and so forth. The task of the subjects is to name, seriatim, the colors in which the color words are printed. Thus, their task is to not be distracted by the content of the word they are seeing. Typically, subjects are slowed down in their

---

[4]It is important to distinguish between what I have called "type-as-label" and "type-as-distinctive form" (Block & Ozer, 1982). Psychologists often label as "types" categories of subjects established by use of a cutting score—all individuals scoring beyond a certain point on a continuum are labeled as a "type" (e.g., "behaviorally inhibited types" versus "behaviorally uninhibited types"). In such circumstances, the term "type" is being used as a casual label, for communicative convenience; it does not meet the sterner and more implicative criteria of "type-as-distinctive-form."

color-naming by the contrasting meaning of the color word they are reading. But there are wide individual differences in the ability to resist this interference effect. In our longitudinal study, for both sexes there are many personality characteristics associated with the ability to resist the Stroop interference effect. However, the constellations of findings are very different for each sex. In young women, ability to resist the Stroop interference effect relates strongly to ego-resilience (Block & Kremen, 1996). In young men, the ability to resist the interference effect relates strongly to ego-overcontrol (Block, 1985).

Furthermore, involvement in drug usage during adolescence seems to be influenced appreciably in young women by exogenous environmental factors, but seems endogenously rather than environmentally influenced in young men (Block, Block, & Keyes, 1988).

It is not only gender differences that indicate the usefulness—even necessity—of working within a typological or taxonic approach. Disregarding gender, neurotic overcontrollers (NOC) and neurotic undercontrollers (NUC) react very differently when anxious and under stress; the former narrow their focus, rigidify, and perseverate while the latter react in unfocused, intense, transitory ways (Block, unpublished research, 1955; the content of the NOC and NUC scales is presented in Dahlstrom, Welsh, & Dahlstrom, 1960).

Within gender, various personality types can be identified manifesting remarkably different developmental paths over very long periods of time (Block, 1971, 1981). Such organized but different life courses cannot be construed in or assimilated to continuistic, variable-emphasizing terms.

Separate from the usefulness of the empirical evidence adduced for a typological or taxonic approach, there is another, less data-based reason why typological thinking is attractive to many personality and developmental psychologists: It provides a way of, in a sense, partaking of the nomothetic approach but in a more idiographic way. On the one hand, the promise of generalizations afforded by the nomothetic approach, which seeks general laws, are scientifically attractive. On the other hand, psychologists are also attracted by the idiographic approach, which seeks understanding of the single case. The weakness of the nomothetic approach to personality has been that the generalizations it has issued are so often expectable, slight, and psychologically bland. The weakness of the idiographic approach is that, although it provides detailed and vivid information about an individual, one cannot have scientific faith in generalizing from the single case. The typological approach, however, lies inbetween the nomothetic and the idiographic approaches and can be viewed as importantly conjoining their respective strengths. Because the nomothetic sample has been typologically articulated, deeper understandings of each resulting cluster of individuals is afforded than otherwise is available for the larger, undifferentiated group. And, because each type has a number of type representatives, one can still apply the necessary statistics to permit generalization across the set of type members.

It is certainly understandable why some, perhaps many, psychologists might prefer not to deal with the consequences of accepting the existence of types—the problems of thinking about and reporting findings would expand geometrically. Certainly, one should be slow to go the typological route; one should remain dimensional or "continuistic" in one's thinking and analyses insofar as possible. Only reluctantly should one embark upon the typological route. However, if research of quality reveals that the reality "out there" indicates the existence of different lines of functioning or developmental paths or *modi vivendi,* it is dereliction of scientific duty to ignore this recognition.

It seems to me that recent empiricism increasingly has been demonstrating the usefulness of thinking in typological or taxonic terms (see, e.g., Asendorpf, this volume; Bergman & Magnusson, 1997; Block, 1971; Caspi et al., 1995; Erlenmeyer-Kimling, Golden, & Cornblatt, 1989; Gangestad & Snyder, 1985; Harris, Rice, & Quinsey, 1994; Hart, Hofman, Edelstein, & Keller, 1997; John, Pals, & Westenberg, 1998; Lenzenweger & Korfine, 1995; Ozer & Gjerde, 1989; Pulkkinen, 1996; Robins, John, Caspi, & Moffitt, 1996; Trull, Widiger, & Guthrie, 1990; Waller, Putnam, & Carlson, 1996; York & John, 1992). The recent volume by Waller and Meehl (1998), which closely considers the conceptual basis for studying taxons or types and offers new, sophisticated methodologies, can be expected to further expand interest in this approach. To the extent this trend represents a move away from a piecemeal, variable-centered psychology toward a more holistic and person-centered psychology, it may be considered salutary in affording more incisive understandings.

## REFERENCES

Bergman, L., & Magnusson, D. (1997). A person-oriented approach in research on developmental psychopathology. *Development and Psychopathology, 9,* 291–319.

Block, J. (1950). *An experimental investigation of the construct of ego-control.* Unpublished doctoral dissertation, Stanford University, Stanford, California.

Block, J. (1955). The difference between Q and R. *Psychological Review, 62,* 356–358.

Block, J. (1965). *The challenge of response sets: Unconfounding meaning, acquiescence and social desirability in the MMPI.* New York: Appleton-Century-Crofts.

Block, J. (1971). *Lives through time.* Berkeley, CA: Bancroft.

Block, J. (1981). Some enduring and consequential structures of personality. In A. I. Rabin, J. Aronoff, A. M. Barclay, & R. A. Zucker (Eds.), *Further explorations in personality* (pp. 27–43). New York: Wiley.

Block, J. (1982). Assimilation, accommodation, and the dynamics of personality change. *Child Development, 53,* 281–295.

Block, J. (1985). *Personality implications of resistance to Stroop interference.* Unpublished manuscript.

Block, J. (1995). A contrarian view of the five-factor approach to personality description. *Psychological Bulletin, 117,* 187–215.

Block, J., Block, J. H., & Keyes, S. (1988). Longitudinally foretelling drug use in adolescence: Early childhood personality and environmental precursors. *Child Development, 59,* 336–355.

Block, J., Gjerde, P. F., & J. H. Block (1991). Personality antecedents of depressive tendencies in 18-year-olds: A prospective study. *Journal of Personality and Social Psychology, 60,* 726–738.

Block, J. & Kremen, A. M. (1996). IQ and ego-resiliency: Conceptual and empirical connections and separateness. *Journal of Personality and Social Psychology, 70,* 349–361.

Block, J., & Ozer, D. J. (1982). Two types of psychologists: Remarks on the Mendelsohn, Weiss, and Feimer contribution. *Journal of Personality and Social Psychology, 42,* 1171–1181.

Block, J. H. (1951). *An experimental study of a topological representation of ego-structure.* Unpublished doctoral dissertation, Stanford University, Stanford, California.

Block, J. H., & Block, J. (1980). The role of ego-control and ego-resiliency in the organization of behavior. In W. A. Collins (Ed.), *The Minnesota Symposia on Child Psychology* (Vol. 13, pp. 39–101). Hillsdale, NJ: Lawrence Erlbaum Associates.

Caspi, A., Begg, D., Dickson, N., Langley, J., and others. (1995). Identification of personality types at risk for poor health and injury in late adolescence. *Criminal Behavior and Mental Health, 5,* 330–350.

Cattell, R. B. (1952). The three basic factor-analytic research designs—their interrelations and derivatives. *Psychological Bulletin, 49,* 499–520.

Cloninger, C. R. (1987). A systematic method for clinical description and classification of personality variants: A proposal. *Archives of General Psychiatry, 44,* 573–588.

Cronbach, L. J. (1953). Correlations between persons as a research tool. In O. H. Mowrer (Ed.), *Psychotherapy: Theory and research* (pp. 376–388). New York: Ronald.

Dahlstrom, W. G., Welsh, G. S., & Dahlstrom, L. E. (1960). *An MMPI handbook: I. Clinical interpretation.* Minneapolis: University of Minnesota Press.

Erlenmeyer-Kimling, L., Golden, R. R., & Cornblatt, B. A. (1989). A taxometric analysis of cognitive and neuromotor variables in children at risk for schizophrenia. *Journal of Abnormal Psychology, 98,* 203–208.

Eysenck, H. J. (1977) Personality and factor analysis: A reply to Guilford. *Psychological Bulletin, 84,* 405–411.

Gangestad, S., & Snyder, M. (1985). "To carve nature at its joints": On the existence of discrete classes in personality. *Psychological Review, 92,* 317–349.

Guilford, J. P. (1975). Factors and factors of Personality. *Psychological Bulletin, 82,* 802–814.

Guilford, J. P. (1977). Will the real factor of extraversion-introversion please stand up? A reply to Eysenck. *Psychological Bulletin, 84,* 412–416.

Harris, G. T., Rice, M. E., & Quinsey, V. L. (1994). Psychopathy as a taxon: Evidence that psychopaths are a discrete class. *Journal of Consulting and Clinical Psychology, 62,* 387–397.

Hart, D., Hofman, V., Edelstein, W., & Keller, M. (1997). The relation of childhood personality types to adolescent behavior and development: A longitudinal study of Icelandic children. *Developmental Psychology, 33,* 195–205.

Hinde, R. A., & Dennis, A. (1986). Categorizing individuals: an alternative to linear analysis. *International Journal of Behavioral development, 9,* 105–119.

John, O. P., Pals, J. L., & Westenberg, P. M. (1998). Personality prototypes and ego development: Conceptual similarities and relations in adult women. *Journal of Personality and Social Psychology, 74,* 1093–1108.

Kelley, T. L. (1927). *Interpretation of educational measurements.* Yonkers, NY: World Book.

Lenzenweger, M. F., & Korfine, L. (1995). Tracking the taxon: On the latent structure and base rate of schizotypy. In A. Raine, T. Lencz, & S. Mednick (Eds.), *Schizotypal personality* (pp. 135–167). New York: Cambridge University Press.

Lewin, K. (1946). Behavior and development as a function of the total situation. In L. Carmichael (Ed.), *Manual of Child Psychology* (pp. 918–970). New York: Wiley.

Magnusson, D. (1990). Personality development from an interactional perspective. In L. Pervin (Ed.), *Handbook of personality: Theory and measurement* (pp. 193–222). New York: Guilford.

Magnusson, D. (1995). Individual development: A holistic, integrated model. In P. Moen, G. H. Elder, & K. Luscher (Eds.), *Examining lives in context: Perspectives on the ecology of human development* (pp. 19–60). Washington, DC: American Psychological Association.

Magnusson, D. (1996). *The life-span development of individuals: Behavioral, neurobiological, and psychosocial perspectives*. Cambridge, UK: Cambridge University Press.

Magnusson, D., & Törestad, B. (1993). A holistic view of personality: A model revisited. *Annual Review of Psychology, 44*, 427–452.

Meehl, P. E. (1992). Factors and taxa, traits and types, differences of degree and differences in kind. *Journal of Personality, 60*, 117–174.

Ozer, D. J., & Gjerde, P. F. (1989). Patterns of personality consistency and change from childhood through adolescence. *Journal of Personality, 57*, 483–507.

Pinero, A. W. (1893). From The Second Mrs. Tanqueray. In *Bartlett's Familiar Quotations* (13th ed.). Boston: Little Brown.

Pulkkinen, L. (1996). Female and male personality styles: A typological and developmental analysis. *Journal of Personality and Social Psychology, 70*, 1288–1306.

Robins, R. W., John, O. P., Caspi, A., & Moffitt, T. E. (1996). Resilient, overcontrolled, and undercontrolled boys: Three replicable personality types. *Journal of Personality and Social Psychology, 70*, 157–171.

Stephenson, W. (1953). *The study of behavior: Q-technique and its methodology*. Chicago: University of Chicago Press.

Stroop, J. R. (1935) Studies of interference in serial verbal reactions. *Journal of Experimental Psychology, 18*, 643–662.

Tellegen, A. (1985). Structures of mood and personality and their relevance to assessing anxiety, with an emphasis on self-report. In A. H. Tuma & J. D. Maser (Eds.), *Anxiety and the anxiety disorders* (pp. 681–706). Hillsdale, NJ: Lawrence Erlbaum Associates.

Tellegen, A., & Lubinski, D. (1983). Some methodological comments on labels, traits, interaction, and types in the study of "femininity" and "masculinity": Reply to Spence. *Journal of Personality and Social Psychology, 44*, 447–455.

Thorndike, E. L. (1904). *An introduction to the theory of mental and social measurements*. New York: Teachers College, Columbia University.

Trull, T. J., Widiger, T. A., & Guthrie, P. (1990). Categorical versus dimensional status of borderline personality disorder. *Journal of Abnormal Psychology, 99*, 40–48.

Underwood, B. J. (1975). Individual differences as a crucible in theory construction. *American Psychologist, 30*, 128–134.

Waller, N. G., & Meehl, P. E. (1998). *Multivariate taxometric methods: Distinguishing types from continua*. Newbury Park, CA: Sage.

Waller, N. G., Putnam, F. W., & Carlson, E. B. (1996). Types of dissociation and dissociative types: A taxonometric analysis of dissociative experiences. *Psychological Methods, 1*, 300–321.

Watson, D., & Clark, L. A. (1993). Behavioral disinhibition versus constraint: A dispositional perspective. In D. M. Wegner & J. W. Pennebaker (Eds.), *Handbook of mental control* (pp. 506–527). Englewood Cliffs, NJ: Prentice-Hall.

York, K. L., & John, O. P. (1992). The four faces of Eve: A typological analysis of women's personality at midlife. *Journal of Personality and Social Psychology, 63*, 494–508.

Zuckerman, M., Kuhlman, D. M., Joireman, J., Teta, P., & Kraft, M. (1994). A comparison of three structural models for personality: The Big Three, the Big Five, and the Alternative Five. *Journal of Personality and Social Psychology, 65*, 757–768.

# 11

# Real and Statistical Parents and Children: The Varied Discoveries of Research

Marian Radke-Yarrow
National Institute of Mental Health

The scientific method possesses persuasive authority among scientists and lay persons. Yet, despite its credentials, it is not a set of golden principles that guarantee validity, or that offer absolute guides for the most critical decisions in research. Systematic and precise modes of inquiry are the passwords. But more is needed.

This is not a new conclusion. It was expressed centuries ago by Leonardo da Vinci: Science and art are inseparable, he wrote. Although he is best known to us as an artist, da Vinci was also a scientist. It would seem that his achievements are recommendations for attending to his convictions, in contemporary science.

What, then, are the qualities of art that lend power to science? It is not difficult to see science in da Vinci's art, and art in his science. He studied water, for example—its texture and movement, the effects of obstructions in its path, the play of sunlight on the spray from the fountain. Through observations from different angles, at varied levels of detail, in altered contexts, and painted with different brushes, the artist scientist brings out features of his subject and opens the mind to new ideas—creating and also constraining.

Is it too broad a leap to read these searching, artistic approaches into methods of scientific inquiry that take seriously the complexity of human behavior and development—ongoing states, multifaceted, multicontextual, and multidetermined? Such a framework encourages study of behavior from diverse perspectives. Its discoveries often do not fit easily into simple generalizations. At the same time, it opens the mind to ways of penetrating the complexity. It influences each stage of research—the questions that are asked, the methods by which they are investigated, and how they are answered. That is the focus of this chapter.

Ideally, research questions, conceptualizations of the phenomena being studied, and methods of investigation are in harmony. With a holistic orientation as the anchor, my objective is to explore points of harmony and disharmony between this orientation and research questions and methods in the study of individual behavioral development.

Kurt Lewin's (1931) basic formulation of behavior and development as a function of the interaction of person and environment states most simply and directly the requirements for questions and methods in a holistic orientation. To prevent drifting into more static and reductionistic views, it may help to keep in mind a circle or spiral of ongoing processes, of behavior, person, and environment in continuing interaction, with a dimension of developmental history, as the phenomena to be investigated. I explore this circle, recognizing the elaborations and extensions by recent theorists (Magnusson, 1985; Magnusson & Bergman, 1988; Magnusson & Cairns, 1996).

As a "laboratory" for this essay, I use a long-term longitudinal study to provide arguments, examples, and challenges in the research enterprise. The interdependencies of parents and children in the developmental process are the focus. The families my colleagues and I have studied are contrasts in risk, by virtue of parental psychiatric wellness or depressive illness (Radke-Yarrow, 1998). Ninety-eight families (mother, father, and two children) have been studied at regular intervals, from children's preschool years to adolescence and young adulthood. The data sources are observations and interviews from multiple situations and informants.

Parents and children in relation to each other are an especially appealing territory in which to examine a holistic–interactionist approach because many facets of interaction are involved, over long periods, in varied contexts. Moreover, because parent and child are environments for each other, they offer a good laboratory for investigating reciprocal processes.

We begin by asking how research questions are formulated, how they are shaped by the investigator's orientation. We compare variable-oriented and person-oriented approaches. Second, we concentrate on behavior in the Lewinian formula. In studies of development, we are often asking, what is the behavior "outcome," how is it best measured in a conceptualization of behavior as ongoing processes? Third, in line with the holistic orientation (Magnusson & Bergman, 1988), we examine some research findings arrived at by variable-based and person-based approaches, using the same data sources.

## WHAT IS THE RESEARCH QUESTION?

Theorists advocating a holistic approach have criticized research in which variables are viewed as if operating independently, without regard to their contexts. The assumption of independence from context is not necessarily explicit in the formulation of the research question; in other instances, these variables are "controlled."

Much of research concerned with parental influences on children has been formulated in a variable-based way, and many variables are associated with child "outcomes." Cairns and Cairns (1995) have critically summarized the state of these findings with the conclusion that "virtually any sane expectation will be 'statistically significant' if the study is competent" (p. 4). The implication is that something more is required of the research questions—as well as of the methods. Research questions, and the perspectives and assumptions on which they rest, deserve priority attention. The research question that is carefully and fully formulated brings conceptualizations and needed methods face-to-face, and conveys the level of answers being sought.

With the data from our research, we compare questions formulated in terms of single variable influences and reformulated with holistic considerations.

### Two Types of Questions, Two Approaches, Two Sets of Findings

Many studies of parental psychopathology and offspring development are formulated in terms of hypothesized main effects of single, isolated variables: What is the influence of a family history of psychopathology (Weissman, Kidd, & Prusoff, 1982), chronicity of parental depression (Keller, Beardslee, Dorer, Lavori, Samuelson, & Klerman, 1986), parents' personality disorders (Rutter & Quinton, 1984), marital and family discord (Emery, Weintraub & Neale, 1982), and more. All have statistically significant effects, as Cairns and Cairns predicted. It must be assumed from the research question that the variable is expected to have its effect across conditions, and across offspring. The offspring remain an undifferentiated "target." Ironically, even though parental influences on children is a developmental topic, par excellence, the research questions have rarely been formulated with reference to the developmental stage of the child. Information on any age-dependent processes (genetic or environmental) is thus sacrificed.

The question of parental psychopathology as a risk to the child is reformulated in our study, in the direction of a holistically oriented research question, taking the context of development into account: How do qualities of parental psychopathology interact with age-dependent capacities and needs of the child in influencing child outcome?

Indeed, we found the developmental context to be important, affecting both amount and kinds of offspring problems. For example, comparing the children of bipolar mothers and well mothers, we found them to be equally competent in social interactions in the preschool years (except for a few very dysfunctional children of bipolar mothers). However, in late childhood and adolescence, the contrast between the groups is marked, with high rates of problems in the children of the ill mothers. Also, what is learned about similarities and differences between children of unipolar depressed and bipolar mothers depends on the developmental context. Children of unipolar depressed mothers manifest problems of anxious, disruptive, and depressive behavior in the preschool years and continue through childhood: This is in contrast to the course of children of bipolar mothers who, as just noted, do reasonably well until later childhood and adolescence, when problems erupt.

Clearly, the research question without the developmental context loses important findings, and runs the risk of erroneous generalization based on mixture of ages. The research question framed developmentally has enriched understanding in a very important way: The new perspectives point to specific directions for further inquiry into processes (genetic and nongenetic) that underlie the observed differences in the timing and content of offspring problems.

In a second example, the influence of investigators' orientations is seen in the question formulation. A familiar question in the same literature is: What is the impact of maternal depression and of marital discord on the development of the children? In this formulation, the variables of diagnosis and discord are viewed as independent influences. The two conditions have been compared almost as competitors in influence (e.g., the relative weight, the effect of one when the other is statistically "held constant"). Findings are persistently inconsistent. Quite clearly this formulation is at odds with the notion of configurations of variables acting together in influencing offspring.

We approached the question of influences of marital discord on children of depressed parents by examining first the pattern of stresses in these families, where stresses are multiple. We found that marital discord is not a condition in isolation. It is significantly correlated with most other stressors in the families of depressed mothers, and embedded very differently in family life, in different families. Hence, "its" effect on offspring can also be the effect of other stressors. To further complicate, marital conflict interacts with depressed mother–child relationships differently in different families (a point made by Engfer, 1988). Spousal problems may bring mother and child into a harmful enmeshing relationship. Another child is rejected by the mother as the father's favorite. In other families, both children are the victims of both parents' anger. Thus, across families, marital conflict has a highly varied role in the lives of individual children, and is not a good constant to weigh in comparison with maternal diagnosis.

In these examples, single-variable and contextual–interactional considerations bring the data to different conclusions and give different directions to further research.

## MEASURES OF BEHAVIOR

In the framework of behavior as ongoing processes, behavioral "stills" or outcomes present inherent problems for measurement. In developmental studies, behavioral snapshots must index a changing (maturing) organism, in changing contexts. The sample that is taken of ongoing behavior, therefore, is a critical consideration in measurement.

How well do we in the developmental disciplines fare in our measures of psychosocial behavior? Two generalizations, in my opinion, characterize the field. In one, about which I will say very little, there are finely tooled, sophisticated, and precise measures of behavior. Measures in long-term programmatic research (such as research by Block & Block, 1980; Cairns & Cairns, 1995; Loeber, 1991; Olweus, 1980; Patterson, 1982) meet these criteria.

The second generalization is that our field is in chaos. Measures are often unique to a study. The problem is not only in the diversity of measures; the problem lies in the fact that there is little cross-measures evaluation, and there are few restraints on what is claimed and generalized from various measures. As an index of mother's behavior, are two minutes of mother–child interaction in solving an experimenter's staged problem equal to a mother's interview report, equal to the home visitor rating? Is differential treatment of siblings equally well estimated in participant reports, laboratory observations, therapist's assessments?

The problem is many-sided. The same labels are used for vastly different behavioral measures. There is tolerance for an amazing range of procedures. The adequacy and theoretical justification of the behavior sample (types of situations, amount of behavior sampled), the units in which behavior is observed or encompassed in reports and interviews, the sophistication of the data-gatherers all vary with the investigator.

These "apples and oranges" do not sum easily, and do not permit fundamental replications and generalizations. The potpourri of existing measures lends support to the perception of behavioral research as the "mushy sciences." Interestingly, problems of measurement do not incite enthusiastic efforts on the part of the disciplines to develop a strong and unified foundation of measurement tools.

Much could be gained from confronting current limitations in the measurement of psychosocial behavior. Should we not treat our measures as objects of research, making explicit the assumptions or evidence on which our choice of tools rests? This "puritanical" critique has, no doubt, been prompted by the kinds of measurement challenges that a long-term developmental study presents. So I turn to our study to illustrate difficult requirements and choices in assessment, and to share some lessons we have learned from our experience.

Our study called for assessment of developmentally changing emotional, cognitive, and social (mal)adaptions of children from age 3 to young adulthood, and synchronized assessment of the family and parent contexts. Foremost as a measurement difficulty is the general unavailability of measures that cross developmental stages. When good measures exist that are applicable to specific ages, there are few translation guides for establishing the comparability across sets of measures at different developmental stages.

Surprisingly, psychiatric classifications, on a number of counts, offered good measurement prospects (surprising because the classifications derive from a nondevelopmental system for classifying adult psychopathology). We found concepts that are applicable and definable across development. Concepts of anxiety, conduct problems of disruptive and oppositional behavior, and depression were relevant in our study. My point here is not so much praise of the psychiatric classification system as it is praise of the process of arriving at the measures. It is for this point that I dwell on the psychiatric measures.

Their virtues include the following:

1. The measures approach a stage of standard definition, arrived at on the basis of long experience and deliberation of experts.
2. A concept represents a pattern of varied behavior elements that cohere within the boundaries of the concept.
3. The raw data are a wide and deep sampling of behavior, drawn from planned, diverse settings. (In this instance the tool is the structured, psychiatric interview.)
4. The expert is involved in obtaining and interpreting the raw data.

On these various counts, the measures are person-oriented and context sensitive. In principle, they have a constancy across investigators and studies.

By psychiatric tradition, the data are converted into an extreme score, a diagnosis, that has the known advantages and limitations of a categorical measure. However, the array of specific, detailed behavior elements (used to arrive at a diagnosis) makes possible another level of analysis, which is very important in developmental study. These elements make it possible to measure behavior as an ongoing process. The specific and varied behavior elements allow one to trace, through repeated assessments over time, the evolution of problems and adaptations within the individual—from emerging signs to full-blown dysfunction or mastery. This second view of the child's development can make a difference in the appearance of continuity and change. One can see progression in the child's problems and also the coping efforts of the child. This self-righting process was pointed out long ago by Murphy and Moriarty (1976), but it is seldom included in investigating developing psychopathology.

I have emphasized the role of experts in the development and implementation of psychiatric measures. In behavioral studies, data collection and the translation of the raw data of research into the categories or ratings that enter analyses, are often not the responsibility of the most highly trained persons on the research team. While this practice may adequately serve many coding needs, it can also result in compromises—in the tailoring of codes to achieve reliability, thereby simplifying or distorting concepts.

We experienced this danger of distortion in attempting observational coding of a complex concept that is of considerable importance in maternal depression. The concept is that of the depressed mother's psychological neediness and dependency, and its expression in her mothering of her child. This concept could not be successfully broken down into simpler components for coding purposes (such as attention to child, affection, warmth, etc.), or arrived at through the addition of these separate variables. Adequate assessment required the intact concept, which required sensitivity to cues of context, qualitative distinctions in appropriateness and timing of the component behaviors, and conceptual integration of the information—all of which require expertise. This is not likely to be a unique example of the need for an expert in measurement procedures.

This combination of praiseworthy measurement qualities in the psychiatric concepts is not available for many of the psychosocial variables that are important in developmental theory. A generalization to carry away is that it will take a motivated discipline to invest concentrated, systematic effort to bring order, comparability, and sophistication into the measurement of behavior. Standardization may be premature, but standards of measurement and integration of existing procedures are not.

## BEHAVIOR AS A FUNCTION OF PATTERNS OF OPERATING FACTORS

In the spirit of comparing research findings based on holistic propositions with findings based on a conventional variable-based orientation, we applied these two approaches to a part of our analyses of depressed mothers as influences in the children's psychopathology. The aim in our study was to conceptualize and measure the mother as an organized unity, comprised of patterns of attributes and behavior that operate jointly in influencing the child. We compared findings from a holistic approach with findings when each variable is examined separately. Magnusson (1985) leads us to expect differences.

## Patterns of Elements Operating Jointly

There is not a ready solution to finding the patterns of elements of the mother that function jointly. Finding them is both the research question and the answer to it. Hinde (1998), in addressing this issue, identified four routes: study of the individual, focus on extremes of one or more dimensions, statistical procedures to distinguish behavior profiles, and theory- or problem-based criteria.

Developmental and clinical knowledge played the primary role in selecting elements for patterns of mothers. In child-rearing research, mothers have most often been represented as techniques of control and training, or in global dimensions of relationships with the child. Characteristics of the mother as a person have been almost nonexistent in the research. In conceptualizing the child's behavioral environment, as represented in the mother, we reasoned that it is important to characterize the mother as a person as well as a "rearing agent," and as an integration of these qualities.

If, over the years, research on parental influences had taken Barker and Wright's (1951) *One Boy's Day* as a methodological guide for conceptualizing environments that mothers provide, we would probably have a different childrearing literature. Would we not have found in a mother's day that mother reveals herself to the child in her moods, her organization of time, her energy, how she interacts with others and how they treat her, how she handles difficulties, what experiences she provides, how she contributes to the day-to-day ambience of the family? Much of this behavior is not directed at the child, but her day would also involve direct interaction with her child, in care, control, teaching, and love.

Reasoning from this hypothetical day, we constructed a mother-totality that includes two perspectives in combination—mother's "person" characteristics and her "techniques" with her child. Our selection of "person" elements draws upon qualities that are accentuated in a depressed person (e.g., negativity, depressive-affect, dependency, self-absorption). As mother's daily functioning expresses these qualities, they enter into the child's life very pervasively. For mother's rearing functions, we included her early regulation of the child's behavior and her provision of a secure base for the child. We composed homogeneous groups of mothers defined by these combined criteria.

But mothers as patterns of variables interact with children who likewise are patterns of variables. Therefore, before comparing analytic approaches to mothers' influences on offspring, we add a quality of the child (easy vs. problematic temperament). We have then the following variables to examine in relation to child problems: mother's "person" qualities, her "techniques" with child, and the child's temperament.

## COMPARING APPROACHES

First, we consider the findings by single variables: Considered separately, mother's negativity, enmeshing behavior, and failure in early regulation of the child have some influence on the child's later disruptive problems. Attachment pattern is not predictive of later disruptive problems. Child's problematic temperament is modestly related to increased disruptive problems in later childhood.

Second, we consider the findings representing mother and child in pattern terms: There are radical changes in associations with attachment, depending on depressed mother's person characteristics. The functions of attachment are influenced by maternal symptomatic and asymptomatic behavior. Secure attachment to a negative, angry mother or an enmeshing mother is a risk for later disruptive disorders, whereas secure attachment to an asymptomatic mother is protective. Children insecurely attached to an asymptomatic mother, and lacking early regulation, are at high risk for later disruptive disorders. Problematic temperament characteristics are a high risk primarily for children with symptomatic mothers. In dyads with symptomatic mother and problem-temperament child, problem behavior of both child and mother increases over time, suggesting a damaging cumulative, reciprocal process.

The sets of findings from the two approaches to the data speak for themselves. The configuration in which a given variable is operating can affect the function of that variable. In the extreme, its properties of risk and protection may be reversed.

Mother as a pattern of variables interacting with systems within the child significantly influences findings in a field that has long relied on associations between single maternal variables and child behavior.

Through analyses of our data in which patterns of variables have been the focus, individual development begins to emerge and the "average" child and parent recede; so, too, the "average" processes. Influences on individual development are seen as multiple and complex, but in their complexity and diversity, an orderliness in processes is revealed.

## CONCLUDING COMMENTS

Individual development in terms of the interdependencies of parent and child is a complex field. The complexities of systems within parent and child, and the larger systems in which they function, leave much still to be learned. Failures in theory and findings have encouraged change in the perspectives and approaches that are brought to continuing study.

The holistic–interactionist approach has much to recommend it for a leading role in this change. It does not offer a theory; it provides a framework that steers perspectives, conceptualizations, and methods into, rather than away from, the multilayered and multiinteracting elements and patterns that are behavioral process. It has consequences not only for what is learned about human development but for what is suggested for further study.

We have used a "case study," our longitudinal study, to illustrate, on a small scale, some consequences of the holistic approach in investigating interactive psychopathological and adaptive processes in parents and their children. The "case" has demonstrated effects at many phases of the research process. This old field of study can no longer be comfortable with a formulation of parental influences on child, in isolation from interactional influences.

Longitudinal studies have been a major agent of change, as findings of diversity in development in relation to person and environmental conditions have brought attention to multiinfluences. New and changing knowledge bases from neighboring fields of science are also contributing to the emphasis on interactional processes. Biobehavioral interdependencies are emphasized in the interplay of early neurobiological and experiential factors (e.g., Schore, 1996). In Elder's work (1997) we are alerted to macrocontexts and historical periods (e.g., The Great Depression, World War II) influencing individual functioning. Patterns of variables at various levels are bringing new science to the study of individual development.

## REFERENCES

Barker, R., & Wright, H. (1951). *One boy's day*. New York: Harper.
Block, J. H., & Block, J. (1980). The role of ego-control and ego-resiliency in the organization of behavior. In W. Collins (Ed.), *Minnesota Symposia on Child Psychology, Vol. 13*. Hillsdale, NJ: Lawrence Erlbaum Associates.
Cairns, R. B., & Cairns, B. (1995). *Lifelines and risks*. New York: Cambridge University Press.
Elder, G. (1997). The life course as developmental theory. *Presidential Address*. Washington, DC: Society for Research in Child Development.
Emery, R. E., Weintraub, S., & Neale, J. (1982). Effects of marital discord on the school behavior of children of schizophrenic, affective disordered, and normal parents. *Journal of Abnormal Child Psychology, 16*, 215–225.

Engfer, A. (1988). The interrelatedness of marriage and the mother–child relationship. In R. Hinde & J. Stevenson-Hinde (Eds.), *Relationships with families* (pp. 104–118). Oxford, UK: Clarendon Press.

Hinde, R. (1998). Through categories towards individuals: Attempting to tease apart the data. In R. B. Cairns, L. R. Bergman, & J. Kagan (Eds.), *Methods and models for studying the individual* (pp. 11–30). Thousand Oaks, CA: Sage.

Keller, M. B., Beardslee, W. R., Dorer, D. J., Lavori, P. W., Samuelson, W., & Klerman, G. R. (1986). Impact of severity and chronicity of parental affective illness on adaptive functioning and psychopathology in children. *Archives of General Psychiatry, 43,* 930–937.

Lewin, K. (1931). Environmental forces in child behavior and development. In C. Murchison (Ed.), *A handbook of child psychology* (2nd ed., pp. 590–625). Worcester, MA: Clark University Press.

Loeber, R. (1991). Questions and advances in the study of developmental pathways. In D. Cicchetti & S. Toth (Eds.), *Rochester symposium on developmental psychopathology.* (Vol. 3, pp. 97–115). New York: Rochester University Press.

Magnusson, D. (1985). Implications of an interactional paradigm for research on human development. *International Journal of Behavioral Development 8,* 115–137.

Magnusson, D., & Bergman, L. R. (1988). Individual and variable-based approaches to longitudinal research on early risk factors. In M. Rutter (Ed.), *Studies of psychological risk: The power of longitudinal data* (pp. 45–60). Cambridge, UK: Cambridge University Press.

Magnusson, D., & Cairns, R. B. (1996). Developmental science: Toward a unified framework. In R. B. Cairns, G. H. Elder, Jr., & Costello, E. J. (Eds.), *Developmental science* (pp. 7–30). New York: Cambridge University Press.

Murphy, L., & Moriarty, A. (1976). *Vulnerability, coping, and growth from infancy to adolescence.* New Haven, CT: Yale University Press.

Olweus, D. (1980). Familial and temperamental determinants of aggressive behavior in boys: A causal analysis. *Developmental Psychology, 16,* 644–660.

Patterson, G. (1982). *Coercive family process.* Eugene, OR: Castalia.

Radke-Yarrow, M. (with Martinez, P., Mayfield, A., & Ronsaville, D.). (1998). *Children of depressed mothers: From childhood to early maturity.* New York: Cambridge University Press.

Rutter, M., & Quinton, D. (1984). Parental psychiatric disorder: Effects on children. *Psychological Medicine, 14,* 855–880.

Schore, A. (1996). The experience-dependent maturation of a regulatory system in the orbital prefrontal cortex and the origin of developmental psychopathology. *Development and Psychopathology, 8*(1), 59–88.

Weissman, M., Kidd, K., & Prusoff, B. A. (1982). Variability in rates of affective disorders in relatives of depressed and normal probands. *Archives of General Psychiatry, 19,* 1397–1403.

# A BIOLOGICAL PERSPECTIVE

# 12

# Understanding Genetic Activity Within a Holistic Framework

Gilbert Gottlieb
Center for Developmental Science
University of North Carolina, Chapel Hill

The new discipline of the genetics of behaviour, to judge by some recent books, is caught in the dogmas of Mendelian genetics without regard to developments in modern genetics during the last ten years, and to modern experimental approaches to the genetic roots of behaviour. Books on the subject usually begin with an account of the principles of Mendelian genetics. The material on behaviour deals mainly with mutated animals and their observed changes in behaviour. That is exactly what genetic principles predict. If an important mutation should not be followed by a change in behaviour—then geneticists would have to worry about the validity of the principles.

What these books fail to pay attention to is the trend in modern genetics which deals with the activation of gene areas, with the influence of external factors on the actualization of gene-potentials and their biochemical correlates in behaviour. . . . I would venture to guess that, apart from the dogma, the main reason for this silence is the fear of even the slightest suspicion that one might misinterpret such facts to mean that a Lamarckian mechanism were at work. (Hydén, 1969, pp. 114–115)

In the ensuing decades since Hydén made the above observation, things have not changed very much. A virtual revolution has taken place in our knowledge of environmental influences on gene expression that has not yet seeped into the social sciences in general and the behavioral sciences in particular, and fits beautifully with a holistic perspective down to the level of molecular biology. Aside from the feared misinterpretation of Lamarckian mechanisms at work, there is an explicit dogma, formulated as such, that does not permit environmental influences on gene activity: the central dogma of molecular biology, first enunciated by Crick in 1958.

Although the central dogma may seem quite remote from psychology, I think it lies behind some psychological and behavioral theories that emphasize the sheerly endogenous construction of the nervous system and early behavior (e.g., Elman et al., 1996; Spelke & Newport, 1998), and the "innate foundation of the psyche" (e.g., Tooby & Cosmides, 1990), independent of experience or functional considerations: the essentially dichotomous view that genes and other endogenous factors construct part of the organism and environment determines other features of the organism. The present essay is an attempt to show how genes and environment necessarily cooperate in the construction of organisms; specifically, how genes require environmental and behavioral inputs to function appropriately during the normal course of individual development.

## PREDETERMINED AND PROBABILISTIC EPIGENESIS

In an earlier article, I described two concepts of epigenetic development: predetermined and probabilistic epigenesis (Gottlieb, 1970). In this early formulation, the difference between the two points of view hinged largely on how they conceived of the structure–function relationship. In predeterminism it was unidirectional (S → F), whereas in probabilism it was bidirectional (S ↔ F). Subsequently, I (Gottlieb, 1976, p. 218; 1983, p. 13; 1991, p. 13) extended the uni- and bidirectionality to include genetic activity:

Predetermined Epigenesis
*Unidirectional Structure–Function Development*
Genetic activity (DNA → RNA → Protein) →
structural maturation → function, activity, or experience

Probabilistic Epigenesis
*Bidirectional Structure–Function Development*
Genetic activity (DNA ↔ RNA ↔ Protein) ↔
structural maturation ↔ function, activity, or experience

As applied to the nervous system, structural maturation refers to neurophysiological and neuroanatomical development, principally the structure and function of nerve cells and their synaptic interconnections. The unidirectional structure–function view assumes that genetic activity gives rise to structural maturation that then leads to function in a nonreciprocal fashion, whereas the bidirectional view holds that there are reciprocal influences among genetic activity, structural maturation, and function. In the unidirectional view, the activity of genes and the maturational process are pictured as relatively encapsulated or insulated, so that they are uninfluenced by feedback from the maturation process or function, whereas the bidirectional view assumes that genetic activity and maturation are affected by function, activity, or experience. The bidirectional or probabilistic view applied to the usual unidirectional formula calls for arrows going back to genetic activity to indicate feedback serving as signals for the turning on and turning off of genetic activity. The usual view, as we shall see below in the central dogma of molecular biology, calls for genetic activity to be regulated by the genetic system itself in a strictly feed-forward manner. In this chapter I (1) present the central dogma as a version of predetermined epigenesis and (2) elaborate on the prior description of probabilistic epigenesis to bring it up to date on what we now know about the details of the bidirectional effects among genetic activity, structural maturation, neural and behavioral function, and experience.

## THE CENTRAL DOGMA

The central dogma asserts that "information" flows in only one direction, from the genes to the structure of the proteins that the genes bring about, through the formula DNA → RNA → Protein. (Messenger RNA [mRNA] is the intermediary in the process of protein synthesis. In the lingo of molecular biology, the DNA → RNA is called transcription and the RNA → Protein is called translation.) After retroviruses—in which RNA reversely transcribes DNA through the enzyme reverse transcriptase—were discovered in the 1960s, Crick (1970) wrote a postscript to his 1958 paper in which he congratulated himself for not claiming that reverse transcription was impossible: "In looking back I am struck not only by the brashness which allowed us to venture powerful statements of a very general nature, but also by the rather delicate discrimination used in selecting what statements to make" (p. 562). He then went on to consider the central dogma formula, DNA → RNA → Protein, in much more explicit detail than in his earlier paper. In particular, he wrote: "These are the three [information] transfers which the central dogma postulates never occur:

Protein → Protein
Protein → DNA
Protein → RNA." (p. 562)

I suppose if one is going to be brash about making proposals in largely unchartered waters it stands to reason one might err, even given the otherwise acknowledged insight of the author regarding other scientific issues. In the present case, Crick was wrong in two of the three central-dogmatic postulates described above. Regarding protein–protein interactions, it is now known that in neurodegenerative disorders such as Creutzfeldt–Jakob disease, "prions" (abnormally conformed proteins) can transfer their abnormal conformation to other proteins ( = Protein → Protein transfer of "information"), without the benefit of nucleic acid participation (RNA or DNA) (Telling et al., 1996). The strength of the dogma that nucleic acids are required for "information transfer" is so compelling that some people believe there must be something like an RNA-transforming virus that brings about the changed protein conformation, even though there is no evidence for such a virus (Chesebro, 1998; Grady, 1996).

Regarding Protein → DNA transfer, there has long been recognized a class of regulative proteins that bind to DNA, serving to activate or inhibit DNA expression (i.e., turning genes on or off) (reviews in Davidson, 1986, and Pritchard, 1986).

With respect to the third prohibited information transfer (Protein → RNA), which would amount to reverse translation, to my knowledge that phenomenon has not yet been observed.

Any ambiguity about the controlling factors in gene expression in the central dogma was removed in a later article by Crick, in which he specifically says that the genes of higher organisms are turned on and off by other genes (Crick, 1982, p. 515). Figure 12.1 shows the central dogma of molecular biology in the form of a diagram.

## The Genome According to Central Dogma

The picture of the genome that emerges from the central dogma is (a) one of encapsulation, setting the genome off from supragenetic influences, and (b) a largely feed-forward informational process in which the genes contain a blueprint or master plan for the construction and determination of the organism. In this view, the genome is not seen as part of the holistic, bidirectional developmental–physiological system of the organism, responsive to signals from internal cellular sources such as the cytoplasm of the cell, cellular adhesion molecules (CAMs), or to extracellular influences such

### Genetic Activity According To Central Dogma

$$\text{DNA} \longrightarrow \text{DNA} \overset{?}{\underset{}{\longleftarrow}} \text{RNA} \longrightarrow \text{Protein}$$

FIG. 12.1. Central dogma of molecular biology. The right-going arrows represent the central dogma. The discovery of retroviruses (represented by the left-going arrow from RNA to DNA) was not part of the dogma but, after the discovery, was said by Crick (1970) to not be prohibited in the original formulation of the dogma (Crick, 1958).

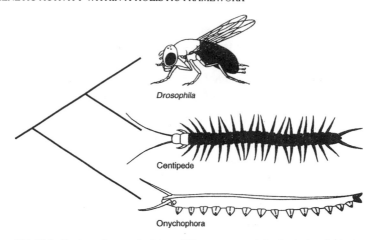

FIG. 12.2. Darkened areas indicate different parts of the body in which the same *Hox* genes are active in three species: abdominal segment in Drosophila, virtually the entire body in centipede, and only the single hindmost segment in Onychophora. (Modified from Grenier et al., 1997, with permission.)

as hormones, and certainly not to extraorganismic influences such as stimuli or signals from the external environment. Witness the well-known biologist Ernst Mayr's view "that the DNA of the genotype does not itself enter into the developmental pathway but simply serves as a set of instructions" (Mayr, 1982, p. 824). Mae-Wan Ho (1984) has characterized this view of the genes as the unmoved movers of development and the masters of the cellular slave machinery of the organism. Ho's own work on the transgenerational effects of altered cytoplasmic influences seriously faults this view, as does the research reviewed by Jablonka and Lamb (1995).

Genes are conserved during evolution; hence some of the same genes are found in many different species. What this has shown us is that there is not an invariable association between the activity of a specific gene and the part of the body in which it is active. One of the nicest demonstrations is the activity of the so-called *Hox* genes that are found in a number of species (Grenier, Garber, Warren, Whitington, & Carroll, 1997). As shown in Fig. 12.2, in fruit flies the *Hox* genes are active only in the abdominal segment of the body, whereas in centipedes the same *Hox* genes are active in all segments of the body except the head. And, in a related worm-like creature, Onychophora, the *Hox* genes are active only in a single segment of the organism, in its hindmost region. Since these are not homologous parts of these three species, this demonstrates that the specific developmental contribution of the same genes varies as a consequence of the developmental system in which they find themselves. Genes that play a role in the abdominal segment of fruit flies are active in virtually all the bodily segments of centipedes, but in only a single segment in Onychophora.

The main point of the present essay is to extend the normally occurring influences on genetic activity to the external environment, thereby further demonstrating that the genome is not encapsulated and is in fact a part of the organism's general developmental–physiological adaptation to environmental stresses and signals: Genes express themselves appropriately only in responding to internally and externally generated stimulation. Further, in this holistic view, although genes participate in the making of protein, protein is also subject to other influences (Davidson, 1986; Pritchard, 1986), and protein must be further stimulated and elaborated to become part of the nervous system (or other systems) of the organism; therefore, genes operate at the lowest level of organismic organization and they do not, in and of themselves, produce finished traits or features of the organism.[1] Thus, there is no correlation between genome size and the structural complexity of organisms (reviewed in Gottlieb, 1992, pp. 154–157), nor is there a correlation between numbers of genes and numbers of neurons in the brains of a variety of organisms (Table 12.1). The organism is a product of epigenetic development, which includes the genes as well as many other supragenetic influences. Since this latter point has been the subject of numerous contributions (reviewed in Gottlieb, 1992, 1997), I shall not deal with it further here, but, rather, restrict this essay to documenting that the activity of genes is regulated in just the same way as the rest of the

---

[1]Among the most scholarly early critiques to make this point was that of G. Stent (1981), who wrote:

> For the viewpoint that the structure and function of the nervous system of an animal is specified by its genes provides too narrow a context for actually understanding developmental processes and thus sets a goal for the genetic approach that is unlikely to be reached. Here too "narrow" is not to mean that a belief in genetic specification of the nervous system necessarily implies a lack of awareness that in development there occurs an interaction between genes and environment, a fact of which all practitioners of the genetic approach are certainly aware. Rather, "too narrow" means that the role of the genes, which, thanks to the achievements of molecular biology, we now know to be the specification of the primary structure of protein molecules, is at too many removes from the processes that actually "build nerve cells and specify neural circuits which underlie behavior" to provide an appropriate conceptual framework for posing the developmental questions that need to be answered. (pp. 186–187)

Stent's critique was taken a step further by Nijhout (1990), who wrote in a general way about the importance of interactions, above the genetic level, in the internal environment of the organism to bring about growth and differentiation (morphogenesis). Nijhout's point was that "genes do not . . . 'cause' or 'control' morphogenesis; they enable it to take place" (p. 443). Even more pertinent to the theme of the present chapter, Nijhout wrote that "the genes whose products are necessary during development are activated by stimuli that arise from the cellular and chemical processes of development. Thus the network or pattern of gene activation does not constitute a program, it is both the consequence of, and contributor to, development" (p. 443). In this chapter I extend this point of view to the external environment.

TABLE 12.1
Approximate Number of Genes and Neurons in the Brains of Organisms in Different Lineages

| Lineages | Genes | Neurons |
|----------|-------|---------|
| Chordates | 70,000 | 40 million |
| *Mus musculus* | | |
| *Homo sapiens* | 70,000 | 85 billion |
| Nematodes | | |
| *Caenorhabdhitis elegans* | 14,000 | 302 |
| Arthropods | | |
| *Drosophila melanogaster* | 12,000 | 250,000 |

From G. L. Gabor Miklos (unpublished). Reprinted by permission. The exact number of neurons in the brain of *C. elegans* in known to be 302.

organism, being called forth by signals from the normally occurring external environment, as well as the internal environment (Nijhout, 1990; Pritchard, 1986). Although this fact is not well known in the social and behavioral sciences, it is surprising to find that it is also not widely appreciated in biology proper (Strohman, 1997). In biology, the external environment is seen as the agent of natural selection in promoting evolution, not as a crucial feature of individual development (van der Weele, 1995). Many biologists subscribe to the notion that "the genes are safely sequestered inside the nucleus of the cell and out of reach of ordinary environmental effects" (Wills, 1989, p. 19).

## Normally Occurring Environmental Influences on Gene Activity

As can be seen in Table 12.2, a number of different naturally occurring environmental signals can stimulate gene expression in a large variety of organisms from nematodes to humans. The earliest demonstration that I could find of this regularly occurring phenomenon in intact organisms is the work of H. Hydén (Hydén & Egyházi, 1962). In this rarely cited study, hungry rats had to learn to traverse a narrow rod from an elevated start platform to an elevated feeding platform—a veritable balancing act. The nuclear base ratios in their vestibular nerve cells were then compared with an untrained control group and a control group given passive vestibular stimulation. The RNA base ratios in the experimental group differed from both the control groups, and there was no difference between the control groups.

I think the Hydén and Egyházi study is rarely cited because the results not only did not fit into any existing paradigm, they seemed to raise the

TABLE 12.2
Normally Occurring Environmental and Behavioral Influences on Gene Activity

| Species | Environmental Signal or Stimulus | Result (alteration in) | Author(s) |
|---|---|---|---|
| Nematodes | absence or presence of food | neuronal *daf-7* gene mRNA expression, inhibiting or provoking larval development | Ren et al., 1996 |
| Fruit flies | transient elevated heat stress during larval development | heat shock proteins and thermotolerance | Singh & Lakhotia, 1988 |
| Fruit flies | light–dark cycle | PER and TIM protein expression and circadian rhythms | Lee et al, 1996; Myers et al., 1996 |
| Various reptiles | incubation temperature | sex determination | reviewed in Bull, 1983; van de Weele, 1995 |
| Songbirds (canaries, zebra finches) | conspecific song | forebrain mRNA | Mello, Vicario, & Clayton, 1992 |
| Hamsters | light–dark cycle | pituitary hormone mRNA and reproductive behavior | Hegarty et al., 1990 |
| Mice | acoustic stimulation | c-*fos* expression, neuronal activity, tonotopy in auditory system | Ehret & Fisher, 1991 |
| Mice | light–dark cycle | c-*fos* mRNA expression in suprachiasmatic nucleus of hypo-thalamus, circadian locomotor activity | Smeyne et al., 1992 |
| Rats | tactile stimulation | c-*fos* expression and number of somatosensory cortical neurons | Mack & Mack, 1992 |
| Rats | learning task involving vestibular system | nuclear RNA base ratios in vestibular nerve cells | Hydén & Egyházi, 1962 |

*(Continued)*

TABLE 12.2
(Continued)

| | | | |
|---|---|---|---|
| Rats | visual stimulation | RNA and protein synthesis in visual cortex | Rose, 1967 |
| Rats | environmental complexity | brain RNA diversity | Uphouse & Bonner, 1975; review in Rosenzweig & Bennet, 1978 |
| Rats | prenatal nutrition | cerebral DNA (cerebral cell number) | Zamenhof & van Marthens, 1978 |
| Rats | infantile handling; separation from mother | hypothalamic mRNAs for corticotropin-releasing hormone throughout life | Meaney et al., 1996 |
| Cats | visual stimulation | visual cortex RNA complexity (diversity) | Grouse et al., 1979 |
| Humans | academic examinations taken by medical students (psychological stress) | interleukin 2 receptor mRNA (immune system response) | Glaser et al., 1990 |

Lamarckian spectre mentioned by Hydén in the opening quotation.[2] If that is the case, there is an elementary misunderstanding. First, environmental stimulation of gene activity in the organ of balance does not mean the genes were necessarily altered in the process or, second, if they were altered, there is no reason to assume that the alteration was passed on to the progeny, as would be required by the way Lamarck used the notion of the inheritance of acquired characters in his theory of evolution.[3] In the Hydén and Egyházi study the most conservative and acceptable explanation is that genes (DNA) were turned on in the experimental group in a way that they were not turned on in the control groups, resulting in an alteration of RNA base ratios in the experimental group.

To understand the findings summarized in Table 12.2, the nongeneticist will need to recall that the sequence of amino acids in proteins is deter-

[2]Due to the great advances in molecular techniques since 1962, some present-day workers may question the results of Hydén and Egyházi on methodological grounds.

[3]Although it is not a popular idea, and it is a separate question, genes can be altered by internal (reverse transcription, for example) and external events during development and, under certain conditions, the activities of these altered genes can persist across generations (Campbell & Perkins, 1983; Campbell & Zimmerman, 1982; Holliday, 1990; Jablonka & Lamb, 1995).

mined by the sequence of nucleotides in the gene that "codes" for it, operating through the intermediary of mRNA. So there are three levels of evidence of genetic activity in Table 12.2: protein expression or synthesis, mRNA activity, and genetic activity itself. A difference in number of brain cells as a consequence of environmental influences—as in the Mack and Mack, and Zamenhof and van Marthens studies—means that DNA activity has been turned on by the environmental stimulation. In the case of the more recent study, Mack and Mack (1992) were able to measure *fos* activity as well as count the number of cortical cells, whereas Zamenhof and van Marthens (1978) were able only to count the number of cerebral cells as evidence of DNA activity.

As Table 12.2 shows, there are important neural and behavioral correlations to genetic activity, even though the activity of the genes is quite remote from these effects. The posttranslational expression of genes beyond the initial synthesis of protein involves the intervention of many factors before the end product of gene activity is realized (review in Pritchard, 1986, p. 179).

The fact that normally occurring environmental events stimulate gene activity during the usual course of development in a variety of organisms means that genes and genetic activity are part of the developmental–physiological system and do not stand outside of that system as some biologists and others have assumed on the basis of the central dogma. The mechanisms by which environmental signals turn on genetic activity during the normal course of development are being actively explored in a number of laboratories, and reviews can be found in Campbell and Zimmermann (1982), Holliday (1990), Morgan and Curran (1991), Rosen and Greenberg (1994), Curran, Smeyne, Robertson, Vendrell, and Morgan (1994), and Jablonka and Lamb (1995). Psychologists may be particularly interested in the fact that environmentally provoked gene expression is thought to be required for long-term memory (review in Goelet, Castellucci, Schacher, & Kandel, 1986).

## FROM CENTRAL DOGMA OF MOLECULAR BIOLOGY TO PROBABILISTIC EPIGENESIS

The main purpose of this chapter is to place genes and genetic activity firmly within a holistic developmental–physiological framework, one in which genes not only affect each other and mRNA but are affected by activities at other levels of the system, up to and including the external environment. This holistic-developmental system of bidirectional, coactional influences is captured schematically in Fig. 12.3. In contrast to the unidirectional and encapsulated genetic predeterminism of the central dogma, a probabilistic view of epigenesis holds that the sequence and outcomes of development are probabilistically determined by the critical operation of various endog-

## BIDIRECTIONAL INFLUENCES

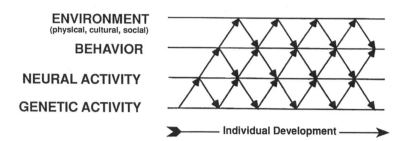

ENVIRONMENT
(physical, cultural, social)

BEHAVIOR

NEURAL ACTIVITY

GENETIC ACTIVITY

Individual Development

FIG. 12.3. Probabilistic–epigenetic framework: Depiction of the completely bidirectional and coactional nature of genetic, neural, behavioral, and environmental influences over the course of individual development. (From *Individual Development and Evolution: The Genesis of Novel Behavior* by Gilbert Gottlieb. Copyright 1992 by Oxford University Press, Inc. Used by permission of Oxford University Press, Inc.)

enous and exogenous stimulative events (Gottlieb, 1970, p. 111; recent review in Gottlieb, 1997).

The probabilistic–epigenetic framework presented in Fig. 12.3 is not only based on what we now know about mechanisms of individual development at all levels of analysis but also derives from our understanding of evolution and natural selection. Natural selection serves as a filter and preserves reproductively successful phenotypes. These successful phenotypes are a product of individual development, and thus are a consequence of the adaptability of the organism to its developmental conditions. Therefore, natural selection has preserved (favored) organisms that are adaptably responsive to their developmental conditions, both behaviorally and physiologically. Organisms with the same genes can develop very different phenotypes under different ontogenetic conditions, as witness the two extreme variants of a single parasitic wasp species, shown in Fig. 12.4, and identical twins reared apart in the human species (Fig. 12.5).[4]

As the probabilistic–epigenetic view presented in Fig. 12.3 does not portray enough detail at the level of genetic activity, it is useful to flesh that out in comparison with the previously described central dogma of molecular biology.

---

[4]This great amount of phenotypic variation observed in identical twins (sharing the same genotype) coordinates well with the enormous degree of phenotypic variation in the human species, in which there is in fact only a very small degree of individual genetic variation at the level of DNA. DNA is composed of two base pairs of nucleotides. There is such a small amount of variation in these base pairs in the human population that any two individuals selected at random from anywhere on earth would exhibit differences in only 3 or 4 base pairs out of 1,000 base pairs (i.e., .3% or .4%!) (Cann, 1988; Merriwether et al., 1991).

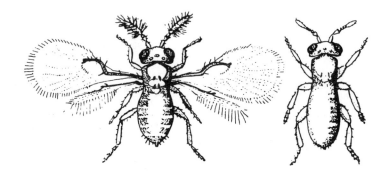

**Butterfly Host**               **Alder Host**

FIG. 12.4. Two very different morphological outcomes of development in the minute parasitic wasp, depending on the host (butterfly or alder fly) in which the eggs were laid. The insects are of the same species of parasitic wasp (*Trichogramma semblidis*). (Modified after Wigglesworth, 1964.)

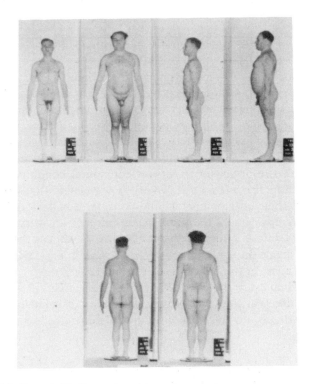

FIG. 12.5. Remarkable illustration of the enormous phenotypic variation that can result when monozygotic (single egg) identical twins are reared apart in very different family environments from birth. (From Tanner, 1978, based on Shields, 1962.)

As shown in Fig. 12.6, the original central dogma explicitly posited one-way traffic from DNA → RNA → Protein, and was silent about any other flows of "information" (Crick, 1958). Later, after the discovery of retroviruses (RNA → DNA information transfer), Crick (1970) did not claim to have predicted that phenomenon, but rather, that the original formulation did not expressly forbid it. In the bottom of Fig. 12.6, probabilistic epigenesis, being inherently bidirectional in the horizontal and vertical levels (Fig. 12.3), has information flowing not only from RNA → DNA but between Protein ↔

## Genetic Activity According To Central Dogma

## Genetic Activity According To Probabilistic Epigenesis

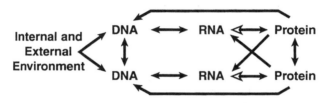

FIG. 12.6.  Different views of influences on genetic activity in the central dogma and probabilistic epigenesis. The filled arrows indicate documented sources of influence, while the open arrow from Protein back to RNA remains a theoretical possibility in probabilistic epigenesis and is prohibited in the central dogma (as are Protein ↔ Protein influences). Protein → Protein influences occur when (1) prions transfer this abnormal conformation to other proteins, and (2) when, during normal development, proteins activate or inactivate other proteins as in the phosphorylation example described in the text. The filled arrows from Protein to RNA represent the activation of mRNA by protein as a consequence of phosphorylation, for example. DNA ↔ DNA influences are termed "epistatic," referring to the modification of gene expression depending on the genetic background in which they are located. In the central dogma genetic activity is dictated solely by genes (DNA → DNA), whereas in probabilistic epigenesis internal and external environmental events activate genetic expression through protein (Protein → DNA), hormonal, and other influences. To keep the diagram manageable, the fact that behavior and the external environment exert their effects on DNA through internal mediators (proteins, hormones, etc.) is not shown; nor is it shown that the protein products of some genes regulate the expression of other genes. (Further discussion in text.)

Protein and DNA ↔ DNA. The only relationship that is not yet supported is Protein → RNA, in the sense of reverse translation (Protein altering the structure of RNA), but there are other influences of Protein on RNA activity (not its structure) that would support such a directional flow. For example, a process known as *phosphorylation* can modify proteins such that they activate (or inactivate) other proteins (Protein → Protein) which, when activated, trigger rapid association of mRNA (Protein → RNA activity). When mRNAs are transcribed by DNA they do not necessarily become immediately active but require a further signal to do so. The consequences of phosphorylation could provide that signal (Protein → Protein → mRNA activity → Protein). A process like this appears to be involved in the expression of "fragile X mental retardation protein" under normal conditions, and proves disastrous to neural and psychological development when it does not occur (Weiler et al., 1997).[5] Hyman and Nestler (1993) provide an excellent overview of the various roles of phosphorylation in the nervous system.

Amplifying the left side of the bottom of Fig. 12.6, gene expression is affected by events in the cytoplasm of the cell, which is the immediate environment of the nucleus and mitochondria of the cell wherein DNA resides, and by hormones that enter the cell and its nucleus. This feed-downward effect can be visualized thusly:

Gene expression influenced by

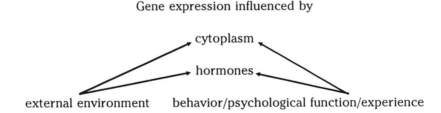

cytoplasm

hormones

external environment        behavior/psychological function/experience

---

[5]The label of "fragile X mental retardation protein" makes it sound as if there is a gene (or genes) that produces a protein that predisposes to mental retardation, whereas it is this protein that is *missing* (absent) in the brain of fragile X mental retardates, and thus represents a failure of gene (or mRNA) expression rather than a positive genetic contribution to mental retardation. The same is likely true for other "genetic" disorders, whether mental or physical: These most often represent biochemical deficiencies of one sort or another due to the lack of expression of the requisite genes and mRNAs to produce the appropriate proteins necessary for normal development. Thus, the search for "candidate genes" in psychiatric or other disorders is most often a search for genes that are not being expressed, rather than genes that are being expressed and causing the disorder. So-called cystic fibrosis genes and manic-depression genes, among others, are in this category. The instances that I know of in which the presence of genes causes a problem are Edward's Syndrome and trisomy 21 (Down syndrome), wherein the presence of an extra, otherwise normal, chromosome—18 and 21, respectively—causes problems because the genetic system is adapted for two, not three, chromosomes at each location. In some cases, it is of course possible that the expression of mutated genes can be involved in a disorder, but, in my opinion, it is most often the lack of expression of normal genes that is the culprit.

According to this view, different proteins are formed depending on the particular factors influencing gene expression. Concerning the effect of psychological functioning on gene expression we have the evidence in Table 12.2 of heightened interleukin 2 receptor mRNA, an immune system response, in medical students taking academic examinations (Glaser et al., 1990). More recently, in an elegant study that traverses all levels from psychological functioning to neural activity to neural structure to gene expression, Cirelli, Pompeiano, and Tononi (1996) showed that genetic activity in certain areas of the brain is higher during waking than during sleep in rats. In this case, the stimulation of gene expression was influenced by the hormone norepinephrine flowing from locus coeruleus neurons that fire at very low levels during sleep, and at high levels during waking and when triggered by salient environmental events. Norepinephrine modifies neural activity and excitability, as well as the expression of certain genes. So, in this case, we have evidence for the interconnectedness of events relating the external environment and psychological functioning to genetic expression by a specifiable hormone emanating from the activity of a specific neural structure whose functioning waxes and wanes in relation to the psychological state of the organism.

## Importance of Behavioral and Neural Activity in Determining Gene Expression, Anatomical Structure, and Physiological Function

Many, if not all, of the normally occurring environmental influences on genetic activity summarized in Table 12.2 involve behavioral and neural mediation. In the holistic spirit of this essay I want to emphasize the contribution of events above the genetic level (the whole organism and environmental context) by way of redressing the balance to the way many think about the overriding importance of molecular biology. The earliest synaptic connections in the embryonic and fetal nervous system are created by spontaneous activity of nerve cells (review in Corner, 1994, and Katz & Shatz, 1996). This early, "exuberant" phase produces a very large array of circuits that is then pared down by the organism's encounters with its prenatal and postnatal environment. In the absence of behavioral and neural activity (e. g., experimentally induced paralysis), cells do not die and circuits do not become pruned in an adaptive way that fits the organism to the demands of its physical, social, and cultural environments (Pittman & Oppenheim, 1979). Until recently, it was thought that the early exuberant phase of neural circuit formation was independent of neural activity but that has been shown to be incorrect: Neural activity is required if the initial circuits are to be in the appropriate area of the brain (Catalano & Shatz, 1998). A recent review of the development and evolution of brain plasticity may be found in Black and Greenough (1998).

(a)                     (b)

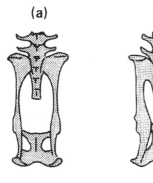

FIG. 12.7. Modification of pelvic and spinal anatomy consequent to bipedalism. (a) Pelvis and lower spine of a normal quadrupedal goat. (b) Pelvis and lower spine of a goat born without forelimbs and which adopted a form of locomotion similar to a kangaroo. (From Pritchard, 1986, after Slijper, 1942.) (Used by permission of Dorian Pritchard.)

Sometimes one reads the perfectly reasonable suggestion that, while genes don't make anatomical, physiological, or behavioral traits, the genes constrain the outer limits of variation in such traits. It is of course the developmental system, of which the genes are a part (Fig. 12.3), and not solely the genes that constrain development. It is not possible to predict in advance what the outcome of development will be when the developing organism is faced with novel environmental or behavioral challenges never before faced by the species or strain of animal. This has been known since 1909 when Woltereck did the first experiments that resulted in the open-ended concept of the norm of reaction, an idea that has been misunderstood by some behavior geneticists who think of genes as setting up a too-narrow *range of reaction* (reviews in Gottlieb, 1995; Platt & Sanislow, 1988).

A very striking example of the role of novel behavior bringing about an entirely new anatomical structure can be seen in Fig. 12.7: Slijper's (1942) goat. This animal was born with undeveloped forelimbs and adopted a kangaroo-like form of locomotion. As a result, its skeleton and musculature became modified, with a pelvis and lower spinal column like that of a biped instead of a quadruped. Thus, while there can be no doubt that genes and other factors place constraints on development, Slijper's goat shows that it is not possible to know the limits of these constraints in advance, even though it might seem quite reasonable to assume, in advance of empirical inquiry, that a quadruped is not capable of bipedality. While an open-ended, empirically based norm of reaction can accommodate Slijper's goat, a narrowly constrained, rationally based range of reaction cannot, no matter how reasonable it seems. It may very well be that all quadruped species cannot adapt bipedally, but we can't know that without perturbing the developmental system.

## SUMMARY AND CONCLUSIONS

While it is tempting to show the nice link between probabilistic epigenesis and an epigenetic-behavioral theory of evolution, that topic has been reviewed in depth in several recent publications (Gottlieb, 1992, 1997), so I will forego that temptation here in favor of sticking to the main point of the essay. The central dogma lies behind the persistent trend in biology and psychology to view genes and environment as making identifiably separate contributions to the phenotypic outcomes of development. Quantitative behavior genetics is based on this erroneous assumption. It is erroneous because animal experiments have repeatedly shown that it is not possible to identify the genetic and environmental components of any phenotype, whether behavioral, anatomical, or physiological (extensive review in Wahlsten & Gottlieb, 1997).[6] While genes no doubt play a constraining role in development, the actual limits of these constraints are quite wide and, most importantly, cannot be specified in advance of experimental manipulation or accidents of nature, as documented in Figs. 12.4, 12.5, and 12.7. (The prenatal environment also plays a constraining role that cannot be known in advance of experimental or manipulative inquiry; Gottlieb, 1971, 1997.) There is no doubt that development is constrained at all levels of the system (Fig. 12.3), not only by genes and environments.

The theoretical crux of this chapter is that the internal and external environments supply the necessary signals to the genes that instigate the eventual production of the requisite proteins under normal as well as unusual conditions of development. There is no genetic master plan or blueprint that is self-actualized during the course of development as was assumed by the central dogma. Undoubtedly there are unusual developmental conditions to which genes cannot respond adaptably, but the range of possible adaptable genetic responses to strange environmental conditions is truly astounding, as when bird oral epithelial cells mixed with mouse oral mesenchyme cells result in the production of a fully enameled molar tooth (Kollar & Fisher, 1980). The saying "Scarce as a hen's tooth" is based on the fact that bird oral epithelial cells never produce teeth when in conjunction with bird oral mesenchyme cells, as would be the case under normal conditions of development. If this finding is "clean" (no mouse oral

---

[6]This is not the same as saying one can't pinpoint the participation of specific genes and specific environments in *contributing* to phenotypic outcomes. However, since genes and environments always collaborate in the production of any phenotype, it is not possible to say that a certain component of the phenotype was caused exclusively by genes (independent of environmental considerations) and some other component was caused exclusively by environment (independent of a genetic contribution). An understanding of developmental phenomena demands a relational or coactive concept of causality as opposed to singular causes acting in supposed isolation (discussed at length in Gottlieb, 1991, 1997). Overton (1998) presents a historical overview on the topic of dualistic conceptions of causality versus the more recent relational or coactive concept of causality. Further, with respect to the erroneous separation of hereditary and environmental contributions to the phenotype by quantitative behavior geneticists, Wahlsten (1990) has shown that the absence of heredity–environment interaction is a statistical artifact stemming from the insufficient power of the ANOVA to detect such interactions, not the empirical absence of such gene–environment interactions.

epithelial cells accidentally contaminating the mix), it involves the appropriate reactivation of a genetic combination that has been latent for 80 million years when birds' last toothed ancestor existed (Pritchard, 1986, pp. 308–309). Also, the finding that a crucial nutriment experimentally deleted from the environment of bacterial cells could lead to the production of that nutriment by a genetic recombination ("adaptive mutation") caused a storm of disbelief in the biological community until it was shown that there was indeed a molecular basis for this "theoretically impossible" finding (Harris, Longerich, & Rosenberg, 1994; Thaler, 1994).

It will be interesting to see how probabilistic epigenesis becomes modified in the ensuing years as more information accrues through the necessarily interdisciplinary and multidisciplinary efforts of future researchers. The contrasting ideas of predetermined and probabilistic epigenesis were first put forward in Gottlieb (1970). While the central dogma as depicted in Fig. 12.6 is consistent with the formulation of predetermined epigenesis, it is too much to claim that the contrasting formulation of probabilistic epigenesis made in 1970 predicted all the details of the relationships in the lower half of Fig. 12.6. One can say only that those relationships are consistent with the bidirectional influences stated in the probabilistic formula Genetic activity ↔ Structure ↔ Function presented in Gottlieb (1976, p. 218; 1983) and elaborated in Gottlieb (1991, see especially Appendix, p. 13). As I have described in detail elsewhere (e.g., Gottlieb, 1992, 1997), the formulation of probabilistic epigenesis built on the writings of Z.-Y. Kuo (1976), T. C. Schneirla (1960), D. S. Lehrman (1970), and Ashley Montagu (1977).

Finally, in response to a concern raised by colleagues who have read this essay in manuscript form, I do hope that the emphasis on normally occurring environmental influences on gene activity does not raise the spectre of a new, subtle form of "environmentalism." If I were to say organisms are often adaptably responsive to their environments, I don't think that would label me an environmentalist. So, by calling attention to genes being adaptably responsive to their internal and external environments, I am not being an environmentalist, but merely including genetic activity within the probabilistic–epigenetic framework that characterizes the organism and all of its constituent parts (Fig. 12.3). The probabilistic–epigenetic view follows the open-systems view of development championed by the biologists Ludwig von Bertalanffy (1933/1962), Paul Weiss (1939/1969), and Sewall Wright (1968). Their writings were based on a highly interactive conception of embryology, and the central dogma simply overlooked this tradition of biological theorizing, resulting in an encapsulated formulation of gene activity at odds with the facts of embryological development. (The current reductionistic theoretical stance of molecular biology continues to disregard epigenetic considerations [Strohman, 1997].) Building on the insights of von Bertalanffy, Weiss, and Wright, the probabilistic–epigenetic view details the cooperative workings of the embryological open-systems view at the genetic and neural levels, prenatal and postnatal behavior, and the external environment. This view fleshes out, at the prenatal and intraorganismic levels of analysis, various other approaches in developmental psychology: ecological (Bronfenbrenner, 1979), transactional (Sameroff, 1983), contextual (Lerner & Kaufman, 1985), interactional or holistic (Johnston, 1987; Magnusson, 1988), individual–sociological (Valsiner, 1997), structural–behavioral (Horowitz, 1987), dynamic systems (Thelen & Smith, 1994), and, most globally speaking, interdisciplinary developmental science (Cairns, Elder, & Costello, 1996).

## ACKNOWLEDGMENTS

The author's research and scholarly activities are supported in part by NIMH Grant MH-52429. I have benefited from discussions with Jaan Valsiner and other members of the Carolina Consortium of Human Development, as well as from the comments of Dorian Pritchard, Lynda Uphouse, Richard C. Strohman, Kathryn Hood, and Nora Lee Willis Gottlieb on earlier drafts of the manuscript. James Black and William Greenough made very helpful substantive suggestions for which I am most grateful. Ramona Rodriguiz provided generous bibliographic assistance. This chapter is based on an article that appeared in the *Psychological Review*, 1998, Vol. 105, pp. 792–802, copyright © 1998 by the American Psychological Association. Adapted with permission.

## REFERENCES

Bertalanffy, L., von. (1962). *Modern theories of development: An introduction to theoretical biology.* New York: Harper. (Originally published in German in 1933.)

Black, J. E., & Greenough, W. T. (1998). Developmental approaches to the memory process. In J. L. Martinez & R. P. Kesner (Eds.), *Learning and memory: A biological view* (3rd ed., pp. 55–88). New York: Academic Press.

Bronfenbrenner, U. (1979). *The ecology of human development: Experiments by nature and design.* Cambridge, MA: Harvard University Press.

Bull, J. J. (1983). *Evolution of sex determining mechanisms.* Menlo Park, CA: Benjamin/Cummings.

Cairns, R. B., Elder, G. H., & Costello, E. J. (Eds.). (1996). *Developmental science.* New York: Cambridge University Press.

Campbell, J. H., & Perkins, P. (1983). Transgenerational effects of drug and hormonal treatments in mammals: A review of observations and ideas. *Progress in Brain Research, 73,* 535–553.

Campbell, J. H., & Zimmermann, E. G. (1982). Automodulation of genes: A proposed mechanism for persisting effects of drugs and hormones in mammals. *Neurobehavioral Toxicology and Teratology, 4,* 435–439.

Cann, R. L. (1988). DNA and human origins. *Annual Review of Anthropology, 17,* 127–143.

Catalano, S. M., & Shatz, C. J. (1998). Activity-dependent cortical target selection by thalamic axons. *Science, 281,* 559–562.

Chesebro, B. (1998). BSE and prions: Uncertainties about the agent. *Science, 279,* 42–43.

Cirelli, C., Pompeiano, M., & Tononi, G. (1996). Neuronal gene expression in the waking state: A role for locus coeruleus. *Science, 274,* 1211–1215.

Corner, M. A. (1994). Reciprocity of structure-function relations in developing neural networks: The odyssey of a self-organizing brain through research fads, fallacies, and prospects. *Progress in Brain Research, 102,* 3–31.

Crick, F. (1958). On protein synthesis. *Symposia of the Society for Experimental Biology: no. 12. The biological replication of macromolecules* (pp. 138–163). Cambridge, UK: Cambridge University Press.

Crick, F. (1970). Central dogma of molecular biology. *Nature, 227,* 561–563.

Crick, F. (1982). DNA today. *Perspectives in Biology and Medicine, 25,* 512–517.

Curran, T., Smeyne, R., Robertson, L., Vendrell, M., & Morgan, J. I. (1994). FoslacZ expression: A transgenic approach to gene activation in the brain. In S. Zalcman, R. Scheller, & R. Tsien (Eds.), *Molecular neurobiology: Proceedings of the Second NIMH Conference* (pp. 165–172). Rockville, MD: National Institute of Mental Health.

Davidson, E. H. (1986). *Gene activity in early development.* Orlando, FL: Academic Press.

Ehret, G., & Fisher, R. (1991). Neuronal activity and tonotopy in the auditory system visualized by *c-fos* gene expression. *Brain Research, 567,* 350–354.

Elman, J. L., Bates, E. A., Johnson, M. H., Karmiloff-Smith, A., Parisi, D., & Plunkett K. (1996). *Rethinking innateness: A connectionist perspective on development.* Cambridge, MA: MIT Press.

Glaser, R., Kennedy, S., Lafuse, W. P., Bonneau, R. H., Speicher, C., Hillhouse, J., & Kiecolt-Glaser, J. K. (1990). Psychological-stress-induced modulation of interleukin 2 receptor gene expression and interleukin 2 production in peripheral blood leukocytes. *Archives of General Psychiatry, 47,* 707–712.

Goelet, P., Castellucci, V. F., Schacher, S., & Kandel, E. R. (1986). The long and short of long-term memory—a molecular framework. *Nature, 322,* 419–422.

Gottlieb, G. (1970). Conceptions of prenatal behavior. In L. R. Aronson, E. Tobach, D. S. Lehrman, and J. S. Rosenblatt (Eds.), *Development and evolution of behavior: Essays in memory of T. C. Schneirla* (pp. 111–137). San Francisco: Freeman.

Gottlieb, G. (1971). *Development of species identification in birds: An inquiry into the prenatal determinants of perception.* Chicago: University of Chicago Press.

Gottlieb, G. (1976). Conceptions of prenatal development: Behavioral embryology. *Psychological Review, 83,* 215–234.

Gottlieb, G. (1983). The psychobiological approach to developmental issues. In M. M. Haith & J. J. Campos (Eds.), *Handbook of child psychology: Vol. 2. Infancy and developmental psychobiology* (4th ed., pp. 1–26). New York: Wiley.

Gottlieb, G. (1991). Experiential canalization of behavioral development: Theory. *Developmental Psychology, 27,* 4–13.

Gottlieb, G. (1992). *Individual development and evolution: The genesis of novel behavior.* New York: Oxford University Press.

Gottlieb, G. (1995). Some conceptual deficiencies in 'developmental' behavior genetics. *Human Development, 38,* 131–141.

Gottlieb, G. (1997). *Synthesizing nature-nurture: Prenatal roots of instinctive behavior.* Mahwah, NJ: Lawrence Erlbaum Associates.

Grady, D. (1996). Ironing out the wrinkles in the prion strain problem. *Science, 274,* 2010.

Grenier, J. K., Garber, T. L., Warren, R., Whitington, P. M., & Carroll, S. (1997). Evolution of the entire arthropod *Hox* gene set predated the origin and radiation of the onychophoran/arthropod clade. *Current Biology, 7,* 547–553.

Grouse, L. D., Schrier, B. K., Letendre, C. H., & Nelson, P. G. (1980). RNA sequence complexity in central nervous system development and plasticity. *Current Topics in Developmental Biology, 16*, 381–397.

Harris, R. S., Longerich, S., & Rosenberg, S. M. (1994). Recombination in adaptive mutation. *Science, 264*, 258–260.

Hegarty, C. M., Jonassent, J. A., & Bittman, E. L. (1990). Pituitary hormone gene expression in male golden hamsters: Interactions between photoperiod and testosterone. *Journal of Neuroendocrinology, 2*, 567–573.

Ho, M.-W. (1984). Environment and heredity in development and evolution. In M.-W. Ho, & P. T. Saunders (Eds.), *Beyond neo-Darwinism: An introduction to the new evolutionary paradigm* (pp. 267–289). San Diego, CA: Academic Press.

Holliday, R. (1990). Mechanisms for the control of gene activity during development. *Biological Reviews, 65*, 431–471.

Horowitz, F. D. (1987). *Exploring developmental theories: Toward a structural/behavioral model of development*. Hillsdale, NJ: Lawrence Erlbaum Associates.

Hydén, H. (1969). Afterthoughts. In A. Koestler & J. R. Smythies (Eds.), *Beyond reductionism: New perspectives in the life sciences* (pp. 114–117). London: Hutchinson.

Hydén, H., & Egyházi, E. (1962). Nuclear RNA changes of nerve cells during a learning experiment in rats. *Proceedings of the National Academy of Sciences, USA, 48*, 1366–1373.

Hyman, S. E., & Nestler, E. J. (1993). *The molecular foundations of psychiatry*. Washington, DC: American Psychiatric Press.

Jablonka, E. & Lamb, M. J. (1995). *Epigenetic inheritance and evolution: The Lamarckian dimension*. Oxford, UK: Oxford University Press.

Johnston, T. D. (1987). The persistence of dichotomies in the study of behavioral development. *Developmental Review, 7*, 149–182.

Katz, L. C., & Shatz, C. J. (1996). Synaptic activity and the construction of cortical circuits. *Science, 274*, 1133–1138.

Kollar, E. J., & Fisher, C. (1980). Tooth induction in chick epithelium: Expression of quiescent genes for enamel synthesis. *Science, 207*, 993–995.

Kuo, Z.-Y. (1976). *The dynamics of behavior development* (enlarged ed.). New York: Plenum.

Lee, C., Parikh, V., Itsukaichi, T., Bae, K., & Edery, I. (1996). Resetting the *Drosophila* clock by photic regulation of PER and a PER-TIM complex. *Science, 271*, 1740–1744.

Lehrman, D. S. (1970). Semantic and conceptual issues in the nature-nurture problem. In L. R. Aronson, E. Tobach, D. S. Lehrman, & J. S. Rosenblatt (Eds.), *Development and evolution of behavior: Essays in memory of T. C. Schneirla* (pp. 17–52). San Francisco: Freeman.

Lerner, R. M., & Kaufman, M. B. (1985). The concept of development in contextualism. *Developmental Review, 5*, 309–333.

Mack, K. J., & Mack, P. A. (1992). Induction of transcription factors in somatosensory cortex after tactile stimulation. *Molecular Brain Research, 12*, 141–147.

Magnusson, D. (1988). *Individual development from an interactional perspective: A longitudinal study*. Hillsdale, NJ: Lawrence Erlbaum Associates.

Mayr, E. (1982). *The growth of biological thought*. Cambridge, MA: Belknap Press of Harvard University Press.

Meaney, M. J., Diorio, J., Francis, D., Widdowson, J., LaPlante, P., Caldji, C., Sharma, S., Seckl, J. P., & Plotsky, P. M. (1996). Early environmental regulation of forebrain glucocorticoid receptor gene expression: Implications for adrenocortical responses to stress. *Developmental Neuroscience, 18*, 49–72.

Mello, C. V., Vicario, D. S., & Clayton, D. F. (1992). Song presentation induces gene expression in the songbird forebrain. *Proceedings of the National Academy of Sciences, USA, 89*, 6818–6822.

Merriwether, D. A., Clark, A. G., Ballinger, S. W., Schurr, T. G., Soodyall, H., Jenkins, T., Sherry, S. T., & Wallace, D. C. (1991) The structure of human mitochondrial DNA variation. *Journal of Molecular Evolution, 33*, 543–555.

Montagu, A. (1977). Sociogenic brain damage. In S. Arieti & G. Chrzanowski (Eds.), *New dimensions in psychiatry: A world view* (Vol. 2, pp. 4–25). New York: Wiley.

Morgan, J. I., & Curran, T. (1991). Stimulus-transcription coupling in the nervous system: Involvement of the inducible proto-oncogenes *fos* and *jun*. *Annual Review of Neurosciences, 14,* 421–451.

Myers, M. P., Wager-Smith, K., Rothenfluh-Hilfiker, A., & Young, M. W. (1996). Light-induced degradation of TIMELESS and entrainment of the *Drosophila* circadian clock. *Science, 271,* 1736–1740.

Nijhout, H. F. (1990). Metaphors and the role of genes in development. *BioEssays, 12,* 441–446.

Overton, W. F. (1998). Developmental psychology: Philosophy, concepts, and methodology. In R. M. Lerner (Ed.), *Handbook of child psychology: Vol. 1. Theoretical models of human development* (5th ed., pp. 107–189). New York: Wiley.

Pittman, R., & Oppenheim, R. W. (1979). Cell death of motoneurons in the chick embryo spinal cord. IV. Evidence that a functional neuromuscular interaction is involved in the regulation of naturally occurring cell death and the stabilization of synapses. *Journal of Comparative Neurology, 187,* 425–446.

Platt, S. A., & Sanislow, C. A. (1988). Norm-of-reaction: Definition and misinterpretation of animal research. *Journal of Comparative Psychology, 102,* 254–261.

Pritchard, D. J. (1986). *Foundations of developmental genetics.* London and Philadelphia: Taylor & Francis.

Ren, P., Lin, C.-S., Johnson, R., Albert, P. S., Pilgrim, D., & Riddle, D. L. (1996). Control of *C. elegans* larval development by neuronal expression of a TGFβ homolog. *Science, 274,* 1389–1391.

Rose, S. P. R. (1967). Changes in visual cortex on first exposure of rats to light: Effect on incorporation of tritiated lysine into protein. *Nature, 215,* 253–255.

Rosen, L. B., & Greenberg, M. E. (1994). Regulation of *c-fos* and other immediate-early genes in PC-12 cells as a model for studying specificity in neuronal signaling. In S. Zalcman, R. Scheller, & R. Tsein (Eds.), *Molecular neurobiology: Proceedings of the Second NIMH Conference* (pp. 203–216). Rockville, MD: National Institute of Mental Health.

Sameroff, A. J. (1983). Developmental systems: Contexts and evolution. In W. Kessen (Ed.), *Handbook of child psychology: Vol. 1. History, theory, and methods* (4th ed., pp. 237–294). New York: Wiley.

Schneirla, T. C. (1960). Instinctive behavior, maturation—Experience and development. In B. Kaplan & S. Wapner (Eds.), *Perspectives in psychological theory—Essays in honor of Heinz Werner* (pp. 303–334). New York: International Universities Press.

Shields, J. (1962). *Monozygotic twins.* London: Oxford University Press.

Singh, A. K., & Lakhotia, S. C. (1988). Effect of low-temperature rearing on heat shock protein synthesis and heat sensitivity in *Drosophilia melanogaster. Developmental Genetics, 9,* 193–201.

Slijper, E. J. (1942). Biologic-anatomical investigations on the bipedal gait and upright posture in mammals, with special reference to a little goat, born without forelegs. II. *Proceedings Series C Biological and Medical Sciences: Koninklijke Nederlandse Akademie van Wetenschappen Amsterdam, 45,* 407–415.

Smeyne, R. J., Schilling, K., Robertson, L., Luk, D., Oberdick, J., Curran, T., & Morgan, J. I. (1992). Fos-lacZ transgenic mice: Mapping sites of gene induction in the central nervous system. *Neuron, 8,* 13–23.

Spelke, E. S., & Newport, E. L. (1998). Nativism, empiricism, and the development of knowledge. In R. M. Lerner (Ed.), *Handbook of child psychology: Vol. 1. Theoretical models of human development* (5th ed., pp. 275–340). New York: Wiley

Stent, G. (1981). Strength and weakness of the genetic approach to the development of the nervous system. *Annual Review of Neuroscience, 4,* 163–194.

Strohman, R. C. (1997). The coming Kuhnian revolution in biology. *Nature Biotechnology, 15,* 194–200.

Tanner, J. M. (1978), *Foetus into man: Physical growth from conception to maturity*. Cambridge, MA: Harvard University Press.

Telling, G. C., Parchi, P., DeArmond, S. J., Cortelli, P., Montagna, P., Gabizon, R., Mastrianni, J., Lugaresi, E., Gambetti, P., & Pruisner, S. B. (1996). Evidence for the conformation of the pathologic isoform of the prion protein enciphering and propagating prion diversity. *Science, 274*, 2079–2082.

Thaler, D. S. (1994). The evolution of genetic intelligence. *Science, 264*, 224–225.

Thelen, E., & Smith, L. B. (1994). *A dynamic systems approach to cognition and action.* Cambridge, MA: MIT Press.

Tooby, J., & Cosmides, L. (1990). The past explains the present: Emotional adaptations and the structure of ancestral environments. *Ethology and Sociobiology, 11*, 375–424.

Uphouse, L. L., & Bonner, J. (1975). Preliminary evidence for the effects of environmental complexity on hybridization of rat brain RNA to rat unique DNA. *Developmental Psychobiology, 8*, 171–178.

Valsiner, J. (1997). *Culture and the development of children's action: A theory of human development* (2nd ed.). New York: Wiley.

Wahlsten, D. (1990). Insensitivity of the analysis of variance to heredity-environment interaction. *Behavioral and Brain Sciences, 13*, 109–120; open peer commentary, 121–161.

Wahlsten, D., & Gottlieb, G. (1997). The invalid separation of nature and nurture: lessons from animal experimentation. In R. J. Sternberg & E. Grigorenko (Eds.), *Intelligence, heredity, and environment* (pp. 163–192). New York: Cambridge University Press.

van der Weele, C. (1995). *Images of development : Environmental causes in ontogeny*. Unpublished doctoral dissertation, Vrije University, Amsterdam.

Weiler, I. J., Irwin, S. A., Klintsova, A. Y., Spencer, C. M., Brazelton, A. D., Miyashiro, K., Comery, T., Patel, B., Eberwine, J., & Greenough, W. T. (1997). Fragile X mental retardation protein is translated near synapses in response to neurotransmitter activation. *Proceedings of the National Academy of Sciences USA, 94*, 5395–5400.

Weiss, P. (1939). *Principles of development: A text in experimental embryology*. New York: Holt, Rinehart & Winston.

Wigglesworth, V. B. (1964). *The life of insects*. Cleveland, OH: World Publishing.

Wills, C. (1989). *The wisdom of the genes: New pathways in evolution*. New York: Basic Books.

Woltereck, R. (1909). Weitere experimentelle Untersuchungen über Artveränderung, speziell über das Wesen quantitativer Artunterschiede bei Daphniden [Further experimental investigations of species modification, particularly the nature of quantitative species differences in daphnia]. *Verhandlungen der Deutschen Zoologischen Gesellschaft, 19*, 110–173.

Wright, S. (1968). *Evolution and the genetics of population: Vol. 1. Genetic and biometric foundations*. Chicago: University of Chicago Press.

Zamenhof, S., & van Marthens, E. (1978). Nutritional influences on prenatal brain development. In G. Gottlieb (Ed.), *Early influences* (pp. 149–186). New York: Academic Press.

# 13

# Lessons From the Wings of Drosophila

Sarnoff A. Mednick
Social Science Research Institute
University of Southern California

Matti O. Huttunen
University of Helsinki, Finland
National Health Institute, Helsinki, Finland

The effects of organ teratogens during fetal development are known to be highly dependent on their timing. In the well-known example in humans, the hypnotic, thalidomide, is only effective as a teratogen during one week of the first trimester of gestation. The resultant teratogenic effects are specific and recognizable. The details of the timing and mechanism of teratogenic events have been most elegantly elucidated in the fruit fly, Drosophila Melanogaster (Schlesinger, Ashburner, & Tissieres, 1982). In this model the most commonly studied teratogen has been heat shock. During a period of rapid gene expression of some bodily part of the larvae (such as the wings or legs), the development of that particular bodily part is highly sensitive to the effects of heat shock. In these critical periods, or developmental windows, the gene expression of the particular part of Drosophila is put on hold by heat shock or other teratogens. When the environmental danger to the cells is past, the genes begin to express normally again, but they do not return to the previous cycle of gene expression to correct omissions or developmental errors. Each part of the body of Drosophila has a narrow developmental window of its own. Thus, if the heat shock is presented during the 37 to 41 hours of the pupal stage, the resultant Drosophila may have no wings, or the wings may be deformed. If the heat shock is presented during the 40 to 44 hours of pupal development, the head will not develop properly. The part of the larva that develops abnormally depends on which part happens to be experiencing a spurt of gene expression and development at the time of the teratogenic event.

Taking as a model the development of the wings of Drosophila, we propose a general theory: The different parts of the developing central nervous system are sensitive to narrowly timed environmental teratogens. We further propose that these environmentally induced, subtle (i.e., not obvious to physical examination at birth) neurodevelopmental omissions and errors play a crucial role in the etiology of psychiatric disorders and their symptom profiles. During fetal development, every area of the brain has its sensitive growth spurts. If the area does not fully develop in those assigned periods, the developing brain does not backtrack in order to compensate; the area is left with a deficit. These environmentally induced deficits in specific brain areas, systems, or circuits are associated with specific mental, behavioral, and cognitive patterns and disorders. Furthermore, a variety of untoward gestational influences may act as neurodevelopmental "heat shocks" in human fetuses and young infants, including maternal viral infections, maternal stress, alcohol ingestion, smoking tobacco, and so on.

In rodents and rhesus monkeys the behavioral, neurochemical, or neuroanatomic teratogenic effects of environmental stress or glucocorticoids are known to be highly time-dependent and time-specific (Alonso, Arevalo, Afonso, & Rodriguez, 1991; Alonso, Navarro, & Rodriguez, 1994; Benes, 1994, 1997; Gould, Tanapat, & Cameron, 1997; Gould, Woolley, & McEwen, 1991; Huttunen, 1971; Joffe, 1969; Sapolsky, 1997; Trejo, Machin, Arahuetes, & Rúa, 1995; Uno et al., 1990, 1994; Weinstock, 1997). When fetal rhesus monkeys are exposed to dexamethasone, at the critical period of hippocampal development, there is a permanent reduction in the hippocampal pyramidal neurons and dendritic processes (Uno et al., 1990, 1994). It is known that reduced uterine blood flow increases significantly fetal plasma concentrations of cortisol (Bocking, McMillan, Harding, & Thorburn, 1986) and that the cortisol-induced apoptosis of developing dentate gyrus can be prevented by NMDA receptor antagonists.

Several epidemiological studies have shown that both prenatal viral infections and maternal stress are able to increase the incidence of adult psychiatric disorders in the offspring (Huttunen & Niskanen, 1978; Machon, Huttunen, & Mednick, 1997; Mednick, Machon, Huttunen, & Bonett, 1988; Mednick, Huttunen, & Machon, 1994; Susser et al., 1996; Van Os & Selten, 1998). Even more interesting, there is growing evidence that the exact timing of the various pre- and perinatal neurodevelopmental insults may be crucial for the phenotype of the resulting adult psychiatric disorder (Mednick et al., 1998). In Finland and Denmark, it has been demonstrated that the maternal influenza infection in the second trimester of gestation can increase a fetus' risk for both adult schizophrenia (Mednick et al., 1988,

1994) and major affective disorder (Machon et al., 1997). In addition, the distribution of the precise times of the maternal influenza infection seems to be different for schizophrenics and for those with affective disorders. While the majority of schizophrenics (in the Finnish study) suffered a maternal influenza infection in the sixth month of gestation, this was true for only 10% of the affective disorder cases. The majority of those with affective disorder were exposed to maternal infection in the fifth month of gestation (Mednick et al., 1998). In Finland, the association of timing of a maternal influenza infection and the violent criminality among this same birth cohort was examined. The Finnish Criminal Register provided the conviction records of all the Helsinki population born in the nine months after the 1957 A-influenza pandemic. There was no relationship between property crime and period of gestation of exposure to the October–November 1957 pandemic. Convictions for violent crimes were, however, significantly associated with the exposure to the 1957 epidemic during the second trimester of gestation. Moreover, there was a tendency for the violent offenders to have been exposed at the cusp of the sixth and seventh months of gestation. Maternal influenza, however, is not the only neurodevelopmental insult whose timing is crucial for the behavioral or psychiatric outcome of the offspring. In a prospective of study of almost two thousand children born in Helsinki between 1975 and 1976, the difficult ("fussiness") temperament of the 6-month-old infant was associated with the maternal emotional stress during the late first trimester of the mother's pregnancy (Noyes, Martin, Wisenbaker, & Huttunen, in press).

Maternal influenza infection can thus act as a teratogen that disrupts the development of the fetal brain. But to increase the risk for adult schizophrenia this disruption must occur during a period (or periods) of development spurt in specific brain regions, and the resulting deficit plays a significant role in that risk. These periods of vulnerability of specific brain regions are probably rather narrow and span a period of a few days or a couple of weeks in the second trimester of gestation. For example, if a failure of development of a subarea or circuit of the prefrontal cortex or thalamus is a risk factor for schizophrenia, then one period of vulnerability might comprise those days of gestation during which the future cells of the prefrontal cortex or thalamus, or both, are most rapidly proliferating or developing. There may thus exist a period (or periods) of fetal brain development during which an environmental insult may increase risk specifically for schizophrenia. If the genetic or teratogenic developmental disruption strikes at a different gestational period, some other brain area is likely to be undergoing rapid development, but the risk for schizophrenia will not be increased. However, if this other brain region is important in the etiology of another mental disorder, then the risk for that disorder would be increased.

The etiology of schizophrenia is largely genetic (Cannon, Kaprio, Lön-quist, Huttunen, & Koskenvuo, 1998), but it is possible that some proportion of schizophrenics are phenocopies. In Drosophila, the heat-shock produced disturbances of development can phenotypically be similar to specific mutant gene defects. The offspring of these phenocopy-Drosophila develop normally (Schlesinger et al., 1982). It is, therefore, highly interesting that the schizophrenics exposed to the 1957 influenza pandemic during the second trimester of fetal development have significantly less schizophrenia among their first-degree relatives than schizophrenics in general or the schizophrenics exposed to influenza during the first or third trimester of fetal development. Thus, it is conceivable that some cases of adult schizophrenia are second-trimester-induced phenocopies.

Symptomatologically schizophrenia is a most heterogenous disease. Even if schizophrenia is a highly genetic disease, there is little consistency in the genetic transmission of the different subclasses or symptom profiles of schizophrenia. Based on the animal and human epidemiological research, it is quite possible that the neurodevelopmental and behavioral effects of differently timed pre- and perinatal insults can explain much of the variance in the symptomatology, as well as in the neuropsychological and neuro-imaging research of major psychiatric disorders. Under even "normal" conditions the pregnant woman may experience many events that can affect the development of the fetal brain. Each area of the brain has its own sensitive period of rapid gene expression that may also overlap with the critical periods of other, functionally unrelated subareas of brain. The timing of some teratogens may result in changes in the neuronal circuitry that are of little functional consequence; the timing of some, however, may result in serious neurofunctional or behavioral consequences. The result of these "random" and partially overlapping neurodevelopmental teratogenic events may have its expression in the variance of the symptoms of schizophrenia and other psychiatric disorders. The schizophrenics exposed to maternal second trimester influenza suffered significantly more often from paranoid symptoms than the schizophrenics exposed to maternal first or third trimester influenza (Machon, Huttunen, Mednick, & LaFosse, 1995). Perinatal hypoxia among genetically high-risk newborns is associated with both an increased risk and chronicity of schizophrenia and a more negative-type symptom profile (Cannon, 1997). It is also important to remember that both the genetically programmed and environmentally induced apoptotic processes continue after the birth of the infant and can thus profoundly and permanently affect the structure and function of a developing child. It is known, for example, that the neuronal recognition patterns for speech sound and prosody develop within the first year of human life (Näätänen et al., 1997). The difficulty some schizophrenics experience in recognizing facial emotions or speech prosody could thus result from the environmentally induced postnatal disturbance of the development of emotion-specific neuronal recognition structures.

The life of an individual pregnant woman can be full of unpredictable, emotionally stressful or traumatic events, or viral infections. Some pregnant women are addicted to alcohol or tobacco. In light of the current animal research and human epidemiological studies, these common life events can profoundly influence the fetal and perinatal development of the human central nervous system. The lottery of life will determine the exact timing of these environmental events, which are potentially able to affect both the temperament of our children and their risk for a variety of psychiatric disorders.

## ACKNOWLEDGMENTS

The authors wish to thank Professor Maria Pelligrini (Keck Foundation, Los Angeles) for sensitizing us to the research on the Drosophila.This research was supported by the National Institute of Mental Health research grant MH37692 and the National Institute of Mental Health grant MH00619, Research Scientist Award to S. Mednick.

## REFERENCES

Alonso, S. J., Arevalo, R., Afonso, D., & Rodriguez, M. (1991). Effects of maternal stress during pregnancy on forced swimming test behavior of the offspring. *Physiology and Behavior, 50,* 511–517.

Alonso, S. J., Navarro, E., & Rodriguez, M. (1994). Permanent dopaminergic alterations in the nucleus accumbens after prenatal stress. *Pharmacology and Biochemistry of Behavior, 49,* 353–358.

Benes, F. M. (1994). Developmental changes in stress adaptation in relation to psychopathology. *Development and Psychopathology, 6,* 723–739.

Benes, F. M. (1997). The role of stress and dopamine-GABA interactions in the vulnerability for schizophrenia. *Journal of Psychiatric Research, 31,* 257–275.

Bocking, A. D., McMillen, I. C., Harding, R., & Thorburn, G. D. (1986). Effect of reduced uterine blood flow on fetal and maternal cortisol. *Journal of Developmental Physiology, 8,* 237–245.

Cannon, T. D. (1997) On the nature and mechanism of obstetric influences in schizophrenia: A review and synthesis of epidemiological studies. *International Reviews of Psychiatry, 9,* 387–397.

Cannon, T. D., Kaprio, J., Lönquist, J., Huttunen, M. O., & Koskenvuo, M. (1998). The genetic epidemiology of schizophrenia in a Finnish cohort: A population-based modelling study. *Archives of General Psychiatry, 55,* 67–74.

Gould, E., Tanapat, P., & Cameron, H. A. (1997). Adrenal steroids suppress granule cell death in the developing dentate gyrus through an NMDA receptor-dependent mechanism. *Developmental Brain Research, 103,* 91–93.

Gould, E., Woolley, C. S., & McEwen, B. S. (1991). The stress hyporesponsive period regulates dentate gyrus development in the rat. *Journal of Comparative Neurology, 304*, 408–418.

Huttunen, M. O. (1971). Persistent alteration of turnover of brain noradrenaline in the offspring of rats subjected to stress during pregnancy. *Nature, 230*, 53–55.

Huttunen, M. O., & Niskanen, P. (1978). Prenatal loss of father and psychiatric disorders. *Archives of General Psychiatry, 35*, 429–431.

Joffe, J. M. (1969). *Prenatal determinants of behavior*, Oxford, England: Pergamon.

Machon, R. A., Huttunen, M. O., & Mednick, S. A. (1997). Adult major affective disorder after prenatal exposure to an influenza epidemic. *Archives of General Psychiatry, 54*, 322–328.

Machon, R. A., Huttunen, M. O., Mednick, S. A., & LaFosse, J. (1995). Fetal viral infection and adult schizophrenia; Empirical findings and interpretattion. In S. A. Mednick & J. M. Hollister (Eds.), *Neural Development and Schizophrenia* (pp. 191–202). New York: Plenum.

Mednick, S. A., Huttunen, M. O., & Machon, R. A. (1994). Prenatal influenza infections and adult schizophrenia. *Schizophrenia Bulletin, 20*, 263–267.

Mednick, S. A., Machon, R. A., Huttunen, M. O., & Bonett, D. (1988). Adult schizophrenia following prenatal exposure to an influenza epidemic. *Archives of General Psychiatry, 45*, 189–192.

Mednick, S. A., Watson, J. B., Huttunen, M. O., Cannon, T. D., Katila, H., Machon, R. A., Mednick, B., Hollister, M., Parnas, J., Schulsinger, F., Sajaniemi, N., Voldsgaard, P., Pyhälä, R., Gutkind, D., & Wang, X. (1998). A two-hit working model of the etiology of schizophrenia. In M. F. Lenzenweger & R. H. Dworkin (Eds.), *Origins and development of Schizophrenia* (pp. 27–66). Washington, DC: American Psychological Association.

Näätänen, R., Lehtokoski, A., Lennes, M., Cheour, M., Huotilainen, M., Ilvonen, A., Vainio, M., Alku, P., Ilmoniemi, R. J., Luuk, A., Allik, J., Sinkkonen, J., & Alho, K. (1997). Language-specific phone representations revealed by electric and magnetic brain responses. *Nature, 385*, 432–434.

Noyes, J., Martin, R. P., Wisenbaker, J. & Huttunen, M. O. (in press). Prediction of early childhood negative emotionality and inhibition from maternal distress during pregnancy. *Journal of Infant Behavior and Develmepment.*

Sapolsky, R. M. (1997). The importance of a well-groomed child. *Science, 277*, 1620–1622.

Schlesinger, M. J., Ashburner, M., & Tissieres, A. (1982). *Heat shock from bacteria to man.* Cold Spring Harbor, Maine: Cold Spring Harbor Laboratory.

Susser E., Neugebauer R., Hoek, H. W., Brown, A. S., Lin, S., Labovitz, D., & Gorman, J. M. (1996). Schizophrenia after prenatal famine. *Archives of General Psychiatry, 53*, 25–31.

Trejo, J. L., Machin, C., Arahuetes, R. M., & Rúa, C. (1995). Influence of maternal adrenalectomy and glucocorticoid administration on the development of rat cerebral cortex. *Anatomy and Embryology, 192*, 89–99.

Uno, H., Lohmiller, L., Thieme, C., Kemnitz, J., Engle, M., Roecker, E., & Farrell P. (1990). Brain damage induced by prenatal exposure to dexamethasone in fetal rhesus macaques. I. Hippocampus. *Developmental Brain Research, 53*, 157–167.

Uno, H., Eisele, S., Sakai, A., Shelton, S., Baker, E., DeJesus, O., & Holden, J. (1994). Neurotoxicity of glucocorticoids in the primate brain. *Hormones and Behavior, 28*, 336–348.

Van Os, J., & Selten, J.-P. (1998). Prenatal exposure to maternal stress and subsequent schizophrenia. The May 1940 invasion of The Netherlands. *British Journal of Psychiatry, 172*, 324–326.

Weinstock, M. (1997). Does prenatal stress impair coping and regulation of hypothalamic-pituitary-adrenal axis? *Neuroscience and Biobehavioral Reviews, 21*, 1–10.

# 14

# Psychobiological Patterns at Adult Age: Relationships to Personality and Early Behavior

Britt af Klinteberg
Stockholm University

In this chapter, empirical studies on aspects of psychobiological functioning in a group of normal male and female subjects within a longitudinal program will be described. The theoretical perspective is holistic and interactionistic; the approach reflecting significant findings from the area of brain research in the understanding of psychological phenomena and processes in individual interaction with the environment. The present main issue concerns risk factors in the development of personality and antisocial behavior.

## AN INTERACTIVE VULNERABILITY MODEL

The focus was on testing an interactive psychobiological vulnerability model, examining associations between psychological and biological indicators of vulnerability for psychosocial disturbances, particularly psychopathy. When we tested the vulnerability model, psychopathic personality and early risk behaviors were treated as *dimensions,* rather than *categories,* as are often used in clinical work. Consequently, the present research was based on the assumption that there are differences among normal subjects as to their vulnerability to externalizing disturbances, antisocial behavior, and psychopathy-related personality traits. Certain of the components in these disorders, whether genetically influenced or due to early environmental causes, are manifested early in life as more subtle disturbances than those seen in clinical disorders. Thus, a dimensional approach made possible the studying of different levels of risk factors in the developmental process. Certain childhood disturbances are found to be precursors of adult psychosocial disturbances and psychopathy: hyperactive behaviors—motor restlessness, impulsivity, and concentration difficulties (Satterfield, 1987; Taylor, 1988; White, 1999). Aggressiveness has sometimes been included in this hyperactive behavior syndrome, but there are arguments for regarding aggressiveness as a separate dimension (af Klinteberg, Magnusson, & Schalling, 1989; af Klinteberg & Oreland, 1995; McBurnett et al., 1993; McGee, Williams, & Silva, 1985). In these behavior precursors, as well as in adult psychopathy, signs of disturbances in neurochemical functions related to serotonergic activity in the central nervous system (CNS) and also in endocrine functions, such as adrenal-medullary activity/reactivity, have been reported (Kruesi et al., 1992; Lidberg, Modin, Oreland, Tuck, & Gillner, 1985; Satterfield, 1987; Zahn, Kruesi, Leonard, & Rapaport, 1994). The activity of the enzyme monoamine oxidase (MAO) in blood platelets, which is assumed to reflect central serotonergic function (for a review, see Oreland, 1993), has been found to be of particular interest in understanding the biological bases for antisocial behavior and psychosocial disorders. Low platelet MAO activity was recently found to be related to persistent criminal behavior over the life span in a group of males with a history of early criminal behavior (Alm et al., 1994). Interestingly, impulsivity-related personality traits, associated with low platelet MAO activity (for a review, see Schalling, 1993), have, in turn, been shown to be useful as intermediates between biological "vulnerability" and disinhibitory disturbances, such as criminal behavior, violence, alcohol problems, and other forms of psychosocial disorders and disinhibitory syndromes (Barratt & Patton, 1983; af Klinteberg, Humble, & Schalling, 1992; White et al., 1994).

## THE LONGITUDINAL PROJECT IDA

The study was performed on a sample from the general population of male and female subjects within the Swedish project "Individual Development and Adjustment" (IDA) (Magnusson, 1988). In the IDA research program, an age cohort of children in a community attending Grade 3 at the time of the first data collection, comprising about 1100 subjects, have been prospectively studied. A representative group of the total sample, which was employed in the biological analyses, consisted of boys ($n = 82$) and girls ($n = 86$) from whom the following data were collected: (a) behavioral data at the age of 10 and 13 years, (b) personality measures, and (c) biological measures from the biological examination at the age of 26 or 27 years. Thus, the same individuals were followed over time from age 10 to early adult life.

From among those boys and girls a specific group was chosen for the analysis of psychobiological patterns (the results of which are reported in this chapter), for which each biochemical measure was analyzed at the same laboratory. A comparison between the total biological sample and the specific group was undertaken for the purpose of testing equality between groups in early behaviors, keeping male and female subjects apart. No significant differences between groups in any of the behaviors were discerned (for information on the groups and the various measures, see af Klinteberg, 1996a; Magnusson, 1988).

In view of the previously mentioned hypothesis of vulnerability, the longitudinal prospective data on this nonclinical sample offered the opportunity to investigate the predictive importance of childhood behaviors on adult personality, relating to the dimension adjustment–maladjustment. A dimensional description of personality was performed, separately for male and female subjects. The personality dimensions obtained were then examined in relation to childhood behaviors, assumed to be differentially reflecting vulnerability to externalizing (outacting) and internalizing (anxiety-related) psychosocial disturbances (af Klinteberg, Schalling, & Magnusson, 1990). Next, the personality dimensions were related to biochemical factors in the representative sample of young male and female subjects within the project. Subjects were then grouped on the basis of their pattern of biochemical factor scores, and childhood behaviors and personality scale scores were studied in relation to psychobiological patterns at adult age.

## ADULT PERSONALITY AS RELATED TO CHILDHOOD BEHAVIORS

The dimensional description of personality was performed on the self-report inventory applied, the Karolinska Scales of Personality (KSP). Scales included in the inventory were designed for the definition of certain vulnerability traits, the constructs of which are derived from theories of biologically based temperament dimensions underlying psychiatric disorders. A description of extreme scorers on these scales is given in Schalling, Åsberg, Edman, and Oreland (1987). Some of the scales were of specific interest for the research described in this chapter: The impulsiveness scale, assumed to reflect tendencies to act on the spur of the moment, lack of planning, rapid decision making, and carefreeness; monotony avoidance, a sensation-seeking-related scale, assumed to reflect a need for novelty and change, preference for strong stimuli, and an adventurous life-style; the socialization scale, reflecting stability in interpersonal relationships and acceptance of social rules and values; the anxiety scales, reflecting symptoms concerning somatic versus cognitive-social anxiety; and finally the detachment scale, reflecting lack of interpersonal warmth (for information about the scales, see af Klinteberg et al., 1990). Scale scores from the KSP inventory were used in the factor analyses, separately for males and female subjects.

In the *male* group, a broad psychopathy-related factor, two anxiety factors (denoted as "cognitive-social anxiety" and "nervous tension and distress"), and an aggressive nonconformity factor were obtained. Low socialization was associated with high impulsivity and monotony avoidance. In *females*, the factors obtained were congruent with the Eysenckian personality structure (Eysenck & Eysenck, 1975), yielding one broad anxiety factor denoted as "negative emotionality," one aggressive nonconformity factor, and one extraversion factor that included three aspects of extraversion—impulsivity, sensation seeking, and sociability. It is noteworthy that, in males, maladjustment in general (low socialization) was associated with high extraversion and psychopathy-related traits, whereas in females it was associated with low extraversion, "dysthymic" vulnerability, and anxiety traits.

The investigation of the relation between the personality factors at adult age and vulnerability indicators from teacher ratings of childhood behavior showed the following results. For *male subjects*, there was a significant positive relation between childhood "externalizing" (hyperactive-aggressive) behavior and the adult personality factor defined by the psychopathy-related scales, assumed to reflect impulsivity, sensation seeking, and low socialization ($p < .01$), as well as a significant positive relation between childhood timidity or shyness and the adult anxiety factors ($p < .05$). Among *females*, there were mixed relations between early behavior and adult personality: Motor restlessness correlated significantly and positively ($p < .01$), whereas aggressiveness tended to show a positive relationship only over time with the extraversion factor. The findings on these normal subjects were consistent with clinical studies, suggesting that there is a high continuity of antisocial, "externalizing" behaviors and personality traits over time, especially among males (af Klinteberg et al., 1990; cf. Robins, 1978).

## Underlying Biological Mechanisms

Considering the character of the present personality scales as assumed indicators of different kinds of vulnerability, it might be possible to link the relative stability of psychopathy-related early behaviors and corresponding personality scales to underlying biochemical bases. Several studies suggest the involvement of neurochemical systems in hyperactive and psychopathy-related behaviors and traits (for reviews, see Hare & Schalling, 1978; Zuckerman, 1991). Although impulsive-aggressive and disinhibited behaviors have been associated with low serotonergic activity in the CNS (Virkkunen & Linnoila, 1993), platelet MAO activity is a more accessible biological indicator. For a review of the possible mechanisms behind the correspondence between platelet MAO activity and processes in the CNS, see Oreland and Hallman (1995). It is noteworthy that in nonlinear examinations of the relation between personality traits and MAO activity in groups of college students (af Klinteberg, Schalling, Edman, Oreland, & Åsberg, 1987), low MAO activity was strongly associated with high scores in impulsivity and sensation-seeking-related scales for males as well as for females. Furthermore, in congruence with earlier findings (Fowler, Tipton, MacKay, & Youdim, 1982; Oreland, 1993), males were found to have significantly lower platelet MAO activity than females.

Other biochemical measures of interest associated with externalizing disturbances and antisocial behaviors are thyroid activity, cortisol, dopamine, noradrenaline, and adrenaline levels. An excess of thyroid functioning was found to be related to a decrease in sympathetic system activity in groups of male subjects with different forms of psychosocial deviancy (Moss, Guthrie, & Linnoila, 1986; Whybrow & Prange, 1981) and cognitive functioning influenced by developmental thyroid hormone imbalance (Gould, Allen, & McEwen, 1990). In a longitudinal study of young lawbreakers, triiodothyronine (the active part of thyroxine) levels were positively related to persistent criminal behavior (Alm et al., 1996), which in turn has been found to be correlated with low sympathetic-adrenal activity (Magnusson, af Klinteberg, & Stattin, 1994). Plasma cortisol levels have been inversely related to impulsivity in healthy volunteers, and low levels of salivary or urinary cortisol are found in groups of conduct-disordered boys and young offenders, and in individuals showing disinhibitory tendencies (McBurnett, Lahey, Capasso, & Loeber, 1996; Schalling, 1993). Furthermore, dopamine and noradrenaline activity were included in the study that this chapter is based on because of their involvement in inhibitory control mechanism and behavior (Rammsayer, Netter, & Vogel, 1993; Tucker & Williamsson, 1984). Because steroid hormones are reported to be related to personality and to certain aspects of human behavior (Dabbs, Hopper, & Jurkovic, 1990; Olweus, 1986), and findings of low MAO are associated with high sensation-seeking-related traits, in turn related to testosterone (Mattson, Schalling, Olweus, Löw, & Svensson, 1980), estimates of plasma levels of the androgens testosterone and dehydroepiandrosterone sulfate (DHEAS), as well as of estradiol, were included in the present study. Finally, prolactin was included for exploratory reasons concerning assumed hormonal influences on psychological development (Gray, Jackson, & McKinlay, 1991).

## A Dimensional Description of Biochemical Variables

Factor analyses according to method Principal Axis Factoring (PAF), varimax, orthogonal rotation, in the Statistical Package for Social Sciences (SPSS, 1990), were carried out for the 10 biochemical measures (for females an additional estrogen measure was included), separately for male and female subjects. The number of factors to be chosen was equal to the number of eigen value exceeding 1.0. The analyses resulted in four factors for the male subjects, and in three factors for females, explaining 66.2% and 49.7%, respectively, of the total variance. For *male* subjects, the first biochemical factor is defined by positive loadings on serum noradrenaline, adrenaline, prolactin, and cortisol (Factor BML1, denoted *the Adrenal-cortisol factor*); the second factor is defined by positive loadings on the platelet MAO activity substrates (Factor BML2, denoted *the MAO factor*); the third factor is defined by positive loadings on dopamine and on the testosterone-related measure DHEAS (Factor BML3, denoted *the Dopamine-androgen factor*); and the fourth factor is defined by positive loadings on testosterone and negative loadings on cortisol (Factor BML4, denoted *the Testosterone-related factor*).

For *female* subjects, the first factor is defined by positive loadings on serum testosterone, estrogen, and adrenaline (Factor BFL1, denoted *the Adrenal-steroid factor*); the second factor is defined by positive loadings on the platelet MAO substrates and on thyroid-stimulating hormone (TSH) (Factor BFL2, denoted *the MAO-thyroid factor*); and the third factor is similar to factor BML3, however defined by *negative* loadings on dopamine and positive loadings on noradrenaline and DHEAS (Factor BFL3, denoted *the Dopamine-androgen-related factor*). The factor structure is different for male and female subjects. The two factors loading on dopamine differ in that the male factor (BML3) has positive loadings and the female factor (BFL3) negative loadings on dopamine together with positive loadings on the androgen measure DHEAS.

## Personality Dimensions as Related to Biochemical Factors

Product-moment correlation coefficients were calculated between the described personality dimensions and biochemical factors based on the biochemical variables included in the study, separately for male and female subjects. Among *males*, there were strong positive relations between the adult psychopathy-related personality dimension and both the Dopamine-androgen factor (BML3) ($p < .01$), and the Testosterone-related factor (BML4) ($p < .001$). Furthermore, there was a trend toward a negative association between the psychopathy-related personality dimension and the Adrenal-cortisol factor (BML1) ($p < .10$). There were no significant relations between personality and the MAO factor (BML2) (Table 14.1). For *female* subjects, there was a trend toward a relation between the extraversion personality dimension and the Dopamine-androgen-related factor (BFL3) ($p < .10$, Table 14.2). There were no significant relationships between personality and the other female biochemical factors. Taken together, these

TABLE 14.1

Product-Moment Correlations Between Personality Factors (KSP Factors: PERSM1–PERSM4) and Factors Based on Biochemical Variables (BML1–BML4) at Age 27 for a Group of Male Subjects ($n = 49$)

| | Biochemical Factors | | | |
| --- | --- | --- | --- | --- |
| Personality Factors | | | | |
| | BML1 | BML2 | BML3 | BML4 |
| PERSM1 | .01 | .20 | -.04 | .18 |
| PERSM2 | .06 | -.02 | -.10 | .13 |
| PERSM3 | -.01 | -.21 | .19 | .02 |
| PERSM4 | -.26+ | -.12 | .38** | .42*** |

Note. PERSM1 = Cognitive-social anxiety; PERSM2 = Nervous tension and distress; PERSM3 = Aggressive nonconformity; and PERSM4 = Impulsive sensation-seeking psychopathy.

BML1 = (z) Noradrenaline +; Adrenaline +; Prolactin +; Cortisol +
BML2 = (z) MAO β-pea +; MAO trypt +
BML3 = (z) Dopamine +; DHEAS +
BML4 = (z) Testosterone +; Cortisol -

Expl var: 66.2%
Fact loadings 0.50 ≤

+$p < .10$. *$p < .05$. **$p < .01$. ***$p < .005$.

results indicated relations between personality and biochemical factors in groups of normals *only* concerning psychopathy-related, and to some extent extraversion-related, personality dimensions.

## Psychobiological Patterns at Adult Age

In the next step of the research, subjects were grouped or clustered on the basis of their factor scores on the obtained biochemical factors, separately for male and female subjects, according to a hierarchical method (WARD), using squared Euclidean distance. Results of multivariate analyses of variance (MANOVA) and Bonferroni tests of pairwise comparisons of the clusters indicated the following: For the *male* subjects, a solution of five clusters (MB1–MB5) differing in the biochemical factors was chosen [$F(4, 44) = 16.49$, $p < .0001$]. The clusters differed significantly ($p < .05$) concerning level. They also differed concerning form; there was a significant overall cluster effect on the biochemical factors [Wilk's lambda: $F(12, 111) = 12.63$, $p < .0001$], with strong interactions, as illustrated especially by clusters MB2 and MB3 in Factors BML2 and BML4 (Fig. 14.1).

TABLE 14.2
Product-Moment Correlations Between Personality Factors (KSP Factors: PERSF1–PERSF3) and
Factors Based on Biochemical Variables (BFL1–BFL3) at Age 27 for a Group of Female Subjects
($n = 48$)

| | Biochemical Factors | | |
|---|---|---|---|
| *Personality Factors* | | | |
| | *BFL1* | *BFL2* | *BFL3* |
| PERSF1 | .03 | -.20 | .03 |
| PERSF2 | -.01 | -.11 | -.16 |
| PERSF3 | -.21 | -.17 | .27+ |

*Note.* PERSF1 = Negative emotionality; PERSF2 = Aggressive nonconformity; PERSF3 = Extraversion

BFL1 = (z) Testosterone +; Estrogen +; Adrenaline +
BFL2 = (z) MAO tryptamine +; MAO β-pea +; TSH +
BFL3 = (z) Dopamine -; Noradrenaline +; *DHEAS* +

Expl var: 49.7%
*Fact loadings 0.45 ≤*
Fact loadings 0.50 ≤

+ $p < .10$

For the *female* subjects, a solution of four clusters (FB1–FB4) differing in the biochemical factors was chosen [$F(3, 44) = 15.20$, $p < .0001$]. Three clusters differed significantly in one of the biochemical factors ($p < .05$). Furthermore, the clusters differed concerning form [Wilk's lambda: $F(6, 86) = 19.99$, $p < .0001$]. Clusters FB2 and FB3 showed strong interactions with clusters FB1 and FB4; they also interacted with each other in Factor BFL3 (Fig. 14.2). The biochemical factors or variables included in the MANOVAs differed in the male group [$F(3, 42) = 4.43$, $p < .01$]; this was not the case in the female group (*ns*).

## Childhood Behavior, Adult Personality, and Psychobiological Patterns

Among *male* subjects, one-way ANOVAs indicated that the cluster MB2, characterized by *low* scores (mean z score: −1.5) on the MAO factor, combined with *high* scores (mean z score: 1.1) on the Testosterone-related factor, was associated with higher childhood concentration difficulties [$F(4, 44) = 3.36$, $p < .02$], aggressiveness [$F(4, 44) = 2.63$, $p < .05$], stable (based on ratings from 10 and 13 years) hyperactive [$F(4, 44) = 2.17$, $p < .10$], and stable aggressive behaviors [$F(4, 44) = 2.46$, $p < .10$]; and with lower adult sociali-

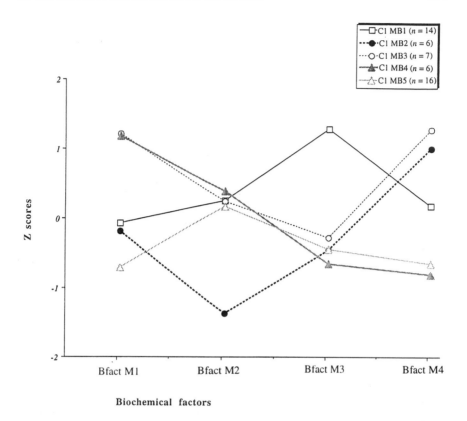

**Biochemical factors**

FIG. 14.1. Biochemical patterns in a group of males at age 27.

zation [$F(4, 44) = 3.20$, $p < .02$] and higher scores on the somatic anxiety factor [$F(4, 44) = 2.46$, $p < .10$], compared with the other clusters. The cluster MB4, characterized by *high* scores (mean z score: 1.2) on the Adrenal-cortisol factor, scores close to the mean on the MAO factor, and significantly *lower* scores on the Testosterone-related factor, displayed lower childhood problem behaviors, in terms of lower concentration difficulties, hyperactive behavior, and aggressiveness ($p < .05$); and a tendency to higher adult socialization ($p < .10$) combined with lower somatic anxiety indications ($p < .05$), compared with the former male cluster (MB2) subjects.

For *females*, the cluster FB3, characterized by *low* scores (mean z score: $-1.2$) on the MAO-thyroid factor, and *high* scores (mean z score: 1.0) on the Dopamine-androgen-related factor, was associated with a tendency to higher childhood concentration difficulties [$F(4, 44) = 2.35$, $p < .10$], and higher adult suspicion [$F(4, 44) = 2.29$, $p < .10$], compared with the other female clusters. In comparison to the "normative" female cluster FB4, characterized by mean z scores within one standard deviation above the mean

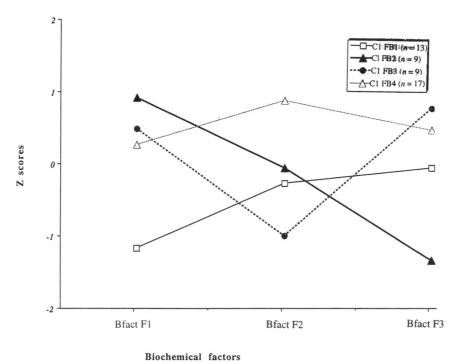

**Biochemical factors**

FIG. 14.2. Biochemical patterns in a group of females at age 27.

in all three biochemical factors, the cluster FB3 females displayed significantly lower adult socialization ($p < .01$), higher somatic anxiety ($p < .05$), and a tendency to higher suspicion scores ($p < .10$). Furthermore, the cluster FB2, characterized by *high* scores (mean $z$ score: 1.0) on the Adrenal-steroid factor, in combination with significantly *lower* scores (mean $z$ score: −1.5) on the Dopamine-androgen-related factor, displayed significantly lower scores on childhood concentration difficulties, lower motor restlessness, lower scores on stable hyperactive behavior (all $p < .05$), and a tendency to lower adult impulsiveness ($p < .10$), than was observed among the FB3 cluster subjects.

Patterns of childhood behavior and psychobiology were studied at the *individual level*, applying configural frequency analyses (CFA) (Bergman & El-Khouri, 1995). The existence of syndromes among dichotomized variables of hyperactive behavior and aggressiveness (high/low) (for cut-points, see af Klinteberg, Andersson, Magnusson, & Stattin, 1993) and a biochemical risk indication variable, based on a combination of scores on factors reflecting the interaction effects in the MANOVAs, was tested, separately for male and female subjects. For male subjects a combination of scores on the MAO ($<$ mean) and the Testosterone-related ($\geq$ mean) factors constituted the risk indication variable; for females a combination of scores on the MAO-thyroid (< mean) and the Dopamine-androgen-related ($\geq$ mean) factors (presence–no presence) yielded the corresponding risk variable. The critical pattern to be investigated was that of high hyperactive behavior, high aggressiveness, and presence of the respective psychobiological risk indication described. In line with expectations, in a binomial probability test, a significant excess of cell frequencies ("types") was found for that pattern in the male (as presented in Table 14.3) and female (Table 14.4) groups, respectively.

## DISINHIBITORY DISTURBANCES— VIOLENT OFFENDING

Earlier findings within the IDA project, in studying the population, highlighted aspects of childhood vulnerability in relation to violent and nonviolent criminal offending (af Klinteberg, 1996a). It was found that, for the *male* subjects, behavior ratings at age 13, assumed to reflect externalizing disturbances, differed significantly between all groups: Violent criminals ($n = 40$) being the higher, noncriminals ($n = 338$) the lower, and nonviolent criminals ($n = 163$) intermediate on aggressiveness [$F(2, 538) = 29.85, p < .0001$] and concentration difficulties [$F(2, 538) = 39.83, p < .0001$]; both violent and nonviolent criminal groups displayed significantly higher mean hyperactive

TABLE 14.3
Configurations of Dichotomized Hyperactive Behavior and Aggressiveness Ratings at Age 13, and Presence–No Presence of a Biochemical Risk Indication Variable, based on a Combination of Scores on the MAO (< mean), and the Testosterone-Related ($\geq$ mean) Factors, for a Group of Normal Male Subjects at the Age of 27 ($n = 48$)

| Pattern | | | Size | | | Level of Sign | |
|---|---|---|---|---|---|---|---|
| Hyperactive Behavior | Aggressive-ness | Biochemical Risk | Obt | Exp | z | p< | Type–Antitype |
| Low | Low | No | 23 | 18.4 | 1.38 | | |
| Low | Low | Yes | 7 | 6.1 | 0.39 | | |
| Low | High | No | 8 | 10.1 | -0.75 | | |
| Low | High | Yes | 0 | 3.4 | -1.92 | .05 | at |
| High | Low | No | 1 | 4.8 | -1.83 | .05 | at |
| High | Low | Yes | 0 | 1.6 | -1.29 | | |
| High | High | No | 4 | 2.7 | 0.82 | | |
| High | High | Yes | 5 | 0.9 | 4.36 | .002 | t |

*Note.* Hyperactive Behavior (Hyp Beh): Combination of rating scores for Motor Restlessness (MR) and Concentration Difficulties (CD); high Hyp Beh = 5–7 on both MR and CD; low Hyp Beh = all other combinations; and Aggressiveness (Agg): high Agg = 5–7; low Agg = 1–4.

TABLE 14.4
Configurations of Dichotomized Hyperactive Behavior and Aggressiveness Ratings at Age 13,
and Presence–No Presence of an Explorative Biochemical Risk Indication Variable, based
on a Combination of Scores on the MAO-thyroid (< mean), and the Dopamine-androgen-related
(≥ mean) Factors, for a Group of Normal Female Subjects at the Age of 27 ($n = 46$)

| Pattern | | | Size | | | | Level of Sign |
|---|---|---|---|---|---|---|---|
| Hyperactive Behavior | Aggressiveness | Biochemical Risk | Obt | Exp | z | p< | Type–Antitype |
| Low | Low | No | 25 | 21.9 | 0.92 | | |
| Low | Low | Yes | 10 | 8.6 | 0.53 | | |
| Low | High | No | 3 | 5.3 | -1.06 | | |
| Low | High | Yes | 0 | 2.1 | -1.48 | | |
| High | Low | No | 2 | 4.6 | -1.28 | | |
| High | Low | Yes | 0 | 1.8 | -1.37 | | |
| High | High | No | 3 | 1.1 | 1.83 | | |
| High | High | Yes | 3 | 0.4 | 4.13 | .01 | t |

*Note.* Hyperactive Behavior (Hyp Beh): Combination of rating scores for Motor Restlessness (MR) and Concentration Difficulties (CD); high Hyp Beh = 5–7 on both MR and CD; low Hyp Beh = all other combinations; and Aggressiveness (Agg): high agg = 5–7; low Agg = 1–4.

behavior ratings than the noncriminals [$F(2, 538) = 37.99, p < .0001$]. For *female* subjects, violent and nonviolent criminals ($n = 50$) being significantly higher on aggressiveness [$F(1, 549) = 30.76, p < .0001$], motor restlessness [$F(1, 549) = 25.58, p < .0001$], and concentration difficulties [$F(1, 549) = 19.04, p < .0001$], compared with the noncriminal females ($n = 501$). The indicator assumed to reflect internalized disturbances at age 13, timidity, did not show differences between groups for the males, or for the females.

Furthermore, personality aspects, as described above, were studied in relation to criminal and violent criminal offending. It was found, that among *male subjects*, violent criminals differed significantly from noncriminals in displaying higher scores on the impulsiveness scale [$F(2, 79) = 6.06, p < .005$] and lower scores on the conformity–nonconformity scale socialization [$F(2, 79) = 10.91, p < .0001$]; nonviolent criminals differed significantly from noncriminals with higher scores on the sensation-seeking-related monotony avoidance scale [$F(2, 79) = 6.00, p < .005$]. Furthermore, the criminal male groups exhibited lower scores on social desirability [$F(2, 79) = 3.11, p < .05$], than noncriminals (see Fig. 14.3). Among *female subjects*, there were no significant differences between the criminal ($n = 6$) and noncriminal groups ($n = 81$) on the introversion–extraversion-related or conformity–nonconformity scales. Interestingly, high self-reported normbreaking behavior in adolescent females was found to be associated with adult impulsiveness

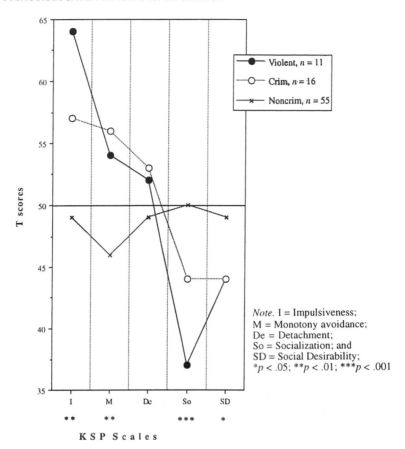

FIG. 14.3. Comparison of mean personality scale scores for violent criminals, nonviolent criminals and noncriminal males, at age 27. (From "Biology, norms, and personality: A developmental perspective," af Klinteberg (1996), *Neuropsychobiology, 34*, 146–154. Reprinted by permission, Karger, Basel)

$[F(2, 76) = 7.24, p < .001]$ and low socialization $[F(2, 76) = 5.70, p < .005]$, as illustrated in Fig. 14.4; as well as signs of low serotonergic activity in terms of low platelet MAO activity for both male and female subjects (af Klinteberg, 1996a, 1996b).

Findings from another longitudinal program "Young Lawbreakers as Adults" (YLA) (af Klinteberg et al., 1992) are in support of the results presented here. A group of males studied exhibited the same pattern of early hyperactive behavior being related to adult psychopathy-related traits; violent offending was significantly related to lower platelet MAO activity $[F(1, 108) = 6.98, p < .01]$ and higher thyroid functioning $[F(1, 121) = 21.63, p < .001]$ compared with nonviolent subjects (af Klinteberg, Alm, Gacono, Humble, & Oreland, 1999). Violent criminals also displayed the person-

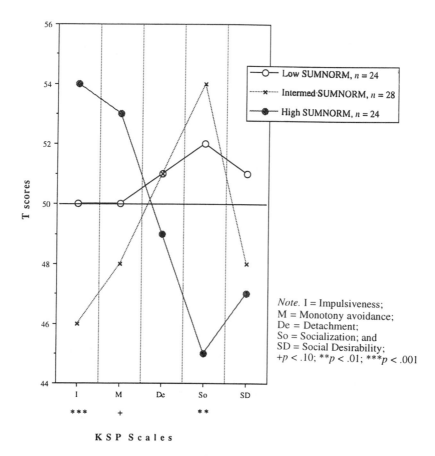

FIG. 14.4. Comparison of mean personality scale scores for female groups with low, intermediate, and high scores of adolescent normbreaking behavior (SUMNORM).

ality profile (Fig. 14.5) found among violent criminal males and to some extent the high normbreaking females in the IDA project. The results support the assumption of underlying psychobiological mechanisms of the maladjustment problems discussed, indicating possible diminished capabilities for the individual to *interact effectively* with the environment in the socialization process, as indicated in disinhibited and impulsive behaviors. An underlying condition of abnormally low arousal and inhibitory levels in the CNS is proposed as being common in disinhibitory syndromes (Gorenstein & Newman, 1980). Taken together, the results presented underscore the possible importance of individual traits in the development of disinhibitory psychosocial disturbances. The results demonstrated psychopathy-related personality traits to be associated with biochemical measure levels,

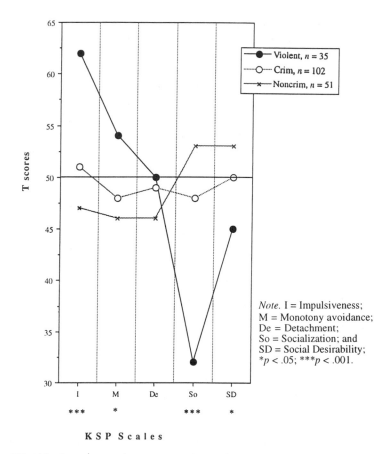

FIG. 14.5.  Comparison of mean personality scale scores for violent criminals, nonviolent criminals and noncriminal males, at age 32–40 years.

especially with low platelet MAO activity, in a group of normals. The results of early childhood externalizing behaviors, criminal and violent offending in the same subjects in the present normal group of males, and the associations between psychopathy-related traits and the psychobiological vulnerability indicator of low platelet MAO activity in the same subjects, are congruent with the assumptions of genetically induced different forms of disinhibitory psychopathology (Oreland, 1993).

## CONCLUDING REMARKS

The present study of normal groups of male and female subjects, showed that individual-related psychobiological patterns were associated with risk for developing psychosocial disturbances as indicated by early behaviors and adult personality traits. In the male group, associations between externalizing childhood behaviors and psychopathy-related personality traits, and between internalizing childhood behaviors and anxiety traits, were found over a period of 14 years. For female subjects, motor restlessness was related over the life span with an extraversion dimension (impulsiveness, monotony avoidance, and sociability). It was suggested that females might be more susceptible to life changes, thus attenuating the prospective influence of childhood behavior on adult personality. There are indications that problem behaviors in girls start at a later stage than the age period studied, often during adolescence (af Klinteberg, 1996b; Robins, 1986), which might explain the present paucity of relations. It is noteworthy that susceptibility to serious life changes was reported earlier to characterize boys in a study on intellectual development (Bergman, 1981). Moreover, in the present longitudinal project, the factors of adult personality indicated that low socialization was related to high scores on impulsiveness and monotony avoidance scales in the male group, whereas among the female subjects it was associated with high scores on anxiety-related scales (af Klinteberg et al., 1990).

In this sample, it was found that typical psychobiological patterns differed as related to childhood behavior and adult personality vulnerability indicators of psychosocial disturbances, among males (as indicated by low socialization and high somatic anxiety) and more weakly among females (as indicated by nonconformity, hostility, and impulsivity). It is noteworthy that low platelet MAO activity characterized one each of the male and female individual-related clusters. This finding is consistent with the assumption that low platelet MAO activity constitutes a vulnerability factor present in normal subjects, as well as in groups of patients and relatives of patients (see Schalling, 1993; Virkkunen & Linnoila, 1993). The neurochemical substrate for disinhibitory behavior, associated with impulsivity and violence, is assumed to involve a weak or unstable serotonergic system (Oreland, 1993; Soubrié, 1986). Thus, in the present study, results illustrated high scores on early risk behaviors, high adult psychopathy-related traits, and low platelet MAO activity in individuals having committed one or more violent offences.

Furthermore, in a person approach, for male subjects a combination of scores on the MAO and the Testosterone-related factors constituted a risk indication; for females a combination of scores on the MAO-thyroid and the Dopamine-androgen-related factors yielded a corresponding risk variable. Presence of the respective psychobiological risk indications together with presence of high hyperactive behavior and high aggressiveness in childhood constituted significant types. This finding underscores the importance of studying the occurrence of different vulnerability markers in the same individuals over time. These *individual risk patterns* might suggest underlying mechanisms, to which the problems might be linked, and have implications for the type of psychopathology that may emerge if there is a combination of disposition and certain types of situational stressors or life events.

In the development of personality and antisocial behavior, individual personality traits, behavioral and biological aspects of human functioning, and psychosocial influences act together in *a continuously ongoing process of interaction* between the individual and his or her environment *over time*. Thus, the holistic integrated view on individual functioning has important implications for intervention and methodological strategy. In the presence of additional risk factors, "vulnerable" subjects might be more dependent than their less vulnerable counterparts on the *quality of environmental support* during the developmental process. It is therefore of crucial importance to be able to follow groups of normal subjects over the life span and to interpret the developmental process, based on an integrated holistic view on individual functioning, within a theoretical framework of interactional psychology (Magnusson, 1988; 1999; Magnusson & Stattin, 1998). This was the approach within the IDA longitudinal project.

## ACKNOWLEDGMENTS

This chapter was made possible by access to data from the longitudinal research program "Individual Development and Adjustment," Sweden. Responsible for the planning, implementation, and financing of the collection of data was Professor David Magnusson. The data collection was originally supported by grants from the Swedish Board of Education. The present research was financially supported by grants from the Swedish Council for Planning and Coordination of Research, and the Swedish Council for Social Research. Special thanks are forwarded to Professor Magnusson for constructive collaboration. Valuable comments on an earlier version from Dr. S. E. Johansson are gratefully acknowledged.

## REFERENCES

Alm, P. O., af Klinteberg, B., Humble, K., Leppert, J., Sörensen, S., Tegelman, R., Thorell, L.-H., & Lidberg, L. (1996). Criminality and psychopathy as related to thyroid activity in former juvenile delinquents. *Acta Psychiatrica Scandinavica, 94*, 112–117.

Alm, P. O., Alm, M., Humble, K., Leppert, J., Sörensen, S., Lidberg, L., & Oreland, L. (1994). Criminality and platelet monoamine oxidase activity in former juvenile delinquents as adults. *Acta Psychiatrica Scandinavica, 89*, 41–45.

Barratt, E. S., & Patton, J. H. (1983). Impulsivity: Cognitive, behavioral, and psychophysiological correlates. In M. Zuckerman (Ed.), *Biological Bases of Sensation Seeking, Impulsivity and Anxiety* (pp. 77–122). Hillsdale, NJ: Lawrence Erlbaum Associates.

Bergman, L. R. (1981). Is intellectual development more vulnerable in boys than in girls? *The Journal of Genetic Psychology, 138*, 175–181.

Bergman, L. R. & El-Khouri, B. M. (1995). *SLEIPNER: A statistical package for pattern-oriented analyses* (User Manual). Stockholm, Sweden: Stockholm University, Department of Psychology.

Dabbs, J. M., Hopper, C. H., & Jurkovic, G. J. (1990). Testosterone and personality among college students and military veterans. *Personality and Individual Differences, 11*, 1263–1269.

Eysenck, S. B. G., & Eysenck, H. J. (1975). *Manual of the Eysenck personality questionnaire*. London: Hodder & Stoughton.

Fowler, C. J., Tipton, K. F., MacKay A. V. P., & Youdim, M. B. H. (1982). Human platelet monoamine oxidase—a useful enzyme in the study of psychiatric disorders? *Neuroscience, 7*, 1577–1594.

Gorenstein, E. E., & Newman, J. P. (1980). Disinhibitory psychopathology: A new perspective and a model for research. *Psychological Review, 87*, 301–315.

Gould, E., Allen, M. D., & McEwen, B. S. (1990). Dendritic spine density of adult hippocampal pyramidal cells is sensitive to thyroid hormone. *Brain Research, 525*, 327–329.

Gray, A., Jackson, D. N., & McKinlay, J. B. (1991). The relation between dominance, anger, and hormones in normally aging men: Results from the Massachusetts male aging study. *Psychosomatic Medicine, 53*, 375–385.

Hare, R. D., & Schalling, D. (1978). *Psychopathic Behavior. Approaches to Research.* Chichester: Wiley.

af Klinteberg, B. (1996a). Biology, norms, and personality: A developmental perspective. *Neuropsychobiology, 34*, 146–154.

af Klinteberg, B. (1996b, August). *The development of antisocial behaviors: Are the psychobiological risk factors the same in groups of female and male subjects?* Paper discussed at the workshop "Life course in female aggression" at the XIVth Biennial ISSBD Conference, Quebec, Canada.

af Klinteberg, B., Alm, P.-O., Gacono, C., Humble, K., & Oreland, L. (1999). *Adult antisocial behavior and biochemical indicators associated with childhood Rorschach risk variables.* Manuscript submitted for publication.

af Klinteberg, B., Andersson, T., Magnusson, D., & Stattin, H. (1993). Hyperactive behavior in childhood as related to subsequent alcohol problems and violent offending: A longitudinal study of male subjects. *Personality and Individual Differences, 15*, 381–388.

af Klinteberg, B., Humble, K., & Schalling, D. (1992). Personality and psychopathy of males with a history of early criminal behavior. *European Journal of Personality, 6*, 245–266.

af Klinteberg, B., Magnusson, D., & Schalling, D. (1989). Hyperactive behavior in childhood and adult impulsivity: A longitudinal study of male subjects. *Personality and Individual Differences, 10*, 43–50.

af Klinteberg, B., & Oreland, L. (1995). Hyperactive and aggressive behaviors in childhood as related to low platelet monoamine oxidase (MAO) activity at adult age: A longitudinal study of male subjects. *Personality and Individual Differences, 19*, 373–383.

af Klinteberg, B., Schalling, D., Edman, G., Oreland, L., & Åsberg, M. (1987). Personality correlates of platelet monoamine oxidase (MAO) activity in female and male subjects. *Neuropsychobiology, 18*, 89–96.

af Klinteberg, B., Schalling, D., & Magnusson, D. (1990). Childhood behaviour and adult personality in male and female subjects. *European Journal of Personality, 4*, 57–71.

Kruesi, M. J. P., Hibbs, E. D., Zahn, T. P, Keysor, C. S., Hamburger, S. D., Bartko, J. J., & Rapoport, J. L. (1992). A 2-year prospective follow-up study of children and adolescents with disruptive behavior disorders. *Archives of General Psychiatry, 49*, 429–435.

Lidberg, L., Modin, I., Oreland, L., Tuck, J. R., & Gillner, A. (1985). Platelet monoamine oxidase activity and psychopathy. *Psychiatry Research, 16*, 339–343.

Magnusson, D. (1988). Individual development from an interactional perspective: A longitudinal study. In D. Magnusson (Ed.), *Paths through life* (Vol. 1). Hillsdale, NJ: Lawrence Erlbaum Associates.

Magnusson, D. (1999). Personality development from an interactional perspective. In L. A. Pervin & O. P. John (Eds.), *Handbook of personality: Theory and research* (pp. 219–247). New York: Guilford.

Magnusson, D., af Klinteberg, B., & Stattin, H. (1994). Juvenile and persistent offenders: Behavioral and physiological characteristics. In R. D. Ketterlinus & M. E. Lamb (Eds.), *Adolescent problem behaviors—Issues and research* (pp. 81–91). Hillsdale, NJ: Lawrence Erlbaum Associates.

Magnusson, D., & Stattin, H. (1998). Person-context interaction theories. In R. Lerner (Ed.), *Handbook of child psychology: Vol. 1. Theoretical models of human development* (5th ed., pp. 685–759). New York: Wiley.

Mattson, Å., Schalling, D., Olweus, D., Löw, H., & Svensson, J. (1980). Plasma testosterone, aggressive behavior, and personality dimensions in young male delinquents. *Journal of the American Academy of Child Psychiatry, 19*, 476–490.

McBurnett, K., Harris, S. M., Swanson, J. M., Pfiffner, L. J., Tamm, L., & Freeland, D. (1993). Neuropsychological and psychophysiological differentiation of inattention/overactivity and aggression/defiance symptom groups. *Journal of Clinical Child Psychology, 22*, 165–171.

McBurnett, K., Lahey, B. B., Capasso, L., & Loeber, R. (1996). Aggressive symptoms and salivary cortisol in clinic-referred boys with conduct disorder. *Annals of the New York Academy of Sciences, 794*, 169–178.

McGee, R., Williams, S., & Silva, P. A. (1985). Behavioral and developmental characteristics of aggressive, hyperactive, and aggressive-hyperactive boys. *Journal of the American Academy of Child Psychiatry, 23*, 270–279.

Moss, H. B., Guthrie, S., & Linnoila, M. (1986). Enhanced thyrotropin response to thyrotropin releasing hormone in boys at risk for development of alcoholism. *Archives of General Psychiatry, 43*, 1137–1142.

Olweus, D. (1986). Aggression and hormones: Behavioral relationship with testosterone and adrenaline. In D. Olweus, J. Block, & M. Radke-Yarrow (Eds.), *Development of antisocial and prosocial behavior* (pp. 51–72). New York: Academic Press.

Oreland, L. (1993). Monoamine oxidase in neuro-psychiatric disorders. In H. Yasuhara, S. H. Parvez, K. Oguchi, M. Sandler, & T. Nagatsu (Eds.), *Monoamine Oxidase: Basic and Clinical Aspects* (pp. 219–247). Utrecht, Holland: VSP Press.

Oreland, L., & Hallman, J. (1995). The correlation between platelet MAO activity and personality—a short review of findings and discussion on possible mechanisms. In P. M. Yu, K. F. Tipton, & A. A. Boulton (Eds.), *Progress in brain research: Vol. 106. Current neurochemical and pharmacological aspects of biogenic amines: their function, oxidative deamination and inhibition* (pp. 77–84). New York: Elsevier.

Rammsayer, T., Netter, P., & Vogel, W. H. (1993). A neurochemical model underlying differences in reaction times between introverts and extraverts. *Personality and Individual Differences, 14*, 701–712.

Robins, L. (1978). Aetiological implications in studies of childhood histories relating to antisocial personality. In R. D. Hare & D. Schalling (Eds.), *Psychopathic behaviour. Approaches to research* (pp. 255–271). Chichester: Wiley.

Robins, L. (1986). The consequences of conduct disorder in girls. In D. Olweus, J. Block, & M. Radke-Yarrow (Eds.), *Development of antisocial and prosocial behavior* (pp. 385–409). New York: Academic Press.

Satterfield, J. H. (1987). Childhood diagnostic and neurophysiological predictors of teenage arrest rates: An eight-year prospective study. In S. A. Mednick, T. E. Moffitt, & S. A. Stack (Eds.), *The causes of crime* (pp. 199–207). Cambridge, UK: Cambridge University Press.

Schalling, D. (1993). Neurochemical correlates of personality, impulsivity and disinhibitory suicidality. In S. Hodgins (Ed.), *Mental disorder and crime* (pp. 208–226). Newbury Park, CA: Sage.

Schalling, D., Åsberg, M., Edman, G., & Oreland, L. (1987). Markers for vulnerability to psychopathology: Temperament traits associated with platelet MAO activity. *Acta Psychiatrica Scandinavica, 76*, 172–182.

Soubrié, P. H. (1986). Reconciling the role of central serotonin neurons in human and animal behavior. *The Behavioral and Brain Sciences, 9,* 319–364.

SPSS. (1990). *Base system user's guide.* Chicago: SPSS Inc.

Taylor, E. (1988). Diagnosis of hyperactivity—A British perspective. In L. M. Bloomingdale & J. Sergeant (Eds.), *Attention Deficit Disorder: Criteria, cognition, intervention* (pp. 141–159). Oxford: Pergamon.

Tucker, D. M., & Williamsson, P. A. (1984). Asymmetric neural control systems in human self-regulation. *Psychological Review, 91,* 185–212.

Virkkunen, M., & Linnoila, M. (1993). Serotonin in personality disorders with habitual violence and impulsivity. In S. Hodgins (Ed.), *Mental disorder and crime* (pp. 227–243). London: Sage.

White, J. D. (1999). Personality, temperament and ADHD: A review of the literature. *Personality and Individual Differences, 27,* 589–598.

White, J. L., Moffitt, T. E., Caspi, A., Bartusch, D. J., Needles, D. J., & Stouthamer-Loeber, M. (1994). Measuring impulsivity and examining its relationship to delinquency. *Journal of Abnormal Psychology, 103,* 192–205.

Whybrow, P. C., & Prange, A. J. (1981). A hypothesis of thyroid-catecholamine receptor interaction. *Archives of General Psychiatry, 38,* 106–113.

Zahn, T. P., Kruesi, M. J. P., Leonard, H. L., & Rapaport, J. L. (1994). Autonomic activity and reaction time in relation to extraversion and behavioral impulsivity in children and adolescents. *Personality and Individual Differences, 16,* 751–758.

Zuckerman, M. (1991). *Psychobiology of Personality.* Cambridge, UK: Cambridge University Press.

# 15

# Social Ecology and the Development of Stress Regulation

Mary Carlson
Felton Earls
Harvard Medical School

In this chapter we outline our commitment to integrative approaches to biological, psychological, and social understanding with child development, along with describing our preliminary findings on the regulation of stress hormone and behavioral development in institutionalized Romanian children. We present the example of these children to illustrate the biological, psychological, and social consequences of a degraded human environment in which the failure to consider the critical role of social contact in the development of basic physiological function (as well as complex behavioral capacities) results in enduring biological and psychological dysfunction. We think that the findings from research in such extreme conditions have implications for the role that parents and other caretakers must play in the lives of children to permit and promote the development of neuroendocrine regulation and behavioral capacities. Our integrative approach benefits from the theoretical and empirical work of Magnusson and his colleagues (Magnusson, 1988), in which the importance of an interactional perspective is so clearly and elegantly illustrated. In this important work, human development is viewed in a holistic perspective that respects the integrity and complexity of the individual, and in a longitudinal framework that appreciates the importance of change through time. From our reading and direct contact with this ongoing research, we have confirmed our own predilection for a dynamic and unified approach to the study of neural and behavioral development.

## MULTILEVEL CONCEPTUAL FRAMEWORK
## FOR CHILD DEVELOPMENT

From the theory and practice of our studies in primate biology and neuro-biology and epidemiological and longitudinal studies of children, our holistic (referred to in modern biology as *organismic*) approach to the study of developmental processes in children is best characterized as an ecological perspective. This perspective is reflected in contemporary, evolutionary approaches to behavior: "The study of behavior is now expanding primarily in two directions. On the one hand it is merging with neurophysiology, on the other hand with ecology: species-specific behavior is studied from the point of view of its selective significance within the niche of the perspective species" (Mayr, 1982, p. 120). We take seriously the understanding of dynamic changes in neural structure and function, in behavioral abilities and propensities, and in the material and social resources within the developmental niche of a child. The organismic and ecological approaches require detailed understanding at each constitutive level of analysis as well as inquiry into the mechanisms through which physiological, behavioral, and social factors interact to shape developmental outcomes. The dynamic nature of the interactive mechanisms that span the developing nervous system and the ecological setting of a developing organism is represented in the statement: "Development cannot be regarded as a self-contained package of activity but as a program of events in which selected parts of the ecological environment form specific components of the epigenetic system" (Williams, 1966, p. 70).

Ours is a developmental perspective that begins with the consideration of the fundamental and intricate transactions that occur within the nucleus and cytoplasm of dividing embryonic cells, as well as the elaborate and decisive transactions that occur among proliferating (and dying) neuronal precursors and migrating and differentiating neurons that lead to the formation of neural structures in the prenatal period (Earls & Carlson, 1995). This perspective is shaped by various epigenetic events that include the trophic and structural processes that guide the formation of neural pathways and the activity-dependent mechanisms that mediate synaptic competition, elimination, stabilization, and elaboration (Carlson, Earls, & Todd, 1988). The ecology of the developing nervous system consists not only of the cascading sequence of multicellular events involved in structural formation and functional activity but also the continuous pattern of stimulation that results in activity-dependent shaping of the developing nervous system. We believe that the development of neuroendocrinological control of the stress hormone, cortisol, illustrates the critical role of the social ecology in the postnatal epigenesis of the nervous system in a compelling way.

Ours is also an evolutionary perspective that recognizes the key role of the selection of diverse ontogenetic processes in the course of phylogenetic development (Gould, 1977). Comparative understanding of ontogenetic processes in brain and behavior in closely related species within the primate order provides a basis from which to consider the possible evolutionary strategies and species-appropriate ecologies of diverse primate lineages (Carlson, 1990; Carlson & Nystrom, 1994). Indeed, our current studies of children raised in institutions stems from earlier research experience with socially deprived macaques and chimpanzees (Randolph & Mason, 1969) in which touch was identified as the critical modality in early social development (Harlow & Harlow, 1965). Two decades of research on the projection to and processing of tactile input in the cerebral cortex in a variety of nonhuman primates failed to detect lasting consequences in cortical organization or sensory capacity of either sensory derivation or cortical damage (Carlson, 1984, 1990, 1991), as has been shown for the development of visual cortex structure and function following early visual deprivation (Carlson, Hubel, & Wiesel, 1986). The failure to detect detrimental neural changes or enduring sensory deficits as a result of early touch deprivation required that we look to other neural systems for clues as to the basis for severe and lasting behavioral deficits following early social or tactile restriction. Recent findings in rodents on the effects of handling on the development of stress hormone regulation, hippocampal function, and related forms of memory provided the impetus to shift from studies on the development of the cerebral cortex to investigation of the adrenal cortex, and to our collaborative effort on the development of infants and young children in the context of extreme social disadvantage.

The ecological perspective we adopt recognizes that human development requires social and economic resources in the form of caring relationships, education, and jobs, and physical settings in which these activities are encouraged and supported. The theoretical contributions of Lewin, Barker, and Bronfenbrenner provide an intellectual base to orient and complement our work, but there has been a major problem in balancing theory, method, and analytical capacity in scientifically advancing this perspective (Earls & Buka, in press). Over the past several years, a major preoccupation of the Project on Human Development in Chicago Neighborhoods (PHDCN) has been to combine theory, methods, and analytical challenges in studying a broad range of urban contexts to examine the impact of neighborhood, family, and school environments on developmental outcomes of children and adolescents. It has demanded that we researchers develop new measures and statistical tools, and to adjust our theoretical thinking about such influences as new findings emerge. The work is ongoing and promising. To date, we have isolated a neighborhood-level process termed "collective efficacy" that we demonstrate in a multilevel analysis to mediate the relationship between residential instability and social disadvantage and violent crime (Sampson, Raudenbush, & Earls, 1997). Having shown that we can measure processes of this nature with satisfactory degrees of precision and validity, we are now pursuing additional analyses that tie together aspects of individual development with social phenomena operating across home, school, neighborhood, and metropolitan settings. To accomplish this, it is essential that bidirectional influences are tested between individuals and the social units they inhabit. As this kind of inquiry proceeds, we keep in mind Lewin's field theory that emphasized the interaction of person and environment (Lewin, 1954). He introduced a set of formal mechanisms in the form of vectors and psychological subsystems, but never submitted these to rigorous empirical testing. His ideas remain inspiring to us and thoroughly congenial to those of the holistic child approach that David Magnusson has introduced and scientifically nurtured over many years.

## REGULATION OF STRESS HORMONE AND DEVELOPMENT

An appreciation of hormonal regulation and development must begin with an emphasis on the distinction between basal levels of hormones (and other metabolic processes) regulated by homeostatic mechanisms and those reactive processes stimulated by particular demands or challenges from the environment. Homeostasis is a state of equilibrium that when destabilized by intrinsic or extrinsic forces immediately initiates a local negative feedback response to limit the response to the perturbation. Within seconds of the destabilization of the stress-related endocrine system, a "fight or flight" reaction will occur, mediated by the catecholaminergic neurotransmitters, epinephrine (EP, or adrenaline) and norepinephrine (NE), and activation of the autonomic nervous system (ANS). The initial stress cascade is one that begins with noradrenergic neurons in the locus coeruleus (LC) and other brain stem regions, followed by release of NE and activation of the sympathetic nervous system (SNS) and finally, release of EP from the medulla of the adrenal gland located atop the kidneys. The peripheral effect of activation of the SNS and release of NE and EP is to redirect blood flow to muscles from skin, kidney, and intestines. Recovery from the short-term SNS activation occurs through activation of the parasympathetic (PNS) component of the ANS, which restores metabolic balance by slowing the heart rate, stimulating digestion, and constricting the pupil (Chrousos & Gold, 1992). Given infrequent short-term exposure to stress, this fast-acting system and the recovery processes it stimulates are adaptive and reversible.

A second, slower acting chain of hormonal and metabolic events follows the initial LC/NE/SNS stress response and also plays a role in restoring homeostatic balance (see Fig. 15.1). This second system, the hypothalamic-pituitary-adrenal (HPA) axis, is activated when signals transmitted to the paraventricular nucleus of the hypothalamus (PVN) result in the secretion of corticotropin-releasing hormone (CRH) and arginine vasopressin (AVP). These peptides are transported from the hypothalamus through portal circulation to the anterior pituitary body where they stimulate the release of an adrenocorticotropic hormone (ACTH), that in turn travels through the general circulation to stimulate release of the glucocorticoid, cortisol (or corticosterone in rodents), from the adrenal cortex. The cortisol released into general circulation produces dramatic effects upon many organ systems as well as upon the HPA axis itself. At the level of the hypothalamus, cortisol inhibits further secretion of CRH and inhibits ACTH release from the pituitary, providing a local homeostatic negative feedback system of containment of this vital component of the stress response. Throughout the body, the active form of cortisol mobilizes energy over the short-term through increased glucose and lipid metabolism and over the longer term through stimulation of feeding behavior. As an apparent energy-saving strategy, other high-energy-demanding metabolic activities such as growth, reproduction, and immune function are inhibited by cortisol. As with the LC/NE/SNS stress axis, the HPA axis has an adaptive function in response to occasional and acute environmental demands. However, when these demands are frequent, unpredictable, or enduring, the HPA axis can exert adverse effects upon the major systems of the body as a result of ensuing dysregulation of the stress system (McEwen & Stellar, 1993).

Homeostasis suggests a mechanism through which systems are tightly regulated to maintain a constant internal environment. Through a simple process of local negative feedback, the regulation of blood oxygen, pH, and body temperature can be maintained within certain limits in spite of endogenous and exogenous perturbations. Yet other systems, such as the HPA, ANS, cardiovascular, and immune systems, respond continuously to physiological and behavioral challenges, such that their parameters must vary dynamically to match fluctuating demands. By contrast to homoeostatically regulated systems, these systems have been described as contained through a strategy of "allostasis" (Sterling & Eyer, 1988). Rather than working simply through local negative feedback confined to peripheral tissues, allostatic systems operate under many levels of neuronal control, through converging pathways that parallel or override the local negative feedback (such as the action of cortisol at the level of the hypothalamus and pituitary). Examples of such neuronal circuitry are forebrain nuclei (amygdala and bed nucleus of the stria terminalis, BST) projections to the PVN that

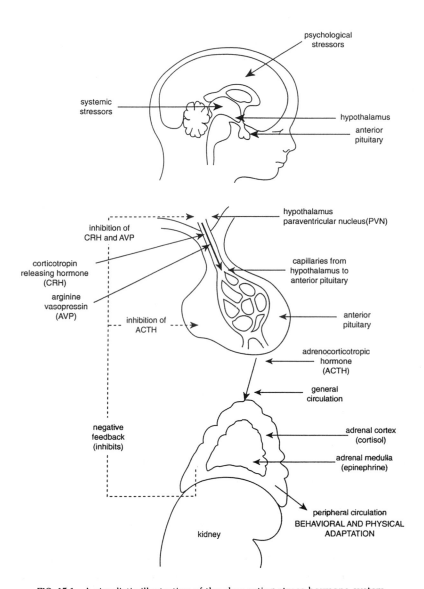

FIG. 15.1. A simplistic illustration of the slow-acting stress hormone system, hypothalamic-pituitary-adrenal axis. Both physical and psychological stressors impact on the HPA axis through connections from higher cortical regions to the HPA axis. Activation of the hypothalamus (PVN) results in release of CRH and AVP, which are transported through the portal circulation to the anterior pituitary, which in turn is activated to release ACTH into the general circulation. Release of cortisol from the adrenal cortex occurs in response to blood levels of ACTH, and subsequently the release of CRH, AVP, and ACTH is inhibited in response to high levels of circulating ACTH. Autoregulation of cortisol occurs through the cascading events in the HPA axis followed by the negative feedback occurring after cortisol release. This simplistic diagram of a homeostatic mechanism of control does not reflect the actual complexity of allostatic control described in the text.

have an excitatory impact on the HPA axis, in contrast to hippocampus and prefrontal cortex projections that inhibit the axis via indirect connections to the PVN (possibly by way of other hypothalamic nuclei and the BST; Herman & Cullinan, 1997).

Both excitatory and inhibitory central pathways to the HPA axis (which may mediate allostatic control) allow for more adaptive characteristics than simple homeostatic mechanisms, as well as for the continuous readjustment of HPA activity that benefits from past experiences, and "learns" to antici- pate adverse conditions. The amygdala has been proposed as the neural structure mediating the anticipatory function in allostatic regulation through its facilitative effects upon HPA activity (Schulkin, McEwen, & Gold, 1994). Yet this same flexibility of endocrine function that the central control of containment affords under conditions of chronic activation or anticipa- tion of negative experiences, can produce "allostatic load" resulting in adverse health outcomes (McEwen & Steller, 1993). Allostatic load is defined as the cost to physiological integrity exacted by repeated reactions to fluctuating environmental demands and stresses. Chronic activation can lead to an extreme allostatic load that may result in a loss of adaptive balance (or dysregulation) resulting in stress-induced disease states.

Before considering the dysregulation that occurs in response to the extreme neglect of institutional care, it is important to consider the normal development of regulation in infants. Basal (or nonstressed) levels of corti- sol are not constant throughout the day; rather, they show a clear diurnal variation, in which levels prior to waking surge to more than 0.6 ug/dL, but drop precipitously to less than 0.2 ug/dL by midmorning in children and adults. Reactivity levels following an acute stressor rise from that level to more than 0.4 ug/dL and fall to basal levels again within 30 to 45 minutes. This single diurnal pattern (with a single morning peak) is lacking in new- born infants whose pattern is characterized by several peaks over a 24-hour period.

In fact, the diurnal regulation of basal levels of HPA activity, showing the characteristic single pattern of elevated morning level and daily low level of cortisol, appears only as infants begin regular cycles of feeding and sleeping through the night at about 12 weeks of age (Price, Close, & Fielding, 1983). The capacity of infants to contain the level of cortisol secretion in response to an acute stress and to return to prestress levels of secretion (reactivity regulation) appears in the first 6 months of age. Research on human infants suggests that social contact with some primary caretaker plays an important role in buffering the psychological response to a poten- tially threatening event (such as a medical exam or immunization) begin- ning at about 4 to 6 months of age (Gunnar, Mangelsdorf, Larson, & Hertsgaard, 1991). That contact with a familiar adult can reduce levels of stress for the child suggests a mechanism of social buffering of stress levels.

More recently, Michael Meaney and his colleagues (Meaney, Aitken, Sharma, Viau, & Sarrieau, 1989; Liu et al., 1997) have shown that touch is critical in organizing the neural pathways that control the regulation of the glucocorticoid stress hormone, corticosterone, in rodents. The amount of tactile stimulation the infant pup receives from the mother prior to weaning influences the level of stress hormone secreted by the adrenal gland in response to stress, an effect that lasts throughout the life of the animal. Those rat pups receiving the most stimulation from the mother had more glucocorticoid receptors in the areas in the hippocampus (which provides a net inhibitory influence on the PVN) that contribute to the regulation of hormone levels along with the hypothalamus and pituitary gland. The investigators demonstrated that those animals receiving less tactile stimulation had fewer receptors for corticosterone in their hippocampus (but not the hypothalamus and pituitary) and thus had a less-effective allostatic control of cortisol regulation. As a result, these pups maintain higher hormone levels in response to stressful events, accompanied by premature degeneration of the same area of the hippocampus that normally shows high levels of these receptors (Bodnoff et al., 1995). In conjunction with this hippocampal degeneration, the unhandled rats as adults suffered from premature spatial memory loss generally associated with the hippocampus. Indeed, the earlier results of this important work led us to examine stress hormones in institutionalized infants.

## NEURAL AND BEHAVIORAL DEVELOPMENT IN THE CONTEXT OF SEVERE SOCIAL DEPRIVATION

Knowledge of the conditions of abandoned infants and children living in state-run institutions for children from birth to 3 years of age (known as *Leagane*, or cradles) in Romania led us to speculate that the profound degree of social deprivation experienced might prevent (or delay or disrupt) the development of regulation of the HPA axis. This hypothesis was informed by the finding in rodents that touch is critical to the development of reactivity regulation. We were fortunate to discover that a colleague, Joseph Sparling of the University of North Carolina, had developed an enrichment program in the *Leagane* in Iasi (in northeast Romania). Once we obtained his interest as a collaborator, we sought permission from the organization responsible for the children in these institutions (Iasi Medical School and Department of Public Health) to collect saliva from these children to examine daily basal levels of cortisol and the regulation of stress activity in response to an acute stressor (a physical exam).

Most of the children residing in these *Leagane* had experienced severe social deprivation since birth due to inadequate funding and training of caretakers in principles of child development. Sparling's program randomly assigned two groups of infants (between 2 and 9 months of age) to either the intervention or control condition. The intervention condition provided social and educational enrichment and a child-to-caretaker ratio of 4:1. The control group received the routine custodial and medical care typical of a Romanian *Leagane*, in which the child-to-caretaker ratio was often 20:1. Unfortunately, the small grant on which the intervention operated was exhausted within 13 months. Thus, by the time we obtained permission to conduct the cortisol study, children in the intervention group had been moved back and had been in the depriving environment of the institution for 6 months, at which time we took saliva samples, along with physical and behavioral assessments.

Salivary samples were taken prior to meals on two consecutive days: at 8 AM, noon, and 7 PM on Day 1, and again at 8 AM and noon, and at three closely spaced intervals in the afternoon and evening (5 PM, 6:30 PM, and 7 PM) on Day 2. The afternoon period corresponded to intervals prior to, and 15 and 45 minutes following, a physical examination, which was introduced as a mild stressor. Although the 30 children in the intervention group had shown significantly accelerated physical growth and mental and motor development compared with the 28 children in the control group by the end of the 13-month period, they lost this advantage within 6 months of the program ending. The measures of weight and height, head, triceps and chest circumference, and mental and motor performance (using the Bayley Scales of Infant Development) all revealed stagnation had occurred in the brisk catch-up development experienced by the intervention group. Most children in both groups were grossly delayed in physical growth (3rd to 10th percentile) and mental and motor indices (60–70% of expected performance) for their chronological age. Our study of diurnal patterns of cortisol secretion and the reactivity of the HPA system to a novel social event questioned whether the intervention might have produced a sustainable beneficial effect, and whether basal and reactivity levels of cortisol bore a relationship to behavioral and physical growth parameters.

The following is a summary of some preliminary reports of the findings from our 3-year study of institutional- and family-reared children in Romania (Carlson et al., 1995, 1997). The examination of basal cortisol levels revealed that morning levels in the 2-year-old *Leagan* children were significantly lower (less than 0.4 ug/dL) than in the same-aged Romanian children at home on the weekend (greater than 0.6 ug/dL). In the PM, when cortisol levels are normally low (around 0.1 ug/dL), levels in both *Leagan* groups remained elevated. When the two *Leagan* groups were examined separately, cortisol levels in the control group were found to be significantly higher at noon (near 0.5 ug/dL) than in the intervention group (around 0.3 ug/dL). Statistically significant correlations were obtained between suppressed AM cortisol levels and poor performance on Bayley Scales for both groups of *Leagan* children, as well as with elevated noon levels and poor performance for the control group. Furthermore, those children in both groups with the highest and most sustained levels of cortisol secretion in response to the physical exam were those who also scored lower on the Bayley Scales. It should be emphasized that as a group the *Leagan* children were strikingly below the Bayley norms and growth norms for their age, although the majority had been of normal birth weight and neonatal maturity upon entry into these institutions. Correlations between cortisol levels and the mental and motor scales of the Bayley were also found for the 2-year-old family-reared Romanian children, who were similar to norms for U.S. children.

Since the original data collection, we have obtained additional measurements from the *Leagan* children, along with measures of 2- and 3-year-old family-reared children at home and in state-run day-care settings. We were surprised to find that both family-reared groups who had normal cortisol profiles at home showed dysregulated basal profiles. The 2-year-old group showed significantly elevated noon levels compared to their home values, and the 3-year-old groups showed significantly suppressed AM values and elevated PM levels compared to home values. When the *Leagan* children were around 3 years of age, the control group continued to show elevated noon levels when compared with the intervention group and the 3-year-old family-reared children at home. Those children in the control group with the most elevated noon levels also demonstrated the lowest behavioral scores at age 2. A unique finding for the intervention group was that those children showing the greatest elevation in hormone levels following the brief physical exam had the lowest mental and motor scores at age 2. Both these profiles—elevated noon levels for the control group and stress and post-stress levels associated with Bayley scores for the intervention group—were found at both ages 2 and 3, indicating sustainable differences relating to their different rearing experiences between 6 to 19 months of age. By age 3, however, after half the children in both groups had several months of pre-school experience, morning values of both groups had risen to near normal levels. Interestingly, those with the lowest AM levels in both groups were still the children with the lowest Bayley scores. A recent report of cortisol profiles in children experiencing the 1988 Armenian earthquake have shown suppressed AM levels as the only difference between those adolescents living close to as opposed to a longer distance from the quake epicenter (Goenjian et al., 1996). Several years after the earthquake, those with the lowest AM cortisol levels displayed the highest frequency of intrusion symptoms characteristic of posttraumatic stress disorder (PTSD). The features of cortisol dysregulation in 2- and 3-year-old socially deprived *Leagan* children (low AM and high noon levels) and traumatized adolescents (low AM levels) appear to be persistent over time and a marker of behavioral difficulties.

When these results are considered in light of the findings from rearing effects on rodents, several issues emerge. The finding that both *Leagan* groups showed abnormally low AM levels at age 2 (as did the 3-year-olds in day care) was not anticipated from the rodent work in which rearing was found to consistently relate to cortisol reactivity and not to basal or diurnal regulation. Moreover, the fact that low AM cortisol levels are strongly related to low Bayley scores contrasts with the finding in rodents of high reactivity corticosterone levels correlating with memory deficits. We do not have clues from the animal literature to indicate through what pathways or by what mechanisms this form of basal dysregulation may occur, nor by what mechanism low AM levels might relate to poor behavioral performance. The abnormally elevated noon values in the control group at ages 2 and 3 (and inverse relation with Bayley scores) suggest long-term consequences of early rearing experiences on basal levels. The possibility that this may be a reactivity to daytime stress or anticipation of meal time should be entertained although it seems unlikely. Another important idea to pursue is that the generally elevated levels at noon and PM in both *Leagan* groups may interfere with the mechanisms that reset the circadian regulation each day, or that high levels of cortisol synthesis at other points of the day may suppress the maximum synthesis of cortisol in the AM. These are issues that will require laboratory studies in nonhuman species to be more fully understood.

## Stress Hormone, Psychiatric, and Memory Disorders

The enduring relation between cortisol levels and general behavioral function in both groups suggest that the positive effects of stimulation, as well as the negative effects of deprivation and stress, may have persistent neural and behavioral consequences for infants and children. We have found that social deprivation in infants and young children due to the poor quality care they receive in residential and day-care institutions in Romania leads to abnormal levels of stress hormone as measured in samples of their saliva. Moreover, those *Leagan* children (and the 3-year-olds in day care) with the most abnormally high or low hormone levels at different times of the day also have the lowest scores on tests of mental and motor ability. Recent clinical work in adults with abnormally high and low cortisol levels (due to psychiatric or other medical conditions) has revealed volume differences in hippocampal formation as seen by neural imaging techniques. These observed changes in the size of this brain region are also associated with deficits in specific memory tasks known to be associated with this limbic cortical region.

Of particular interest for the *Leagan* results are the studies of children with PTSD symptoms (Goenjian et al., 1996), and the results of behavioral and neural imaging studies of adults with PTSD (Sapolsky, 1996). Adults with this disorder show low levels of 24-hour urinary cortisol compared to normal individuals with similar experiences (Yehuda, Kahana, et al., 1995). From these data it is not possible to determine if the low averages are due to a selective suppression of AM levels as in children and adolescents. Adults with PTSD have also been shown to display a specific deficit in verbal memory thought to be mediated by the hippocampus (delayed free recall) in comparison with an unaffected matched control group (Yehuda, Keefe, et al., 1995). The finding of low cortisol levels in PTSD patients, along with the report of significant shrinkage of the hippocampus as revealed by neural imaging (magnetic resonance imaging, MRI) reported for patients with PTSD, and smaller hippocampal formation in PTSD patients following childhood abuse (Bremner et al., 1997) seems at first paradoxical. Yet, an active debate continues on whether the low cortisol associated with PTSD follows a period of elevated levels immediately following the traumatic exposure, implying that abnormally low levels are a second phase of response to stress (Sapolsky, 1996, 1997; Yehuda, 1997) The mechanisms and possible central pathways contributing to abnormally low levels of cortisol (whether in the AM or averaged across a 24-hour period) remain to be explained. Nevertheless, low cortisol may be a marker, but perhaps not a direct cause, of hippocampal structural changes and associated memory deficits. The detrimental effects of short-term, exogenously suppressed cortisol on memory function was shown in normal young adults receiving dexamethasone suppression for a 4-day period. A selective decrement in declarative memory performance (paragraph recall task) was seen over that extended period which washed out over the next 7-day period, suggesting that suppressed levels can reversibly affect verbal memory performance (Newcomer, Craft, Hershey, Askins, & Bardgett, 1994).

The evidence that abnormally elevated cortisol levels are associated with hippocampal and memory changes is more straightforward and less controversial. Both MRI changes in hippocampal volume (right hemisphere) and deficits in verbal memory (paired associate learning and verbal recall corrected for full-scale IQ) have been associated with the level of cortisol elevation in Cushing's syndrome in which chronic elevated cortisol levels result from neoplastic or metabolic disease (Starkman, Gebarski, Berent, & Schteingart, 1992). A significant, positive correlation was found between hippocampal volume (determined by MRI measures) and verbal memory (percent retention). Both the hippocampal shrinkage and memory deficit have been found to be reversible following treatment for high cortisol levels. The elevated levels of cortisol seen in many depressed adults and adolescents are associated with verbal memory impairment (Dahl et al., 1991; Rubinow, Post, Savard, & Gold, 1984). Elevated levels of exogenous glucocorticoids administered for treatment of asthma have been shown to produce verbal memory (long-term storage and retrieval) deficits and mood changes (worry, anxiety) in children (Bender, Lerner, & Kollasch, 1988). A recent study has shown reduced hippocampal volumes in depressed adults currently in remission compared with matched controls. The correspondence between the accumulated duration of previous depressive episodes and hippocampal volume provides convincing evidence for a persistent neural change associated with assumed past elevated levels of cortisol (Sapolsky, 1996). Together these clinical findings of cortisol dysregulation and hippocampal and memory deficits intensify the concern for quality of care and social stimulation that infants and young children receive in the first years of life.

## ETHICAL CONSIDERATIONS AND FUTURE DIRECTIONS

In a previous publication we have argued that it is an ethical (as well as a scientific) necessity to consider the social ecology in the study of disadvantaged children (Carlson & Earls, 1997). The study of the social ecology of the disadvantaged child requires consideration of patterns of economic disparity and social exclusion that determine the distribution of material and social resources necessary for normative development, in contrast with the advantaged child for whom resources may range from adequate to excessive. Within an ecological framework, the distribution of finite resources can be examined in such a manner as to understand the reciprocal relationship between the emerging capacities of the child and the nutritional and social inputs required for stabilization and elaboration of neural and behavioral competencies. The design of behavioral studies can be expanded within an ecological framework to incorporate important strategic principles such as prevention, treatment, and rehabilitation of individuals experiencing developmental attrition and disorders. We believe that research on disadvantaged populations in which children are viewed as a "natural experiment" is unethical unless that research is designed and conducted with a concern for how the outcome of the research can be used to inform the analysis and to make recommendations for the protection and rehabilitation of those children who suffer in that "natural experiment."

Ethical principles to guide adults acting on behalf of children and the rights of children as citizens are stated in the United Nations Convention on the Rights of the Child (CRC), which has been ratified by all UN members except the U.S. and Somalia. We use the ethical framework of this remarkable document as a guide for our work in the U.S., Romania, and the other UN member states. This document specifies that all actions be guided by "the best interests of the child," along with specifying the responsibilities of families, states, and the international community in promoting the development of children. Although the importance of touch and other forms of early stimulation for normal human development has been known for most of this century, a number of East European and former Soviet Union countries have continued to provide an inadequate form of care for indigent, abandoned, and orphaned children. Among these countries, Romania has received the greatest attention because of the large number of children raised in institutions (about 2% of the child population) and the severe deprivation that many experience due to the inadequate number and training of caretakers. Our research was originally conceived to use contemporary findings from developmental neuroendocrinology to show how the violation of the fundamental social rights of children could adversely impact basic physiological homeostatic and regulatory functions and thereby strengthen the empirical basis for such claims for children. As we have learned more about the history and current policy debates within Romania, we have become more aware of how our findings can assist in the reformulation of polices for children at risk of abandonment and institutionalization. We have worked closely with Romanian pediatricians and colleagues and have published these results jointly (Carlson et al., 1995, 1997). We have worked with the Romanian office of UNICEF and other child advocacy organizations concerned with the rehabilitation of abandoned children and the promotion of alternatives to institutionalized care that are being considered to bring Romania into compliance with the CRC. These individuals and organizations believe that our research and the presentation of our findings to medical groups and governmental ministries can encourage the government and parents to seek alternatives to institutionalization of children from families experiencing economic and social challenges.

The most remarkable insight we have gained from our work in Romania is that social deprivation results in detrimental consequences across multiple physiological and behavioral domains in early development. By extending the analysis of early deprivation into the realm of the neurobiology of the HPA axis, we propose not only another way of confirming the serious effects that are the consequence of high levels of stress and deprivation, but also to introduce a system in which social environmental events affect specific brain functions and reduce the body's capacity to respond to challenges of many different types. These challenges range from diminished immune response and dysregulation of glucose metabolism to abnormalities in social and emotional behavior (Chrousos & Gold, 1992; McEwen & Stellar, 1993). This added knowledge assists us in understanding the degree to which development is directed by social-environmental conditions. To a large extent these are conditions that can be influenced, if not controlled, by human industry. The social ecology of schools, day-care centers and other forms of surrogate parenting are all well within the domain of man-made environments. It has been important to begin this analysis of early social influences of HPA regulation in a situation in which the severity of social deprivation is undeniable and completely indefensible.

It came as a great shock for us to return to the U.S. after the first visit to Romania in 1994 to find a number of politicians, policy makers, and journalists recommending a return to orphanages as an answer to persisting poverty in American families (Frank, Klass, Earls, & Eisenberg, 1996). The current welfare reform policy now in effect requires steady labor force participation of millions of low-income and unemployed parents without advanced assurance of an adequate supply of quality day care for their dependent children, which will require that many children be left in questionable care arrangements. In Romania, we found that family-reared children in poor quality day-care centers have abnormal cortisol profiles during the week, but not at home on weekends. These findings under less extreme conditions than the *Leagane* have significance for the large numbers of children about to enter inadequate nonfamilial care in the United States. The consistent relation between abnormal cortisol profile for children in residential institutions and in low-quality day care causes us to raise the question: What are we doing in the U.S. to assure that many of our most vulnerable children are not subjected to the type of depriving experience of custodial care in Romania that has been demonstrated to result in enduring consequences for neural, hormonal, and behavioral development?

The HPA system may reflect not only current adaptive pressures, but also the history of such experiences in the organism, particularly when stress or deprivation has been chronic. In this connection the concept of allostatic load as reflecting the dysfunction that may occur from repeated efforts to adapt to a chronically challenging environment is of interest. If, as hypothesized, lesser degrees of control are reflected in higher levels of allostatic load, then the HPA system may indeed prove to be of pivotal importance in disease pathogenesis (Schulkin et al., 1994). But by the same token, an ecological setting that is predictable and allows for a sense of control can promote and sustain good health and development from the early years onward. A final illustration represents a synthesis of science and ethics that has always been our pursuit (see Fig. 15.2). The HPA system sits at the center of a complex array of social and biological processes that determine states of well-being. By presenting it in this comprehensive fashion we authors hope to stimulate research that links the physiology of a complex neurobiological system to the even greater complexity of the social ecology to which it is tuned. We emphasize that the invalid and regressive distinction of nature–nurture that continues to dominate much of child development conceptualization must be modified to recognize the role of children themselves as agents in seeking and engaging resources as well as detecting and avoiding aversive conditions.

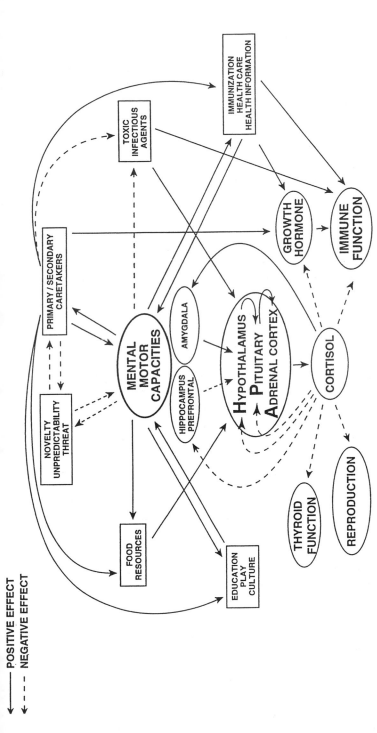

POSITIVE EFFECT
NEGATIVE EFFECT

FIG. 15.2. An illustration of HPA axis and behavioral regulation in the context of social support (e.g., caretakers), resources (e.g., food, education, and health care), and environmental threats (e.g., unpredictability, toxins). The interactions between emerging mental and motor capacities, central nervous system regions (hippocampus, amygdala), and the HPA axis are illustrated relative to other critical metabolic systems (e.g., growth, immune) that are reciprocally interactive with neuroendocrine regulation of cortisol. The U.N. Convention on the Rights of the Child contains 41 articles that are classified into survival (e.g., nutrition, health care), protection (e.g., caretakers and states protecting from violence and exploitation), and participation rights (e.g., to information, to expression, and to association). The rights perspective requires that the active role of the child is considered in addition to the role that caretakers and service providers play in the child's survival, care, and protection. This depiction of the complexity of interactions within physiological systems (nature) and within the material and social contexts (nurture) is intended to take discussion of child development beyond the simplistic and contentious nature–nurture debate to include the child as an active agent in a system that does not yield to reductionistic explanatory strategies.

Perhaps the most profound insight that has come from the past 3 years of working with children of the *Leagane* has been the recognition of the vast importance of agency in the lives of normal infants and toddlers. The social withdrawal, passivity, lack of movement, and vocalization by infants in *Leagane* as young as 3 months portray the fragility of this most human quality and speak to the importance of respecting, protecting, and encouraging agency even in the first 3 years. These children's lack of agency can be construed as a violation of their right to participate in their own development. In addition to rights of survival, care, and protection based on adults' responsibilities to children, the CRC gives special attention to the rights (and capacities) of children to be active agents at all ages. These participation rights include the right to form associations, to obtain information, and to express an opinion about practices that impact their development and well-being. We argue that deterministic approaches to the study of child development, whether from the perspective of nature or nurture, are scientifically and ethically invalid. The complex biosocial systems approach that is necessary to understand child development must include the concept of the child as an agent, in the same way that the study of living systems cannot be reduced to the simple mechanics of inorganic matter.

## ACKNOWLEDGMENTS

The research described in this chapter was carried out in collaboration with Marie Farrell, Megan Gunnar, Pia Nystrom, and Joseph Sparling from the U.S. and Melania Cuiperca, Cristiana Dragomir, Carmen Grigoras, Olimpia Macovei, and Gina Scripcaru from Romania. The contribution of each is respectfully recognized. We are grateful for the funds from the Milton Fund of Harvard University and the Bunting Institute of Radcliffe College; and the NIH grant MH40157 to M.C., as well as grants from the John D. and Catherine T. MacArthur and the Irving B. Harris Foundations to F.E., which have all made the collection and analysis of these data possible.

## REFERENCES

Bender, B. G., Lerner, J. A., & Kollasch, E. (1988). Mood and memory changes in asthmatic children receiving corticosteroids. *Journal of the American Academy of Child and Adolescent Psychiatry, 27*, 720–725.

Bodnoff, S. H., Humphreys, A. G., Lehman, J. C., Diamond, D. M., Rose, G. M., & Meany, M. J. (1995). Enduring effects of chronic corticosterone treatment on spatial learning, synaptic plasticity, and hippocampal neuropathology in young and mid-aged rats. *Journal of Neuroscience, 15*, 61–69.

Bremner, J. D., Randall, P., Scott, T. M., Bronen, R. A., Seiby, J. P. L., Southwick, S. M., Delaney, R. C., McCarthy, G., Charney, D. S., & Innis, R. B. (1995). MRI-based measurement of hippocampal volume in patients with combat-related posttraumatic stress disorder. *American Journal of Psychiatry, 152*, 973–981.

Bremner, J. C., Randall, P., Vermetten, E., Staib, L., Bronen, R. A., Mazure, C., Capelli, S., McCarthy, G., Innis, R. B., & Charney, D. S. (1997). Magnetic resonance-image based measurement of hippocampal volume in posttraumatic stress disorder related to childhood physical and sexual abuse—a preliminary report. *Biological Psychiatry, 41*, 23–32.

Carlson, M. (1984). Development of tactile discrimination capacity in *Macaca mulatta*. I. Normal infants. *Developmental Brain Research, 16*, 69–82.

Carlson, M. (1990). Role of somatic sensory cortex in tactile discrimination in primates. In E. G. Jones & A. Peters (Eds.), *Cerebral Cortex, Vol. 8B* (pp. 451–486). New York: Plenum.

Carlson, M. (1991). Ontogenetic and phylogenetic perspectives on somatic sensory cortex and tactile discrimination. In O. Franzén & J. Westman (Eds.), *Informational Processing in the Somatosensory System, Wenner-Gren International Symposium Series, Vol. 57* (pp. 177–192). Hampshire, UK: Macmillian.

Carlson, M., Dragomir, C., Earls, F., Farrell, M., Macovei, O., Nystrom, P., & Sparling, J. (1995). Effects of social deprivation on cortisol regulation in institutionalized Romanian infants. *Society for Neuroscience Abstracts, 218.12.*

Carlson, M., Dragomir, C., Earls, F., Farrell, M., Macovei, O., Nystrom, P., & Sparling, J. (1997). Cortisol regulation in home-reared and institutionalized Romanian children. *Society for Neuroscience Abstracts, 698.1.*

Carlson, M., & Earls, F. (1997). Psychological and neuroendocrinological sequelae of early social deprivation in institutionalized children in Romania. *Annals of New York Academy of Science, 807*, 419–428.

Carlson, M., Earls, F., & Todd, R. D. (1988). The importance of regressive changes in the development of the nervous system: Towards a neurobiological theory of child development. *Psychiatric Developments, 6*, 1–22.

Carlson, M., Hubel, D. H., & Wiesel, T. N. (1986). Effects of monocular exposure to oriented lines on monkey striate cortex. *Developmental Brain Research, 25*, 71–81.

Carlson, M., & Nystrom, P. (1994). Tactile discrimination capacity in relation to size and organization of primary somatic sensory cortex in primates: I. Old World prosimian, *Galago*; II. New World anthropoids, *Saimiri* and *Cebus*. *Journal of Neuroscience, 14*, 1516–1541.

Chrousos, G. P., & Gold, P. W. (1992). The concept of stress and stress system disorders: overview of physical and behavioral homeostasis. *Journal of the American Medical Association, 267*, 1244–1252.

Dahl, R. E., Ryan, N. D., Puig-Antich, J., Nguyen, N., al-Shabbout, M., Meyer, V. A., & Perel, J. (1991). 24-hour cortisol measures in adolescents with major depression: a controlled study. *Biological Psychiatry, 30*, 25–36.

Earls, F., & Buka, S. (in press). Measurement of community characteristics. In S. J. Meisels & J. P. Shonkoff (Eds.), *Handbook of Early Childhood Intervention* (2nd edition).

Earls, F., & Carlson, M. (1993). Towards sustainable development for American families. *Daedalus, 122*, 93–121.

Earls, F., & Carlson, M. (1995). Promoting human capability as an alternative to early crime prevention. In P.-O. Wiktrom, R. V. Clarke, & J. McCord (Eds.), *Integrating Crime Prevention Strategies* (pp. 141–168). Stockholm: National Council for Crime Prevention.

Frank, D. A., Klass, P. E., Earls, F., & Eisenberg, L. (1996). Infants in Orphanages? A View from Pediatrics and Child Psychiatry. *Pediatrics, 97*, 569–578.

Goenjian, A. K., Yehuda, R., Pynoos, R. S., Steinberg, A. M., Tashjian, M., Yang, R. K., Najarian, L. M., & Fairbanks, L. A. (1996). Basal cortisol, dexamethasone suppression of cortisol and MHPG in adolescents after the 1988 earthquake in Armenia. *American Journal of Psychiatry, 153*, 929–934.

Gould, S. J. (1977). *Ontogeny and Phylogeny*. Cambridge, MA: Harvard University Press.

Gunnar, M., Mangelsdorf, S., Larson, M., & Hertsgaard, L. (1995). Dampening of behavioral and adrenocortical reactivity during infancy: Normative changes and individual differences. *Child Development, 67*, 877–889.

Harlow, H. F., & Harlow, M. K. (1965). The Affectional systems. In H. F. Harlow & F. Stolnitz (Eds.), *Behavior of Nonhuman Primates: Vol 2* (pp. 287–334). New York: Academic Press.

Herman, J. P., & & Cullinan, W. E. (1997). Neurocircuitry of stress: central control of the hypothalamic-pituitary-adrenocortical axis. *Trends in Neuroscience, 20*, 78–84.

Lewin, K. (1954). Behavior as a function of the total situation. In L. Carmichael (Ed.), *Manual of Child Psychology* (pp. 918–970). New York: Wiley.

Liu, D., Diorio, J., Tannebaum, B., Caldji, C., Francis, D., Freedman, A., Sharma, S., Pearson, D., Plotsky, P. M., & Meaney, M. J. (1997). Maternal care, hippocampal glucocorticoid receptors, and hypothalamic-pituitary-adrenal responses to stress. *Science, 277*, 1659–1662.

Magnusson, D. (1988). *Individual development from an interactional perspective: A longitudinal study*. Hillsdale, NJ: Lawrence Erlbaum Associates.

Mayr, E. (1982). *The growth of biological thought: Diversity, evolution and inheritance* (p. 120). Cambridge, MA: Belknap/Harvard University Press.

McEwen, B. S., & Stellar, E. (1993). Stress and the individual: Mechanisms leading to disease. *Archives of Internal Medicine, 153*, 2093–2101.

Meaney, M. J., Aitken, S., Sharma, S., Viau, S., & Sarrieau, A. (1989). Postnatal handling increases hippocampal glucocorticoid receptors and enhances adrenocortical negative feedback efficacy in the rat. *Neuroendocrinology, 50*, 597–604.

Newcomer, J. W., Craft, S., Hershey, T., Askins, K., & Bardgett, M. E. (1994). Glucocorticoid-induced impairment in declarative memory performance in adult humans. *Journal of Neuroscience, 14*, 2047–2053.

Price, D. A., Close, G. C., & Fielding, B. A. (1983). Age of appearance of circadian rhythm in salivary cortisol values in infancy. *Archives of Disease in Childhood, 58*, 454–456.

Randolph, M. C., & Mason, W. A. (1969). Effects of rearing conditions on distress vocalization in chimpanzees. *Folia Primatologica, 10*, 103–112.

Rubinow, D. R., Post, R. M., Savard, R., & Gold, P. W. (1984). Cortisol hypersecretion and cognitive impairment in depression. *Archives of General Psychiatry, 41*, 279–283.

Sampson, R., Raudenbush, S., & Earls, F. (1997). Neighborhoods and violent crime: A multilevel study of collective efficacy. *Science, 277*, 918–924.

Sapolsky, R. M. (1996). Why stress is bad for your brain. *Science, 273*, 749–750.

Sapolsky, R. M. (1997). Reply to Yehuda. *Science, 275*, 1662–1663.

Schulkin, J., McEwen, B. S., & Gold, P. W. (1994). Allostasis, amygdala, and anticipatory angst. *Neurocsci. Behav. Revs., 18*, 385–396.

Sheline, Y. I., Wang, P. W., Gado, M. H., Csernansky, J. G., & Vannier, M. W. (1996). Hippocampal atrophy in recurrent depression. *Proc. Natl. Acd. Sci., 93*, 3908–3913.

Stansbury, K., & Gunnar, M. L. (1994). Adrenocortical activity and emotional regulation. *Monographs. Soc. Res. Child Develop., 59*, 108–134.

Starkman, M. N., Gebarski, S., Berent, S., & Schteingart, D. E. (1992). Hippocampal formation volume, memory dysfunction and cortisol levels in patients with Cushing syndrome. *Biol. Psychiatry, 32*, 756–765.

Sterling, P., & Eyer, J. (1988). Allostasis: A new paradigm to explain arousal pathology. In S. Fisher & J. Reason (Eds.), *Handbook of life stress, cognition and health* (pp. 629–649). New York: Wiley.

Williams, G. C. (1966). *Adaptation and natural selection: A critique of some current evolutionary thought*. Princeton, NJ: Princeton University Press.

Yehuda, R. (1997). Stress and Glucocorticoid. *Science, 275*, 1662.

Yehuda, R., Kahana, B., Binder-Brynes, K., Southwick, S. M., Mason, J. W., & Giller, E. L. (1995). Low urinary cortisol excretion in holocaust survivors with posttraumatic stress disorder. *American Journal of Psychiatry, 152,* 982–986.

Yehuda, R., Keefe, R. S. E., Harvey, P. D., Levengood, R. A., Gerber, D. K., Geni, J., & Siever, L. J. (1995). Learning and memory in combat veterans with posttraumatic stress disorder. *American Journal of Psychiatry, 152,* 137–139.

# PERSONALITY

# 16

# The Four Cs of Personality: Context, Consistency, Conflict, and Coherence

### Lawrence A. Pervin
Rutgers University

David Magnusson has articulated the key elements of a person approach to personality and developmental psychology, thereby pointing the way toward future bridges between the two fields (Magnusson, 1990, 1996; Magnusson & Stattin, 1998; Magnusson & Törestad, 1993; Stattin & Magnusson, 1996). The key elements of such an approach are a holistic, interactionist view that emphasizes a dynamic systems perspective, patterns of relationships among variables or parts of the system, and nonlinear as well as linear relationships. The person is viewed as an active, purposeful agent interacting with an environment that includes externally created and self-created affordances.

As a personality psychologist, I am very sympathetic to this point of view. As a graduate student, I was influenced by Murray's (1938) approach to the intensive study of individuals and his emphasis on individual–environment transactions (Pervin, 1967, 1968). As a clinician trained within a psychodynamic framework, I am sympathetic to the value of idiographic research and a dynamic systems perspective (Pervin, 1984, 1989). From this perspective, I think that the fundamental issue for the personality psychologist is an understanding of the *coherence of personality*, that is, an understanding of the ways in which the different parts of the personality system interact with one another, and with external contexts, to produce adaptive and maladaptive functioning (Pervin, 1990).

In this chapter I will consider the importance of stable individual differences in self-conceptions and motives-goals as well as the variability within individuals of these self-conceptions and motives as a function of specific contexts. In doing so, I will be addressing an issue of historic concern to personality psychologists, highlighted in an unfortunate way in the person–situation controversy, and one that I most specifically attempted to address in my *Nebraska Symposium on Motivation* paper on the stasis and flow of personality (Pervin, 1983). In that paper I emphasized that stability and variability are each aspects of personality functioning and that the task for us as personality psychologists is to develop a conceptualization that accounts for both. The issue of concern to me is one of understanding the coherence of personality in the presence of both consistency and contextual specificity. Thus, one may ask the following question: How does a complex system adapt to changing circumstances while maintaining a cohesive structure? I believe that the issues of concern relative to individual functioning across situations parallels those of stability, change, and coherence from a developmental, longitudinal perspective.

## THE GENERAL AND THE CONTEXTUAL: SELF AND GOALS

Currently there is a great deal of interest in the phenomenon of multiple personality disorders or, as currently termed, dissociative identity disorders. If, as social cognitive theorists suggest, the self is contextually variable, what is it that gives us a sense of self? If we play many different roles in varied situations, what is it that gives us a sense of self-coherence? If the self is to a great extent contextual, why don't we all experience ourselves as multiple personalities? In social-cognitive terms, what is it that gives us the sense of a family of selves as opposed to unrelated individuals (Cantor & Kihlstrom, 1987)?

Some of my early research on the issue of consistency and variability in personality functioning focused on the self-concept, although it was not framed within that context. In that research individuals selected situations in their daily lives, developed lists of situation characteristics, feelings in situations, and behaviors in situations, and then rated the relevance of the situation characteristics, feelings, and behaviors to each situation (Pervin, 1976). The research was idiographic in that all situations, situation characteristics, feelings, and behaviors were generated by the individual subject. The question addressed was the following: In what ways is the person stable and in what ways does the person vary as a function of which situational characteristics? As indicated in the title of this chapter, the research was construed as a free-response approach to the analysis of person–situation interaction. To consider the results of one subject, Jennifer reported that she almost always was sensitive, vulnerable, and insightful, and almost always friendly, warm, and accepting. However, many aspects of her functioning varied according to such situational contexts as home, school, and with friends, each associated in her mind with specific situational characteristics. Thus, for example, she described herself as caring and concerned but also confused and suppressed in volatile home situations; as determined, cool, and compulsive in school and work situations where she experienced pressure to perform; and as concerned, caring, emotional, and responsive in relaxed situations with friends.

During the past semester I have engaged a group of students in comparing various approaches to personality through studying themselves as individual cases. Each student takes personality tests associated with various theoretical approaches to personality and then considers relations among the theories and data in terms of his or her own personality. The model for this is the case of Jim, presented in my personality text (Pervin & John, 1997). In one part of this research the students rated themselves on 24 semantic differential scales, each scale containing seven points. This constitutes the *General Self*. Following this, students briefly described representative situations in each of the following categories: Home, School, Work, Peers-Recreation, Self at Best, Self at Worst. One representative situation was given for each of the first four categories and two for the Self at Best and Self at Worst. Students then rated themselves on the same seven-point semantic differential scales for each of the eight situations. The first four contexts were selected because they repeatedly come up as important situation categories, the latter two because of my interest in understanding the relation between adaptive and maladaptive functioning within the individual.[1] As a clinician I am impressed with just how discrepant individual adaptive and maladaptive functioning can be. As a personality psychologist I am impressed with the extent to which some theories and associated data tend to emphasize maladaptive functioning (e.g., psychoanalytic theory and Rorschach data) whereas other theories tend to emphasize adaptive personality functioning (e.g., social-cognitive theory and self-efficacy beliefs or life-task pursuits). Finally, students rated themselves on the semantic differ-

---

[1]Although these categories are common and reasonable to use, as I have indicated elsewhere I am not optimistic concerning the potential utility of a taxonomy of situations (Pervin, 1981). My sense is that individuals are very idiosyncratic in their organization of situations. Thus, many categories presented to them will not fit their idiosyncratic organization, and situations grouped together to fit the researcher's categories may not go together in terms of the person's more idiosyncratic organization of the environment. In addition, I have found that subjects have multiple ways of categorizing situations, shifting their organization of categories to fit their goals and the contingencies of the moment. In sum, just as a static picture of the person ignores the dynamic processes that are so basic to human functioning, so too does a static picture of situation categories ignore the dynamic processes involved in engagement with the environment. Of course, this does not preclude the utility of using some situation categories for specific research purposes.

ential scales for the concepts Ideal Self, Ought Self, and Undesired Self (Higgins, 1987; Ogilvie, 1987). The specific issues to be addressed in this research were not known to the students prior to their completing the task. It was presented to them as a study of the self in relation to the personality theory of Carl Rogers.

The first point to be made is that the students had no difficulty completing the task, done over the course of a week. In other words, the students had no difficulty rating themselves in general as well as in specific contexts. The second point is that there is clear evidence of variability of self-ratings by context (Home, School, Work, Recreation) and between Self at Best and Self at Worst. To illustrate the variation in self-ratings by context, we can analyze the ratings on five scales associated with the five-factor model of personality: relaxed–tense (Neuroticism), introverted–extraverted (Extraversion), uncreative–creative (Openness), uncooperative–cooperative (Agreeableness), and disorganized–organized (Conscientiousness). Mean scores for 10 subjects on these seven-point scales for the contexts Home, School, Work, and Peers are presented in Table 16.1. Also presented are the mean ranges of ratings for the 10 subjects across the four contexts. Since ratings were made on a seven-point scale, the maximum possible range was 6. These scores clearly indicate considerable variability by context, but they mask the even greater individual variability embedded in mean scores, captured to some extent in the mean range figures. For example, for the relaxed–tense scale the mean range of individual scores across the four contexts was 3.1, with one subject's ratings ranging between 1 and 6, and another subject giving self-ratings of 3 in all four contexts.[2] Not surprisingly, analysis of such individual ratings indicates that some subjects see themselves as generally stable or consistent across contexts and others as quite varying across contexts, some as consistent on some traits and variable on others, and some as consistent across some contexts and varying in other contexts. Some subjects see themselves as quite stable or consistent across the four contexts but as quite variable between Self at Best and Self at Worst, suggesting that the latter categories cut across the four contexts or are associated with contexts not otherwise explored in the study.

The data for Self at Best and Self at Worst (Table 16.1) present a very similar picture of considerable general variability by context as well as individual variation in the magnitude of the best–worst difference, both in terms of any one scale and across the five scales. Whereas some subjects report little difference between themselves at their best and their worst, others report large best–worst differences and some report small differences on one scale but large differences on another. The five scales repre-

---

[2]Note should be made that ratings appeared to be most variable on this scale, which relates to affect. Previous research has suggested that subjects rate themselves as more variable in affect than in behavior in response to situational variability (Pervin & Furnham, 1987).

TABLE 16.1
Mean Scores for four Contexts on five Trait Scales and Mean Ranges for Individuals Across
the Four Contexts ($N = 10$)

| SCALE: *Relaxed–Tense* | | | SCALE: *Introverted–Extroverted* | | |
|---|---|---|---|---|---|
| Context Means: | *Home* | 2.0 | Context Means: | *Home* | 4.3 |
| | *School* | 4.5 | | *School* | 3.4 |
| | *Work* | 3.1 | | *Work* | 5.6 |
| | *Peers* | 2.5 | | *Peers* | 5.4 |
| | *Mean Range* | 3.1 | | *Mean Range* | 3.5 |
| | *Self at Best* | 2.1 | | *Self at Best* | 5.4 |
| | *Self at Worst* | 6.5 | | *Self at Worst* | 2.1 |
| | *Mean Range* | 4.9 | | *Mean Range* | 3.3 |

| SCALE: *Uncreative–Creative* | | | SCALE: *Uncooperative–Cooperative* | | |
|---|---|---|---|---|---|
| Context Means: | *Home* | 5.5 | Context Means: | *Home* | 5.0 |
| | *School* | 5.0 | | *School* | 5.7 |
| | *Work* | 5.0 | | *Work* | 6.6 |
| | *Peers* | 5.2 | | *Peers* | 5.6 |
| | *Mean Range* | 1.9 | | *Mean Range* | 2.3 |
| | *Self at Best* | 6.1 | | *Self at Best* | 5.7 |
| | *Self at Worst* | 2.9 | | *Self at Worst* | 2.8 |
| | *Mean Range* | 4.0 | | *Mean Range* | 3.8 |

| SCALE: *Disorganized–Organized* | | |
|---|---|---|
| Context Means: | *Home* | 5.3 |
| | *School* | 5.5 |
| | *Work* | 6.2 |
| | *Peers* | 4.7 |
| | *Mean Range* | 2.4 |
| | *Self at Best* | 6.2 |
| | *Self at Worst* | 2.9 |
| | *Mean Range* | 4.0 |

sented in Table 16.1 tend to have a social desirability element to them, as is true for the Big-Five factors.[3] Therefore, it is not surprising that generally

---

[3]One of the problems with the use of semantic differential is the challenge of developing scales that are not skewed in terms of social desirability but still provide for variability of response. Many scales that are equally positive or negative at both ends result in ratings in the middle of the scale for a great majority of the subjects, indicating that many subjects refuse

the Self at Best ratings tend toward the more desirable end of the scale and the Self at Worst toward the other end. However, it should be noted that there were a few individual exceptions to this pattern, with one subject reporting being more creative and another more cooperative in Self at Worst than in Self at Best. More generally, one can see evidence of individual differences on many of the scales that are less clearly defined in terms of the Big Five. For example, some subjects viewed themselves as too dependent at their worst whereas others viewed themselves as too independent, some as too submissive and others as too dominant. The suggestion may be made that individuals differ in their pattern of best–worst functioning, reflecting the interplay between adaptive and maladaptive resources, and that this pattern reflects an important component of their personality.

The variability in ratings by context raises questions concerning a pure trait view of personality functioning. Although one could argue that the data reflect unreliability due to single scales and single situations being involved, I am confident that they reflect the true nature of personality functioning and that the results would be maintained with the inclusion of more scales and situation ratings for each trait. They are consistent with the data reported in my (1976) free-response study, with Cervone's (1997) study of self-efficacy beliefs, and with the behavioral observations reported by Shoda, Mischel, and Wright (1994). Such data support the view stated by Roberts and Nesselroade (1986) that the trait assumption of stability is "risky" and, as Kagan (1996) notes, question the "pleasing idea" of broad generalizability of personality characteristics across contexts.

A point to consider is the meaning of the rating of the General Self; that is, when subjects rate their overall self, what is it that they are representing? Does this self reflect the ways in which one is consistent across situations, as one trait theorist suggested to me? Does this self reflect a prototypic self as social-cognitive psychologists might suggest? Does this self represent reflected appraisals or a historical narrative, as others might suggest? At this point it is unclear how individuals derive an overall conceptualization of the self. One of the most striking things about the ratings of the General Self is that although in many cases they appear to reflect some combination of the ratings across the four contexts or the best and worst of functioning, in other cases they do not appear to follow any identifiable pattern. For example, in some cases individuals rate the General Self as higher or lower on a scale than they rate the self in any of the specific contexts, a response that is understandable within the Gestalt emphasis on the whole as different

---

to select either alternative and do not find that format conducive to making their ratings. Of course, for some subjects a rating in the middle indicates that they perceive themselves between the two extremes. However, from the ratings there is no way of distinguishing between the two types of response.

from the sum of the parts, but perhaps difficult to otherwise comprehend. Given these data, the General Self appears to express an idiosyncratic combination of representations across current and past contexts. In other words, there may be no laws regulating the formulation of the General Self that are expressed in individual ratings on self inventories.

The evidence of variability of contextual self-ratings may also make one wonder about the meaning of reported significant self–observer correlations for trait ratings (Funder, 1980; John & Robins, 1994; Kenny, 1994; McCrae & Costa, 1990). If the person is tracking their behavior over many situations in the course of days, weeks, or months, this represents a monumental task in information processing. Such a task may be compared to that of the clinician who has been found to fare so poorly relative to actuarial approaches (Grove & Meehl, 1996; Meehl, 1954). In addition, we have the problem of contextual variability. Given such variability, how are we to account for the reported statistical correlations between self and observer ratings, including observers from different contexts?

First, it is important to note that the reported self–observer correlations are on the order of .40, leaving considerable room for self–observer and observer–observer disagreement to be due to differences in contextual observation. Second, differences in contextual observations are important. In a study of the issue, Funder, Kolar, and Blackman (1995) attempted to rule out the contribution of context overlap between self and observer by comparing self-ratings with those of parents, college friends, and hometown friends. They concluded:

> The results show that judges who see the target in different contexts agree with each other about what the target is like, although those who know the target in the same context agree even better. It seems that the parents, hometown acquaintances, and college acquaintances all know the target as more or less the same person. (p. 661)

The data in this well-done study leave room, however, for disagreement as to what constitutes knowing "more or less" the same person. Context clearly made a difference in self–observer agreement in ratings. The mean same-context correlation for the Big Five was .50 whereas that for different contexts was .29. Observer judges on the whole showed agreement with one another in their ratings of the same person but much of this agreement came from judges in the same context. Although the authors concluded that viewing the target in the same context is not necessary for interjudge agreement, they described it as "surely helpful" and recognized that "these results indicate that judges who know a target in the same context agree better about his or her personality than do judges who know him or her in different contexts" (p. 660). Further, although emphasizing self–other agreement, Kenny (1994) suggested that such agreement need not reflect "how the person truly is" (p. 202) and concluded that the data "should lead researchers to question seriously the orientation that views personality as the study of self-report inventories" (p. 194). As with trait ratings generally, reports of self–observer agreement appear to pick up the most general consistency in personality functioning that can be found across individuals and contexts, consistency that cannot be ignored in personality assessment. However, such reports of self–observer agreement also appear to fail to recognize evidence of considerable contextual specificity in personality functioning.

Turning to the study of goal system functioning, students were given a list of 24 goals and invited to add up to 3 more goals that were important to them and missing from the list. The list of goals was derived from the factor analysis of goal ratings provided in earlier research where free-response procedures were used (Pervin, 1983). Half the goals were written as "approach goals" (e.g., develop competence, increase intimacy) and half as "avoidance goals" (e.g., avoid blame or criticism, avoid rejection). Subjects were first asked to rate, on a four-point scale, the general importance of each goal to them. They then were asked to rate the importance of each goal in the home, school, work, and peer situations used in the self-ratings procedure described above, as well as in one of the Self at Best and Self at Worst situations. Thus, each subject rated the 24 goals, in addition to any others provided, on a four-point scale in terms of how important each goal was in general as well as in each of six situations. Following this they rated each goal in general and in relation to the same six specific situations in terms of the perceived affordance provided for meeting that goal. In other words, for each goal they related the extent to which the environment in general and each of the six specific contexts offered the potential for goal attainment. In sum, general goal-importance ratings could be compared with specific situation or context ratings, general affordance ratings could be compared with specific situation affordance ratings, and analyses could be conducted of general and contextual relations between goals and affordances. As with the self-ratings, there was interest in the relation of general ratings to contextual ratings. In addition, in this case there was an interest in perceived affordances in the environment in relation to perceptions of one's own goals.[4]

Analysis of these ratings provides a picture of consistency and variability not unlike that found in relation to the self-ratings: considerable individual variability in the ratings of general importance of goals and presence of goal

---

[4]These data provided the opportunity for other analyses as well, including the possible importance of ratios of approach to avoidance goals and the relation of goals to traits as measured later in the semester in relation to trait theory.

affordances, considerable variation in the extent to which goals are seen as applicable to situations and potentially met in situations (i.e., affordances), both in terms of the same goals generally being more relevant to some situations than other situations and in terms of individual differences in the relevance of goals and affordances to specific situations. Finally, once more there are the occasions where a goal is rated as more (or less) important generally than in any of the specific situations, and the environment is rated as generally higher (or lower) in affordance than in relation to any of the specific situations. Although these data are still being analyzed, two observations can be reported. First, Self at Best situations can be distinguished from Self at Worst situations in terms of the presence of more goals and the presence of approach goals relative to avoidance goals (i.e., more approach than avoidance in Self at Best situations and more avoidance than approach in Self at Worst situations). Second, Self at Best situations can be distinguished from Self at Worst situations in terms of the perceived affordance for goal attainment, both for approach goals and for avoidance goals. This difference held for every one of the subjects. Differences in goal affordance ratings between best and worst situations appeared to be even more striking than corresponding differences for goal importance differences. Thus, the data suggest the possibility that even more important than individual differences in ratings of goal importance are ratings of goal affordance; that is, perceptions of opportunities for attaining goals in terms of environmental affordances may be even more important for personality functioning than perceptions of the presence of goals.

## CONFLICT AND INTEGRATION WITHIN THE SYSTEM: SELF AND GOALS

In this section I will consider relations between various conceptions of the self as well as aspects of goals system functioning. As noted earlier, subjects rated themselves on the concepts Ideal Self, Ought Self, and Undesired Self. Higgins (1987) has emphasized the importance of self-discrepancies in relation to the first two in terms of the affects of depression and anxiety, and Ogilvie (1987) has emphasized the importance of Self–Undesired Self discrepancies for emotional well-being. As a measure of such relationships, for each individual discrepancy scores on the semantic differential scales were computed for the relevant concepts (e.g., Self–Ideal Self, etc.). As a further measure of psychological functioning, a measure was obtained of how close the individual's self-ratings were to the Self at Best ratings, compared with how close they were to the Self at Worst ratings. The assumption was that a more positive view of the self would be reflected in self-ratings closer to Self at Best ratings relative to Self at Worst ratings. Finally, the discrepancy

TABLE 16.2
Rank Order Correlations Between Self-Discrepancy Scores and Neuroticism ($N = 10$)
and between Measures of Goal System functioning and Neuroticism ($N = 13$)

| Self-Discrepancy Scores | Eysenck N |
|---|---|
| 1. Self–Ideal Self | .49 |
| 2. Self–Ought Self | .20 |
| 3. Self–Undesired Self | -.29 |
| 4. Self to Best Relative to Worst | -.38 |
| 5. Best–Worst | .53 |

| Goal System Functioning | |
|---|---|
| 1. Approach/Avoidance Goals | -.36 |
| 2. Perceived Affordance | -.45 |
| 3. Goal Conflict | .44 |

between the Self at Best and Self at Worst ratings was calculated.[5] This follows from a study by Brownfain (1952) of what he called "stability of the self-concept" in which individuals with stable self-concepts (i.e., small differences between positive self and negative self) were found to have higher self-esteem than individuals with unstable self-concepts. In this study stability was assumed to reflect an integrative function rather than rigidity.

The relevant discrepancy scores were related to neuroticism scores derived from the Eysenck Personality Inventory. Rank order correlations between the various self discrepancy measures and the neuroticism scores are presented in Table 16.2. Although none of the relationships is statistically significant, given the extremely high correlations required by the small number of subjects, they show a consistent pattern of results. The closer the General Self is to the Ideal Self, Ought Self, and Best Self, the lower the neuroticism score. Similarly, the further the General Self is from the Undesired Self, the lower the neuroticism score. Finally, in accord with Brownfain's (1952) finding, the greater the discrepancy between the Best Self and Worst Self, the higher the neuroticism score. In sum, there is evidence that dissatisfaction with the self, in terms of the relation of the general self-concept to other self-representations, is related to a self-report measure of neuroticism.

Turning to the study of goals, three measures of goal system functioning were related to the measure of neuroticism. First, the relative importance

---

[5]This followed a suggestion by Jack Block after discussion of an earlier draft of the paper. My appreciation to him for bringing the Brownfain (1952) reference to my attention.

of approach goals to avoidance goals was considered. For each subject the sum of the general rating of the 12 approach goals was calculated relative to the sum of the general rating of the 12 avoidance goals. Second, the sum of the general affordance ratings for the 24 goals was calculated for each subject. Third, subjects were given a list of 20 goal conflicts (e.g., Express anger vs. Avoid conflict, Relax vs. Do what "should" do, Get close vs. Risk betrayal), derived from earlier free-response research (Pervin, 1983), and asked to rate the importance of each on a 10-point scale. The sum of the ratings for the 20 conflicts was used as a measure of overall goal conflict. The relation of these three measures of aspects of goal system functioning to the neuroticism measure is presented in Table 16.2. Again, none of the relationships is statistically significant. However, there is clear evidence of a relation between the presence of approach goals relative to avoidance goals and low neuroticism, between perceived goal affordance and low neuroticism, and between goal conflict and high neuroticism. In sum, there is evidence of a relation between aspects of goal system functioning and subjective well-being.

## CONSISTENCY, CONTEXT, CONFLICT, AND COHERENCE IN PERSONALITY FUNCTIONING

The results presented give clear evidence of both consistency and variability in personality functioning, at least in terms of self-ratings in two areas of personality functioning. They further suggest that individuals can have general representations of the self that are different from the representations of the self in specific contexts, at least insofar as such contexts were measured in this research. In other words, representations of the general self can be greater or less than the sum of the parts. A similar picture emerges in terms of the representation of goals and environmental affordances; that is, not only do goals and affordances vary by context, as would be expected, but general ratings can be greater or less than the specific context ratings. The data also suggest that relations between representations of the self as well as relations between aspects of goal system functioning can have important implications for emotional well-being. Finally, the data suggest that an important aspect of personality functioning may be the perceptions individuals have of affordances in the environment. Such perceptions may be at least as important as perceptions of one's goals or self-efficacy beliefs.

But what can be said concerning the issue of coherence? I have touched upon this issue in relation to discrepancies between representations of the general self and contextual selves, and in relation to discrepancies between representations of the self and such concepts as Ideal Self, Ought Self, Undesired Self, Self at Best and Self at Worst. In addition, there was discussion of perceived relations between goals and affordances and perceived conflict between goals. However, I am not sure how far we researchers have come in addressing the issue of coherence. Perhaps what is most lacking is an understanding of how the various conceptions of the self and various goal ratings relate to one another, that is, how they function as part of a system.

Further, the issue of how different parts of the system (e.g., self-representations, goals, beliefs) relate to one another has not been addressed. In the case of Jim presented in my personality text (Pervin & John, 1997), it is clear that the data obtained from different approaches to assessment give different pictures of Jim's personality. How are we to understand relations among such different pictures? A patient presents himself as a very inhibited, shy, unaggressive, and unsexual person, yet his fantasies and television viewing focus on sex and aggression. Are these to be understood as separate, independent aspects of his functioning or are they to be understood as representing the varying interplay among parts of his personality? McClelland (1980) has suggested that operant and respondent personality measures tap into different aspects of personality functioning. Are these aspects independent of one another or are they related to one another as parts of the same system? These are issues fundamental to that of coherence and clearly issues that need to be addressed in the future. In sum, what is being suggested is that there is a need for more research in the area of system functioning, both in terms of the organization of personality functioning across contexts and the organization of the various components or units of personality functioning; that is, there is the need for more research in the area of personality coherence. In terms of Magnusson's holistic perspective, there is an analogous need for research into the question of personality coherence over time; that is, how the individual maintains a relatively stable, adaptive personality structure given the interplay between continuity and change that occurs over the life course.

## REFERENCES

Brownfain, J. J. (1952). Stability of the self-concept as a dimension of personality. *Journal of Abnormal and Social Psychology, 47,* 957–606.

Cantor, N., & Kihlstrom, J. F. (1987). *Personality and social intelligence.* Englewood Cliffs, NJ: Prentice-Hall.

Cervone, D. (1997). Social-cognitive mechanisms and personality coherence. *Psychological Science, 8,* 43–50.

Funder, D. C., (1980). On seeing ourselves as others see us: Self-other agreement and discrepancy in personality ratings. *Journal of Personality, 48,* 473–493.

Funder, D. C., Kolar, D. C., & Blackman, M. C. (1995). Agreement among judges of personality: Interpersonal relations, similarity, and acquaintanceship. *Journal of Personality and Social Psychology, 69,* 656–672.

Grove, W. M., & Meehl, P. E. (1996). Comparative efficiency of informal (subjective, impressionistic) and formal (mechanical, algorithmic) prediction procedures: The clinical-statistical controversy. *Psychology, Public Policy, and Law, 2,* 293–323.

Higgins, E. T. (1987). Self-discrepancy: A theory relating self and affect. *Psychological Review, 94,* 319–340.

John, O. P., & Robins, R. W. (1994). Accuracy and bias in self-perception: Individual differences in self-enhancement and the role of narcissism. *Journal of Personality and Social Psychology, 66,* 206–219.

Kagan, J. (1996). Three pleasing ideas. *American Psychologist, 51,* 901–908.

Kenny, D. A. (1994). *Interpersonal perception: A social relations analysis.* New York: Guilford.

Magnusson, D. (1990). Personality development from an interactional perspective. In L. A. Pervin (Ed.), *Handbook of personality: Theory and research* (pp. 193–222). New York: Guilford.

Magnusson, D. (1996). *The logic and implications of a person approach* (Rep. No. 817). Stockholm, Sweden: Stockholm University, Department of Psychology.

Magnusson, D., & Stattin, H. (1998). Person-context interaction theories. In R. M. Lerner (Ed.), *Handbook of child psychology Vol. 1: Theoretical models of human development* (5th ed., pp. 685–759). New York: Wiley.

Magnusson, D., & Törestad, B. (1993). A holistic view of personality: A model revisited. *Annual Review of Psychology, 44,* 427–452.

McClelland, D. C. (1980). Motive dispositions: The merits of operant and respondent measures. *Review of Personality and Social Psychology, 1,* 10–41.

McCrae, R. R., & Costa, P. T., Jr. (1990). *Personality in adulthood.* New York: Guilford.

Meehl, P. E. (1954). *Clinical versus statistical prediction.* Minneapolis: University of Minnesota Press.

Murray, H. A. (1938). *Explorations in personality.* New York: Oxford University Press.

Ogilvie, D. M. (1987). The undesired self: A neglected variable in personality research. *Journal of Personality and Social Psychology, 52,* 379–385.

Pervin, L. A. (1967). A twenty-college study of student-college interaction using TAPE (Transactional Analysis of Personality and Environment): Rationale, reliability, and validity. *Journal of Educational Psychology, 58,* 290–302.

Pervin, L. A. (1968). Performance and satisfaction as a function of individual-environment fit. *Psychological Bulletin, 69,* 56–68.

Pervin, L. A. (1976). A free-response description approach to the analysis of person-situation interaction. *Journal of Personality and Social Psychology, 34,* 465–474.

Pervin, L. A. (1981). The relation of situations to behavior. In D. Magnusson (Ed.), *The situation: An interactional perspective.* Hillsdale, NJ: Lawrence Erlbaum Associates.

Pervin, L. A. (1983). The stasis and flow of behavior: Toward a theory of goals. In M. M. Page (Ed.), *Personality: Current theory and research* (pp. 1–53). Lincoln: University of Nebraska Press.

Pervin, L. A. (1984). Idiographic approaches to personality. In N. Endler & J. McV. Hunt (Eds.), *Personality and the Behavioral Disorders* (2nd ed., pp. 261–282). New York: Wiley.

Pervin, L. A. (1989). Psychodynamic-systems reflections on a social intelligence model of personality. *Advances in Social Cognition, 2,* 153–161.

Pervin, L. A. (Ed.). (1990). *Handbook of personality: Theory and research.* New York: Guilford.

Pervin, L. A., & Furnham, A. (1987). Goal-based and situation-based expectations of behavior. *European Journal of Personality, 1,* 37–44.

Pervin, L. A., & John, O. P. (1997). *Personality: Theory and research* (7th ed.). New York: Wiley.

Roberts, M. L., & Nesselroade, J. (1986). Intraindividual variability in perceived locus of control in adults: P-technique factor analyses of short-term change. *Journal of Research in Personality, 20,* 529–545.

Shoda, Y., Mischel, W., & Wright, J. C. (1994). Intra-individual stability in the organization and patterning of behavior: Incorporating psychological situations into the idiographic analysis of personality. *Journal of Personality and Social Psychology, 67,* 674–687.

Stattin, H., & Magnusson, D. (1996). Antisocial behavior—a holistic perspective. *Development and Psychopathology, 8,* 617–645.

# 17

# Self-Description and Personality Styles

Lea Pulkkinen
Kaisa Männikkö
Jari-Erik Nurmi
University of Jyväskylä, Finland

In this chapter, which is based on an ongoing longitudinal study, we made an effort to combine three quite different ways to conceptualize and investigate personality. First, free descriptions of personality characteristics were studied idiographically. Second, a nomothetic Five-Factor Model was applied to the analysis of idiographic data. Third, a holistic approach to the analysis of the patterns of personality characteristics was adopted, following the lines of holistic personality theory laid down by Magnusson (1998).

Our first aim was to examine the ways in which individuals describe their personality when they are asked what makes them different from other people. In this context, we relied on Allport's (1937) notion of personality as a "dynamic organization within the individual of those psychophysical systems that determine his unique adjustments to his environment" (p. 48). He further described the structure of personality in terms of traits—a trait is a determining tendency or a predisposition to respond. Allport argued that, fundamentally, all traits are individual: No two individuals ever have exactly the same traits. Consequently, our hypothesis was that individuals would describe themselves with a unique set of characteristics.

Despite the uniqueness of self-descriptions, we assumed that they might be conceptualized and categorized in terms of nomothetic traits. Although Allport distinguished between individual or unique, and common or nomothetic types of traits, he stated that individual traits have common aspects, and that there are similarities in the trait structure across individuals. Those similarities are due to the community of common influences involved in a shared culture, and also to species similarities. Allport also suggested a distinction between various types of trait. A cardinal trait is very dominant and makes it possible to trace most activities directly or indirectly to the influence of the single cardinal trait. More typical are the central traits (perhaps 5 to 10 for an individual). They represent tendencies that are highly characteristic of the individual and very easy to infer. A secondary trait is more limited in its occurrence and is less crucial to a description of the personality (Hall & Lindzey, 1957, p. 266).

Personality traits have recently been conceptualized in terms of a Five-Factor Model (Digman, 1990; Goldberg, 1981, 1993; John, 1990; John, Angleitner, & Ostendorf, 1988; Pulver, Allik, Pulkkinen, & Hämäläinen, 1995; Wiggins & Pincus, 1992). The five major dimensions are: (I) Extraversion, (II) Agreeableness, (III) Conscientiousness, (IV) Emotional Stability or Neuroticism, and (V) Intellect or Openness to Experience. We assumed that individuals' conceptions of their personality concentrate on a few central dimensions that can be categorized in terms of the Five-Factor Model. We also assumed that the ways in which people describe themselves have implications for their well-being. Our hypothesis was that a positive self-description is related to high self-esteem and psychological well-being, whereas a negative self-description is associated with low self-esteem and problems in psychological well-being.

Our second aim concerned a correspondence between self-descriptions categorized in terms of the Five-Factor Model, and responses to a five-factor inventory. In our longitudinal study, we had two types of data about individuals' personality: a standard, nomothetic personality questionnaire—the NEO Personality Inventory (NEO-PI; Costa & McCrae, 1985)—and an idiographic self-description instrument. These instruments were employed 3 years apart. Considering the stability of personality characteristics in adult individuals over time (Block, 1971; McCrae & Costa, 1990), we hypothesized that individuals' self-descriptions coded into five factors would correlate with the NEO-PI scales.

In addition to the variable-oriented approach, we applied a person-oriented approach to the study of the correspondence between findings with different instruments as suggested by Bergman and Magnusson (1997). Three major clusters for personality types have recently been identified with a sample of children (Robins, John, Caspi, Moffitt, & Stouthamer-Loeber, 1996), female students (Asendorpf, chap. 18, this volume), and adult men (Pulkkinen, 1996), representing undercontrolled, overcontrolled, and adjusted individuals. We expected that the clusters for overcontrolled, undercontrolled, and adjusted would emerge both in the self-descriptions and the personality inventory. The clusters were also expected to differ with respect to the external criteria of behavioral control and social adjustment.

## METHOD

### Participants

The study was part of the ongoing Jyväskylä Longitudinal Study of Personality and Social Development. The same individuals (originally 173 females and 196 males) have been studied since 1968, when they were 8 years old. From the extensive longitudinal study, data collected at ages 33 and 36 were used for the present investigation. At 33 years of age, 106 women and 96 men filled in a personality inventory that had been mailed to them. At 36 years of age, 137 women and 146 men were interviewed for 2 to 4 hours. The sample fairly represented the whole age cohort born in 1959 in terms of marital status, education, and employment.

### Measures and Variables

*Age 33.* The personality inventory (Pulver et al., 1995), which was mailed to the participants, is an authorized adaptation of the NEO-PI. About one fourth of its items are substitutes for the original American items. Cronbach's alphas were as follows: Neuroticism, .84; Extraversion, .72; Agreeableness, .79; Conscientiousness, .82; and Openness to Experience, .78.

*Age 36.* The task of self-description was included in an interview by giving the participants the following instruction: We all have some central characteristics which make us different from other people. What characteristics are typical of you? In most cases, responses to this question consisted of individual adjectives. The adjective lists of Goldberg (1990), De Raad (1992), Saucier and Goldberg (1996), and Trapnell and Wiggins (1990) were utilized in coding these descriptors within the framework of the Five-Factor Model. For each factor, three categories were set up; one for each end of the factor and one for ambiguous or ambivalent responses. In addition, categories for appearance and skills were formed.

For the analysis of self-description, several variables were created:

1. The number of descriptors provided by each participant was counted.
2. For each of the five personality factors, a variable was made up by calculating a difference score of the number of descriptors given by the participant for each end of a factor (e.g., 3 descriptors for Emotional Stability minus 1 descriptor for Neuroticism makes 2 for Emotional Stability). People whose difference score was zero, and those who did not describe themselves along this particular dimension were given the value "zero."

3. A variable for positive self-description was formed by computing the sum score of Emotional Stability, Extraversion, Agreeableness, Conscientiousness, and Openness to Experience.

4. Correspondingly, a variable for negative self-description was formed by computing a sum score for Neuroticism, Introversion, Aggressiveness, Nonconscientiousness, and Nonopenness to Experience.

5. A variable for the versatility of self-description was formed to depict the number of factors covered by the descriptors that a participant gave for self-description.

**Well-Being Measures at Age 36.** The semistructured interview also included inventories measuring psychological well-being:

1. Self-esteem was measured using Rosenberg's (1965) Self-Esteem Scale. It consists of 10 items measuring individuals' approving or disapproving attitude towards themselves. Responses were given on a 4-point scale (*1 = strongly disagree, 4 = strongly agree*). Cronbach's alpha was .75.

2. Health problems were based on a 20-item list of different pains and symptoms experienced during the last 6 months (Aro & Hänninen, 1984). Responses were given on a 4-point scale (*1 = never, 2 = now and then, 3 = quite often, 4 = often*). Cronbach's alpha was .71.

3. Depression was measured using a shortened (16-item) version of the Depression scale of the General Behavior Inventory (Depue, 1987). Responses were given on a 4-point scale (*1 = never or very seldom, 4 = very often*). Cronbach's alpha was .91.

4. Anxiety was measured by means of the Karolinska Scales of Personality (af Klinteberg, Schalling, & Magnusson, 1990) as the composite score of three subscales: somatic anxiety, psychic anxiety, and muscular tension. Cronbach's alpha was .89.

**Behavioral Control and Social Adjustment at Age 36.** Four external criteria were used for the comparison of the clusters:

1. Career line coded as follows: *1 = unstable career line* (including long-term unemployment), *2 = changeable career line*, and *3 = stable career line* (Rönkä & Pulkkinen, 1995).

2. Problem drinking coded as follows: *1 = no problem drinker, 2 = presumptive problem drinker*, and *3 = problem drinker* (based on alcoholism screening tests, consequences of drinking, and the frequency of drinking and intoxication).

3. Criminality based on the number of registered criminal arrests.

## RESULTS

### How Do People Describe Themselves?

*Uniqueness of Self-Descriptions.* The participants invoked a great variety of characteristics in the free description of their personality. They used mostly single descriptors, although a few longer characterizations also emerged. A qualitative inspection of the individual self-descriptions revealed that they were quite unique for every individual and no pair of similar descriptions appeared in the data. This confirmed our hypothesis about the uniqueness of self-descriptions. The number of descriptors used ranged from 0 to 10 for women ($M = 4.87, SD = 1.39$) and from 0 to 9 for men ($M = 4.37, SD = 1.63$).

*Self-Descriptions and the Five-Factor Model.* The descriptors people used to describe their personalities were coded in terms of the Five-Factor Model. Table 17.1 shows, for example, that 68 women (49.6% of women participants) had mentioned a descriptor that could be coded into the factor for Emotional Stablity versus Neuroticism: 25 women had given a descriptor that could be coded as Emotional Stability and 47 women had given a descriptor coded as Neuroticism. The table also shows that these 68 women had mentioned a total of 94 descriptors coded into the factor for Emotional Stability versus Neuroticism. There were only a few descriptors that could not be coded within the Five-Factor Model.

*Agreeableness—The Most Common Underlying Factor.* The factor that emerged most often in the free descriptions of personality provided by both women and men was Agreeableness (Table 17.1). Altogether, 242 of the descriptors provided by women (225 by men) were coded into the factor for Agreeableness. Among these, 85 different descriptors emerged in women's responses and 86 different descriptors in men's responses. The most frequently mentioned descriptors were the same for men and women, such as calm, honest, and reliable; but most of the descriptors were used by only either women (49) or men (50). They were different in a gender-stereotypical way. An agreeable woman described herself as yielding her control over activities to another person, that is, as being compliant; unable to say "no," and helpful. In contrast, an agreeable man described himself as having nice characteristics but maintaining his control of activities, for instance, as being generous, loving, and conciliatory. A nonagreeable woman described herself as being mean: for instance, nagging, sarcastic, and unforgiving, whereas a nonagreeable man described himself as being domineering, for instance, cold, intolerant, and disputatious.

TABLE 17.1
The Distribution of Descriptors

| Category[1] | Women (n = 137) | | | Men (n = 146) | | |
|---|---|---|---|---|---|---|
| | fr | % | Descriptors (fr) | fr | % | Descriptors (fr) |
| **Emotional stability** | **68** | **49.6** | **94** | **57** | **39.0** | **80** |
| Emotional stability | 25 | 18.3 | 27 | 35 | 24.0 | 37 |
| Neuroticism | 47 | 34.4 | 67 | 30 | 20.5 | 40 |
| **Extraversion** | **92** | **67.2** | **160** | **94** | **64.4** | **169** |
| Extraversion | 81 | 59.1 | 137 | 76 | 52.1 | 125 |
| Introversion | 17 | 12.4 | 20 | 29 | 19.9 | 40 |
| **Agreeableness** | **120** | **87.6** | **242** | **113** | **77.4** | **225** |
| Agreeableness | 109 | 79.6 | 199 | 102 | 69.9 | 185 |
| Nonagreeableness | 34 | 24.8 | 41 | 32 | 21.9 | 40 |
| **Conscientiousness** | **88** | **64.2** | **136** | **76** | **52.1** | **119** |
| Conscientiousness | 76 | 55.5 | 114 | 67 | 45.9 | 102 |
| Nonconscientiousness | 17 | 12.4 | 21 | 12 | 8.2 | 17 |
| **Openness to experience** | **26** | **19.0** | **32** | **29** | **19.9** | **37** |
| Openness to experience | 26 | 19.0 | 32 | 25 | 17.1 | 33 |
| Nonopenness to experience | 0 | 0.0 | 0 | 4 | 2.7 | 4 |

*Note.* The number of participants may be smaller than the sum of the number of participants for subcategories, because a participant might have described him or herself using adjectives for different subcategories of the same factor.
[1]A subcategory for ambiguous responses was deleted from each personality trait because of its small frequency (0–4) for each factor; for instance, 3 for male Emotional stability.

**Versatility of Self-Description.** Altogether, 23 combinations of underlying factors emerged in self-descriptions of women and 28 combinations in those of men, confirming our hypothesis about the unique nature of self-descriptions.

In most cases, however, participants used self-descriptors that could be categorized into three out of the five factors (45% of women and 37% of men). The most frequently emerging combination of factors was Agreeableness, Extraversion, and Conscientiousness, which was found in the self-descriptions of 19% of women and 16% of men. All five factors were represented in the self-descriptions of 2.2% of women and 1.4% of men, and one factor only in the self-descriptions of 4% of women and 9% of men.

## Self-Descriptions and Psychological Well-Being

The correlations between self-description scores and the psychological well-being variables also fit in well with our hypothesis. A positive self-description correlated with high self-esteem in both sexes (.36 for women and .28 for men, $p < .001$ for each), and a negative self-description with low self-esteem ($-.24$ for women and $-.31$ for men, $p < .01$ and .001, respectively). A negative self-description was also indicative of health problems (.22, $p < .01$), depression (.21, $p < .05$), and anxiety (.21, $p < .05$) in men; but not in women. This was mainly due to Neuroticism, which was related to low self-esteem ($r = -.29$, $p < .001$), depression (.30, $p < .001$), anxiety (.40, $p < .001$), and health problems (.34, $p < .001$) in men; but again, not in women. Although female Extraversion correlated with high self-esteem (.29, $p < .001$), it also correlated with health problems (.18, $p < .05$); female introversion correlated with anxiety (.19, $p < .05$). For other factors correlations were low.

## Stability of Personality Structure: Comparison of the Free Self-Descriptions and the NEO Personality Inventory

To follow first a variable-oriented line of thinking, correlation coefficients between the difference scores of self-descriptions and the NEO-PI scales were computed. The intercorrelations revealed (Table 17.2) that except for female Neuroticism, all difference scores of personality factors correlated with the corresponding NEO-PI factors. Some of the correlations were high. For instance, men who described themselves as being extravert had received high scores in the scale for Extraversion 3 years earlier ($r = .53$, $p < .001$). The corresponding correlation for male Openness to Experience was .47 ($p < .001$). For women and men, Openness to Experiences correlated with low Conscientiousness.

To complement this analysis with a person-oriented approach, a cluster analysis was carried out separately for men and women. Five difference scores, one for each of the five factors of personality, and standardized separately for men and women, were used as clustering variables. The cluster analysis examined whether a typical three-cluster solution of personality styles, as suggested by Asendorpf (chap. 18), could be identified in this sample. A hierarchical cluster analysis (Ward method, Euclidean distances) was calculated to determine initial cluster centers for SPSS (Statistical Package for Social Sciences) K-Means Cluster Analysis. Each case was assigned to the nearest cluster with the nearest centroid sorting. Each cluster mean was compared with its complement (i.e., with the mean of all other same-sex participants) in the clustering variables, using a $t$ test; and

TABLE 17.2

The Stability of Personality Factors Across Time and Different Instruments

| Self-Descriptions Coded Into Factors (Age 36) | NEO-Personality Inventory (Age 33) | | | | | | | | | |
| --- | --- | --- | --- | --- | --- | --- | --- | --- | --- | --- |
| | Neuroticism | | Extraversion | | Agreeableness | | Conscientiousness | | Openness to Experience | |
| | F | M | F | M | F | M | F | M | F | M |
| Neuroticism | 08 | 27*** | 13 | -04 | -02 | 05 | -14 | 02 | 11 | 03 |
| Extraversion | -03 | 07 | 32*** | 53*** | 01 | -18 | 15 | -04 | 11 | 24* |
| Agreeableness | -17 | -06 | 07 | -09 | 26** | 26** | -06 | 04 | 01 | 07 |
| Conscientiousness | -07 | -06 | -16 | -06 | -06 | -15 | 33*** | 28** | -26** | 16 |
| Openness to Experience | 04 | 13 | 02 | 02 | -05 | -08 | -13 | -33*** | 29** | 47*** |

Note. *p < .05. **p < .01. ***p < .001.

labeled on the basis of the discriminating factors. A corresponding cluster analysis was also performed with the NEO-PI scales for the comparison of clusters extracted from the two different data sets. The profiles of the clusters were compared to those obtained by Asendorpf (chap. 18).

## Men

Figure 17.1 shows the three-cluster solution profiles obtained for men for the NEO-PI scales. The clusters that emerged were very similar to those obtained in the Asendorpf study for female students. Consequently, the clusters were labeled as the *Overcontrolled* ($n = 35$; 38% of the men), the *Undercontrolled* ($n = 27$; 29%), and the *Adjusted* ($n = 31$; 33%). For the Overcontrolled, small differences in emphasis between the different factors emerged, such as lower Neuroticism among the Finnish overcontrolled men than among the German overcontrolled women.

**Self-Description.** Figure 17.1 also shows the three-cluster solution for the self-descriptions. The *Resilient* ($n = 67$; 46% of the men) had a profile very similar to the cluster for the Adjusted. The *Inhibited* ($n = 55$; 38%) resembled the cluster for the Overcontrolled, although Conscientiousness was less important in it than it was in the Overcontrolled men. The *Open to Experiences* ($n = 24$; 16%) resembled the cluster for the Undercontrolled, although Conscientiousness and Emotional Stability were higher in the former than in the Undercontrolled men.

## Women

Figure 17.2 shows the three-cluster solution profiles obtained for women for the NEO-PI scales. The results revealed that there were some similarities between the clusters that emerged, based on the NEO-PI scales for the Finnish women and the clusters obtained by Asendorpf with the German female students. For example, Openness to Experiences and Extraversion characterized the cluster that was labeled as the *Undercontrolled* ($n = 29$; 32% of the women). A second cluster had high levels of Conscientiousness and Emotional Stability and a low level of Openness to Experiences, as in the cluster for the Adjusted in the Asendorpf study. It was labeled accordingly as the *Adjusted* ($n = 47$; 52%). A third cluster was low in Extraversion, Emotional Stability, and Openness to Experiences, as in the Overcontrolled in the Asendorpf study, and it was identified as the *Overcontrolled* women ($n = 14$; 16%). The latter cluster differed from that obtained for the German students in including lower Conscientiousness. The major difference between the NEO-PI clusters in our study and those in the Asendorpf study was that Agreeableness did not differentiate the female clusters.

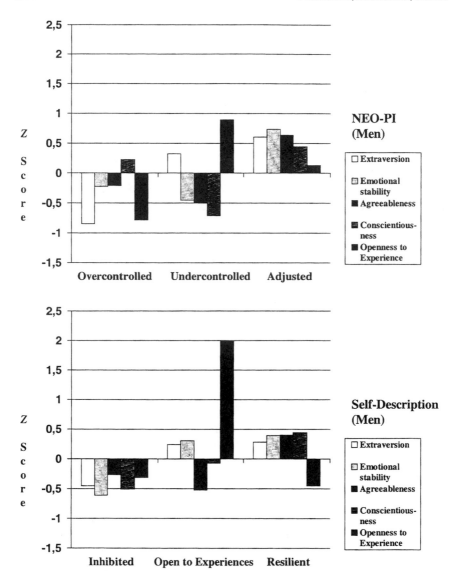

FIG. 17.1. Three clusters extracted for men with difference scores of self-descriptions and NEO-PI scales as clustering variables.

*Self-Description.* Figure 17.2 also shows the three-cluster solution profiles obtained for the self-descriptions of women. High Agreeableness characterized the *Agreeable* ($n$ = 45; 33% of the women), and low Agreeableness the *Extravert* ($n$ = 69; 50%); they did not resemble any of the clusters in the

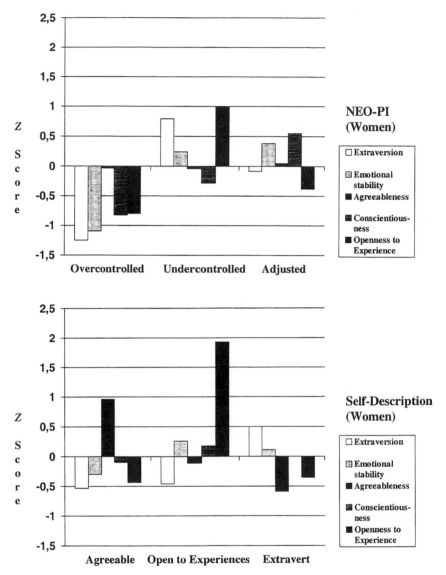

FIG. 17.2. Three clusters extracted for women with difference scores of self-descriptions and NEO-PI scales as clustering variables.

Asendorpf study or any of our own clusters that were based on the NEO-PI scales. The profile of the *Open to Experiences* (*n* = 23; 17%) corresponded slightly to that of the cluster for the Undercontrolled obtained from the NEO-PI scales.

## Comparison of the Clusters in the Case
## of External Criteria

The three-cluster solutions were also compared for the variables for social adjustment and psychological well-being. The results for the male NEO-PI clusters (Table 17.3) fit in well with the labels given to the clusters: the Adjusted men were characterized by high self-esteem, stable career line, low problem drinking, and low psychosocial problems. The Undercontrolled men were characterized by problem drinking, unstable career, low self-esteem, depression, and anxiety. The Overcontrolled men showed anxiety, low self-esteem, low problem drinking, and high career stability.

The differences between the male self-description clusters went in a similar direction as the clusters for the Open to Experiences and the Resilient (Table 17.3). The Open to Experiences men had similar characteristics to the Undercontrolled men, whereas the Resilient men had characteristics similar to the Adjusted men. These two groups differed also in health problems: The Resilient men had fewer health problems. A clear difference between the findings obtained by the NEO-PI scales and the self-descriptions was that compared to the Overcontrolled men, the self-described Inhibited men had fewer characteristics typical of the Resilient and Adjusted men. Self-descriptions in Inhibited men were related to low career stability, problem drinking, depression, and health problems. These characteristics were also typical of the Open to Experiences men.

For the female NEO-PI clusters (Table 17.3), the Adjusted women had stable career lines, low problem drinking, high self-esteem, and few psychosocial problems (as was found for the Adjusted men). The most problematic group was the Overcontrolled women: They were depressed and anxious, and had low self-esteem, unstable career lines, and the highest problem drinking. The Undercontrolled women, on the other hand, differed from the Adjusted women only in having a higher level of problem drinking.

The results for the self-description clusters were meagre (Table 17.3). They showed that the Extravert women had more problem drinking and health problems than the Agreeable women, in particular.

## DISCUSSION

People describe themselves as being different from other people. Adults typically use about five personality characteristics to describe themselves. This is about the same as the number of central traits suggested by Allport (1937). Although most of the descriptors used by participants in our study fit the Five-Factor Model, the underlying factors in individuals' self-descriptions were unique, as evidenced in both the number of factors and their

TABLE 17.3
Male and Female NEO-PI and Self-Description Clusters Compared (one-tailed *t* test)

| Clusters | Career Stability | Problem Drinking | Criminality | Anxiety | Self-Esteem | Health Problems | Depression |
|---|---|---|---|---|---|---|---|
| **Men** | | | | | | | |
| NEO-PI | | | | | | | |
| 1. Overcontrolled | 0.30 | -0.13 | 0.02 | 0.39 | -0.17 | 0.16 | -0.04 |
| 2. Undercontrolled | -0.46 | 0.38 | 0.33 | 0.27 | -0.12 | 0.01 | 0.21 |
| 3. Adjusted | 0.06 | -0.15 | -0.06 | -0.55 | 0.31 | -0.05 | -0.21 |
| *t* test | 1,3 > 2 | 2 > 1,3 | | 1,2 > 3 | 3 > 1,2 | | 2 > 3 |
| Self-Description | | | | | | | |
| 1. Inhibited | -0.16 | 0.24 | 0.19 | 0.41 | -0.28 | 0.19 | 0.12 |
| 2. Open | -0.22 | 0.26 | 0.02 | 0.14 | -0.07 | 0.03 | 0.16 |
| 3. Resilient | 0.21 | -0.29 | -0.16 | -0.38 | 0.19 | -0.15 | -0.23 |
| *t* test | 3 > 1,2 | 1,2 > 3 | 1 > 3 | 1,2 > 3 | 3 > 1,2 | 1,2 > 3 | 1,2 > 3 |
| **Women** | | | | | | | |
| NEO-PI | | | | | | | |
| 1. Overcontrolled | -0.51 | 0.83 | 0.14 | 1.00 | -0.54 | 0.06 | 0.53 |
| 2. Undercontrolled | -0.00 | 0.08 | 0.03 | -0.46 | 0.27 | -0.04 | -0.09 |
| 3. Adjusted | 0.35 | -0.46 | -0.03 | -0.18 | 0.15 | -0.07 | -0.14 |
| *t* test | 3 > 1,2 | 1 > 2 > 3 | | 1 > 2,3 | 2,3 > 1 | | 1 > 2,3 |
| Self-Description | | | | | | | |
| 1. Agreeable | 0.03 | -0.21 | 0.57 | 0.09 | -0.01 | -0.08 | 0.06 |
| 2. Open | 0.13 | -0.25 | 0.55 | -0.11 | 0.08 | -0.02 | 0.06 |
| 3. Extravert | -0.06 | 0.22 | -0.07 | -0.02 | 0.04 | 0.06 | 0.02 |
| *t* test | 3 > 1,2 | 3 > 1,2 | | | | 3 > 1 | |

combinations. Thus our hypothesis about the uniqueness of self-descriptors was confirmed.

The Five-Factor Model was applicable in the context of the idiographic description of personality characteristics. People typically used self-descriptions that reflected three out of five major personality factors. The most frequently emerging combination of factors was Agreeableness, Extraversion, and Conscientiousness; the most frequently used factor was Agreeableness. The scores of free personality descriptions in terms of the Big-Five dimensions (Goldberg, 1981) were closely associated with the same NEO-PI scores obtained 3 years earlier, suggesting stability in personality characteristics across time (Block, 1971; McCrae & Costa, 1990).

People typically describe their personality in terms of positive rather than negative attributes. Positive self-descriptions are also related to high self-esteem. This fits in well with our hypothesis, and with earlier research, revealing that a positive self-image (Harter, 1990), and even illusions (Taylor & Brown, 1988), are important for the maintenance of a well-adapted personality. Among men, Neuroticism, in particular, is related to low self-esteem and a high level of physiological symptoms and depression.

Magnusson (1998) recently emphasized a need for a holistic approach in which an individual is described in terms of an organized whole, functioning and developing as a totality. Following his line of thinking, we identified three clusters on the basis of both the self-descriptions and the NEO-PI scales. Our results confirmed the findings of Asendorpf (chap. 18); we were able to identify clusters for Adjusted, Overcontrolled, and Undercontrolled individuals from the NEO-PI scales, for both men and women. The three clusters identified from the male self-descriptions are quite similar to the clusters extracted from the NEO-PI scales, whereas the female self-description clusters provide quite a different view. Differences between the male and female clusters also formed in an earlier analysis of the data (Pulkkinen, 1996): Social roles affect the differences between women when grouping is not limited to personality-test data.

Our interpretation of the clusters is confirmed by the differences of the clusters in external criteria for social adjustment and psychological well-being. The clusters extracted from the self-descriptions and the NEO-PI scales differ, however, for males in that adjustment problems are more strongly related to self-described inhibition than to overcontrol based on the NEO-PI scales. This is in accordance with the finding that Conscientiousness is more characteristic of the Overcontrolled than the Inhibited. There is also a gender difference in social adjustment problems: for men, these problems are typical of the Undercontrolled, but for women, they are typical of the Overcontrolled. This difference is in accordance with earlier research findings (Zoccolillo, 1993; Bird, Gould, & Stachezza, 1993). The Undercontrolled women do not differ from the Adjusted women in career stability, self-esteem, anxiety, and depression. It is possible that the Openness to Experiences, which is characteristic of the Undercontrolled women, may have different contents and consequences for women than for men.

## ACKNOWLEDGMENT

This study was financially supported by the Academy of Finland.

## REFERENCES

Allport, G. W. (1937). *Personality: A psychological interpretation.* New York: Holt.

Aro, S., & Hänninen, V. (1984). Life events or life processes as determinants of mental strain? A 5-year follow-up study. *Social Science and Medicine, 18*, 1037–1044.

Bergman, L. R., & Magnusson, D. (1997). A person-oriented approach in research on developmental psychopathology. *Development and Psychopathology, 9*, 291–319.

Bird, H. R., Gould, M. S., & Stachezza, B. M. (1993). Patterns of diagnostic comorbidity in a community sample of children aged 9 through 16. *Journal of the American Academy of Child and Adolescent Psychiatry, 32*, 361–368.

Block, J. (1971). *Lives through time.* Berkeley, CA: Bancroft.

Costa, P. T., Jr., & McCrae, R. R. (1985). *The NEO Personality Inventory Manual.* Odessa, FL: Psychological Assessment Resources.

Depue, R. (1987). *General Behavior Inventory.* Department of Psychology, Cornell University, Ithaca, NY.

De Raad, B. (1992). The replicability of the Big Five personality dimensions in three word-classes of the Dutch language. *European Journal of Personality, 6*, 15–29.

Digman, J. M. (1990). Personality structure: Emergence of the Five Factor Model. *Annual Review of Personality, 41*, 417–440.

Goldberg, L. R. (1981). Language and individual differences: The search for universals in personality lexicons. In L. Wheeler (Ed.), *Review of personality and social psychology, Vol. 2* (pp. 141–165). Beverly Hills, CA: Sage.

Goldberg, L. R. (1990). An alternative "description of personality": The Big Five factor structure. *Journal of Personality and Social Psychology, 59*, 1216–1229.

Goldberg, L. R. (1993). The structure of phenotypic personality traits. *American Psychologist, 48*, 26–34.

Hall, C. S., & Lindzey, G. (1957). *Theories of personality.* New York: Wiley.

Harter, S. (1990). Process underlying adolescent self-concept formation. In R. Montemayor, G. R. Adams, & T. P. Gullotta (Eds.), *From childhood to adolescence: A transitional period* (pp. 205–239). Newbury Park, CA: Sage.

John, O. P. (1990). The "Big Five" factor taxonomy: Dimensions of personality in the natural language and in questionnaires. In L. A. Pervin (Ed.), *Handbook of Personality: Theory and Research* (pp. 66–100). New York: Guilford.

John, O. P., Angleitner, A., & Ostendorf, F. (1988). The lexical approach to personality: A historical review of trait taxonomic research. *European Journal of Personality, 2*, 171–205.

af Klinteberg, B., Schalling, D., & Magnusson, D. (1990). Childhood behavior and adult personality in male and female subjects. *European Journal of Personality, 4*, 57–71.

Magnusson, D. (1998). The logic and implications of a person approach. In R. B. Cairns, L. R. Bergman, & J. Kagan (Eds.), *Methods and models for studying the individual* (pp. 33–63). Thousand Oaks, CA: Sage.

McCrae, R. R., & Costa, P. T., Jr. (1990). *Personality in adulthood.* New York: Guilford.

Pulkkinen, L. (1996). Female and male personality styles: A typological and developmental analysis. *Journal of Personality and Social Psychology, 70,* 1288–1306.

Pulver, A., Allik, J., Pulkkinen, L., & Hämäläinen, M. (1995). A Big-Five personality inventory in two non-Indo-European languages. *European Journal of Personality, 9,* 109–124.

Robins, R. W., John, O. P., Caspi, A., Moffitt, T. E., & Stouthamer-Loeber, M. (1996). Resilient, overcontrolled, and undercontrolled boys: Three replicable personality types. *Journal of Personality and Social Psychology, 70,* 157–171.

Rönkä, A., & Pulkkinen, L. (1995). Accumulation of problems in social functioning in young adulthood: A developmental approach. *Journal of Personality and Social Psychology, 69,* 381–391.

Rosenberg, M. (1965). *Society and the adolescent self-image.* Princeton, NJ: Princeton University Press.

Saucier, G., & Goldberg, L. R. (1996). Evidence for the Big Five in analyses of familiar English personality adjectives. *European Journal of Personality, 10,* 61–77.

Taylor, S. E., & Brown, J. (1988). Illusion and well-being: A social psychological perspective on mental health. *Psychological Bulletin, 103,* 193–210.

Trapnell, P. D., & Wiggins, J. S. (1990). Extension of the interpersonal adjective scales to include the Big Five dimensions of personality. *Journal of Personality and Social Psychology, 59,* 781–790.

Wiggins, J. S., & Pincus, A. L. (1992). Personality: Structure and assessment. *Annual Review of Psychology, 43,* 473–504.

Zoccolillo, M. (1993). Gender and the development of conduct disorder. *Development and Psychopathology, 5,* 65–78.

# 18

# A Person-Centered Approach to Personality and Social Relationships: Findings From the Berlin Relationship Study

Jens B. Asendorpf
Institute for Psychology
Humboldt University, Berlin

Over the past 20 years, dynamic interactionism has been the main paradigm for the study of personality development. It is assumed that individuals develop in a dynamic, continuous, and reciprocal process of interaction, or *transaction*, with their environment (Caspi, 1998; Magnusson, 1988, 1990; Sameroff, 1983). In terms of social relationships, it is hypothesized that, over time, personality affects the environment and the environment affects personality (Asendorpf & Wilpers, 1998). Whereas this assumption seems justified in childhood, it is less obvious in young adulthood. Is personality already so much crystallized at the end of adolescence that it is immune to future experiences in social relationships with parents and peers? Or do important life transitions (Elder, 1985) such as the transition to the new social world of university change personality through new experiences with peers and the decreasing contact with one's family? If students' social relationships are destabilized during such a life transition, is the reorganization of their relationships influenced by their personality?

## THE BERLIN RELATIONSHIP STUDY: VARIABLE-CENTERED APPROACH

The Berlin Relationship Study (Asendorpf & Wilpers, 1998) was designed to answer these questions empirically through an intensive longitudinal study of both the personality and the social relationships of 132 students during their transition to university. The participants' Big-Five factors of personality (NEO-FFI; Costa & McCrae, 1989) were assessed four times, and their network of social relationships seven times, over the first 18 months at university. Personality was assessed less often because we assumed that it shows less developmental change than the social network. The results strongly confirmed this asumption: The 18-month stability of the Big-Five scales varied between .72 (Neuroticism) and .79 (Extraversion). Much of the instability could be attributed to measurement error: stabilities corrected for attenuation varied between .87 (Openness) and .95 (Extraversion).

In contrast, the number and quality of the participants' social relationships were less stable; for example, the stability of the number of peer relationships dropped from an initially high 3-month stability of .86 to a very low stability of .30 over 18 months. The 18-month stabilities for various aspects of the participants' relationship quality (e.g., conflict with peers, emotional support from peers, contact with the mother) were moderate at best (.28–.62). Thus, the personality traits were much more stable than the relationship qualities during this life transition.

Reciprocal influences between personality traits and relationship quality were studied by path analyses (Rogosa, 1980) and by hierarchical linear modeling of individual growth curves (HLM; Bryk & Raudenbush, 1992). The results of these analyses are described in detail by Asendorpf and Wilpers (1998), and are easily summarized: Personality traits influenced social relationships but not vice versa. When the initial correlation between a trait and a relationship quality was statistically controlled, Extraversion, Agreeableness, and Conscientiousness significantly predicted relationship change but not vice versa, and personality change was completely unrelated to relationship change.

## ALTERNATIVE: A HOLISTIC PERSON-CENTERED APPROACH

The results of the Berlin Relationship Study were obtained through a traditional variable-centered approach to personality and relationships. The effects of personality on relationships and vice versa were studied trait by trait. It has been repeatedly pointed out throughout the history of personality psychology that such a variable-centered approach may miss important aspects of personality (Allport, 1937, 1961; Block, 1971; Magnusson, 1988, 1990). As early as 1911, William Stern (who many, including myself, consider to be the founder of personality psychology) suggested complementing the variable-centered approach with a more holistic person-centered approach where individual patterns in many traits are the units of analysis. Stern (1911) illustrated this complementary nature of the variable- and the person-centered approach with a figure (Fig. 18.1; translated from German by the author).

In the figure, small letters designate variables, large letters, persons. Stern distinguished among four "disciplines of differential psychology": "Variationsforschung" (variation research) studies interindividual differences in one variable, and "Korrelationsforschung" (correlation research) is based on correlations between variables over persons. Figure 18.1 nicely illustrates that these two variable-centered approaches are complemented by two person-centered approaches generated from the variable-centered

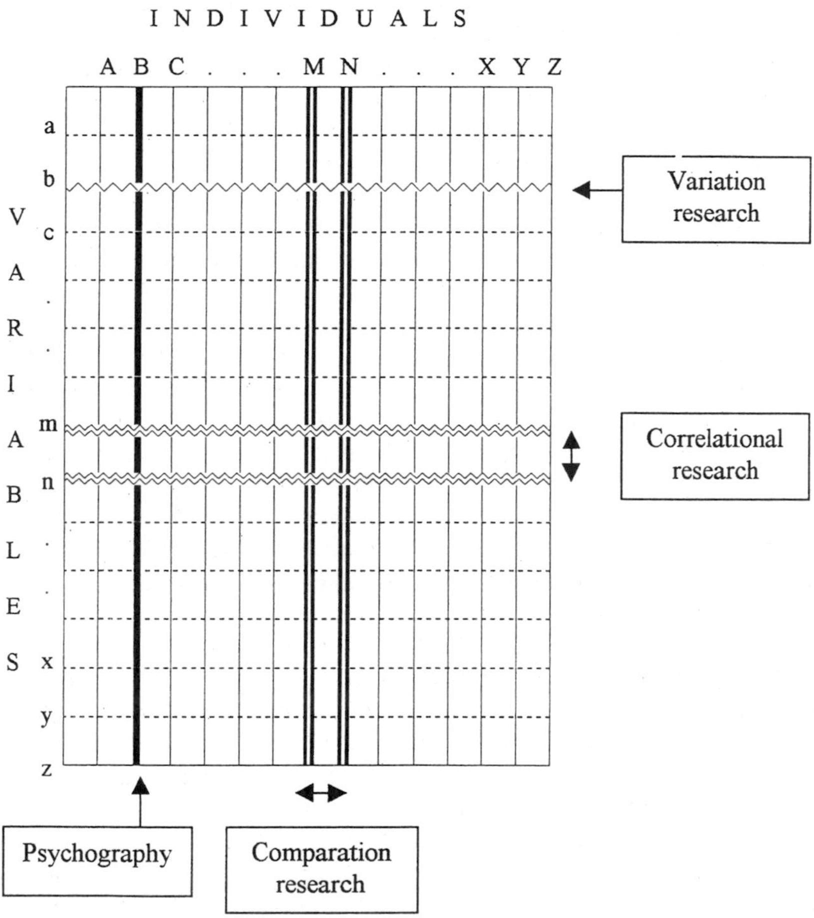

FIG. 18.1. Four disciplines of differential psychology according to William Stern (1911).

approaches by a switch of 90 degrees (and vice versa). "Psychographie" (psychography) studies intraindividual differences in one person, and "Komparationsforschung" (comparation research) is based on correlations between persons over variables.

Unfortunately, Allport did not take up Stern's view that these two approaches were complementary, although he spent some time with Stern in Hamburg, Germany; and Stern's eminent book of 1911 was never translated into English. Therefore, it took decades until Stern's approach was rediscovered and generalized into a three-dimensional covariation chart with persons, tests, and occasions by Cattell (1946), who nevertheless remained predominantly variable-centered in his work. For a long time, Block (1955, 1961, 1971) swam against the current of the variable-centered mainstream. Although he and his wife (Block & Block, 1980) showed how a person-centered approach based on Q-sort ratings can be successfully implemented in the longitudinal study of personality in both childhood and adulthood, the payoff of this groundbreaking work came slowly.

But it came. In recent years there has been an upsurge of interest in a more holistic person-centered approach to personality patterns (Asendorpf & van Aken, 1999; Caspi & Silva, 1995; Hart, Hofmann, Edelstein, & Keller, 1997; Magnusson, 1988; Ozer & Gjerde, 1989; Pulkkinen, 1996; Robins, John, Caspi, Moffitt, & Stouthamer-Loeber, 1996; York & John, 1992). In this research there is evidence for at least three personality types that are found again and again in studies ranging from behavioral ratings of 3-year-old New Zealand children to self-reports of 27-year-old Finnish men and women: a large group of *Adjusted* persons, complemented by two major maladjusted types: *Overcontrolled*, characterized by high impulse control, high anxiety, and low open aggressiveness; and *Undercontrolled*, characterized by low impulse control, low trustworthiness, and open aggressiveness. In childhood, the two maladjusted types are often described as exhibiting internalizing versus externalizing problems (Achenbach & Edelbrock, 1981).

The consistency of personality types across different studies is far from perfect, however (e.g., contrast Block, 1971, with Pulkkinen, 1996). A high consistency cannot be expected because the personality types found in a particular study depend on (a) the level of abstraction (How many types? At the extremes, all individuals are human, or each individual represents his or her own type), (b) the traits on which the types are based, (c) the age and the genetic and environmental characteristics of the population, and (d) the method of deriving types from individual patterns of traits; small, selective samples further threaten the replicability of types across studies. Given these limitations, it is encouraging to notice that there is now considerable agreement at least at the level of the three types (see also Caspi, 1998).

## THE PRESENT STUDY

The purpose of this study was to reanalyze the data of the Berlin Relationship Study from a holistic, person-centered view. First, I tried to confirm the three major personality types that were found in earlier studies. If successful, I then wanted to compare the social relationships among these three personality types, and to explore whether subtypes of the three major personality types showed different kinds of relationships. Such a discriminant validity of subtypes would suggest that finer-grained type definitions would be useful. Because the types were based on patterns of responses to a personality inventory rather than on Q-sorts, I used cluster analysis to derive the types from the questionnaire responses (see Caspi & Silva, 1995, and Pulkkinen, 1996, for a similar approach).

Because no effects of the initial relationship status or the relationship change on the Big-Five personality traits were found in the variable-centered analyses, I did not expect such effects on the personality types either. Thus, I could try to strengthen the classification of types by reducing measurement error through aggregating the personality assessments across time. Also, I could use the multiple assessments for a study of the stability of the personality types across time.

The sample reported by Asendorpf and Wilpers (1998) consisted of 92 females and 40 males. Preliminary analyses suggested that there were important sex differences in the personality types, which is consistent with earlier studies (Block, 1971; Pulkkinen, 1996). Because the male sample was too small for a meaningful type analysis, I report here only the findings for the female sample.

### Methodology of Deriving Personality Types

A type approach seems to be the king's road to the study of personality from a lay-psychological point of view. In everyday life, someone's personality is described by comparing the observed pattern of behavior with a prototypic pattern that represents a personality type (Stern's "Komparationsforschung"). Why has this main road for lay psychologists been such a long, bumpy road for personality psychologists? In my view, the major reason is that all other disciplines of psychology have fared well with the variable-centered approach until now. Students of psychology are so trained to represent psychological data in terms of a persons × variables matrix that most of them have considerable difficulties in following Stern's 90 degree switch to a variables × persons matrix.

One unfortunate consequence of this difficulty is that many researchers interested in personality types follow a blind alley. They try to define types by extreme scores in a single, continuously distributed trait. The problem with this approach is that, for an assortment of people there is no natural division between types and nontypes. As first Gauß observed, any outcome of multiple, independent causes will be more normally distributed, the more causes there are. Because personality traits are the outcome of many causes, they tend to be normally distributed, and for such distributions it is completely arbitrary which scores are considered extreme and which are not. Therefore, the extreme group approach is not a viable procedure for "carving nature at its joints" (Gangestad & Snyder, 1985) simply because the joints join traits, not persons.

If the joints join traits, multiple traits must be studied within a person; there is no way around Stern's 90 degree switch. Thus, personality types must be derived from individual patterns of traits. These patterns can be assessed either by person-centered procedures such as the Q-sort method where many items are rank-ordered for their typicality for one person, or by variable-centered procedures such as personality questionnaires, test batteries, and observations of multiple traits. In the Q-sort approach, the overall mean and variability of the items are fixed. Thus, the patterns of different persons differ only in their shape, not in their elevation. Hence, the correlation between the individual patterns is an appropriate measure of the similarity of the patterns (Cronbach, 1955); personality types can then be identified by inverse factor analysis (Block, 1961; Hart et al., 1997; Robins et al., 1996; York & John, 1992).

If patterns are based on items derived from a variable-centered approach, as is the case here, great care must be exercised because there exist numerous options on how to cluster personality patterns. As with structural equation modeling, thoughtless choice of options can result in misleading solutions and false interpretations of substantive issues. The methodological decisions I made, and my reasons for them, follow.

In the Berlin Relationship Study, personality traits were assessed by questionnaire. The personality patterns were defined on the basis of scales, not items, to increase the reliability of the within-subject trait differences. I used cluster analysis to define types consisting of persons with similar patterns of scale scores (see Caspi & Silva, 1995, and Pulkkinen, 1996, for similar approaches). I standardized the scales between subjects to avoid the greater influence of scales with higher variance on the similarity of the patterns, and hence on the definition of the clusters. I reversed the neuroticism scores to allow a meaningful interpretation of the within-subject scale mean; after this correction, this mean reflected the overall social desirability of the individual's personality.

As a measure of pattern similarity I used the squared Euclidean distance because it is sensitive both to the within-subject mean and the within-subject differences among the scales. I applied a hierarchical clustering procedure to make sure that a three-cluster solution can be found that can be compared with the three personality types identified in the literature, and to explore whether splits of the three clusters into subgroups would result in meaningful subtypes. Ward's procedure was used to define initial cluster solutions of similar size. These initial solutions were then optimized by iterative nearest centroid sorting at each level of clustering (this procedure changes the centers only slightly but minimizes the distance between the individual patterns and the center of their cluster).

It was important to evaluate the replicability of the cluster structure by splitting either items or the sample into halves or by comparing clusters across time. The first two possibilities were not appropriate, given that there were only 12 items for each scale, and only 92 subjects. Thus, the stability of the clusters was studied over time, searching for replicability at least between adjacent assessments.

Table 18.1 summarizes the methodology used. It makes clear that many methodological decisions are involved in deriving meaningful personality types. Indeed, thanks to fast computers, I played around with these decisions and arrived at very different personality types according to the particular pattern of decisions. It is important to note, however, that this does not mean that "anything goes" in deriving types from patterns. There was always a preference for one option based on a priori theorizing.

TABLE 18.1
Decisions in the derivation of Personality Types From Personality Patterns

| Decision | Berlin Relationship Study |
| --- | --- |
| Derivation of patterns | |
| Population (age) | Female university students aged 18–21 years |
| Trait measures | 5 NEO–FFI scales |
| Trait distribution | Standardized between individuals ($z$ scores) |
| Sign of trait scores | High = socially desirability score |
| Derivation of types from patterns | |
| General approach | Cluster analysis |
| Measure of profile similarity | Squared Euclidean distance |
| Initial method | Hierarchical |
| Cluster sizes | Similar: Ward's method |
| Optimization | Iterative nearest centroid sorting |
| Evaluation of cluster replicability | Across time |

## Continuity and Stability of Personality Types

Within the variable-centered approach to personality development, an important distinction can be made between the continuity of a construct and the stability of a particular operationalization of the construct at the empirical level. The observed stability can be low despite perfect continuity of the construct if (a) the person's personality changed at the construct level, (b) one or both assessments are not reliable, or (c) one or both assessments have low construct validity. If the construct level is not clearly distinguished from the empirical level, instability will be attributed to (a) or (b), ignoring (c) (see Asendorpf, 1992a, 1992b; Kagan, 1980).

When these distinctions are applied to personality types, two very different kinds of stability must be distinguished: The stability of the cluster centers that represent the prototypic pattern of the type, and the stability of the membership of persons for a type with a particular center. If persons are independently clustered at different assessments, the similarity of the resulting clusters across time (the cluster overlap) confounds both kinds of stability. Persons may switch their membership because the clusters' centers changed, or because their personality shifted to another type. In the first case, the clusters change their meaning over time; in the second case, the clusters have the same meaning but the members of the clusters change. To clearly distinguish between these two aspects of the cluster overlap, the stability of the clusters' centers may be called the *continuity* of the clusters, and the stability of the membership of individuals for continuous clusters may be called the *stability* of the clusters.

The distinction between continuity and stability turned out to be important for the Berlin Relationship Study. As Table 18.2 indicates, the stability of the individual patterns was high for short retest intervals and did not decrease much for longer ones. But the overlap of the clusters based on separate 3-cluster solutions for each of the four assessments (nonfixed centers) was high only over brief periods of time, and then decreased considerably. Was this strong decrease in the cluster overlap due to a low continuity of the clusters or due to a low stability of highly continuous clusters?

One way to distinguish between these alternatives was to fix the clusters' centers of the four assessments. Fixing the centers made the clusters continuous; the remaining nonoverlap was due only to a low stability. I fixed each assessment's center to the centers of the 3-cluster solution found when all four assessments of the NEO-FFI were aggregated and then $z$-transformed over individuals. Thus, all clusters had the same prototypic Big-Five pattern. Then I computed separately for each assessment each person's cluster membership by noniterative nearest centroid sorting (SPSS procedure Quick Cluster, method Classify). This Procrustean procedure made sure

TABLE 18.2
Temporal Stability of Personality Patterns and clusters

| Assessment | Mean Stability of Individual Patterns | | | Stability of Clusters (Nonfixed Centers) | | | Stability of Clusters (Fixed centers) | | |
| --- | --- | --- | --- | --- | --- | --- | --- | --- | --- |
| | *2* | *3* | *4* | *2* | *3* | *4* | *2* | *3* | *4* |
| 1 | .74 | .70 | .62 | .69 | .43 | .28 | .71 | .65 | .62 |
| 2 | | .76 | .71 | | .54 | .35 | | .66 | .69 |
| 3 | | | .79 | | | .56 | | | .71 |

*Note. N* = 92. The stability of the individual patterns is measured by the intraclass correlation, the stability of clusters by Cohen's K. The mean of the intraclass correlations over individuals was computed using Fisher's *r* to *Z* transformation.

that the resulting centers for each assessment were as similar as possible to the centers based on the aggregated assessments.

Table 18.2 shows that this method resulted in a cluster overlap that was slightly higher for short periods of time but considerably higher for longer retest intervals than the cluster overlap for separate cluster solutions (non-fixed centers). Thus, the decreasing overlap found with the first method of separate cluster analysis for each assessment seems to be due to a *low continuity* of the clusters. A very similar result was found for 4- and 5-cluster solutions.

Because it is not plausible that personality types change at the construct level within a few months of adult development, the low continuity of the clusters can be attributed to measurement error produced by the method of clustering. Indeed, methods that generate discrete classes are more susceptible to measurement error than are linear methods because small differences between individual patterns can result in different cluster memberships that, in turn, contribute to different cluster centers. It is very important, therefore, to reduce measurement error in the clusters by increasing the reliability of the patterns on which the clusters are based. I did this by considering only clusters of patterns that were based on aggregates of all four assessments of the NEO-FFI.

It could be argued that such an approach is developmentally insensitive because possible developmental changes are "aggregated away." However, the high stability of the continuous clusters (note that stabilities are kappas; a kappa of .60 roughly corresponds to a correlation of .80) indicated that the personality types were stable over time, and in this case aggregation was appropriate.

## Female Personality Types

On the basis of these stability analyses, I generated clusters based on the individual patterns of the $z$-transformed, cross-time aggregates of the NEO-FFI scale scores. As previously described, I used Ward's algorithm, followed by iterative nearest centroid sorting. Because I expected that the 3-cluster solution would resemble the Adjusted, Overcontrolled, and Undercontrolled personality types, and because this expectation was strongly confirmed by the results, I describe the findings by starting at this level, and then move up to the two-cluster solution and down to the 4- and 5-cluster solutions.

Figure 18.2 shows the 3-cluster solution. The cluster centers are displayed for each cluster, and because they are measured in terms of $z$ scores, effect sizes of the differences between the clusters are evident. The largest cluster consisted of half of the sample. As Fig. 18.2 indicates, members of this cluster reported more socially desirable scores than the other two clusters except for Openness to Experience. This exception can be attributed to the fact that the sample as a whole had slightly higher scores in Openness than the normative German female sample reported by Borkenau and Ostendorf (1993) (an effect size of .22 standard deviations).

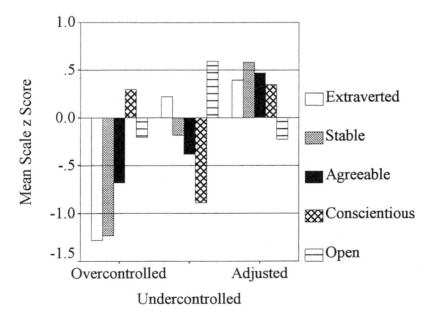

Final Clusters

FIG. 18.2. Cluster centers for the final 3-cluster solution.

Thus, the slightly negative mean $z$ score in Openness of this cluster corresponds to an average Openness score in the female population. Considering this fact, the interpretation of this cluster was straightforward: Females who described themselves not as undesirable but also not as exceptionally desirable in a particular trait. *Adjusted* seemed to be an appropriate label for this personality type ("well-adjusted" or "resilient" do not really apply because these labels have stronger positive implications).

The other two clusters had a similar size and were immediately recognizable as Overcontrolled and Undercontrolled females. Compared with the Adjusted group, the *Overcontrolled* cluster had lower scores in Extraversion, Emotional stability, and Agreeableness. This pattern is characteristic for anxious, shy females. The *Undercontrolled* cluster had lower scores in Conscientiousness, Agreeableness, and Emotional stability, and higher scores in Openness than the adjusted group; also, they reported higher Emotional Stability than the overcontrollers. This pattern is characteristic for Undercontrolled females ("aggressive" does not seem appropriate because it would imply lower Agreeableness and Openness). All in all, the three personality types reported in the recent literature were clearly confirmed.

This 3-cluster solution was derived from an initial 2-cluster solution that consisted of the Adjusted cluster plus a cluster with mirrored centers that can be simply described as *maladjusted*. Thus, the first split in the hierarchical analysis separated Adjusted from maladjusted women, and the second split distinguished between Overcontrolled and Undercontrolled maladjusted types. Moving down the cluster hierarchy, the next two splits occurred within the Adjusted cluster. Thus, the Over- and Undercontrolled clusters were fairly homogeneous.

The first split within the Adjusted cluster resulted in a larger group of 31 females with a center similar to the Adjusted cluster except for higher Openness scores, labeled the *resilient* type. The second Adjusted subtype consisted of 13 women with very low scores in Openness (mean $z = -1.5$) and lower scores than the resilient type in Conscientiousness, tentatively called *passive*. The combination of low Openness and low Conscientiousness was difficult to interpret, particularly because there were virtualy no differences between this type and the resilient type in any relationship variable in the analyses, described in the next section.

A similar problem applied to the next split that occurred within the resilient group and resulted in two equally large subtypes. One was characterized by slightly negative scores in Agreeableness along with high scores in Extraversion and Emotional Stability; it may be called *assertive*. The other type had high scores in Agreeableness and Conscientiousness along with Extraversion and Emotional Stability scores close to zero; this type may be called *agreeable*. Again, however, there were no significant differences between these two adjusted subtypes for any relationship variable. Because of the lack of discriminant validity of the three identified subtypes of Adjusted women for their relationship development, I report only the results for the 3-cluster solution.

## Relationship Development of the Three Personality Types

Differences between Overcontrolled and Undercontrolled females and the Adjusted group were studied for various kinds of relationship variables: number of peers (defined as nonsiblings aged 18–27 years), frequency of contact with the parents, perceived available support from a best peer friend and from the parents, and conflict with peers and with the parents.

Differences between the three personality types in the overall relationship status (mean of a relationship variable across all 7 assessments) and the relationship change (within-subjects factor time) were tested for significance by a repeated-measures ANOVA for each relationship variable, followed by post hoc comparisons between the Overcontrolled and Undercontrolled types and the Adjusted type. Similarly, type differences in relationship change were tested by interactions between type and time, followed by tests of interactions between type and polynomial contrasts in time that, if significant, were followed by post hoc comparisons between the Overcontrolled and Undercontrolled types and the Adjusted type. All effects discussed later are based on significant type effects and at least marginally significant post hoc comparisons. Two variables showed type by time interactions (see Fig. 18.3).

All three types reported an increasing number of peers in their network but both maladjusted types reported fewer peers overall; in addition, the Overcontrolled type showed a stronger increase in the number of peers than the Adjusted type. Figure 18.3a shows that the Overcontrolled participants began with a smaller peer network but reported a faster growth; after 18 months, they had as many peer relationships as their adjusted fellows. In contrast, the Undercontrolled type began with a similar peer network size as the Adjusted type and showed initially a similar increase in size. After 3 months, however, the Undercontrolled type's peer network had already reached a maximum and subsequently decreased slightly, whereas the Adjusted type reached the maximum 6 months later. Consequently, the Undercontrolled type ended up with a smaller peer network than the two other types.

The initial deviation of the Overcontrolled type from the other types concerned not only the sheer number of peers but also the emotional support that was received from them. As Fig. 18.3b shows, both the Adjusted and the Undercontrolled types reported high support from at least one peer right from the beginning (nearly a ceiling effect because the

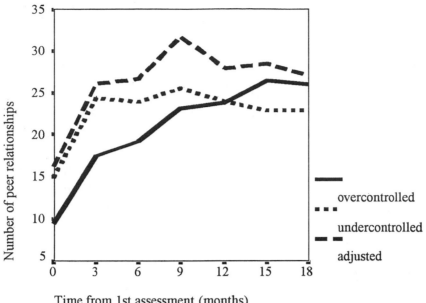

overcontrolled
........
undercontrolled
- - -
adjusted

Time from 1st assessment (months)

a

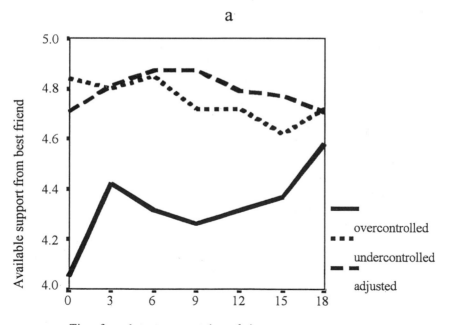

overcontrolled
........
undercontrolled
- - -
adjusted

Time from 1st assessment (months)

b

FIG. 18.3. Changes in peer relationships of the three personality types. (a) Number of peer relationships. (b) Available support from best friend.

maximum score on the response scale was 5). The Overcontrolled type reported initially less support from a best peer friend, but later overcame this disadvantage completely.

The remaining results concerned overall type effects without type by time interactions. As one would expect, the Undercontrolled type reported more conflict with parents and peers than the Adjusted type whereas the Overcontrolled type did not. Complementing the findings for peers, the Over-controlled type reported less emotional support from parents, and the Undercontrolled type reported less frequent contact with parents. Analyses of the living conditions of the three types showed a striking difference that explained the contact ratings to a great extent: Undercontrolled females lived (at the beginning of the study) together with their family significantly less often (16%) than the two other groups (Overcontrolled, 42%; Adjusted, 43%). North-American readers should note that German students begin university at an older age than in North America but nevertheless more often live at home, particularly if they study in their home town, because dormitory rooms are less available and considered to be of a poor standard; most students who leave home live in private apartments.

Because of the substantial attrition rate (47% of the initial subjects dropped out during the course of the study), the influence of personality type on attrition was also analyzed. The same logic was applied as for the stability analyses: To make the longitudinal types comparable with types for the initial full sample, the centers of the 3-cluster solution of the first assessment of the full sample was forced to be equal to those of the longitudinal types; the clusters were then formed by noniterative nearest centroid sorting. This procedure made sure that the types identified for the full initial sample were directly comparable to those based on the longitu-dinal sample.

As one can expect on the basis of motivational considerations, the two maladjusted types had marginally higher dropout rates than the Adjusted type (Undercontrolled, 55%; Overcontrolled, 48%; Adjusted, 39%). Dropouts within a type did not have significantly higher or lower scores in any of the 5 scales than the other members of the same type who continued until the end of the study. Thus, the expected selective effects for types were found, but they were not strong, and the results were not much influenced by selective dropout effects within types.

All in all, these findings strongly confirmed the interpretation of the three types. Overcontrolled females had particular problems in new social environments due to a high inhibition when confronted with the unfamiliar (Kagan, Reznick, Clarke, Snidman, & Garcia-Coll, 1984). As Caspi, Elder, and Bem (1988) observed, shy children show delayed development with regard to various life tasks in adulthood but do not exhibit problems in the long run; for example, they marry later and have their first child later, but have at least as stable marriages and as many children as their nonshy fellows. In the Berlin Relationship Study, Overcontrolled females overcame their disadvantage in terms of peer relationships within 18 months. It should be noted that this rosy picture may not be generally applicable to the whole population of students because of the self-selection of the subjects for the study.

Undercontrolled females had more conflictual relationships with their parents and peers. The conflicts with parents might have had some history before the study began. This, in turn, would explain why the Undercontrolled women left their family earlier and therefore had less frequent contact with their parents. But their conflicts were not restricted to parents; their conflicts with peers were even stronger relative to the Adjusted participants. Also, these Undercontrolled women tended to drop out from the study more than others. Together, these finding were consistent with the picture of a young woman who acts impulsively and is less reliable in her social relationships, giving rise to frequent interpersonal conflict.

Adjusted females presented themselves as more socially desirable in virtually every aspect of their personality and social relationships than the maladjusted types, as well as having a lower dropout rate from the study. It is difficult to believe that this highly consistent style was due only to a differential tendency of the Adjusted types to present themselves more favorably to others. The more parsimonious interpretation is that most of them did have a more socially desirable personality, although it cannot be excluded that there was a subgroup consisting of defensive self- or other-deceptors (Paulhus, 1984), who tended to enhance themselves and their relationships. Because it was not possible to include ratings from acquaintances, this question remains open.

## DISCUSSION

These person-centered analyses show that (a) the expected three personality types of Overcontrolled, Undercontrolled, and Adjusted women are confirmed, (b) there is no evidence for an incremental validity for a more refined typology consisting of four or five types, and (c) the three personality types follow distinct paths of relationship development. The findings are consistent with the general conclusion of Asendorpf and Wilpers (1998) that personality shapes the development of social relationships in predictable, meaningful ways.

These results are based on a female sample. Although similar types can also be identified for males (see Block, 1971, and Pulkkinen, 1996), the male sample was too small for a meaningful analysis, and it is not clear to what extent the findings for women can be generalized to men.

The hierarchical cluster analyses identified 3-, 4- and 5-cluster solutions that were initially not highly stable over time. However, when the cluster centers were fixed to the same prototypic Big-Five pattern, the cluster membership of the subjects was found to be stable across the 18 months of the study. This result highlights the importance of a clear distinction between continuity and stability in the study of personality development. Deriving types by cluster analysis is not a very robust procedure because it tends to produce cluster solutions that are sensitive to slight variations in the similarity structure of the personality patterns due to measurement error. Care must be exercised not to confuse the resulting instability of the clusters with an instability of the personality types at the construct level. The Procrustean method I used in this study seems to provide a solution to this problem for short-term longitudinal studies where it is highly improbable that types are discontinuous at the construct level. For long-term studies such as the study reported by Bergman and Magnusson (1991) however, the assumption that types do not change at the construct level cannot be made. In that case, different methods are needed in order to reduce measurement error, such as the aggregation of the data across assessments close in time.

When the findings of the person-centered approach are contrasted with the results of the variable-oriented approach, it may be objected that the person-centered results only describe the same coin from a different side; they were based on the same set of data, after all. Are these findings, however, redundant when I already have the variable-centered results? Although some of the differences between the types also emerged from the variable-centered analyses, not all of them were detected in these analyses. The relationship characteristics of Overcontrolled women were also found when a low-Extraverted group was compared with a high-Extraverted group, and the infrequent contact with family members was also found when a low-Conscientious group was compared with a high-Conscientious group. This is not surprising because Extraversion distinguished best between Overcontrolled and other females, and Conscientiousness best separated Undercontrolled from other women.

But the conflict pattern was not as clear from the variable-centered view: Conflict with peers was more related to low Agreeableness whereas conflict with parents was more associated with low Conscientiousness. Because the Undercontrolled type combined both characteristics, the results were clearer. Also, the early leveling-off of the growth of the peer network was observed neither for low-Agreeable nor for low-Conscientious participants.

These findings illustrate a general principle: The better a variable distinguishes one personality type from others, the more the variable- and the person-centered approaches yield the same results with regard to this type. Because it is always possible to construct variables that represent types well, a person-centered approach is not generally superior to a variable-centered approach with regard to this criterion.

However, a person-centered approach seems necessary to separate meaningful personality traits that capture the prototypic meaning of a particular personality type from artificial constructs that are not related to any type that occurs with some frequency in the population of interest. From this point of view, a person-centered approach is most useful as an intermediate step in the construction of efficient measures of personality types. Start with a large sample of traits, cluster or factor them within a person-centered approach, and finally construct efficient scales that represent each personality type. In this sequence, the variable-centered and the person-centered approaches to personality are both indispensable and they complement one another.

## ACKNOWLEDGMENTS

This research was supported by a grant from the German Research Foundation to Jens B. Asendorpf (As 59/4). Special thanks to Susanne Wilpers who carried out the Berlin Relationship Study and ran many preliminary variable-centered analyses.

## REFERENCES

Achenbach, T. M., & Edelbrock, C. S. (1981). Behavioral problems and competencies reported by parents of normal and disturbed children aged four through sixteen. *Monographs of the Society for Research in Child Development, 46,* (Serial No. 188).

Allport, G. W. (1937). *Personality: A psychological interpretation.* New York: Holt, Rinehart & Winston.

Allport, G. W. (1961). *Pattern and growth in personality.* New York: Holt, Rinehart & Winston.

Asendorpf, J. B. (1992a). A Brunswikean approach to trait continuity: Application to shyness. *Journal of Personality, 60,* 53–77.

Asendorpf, J. B. (1992b). Continuity and stability of personality traits and personality patterns. In J. B. Asendorpf & J. Valsiner (Eds.), *Stability and change in development: A study of methodological reasoning* (pp. 116–142). Newbury Park, CA: Sage.

Asendorpf, J. B., & van Aken, M. A. G. (1999). Resilient, overcontrolled and undercontrolled personality prototypes in childhood: Replicability, predictive power, and the trait/type issue. *Journal of Personality and Social Psychology.*

Asendorpf, J. B., & Wilpers, S. (1998). Personality effects on social relationships. *Journal of Personality and Social Psychology, 74,* 1531–1544.

Bergman, L. R., & Magnusson, D. (1991). Stability and change in patterns of extrinsic adjustment problems. In D. Magnusson, L. R. Bergman, G. Rudinger, & R. Törestad (Eds.), *Problems and methods in longitudinal research: Stability and change* (pp. 323–346). Cambridge, UK: Cambridge University Press.

Block, J. (1955). The difference between Q and R. *Psychological Review, 62,* 356–358.

Block, J. (1961). *The Q-sort method in personality assessment and psychiatric research.* Springfield, IL: Thomas.

Block, J. (1971). *Lives through time*. Berkeley, CA: Bancroft.

Block, J. H., & Block, J. (1980). The role of ego-control and ego-resiliency in the organization of behavior. In W. A. Collins (Ed.), *Minnesota Symposium on Child Psychology, Vol. 13* (pp. 39–101). Hillsdale, NJ: Lawrence Erlbaum Associates.

Borkenau, P., & Ostendorf, F. (1993). *NEO-Fünf-Faktoren Inventar (NEO-FFI)* [NEO five-factor inventory]. Göttingen, Germany: Verlag für Psychologie.

Bryk, A. S., & Raudenbush, S. W. (1992). *Hierarchical linear models*. Newbury Park, CA: Sage.

Caspi, A. (1998). Personality development across the life course. In N. Eisenberg (Ed.), *Handbook of child psychology: Vol. 3. Social, emotional, and personality development* (5th ed., pp. 311–388). New York: Wiley.

Caspi, A., Elder, G. H., & Bem, D. J. (1988). Moving away from the world: Life-course patterns of shy children. *Developmental Psychology, 24*, 824–831.

Caspi, A., & Silva, P. A. (1995). Temperamental qualities at age three predict personality traits in young adulthood: Longitudinal evidence from a birth cohort. *Child Development, 66*, 486–498.

Cattell, R. B. (1946). *The description and measurement of personality*. Yonkers, NY: World Book.

Costa, P. T., & McCrae, R. R. (1989). *The NEO PI/FFI manual supplement*. Odessa, FL: Psychological Assessment Resources.

Cronbach, L. J. (1955). Processes affecting scores on "understanding others" and "assumed similarity." *Psychological Bulletin, 52*, 177–193.

Elder, G. H., Jr. (1985). Perspectives on the life course. In G. H. Elder, Jr. (Ed.), *Life course dynamics: Trajectories and transitions, 1968–1980* (pp. 23–49). Ithaca, NY: Cornell University Press.

Gangestad, S., & Snyder, M. (1985). "To carve nature at its joints": On the existence of discrete classes in personality. *Psychological Review, 92*, 317–349.

Hart, D., Hofmann, V., Edelstein, W. & Keller, M. (1997). The relation of childhood personality types to adolescent behavior and development: A longitudinal study of Icelandic children. *Developmental Psychology, 33*, 195–205.

Kagan, J. (1980). Perspectives on continuity. In O. G. Brim, Jr. & I. Kagan (Eds.), *Constancy and change in human development* (pp. 26–74). Cambridge, MA: Harvard University Press.

Kagan, J., Reznick, J. S., Clarke, C., Snidman, N., & Garcia-Coll, C. (1984). Behavioral inhibition to the unfamiliar. *Child Development, 55*, 2212–2225.

Magnusson, D. (1988). *Individual development from an interactional perspective: A longitudinal study*. Hillsdale, NJ: Lawrence Erlbaum Associates.

Magnusson, D. (1990). Personality development from an interactional perspective. In L. A. Pervin (Ed.), *Handbook of personality: Theory and measurement* (pp. 193–222). New York: Guilford.

Ozer, D. J., & Gjerde, P. F. (1989). Patterns of personality consistency and change from childhood through adolescence. *Journal of Personality, 57*, 483–507.

Paulhus, D. L. (1984). Two-component models of socially desirable responding. *Journal of Personality and Social Psychology, 46*, 598–609.

Pulkkinen, L. (1996). Female and male personality styles: A typological and developmental analysis. *Journal of Personality and Social Psychology, 70*, 1288–1306.

Robins, R. W., John, O. P., Caspi, A., Moffitt, T. E., Stouthhamer-Loeber, M. (1996). Resilient, overcontrolled, and undercontrolled boys: Three replicable personality types. *Journal of Personality and Social Psychology, 70*, 157–171.

Rogosa, D. (1980). A critique of cross-lagged correlation. *Psychological Bulletin, 88*, 245–258.

Sameroff, A. J. (1983). Developmental systems: Contexts and evolution. In W. Kessen (Ed.), *Handbook of child psychology: Vol. 1. History, theory, and methods* (4th ed., pp. 237–294). New York: Wiley.

Stern, W. (1911). *Die differentielle Psychologie in ihren methodischen Grundlagen* [Methodological foundations of differential psychology]. Leipzig, Germany: Barth.

York, K. L., & John, O. P. (1992). The four faces of Eve: A typological analysis of women's personality at midlife. *Journal of Personality and Social Psychology, 63*, 494–508.

# 19

# Personality and Organizational Destructiveness: Fact, Fiction, and Fable

Sigrid B. Gustafson
American Institutes for Research

The underlying assumption in leadership research has generally been that "bad" leaders either lack (or are perceived to lack) the attributes of "good" leaders, or that they suffer from situational constraints that prevent effective performance, or both. In contrast, I argue that at least one specific kind of bad leader—with bad connoting evil rather than incompetent—is characterized by a predictable. pattern of personality and personality-driven behavior. I call these individuals *aberrant self-promoters* (ASPs), and I suggest that empowering destructive leaders of this type, by granting them control over human and material resources, inevitably leads to negative organizational consequences, including impaired mental health of subordinates and eventual system dysfunction. Moreover, in the course of this chapter, I attempt to dispel the commonly held notion that leaders referred to as "Machiavellians" necessarily fall into the category of destructive leaders. Finally, I offer a new method for identifying ASPs from a holistic person perspective.

This line of research began when Gustafson and Ritzer (1995) proposed and validated a subclinical syndrome called aberrant self-promotion. The concept of aberrant self promotion is consistent with Hare's (e.g., Harpur, Hare, & Hakstian, 1989) two-factor definition of psychopathy, with Factor 1 reflecting personality characteristics, such as exploitativeness, entitlement, grandiosity, superficial charm, and lack of empathy or guilt, and Factor 2 reflecting antisocial behavior. However, representing a less severe form of psychopathy, ASPs differ from psychopaths only in degree, not in kind.

**299**

Individuals are diagnosed as psychopaths only when they display an entire constellation of characteristics that are embedded in the two general factors. Similarly, aberrant self-promoters were first defined according to a person-oriented pattern that combined a narcissistic personality configuration (cf. Raskin, Novacek, & Hogan, 1991)—high self-esteem, high narcissism, and low concern for giving socially desirable responses—with a high degree of antisocial behavior.

## STUDY I

### Methods

The initial effort towards establishing the validity of aberrant self-promotion as an identifiable psychological syndrome revealed the existence of the ASP pattern in two separate samples of university undergraduates ($N$'s = 214 and 367), using three methods: cluster analysis using five total-instrument scores as indicators, factor analysis at the item level, and factor analysis of persons instead of items. The study employed a 179-item questionnaire, composed of five personality instruments (Gustafson & Ritzer, 1995):

1. The 40-item Narcissistic Personality Inventory (NPI; Raskin & Hall, 1979, 1981).
2. The 54-item Socialization subscale of the California Psychological Inventory (CPI; Gough, 1987).
3. The 10-item version (M-C 1 (10); Strahan & Gerbasi, 1972) of the Marlowe-Crowne Social Desirability Scale (Crowne & Marlowe, 1960).
4. An 11-item self-esteem measure taken from the Organizational Climate Questionnaire (OCQ; Jones & James, 1979).
5. The 58-item Self-Report of Psychopathy II (SRP II; Harpur & Hare, 1989) (Table 19.1).

Six additional items developed specifically for this study were also employed. The expected "ASP pattern" was defined as high on narcissism, self-esteem, and self-reported psychopathy and low on socialization and social desirability.

### Results

The three methods, each of which was based on participants' patterns across different sets of items, targeted virtually the same persons as ASPs. In Sample 1 the three methods demonstrated a convergence of 92%; in

TABLE 19.1
Means, Standard Deviations, and Alphas for Scale–Score Composites: Samples 1 and 2

| Composite | Sample 1 (N = 214 | | | Sample 2 (N = 367 | | |
|---|---|---|---|---|---|---|
| | Mean | SD | Alpha | Mean | SD | Alpha |
| NPI | 16.01 | 7.24 | .85 | 15.93 | 7.15 | .86 |
| CPI | 34.85 | 6.17 | .79 | 35.29 | 6.33 | .79 |
| M–C (10) | 3.40 | 1.91 | .60 | 3.69 | 1.91 | .57 |
| SE | 41.76 | 7.34 | .91 | 41.53 | 7.17 | .90 |
| SRP | 180.50 | 20.62 | .89 | 178.55 | 22.81 | .90 |

*Note.* NPI = Narcissistic Personality Inventory total. CPI = total for the Socialization subscale of the California Psychological Inventory. M–C (10) = total for the short form of the Marlowe–Crowne Social Desirability Scale. SE = total for the self-esteem scale of the Organizational Climate Questionnaire. SRP = Self-Report of Psychopathy II total.

Sample 2 the convergence rate was 94% (Gustafson & Ritzer, 1995). Moreover, the prevalence was higher than Cleckley's (1976) estimated 2% of psychopaths in the population; prevalence rates were 11% in the first sample and 6% in the second.

Having verified that ASPs could be among late adolescents, the next step was to demonstrate that they differed predictably from non-ASPs on relevant behavioral criteria. Thus, the following study sought to differentiate the ASPs targeted in the earlier investigation from a group of participants whose patterns of personality and behavior exhibited high self-esteem without the negative characteristics that define the ASP.

## STUDY 2

Because the aberrant self-promotion pattern is conceptualized as functionally similar to psychopathy, one obvious domain in which ASPs should differ from non-ASPs is their scores on Hare's Revised Psychopathy Checklist (PCL-R; Hare, 1991; Hare et al., 1990), the most widely used instrument in the world for assessing psychopathy. Therefore, having identified specific individuals who manifested the hypothetical ASP pattern, the first hypothesis was that these targeted ASPs would score significantly higher on the PCL-R than would the non-ASP comparisons, although the ASPs' scores were not expected to meet the criterion for psychopathy. Another set of hypotheses was that the ASPs would have engaged in significantly more antisocial behavior, as indicated by university records, than would have the non-ASPs.

## Methods

The participants for the second study, which first involved an interview, came from both Sample 1 ($N$ = 214, 60% female) and Sample 2 ($N$ = 367, 70% female) of the first study. The putative ASPs were 32 participants targeted by all three methods described in the first study. Thirty comparison (i.e., non-ASP) participants were also drawn for interview from Sample 1 and Sample 2. These comparison participants were characterized by a non-ASP pattern that reflected high self-esteem and average social desirability, in combination with low levels of narcissism, self-reported psychopathy, and antisocial behavior.

A discriminant analysis was conducted to compare the 32 putative ASPs with the remainder of Sample 1 and Sample 2, minus all interviewed participants, using as the discriminating variables the five inventory totals on which the cluster analysis had been performed. A second discriminant analysis compared the 30 non-ASPs to the 32 targeted ASPs. All differences were significant in the expected directions: The 32 targeted ASPs were higher than the rest of the combined samples ($N$ = 519) and higher than the 30 comparison participants on narcissism, self-esteem, and self-reported psychopathy and lower on socialization and social desirability. All differences between the targeted ASPs and the comparison participants were significant either at an alpha level of less than .0001 (narcissism, socialization, social desirability, self-reported psychopathy) or at an alpha level of .001 (self-esteem). Although the targeted ASPs were significantly higher than the comparisons on self-esteem (a variable that later proved not to be an indicator of aberrant self-promotion), the comparisons' self-esteem mean was still a half a standard deviation above the overall sample mean. All differences between the targeted ASPs and the rest of the sample were significant at an alpha level of .0001.

## Results

*PCL-R Interview.* The interview protocol was modified somewhat, to inquire into issues related to college life. Also, because the last 3 of the 20 original PCL-R items assessed aspects of criminal activity per se, these items were not scored (see the last 3 items measuring Factor 2 in Table 19.2).

As expected, the ASPs scored significantly higher than the comparisons on the PCL-R total score and did not meet the PCL-R criterion for a diagnosis of psychopathy, that, in this version of the interview, would have required a total score of 25. Three $t$ tests, comparing the overall PCL-R mean totals, the Factor 1 mean totals, and the Factor 2 mean totals of the targeted ASPs with those of the comparison participants, were all significant at an alpha level of less than .0001. These results are depicted in Table 19.3. (It was also

## TABLE 19.2
### Revised Psychopathy Checklist (PCL–R) Items

| Factor 1 Items | Factor 2 Items |
| --- | --- |
| Glibness/superficial charm | Need for stimulation/proneness to boredom |
| Grandiose sense of self-worth | Parasitic lifestyle |
| pathological lying | Poor behavioral controls |
| Conning/manipulative | Promiscuous sexual behavior |
| Lack of remorse or guilt | Early behavioral problems |
| Shallow affect | Lack of realistic, long-term goals |
| Callous/lack of empathy | Impulsivity |
| Failure to accept responsibility for own actions | irresponsibility |
| | Many short-term marital relationships[a] |
| | Juvenile delinquency[b] |
| | Revocation of conditional release[b] |
| | Criminal versatility+ |

*Note.* [a]Changed to "Many living-together or spending-virtually-every-night-together relationships" for this study. [b]These items not scored in the study.

## TABLE 19.3
### Difference Between ASPs and Comparisons on PCL–R Mean Scores

| Group | Mean | Standard Deviation | d.f. | t-Value |
| --- | --- | --- | --- | --- |
| | | PCL–R Total Score | | |
| ASPs ($n = 32$) | 12.56 | 5.71 | | |
| Comparisons ($n = 30$) | 3.75 | 4.23 | 60 | 6.86* |
| | | Factor 1 Total Score | | |
| ASPs ($n = 32$) | 6.89 | 3.73 | | |
| Comparisons ($n = 30$) | 1.67 | 2.44 | 60 | 6.45* |
| | | Factor 2 Total Score | | |
| ASPs ($n = 32$) | 5.00 | 2.59 | | |
| Comparisons ($n = 30$) | 1.78 | 1.85 | 60 | 5.59* |

* $p < .0001$.

noteworthy that there were no significant gender differences among the ASPs on PCL-R mean scores.)

**Antisocial Behavior Criteria: ASPs Versus Non-ASPs.** We next compared the ASPs to the non-ASPs on a number of antisocial behavior criteria. First, 29 ASPs and 29 non-ASPs allowed us access to their university transcripts. On a grade point scale of 0 to 5, the mean grade point average of the ASPs was 2.59. In contrast, the non-ASPs' mean grade point average of 3.03 was significantly higher ($t(56) = 3.02, p < .01$). This result supported our hypothesis that because of their impulsivity and their failure to develop and implement realistic long-term goals or to take responsibility for their actions, the ASPs' grades would not be as high as those of their more conscientious counterparts.

ASPs also exhibited greater involvement in self-reported illegal acts than did non-ASPs. Twenty-six of the 32 ASPs (81%) admitted to committing at least one crime—other than underage drinking, in which almost all participants had engaged—for which they would probably have been arrested if caught. These acts included stealing, vandalizing property, experimenting with explosives, forging a prescription, using illegal drugs, driving while intoxicated, creating a public disturbance, and carrying falsified identification. The ASPs' widespread self-reporting of illegal acts underscored their low concern for giving socially desirable responses.

In contrast, 14 of the 30 non-ASPs (47%) admitted to committing at least one offense, other than underage drinking, for which they probably would have been arrested. A 2 (ASPs vs. non-ASPs) × 2 (offenses vs. no offenses) chi-squared test demonstrated that reporting the commission of offenses was significantly associated with exhibiting the aberrant self-promotion pattern (chi-squared $(1) = 8.09, p < .01$).

We also hypothesized that, because of their feelings of "entitlement," which are characteristic of narcissism, and because of their general disregard for rules that inconvenience them, the ASPs would have garnered significantly more parking tickets, compared with the non-ASPs. Of 23 ASPs with cars registered at the university, 19 had received a combined total of 133 tickets. In contrast, among 27 non-ASPs with cars registered over the same 2-year period, 18 had received a total of 43 tickets. Astonishingly enough, one ASP had received 68 tickets. When the 68-ticket offender was removed from the analysis, the mean of the ASPs ($2.95, SD = 2.64$) significantly exceeded that of the non-ASPs ($1.59, SD = 1.93; t(47) = 2.08, p < .05$).

The next criterion was the number of judicial reprimands our participants had received. Since their admission to the university, 10 of the participants interviewed had received judicial reprimands. The reprimands had been issued for consuming alcohol in the university residence halls, for vandalism, for setting off fire alarms, and for making obscene telephone

calls. Among the 32 ASPs, 7 (22%) had received a total of 15 judicial reprimands. In contrast, three (10%) of the non-ASPs had received a total of four
reprimands. It should be noted that issuing judicial reprimands is a fairly
infrequent event for this university, affecting only about 6% of 19,000 undergraduates each year; nevertheless, the result of a $t$ test comparing the mean
number of reprimands incurred by the ASPs (0.47, $SD$ = .98) to the mean
number incurred by the non-ASPs (0.14, $SE$ = .44), was significant at an alpha
level of less than .10 ($t(59)$ = 1.72).

The base rate of arrests for undergraduates by the university police is
also quite low, about 1% of the undergraduates in a given year. None of the
non-ASPs had been arrested; however, records showed that three of the
ASPs had been, one for theft and two for public drunkenness. A 2 (ASP vs.
non-ASP) × 2 (arrests vs. no arrests) chi-squared analysis showed being
arrested to be associated with exhibiting the pattern of aberrant self-promotion (chi-squared (1) = 2.96, $p$ < .10).

Finally, the base rate of honors investigations and sanctions is even
lower than the base rate of arrests by the university police force. Nonetheless, one individual from the ASP group was currently under investigation.

## Coda: Later Investigation of an Anomaly

As the result of an anomaly discovered in a related investigation (Holloway,
1995), we reexamined the necessity of including high self-esteem in the
overall pattern of aberrant self-promotion. PCL-R interviews were conducted
with 32 more individuals who manifested high narcissism, high antisociality,
and low social desirability, but whose self-esteem scores ranged from low
to high (10 low, 10 average, 12 high—with the high group being more than
half a standard deviation above the mean and the low group being more
than half a standard deviation below the mean). Thirteen non-ASPs, representing a full range of self-esteem scores, were also interviewed as controls.
The PCL-R mean score across the ASPs was comparable to that obtained
for the ASPs in the previous study. Moreover, the results of an ANOVA
across the three levels of self-esteem demonstrated no significant differences
in PCL-R scores among the ASPs. Finally, when the ASPs' PCL-R scores (total,
Factor 1, and Factor 2) were regressed on self-esteem, none of the three
regression weights for self-esteem were significant. As a result of this finding,
I no longer use self-esteem as an indicator of the ASP pattern.

That highly narcissistic (and antisocial) individuals could not be differentiated from one another on a psychopathy diagnostic interview, regardless of whether their traditionally measured self-esteem was high, average,
or low, was intriguing. One interpretation may be that some narcissists do
not report high self-esteem on items like "On the whole I am satisfied with
myself" because they are, in fact, dissatisfied with the extent to which their
self-perceived superiority has been acknowledged and rewarded by others.

## DISCUSSION

Babiak's (1994) case study of an organizational psychopath's destructiveness, as well as the information provided by ASPs through interview and through their performance on external antisocial behavior criteria, underscore the similarity of ASPs to psychopaths. Moreover, ASPs can be expected to extend to the workplace the same destructive behavior that has been documented in the context of undergraduate life. They can be expected to present others' ideas as their own, to lie to superiors and subordinates alike, to mismanage organizational resources, to subvert organizational policy or even to ignore legal restraints in the service of their own self-interests, to threaten any coworker who seeks to limit their power, and to refuse to accept accountability for the negative consequences their behavior engenders.

## STUDY 3

Now on to my next proposition: A Machiavellian is not necessarily an ASP. In discussing the "dark side of charisma," researchers have frequently identified Machiavellianism as a key characteristic of self-centered or "unsocialized" leaders, like aberrant self-promoters. In contrast, I believe that Machiavellians have been unjustly represented as ruthlessly exploitative individuals who routinely sacrifice ethics in the service of expediency and personal ambition. There is no doubt that "Machiavellians"—as Machiavelli himself depicted them in his most famous work, *The Prince*—can be shrewd, calculating, and manipulative. However, extensive biographic analyses of Machiavelli's actual philosophy, as revealed through his poetry, plays, letters, and treatises other than *The Prince* and *The Discourses* (De Grazia, 1989; Masters, 1996), have recently revealed Machiavelli to have been an exceedingly moral man for whom the two cardinal sins were ambition and greed. In fact, he advocated his precepts exclusively in the context of achieving or maintaining the "common good." In many ways, he can legitimately be considered the first "modern" political scientist, in that his teaching comprised the first scientific approach to human nature and politics, with parallels in game theory and in neo-Darwinian evolutionary theory.

Recent research (Russell, 1996; Russell & Gustafson, 1997) has involved an experimental study contrasting the behavior of ASPs with the behavior of Machiavellians who do not meet the ASP criteria—in a situation designed to elicit the behavioral differences between them. Specifically, the selected task had been used in 1970 by Geis, Weinheimer, and Berger to differentiate "high Mach" from "low Mach" behavior. The task offered the three components that Geis and Christie had identified in 1970 as necessary for Machiavellians to demonstrate their prowess in persuasiveness: face-to-face interaction, latitude for improvisation, and the presence of emotional issues that need to be ignored to accomplish the task at hand.

## Methods

The experimental task was a "legislative game" in which each player represented a particular constituency, in this case a state in the United States. The winning player was the one who garnered the most points from successfully championing any legislation that was favored by his or her constituency and from successfully defeating any legislation opposed by his or her constituency. Each player's constituency had a strong position (for or against) two issues, a moderate position (for or against) two other issues, and no opinion on three more issues. Strong positions carried 30,000 points, and moderate positions carried 20,000 points. Although all seven of these issues were given to every player, every player had a different constituency "mandate," in terms of what legislation should be passed and what should be defeated. Finally, each state wanted to pass what is called a "pork barrel" issue that benefited only that state. This issue was unique to each state and carried 20,000 points. Thus, if players were convincing and clever enough, they could "wheel and deal" on the two issues their states did not care about, as well as on the "pork barrel" issue, to gain maximum support for their constituency's positions.

The game was played twice, with two different sets of issues that were counterbalanced in the order of presentation. One set of issues was designed to elicit an emotional reaction; that is, the issues were "affect-laden." Examples included proposals to "implement universal health care coverage supported by higher income taxes," to "outlaw abortion," to "establish universal military conscription for both sexes," and to "raise the national drinking age from 21 to 25." The other set was affectively neutral. Issues included such propositions as "changing the specifications for sewer pipes," "relocating the National Bureau of Standards," "endorsing the proposed job descriptions for civil service employees," and "approving the appointment of the new ambassador to Guatemala." The results of manipulation checks showed that the two sets of issues differed significantly in the degree of affect they engendered in the players before the players knew their constituencies' wishes.

The initial Geis et al. (1970) study was modified to include ASPs as well as Machiavellians and comparison participants in the groups. The groups, which were always composed of same-sex players, comprised seven members—two ASPs, two "high Machs," and three comparisons. The ASPs were selected through cluster analysis, on the basis of their exhibiting the same pattern as before, except that self-esteem was not used as a pattern indicator. The Machiavellian score was not considered in selecting ASPs because a previous study had demonstrated that ASPs who were also high in Machiavellianism behave like prototypical ASPs (Holloway, 1995). The high Machs were chosen in a "top down" manner, based on their scores on the Mach IV (Geis & Christie, 1970) and on their not displaying the ASP pattern. The comparisons were neither ASPs nor high Machs. Finally, all 438 participants initially screened for the game were administered the Wonderlic Personnel Test (Wonderlic, 1983) so that the members of each group could be matched on cognitive ability.

Fourteen game sessions were conducted. After the instructions were understood, each group member had 30 seconds to present his or her arguments. A 10-minute free-bargaining session then ensued, during which players tried to work out voting alliances that would most benefit them, and after which the group reconvened. Each issue was read aloud by one of the issue's strong proponents, who was given 15 seconds to defend the legislation. One of the same issue's strong opponents was then afforded 15 seconds to rebut the first speaker's arguments. After the rebuttal, the vote was taken. This voting procedure was repeated for all seven issues. Finally, the entire process was repeated for the second set of issues.

### Results

The primary hypothesis was that the Machs, the ASPs, and the comparisons would all win about the same number of points across games in the neutral-issues condition because no one would be distracted by emotions irrelevant to winning the game when faced with issues like relocating the Bureau of Standards. The obvious strategy would be to trade votes with people whose constituency was neutral on issues to which your state was strongly or moderately committed and, in addition, to bargain with your "pork barrel" vote. Thus, only a significant interaction was predicted: Specifically, in the affect-laden condition, the Machs were expected to outscore both the ASPs and the comparisons. As Fig. 19.1 shows, this interaction is exactly what was observed. (Because the comparisons' scores did not differ significantly across conditions and because their responses were not of theoretical interest to the present study, their performance is not represented graphically, although their mean performance in each condition is displayed numerically.)

Moreover, because interpersonal liking among the players was also measured after each set of issues had been voted on, it was clear that the Machs had won without incurring the dislike of their fellow players. In contrast, the degree to which the ASPs were liked decreased significantly from the first set of issues to the second—despite the fact that the ASPs' winnings, in terms of points, did not differ significantly across condition or time. Further, given that liking for the ASPs decreased across time, but not

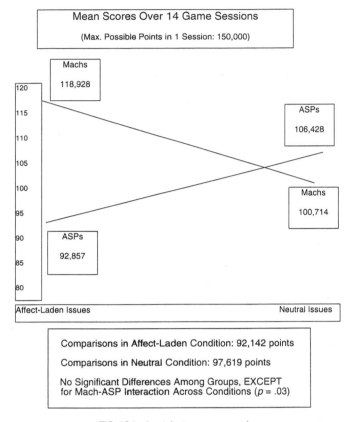

FIG. 19.1.  Legislative game results.

across condition (the conditions were counterbalanced in presentation), other players seemed to "get their number" as the game progressed. Indeed, when it came time to vote, a number of the ASPs reneged on bargains they had made. In fact, some reneged twice (i.e., in both conditions), and, in a couple of cases, an ASP reneged on the same person in both conditions. Conversely, Machiavellians kept their promises.

The results of this study support the interpretation of Machiavellianism as a personality characteristic, expressed through rational, goal-oriented behaviors involving the effective use of influence tactics that do not necessarily place the target of influence at a disadvantage. Thus, in an organizational setting, the Machiavellian, unlike the ASP, may serve collective, as well as individualistic, concerns and aims. Furthermore, the Machiavellian selectively uses influence tactics to attain a particular goal in a particular situation. Machiavellianism can be turned on and off at will because, unlike aberrant self-promotion, it does not reflect or define the person-as-a-whole; in contrast, ASPs are ASPs wherever they go.

## DEVISING A TEST OF ABERRANT
## SELF-PROMOTION

The studies mentioned heretofore have identified ASPs through their profiles across standard personality tests. This method is too long, too intrusive in its items, and (despite the ASP's lack of concern for social desirability) too transparent to be used by organizations in making personnel decisions. However, I am in the last stage of developing a single, easily administered and scored instrument that I believe will assess aberrant self-promotion holistically.

The new instrument appears to test respondents' ability to draw logical inferences and to evaluate logical arguments. To facilitate respondents' belief that they are taking a test of reasoning ability, many of the items are modeled after the "Logical Thinking" sections of standardized achievement tests like the Graduate Record Exam. In fact, the test is actually designed to let the implicit (i.e., the unarticulated, even to themselves) assumptions and biases that underlie the ASP personality lead ASPs to select responses that have been developed specifically to tap these assumptions.

The instrument is based on the concept that the aberrant self-promoter, like the psychopath, brings his or her combination of high narcissism (including grandiosity, lack of empathy, callousness, superiority, dominance, etc.) and antisocial behavior (e.g., impulsiveness, irresponsibility, poor behavioral controls, sensation-seeking, etc.) to virtually every environmental encounter. The first step in developing the instrument has been to state explicitly, for my own guidance in item construction, the tacit assumptions by which the ASP lives and through which ASPs implicitly justify their behavior.

Everyone views his or her own reality through a perceptual lens. From the view of accepted social norms, what elements so distort the ASP's lens that he or she can behave destructively and feel no remorse? I began by articulating the tacit assumptions that I believe to underlie the observable behaviors scored in Hare's Revised Psychopathy Checklist interviews. I submit that the ASP's overarching tacit assumption or implicit bias is that he or she is superior to ordinary human beings in virtually every domain—that he or she has a special destiny. ASPs believe that their pursuit of this destiny excuses them from any responsibility towards others. In fact, their "moral code" is reversed, in that they believe they are obligated not to care about others, lest personal attachments derail their own destiny. They make no apologies for who they are or what they do. In fact, they believe others would be just like them if they had the guts to be.

Furthermore, in the PCL-R interview, they use the language of psychology to support their worldview. For example, one young man was in therapy to "learn more about himself." It also happened that his girlfriend had tried to commit suicide when he broke up with her. When the interviewer asked how that incident had affected him, he said, without apparent emotion, that he had felt bad at first but that his therapist had told him he "mustn't blame himself." (The therapist probably did say that; however, it is doubtful that she meant he should regard the incident with quite so much detachment.) Later, he was asked how he would rate his self-esteem on a scale of 1 to 10. He gave himself "only" a 6 because, he said, "I still have a lot of things to work on in myself." When asked what those areas of improvement might be, he replied, "Sometimes I think I'm just too hard on myself."

The overarching principle of superiority can be subdivided into two main domains—biases used to justify a narcissistic worldview and biases used to justify antisocial behavior. In turn, each of these domains comprises a number of constructs defined by assumptions and biases relevant to those constructs, as guided by the PCL-R items (Table 19.2). For example, the construct of grandiosity falls into the domain of a narcissistic lifestyle. Examples of biases that maintain grandiosity include assumptions like "Superior people don't need to know more than a little jargon to understand the gist of things in virtually any discipline; given their mental ability, they can pick up the essence of the material, without formal training." Or, "Because people enjoy the opportunity to compliment superior people on being informed, intelligent, and interesting, superior people should give others plenty of chances to do so."

Another assumption, one that underlies the construct of manipulativeness in the narcissistic lifestyle domain, is "The superior person is strong enough to resist the conventional prohibition against manipulating family members and/or friends to his or her own advantage." Two more examples, related to the construct of sensation-seeking (part of the antisocial domain), are "Superior people 'prove their mettle' by participating in activities that most people think are too risky to try" and "Drugs and alcohol keep superior people from being chained to a mundane world when operating in alternate realities provides them with valuable life experience."

A couple of examples should help to illustrate how these assumptions can be used to assess personality. James (1998), who has successfully used this method to measure achievement motivation, calls it an assessment of "conditional reasoning." That is, the answer respondents choose as the rational, logical implication of an item stem is "conditional" on their implicit assumptions and biases. It should also be noted that the scores on James' achievement motivation measures are uncorrelated with cognitive ability scores (L. R. James, personal communication, January 1997).

I am attempting to take James' approach one step further by developing individual items, each of which captures more than one aspect of the "person," instead of a single trait. Thus, in a sense, I am attempting to construct items that, taken together, reflect a person-oriented pattern. Table 19.4 shows three sample items; the "ASP" response is starred.

TABLE 19.4
Sample Conditional Reasoning Items for Identifying ASPs

---

I.   "To the victor go the spoils" is a well-known saying. Which of the statements below most logically follows from it?

   1. Media coverage does not address who wins and who loses.
   2. Winners usually do not know those they defeat.
   3. Winners are not responsible for helping losers recover their dignity.*
   4. It is not good policy for winners to gloat over those they have defeated.

II.  There has been along and heated debate in Senator Johnson's state over legalizing marijuana. A new piece of legislation, proposing that the use of marijuana be made legal, has just come to the Senate for a vote. The senator has decided that he can best represent those who elected him by voting *for* this proposed law, thereby making marijuana use legal.

   Assume all of the following statements are true. Which of them presents the strongest support for Senator Johnson's position?

   1. Most marijuana sold in the United states comes from other countries.
   2. Senator Johnson's position means that individuals who use marijuana to increase their creativity will no longer risk arrest in pursuit of their art.*
   3. Senator Johnson's position means that people who have glaucoma (an eye disease that might be hereditary) will be able to use marijuana as prescribed by their doctors.
   4. If people start smoking marijuana, it's only a matter of time before they use other drugs.

---

*ASP response.

The instrument currently being validated is called the Logical Inference Exercise (LIE). A respondent receives a point for the item only if he or she selects the ASP response; otherwise, the score for the item is zero. To date, approximately 500 university undergraduates have completed the LIE; not even one of them has questioned its being a test of reasoning ability. If this strategy succeeds, it will hopefully provide organizations with a means to protect themselves from at least one type of destructive individual.

## REFERENCES

Babiak, P. (1994). When psychopaths go to work: A case study of an industrial psychopath. *Applied Psychology: An International Review, 44*, 171–188.

Cleckley, H. (1976). *The mask of sanity* (5th ed.). St. Louis, MO: Mosby.

Crowne, D. P., & Marlowe, D. (1960). A new scale of social desirability independent of psychopathology. *Journal of Consulting Psychology, 24*, 349–354.

De Grazia, S. (1989). *Machiavelli in hell*. Princeton, NJ: Princeton University Press.

Geis, F. L., & Christie, R. (1970). Overview of experimental research. In R. Christie & F. L. Geis (Eds.), *Studies in Machiavellianism* (pp. 285–313). New York: Academic Press.

Geis, F. L., Weinheimer, S., & Berger, D. (1970). Playing Legislature: Cool heads and hot issues. In R. Christie & F. L. Geis (Eds.), *Studies in Machiavellianism* (pp. 190–209). New York: Academic Press.

Gough, H. G. (1987). *California Psychological Inventory*. Palo Alto, CA: Consulting Psychologists Press.

Gustafson, S. B., & Ritzer, D. R. (1995). The dark side of normal: A psychopathy-linked pattern called aberrant self-promotion. *European Journal of Personality, 9*, 147–183.

Hare, R. D. (1991). *The Hare Psychopathy Checklist–Revised: Manual*. North Tonawanda, NY: Multi-Health Systems, Inc.

Hare, R. D., Harpur, T. J., Hakstian, A. R., Forth, A. E., Hart, S. D., & Newman, J. P. (1990). The revised psychopathy checklist: Reliability and factor structure. *Psychological Assessment: A Journal of Consulting and Clinical Psychology, 2*, 338–341.

Harpur, T. J., & Hare, R. D. (1989). *Self-report of psychopathy II*. Unpublished instrument.

Harpur, T. J., Hare, R. D., & Hakstian, A. R. (1989). Two-factor conceptualization of psychopathy: Construct validity and assessment implications. *Psychological Assessment: A Journal of Consulting and Clinical Psychology, 1*, 6–17.

Holloway, A. E. (1995). *Aberrant self-promotion versus Machiavellianism: A discriminant validity study*. Unpublished master's thesis, Virginia Polytechnic Institute and State University, Blacksburg.

James, L. R. (1998). Measurement of relative motive strength via conditional reasoning. *Organizational Research Methods Journal, 1*, 131–163.

Jones, A. P., & James, L. R. (1979). Psychological climate: Dimensions and relationships of individual and aggregated work environment perceptions. *Organizational Behavior and Human Performance, 23*, 201–250.

Masters, R. D. (1996). *Machiavelli, Leonardo, and the science of power*. Notre Dame, IN: University of Notre Dame Press.

Raskin, R., & Hall, C. S. (1979). A narcissistic personality inventory. *Psychological Reports, 46*, 55–60.

Raskin, R., & Hall, C. S. (1981). The narcissistic personality inventory: Alternate form reliability and further evidence of construct validity. *Journal of Personality Assessment, 45*, 159–162.

Raskin, R., Novacek, J., & Hogan, R. (1991). Narcissistic self-esteem management. *Journal of Social and Personality Psychology, 60*, 911–918.

Russell, D. (1996). *Aberrant self-promotion versus Machiavellianism: A differentiation of constructs*. Unpublished master's thesis, Virginia Polytechnic Institute and State University, Blacksburg.

Russell, D. & Gustafson, S. B. (1997). *Aberrant self-promoters versus Machiavellians: A contrast in organizational destructiveness*. Manuscript in preparation.

Strahan, R., & Gerbasi, K. C. (1972). Short, homogeneous versions of the Marlowe-Crowne Social Desirability Scale. *Journal of Clinical Psychology, 28*, 191–193.

Wonderlic, E. F. (1983). *Wonderlic Personnel Test Manual*. Northfield, IL: E. F. Wonderlic & Associates.

# DEVELOPMENTAL PATHS OF ADJUSTMENT

# 20

# Studying the Etiology of Crime and Violence Among Persons With Major Mental Disorders: Challenges in the Definition and the Measurement of Interactions

Sheilagh Hodgins
University of Montréal

Most of the research on crime and mental disorder has been limited to studies of the prediction of "dangerousness." This is not surprising because mental health professionals are regularly required by law to assess the risk that a patient presents of behaving violently or of committing other illegal acts. Inaccurate predictions can lead to horrific human tragedies or unwarranted confinement for the patient. Accurate predictions, on the other hand, can lead to placing patients in community treatment programs that effectively prevent crime and violence. To date, the accuracy of these predictions has not been good (Borum, 1996). In order to increase the accuracy of these predictions, it is essential that they be based on results of empirical research. However, on what type of research should these procedures for clinical prediction be based? Presently, the literature on the prediction of "dangerousness" among the mentally disordered consists of studies of variables, easily ratable in a clinical situation, that were entered into a linear regression model and found to account for a "significant proportion of the variance." These types of studies are inadequate, both conceptually and methodologically, and consequently their results may be misleading. In order to improve the accuracy of these clinical predictions of dangerousness, their scientific basis must be made sound. This requires abandoning variable-oriented investigations that presume the same predictors apply in the same way to all patients (Brown, Harris, & Lemyre, 1991) and developing prediction procedures based on a more general understanding of the development of individuals who as adults suffer from major mental disorders and commit crimes.

It is not only criminal and violent behavior on the part of persons suffering from major mental disorders that is difficult to predict. As noted by Magnusson and Stattin (1998):

> Given the complex, often non-linear interplay of mental, biological and behavioral subsystems within the individual and an environment, operating in a probabilistic, sometimes very uncertain and unpredictable way, it is unrealistic to hope for accurate prediction of individual functioning across environmental contexts of differing character or over the life span. . . . The final criterion for success in our scientific endeavours is not how well we can predict individual behaviour across situations of different character or across the life course, but how well we succeed in explaining and understanding the processes underlying individual functioning and development. (Magnusson & Stattin, 1998, p. 687)

The scientific goal as noted by these authors is to identify the factors operating in human functioning and ontogeny, and to identify and understand the mechanisms. Thus, although the prediction of behavior is necessary in clinical situations in order to prevent violent and other criminal behavior, prediction is an inappropriate scientific goal. Rather, the procedures used to make predictions of behavior in clinical situations will increase in accuracy only if they are based on a more fundamental understanding of the patients whose behavior is in question.

A more fundamental understanding of such persons can be achieved by adopting the perspective of holistic interactionism. This perspective rests on four basic propositions:

1. The individual functions and develops as a total, integrated organism.
2. Individual functioning within existing mental, biological, and behavioral structures, as well as developmental change, can best be described as complex, dynamic processes.
3. Individual functioning and development are guided by processes of ongoing, reciprocal interaction among mental, behavioral, and biological aspects of individual functioning and social, cultural, and physical aspects of the environment.
4. The environment functions and changes as an ongoing process of reciprocal interaction among social, economic, and cultural factors (Magnusson & Stattin, 1998).

This approach implies identifying homogenous subtypes of individuals among the population of interest and identifying how the types interact differently with both their immediate and larger social environments. This approach has implications for the theoretical framework that is used to conceptualize a problem and to interpret the relevant available findings, for the research strategy adopted to advance knowledge of the problem, and for the statistical models used to analyse the data (Magnusson, 1998). Both at a theoretical and a practical level this approach is of interest in attempting to understand criminal and violent behavior of persons who suffer from major mental disorders.[1] Although the advantages of this approach in general are numerous and well described elsewhere (see, e.g., Bergman & Magnusson, 1997; Magnusson & Bergman, 1998), the advantages of the approach in studying this particular problem remain to be demonstrated.

## PREVALENCE AND PATTERNS OF CRIMINALITY AMONG PERSONS WHO DEVELOP MAJOR MENTAL DISORDERS

There is now compelling evidence that individuals who develop major mental disorders in adulthood are at increased risk, compared with persons with no mental disorder, to commit crimes and acts of violence. Three lines of evidence support this conclusion:

1. Investigations of large birth cohorts that compare the criminality of subjects who develop a major mental disorder and subjects with no mental disorder.
2. Studies that compare the criminality of persons with major mental disorders who are discharged from a psychiatric ward to that of nondisordered subjects living in the same community.
3. Studies of the prevalence of major mental disorders among persons convicted of criminal offenses.

An investigation of an unselected birth cohort composed of all 15,117 persons born in Stockholm in 1953 and still living there in 1963 showed that subjects who developed major mental disorders were at significantly increased risk for criminality compared with nondisordered persons. Among the male subjects, 31.7% of those with no mental disorder and no retardation, compared with 50% of those who developed major disorders, were registered for a criminal offense by the age of 30. Among the female subjects, 5.8% of the nondisordered and 19% of those who developed major

---

[1]Throughout this chapter the terms "major mental disorders" and "mental illness" will be used interchangeably to refer to schizophrenia, schizoaffective disorder, bipolar disorder, major depression, delusional disorder, and atypical (nonalcohol or -drug induced) psychoses.

mental disorders were registered for a criminal offense by age 30. Both the men and the women who developed major disorders were found to be at even greater risk for violent crime than for nonviolent crime. The offenders with major mental disorders committed, on average, as many or more offenses than the nondisordered offenders. They committed all types of crimes (Hodgins, 1992; Hodgins & Janson, in press).

An examination of the ages at first conviction strongly suggests that the offenders with major mental disorders did not constitute a homogenous group. Among the men who developed a major mental disorder, it was found that 15.9% were first convicted before age 15, 15.9% between the ages of 15 and 18 years, 6.1% between the ages of 18 and 21 years, and 12.2% between the ages of 21 and 30. Among the women with major mental disorders, 5.1% were convicted before age 15, 2.5% between the ages of 15 and 18 years, 5.1% from ages 18 to 21, and 6.3% after age 21. These data suggest that there are two groups of offenders with major mental disorders: one group, the early starters, begins offending in childhood or adolescence before the symptoms of the mental disorder would be present, whereas the second group, the late starters, begins offending in adulthood when symptoms of the disorder are likely to be present. The early starters constitute a larger proportion of the male offenders and the late starters constitute a larger proportion of the female offenders. This observation may be of importance because among nondisordered persons, age at first crime identifies subgroups of offenders who differ as to the types and numbers of crimes they commit, the longevity of their criminal careers, and both early childhood and adolescent antecedents (Kratzer & Hodgins, 1999; Moffitt, 1993; 1994).

The results from this epidemiological study of criminality among persons who develop major mental disorders have been replicated in a much larger cohort composed of all the persons born in Denmark in 1944 through 1947. In 1990, when the subjects were between 43 and 46 years of age, the psychiatric and the police registers were screened to identify files of those who were still alive and living in Denmark. Because the police changed the way in which they recorded offenses in 1978, information collected before and after this date was treated separately. Again it was found that, compared with those who were never admitted to a psychiatric ward, proportionately more of the men and women who developed a major mental disorder had been convicted of at least one criminal offense. Although the proportions of subjects, both disordered and nondisordered, who were convicted for criminal offenses differed in the Danish and Swedish cohorts, the relative risk estimates that take account of the prevalence of criminality in the population are similar (see Table 20.1). As in the Swedish Metropolitan study, the offenders with major mental disorders were convicted, on average, for as many or more offenses than the nondisordered subjects. Also,

TABLE 20.1
Relative Risk Extimates for Crime and Violence

|  | Swedish Metropolitan Project $n = 14,401$ | | Danish Project $n = 324,401$ | | | |
|  | Men | Women | Men | | Women | |
|  | to age 30 | to aage 30 | to agae 30–33 | to age 43–46 | to age 30–33 | to aage 43–46 |
|---|---|---|---|---|---|---|
| *Any Crime* | | | | | | |
| No hospitalization | 1 | 1 | 1 | 1 | 1 | 1 |
| Major mental disorder | 2.15 (1.39–3.33) | 3.78 (2.13–6.69) | 2.29 (2.13–2.49) | 3.74 (3.49–3.99) | 3.37 (2.89–3.93) | 4.50 (4.06–4.99) |
| *Violent Crime* | | | | | | |
| No hospitalization | 1 | 1 | 1 | 1 | 1 | 1 |
| Major mental disorder | 4.74 (2.84–7.91) | 11.18 (4.30–29.13) | 2.42 (2.06–2.84) | 4.48 (3.91–5.14) | 5.86 (3.57–9.62) | 8.66 (6.04–12.43) |

*Note.* Numbers in parentheses are the 95% confidence intervals.

as had been found in the Swedish Metropolitan study, the offenders with major mental disorders were convicted of all types of crimes, but the differences between the men and women with and without major mental disorders was greater for violent crimes than for nonviolent crimes. Surprisingly, 34% of the men and 67% of the women with major mental disorders committed their first offence after age 30. These findings suggest that the estimates of criminality obtained in the Swedish cohort are low (Hodgins, Mednick, Brennan, Schulsinger, & Engberg, 1996).

In interpreting the findings from the birth cohort studies, it is important to remember that subjects who had been admitted to a psychiatric ward were assigned to a diagnostic group, regardless of when they developed the disorder. Criminal convictions were then examined. By applying this procedure, we examined criminal convictions of individuals who have been hospitalized for a major mental disorder before the end of the data collection period, without any reference to the time of onset of the major mental disorder. We examined the co-occurrence of a major mental disorder and criminality in the same person. Underlying this approach is a presumption that persons who eventually develop a major mental disorder are different in some way, from conception through adulthood, from persons who do not develop these disorders.

Since the mid-1960s, studies have been conducted in a number of different Western industrialized countries comparing the criminality of persons with major mental disorders who were discharged from psychiatric wards and the criminality of persons with no mental disorder. Despite methodological limitations (Hodgins, 1993), these studies have consistently found that more of the former patients than the nondisordered persons living in the same community were convicted of offenses. Again, the greatest difference between the subjects with major mental disorders and those without related to the proportions of subjects in each group who committed violent crimes.

Given these results it is not surprising that investigations of representative samples of convicted offenders in these countries have documented prevalence rates of the major mental disorders that far exceed those for age and gender matched samples of the general population (Hodgins & Côté, 1990; 1995). Further, six studies of unbiased samples of homicide offenders have documented rates for the major mental disorders varying from 20% to 53% (Hodgins, 1994).

## Conclusion

The results of investigations of birth cohorts are consistent with findings from recent follow-up studies of persons with major mental disorders living in the community, and North American studies of mental disorder among incarcerated offenders, in demonstrating that greater proportions of individuals who develop major mental disorders than those who do not are convicted of at least one criminal offense. Although greater proportions of men than women were found to have committed crimes, the presence of a major mental disorder was associated with a greater increase in the risk of criminality among women than among men and a greater risk for violent than for nonviolent crime. On average, the offenders with major mental disorders committed as many or more offenses than did the nondisordered offenders.

Two of these findings have implications for the designs of future studies. First, the largest of the birth cohort studies indicated that many persons with major mental disorders committed their first crime after the age of 30. Consequently, future investigations need to follow subjects well into their 40s in order to make accurate estimates of the prevalence of criminality in this population. Second, the persons who developed major mental disorders in adulthood and who committed crimes did not constitute a homogenous group. As among offenders without major mental disorders, the age at first offence distinguished one group that began offending in childhood or early adolescence before the symptoms of the mental disorder would have been apparent, and a second group who began offending only in adulthood, at about the time the symptoms of the disorder would have manifested.

## EXPLANATIONS OF CRIMINALITY AMONG PERSONS WITH MAJOR MENTAL DISORDERS

### Contextual Factors

No doubt many factors contribute to the criminality of persons with major mental disorders. Some of these factors relate to the context or environment in which mentally disordered persons live, whereas others relate to their behaviors. Consider first the social context.

The proportion of either antisocial or aggressive behaviors, or both, that leads to arrest and prosecution varies as a function of the intensity and quality of policing, the ease with which the police can have a mentally ill suspect admitted to hospital (and thereby divert him or her from the criminal justice system), and the severity of the offense. The importance of this factor in explaining the crime rate among the mentally ill varies, no doubt, from one jurisdiction to another and from one time period to another.

A second characteristic of the social context in which mentally ill persons find themselves and that contributes to illegal behaviors is the type and intensity of treatment services, and particularly of outpatient treatment services provided to them. Since the policy of deinstitutionalization has been implemented in the mental health field, many persons with major mental disorders live in the community and receive little or no treatment. Studies conducted in the United States document that as soon as this policy was implemented rates of criminality among persons with major mental disorders began to rise. During this period, laws and regulations concerning involuntary hospitalization were changed, restricting the circumstances in which patients could be held against their will and limiting the length of time that they could be detained. As well, patients' rights to refuse treatment were strengthened (for further discussion, see Hodgins & Lalonde, 1999).

The policy of deinstitutionalizing mental health care, limiting involuntary hospitalization, and increasing patients' rights to refuse treatment was implemented somewhat later in Sweden than elsewhere, but it would have had a direct effect on the subjects in the Metropolitan cohort who developed major mental disorders (Ågren, personal communication, 1996; Munk-Jørgensen, Lehtinen, Helgason, Dalgard, & Westrin, 1995). The few studies of criminality of subjects with major mental disorders conducted at the same time as the Metropolitan study indicated increased criminality and violence among subjects with major mental disorders compared with the nondisordered subjects. For example, a follow-up study of 644 patients with schizophrenia, discharged from hospitals in Stockholm in 1971 and followed for 14 years, found increased rates of nonviolent and violent criminality among the female schizophrenics compared with the general female population, and increased rates of violent crime among the male schizophrenics compared with the general male population (Lindqvist & Allebeck, 1990). An investigation of all homicides in Northern Sweden from 1970 to 1981 found that 53% of the offenders suffered from a major mental disorder (Lindqvist, 1986).

The hypothesis that inadequate or inappropriate treatment contributes to criminality among persons with major mental disorders is further supported by findings showing that specialized forensic community programs succeed in keeping crime and violence to a minimum even among high-risk patients (Heilbrun & Peters, in press; Hodgins, Lapalme, & Toupin, in press; Müller-Isberner, 1996; Wiederanders, 1992; Wilson, Tien, & Eaves, 1995). Since the policy of deinstitutionalization has been implemented, few mentally ill persons receive such treatment.

**Individual Adult Characteristics**

Although the criminality of persons with major mental disorders is partially explained by characteristics of the environment in which they live, it is also explained by patterns of behavior that are more common among them than among persons who do not suffer from these disorders. One study, and much clinical lore, has suggested that the mentally ill who commit crimes may be more easily detected by police and convicted than are nondisordered persons simply because they often commit a crime in front of a witness and either stay at the scene of the crime until the police arrive or confess to the police, or both (Robertson, 1988). However, two U.S. investigations found that the mentally ill were not more likely than other offenders to be officially accused of crimes and prosecuted (Link, Andrews, & Cullen, 1992; Steadman & Felson, 1984).

A second individual factor related to the criminality of the mentally ill is alcohol and drug abuse. A large number of investigations demonstrate that substance-use disorders increase the risk of criminality and violence among subjects with major mental disorders just as they do among subjects without these disorders (Hodgins & Janson, in press). This point is well illustrated by a study conducted in Finland of 1,423 homicide offenders. Schizophrenia, without a secondary diagnosis of an alcohol-use disorder, was found to have increased the risk of homicide 6.4 times among men and 5.3 times among women. Schizophrenia plus alcoholism increased the risk of homicide to 16.6 times among men, and 84.8 times among women (Eronen, Tiihonen, & Hakola, 1996).

However, most investigations indicate that only about half of the offenders with major mental disorders have a comorbid alcohol- or drug-use disorder. In the Metropolitan cohort, 51.2% of the male offenders with a major mental disorder (not of the men with a major mental disorder), and 60% of the female offenders with a major mental disorder (not of the female subjects with a major mental disorder), had secondary diagnoses of either alcohol-use or drug-use disorders, or both.

In recent years, a number of studies conducted in different countries have documented higher rates of alcohol- and drug-use disorders among persons with major mental disorders than among persons in the same community without these disorders (see for example, Helzer & Przybeck, 1988). In the Swedish Metropolitan cohort, 32.9% of the men and 10% of the women with major disorders were diagnosed with either alcohol-use or drug use disorders, or both. The prevalence is very high given that these were file diagnoses made during a period when little or no attention was paid by clinicians to co-occurring disorders.

Not only are persons with major mental disorders at greater risk than persons without these disorders to develop alcohol- and drug-use disorders in adulthood, our findings indicate that they are at increased risk during childhood as well. In the Metropolitan cohort, among the males who developed a major mental disorder, 22% had been identified for substance abuse as children, compared with 7.1% of the nondisordered men. Similarly, among the mentally ill females 8.9% had been identified in childhood for substance abuse, compared with 2% of the nondisordered women. Moreover, the risk of illegal behavior among the subjects who developed major mental disorders in adulthood was found to be increased to a greater extent by substance abuse in childhood rather than in adulthood. The presence of substance abuse in childhood among the men who developed major mental disorders increased the risk of crime 10.8 times (95% confidence interval 3.12–37.25) and increased the risk of violent crime 23.1 times (95% confidence interval 8.90–59.80). By contrast, substance abuse in adulthood increased the risk of crime 6.2 times (95% confidence interval 2.60–14.6) and the risk of violent crime 8.6 times (95% confidence interval 3.93–18.97) (Hodgins, 1993; Hodgins & Janson, in press).

Substance abuse in childhood may be only one feature of a more general pattern of antisocial behavior. It has been shown, for example, that children who display a stable pattern of antisocial behavior are exposed earlier than other children to alcohol and drugs (Robins & McEvoy, 1990). Interestingly, persons who develop major mental disorders in adulthood are more likely than those who do not to present a stable pattern of antisocial behavior in childhood. The diagnosis of antisocial personality disorder (ASPD) requires evidence of consistent antisocial behavior before and after the age of 15. Several clinical studies of persons with schizophrenia have documented rates of ASPD, among both men and women, that far exceed the 3.9% to 4.9% documented in the general population. For example, in a sample of 30 male and 30 female schizophrenics treated in outpatient clinics of general hospitals, it was found that the prevalence of ASPD was 23% among the men and 16.7% among the women (Léveillée, 1994). Among persons suffering from schizophrenia who are accused or convicted of crimes, the prevalence of ASPD is estimated to be between 37% and 62% (Hodgins, Toupin, & Côté, 1996) and similar estimates have been documented for subjects with major affective disorders (Hodgins, Lapalme, & Toupin, in press).

This evidence strongly suggests that the proportion of persons who show stable patterns of antisocial behavior across their lifetime is greater among the mentally ill than the nonmentally ill. This conclusion is consistent with results of studies of the development of schizophrenia that have consistently identified a subgroup who display aggressive and antisocial behavior as children (see for example, Cannon, Mednick, & Parnas, 1990; Walker, Neumann, Baum, Davis, DiForio, & Bergman, 1996). Further, a similar subgroup has been identified among those who develop major affective disorders (Carlson & Weintraub, 1993; Harrington, Rutter, & Fombonne, 1996).

## Conclusion

Both contextual factors and individual factors influence criminality and violence by persons who develop major mental disorders. The principal contextual factors include police and judicial policies and practices, the availability of appropriate, effective, long-term community treatment services, and laws governing involuntary hospitalization and rights to refuse treatment. The individual factors include the tendency of the mentally ill to stay at the scene of a crime or to confess, alcohol and drug use, and a stable pattern of antisocial behavior across the lifespan. We have hypothesized that both the contextual and individual factors differentially characterize two subgroups of persons who will develop major mental disorders in adulthood and commit crimes (Hodgins, Côté, & Toupin, 1998). The early starters, who display a stable pattern of antisocial behavior from childhood through adulthood, live in a subculture in which learning to avoid arrest and prosecution are high priority. This would not be true of the late starters, those who begin offending in adulthood, who would have no experience with police and the courts. The early starters generally refuse treatment, and benefit from care—either in the community or in hospital or prison— only if it is ordered by the court. The refusal to take medication leads to repeated episodes of acute psychosis. The late starters, by contrast, are more likely to comply with treatment. However, in most places specialized care for persons with these disorders who are at risk for illegal behavior is not available. Not only does the significance of the contextual factors vary for each subgroup, but also the meanings of the individual characteristics. For example, the early starters would be experienced at fleeing the scene of a crime whereas the late starters would be more apt not to flee. The early starters would have used alcohol and drugs from a young age as part of their antisocial lifestyle. By contrast, the late starters are less likely to abuse drugs, and if they abuse alcohol this habit develops at a later age. Intoxication, as opposed to abuse, may be more important in the offending of the late starters than the early starters and may be associated with an increase in psychotic symptomatology.

## BEGINNING TO INVESTIGATE THE DEVELOPMENT OF EARLY- AND LATE-START OFFENDERS WITH MAJOR MENTAL DISORDERS

As has been found among nondisordered offenders (Kratzer & Hodgins, 1999; in press; Moffitt, 1994), among subjects who developed major mental disorders the prevalence of early starters is greater among the men than among the women. Further, as has also been documented among nondisordered offenders, the early starters commit more crimes than do the late starters, and are distinguished primarily by the number of nonviolent crimes that they commit. Comparisons of mentally ill and nondisordered early-start offenders revealed that the mentally ill early starters were more often convicted of criminal offenses than were the nondisordered early starters. Comparisons of mentally ill and non-disordered late-start offenders revealed that greater proportions of male and female mentally ill late starters than nondisordered late starters were convicted of violent offenses.

In an effort to begin to understand the developmental trajectories of mentally ill offenders, we examined a number of childhood factors. Because of the lack of research on childhood factors associated with offending among the mentally ill, we turned to reports from longitudinal studies that identified childhood characteristics that distinguish adult offenders from nonoffenders. Most of these investigations focused on the childhood characteristics of nondisordered men. Based on this literature review, we identified 11 childhood factors previously associated with adult offending. From our data, we constructed 11 indices of childhood problems. Each index was a composite variable composed of many variables. A total score was calculated for each index indicating the number and severity of the problems. The 11 indices are: socioeconomic status of the family of origin, pregnancy complications, birth complications, birth weight, family problems identified by the child social welfare agency, individual problems of the child other than conduct problems identified by the child social welfare agency, conduct problems identified in the community by age 12, intelligence test scores obtained at age 13, marks obtained in grades 6 and 9, behavior rated by teachers in grades 6 and 9, and conduct problems in the community from ages 13 to 18. (Details of the construction of these indices are provided in Kratzer & Hodgins, 1999.)

These exploratory analyses were limited to men. Among the nondisordered men the indices distinguish between the early- and late-start offenders. The early-start offenders compared with the late-start offenders, came from families of lower socioeconomic status, they had more individual problems other than conduct problems, they obtained lower scores on an intelligence test at age 13, lower marks in grades 6 and 9, ratings of problematic behavior at school, and were identified for conduct problems in the community from ages 13 to 18. Among the men who developed major mental disorders and offended, none of the comparisons between the early and late starters are statistically significant. However, the average scores obtained by the early starters are all indicative of more severe problems than those obtained by the late starters. The average total score obtained by the early starters is much higher, and statistically significantly different, from that obtained by the late starters. In other words, among a group of males who all developed major mental disorders in adulthood and committed crimes, those who began offending earlier had more varied and more severe childhood problems. Further, the mentally ill early starters obtained a much higher average total score of childhood problems than did the nondisordered early starters.

When the percentages of offenders were plotted against the total scores on the indices of childhood problems, among the males, the distribution was bimodal. One group of offenders had high scores and one group had low scores. The high scorers were those who began their criminal careers before age 18, whereas those with few childhood problems had committed their first crimes as adults. Among the women, most offenders had low scores on the indices of childhood problems (Hodgins, Côté, & Toupin, 1998).

In conclusion, the person approach appears well suited to the task at hand. It has allowed us to conceptualize and organize the available findings about the development of the ciminality of persons who develop major mental disorders into testable hypotheses. It provides a framework for the integration of both contextual and individual characteristics of the subjects and the interactions of these factors over the lifespan. Finally, this approach encouraged us to investigate the subgroups among the offenders with major mental disorders. It is important to also note that precisely because this approach focuses on individuals, it is likely to produce findings that will be useful for intervention. However, as stated at the beginning of this chapter, a person-oriented approach and a holistic perspective imply not only a framework for interpreting available findings and developing hypotheses, but also a specific methodology for testing these hypotheses.

## OBSTACLES TO APPLYING THE PERSON APPROACH IN ORDER TO UNCOVER THE ETIOLOGY OF CRIMINALITY AMONG PERSONS WHO DEVELOP MAJOR MENTAL DISORDERS

The subsequent sections of this chapter discuss the obstacles encountered, both at the theoretical and the practical levels, in attempting to apply this approach to understanding why some mentally ill persons repetitively commit numerous serious crimes whereas others who suffer from the same disorders harm no one. Some of the obstacles discussed are common to many areas of study, and others are particular to the study of persons who develop major mental disorders and to our data set.

### Theoretical Framework

In applying this theoretical framework to the study of crime and violence among persons with major mental disorders, two conceptual issues need to be addressed. The first is how to separate antecedents from consequences. For example, our own findings as well as those from previous studies indicate that intelligence, academic performance, and conduct problems may be antecedents of later delinquency that in turn precedes adult criminality. But hereditary factors, perinatal factors, and parental practices, among others, may well be antecedents of intelligence, academic performance, and conduct problems. Depending on the stage of development when data are first collected, an antecedent may appear to be a consequence.

The second conceptual issue relates to this fact: Individuals who will develop a major mental disorder in adulthood cannot be accurately identified at conception or in early childhood. Consequently, it is difficult, if not impossible, to document their development and—as we want to do—to distinguish the developmental trajectories of those who will either behave violently or commit crimes, or both, as they get older. Although the evidence is clear that each major mental disorder is associated with a particular genetic vulnerability, the specific combinations of genes associated with each disorder remain unknown, as do the mechanisms or processes by which these genes increase the risk of developing a mental disorder. Presently, there are two rather unsatisfactory solutions to this problem. The first is to conduct a longitudinal study, wait until subjects have passed through the period of risk for a major mental disorder (age 45), and then examine the childhood data to identify the factors that distinguish those who developed the disorder. Not only is this strategy very expensive, it takes more years than most researchers have. In addition, it is quite inadequate for it fails to identify the individuals who do not develop a major mental disorder even though they carry the genetic vulnerability for the disorder. The second option is to identify fetuses or children that are at risk for a major mental disorder. Presently, depending on the disorder in question, this can be done only with relative inaccuracy for a subgroup of children by using family history of the disorder. It will be a long time before this problem is resolved. In the mean time, the first set of factors in the developmental chain, those that distinguish the subjects of interest, cannot be measured. Further, because we cannot identify the fetuses or children who have inherited a vulnerability for a major mental disorder, we cannot study how they interact with their environments. One possibility is that the genes associated with a major mental disorder alter the individual's biological, cognitive, or emotional sensitivity to specific biological, psychological, or social events. Consequently, an event may have great importance to the development of a small minority of subjects, and little or no importance to the development of the large majority of subjects. Given that we cannot identify individuals who have inherited the vulnerability for a specific disorder, it is presently very difficult, if not impossible, to identify such events.

## Sampling Problems

**A Cohort Effect?**  Even large birth cohorts such as the Metropolitan cohort are samples in time and space and thereby biased. The possibility that the increased prevalence of criminality among the men and women who developed major mental disorders is a cohort effect cannot be presently ruled out. It may be that the increased risk of criminality identified among the mentally ill is limited to subjects born in the late 1940s and early 1950s. There may be both individual and contextual characteristics of these birth cohorts that explain the increased prevalence of criminality among those who developed major mental disorders. Individuals born in the late 1940s and early 1950s may have experienced certain specific pregnancy and birth complications more often than persons born prior or subsequent to this period. For example, certain behaviors of their mothers that were more common then than in preceding or subsequent generations—specifically smoking and drinking—have both been found to be associated with individual characteristics such as conduct disorder, impulsivity, concentration problems, and attention difficulties that are in turn associated with criminality (see for example, Fergusson, Grekin, & Horwood, 1998; Hunt, Streissguth, Kerr, & Olson, 1995; Lagerström, Bremme, Eneroth, & Magnusson, 1990; Milberger, Biederman, Faraone, Chen, & Jones, 1996). The subjects in these cohorts may have developed certain problems that increased their risk for illegal behavior, not only because of their mothers' behavior during their pregnancies but also because of obstetrical practices current at the time they were born. For example, men whose mothers were given phenobarbital while they were in utero, a practice at the time, have been found to have lower verbal intelligence than the norm. The effect of the phenobarbital on adult verbal intelligence scores was found to be increased among men whose mothers had low socioeconomic status and who did not want to be pregnant (Reinisch, Sanders, Mortensen, & Rubin, 1995). Lower than average verbal intelligence has been associated with early-onset antisocial behavior (Moffitt, 1990).

Subjects born in the mid-1940s and early 1950s may be distinctive not only because of the factors that affected their development in the perinatal period, but also because of those that affected them during early childhood. They may have been exposed, more than previous generations, to certain environmental pollutants that damage the central nervous system in such a way as to limit self-control. For example, a cumulation of lead in the bones of young boys has been found to be associated with aggressive behavior and delinquency (Needleman, Riess, Tobin, Biesecker, & Greenhouse, 1996). Subjects in the Metropolitan study and in the other investigations that documented an increased risk of criminality and violent behavior among the mentally ill were the first generation to grow up with automobiles. Until recent environmental controls were made mandatory, cars, trucks, and buses that, during the early years of the subjects' lives became common in urban centers, emitted fumes full of lead. Such perinatal factors and environmental pollutants may have increased the prevalence of antisocial behavior in these cohorts generally. This proposition is consistent with findings from the Epidemiological Catchment Area (ECA) study in the United

States that found an increase in antisocial behavior during this century, and it may be the basis for the increase in crime rates in most countries during the same period (Robins, Tipp, & Przybeck, 1991). Consequently, it may be that as the prevalence of persistent antisocial behavior increased generally, so did the proportion of mentally ill persons who were also antisocial.

However, it could also be that such factors differentially affected individuals at genetic risk for a major mental disorder. Either way, the individual characteristics of some proportion of subjects with major mental disorders in these cohorts increased their risk of antisocial and violent behavior. In a context where mental health care was largely voluntary and limited to antipsychotic medications and where alcohol and drugs were readily accessible, they committed crimes. If the factors—mothers' behavior during pregnancy, obstetrical practices, environmental pollutants—that could lead to the development of the distinctive individual characteristics that are associated with their criminal behavior, or the contextual factors—inadequate and inappropriate treatment—have changed or are changed, the risk of criminality among persons with major mental disorders may diminish or even disappear. This speculative hypothesis applies most clearly to those we have called early starters. By contrast, the context—deinstitutionalization of services, increased patients' rights to refuse treatment, strictly limited involuntary care—and the consequences of the context—substance use and psychotic symptoms—may well be sufficient to explain the criminality of the late starters.

**Validity of Subject Groupings.**   The Metropolitan study is a very impressive set of data on a birth cohort of 15,117 subjects that includes information from pregnancy to age 30 (Hodgins & Janson, in press). However, although the methodological rigor, the size of the cohort, and the broad range of prospectively collected objective data attest to the excellence of the project, it may be insufficient for studying the criminality of persons who develop major mental disorders. The results of the cohort study in Denmark (Hodgins, Mednick, Brennan, et al., 1996) demonstrated that significant numbers of persons who developed major mental disorders committed their first crime after age 30. Consequently, in the Metropolitan Project such subjects were classified as nonoffenders, some in the major mental disorder group and some in the nondisordered group. Attempts to identify characteristics that distinguish the subgroups of offenders with major mental disorders are consequently based on inaccurate classification of the subjects. This problem is made worse by the small numbers of subjects in each group.

**Size of the Subgroups.**   The second reason why our data set, the Metropolitan Project, may not be ideal for the task at hand is that the cohort is not large enough. The data strongly suggest that there are subgroups among the offenders with major mental disorders that have different patterns of criminality with distinct etiologies. However, even though we began with a birth cohort of 15,117 persons, there were only 82 men and 79 women who developed a major mental disorder, of whom 41 men and 15 women committed crimes. If the offenders are divided into subgroups based on age at first crime, the numbers in each group are extremely small. The effect of missing data from early childhood becomes a major problem because of the small number of subjects. This problem is of course compounded by the fact that data collection ended at age 30. The period of risk for the major mental disorders extends to age 45 and consequently, had data collection continued for 15 more years, the group of subjects with major mental disorders would have been larger and the group classification more accurate.

## Measures

*The Measures Are as Old as the Subjects!* The measures of perinatal and early childhood factors are more than 40 years old. Consequently, they do not include some factors that presently are known to be important and the factors were not measured with the same precision and rigor as could be done today.

*Macrosociological Variables.* The meanings of such variables as socioeconomic status are poorly understood. However, we have found that even in Sweden (which at the time our subjects were young had a much lower range of incomes than other countries in the Western industrialized world and an extensive social welfare system—for further discussion, see Hodgins & Janson, in press) this variable appears to be important for distinguishing individuals with early-onset antisocial behavior that persists across the life span and is strongly related to perinatal factors. This variable characterizing the subjects' parents is obviously indexing other factors more directly related to their stable antisocial behavior.

*Factors Plus Timing.* There is much evidence available now to suggest that it is necessary to measure not only the occurrence of events but also the time during development when they affect the subject. There is evidence suggesting that this may be even more important for subjects who have inherited a vulnerability for a major mental disorder than for others. The period of time during which a factor has an effect may be relatively short. For example, research on schizophrenia suggests that events occurring during the second trimester of pregnancy appear to significantly modify the structure of the developing brain, whereas the same event occurring during either the first or third trimester of pregnancy has no effect (see chapter 13, this volume). Similarly, it is hypothesized that stress experienced by children who are genetically vulnerable to depression at certain periods in early development modifies the hypothalamic-pituitary-adrenal axis and renders them more sensitive to negative events throughout the rest of their lives (Post, Weiss, & Leverich, 1994).

## Conclusion

The person approach and holistic perspective provide a theoretical framework that allows researchers to integrate current knowledge about the factors influencing criminality and violence among individuals who develop major mental disorders. Using this approach, the continual interaction of individual factors and contextual factors during development are hypothesized to determine illegal behavior. Further, the approach incites and encourages the search for subgroups of offenders, distinctive not only in their patterns of criminality but also in the patterns of individual and contextual factors over the life span that lead to the criminality. Although the person approach contributes to the elaboration of a rich hypothesis to explain criminality and violence among the mentally ill, its application requires the resolution of a number of problems relating to sampling and measurement. The person approach will permit detailed investigation of the hypothesis that the increased risk of criminality observed among persons born in the late 1940s and 1950s who developed major mental disorders is a cohort effect by identifying the specific patterns of factors that contribute to the development of the criminality. The person approach cannot, of course, alter the length of the follow-up period in our study nor the number of subjects in each subgroup. However, it is less limited by the use of small numbers of subjects, and although the approach cannot improve on data collected over 40 years ago, it does provide a framework for breaking down macrosociological variables into factors that are psychologically meaningful to the individual, and taking account, simultaneously, of the presence and timing of a variable. The next step is to do it! Then, and only then, will we contribute to advancing knowledge about the etiology of criminality and violent behavior among persons with major mental disorders, and in so doing, provide a sound scientific basis for clinical predictions of "dangerousness."

## REFERENCES

Bergman, L. R., & Magnusson, D. (1997). A person-oriented approach in research on developmental psychopathology. *Development and Psychopathology, 9,* 291–319.
Borum, R. (1996). Improving the clinical practice of violence risk assessment: Technology, guidelines, and training. *American Psychologist, 51,* 945–956.
Brown, G. W., Harris, T. O., & Lemyre, L. (1991). Problems and methods in longitudinal research: Stability and change. In D. Magnusson, L. R. Bergman, G. Rudinger, & B. Törestad (Eds.),

*Now you see it, now you don't—some considerations on multiple regression* (pp. 67–94). Cambridge, UK: Cambridge University Press.

Cannon, T. D., Mednick, S., & Parnas, J. (1990). Antecedents of predominantly negative and predominantly positive symptom schizophrenia in a high risk population. *Archives of General Psychiatry, 47,* 622–632.

Carlson, G. A., & Weintraub, S. (1993). Childhood behavior problems and bipolar disorder—relationship or coincidence? *Journal of Affective Disorders, 28,* 143–153.

Eronen, M., Tiihonen, J., & Hakola, P. (1996). Schizophrenia and homicidal behavior. *Schizophrenia Bulletin, 22,* 83–89.

Fergusson, D. M., Grekin, E. R., & Horwood, L. J. (1998). Maternal smoking during pregnancy and psychiatric adjustment in late adolescence. *Archives of General Psychiatry, 56,* 215–219.

Harrington, R., Rutter, M., & Fombonne, E. (1996). Developmental pathways in depression: Multiple meanings, antecedents, and endpoints. *Development and Psychopathology, 8,* 601–616.

Heilbrun, K., & Peters, L. (in press). The efficacy of community treatment programmes. In S. Hodgins & R. Müller-Isberner (Eds.), *Violence, crime and mentally disordered offenders: Concepts and methods for effective treatment and prevention.* London: Wiley.

Helzer, J. E., & Przybeck, T. R. (1988). The co-occurrence of alcoholism with other psychiatric disorders in the general population and its impact on treatment. *Journal of Studies on Alcohol, 49,* 219–224.

Hodgins, S. (1992). Mental disorder, intellectual deficiency and crime: Evidence from a birth cohort. *Archives of General Psychiatry, 49,* 476–483.

Hodgins, S. (1993). The criminality of mentally disordered persons. In S. Hodgins (Ed.), *Mental Disorder and Crime* (pp. 1–21). Newbury Park, CA: Sage.

Hodgins, S. (1994). Schizophrenia and violence: Are new mental health policies needed? *Forensic Psychiatry, 5,* 473–477.

Hodgins, S., & Côté, G. (1990). The prevalence of mental disorders among penitentiary inmates. *Canada's Mental Health, 38,* 1–5.

Hodgins, S., & Côté, G. (1995). Major mental disorder among Canadian penitentiary inmates. In L. Stewart, L. Stermac, & C. Webster (Eds.), *Clinical criminology: Toward effective correctional treatment* (pp. 6–20). Toronto: Ministry of the Solicitor General and Correctional Services of Canada.

Hodgins, S., Côté, G., & Toupin, J. (1998). Major mental disorders and crime: An etiological hypothesis. In D. Cooke, A. Forth, & R. D. Hare (Eds.), *Psychopathy: Theory, research and implications for society* (pp. 231–256). Dordrecht, Netherlands: Kluwer.

Hodgins, S., & Janson, C.-G. (in press). *Criminality and violence among the mentally disordered: The Stockholm Metropolitan Project.* Cambridge, UK: Cambridge University Press.

Hodgins, S., & Lalonde, N. (1999). Major mental disorders and crime: Changes over time? In P. Cohen, L. Robins, & C. Slomkowski (Eds.), *Where and when: Geographical and historial aspects of psychopathology* (pp. 57–83). Mahwah, NJ: Lawrence Erlbaum Associates.

Hodgins, S., Lapalme, M., & Toupin, J. (in press). Criminal activities and substance use of patients with major affective disorders and schizophrenia: A two year follow-up. *Journal of Affective Disorders.*

Hodgins, S., Mednick, S. A., Brennan, P., Schulsinger, F., & Engberg, M. (1996). Mental disorder and crime: Evidence from a Danish birth cohort. *Archives of General Psychiatry, 53,* 489–496.

Hodgins, S., Toupin, J., & Côté, G. (1996). Schizophrenia and antisocial personality disorder: A criminal combination. In L. B. Schlesinger (Ed.), *Explorations in criminal psychopathology: Clinical syndromes with forensic implication* (pp. 217–237). Springfield, IL: Thomas.

Hunt, E., Streissguth, A. P., Kerr, B., & Olson, H. C. (1995). Mothers' alcohol consumption during pregnancy: Effects on spatial-visual reasoning in 14-year-old children. *Psychological Science, 6,* 339–342.

Kratzer, L., & Hodgins, S. (1999). A typology of offenders: A test of Moffitt's Theory among males and females from childhood to age 30. *Criminal Behaviour and Mental Health, 9,* 57–73.

Kratzer, L., & Hodgins, S. (1997). Adult outcomes of child conduct problems: A cohort study. *Journal of Abnormal Child Psychology, 25,* 65–81.

Lagerström, M., Bremme, K., Eneroth, P., & Magnusson, D. (1990). Behavior at 10 and 13 years of age for children with low birth weight. *Perceptual and Motor Skills, 71,* 579–594.

Léveillée, S. (1994). *Évaluation multidimensionnelle du support social des sujets schizophrènes.* Unpublished doctoral dissertation, Université de Montréal.

Lindqvist, P. (1986). Criminal homicide in Northern Sweden 1970–1981: Alcohol intoxication, alcohol abuse and mental disease. *International Journal of Law and Psychiatry, 8,* 19–37.

Lindqvist, P., & Allebeck, P. (1990). Schizophrenia and crime: A longitudinal follow-up of 644 schizophrenics in Stockholm. *British Journal of Psychiatry, 157,* 345–350.

Link, B. G., Andrews, H., & Cullen, F. T. (1992). The violent and illegal behaviour of mental patients reconsidererd. *American Sociological Review, 57,* 275–292.

Magnusson, D. (1998). The logic and implications of a person approach. In R. B. Cairns, L. R. Bergman, & J. Kagan (Eds.), *Methods and models for studying the individual* (pp. 33–63). Thousand Oaks, CA: Sage.

Magnusson, D., & Stattin, H. (1998). Person-context interaction theories. In D. Damon & R. M. Lerner (Eds.), *Theoretical models of human development* (pp. 685–759) New York: Wiley.

Milberger, S., Biederman, J., Faraone, S. V., Chen, L., & Jones, J. (1996). Is maternal smoking during pregnancy a risk factor for attention deficit hyperactivity disorder in children? *American Journal of Psychiatry, 153,* 1138–1142.

Moffitt, T. E. (1990). The neuropsychology of delinquency: A critical review of theory and research. In N. Morris & M. Tonry (Eds.), *Crime and justice* (Vol. 12, pp. 99–169). Chicago: University of Chicago Press.

Moffitt, T. E. (1993). Adolescence-limited and life-course-persistent antisocial behavior: A developmental taxonomy. *Psychological Review, 100,* 674–701.

Moffitt, T. E. (1994). Natural histories of delinquency. In E. G. M. Weitkamp & H. J. Kerner (Eds.), *Cross-national longitudinal research on human development and criminal behavior* (pp. 3–61). Dordrecht, Netherlands: Kluwer.

Müller-Isberner, J. R. (1996). Forensic psychiatric aftercare following hospital order treatment. *International Journal of Law and Psychiatry, 19,* 81–86.

Munk-Jørgensen, P., Lehtinen, V., Helgason, T., Dalgard, O. S., & Westrin, C. G. (1995). Psychiatry in the five Nordic countries. *European Psychiatry, 10,* 197–206.

Needleman, H. L., Riess, J. A., Tobin, M. J., Biesecker, G. E., & Greenhouse, J. B. (1996). Bone lead levels and delinquent behavior. *Journal of American Medical Association, 275,* 363–369.

Post, R. M., Weiss, B. R. S., & Leverich, S. G. (1994). Recurrent affective disorder: Roots in developmental neurobiology and illness progression based on changes in gene expression. *Development and Psychopathology, 6,* 781–813.

Reinisch, J. M., Sanders, S. A., Mortensen, E. L., & Rubin, D. B., (1995). In utero exposure to phenobarbital and intelligence deficits in adult men. *Journal of American Medical Association, 274,* 1518–1525.

Robertson, G. (1988). Arrest patterns among mentally disordered offenders. *British Journal of Psychiatry, 153,* 313–316.

Robins, L. N., & McEvoy, L. (1990). Conduct problems as predictors of substance abuse. In L. N. Robins & M. Rutter (Eds.), *Straight and deviant pathways from childhood to adulthood* (pp. 182–204). Cambridge, UK: Cambridge University Press.

Robins, L. N., Tipp, J., & Przybeck, T. (1991). Psychiatric disorders in America: The epidemiologic catchment area study. In L. N. Robins & D. A. Regier (Eds.), *Antisocial personality* (pp. 258–290). New York: The Free Press.

Steadman, H. J., & Felson, R. B. (1984). Self-reports of violence—Ex-mental patients, ex-offenders, and the general population. *Criminology, 22,* 321–342.

Walker, E. F., Neumann, C. C., Baum, K., Davis, D. M., DiForio, D., & Bergman, A. (1996). The developmental pathways to schizophrenia: Potential moderating effects of stress. *Development and Psychopathology, 8,* 647–665.

Wiederanders, M. R. (1992). Recidivism of disordered offenders who were conditionally vs. unconditionally released. *Behavioral Sciences and the Law, 10,* 141–148.

Wilson, D., Tien, G., & Eaves, D. (1995). Increasing the community tenure of mentally disordered offenders: An assertive case management program. *International Journal of Law and Psychiatry, 18,* 61–69.

# 21

# Swedish Child and Adolescent Psychiatry and a Holistic Approach to the Study of Child Development

P.-A. Rydelius

Karolinska Institutet, Stockholm

## INTRODUCTION

In Sweden, child and adolescent psychiatry developed as a medical discipline from four different sources with a common interest in children's development, their social adjustment, and their mental health. These origins, in pediatrics, education, psychology, social work, and psychiatry may well explain why the embryo of a multidisciplinary view already existed on child development during the 1930s with the establishment of psychiatric teams. In these teams a teacher, a psychologist, a social worker, and a doctor (a pediatrician or a psychiatrist) worked together in evaluating children's psychopathology. In the course of treatment a multidisciplinary view was established. This was influenced by "curative education," the first paradigm of Swedish child and adolescent psychiatry.

Most probably this early multidisciplinary view was the result of Ellen Keys' books (Key, 1909) proclaiming the 20th century "the Century of the Child." In Sweden, her books resulted in a stimulating intellectual discussion on how to improve children's health and social adjustment. Major efforts on these matters during the first decades of this century were exemplified by the proposal of child psychiatry as a "new" medical discipline, a school reform, and a law on child social welfare passed by the Parliament in 1924. This Act forced all Swedish communities to institute a Child Welfare Committee whose main task was to develop programs supporting the social needs of children.

In 1915, Isak Jundell, professor in pediatrics at the Karolinska Institute in Stockholm, published his pamphlet "Broken Minds," in which he argued for better knowledge on matters relating to children's mental health. He wrote (Rydelius, 1993):

> Studies on children's mental characteristics show that mental disturbances in children are unreasonably common—indeed, very much commoner than people have believed. Phenomena that were interpreted as laziness, disobedience, impudence, mendacity, criminality or sexual aberrations in the child have been found in many cases, to be due to mental diseases of various kinds. . . . The main principle in the treatment provided for such cases concerns a kind of mental and physical education adapted with extreme care in each case to the children's organic diseases, abilities, intelligence, instincts, urges and feelings. This upbringing of children with mental and nervous diseases using a medical pedagogic teaching, however, can achieve substantial results only when the precise nature of the disease has been determined in each case. To determine exactly the nature of the disease is here, as in all medical treatment, the first and most important requirement. Consequently, we must offer medical students and physicians opportunities to study mental and nervous diseases in children (in special hospital institutions). For the school physician, knowledge of the child's psychopathology is undoubtedly as important as a knowledge of the child's spinal problems, anaemia and myopia. It is also clear that teachers in our higher and lower schools should develop insight, through use of the hospital cases, into the main features of the discipline of pediatric psychiatry. The increasing criminality among children and adolescents and its close connections with mental disease in the young indicates that lawyers also must have a knowledge of the child's mind in health and in disease. All groups in the community whose task is to bring up children in a sound and healthy manner thus are in need of knowledge in medical pedagogics and in pediatrics. The extent of their knowledge decides the fate of so many children. And on the fate of children depends their parents' happiness and the welfare of the community. (p. 396)

## THE PARADIGM OF CURATIVE EDUCATION—HOW TO UNDERSTAND AND TREAT PSYCHOPATHOLOGICAL BEHAVIOR IN CHILDREN

During the first decades of Swedish child and adolescent psychiatry, 1910 to 1930, the influences from pedagogy and psychology in Central Europe and Vienna were important contributors to the current opinions of those days. A strong influence from Häilpedagogie, originating in Austria and Switzerland, made curative education the first scientific paradigm of Swedish child and adolescent psychiatry, as shown by Jundell's translation of

Häilpedagogie into Swedish as "medical pedagogic teaching." The basic principles of curative education were to observe the child and then to provide him or her with the different social, medical, psychological, and educational support that the observations revealed were needed.

However, the origin of Swedish child and adolescent psychiatry in pediatrics, where longitudinal designs were used to follow the growth of children, also meant that longitudinal prospective designs were already of interest to the Swedish pioneers in child psychiatric research.

This is exemplified by the work of Alfhild Tamm and Alice Hellström, two female physicians from the period. They were both closely connected to pedagogy (Hellström was formally educated both as a teacher and as a physician) and interested in children's capacities to adjust well in school. In 1926, Tamm published an article describing her 13 years of experience as a school psychiatrist supporting children with reading and spelling difficulties, at that time called *congenital word-blindness*. She found that children with these difficulties often showed both psychiatric symptoms and deficits in their language and speech capacities. Working with them in language and speech training, she noticed that they improved their reading and spelling capacities while their psychiatric symptoms diminished. The article from 1926 is still pertinent in today's debate on dyslexia. Tamm's overall work resulted in the establishment of special school clinics for speech therapy in Stockholm in 1932, and school psychiatrist positions in Sweden in the 1940s. From the start, the school psychiatrists' main activities were to diagnose children with intellectual, cognitive, and behavioral problems and to help them adjust better during school.

In 1928, Hellström opened the Mellansjö School Home, an institution for treating and supporting psychopathic children. She also started and conducted the first Swedish longitudinal prospective child psychiatric study relating to delinquent behavior in children and youths. She successively described the admittance, stay, and adult adjustment of over 600 treated children between 1928 and 1969.

Although Hellström was not able to complete her study before she died, it was completed during the 1990s (Fried, 1995). The main question concerned later criminality and alcoholism. It was found that boys admitted to Mellansjö with a history of paternal psychiatric illness, criminality, or alcoholism, and a personal history of reading and spelling difficulties and theft, showed a 91% risk for later Temperance and Criminal Registers despite treatment. In a note from the 1980s, Hellström herself wrote about the long-term significance of prospective longitudinal research covering several decades. She wrote: "Although society has changed a lot since the 1920s it seems to me as if the children coming to Mellansjö in those days were in essential parts very similar to the children of today" (p. 32).

## THE PARADIGM BASED ON GENETICS
## AND RACIAL BIOLOGY

From the 1920s until today one may identify some important shifts of paradigms used in Swedish child and adolescent psychiatric research to understand deviant child development. These shifts constitute the building blocks
of today's multidisciplinary holistic view. However, during these shifts, the
longitudinal prospective design was not abandoned as it proved to be of
increasing interest and importance.

Curative education was replaced in the 1930s by current opinions from
genetics and racial biology. During this period, personality traits, intelligence, behavior, psychopathology, and the like were looked upon as human
variables mainly explained by genetics. This was also true when comparing
different races and nationalities. In many countries, the establishment of
these ideas and views resulted in the passage of legislation on eugenics by
governments and parliaments so that "bad genes" would not be transferred
to future generations. In Sweden, an Act on sterilization, abortion, and
castration was passed by the Parliament in 1933 and with some changes,
persisted until 1976. However, the results from research in human behavior
created new influences that replaced the paradigm of genetics and racial
biology.

Among these new studies there were four important child psychiatric
theses, all showing that a more comprehensive view on human development than that offered by genetics was essential in understanding child
development and delinquency.

In 1941, Sven Ahnsjö, who later held the chair in child and adolescent
psychiatry at the Karolinska Institute from 1958 to 1972, defended his thesis
"Delinquency in girls and its prognosis." His results indicated that a social-
psychiatric perspective was needed in research concerning child and adolescent psychiatry. These findings were further stressed by the results of
Otterström and Ramer when presenting their theses "Delinquency and children from bad homes" (Otterström, 1946) and "The prognosis of the mentally retarded children" (Ramer, 1946). The results formed the basis for
Jonsson's later (1967) hypothesis on a "social inheritance" to explain and
understand how deviant behavior is transferred from generation to generation. His hypothesis also generated ideas on the possible prevention of
delinquency. However, concerning the understanding of dyslexia, genetics
were found to be of importance as shown by Hallgren (1950) in his thesis
"Specific dyslexia—a clinical and genetic study."

These earlier findings are also of interest for today. Now, at the end of
the century, a new discussion seems to be emerging on the importance of
genetics for understanding normal and deviant human behavior. However,
there has recently been a discussion on the long-term well-being of, and

possible negative effects on, Swedish women sterilized during the eugenics period. This discussion has raised considerable concern on genetics in relation to human behavior. In 1997, the Swedish Government decided to undertake a thorough investigation on the scientific, political, and cultural background for the paradigm of eugenics and racial biology and its consequences (Committee Terms of Reference, 1997). One question it addressed was how the surviving victims from "compulsory sterilization" should be compensated. In my opinion, it is necessary to keep the period of eugenics and racial biology in mind when genetics are discussed in today's medicine and behavioral sciences.

## THE PARADIGM OF BRAIN DAMAGE AND BRAIN DYSFUNCTION

The results from the pioneering research previously commented on point to the need of a social-psychiatric view to understand deviant child development. Moreover, another thesis *Personlighetsutveckling på avvägar* (Deviant development of personality) presented by Nycander (1950) also indicated the need to include psychodynamics as a relevant hypothesis in this field. In spite of this, the dominant paradigm of the late 1940s and the 1950s was neuropsychiatry, including theories on brain damage and brain dysfunction.

The more important child psychiatric studies from this period were Annell's (1953) thesis "Pertussis in infancy as a cause of behavior disorders in children," Uddenborg's (1955) thesis "Diagnostic studies in prematures," and Müller and Nylander's study on "Sequele of primary aseptic meningo-encephalities—a clinical, sociomedical, electroencephalografic and psychological study" (Müller, Nylander, Larsson, Widén, & Frankenhaeuser, 1958). These studies were followed by studies on the long-term consequences of serious brain damage (Hjern & Nylander, 1964) and on acute head injuries in children (Rune, 1970).

The results from these studies indicated that theories on brain damage and dysfunction were of limited importance in understanding common child psychiatric symptoms and deviant child behavior.

## TODAY'S MULTIDISCIPLINARY VIEW

From the 1950s until today, comprehensive models using multidisciplinary views and longitudinal prospective designs for research have successively been established in Swedish child and adolescent psychiatry. The more important studies from this period are Nylander's (1960) thesis on children of alcoholic fathers, where he tested a hypothesis on emotional stress explaining nervous symptoms in children due to mental health problems among their fathers; Jonsson's (1967) thesis in which he put forward his hypothesis on a "social inheritance" explaining the development of delinquent behavior; Cederblad's (1968) thesis on Sudanese Arab children; Bohman's (1970) thesis on adopted children and their families; and Klackenberg's (1971) thesis "A prospective longitudinal study of children."

## THE LONGITUDINAL PROSPECTIVE PERSPECTIVE

The need for a more comprehensive holistic view to understand deviant child behavior was also influenced by some projects from the 1940s and 1950s done in the United States. Most important in these respects are Gesell and Ilg's (1946, 1956) studies on child development, together with Glueck and Glueck's (1950) study "Unrevealing juvenile delinquency." Macfarlane's (1938) monograph on studies in child guidance and her Berkeley study on the development of normal child behavior (Macfarlane, Allen, & Honzik, 1954) have had a major influence on Swedish child psychiatry. Some important Swedish studies have since used similar designs. Macfarlane's child-behavior checklist formed the basis for the description of 2000 patients at the Stockholm Child Guidance Clinics from 1953 to 1955, and the successive 10- and 20-year follow-ups presented by Curman and Nylander (1976; Nylander, 1979). Her behavior checklist was translated and adapted to Swedish conditions by Kälvesten and Jonsson (1964) and used in their description of 222 Stockholm boys that included an 18-year follow-up (Anderson, Jonsson, & Kälvesten, 1976). A modern version of this behavior check-list was developed by Cederblad & Höök (1991) for an investigation of mental health in children and teenagers living in Middle Sweden.

In 1981, Mednick and Baert described ongoing longitudinal prospective research. They found five studies relating to Swedish child and adolescent psychiatric research: Klackenberg's "Solna Study" (1981), Curman and Nylander's "Child Guidance Study" (1981), Rydelius' studies on drunkenness and alcohol abuse in children and youth (1981a, 1981b) and children of alcoholic fathers (1981c, 1981d). Although Klackenberg's study covers children's general development, the other studies employed a longitudinal, prospective approach to describe patients and children at special risk.

A review of the different paradigms that have guided research in Swedish child and adolescent psychiatry over the past 70 years, and the more important projects from the same period, identifies two important trends. One is the need for a multidisciplinary view that combines knowledge from different sciences in order to better understand normal and deviant behavior in childhood and during the transition into adulthood. The second is to improve and invent new longitudinal prospective techniques for studying and measuring individual change over time.

The close links between Swedish research interests in child and adolescent psychiatry and developmental psychology, best exemplified by the research of Magnusson (1988) and his group, go back to the shared interest in understanding both normal and deviant child behavior. This in turn can be traced to a common research area at the borderline between behavioral sciences and medical sciences represented by the interest in school children's well-being.

Influenced by the paradigm of *Häilpedagogie* (curative education), school psychiatry developed as a special branch of child and adolescent psychiatry in Sweden. The aim was to support children with intellectual handicaps, cognitive problems, reading, spelling, and arithmetic difficulties and eliminate behavioral and psychiatric problems in school. As a result of these activities, and in order to improve the overall mental health of the pupils, the Swedish school system was changed according to the principles of curative education during the 1930s and 1940s. From that time on, every child was required to pass a school-maturation test at the age of 6 years that was used to plan his or her school start. Children with mental retardation, cognitive deficits, dyslexia, late maturation and the like were identified through this procedure. Their school days and their need for special educational support were then planned on an individual basis in order to give every child the opportunity for maximum academic achievement. An important part of this planning was to avoid stress reactions in the child by minimizing any overwhelming demands. This Swedish school system existed until the end of the 1960s, and is referred to as the period with a "differentiated Swedish school."

During the 1950s, educators and psychologists debated the existing school system, arguing for an integrated school. They regarded the "differentiated school" as a threat to the future health and well-being of the children who might risk becoming stigmatized. The "medical" influence from school psychiatry on the school system was equally debated and a school reform introducing an "integrated school" was recommended.

In this discussion, the results from the longitudinal and prospective studies by Gesell and Ilg (1946, 1956) and Macfarlane (1954), as well as Olson's study (1949, 1959) on child development, were used as arguments by Husén and other distinguished Swedish educators and psychologists of that time (Elmgren, Husén, Sjöstrand, & Trankell, 1959) to favor a school reform. Willard C. Olson's (1959) book on child development, especially the chapter on the "Development of educational achievement" and the case of the growth of a slow-maturing boy who surprised investigators by his later achievements in the chapter of "The child as a whole," were of special interest in the debate. Because the results from longitudinal prospective approaches in research indicated great changes on group levels and within individuals, Husén and his colleagues argued for a school system without school maturation tests and differentiation. In the debate, Ramer (1965), the senior Swedish school psychiatrist at that time, argued for the differentiated school as being the best for children with handicaps and cognitive deficits and for children from unfavorable social conditions, whereas a "new" school, in his opinion, would only favor normally developing children from good homes. Viewed from today, it is hard to decide who was right. However, in summing up his chapter on "the child as a whole," Olson (1959) gives the following advice: "In practice it is always desirable to take a global or "holistic" view of the child in order to treat him with the maximum of wisdom" (p. 221).

It is fascinating to see how the same longitudinal prospective studies were influencing child and adolescent psychiatry and education psychology in different ways. Among child and adolescent psychiatrists the prospective research was useful in understanding deviant behavior and psychopathology, whereas the key interest for psychologists and educators was in learning to understand normal behavior and development.

From this standpoint, it is obvious that Magnusson's (1988) research and the results of his IDA project are very important. The IDA project indicates that the time has now come for a holistic approach to child development, regardless of whether key interest is on normality or abnormality. According to Magnusson's visionary ideas, this approach includes research in the border area of different sciences. Perhaps the first step in this process is to defeat the traditional faculty borders within universities that divide science into medical, behavioral, and other "subsciences."

## REFERENCES

Ahnsjö, S. (1941). Delinquency in girls and its prognosis. *Acta Paediatr Scand* (Suppl 3).

Anderson, M., Jonsson, G., & Kälvesten, A.-L. (1976). *Hur går det för 50-talets Stockholmspojkar?* [How will it go for the Stockholm boys from the 50s?] Stockholm: Handbokskommittén.

Annell, A.-L. (1953). *Pertussis in infancy as a cause of behavior disorders in children.* Stockholm: Almqvist & Wiksell.

Bohman, M. (1970). *Adopted children and their families.* Proprius, Stockholm.

Cederblad, M. (1968). A child psychiatry study on Sudanese arab children. *Acta Psychiatrica Scand* (Suppl 200).

Cederblad, M., & Höök, B., (1991). Östgötastudien. *Stressreaktioner och beteendestörningar hos barn på 80-talet i Östergötland.* Stockholm: Rädda Barnen.

Committee Terms of Reference. (1997). *Sterilisations.* Swedish Government, 1997:100.

Curman, H., & Nylander, I. (1976). A 10-year prospective follow-up study of 2,268 cases at the child guidance clinics in Stockholm. *Acta Paediatr Scand* (Suppl 260).

Curman, H., & Nylander, I. (1981). A 10-year prospective follow-up study of 2,268 cases at the child guidance clinics in Stockholm, Sweden. In S. A. Mednick & A. E. Baert (Eds.), *Prospective*

*Longitudinal Research. An empirical basis for the primary prevention of psychosocial disorders.* New York: Oxford University Press.

Elmgren, J., Husén, T., Sjöstrand, W., & Trankell, A. (1959). *Skolan och differentieringen.* Fyra professorer har ordet. Stockholm: Almqvist & Wiksell.

Fried, I. (1995). Mellansjö school-home. Psychopathic children admitted 1928–1940, their social adaptation over 30 years: a longitudinal prospective follow up. *Acta Paed* (Suppl 408).

Gesell, A., & Ilg, F. L. (1946). *The child from five to ten.* London: Harper.

Gesell, A., & Ilg, F. L. (1956). *Youth: The years from ten to sixteen.* London.

Glueck, S., & Glueck, E. (1950). *Unraveling juvenile delinquency.* New York: Commonwealth Fund and Cambridge, MA: Harvard University Press.

Hallgren, B. (1950). Specific Dyslexia ("Congenital Word-Blindness"). A clinical and genetic study. *Acta Psychiatrica et Neurologica* (Suppl 65).

Hjern, B., & Nylander, I. (1964). Acute head injuries in children. Traumatology, therapy and prognosis. *Acta Paediatrica Scandinavica* (Suppl. 152).

Jonsson, G. (1967). Delinquent boys, their parents and grandparents. *Acta Psychiatrica Scandinavica* (Suppl. 195).

Jundell, I. (1915). *Brustna Sinnen* [Broken Minds]. Stockholm: Barnens Dagblad.

Kälvesten, A.-L., & Jonsson, G. (1964). *222 Stockholmspojkar.* Stockholm: Almqvist & Wiksell.

Key, E. (1909). *Barnets Århundrade - studie.* Stockholm: Bonnier.

Klackenberg, G. (1971). *A prospective longitudinal study of children.* Stockholm: Lindeparkens Boktryckeri.

Klackenberg, G. (1981). The development of children in a Swedish urban community: a prospective longitudinal study. In S. A. Mednick & A. E. Baert (Eds.), *Prospective longitudinal research. An empirical basis for the primary prevention of psychosocial disorders.* New York: Oxford University Press.

Macfarlane, J. W. (1938). Studies in child guidance. I. Methodology of data collection and organization. *Monographs of the Society for Research in Child Development, 3,* vii–254.

Macfarlane, J. W., Allen, L., & Honzik, M. P. (1954). *A developmental study of the behavior problems of normal children between twenty-one months and fourteen years.* Berkeley, CA: University of California Press.

Magnusson, D. (1988). Individual development from an interactional perspective. A longitudinal study. In D. Magnusson (Ed.), *Paths through life* (Vol. 1). Hillsdale, NJ: Lawrence Erlbaum Associates.

Mednick, S. A., & Baert, A. E. (1981). *Prospective longitudinal research. An empirical basis for the primary prevention of psychosocial disorders.* New York: Oxford University Press.

Müller, R., Nylander, I., Larsson, L.-E., Widén, L., & Frankenhaeuser, M. (1958). Sequelae of primary aseptic meningo-encephalitis. A clinical, sociomedical, electroencephalographic and psychological study. *Acta Psychiatrica et Neurologica Scandinavica, 33* (Suppl. 126).

Nycander, G. (1950). *Personlighetsutveckling på avvägar.* Stockholm: Tidens förlag.

Nylander, I. (1960). Children of alcoholic fathers. *Acta Paediatrica Scandinavica 49* (Suppl. 121).

Nylander, I. (1979). A 20-year prospective follow-up study of 2,164 cases at the Child Guidance Clinics in Stockholm. *Acta Paediatrica Scandinavica* (Suppl, 276).

Olson, W. (1949). *Child development.* Boston: D. C. Heath.

Olson, W. (1959). *Child development.* Boston: D. C. Heath.

Otterström, E. (1946). Delinquency and children from bad homes. *Acta Paediatrica Scandinavica* (Suppl 5).

Ramer, T. (1946). *The prognosis of mentally retarded children.* Stockholm: AB Bennel & Co Boktryckeri

Ramer, T. (1965). Högstadiet ökar svårigheterna för de handikappade. *Läkartidningen, 62*(4).

Rune, V. (1970). Acute head injuries in children. An epidemological, childpsychiatric and encephalographic study on primary school children in Umeå. *Acta Paediatrica Scandinavica* (Suppl. 209).

Rydelius, P.-A. (1981a). Relapse of drunkenness. In S. A. Mednick & A. E. Baert (Eds.), *Prospective longitudinal research. An empirical basis for the primary prevention of psychosocial disorders.* New York: Oxford University Press.

Rydelius, P.-A. (1981b). The Umeå investigation: child psychiatric care of young alcoholics. In S. A. Mednick & A. E. Baert (Eds.), *Prospective longitudinal research. An empirical basis for the primary prevention of psychosocial disorders.* New York: Oxford University Press.

Rydelius, P.-A. (1981c). Children of alcoholic fathers: A longitudinal prospective study. In S. A. Mednick & A. E. Baert (Eds.), *Prospective longitudinal research. An empirical basis for the primary prevention of psychosocial disorders.* New York: Oxford University Press.

Rydelius, P.-A. (1981d). Children of alcoholic fathers. Their social adjustment and their health status over 20 years. *Acta Paediatrica Scandinavica* (Suppl. 286).

Rydelius, P.-A. (1993). Broken minds. *Nord J Psychiatry, 47*(6), 395–404.

Tamm, A. (1926). *Medfödd ordblindhet och därmed besläktade rubbningar hos barn.* Tidskrift för barnavård och ungdomsskydd. Årg 1; No. 4, pp. 113–118, Stockholm: Svenska fattig- och barnavårdsförbundet.

Uddenborg, G. (1955). Diagnostic studies in prematures. *Acta Psychiatrica et Neurologica Scandinavica* (Suppl. 104).

# 22

# When Do Preschool Conduct Problems Link to Future Social Adjustment Problems and When Do They Not?

Håkan Stattin
Kari Trost
University of Örebro, Sweden

## THE PERSON–ENVIRONMENT SYSTEM

A basic proposition underlying contemporary development models is that the individual develops and functions as part of a person–environment system. Behavior, one of the most widely used words in scientific psychology for describing the individual, is partially an environmental term.

Despite the agreement between developmental models in principle that an individual's development and ongoing functioning obtain their meaning from the context in which they take place, behavior is measured with only vague reference to context in much developmental research. The focus of interest in many empirical studies is on a single behavior, or on a single combination of behaviors, their interrelations, their stability, and their relations to particular criteria. The same behavioral focus applies in the case of common diagnostic classifications of mental disorders. These tend to be based on statements about specific behaviors or combinations of behaviors, and environmental descriptions play only a subordinate role.

There is an increased awareness that child behavior and developmental contexts function together in an organized and holistic manner (Magnusson, 1995, 1996), and that the patterning or configuration of individual and environmental characteristics constitutes a fundamental unit of analysis. In the area of developmental psychopathology, Cicchetti (1993) has articulated this view as follows:

I contend based on the developmental considerations raised in this paper that progress toward a process level understanding of psychopathology will require research designs and strategies that allow for a simultaneous assessment of multiple domains of variables within and outside each individual. In this regard, I believe that organizational theories will play an important role because they advocate the study of the "whole person" in context, thereby minimizing fragmentation of individual functioning. (p. 495)

Further, Emde (1994), while discussing diagnostic classifications in early childhood, has stated that "current diagnostic classification schemes for this age group were inadequate because of limited coverage and because such schemes did not pay sufficient attention to individuals in context" (p. 72). In a similar vein, Magnusson and Stattin (1998) have concluded that the "fundamental implication for future psychological research is that we have to change the object of theorizing and empirical research from a context-free individual to a person who functions and develops as an active part of an integrated, complex person–environment system" (p. 686).

## ANTISOCIAL DEVELOPMENT

In this chapter, with reference to the holistic, interactionistic position just outlined (Magnusson, 1995; Magnusson & Stattin, 1998), we wish to illustrate the person–context issue by means of a study of antisocial development—one that treats some of the early risk conditions relevant to later social adjustment problems.

Usually, forecasts of future social maladjustment from childhood information have been made from two perspectives: in terms of characteristics of the child, and in terms of characteristics of the surrounding upbringing context (Buka & Earls, 1993; Loeber & Dishion, 1982). In searching for factors related to the child that may provide for early identification of children at risk of future social adjustment problems, externalizing behaviors and conduct disturbances have consistently emerged in longitudinal and retrospective studies as early problem precursors, whether the outcome concerned is delinquency, drinking problems, drug use, or violence. Such early externalizing behaviors and conduct disturbances include antisocial behavior, unsocialized aggression, conduct problems, extrapunitive behavior, oppositional disorder, and disorders of undercontrol, and are generally characterized by aggressiveness, impulsivity and overactivity, tempers, uncooperativeness, restlessness, defiance, and management problems.

Information about child problem behavior is certainly of vital importance for any study concerned with identifying early precursors of later social maladjustment, or with explaining the mechanisms linking early detected individual characteristics to later social maladjustment. But children's behavior problems are not isolated from the environments in which they live. Such problems are embedded in overall family functioning, being both affected by and having an impact on the family system (Bell, 1968, 1971; Minuchin, 1993). The issues of monitoring, supervision, and parents' disciplinary practices during early childhood have been widely investigated with regard to antisocial behavior of individuals in late childhood and adolescence. For children of younger ages, there is empirical support, gathered over the years, demonstrating the important role in antisocial development played by affective family interaction: emotional parent–parent and parent–child interaction (e.g., parental discord, parental disinterest, rejection, and neglect of the child, parental insensitivity to the child, etc.), management techniques (e.g., punitive disciplinary practices, lack of supervision, etc.), and lack of a consistent pattern of simple rules for family life. Disturbed parent–child relations have been reported to be critical antecedents of delinquent behavior (Farrington, 1978; Hirschi, 1969; Lösel & Bliesner, 1994; McCord & McCord, 1959; Nye, 1958; Olofsson, 1973; Stattin & Klackenberg-Larsson, 1990; Wasserman, Miller, Pinner, & Jaramillo, 1996), of deviant peer involvement (Patterson & Yoerger, 1995), of depressive symptoms (Pike et al., 1996), of conduct problems and antisocial behavior (Cuccaro, Holmes, & Wright, 1993; Kandel & Wu, 1995; Vuchinich, Bank, & Patterson, 1992), and also of aggressiveness and fighting (Haapaslo & Tremblay, 1994; Lobitz & Johnson, 1975; Olweus, 1979; Sears, Maccoby, & Levin, 1957; Widom, 1994).

Coercion theory (Patterson, 1982; Patterson, Reid, & Dishion, 1992) has attempted to clarify the link between family functioning and child problem behavior. According to this model, coercive tactics during disciplinary encounters between parents and the child increase the risk of continuing and increasing aggressive behavior on the part of the child. Hence, family interaction, especially if it is abusive by nature, can "train" a child towards deviant behaviors at later developmental stages. It can also act as a stabilizer of family problems themselves. Patterson (1996) posits that family environment, especially the parent–child relationship, can be a breeding ground for pathological familial characteristics that are then enacted by the child through conduct problems.

Despite the almost self-evident truth of, and well-grounded empirical support for, the assertion that attention has to be paid to the child in context, child and environmental characteristics have normally been analyzed separately and independently in actual research. Statistical analyses have typically been accomplished by means of linear-regression techniques where the prognostic utility of each variable (describing the individual or his or her context) is ascertained relative to other predictive measures in the equation. Rarely, if ever, are child characteristics and context addressed as a unitary whole.

## THE HOLISTIC POSITION

Perhaps the most forceful proponent of a stronger holistic orientation in scientific psychological research has been David Magnusson at Stockholm University. Magnusson has argued for empirical studies that aim at analyzing which pattern configurations of functioning are connected with specific later outcomes. He has also emphasized the importance of new method development—of creating appropriate empirical tools for attempting to discover the distinctive configurations of psychological and social factors that characterize any one person.

According to a holistic, integrated model of individual functioning (Magnusson, 1995; Magnusson & Stattin, 1998), the individual is an active, purposeful part of an integrated and dynamic person–environment system. The individual's characteristic patterning of structures and functioning, operationalized in terms of patterns or configurations of values for the variables under study, is a critical unit of analysis by means of which the holistic organization can be tapped. The study of such configurations has been encapsulated in the phrase "a person approach" (Bergman & Magnusson, 1987; Magnusson, 1996). Rather than studying relations between variables across individuals, which is the usual approach in statistical analyses, specific problems are formulated in terms of configurations of persons. Various methodological tools have proved helpful for the analysis of individual functioning in terms of patterns: cluster analysis, Q-sort, configural frequency analysis, latent transition analysis, and so forth (Bergman, 1998). Applications of such methods can now be found in numerous studies in the arena of developmental psychology conducted by the research group in Stockholm (Bergman, 1993; Bergman & Magnusson, 1987, 1997; Magnusson & Bergman, 1990).

From the general perspective that the individual and his or her environment function as a total system, the question addressed in this chapter can be formulated in pattern terms: Which early behavior or environment constellations are likely to be associated with future social adjustment problems and which are not?

The goal is to understand a child's development in the proximal context of the support and constraints of the home environment. Families with the emotional and cognitive resources to cope with problems on the part of children are in a better position to prevent conduct problems from spreading outside the family environment than families characterized by discord, inadequate communication, and poorly functioning disciplinary practices. In the latter families, lack of adequate role models, cohesion, planning and organization, emotional support, and parental guidance may have the consequence that the child will not learn how to act in a prosocial manner. On this view, for future social adjustment it might be expected that whether conduct problems occur in the context of an otherwise well-functioning family system makes a profound difference. In daily interaction between parent and child, it is particularly in more dysfunctional families that behavioral problems on the part of the child can be expected to grow and extend into new domains. In such families, reactions on the part of both child and parents may expand from initial, minor behavioral problems into long-term detrimental maladjustments.

## IMPLICATIONS FOR THE PRESENT STUDY

In this chapter we propose, first, that behavioral problems on the part of the individual child have limited long-term implications in otherwise normally functioning families. By contrast, when conduct problems co-occur with poor parent–child relationships, the risk of future social adjustment problems is far greater. If such amplification is a general developmental factor, we would expect it to apply to both boys and girls.

We have followed a group of children and their parents from birth up to adult age (a random sample from the general population). We analyzed preschool information about the individual child (gathered at the ages of 4 and 5) and parent–child relationships. We looked at different child characteristic and context configurations rather than treat behavior and family-environment aspects as separate variables. We operationalized the child's problem behavior and his or her parental relationships in terms of four patterns. One such broad behavior or environment pattern is where there are no indications of pronounced behavior problems on the part of the child and no indications of a disturbed parent–child relationship. Another applies to children with pronounced behavior problems but with adequate parent–child relationships. A third, the "risk" pattern in our analyses, refers to cases of pronounced behavior problems on the part of the child combined with an evidently disturbed parent–child relationship. To complete the picture, we examined cases with no indications of behavior problems on the part of the child but where there is clear evidence of a disturbed parent–child relationship. In brief, we formulated the problem addressed by the study and operationalized our measures in person terms; and we analyzed the future development of individual children with reference to four well-defined subgroups.

Note that our hypothesis refers to the starting configuration in what can be called a "snowball model" (see Table 22.1; cf. Caprara & Zimbardo, 1996; Rönkä & Pulkkinen, 1995). Adjustment problems are seldom distributed evenly in a population. Concurrently, the individual who constitutes a high-risk subject for a particular type of problem is often the same individual who is at high risk for another. Developmentally, social adjustment prob-

TABLE 22.1
The Snowball Effect

| Preschool | Early School Age | Adolescence | Early Adulthood |
|---|---|---|---|
| Conduct problems | Low school motivation | Juvenile delinquency | Mortality |
| Familial discord | School conduct problems | Heavy drinking | Criminality |
| | Familial discord | Drug abuse | Alcohol abuse |
| | Poor peer relations | School conduct problems | Drug abuse |
| | | Low school motivation | Low level of education |
| | | Truancy | Unstable work |
| | | Poor peer relations | Unemployment |
| | | Familial discord | Poor finances |
| | | Early sexuality/pregnancy | Marital problems |
| | | Early age at leaving home | Divorce |
| | | | Poor social support |
| | | | No participation in community life |

lems tend to co-occur in certain individuals over time. It is commonly observed that the child who at early school age has learning difficulties and peer problems at school becomes the adolescent who drinks heavily and is involved in criminal activity, and the young adult who is unemployed and has marital problems. For this subsample of the population, new social adjustment problems tend to develop successively over time and become what is considered a "snowball effect." "Snowballing," then, entails an increasingly stronger likelihood of developing new problems. It has been observed that the accumulation, rather than the frequency of single problems, has a prime explanatory value for future personal and social maladaptation (Magnusson & Stattin, 1998; Stattin & Magnusson, 1996).

The first issue addressed by this study concerned the basic configuration of the snowball model. The hypothesis tested was whether future problems at different points in time during development are likely to be particularly concentrated among persons for whom there was a co-occurrence of child behavior problems and poor parent–child relationships at preschool age.

A second issue that we addressed concerns behavior stability. Although people often view problem behavior as something a child will "grow out of," behavioral problems tend to be substantially stable over time, at least when they are measured in the same context (Richman, Stevenson, & Graham, 1982; Verhulst, Koot, & Berden, 1990). Often cited in this context is Olweus' (1979) review of aggression studies, that suggested the longitudinal stability of aggression nearly equals that of general intelligence. In his review of 16 studies with assessment intervals varying from half a year to 18 years, Olweus reported stability coefficients of 0.76 and 0.69 for intervals of 1 and 5 years respectively. (The longitudinal study with the longest period between assessments [Kagan & Moss, 1962] produced a correlation of 0.36 between ages 2 and 21.)

Later studies tend to confirm the results of Olweus' meta-analysis. Using Achenbach's Child Behavior Checklist, Verhulst, Koot, and Berden (1990) found stability coefficients over 4 years of 0.65 for externalizing problems in a sample of 4- to 11-year-olds. Moskowitz, Schwartzman, and Ledingham (1985) found moderate to high stability (0.42 to 0.65) over 3 years for 9- and 12-year-olds. Esser, Schmidt, and Woerner (1990) reported rather high persistence of conduct disorders for 8-year-old children retested 5 years later. In a longitudinal study of 4- to 11-year-olds, conducted on the basis of parent-reported externalizing problems, Verhulst and van der Ende (1991) reported that of the children in the top 10% on an externalizing-problem scale, 32% of those with externalizing problems on the first occasion of measurement were among the 10% highest 6 years later. The probability of being among the highest on externalizing problems at the end of the 6-year interval was 9.5 times higher for children who were initially among the highest than for the rest of the children. In summary, available evidence suggests that externalizing problems demonstrate quite high stability over time when measured in a specific context. However, even when taking only the most extreme cases, there are usually substantial errors in prediction (Cairns, Gariépy, & Hood, 1990); moreover, earlier-age measures of antisocial behavior seem to have limited prognostic utility with regard to specific aspects of deviance in adulthood (Andersson, 1988; Cairns & Cairns, 1994; Stattin & Magnusson, 1996).

In the light of previous findings on behavior stability, we expected high temporal stability of behavioral problems in the home environment, whether or not they co-occur with other types of problems in the family. On the other hand, we did not expect such problems to spread to other areas (outside the home) in the case of behavior-disordered children with adequate parent–child relationships. What we call "problem spread" was expected particularly to characterize children with both behavioral problems and disturbed parent–child relationships.

## THE SAMPLE

Our analyses were based on data from a Swedish longitudinal study embarked on in the mid-50s. The Solna project is a longitudinal study of a normal group of Swedish subjects and their parents. Every fourth pregnant mother at the Solna prenatal clinic (in a suburb of Stockholm) from April 1955 to April 1958 was invited to participate in a long-term pediatric study. (In Sweden virtually all pregnant women receive regular care at prenatal clinics.) Of all mothers asked, only 3% refused an invitation to participate, thus, 212 children, 122 boys and 90 girls, came to take part in the study. Comparisons on many relevant variables have shown the sample to be representative of subjects in Swedish urban communities. Extensive information about the subjects has been collected over the years by means of (a) somatic registrations, (b) medical examinations, (c) interviews, inventories, and ratings, (d) objective tests, (e) sociometric methods, and (f) projective techniques. On each occasion of data collection, the aim was, as thoroughly as possible, to map the subjects' somatic, psychological, and social development. The somatic development of the children in the cohort has been summarized in the form of growth charts for various bodily measurements. The values obtained have been used as reference measures in daily child-health and child-clinical work in Sweden since 1973.

The children were examined six times during their first year, twice during the second year, and thereafter annually up to the age of 18. Collections of data were also made at the ages of 21, 25, and 37 years. Up to the age of 18, in order to control for differences in chronological age, all subjects were tested as closely as possible to the age points referred to: The limit applied below 1 year was ± 2 weeks, and it was ± 4 weeks for tests conducted at 18 months and over subsequent years.

## MEASURES AND SUBGROUPS

With respect to child problem behavior, our intention in this study was to identify children who showed oppositional behavior at home, violated rules, and were destructive, aggressive, and acting-out. Questions about such specific behaviors on the part of the child were put to the mothers.[1] Descriptions were worded so that these behaviors would be easily recognizable by the mother in her everyday interaction with the child.

To capture disturbances in parents' relationship with the child, we followed two paths. First, we picked out the children whose mothers perceived their relationship with the child to be severely disturbed. Second, we selected children of the mothers with the most severe punitive practices. We had obtained high correlations between child problem behavior and physical punishment in earlier studies based on this sample (Stattin, Janson, Klackenberg-Larsson, & Magnusson, 1995). Hence, our measure of discordant mother–child relationships is based on a combination of mother's view on relationship and mother's account of punitive practices.

We performed a subgroup differentiation of the children at the ages of 4 and 5 years into subjects with low conduct problems and little evidence of discordant mother–child relationships (the reference group; $n = 78$), subjects with discordant mother–child relationships only ($n = 23$), subjects with high conduct problems only ($n = 46$), and subjects with both high conduct problems and mother–child discord ($n = 54$).

---

[1]We distinguished first between the 50% highest and the 50% lowest on a broad behavior-problem scale, including items based on the following questions to the mother: "Is he or she a noisy child?"; "Ever take things without permission?"; "Ever hurt anybody?"; "Ever tell an untruth?"; "Does he or she often get into a tantrum? (really marked temper)?"; "Is he or she a destructive child?"; "Is he or she ever spiteful (real intention to hurt)?"; "Can you trust him or her not to touch things if you have told him or her not to?"; "Does he or she pester you to get his or her own way?"; and "Is he or she often disobedient?" Alpha reliability was .76 for the total scale.

Second, our measure of discordant mother–child relationships was based on information about severe maternal punitive practices and the view of mothers that they do not get along well with their children. From responses to a direct question posed at the ages of 4 and 5 ("How do you and your son (daughter) get along together?"), we selected mothers who reported "bad" relationships with their children. We also selected the children who were subjected to the most severe physical punishment. At the ages of 4 and 5, questions were posed to mothers on whether (and how often) they smacked (spanked, slapped) their child. We selected the children higher than 1 standard deviation on a maternal-discipline-practice scale, combining ages 4 and 5. In total, 77 children were reported to have either gotten along badly with their mothers or were subjected to severe punitive practices, or both.

Note that our data come from one source, the mother. All information consists of maternal reports of child behavior and mother's relationship with the child. This is a limitation of the study (Yarrow, Campbell, & Burton, 1968), but was also a deliberate choice. Parents normally provide initial information about their children in clinical situations, and are usually the prime informants in preschool screenings of children's social behavior and mental health. Knowledge about the empirical utility for future adjustment of parent-reported child behaviors and surrounding environment characteristics is very much needed.

## Temporal Stability

We first considered the issue of stability solely in terms of behavior. To provide a broad picture we aggregated annually obtained data (from the age of 18 months to 16 years) on mother-reported behavioral problems on the part of the child into broader age categories. Seven age periods were used, each covering about 2 years: 18 months–3 years, 4 and 5 years, 6 and 7 years, 8 and 9 years, 10, 11, and 12 years, 13 and 14 years, and 15 and 16 years. Reliabilities for the different age periods were estimated by Cronbach's alpha, and found to range from .70 to .90 (median .85).

The question posed was: Are children's behavior problems, as viewed by mothers, stable over time from early age up into adolescence, or are these problems transient? In order to examine the issue of temporal stability, correlation coefficients were computed between the seven age periods. These correlations are shown in Table 22.2 (boys above, and girls below the diagonal).

The results displayed in the table show that conduct problems were quite stable over time. Results were similar for boys and girls. Stability coefficients between adjacent age periods ranged from .54 to .84 with an average stability of .74 for females, and from .55 to .80 with an average period-to-period stability of .71 for males (uncorrected coefficients). Stability fell with larger intervals between age periods. However, for males the earliest measures of conduct problems still correlated significantly with the same problems almost 15 years later. Apparently, as an aspect of the child regarded in isolation, behavior problems show substantial continuity over time—at least as perceived by the mother, and as these are perceived in the home environment.

We now move to analyses of stability for children with different constellations of parent–child discord and child problem behavior. In order to perform a straightforward analysis, the following procedure was adopted. In a manner identical to that for the ages 4 and 5, we made a pattern classification on the basis of the same type of information collected at the

TABLE 22.2
Temporal Stability (Uncorrected Coefficients) for Behavioral Problems

| | 18 mos to 3 yrs | 4 & 5 years | 6 & 7 yrs | 8 & 9 yrs | 10 to 12 yrs | 13 & 14 yrs | 15 & 16 yrs |
|---|---|---|---|---|---|---|---|
| 18 mos to 3 yrs | | 55*** | 48*** | 46*** | 37*** | 36*** | 25* |
| 4 & 5 years | 54*** | | 61*** | 60*** | 48*** | 39*** | 33*** |
| 6 & 7 yrs | 44*** | 68*** | | 77*** | 66*** | 57*** | 47*** |
| 8 & 9 yrs | 36*** | 65*** | 84*** | | 77*** | 64*** | 51*** |
| 10 to 12 yrs | 25* | 46*** | 73*** | 76*** | | 77*** | 67*** |
| 13 & 14 yrs | 22[a] | 39*** | 59*** | 58*** | 81*** | | 80*** |
| 15 & 16 yrs | 23[a] | 37*** | 53*** | 54*** | 74*** | 83*** | |

Note. Males above and females below the diagonal. Decimals have been omitted.
[a] p < .10. *p < .05. **p < .01. ***p < .001. (two-tailed tests of significance).

ages of 9 to 12. We cross-tabulated preschool and early school-age discord and conduct constellations.

As shown in Table 22.3, most of the subjects in the reference configuration at the age of 4 and 5 years belonged to the same configuration in early school age. This was also true of subjects with conduct problems only, and of subjects with both conduct problems and mother–child discord. An Exacon analysis (Bergman & El-Khouri, 1998) showed that belonging to the same configuration later at school age for subjects in the reference group, conduct problems, and conduct problems & mother–child discord categories was a "type", that is, this occurred more often than could be expected by chance. There were also atypical developmental paths. It occurred less often than expected from a random model that the reference group of subjects later were classified into the two conduct-problem categories, and it was an atypical path that the conduct-problem subjects at the ages of 4 and 5 were rated as showing the reference pattern at the ages of 9 to 12.

It should be noted that about one in two of the subjects with conduct problems at the ages of 4 and 5 showed the same configuration at school

TABLE 22.3
A Cross-Tabulation of Discord and Conduct Categories Between 4 & 5 Years and 9 to 12 Years
(Expected Number of Subjects Within Parentheses)

|  | *Age 9–12* | | | |
|  | *Reference Group* | *Discord* | *Conduct* | *Discord & Conduct* |
| --- | --- | --- | --- | --- |
| Age 4 & 5 yrs | | | | |
| Reference group | 53 | 9 | 6 | 4 |
|  | (28) | (9) | (17) | (18) |
|  | Type ** |  | Antitype** | Antitype** |
| Discord | 8 | 6 | 1 | 7 |
|  | (9) | (3) | (5) | (7) |
| Conduct | 8 | 4 | 19 | 10 |
|  | (16) | (5) | (9) | (11) |
|  | Antitype* |  | Type** |  |
| Discord & Conduct | 3 | 3 | 16 | 26 |
|  | (19) | (6) | (11) | (12) |
|  | Antitype** |  |  | Type** |

*Note.* Bonferroni corrected *p*-values.

age (46% of the subjects with conduct problems only, and 54% of those with both conduct problems and mother–child discord), and that only a minority of these subjects (20% and 6%, respectively) were reported as being without behavioral problems or mother–child discord later on.

All in all, for the two preschool groups of subjects with conduct problems, we witnessed quite high temporal stability with regard to the reappearance of conduct problems at school age. This was somewhat less true for subjects with discordant mother–child relations only.

It should be observed that both the values for the temporal stability of single measures and those resulting from the contingency analysis are inflated. Both are based on maternal reports and overestimate "true" stability (to an unknown extent). Measured stability in this case reflects both actual stability in behavior and behavior and environment conditions, and stability in mothers' perceptions of these conditions.

### Children With Disturbed Mother–Child Relations

On a superficial level, one of our four child-context patterns appears anomalous. The group contains children who either had been subjected to strong punitive practices or had strongly discordant relations with their mother but who, according to their mothers, were not behaviorally disordered. Further, as reported in Table 22.3, the temporal stability for these subjects was found to be low. Only a minority of the children who belonged in this category at the ages of 4 and 5 were similarly classified at the ages of 9 to 12. To shed further light on children showing this pattern, we examined information from independent sources.

When the child was 4 years of age, a psychologist rated mother–child interaction on a number of dimensions. Such rating was performed in connection with the child being examined at the clinic (Stattin & Klackenberg-Larsson, 1990). The procedure was, in most cases, as follows. First, the child's health status was determined, and different physical measures were taken. The child was x-rayed and photographed. Thereafter, the child and his or her mother were taken to a room equipped with a sand box. The child's behavior in relation to play figures in the sand box was rated according to a structured schema (applying the Moore and Ucko doll-play technique; Moore & Ucko, 1961). Mother's interaction with the child in this test situation was noted by the psychologist. Afterwards, an interview was held with the mother. The total length of the visit to the clinic lasted 2 and a half to 3 hours. The testing situation and the interview with the mother lasted approximately 90 minutes.

Three of the psychologist-rated measures of mother–child interaction reflected discipline practices. As is shown in Fig. 22.1, mothers of children in the "mother–child discord" and "conduct problems & mother–child discord" categories were perceived as more ready to punish their children and to punish their children more severely. There was also a tendency for these mothers to be more dominating than other mothers. Overall, our empirically based view that both the groups of children classified as having disturbed mother–child relationships (with and without child behavioral problems) had mothers with a more punitive attitude was supported.

That some mothers had more severe punitive disciplinary practices (despite the fact that these were not accompanied by the reporting of greater problem behavior among their children) may mirror parents' own disciplinary histories and their disciplinary attitudes.

To examine this, information about disciplinary history and attitudes provided by both mothers and fathers was analyzed. Two measures made up what we call "Parents' disciplinary histories." One was based on the question, "Were you smacked (spanked) as a child?"; the other on the question, "Were you brought up more or less strictly than people in general?" These questions were posed to mothers when their child was 3 years old, and to fathers when the child was 4.

"Parents' disciplinary attitudes" encompassed two factor-dimensions from Schaefer and Bell's Parental Attitude Research Instrument (Schaefer &

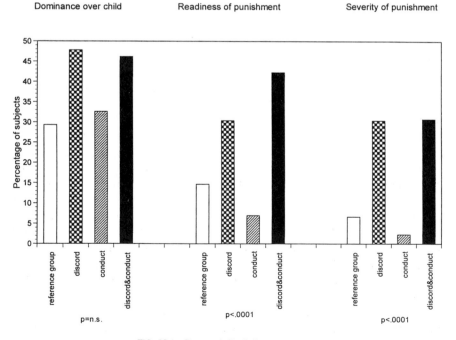

FIG. 22.1. Parents' disciplinary patterns.

Bell, 1958), and was based on questions answered separately by the mother and father when the child was 4 years of age. Two of the scales of this instrument focus on disciplinary issues—"Breaking the will" and "Strictness." Points on these scales were aggregated on one dimension, labeled "Strict disciplinary attitude." The second dimension comprised Schaefer and Bell's "Irritability" factor. It is better described as "Lack of tolerance for annoyance," and consists of five items. In the case of mothers, it is based on agreement or disagreement with statements such as: "Children will get on any mother's nerves if she has to be with them all day," "Mothers very often feel that they can't stand their children a moment longer," and "It's natural for a mother to 'blow her top' when children are selfish and demanding" (see Stattin, Janson, Klackenberg-Larsson, & Magnusson, 1995 for further information).

No differences were detected for father's disciplinary history and disciplinary attitudes between the four groups of subjects. In the case of mothers, significant differences appeared with regard to whether they had been smacked (spanked) as a child. Mothers of the children in the discord and conduct problems & mother–child discord categories reported having been smacked more frequently during upbringing than did other mothers. The most marked difference appeared between the conduct problems and the conduct problems & mother–child discord groups of subjects. In the former group, only 2% of the mothers reported having been spanked as a child in comparison with 40% of the latter. Thirty percent of the mothers of the discord children reported having been spanked as a child in comparison with 18% of the mothers of the reference group of children.

Planned comparisons concerning the question of whether the mother had been brought up more or less strictly than people in general, designed to test differences between the two discord configurations of children and other children, showed that mothers who reported problematic child relationships had been brought up more strictly than other mothers. With regard to disciplinary attitudes, planned comparisons showed that mothers with discordant child relationships reported significantly stricter disciplinary attitudes than mothers without discordant relationships with their child. Finally, planned comparisons produced significant differences between the two groups with regard to mother's tolerance for annoyance; the mothers in the two discord categories showed less tolerance.

In summary, disturbed mother–child relationships seem to be accompanied by a history of more severe punitive disciplinary practices in the mother's own upbringing, and by a stricter disciplinary attitude on the part of these mothers (as rated by an outside observer). Questions surrounding the direction of any causal link, that is, whether mother's disciplinary history directly affects parenting of the child, or whether her practice is actualized by the behavior of the child (and justified by the child's behavior), or both, cannot be answered from the present data. But what can be detected among the two groups of children subjected to relatively severe physical punishment is the persistence over time of the pattern of co-occurrence of child problem behavior and mother's severe punishment. No such stability was found for the group of children with severe maternal punishment only, despite the fact that both groups of children were characterized by having mothers with a severe-punishment upbringing.

## Problem Spread

We now turn to the main analyses. The hypothesis tested was whether it is predominantly when a child's conduct problems co-occur with disturbed parent–child relationships that future adjustment problems can be expected; or, conversely, whether conduct problems not co-occurring with problematic mother–child relationships can be expected to have more limited implications for future social adjustment.

Tables 22.4, 22.5, and 22.6 show the results of analyses covering issues of future (a) education and family, (b) social adjustment problems, and (c) aggressiveness, impulsivity, and concentration difficulties. We report the findings separately for males and females. We have consistently contrast-tested the three so-called risk groups against the reference group of children.

*Education and Family.* As reported in Table 22.4, for the majority of measures covering future education and family, and in accordance with our hypothesis, it was subjects with both conduct problems and discordant mother–child relationships who differed from the reference subjects. This was the case for both males and females. Males with preschool relational and behavioral difficulties had more adjustment problems at school start, showed lower school achievement at the ages of 10 and 13, were more often tired of school at the age of 15, and had more school-adjustment problems at this age. At adult age they had a lower level of education. Females with preschool relational and behavioral difficulties showed somewhat lower school achievement at the ages of 10 and 13, were more often tired of school at the age of 15, and had more school-adjustment problems at this age. They left home earlier than the reference group of females, and more of them bore children at an early age.

The differences between the four groups are illustrated in Fig. 22.2a in the case of adjustment during first year at school. The measure was based on a combination of mother and teacher reports of school problems. As shown in the figure, adjustment problems were particularly characteristic

TABLE 22.4
Implications of Childhood Mother–Child Discord and Conduct Problems for Future Education and
Family (Source of Report and Age Within Parentheses)

| Education and Family | F | p | 2 v. 1 | 3 v. 1 | 4 v. 1 |
|---|---|---|---|---|---|
| *Males* | | | | | |
| Adjustment problems at school start (M+T, 8) | 3.29 | * | — | — | ** |
| Low school achievement (T, 10) | 2.41 | a | — | — | ** |
| Low school achievement (T, 13) | 2.10 | a | — | — | * |
| Tired of school (M+T, 15) | 2.39 | a | — | — | * |
| School-adjustment problems (M, 15) | 4.32 | ** | — | — | * |
| Early age at leaving home (S, 25) | 0.31 | ns | — | — | — |
| Low adult level of education (S, 25) | 4.68 | ** | — | ** | *** |
| Early childbearing (S, 21) | 0.63 | ns | — | — | — |
| Early marriage (S, 21) | 0.60 | ns | — | — | — |
| *Females* | | | | | |
| Adjustment problems at school start (M+T, 8) | 1.13 | ns | — | — | — |
| Low school achievement (T, 10) | 2.02 | ns | — | — | a |
| Low school achievement (T, 13) | 1.42 | ns | — | — | a |
| Tired of school (M+T, 15) | 5.41 | ** | — | — | ** |
| School-adjustment problems (M, 15) | 6.76 | *** | — | — | *** |
| Early age at leaving home (S, 25) | 6.78 | *** | — | — | *** |
| Low adult level of education (S, 25) | 1.29 | ns | — | — | — |
| Early childbearing (S, 21) | 3.70 | * | — | — | ** |
| Early marriage (S, 21) | 0.65 | ns | — | — | — |

*Note.* M = Mother reports, T = Teacher reports, S = Self-reports.
***$p < .001$. **$p < .01$. *$p < .05$. $^a p < .10$.

of boys and girls with preschool evidence of disturbed mother–child relationships and conduct problems. As shown in Fig. 22.2b, school-adjustment problems at the age of 15 were also more characteristic of these children than other children.

Age at leaving home was not related to our preschool categorization in the case of males, but was for girls (see Fig. 22.2c). Females with both preschool conduct problems and disturbed mother–child relationships moved away from home at an earlier age than other females.

The females with both early conduct problems and disturbed mother–child relationships also had children of their own earlier. This is shown, for age 21, in Fig. 22.2d. At this age, few of the males in our study group had children of their own.

TABLE 22.5
Implications of Childhood Mother–Child Discord and Conduct Problems for Future Social
Adjustment Problems (Source of Report and Age Within Parentheses)

| Social-Adjustment Problems | F | p | 2 v. 1 | 3 v. 1 | 4 v. 1 |
|---|---|---|---|---|---|
| *Males* | | | | | |
| Smoking (S, 15) | 1.25 | ns | — | — | — |
| Drinking (S, 18) | 2.32 | a | — | — | * |
| Drinking (S, 25) | 1.34 | ns | — | — | a |
| Conflicts about alcohol (S, 25) | 2.94 | * | — | — | * |
| Drug abuse (S, 17) | 3.73 | * | — | — | * |
| *Females* | | | | | |
| Smoking (S, 15) | 4.11 | ** | — | * | * |
| Drinking (S, 18) | 1.66 | ns | — | — | a |
| Drinking (S, 25) | 1.03 | ns | — | — | — |
| Conflicts about alcohol (S, 25) | 0.77 | ns | — | — | — |
| Drug abuse (S, 17) | 2.33 | a | — | — | a |

*Note.* S = Self-reports.
***$p < .001$. **$p < .01$. *$p < .05$. [a]$p < .10$.

**Social Adjustment Problems.** Similar findings to those reported for education and family appear for the different measures of future social adjustment problems (Table 22.3).

Males with preschool relational and behavioral difficulties drank more heavily at the age of 18, also somewhat more at the age of 25, and had more conflicts at home about alcohol than members of the reference group of males. They also used more drugs at the age of 17. Females with preschool relational and behavioral difficulties smoked more at the age of 15, and there were observed tendencies for them to use more drugs at the age of 17 and drink more at the age of 18.

This is illustrated for a measure of heavy drinking at the age of 18 in Fig. 22.3a. For both males and females, heavy drinking occurred most often among subjects with preschool evidence of conduct problems and disturbed mother–child relationships.

One exception to the general tendency is presented in Fig. 22.3b, which shows experience of drug use by the age of 17. In the case of females, both categories of children with preschool conduct problems differed from the other children. By contrast, male drug use was primarily concentrated among subjects with both early conduct problems and mother–child discord.

TABLE 22.6
Implications of Childhood Mother–Child Discord and Conduct Problems for Future Aggressiveness,
Impulsivity, and Concentration Problems (Source of Report and Age Within Parentheses)

| Aggressiveness, Impulsivity, Concentration Problems | F | p | 2 v. 1 | 3 v. 1 | 4 v. 1 |
|---|---|---|---|---|---|
| **Males** | | | | | |
| Aggressiveness (S, 25) | 1.05 | ns | — | — | — |
| Aggressiveness (P, 25) | 0.59 | ns | — | — | — |
| Careless (T, 10) | 2.48 | a | — | * | * |
| Careless (T, 13) | 1.04 | ns | — | — | — |
| Careless (S, 25) | 4.74 | ** | — | — | ** |
| Careless (P, 25) | 3.88 | * | — | — | * |
| Concentration problems (T, 10) | 3.27 | * | — | — | ** |
| Concentration problems (T, 13) | 3.34 | * | — | — | ** |
| Impulsiveness (P, 25) | 3.90 | * | — | — | ** |
| **Females** | | | | | |
| Aggressiveness (S, 25) | 1.88 | ns | — | a | a |
| Aggressiveness (P, 25) | 3.38 | * | — | — | ** |
| Careless (T, 10) | 3.01 | * | — | a | — |
| Careless (T, 13) | 1.03 | ns | — | — | — |
| Careless (S, 25) | 0.66 | ns | — | — | — |
| Careless (P, 25) | 1.00 | ns | — | — | — |
| Concentration problems (T, 10) | 2.20 | * | — | — | * |
| Concentration problems (T, 13) | 1.63 | ns | — | — | * |
| Impulsiveness (P, 25) | 0.47 | ns | — | — | — |

*Note.* P = Psychologist reports, T = Teacher reports, S = Self-reports.
***$p < .001$. **$p < .01$. *$p < .05$. $^a p < .10$.

***Aggressiveness, Impulsivity, and Concentration Difficulties.*** Table 22.4
covers different aspects of aggressiveness, impulsivity, and concentration
difficulties. With few exceptions, it was the subjects in the fourth group who
differed from subjects showing the reference pattern. Males with preschool
relational and behavioral difficulties were rated by their teachers as more
careless at the age of 10, perceived themselves as more careless at the age
of 25, and were rated by psychologists as more careless at the same age.
These males had more concentration problems. They were rated as having
more concentration disturbances by their teachers at the age of 10 and 13,
and by psychologists at the Solna clinic at the age of 25. There were fewer
differences between the four groups of females on these measures. However, females with preschool relational and behavioral difficulties were

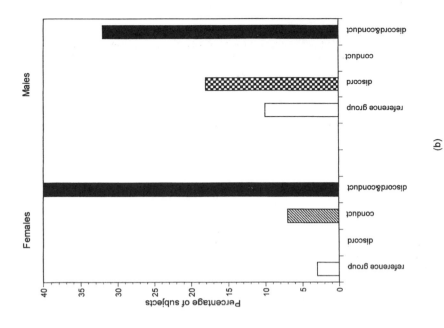

(b)

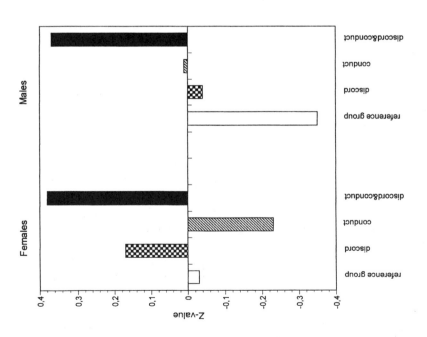

(a)

FIG. 22.2. (a) Adjustment problems at school start, (b) school adjustment problems at age 15, (c) age at moving away from home: females, (d) own children at the age of 21.

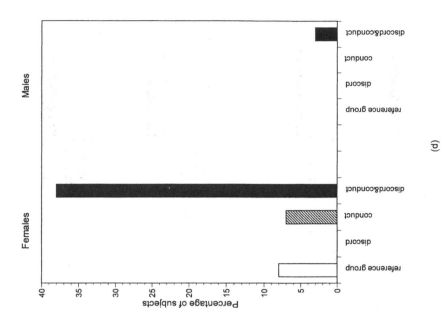

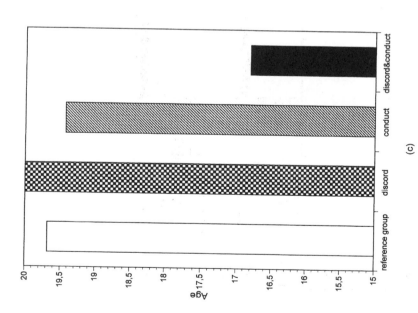

FIG. 22.2. (Continued)

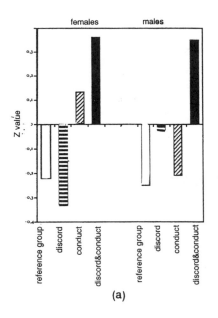

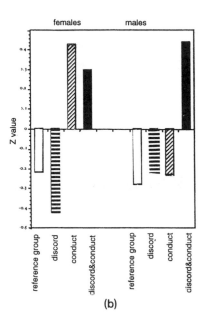

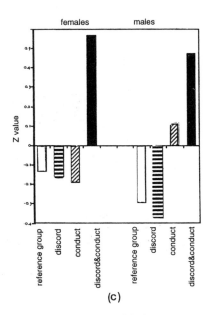

FIG. 22.3. (a) Heavy drinking at age 18, (b) drug use up to age 17, (c) concentration problems at age 10.

found to be somewhat more aggressive at the age of 25 on the basis of self-reports and psychologists' ratings. They also had more concentration problems (according to their teachers) at the ages of 10 and 13.

An illustration of the findings is presented in Fig. 22.3c. It shows the results of teachers' rating of concentration difficulties at the age of 10. Concentration problems are primarily concentrated among males and females with preschool relational and behavioral difficulties.

## CONCLUSIONS

For this study we have analyzed information provided by mothers about their children during the preschool period. The mother in the family reported on her child's behavior and about her relationship with the child. We found that mothers' reports at this age show rather substantial predictive utility for child's future personal and social adjustment. The findings also support the conclusion that attempting to understand future life-course on the basis of childhood information on child problem behavior without simultaneously paying attention to the context of the child's behavior is an ineffective strategy.

We tested the proposition that childhood conduct problems have limited implications for future social adjustment problems unless they are accompanied by poor parent–child relationships. The findings generally support this hypothesis. Co-occurrence of child problem behavior and disturbed mother–child relationships was associated with later problem spread. Child problem behavior without disturbed mother–child relationships was not much of a better indicator of future risk than nonproblematic child behavior with or without disturbed mother–child relationships.

Our study also indicates that conduct problems at home are quite stable over time. Conduct problems, in the age period 18 months to 3 years, were significantly associated with conduct problems at the age of 15 and 16 for males. Moreover, the children classified as high in conduct problems at the ages of 4 and 5 years, regardless of whether mother–child discord was present, were often perceived to display conduct problems in early adolescence. A majority of these children with high conduct problems at the ages of 4 and 5 were later (at the ages 9 to 12) classified as belonging to the conduct-problem group on the same type of criterion measures. It was an atypical developmental path for them to have no mother–child discord or conduct problems in early adolescence.

Stability of behavioral problems over time, either explicitly or implicitly, has been taken as a justification for expecting other types of adjustment problems to emerge. But, although our study provides empirical support for high temporal stability of conduct problems, this does not provide an argument for expecting problem-spread later on. In order for broader social adjustment problems to emerge in the future, it makes a great difference whether a child's problem behavior co-occurs with a poor mother–child relationship. When it does not, "problem children" do not differ much from children without preschool relational and behavioral difficulties. But when preschool conduct problems are accompanied by mother–child discord, the risk of various future social adjustment problems is amplified. We found this to be true both for males and females.

Although, at least to some extent, we obtained similar findings for the genders, there are also some differences worth pointing to. The impact of preschool conduct problems and mother–child discord was more consistent among males than females in the areas of aggressiveness, concentration difficulties, and impulsivity. Among females, there was a greater impact with regard to leaving home and childbearing.

Our findings clearly indicate that there are differences in future adjustment between children with conduct problems only and children with both problematic mother–child relationships and conduct problems. There are also other differences, with regard to parents' own disciplinary upbringing and their disciplinary attitudes. We found that the mothers in the group of children with both problematic mother–child relationships and conduct problems had had a more punitive upbringing and that they expressed more punitive disciplinary attitudes than the mothers of children with behavioral problems where there were no problematic mother–child relationships. A more punitive upbringing and stricter disciplinary attitudes were also found among mothers who reported problematic child relationships but no conduct problems on the part of their child. It seems that we have to take into account the historical context of parenting dimensions; experiences of child rearing may be passed from one generation to the next.

Taken as a whole, our findings suggest that it is the constellation of early behavioral and relational problems, not behavioral and relational problems in isolation, that is prognostic of future adjustment problems. The results suggest that we have to look more closely at the holistic patterning of early problems to understand what we have called the "snowballing" of problems into the future. If this study had had a correlational design, we would have obtained significant correlations between childhood conduct problems and many of the later outcome measures. We also would have obtained significant associations between the measures of early discordant mother–child relationships and later adjustment outcomes. These correlations tell us something about the interrelatedness of interindividual differences over time in general. However, such correlations, based as they are on the total population, mask the existence of differential pathways to the future. For some children with conduct problems, even if these behavioral problems prevail over time, we find limited evidence of problem spreading. For other children with conduct problems, where these problems co-occur with family relational problems, the risk of future adjustment problems are more marked. Accordingly, the issue of problem spread over time cannot be discussed and analyzed once and for all on the basis of a population-general, correlational design. We have to take account of different developmental progressions for subgroups of the larger population, and we have to assess the prognostic utility not only of single risk conditions but also of the broader pattern of early interacting factors.

## ACKNOWLEDGMENTS

This research was supported by grants from Axel and Margaret Ax:son Johnson Foundation, the Swedish Council for Planning and Coordination of Research and the Swedish Council for Research in the Humanities and Social Sciences.

## REFERENCES

Andersson, T. (1988). *Alkoholvanor i ett uyvecklingsperspektiv* [Drinking habits in a developmental perspective]. Unpublished doctoral dissertation, University of Stockholm.

Bell, R. Q. (1968). Reinterpretation of the direction of effects in studies of socialization. *Psychological Review, 75*, 81–95.

Bell, R. Q. (1971). Stimulus control of parent or caretaker by offspring. *Developmental Psychology, 4*, 63–72.

Bergman, L. R. (1993). Some methodological issues in logitudinal research: Looking ahead. In D. Magnusson & P. Casaer (Eds.), *Longitudinal research on individual development* (pp. 217–241). Cambridge, UK: Cambridge University Press.

Bergman, L. R. (1998). A pattern-oriented approach to studying individual development: Snapshots and processes. In R. B. Cairns, L. R. Bergman, & J. Kagan (Eds.), *Methods and models for studying the individual* (pp. 83–121). Thousand Oaks, CA: Sage.

Bergman, L. R., & El-Khouri, B. (1998). *Sleipner. A statistical package for pattern oriented analyses.* Version 2.0. Department of psychology, Stockholm University.

Bergman, L. R., & Magnusson, D. (1987). A person approach to the study of the development of adjustment problems: An emprical example and some research strategy considerations. In D. Magnusson & A. Ohman (Eds.), *Psychopathology: An interactional perspective* (pp. 383–401). Orlando, FL: Academic Press.

Bergman, L. R., & Magnusson, D. (1997). A person-oriented approach in research on developmental psychopathology. *Development and Psychopathology, 9*, 291–319.

Buka, S. & Earls, F. (1993). Early determinants of delinquency and violence. Determinants of violence. *Health Affairs*, 46–64.

Cairns, R. & Cairns, B. (1994). *Lifelines and risks: Pathways of youth in our time.* Cambridge, UK: Cambridge University Press.

Cairns, R., Gariépy, J. L., & Hood, K. E. (1990). Development, microevolution, and social behavior. *Psychological Review, 97*, 49–65.

Caprara, G. V., & Zimbardo, P. G. (1996). Aggregation and amplification of marginal deviations in the social construction of personality and maladjustment. *European Journal of Personality, 10,* 79–110.

Cicchetti, D. (1993). Developmental psychopathology: Reactions, reflections, projections. *Developmental Review, 13,* 471–502.

Cuccaro, M., Holmes, G. R., & Wright, H. (1993). Behavior problems in preschool children: A pilot study. *Psychological Reports, 62,* 1044–1052.

Emde, R. (1994) Individuality, context, and the search for meaning. *Child Development, 65,* 719–737.

Esser, G., Schmidt, M. H., & Woerner, W. (1990). Epidemiology and course of psychiatric disorders in school age children: Results of a longitudinal study. *Journal of Child Psychology and Psychiatry and Allied Disciplines, 31,* 243–263.

Farrington, D. P. (1978). The family background of aggressive youths. In L. A. Hersov, M. Berger, & D. Schaffer (Eds.), *Aggression and Antisocial Behavior in Childhood and Adolescence* (pp. 73–93). Oxford, UK: Pergamon.

Haapasalo, J., & Tremblay, R. E. (1994). Physically aggressive boys from ages 6 to 12: Family background, parenting behavior, and prediction of delinquency. *Journal of Consulting and Clinical Psychology, 62,* 1044–1052.

Hirschi, T. (1969). *Causes of Delinquency.* Berkeley: University of California Press.

Kagan, J., & Moss, H. A. (1962). *Birth to maturity. A study on psychological development* New York: Wiley.

Kandel, D. B., & Wu, P. (1995). Disentangling mother-child effects in the development of antisocial behavior. In J. McCord (Ed.), *Coercion and punishment in long term perspectives* (pp. 106–123). New York: Cambridge University Press.

Lobitz, C. W. & Johnson, S. M. (1975). Parental manipulation of the behavior of normal and deviant children. *Child Development, 46,* 719–726.

Loeber, R. & Dishion, T. J. (1982). Early predictors of male delinquency: A review. *Psychological Bulletin, 94,* 68–99.

Lösel, F., & Bliesner, T. (1994). Some high-risk adolescents do not develop conduct problems: A study of protective factors. *International Journal of Behavioral Development, 17,* 753–777.

Magnusson, D. (1995). Individual development: A holistic integrated model. In P. Moen, G. H. Elder, & K. Luscher (Eds.), *Linking lives and contexts: Perspectives on the ecology of human development* (pp. 19–60). Washington, DC: American Psychological Association.

Magnusson, D. (1996). *The life-span development of individuals: Behavioral, neurobiological and psychosocial perspectives.* Cambridge, UK: Cambridge University Press.

Magnusson, D., & Bergman, L. R. (1990). A pattern approach to the study of pathways from childhood to adulthood. In L. N. Robins & M. Rutter (Eds.), *Straight and devious pathways from childhood to adult hood* (pp. 101–115). Cambridge, UK: Cambridge University Press.

Magnusson, D. & Stattin, H. (1998). Person-context interaction theories. In W. Damon & R. M. Lerner (Eds.), *Handbook of child psychology: Vol. 1. Theoretical models of human development* (pp. 685–759). New York: Wiley.

McCord, W., & McCord, J. (1959). *Origins of crime: A new evaluation of the Cambridge-Somerville study.* New York: Columbia University Press.

Minuchin, S. (1993). *Family Healing.* New York: The Free Press.

Moore, T. & Ucko, L. G. (1961). Four to six: Constructiveness and conflict in meeting dollplay problems. *Journal of Child Psychology and Psychiatry, 3,* 21–47.

Moskowitz, D. S., Schwartzman, A. E., & Ledingham, J. E. (1985). Stability and change in aggression and withdrawal in middle childhood and early adolescence. *Journal of Abnormal Psychology, 94,* 30–41.

Nye, F. I. (1958). *Family relations and delinquent behavior.* New York: Wiley.

Olofsson, B. (1973). *Young delinquents: III. Home upbringing, education and peer relation as reflected in interview and follow-up data (25).* Stockholm: Statens offentliga Utredningar.

Olweus, D. (1979). Stability of aggressive reaction patterns in males: A review. *Pychological Bulletin, 86*, 852–875.

Patterson, G. R. (1982). *Coercive family process: A social learning approach* (Vol. 3). Eugene, OR: Castalia.

Patterson, G. R. (1996, December). *Developmental models for early and late onset delinquency: Implications for prevention.* Paper presented at the International Early Prevention Seminars, Solna, Sweden.

Patterson, G. R., Reid, J. B., & Dishion, T. J. (1992). *Antisocial boys.* Eugene, OR: Castalia.

Patterson, G. R., & Yoerger, K. (1995). Two different models for adolescent physical trauma and for early arrest. *Criminal Behavior and Mental Health, 5*, 411–423.

Pike, A., McGuire, S., Hetherington, M., Reiss, D., & Plomin, R. (1996). Family environment and adolescent depressive symptoms and antisocial behavior. *Developmental Psychology, 32*, 574–589.

Richman, N., Stevenson, J., & Graham, P. J. (1982). Pre-school to school: A behavioural study. *Behavioural Development: A Series of Monographs, 228.*

Rönkä, A., & Pulkkinen, L. (1995). Accumulation of problems in social functioning in young adulthood: A developmental approach. *Journal of Personality and Social Psychology, 69*, 381–391.

Schaefer, E. S., & Bell, R. Q. (1958). Development of a parental attitude research instrument. *Child Development, 29*, 339–361.

Sears, R. R., Maccoby, E. E., & Levin, H. (1957). *Patterns of childrearing.* Evanston, IL: Row Peterson

Stattin, H., Janson, H., Klackenberg-Larsson, I., & Magnusson, D. (1995). Corporal punishment for everyday life. In J. McCord (Ed.), *Coercion and punishment in long-term perspectives* (pp. 315–347). New York: Cambridge University Press.

Stattin, H. & Klackenberg-Larsson, I. (1990). The relationship between maternal attributes in the early life of the child and the child's future criminal behavior. *Development and Psychopathology, 2*, 99–111.

Stattin, H., & Magnusson, D., (1996). Antisocial behavior—A holistic perspective (Special Issue). *Development and Psychopathology, 8*(4), 617–645.

Verhulst, F. C., Koot, H. M., & Berden, G. F. (1990). Four year follow-up of an epidemiological sample. *Journal of the American Academy of Child and Adolescent Psychiatry, 29*, 440–448.

Verhulst, F. C. & Van der Ende, J. (1991). Four year follow up of teacher reported problem behaviours. *Psychological Medicine, 21*, 965–977.

Vuchinich, S., Bank, L., & Patterson, G. R. (1992). Parenting, peers and the stability of antisocial behavior in preadolescent boys. *Developmental Psychology, 28*, 510–521.

Wasserman, G., Miller, L., Pinner, E., & Jaramillo, B. (1996). Parenting predictors of early conduct problems in urban, high risk boys. *Journal of the American Academy of Child and Adolescent Psychiatry, 35*, 1227–1236.

Widom, C. S. (1994). "Does violence beget violence? A critical examination of the literature": Clarification of publishing history. *Psychological Bulletin, 115*, 287.

Yarrow, M. R., Campbell, J. D., & Burton, R. V. (1968). *Child rearing: An inquiry into research methods.* San Francisco: Jossey-Bass.

# 23

# Developmental Patterns and the Dynamics of Alcohol Problems in Adolescence and Young Adulthood

Tommy Andersson
Stockholm University

Alcohol abuse and alcohol-related harm are widespread and serious problems in many countries today. Despite the very large amount of alcohol research, efforts to reduce these problems have attained only limited success. One obvious reason for this is that existing scientific knowledge cannot always be transformed into effective alcohol policy strategies due to the concurrence of other political and economic interests. Another important reason is the "logistic" difficulties in implementing scientifically based strategies for regulation, prevention, and rehabilitation. A third, and very basic, reason is that despite the enormous amount of existing and ongoing alcohol research, it is still not fully understood why some people become alcoholics or generate alcohol-related harm but most people do not. In general, scientific theories about alcohol abuse focus either on the social perspective, the biological perspective, or the psychological perspective, approaches generating different explanations for the problems, and consequently different solutions (Glanz & Pickens, 1992). Although all of these theoretical approaches have generated important knowledge, none of them has found the "alcohol gene" or the ultimate solution to the problem.

An alternative and promising approach to a closer understanding of development of drinking habits and alcohol abuse is to regard individual functioning, including drinking habits and alcohol abuse, as generated by a continuous interaction over time between biological and psychological factors within the individual, and the macro- and microsocial conditions characterizing an individual's environment. Focusing on individual development and functioning in general, such a holistic and developmental approach has been proposed by, among others, Magnusson (1995) and Cairns and Cairns (1994). With a special focus on the development of drinking habits and alcohol abuse, the interaction between characteristics within the individual and characteristics in his or her social and physical environment has been emphasized by, for instance, Donovan, Jessor, and Jessor (1983), Schulenberg, O'Malley, Bachman, Wadsworth, and Johnston (1996), and Wagenar and Perry (1994).

From a holistic and developmental perspective it seems natural that a number of various developmental processes can generate alcohol abuse, processes in which biological, psychological, and social components interact in different ways in ongoing processes ending up in alcohol abuse. An initially genetic disposition for alcohol abuse followed by poor parenting in an unfavorable socioeconomic context, serious conduct problems in childhood and achievement problems in school could, for instance, be one characteristic pathway to early manifested alcohol abuse. Another, perhaps less common, developmental pathway to early manifested alcohol abuse can begin in a problematic adolescence including divorce by the parents, moving to a new area and school, getting involved with the wrong kind of peers, minor criminality, testing drugs, unemployment, and the like.

A holistic approach is relevant for understanding the background of alcohol abuse. In congruence with such a perspective, manifested alcohol abuse is just one ingredient in an individual's total life situation. Alcohol abuse can be one ingredient in a generally antisocial way of functioning of a 20-year-old man, and it can also be an ingredient in the total life situation characterizing a traditional and well-adjusted 60-year-old upper-class woman or a 40-year-old "normal" husband and father in the middle of his career as a salesman or writer. As well as it's reasonable to assume that different developmental processes can generate similar types of alcohol abuse, it's also reasonable to assume that some developmental processes are more common than others depending on the holistic context in which the alcohol abuse is one part.

An obvious consequence of such a perspective is that a single, isolated variable—biological, psychological, or social—present in childhood, adolescence, or adulthood cannot alone be expected to explain more than a minor part of the total variance with respect to the development of alcohol abuse, a consequence well in line with empirical results. Based on experience and empirical results from traditionally variable-oriented research within specific scientific fields, it might be fruitful to, as a next step, apply a holistic perspective and focus on the existence and characteristics of different developmental patterns generating different types of alcohol abuse.

There is one component common to all types of alcohol abuse and in all developmental processes leading to alcohol abuse. The individual starts to drink alcohol. Alcohol drinking usually begins in early adolescence and escalates in the early twenties, whereafter the alcohol consumption normally declines and stabilizes (Fillmore, Hartka, Johnstone, Leino, Motoyoshi, & Temple, 1996). An early advanced drinking habit is seen as a very serious risk factor, perhaps the single most important risk factor with respect to the development of later alcohol problems, and the risk for later alcohol problems is probably the main argument for societal restrictions on alcohol drinking in early adolescence as well as for targeting an alcohol-free childhood and adolescence as an important goal in public health policy. Empirical studies focusing on the relation between drinking habits in adolescence and in young adulthood are few, but do confirm that there is a significant relation between early advanced drinking habits and later alcohol drinking and alcohol problems (Andersson & Magnusson, 1988; Pape & Hammer, 1996). However, although statistically significant, the relation found is normally quite weak and does not exclude a great deal of instability over the adolescent and early adulthood period (Andersson & Magnusson, 1988; Donovan et al., 1983). That is, from a traditional variable and risk factor perspective, early advanced drinking habits are a significant risk factor that explain a small part of the variance with respect to later drinking habits and alcohol problems. In trying to understand the development of early manifested alcohol abuse, a large number of childhood characteristics have also been reported as significant risk factors, individual as well as environmental. Conduct problems, hyperactivity, sensation seeking, and low school performance are a few of the individual characteristics and low socio-economic standard (SES), poor parenting, divorces, and alcohol problems in the family are a few risk factors in the social environment (Clayton, 1992; Donovan et al., 1983; Schulenberg et al., 1996).

Against this basic frame of reference it is important to learn more about the interaction over time between social and individual conditions in late childhood, adolescent drinking habits, and the development of early manifested alcohol problems, and about the existence and characteristics of a specific developmental pattern.

## Purpose

The purpose of this study is to investigate the development of drinking habits and alcohol problems in a representative cohort of 446 Swedish boys, prospectively followed from childhood to adulthood. The developmental interaction between socio-economic and individual aspects of late childhood conditions, adolescent drinking habits, and alcohol problems in early adulthood has been analyzed from a traditional correlational perspective and when using methodology demonstrating the existence and characterics of developmental patterns.

## Method

The study was performed within the Individual Development and Adjustment (IDA) research program. The basic purpose of this research program is to study individual development and adjustment from a longitudinal, interactionist, and developmental perspective (Magnusson, 1988; Magnusson, Dunér, & Zetterblom, 1975). The study cohort consists of all boys and girls in a mid-Swedish community who attended Grade 3 (age 10) in 1965. The cohort has been prospectively followed from childhood to adulthood and has been shown to be representative for the Swedish age cohort in general in a number of aspects (Bergman, 1973; Magnusson et al., 1975; Stattin, Magnusson, & Reichel, 1989).

## Subjects

The subjects in this study consisted of those 446 boys from the cohort who participated in the data collections made at age 13 and at age 15. The attrition was restricted to the 12% of the boys who were not attending school the day of one or both of these data collections.

## Data

Data included information about socioeconomic conditions and individual characteristics in late childhood, drinking habits in early adolescence, and alcohol problems in early adulthood.

As an indicator of socioeconomic standard, information about the parents' occupations and educational status were used. These data were collected by questionnaires filled in by the parents when the subjects were 13 years of age. The information was coded on a 4-point scale where occupation normally requiring academic education was coded as scale value 1 and unskilled work as scale value 4.

As one aspect of individual functioning in late childhood, information from teacher ratings about aggressive behavior, motor restlessness, and impulsivity were used to measure symptoms of conduct problems and attention deficit and hyperactivity disorder (CD/ADHD). The teacher rated each subject in each of the three aspects on 7-point scales where scale value 7 represented high aggressiveness, motor restlessness, and impulsivity. These original values were summarized and transformed into a 4-point scale. Summary scale values 3 to 8 were recoded to scale value 1, representing almost no problems in this aspect. Summary scale values 18 to 21 were recoded to scale value 4, representing severe problems in this aspect of individual functioning.

Another indicator of individual functioning in late childhood focuses on the subject's leisure time activities during the evenings and was measured by self-reports about the frequency of hanging around with peers at public youth centers. These data were collected when the subjects were 13 years of age. "Never" or "almost never" were coded as scale value 1, and visiting youth centers at least 3 evenings a week was coded as scale value 4.

The last indicator representing individual functioning in late childhood was school achievement, measured by the grades in Swedish (language) and mathematics. The original 5-point scales were summarized and transformed into a 4-point scale. Scale value 1 represents the positive end and was assigned subjects with values 2 to 3 on the summary scale; and scale value 4 represents the negative end and was assigned subjects with values 9 to 10 on the summary scale.

The distribution of the four indicators of socioeconomic and individual conditions in late childhood is presented in Table 23.1. A more comprehensive description of this data has been presented by Magnusson et al. (1975).

The data for drinking habits at age 15 were obtained from self-reported information collected in a school survey. The subjects were asked how many times they had drunk so much alcohol that they felt intoxicated. The information was coded on a 4-point scale where scale value 1 represents "never been drunk" (49%) and scale value 4 "been drunk 10 times or more" (7%).

The information about alcohol problems in young adulthood refers to having a psychiatric alcohol diagnosis according to *DSM–III* (APA, 1980), having been under treatment in accordance with the temperance law, or having been registered by the police for drunken driving or public drunkenness (or some combination of the three). Information was obtained by records from the psychiatric care, the social authorities, and the police authorities. These data are nationwide and cover the period of 18 to 24 years of age. Scale value 1 represents no registration for alcohol problems (87%), scale value 2 one registration for public drunkenness or drunken driving (8%), and scale value 3 at least two such incidences and psychiatric

TABLE 23.1
The Distribution of Values for the Age 13 Characteristics Included in the Study
(percentages; $N = 446$)

| Value | Socioeconomic Standard | Visiting Youth Center | CH/ADHD Symptoms | School Achievement |
|-------|-----------------------|----------------------|------------------|--------------------|
| 1 | 9 | 58 | 24 | 12 |
| 2 | 37 | 10 | 43 | 50 |
| 3 | 37 | 22 | 22 | 31 |
| 4 | 17 | 10 | 11 | 7 |
| Total | 100 | 100 | 100 | 100 |

or social care for alcohol problems (5%). Results concerning the development of drinking habits and alcohol problems in this cohort have been presented earlier by Andersson and Magnusson (1988).

## Results

As a starting point, the rank correlation between socioeconomic and individual characteristics at age 13 on the one hand, and drinking habits at age 15 and alcohol problems at age 18 to 24 on the other hand, were calculated. As can be seen in Table 23.2, the results show that indicators of individual functioning in late childhood, especially CD/ADHD symptoms, were significantly related to advanced drinking habits at age 15 whereas social conditions in terms of SES were not. All of the studied characteristics of the late childhood situation were significantly related to alcohol problems in young adulthood. CD/ADHD symptoms were more strongly related to adolescent drinking than to alcohol problems in young adulthood, and the socioeconomic standard in late childhood, not significantly related to adolescent drinking, was significantly related to alcohol problems in young adulthood.

When applying a stepwise regression model to these data (Table 23.3), the results generated a final Multiple $R = .34$ ($p < 0.001$) with respect to adolescent drinking habits and Multiple $R = .30$ ($p < 0.001$) with respect to alcohol problems in early adulthood. After including CD/ADHD symptoms, none of the remaining indicators had an additional significant effect with respect to adolescent drinking habits. With respect to alcohol problems in young adulthood, visiting youth centers and SES had small but significant additional effects beyond the effect of CD/ADHD symptoms. The small additional effects generated by variables other than CD/ADHD point to a high intercorrelation between the variables included in the analyses.

The relation between drinking habits at age 15 and alcohol problems in early adulthood is shown in Table 23.4. Boys with the most advanced drinking habits at age 15 ran a significantly higher risk for later alcohol problems

TABLE 23.2
The Correlations Between Characteristics at Age 13 and Drinking Habits at Age 15 and Alcohol Problems at Age 18 to 24 ($N = 446$)

| Characteristics at Age 13 | Drinking Habits at Age 15 | | Alcohol Problems at Age 18–24 | |
|---|---|---|---|---|
| Socioeconomic standard | .04 | *n.s.* | .15 | .001 |
| Visiting youth center | .16 | .001 | .21 | .001 |
| CH/ADHD symptoms | .32 | .001 | .23 | .001 |
| School Achievement | .15 | .005 | .12 | .05 |

TABLE 23.3

Stepwise Regression Between Characteristics at Age 13 and Drinking Habits at Age 15 and Alcohol Problems at Age 18 to 24 ($N = 446$)

|  | | *Increase in Multiple R* | |
| --- | --- | --- | --- |
|  | *Drinking Habits at Age 15* |  | *Alcohol Problems at Age 18–24* |
| CD/ADHD symptoms (sign) | .31 | CD/ADHD symptoms (sign) | .24 |
| + Visiting youth center (n.s.) | .32 | + Visiting youth center (sign) | .28 |
| + School achievement (n.s.) | .34 | + Socioeconomic standard (sign) | .30 |
| + Socioeconomic standard (n.s.) | *.34* | + School achievement (n.s.) | *.30* |

TABLE 23.4

The Relationship Between Drinking Habits at Age 15 and Alcohol Problems at Age 18 to 24 ($N = 446$)

|  | *Percent with Alcohol Problems, Age 18–24* | | |
| --- | --- | --- | --- |
| *Frequency of Drunkenness, Age 15* | *No Registered Alcohol Problem* | *Registered Once* | *Registered at Least Twice* |
| Never drunk ($n = 216$ | 92 | 6 | 2 |
| 1–3 drunkenness occasions ($n = 146$) | 85 | 9 | 6 |
| 4–10 drunkenness occasions ($n = 51$) | 82 | 8 | 10 |
| > 10 drunkenness occasions ($n = 33$) | 76 | 9 | 15 |
| Total | 87 | 8 | 5 |

*Note.* $r = 15, p < .001$.

compared with boys reporting less-advanced drinking habits at age 15. But, 76% of the boys who had been drunk at least 10 times at age 15 did not develop later alcohol problems (as measured by register data) compared with 24% (7 boys) who did. Of those (216 boys) who had never been drunk at age 15, only 8% (17 boys) developed later alcohol problems. Thus, despite the significant relationship shown in the table, most subjects with early advanced drinking habits did not develop alcohol problems (as measured by register data) and most subjects with alcohol problems in young adulthood did not show advanced drinking habits in early adolescence.

In a further step, the information about drinking habits at age 15 were included in the stepwise regression, after the age 13 indicators (Table 23.5).

TABLE 23.5
Stepwise Regression Including Drinking Habits at Age 15 After the Entrance of Age 13
Characteristics, With Respect to Alcohol Problems at Age 18 to 24 ($N = 445$)

|                                   | Increase in Multiple R |
| --------------------------------- | ---------------------- |
| CD/ADHD symptoms (sign)           | .24                    |
| + Visiting youth center (sign)    | .28                    |
| + Socioeconomic standard (sign)   | .30                    |
| + School adjustment (n.s.)        | .30                    |
| *+ Drinking habits, age 15 (n.s.)* | *.31*                 |

The results show that the additional information about drinking habits at age 15 increased the Multiple R with less than 1% (*ns*) with respect to alcohol problems in young adulthood. Thus, given the information about conditions at age 13, knowledge about drinking habits at age 15 did not substantially increase the possibility of predicting alcohol problems in young adulthood.

An alternative approach for analyzing the relationship between late childhood conditions, early adolescent drinking habits, and alcohol problems in young adulthood is to look for longitudinal developmental patterns. For that purpose, a cluster analysis was initially applied to the data representing age 13 conditions in searching for different characteristic patterns of living conditions in late childhood. The results are shown in Table 23.6.

The figures in the table refer to the 4-point scales mentioned earlier and represent the mean values in each indicator for each of the six clusters of boys. Value 1 represents the most favorable situation and value 4 represents the least favorable situation. Values less than 2 represent a mainly very good situation and have been omitted.

As can be seen in the table, the largest cluster (Cluster 1) includes 28% of the boys and is characterized by a generally good situation, represented by values below 2 in each of the four indicators of late childhood conditions. Cluster 2 was mainly characterized by a good situation, with the exception of a fairly low SES. Cluster 3 comprises a group of boys for whom low SES was combined with low school achievement. The fourth cluster includes boys characterized by high values in CD/ADHD symptoms and around average values in SES and school achievement. In Cluster 5, the group of boys is characterized by frequently visiting youth centers and a fairly good situation in the remaining indicators. Finally, Cluster 6 comprises a group of boys characterized by high values in CD/ADHD symptoms and in visiting youth centers and also by values above average in SES and school achievement. In summary, the results from this analysis clearly demonstrate the

TABLE 23.6
Patterns of Characteristics at Age 13

| Pattern | N | % | Socio-ecomonic Standard | Visiting Youth Center | CD/ADHD Symptom | School Achieve-ment |
|---|---|---|---|---|---|---|
| 1. A generally good situation | 126 | 28 | — | — | — | — |
| 2. Low socioeconomic standard | 65 | 15 | 3.3 | — | — | — |
| 3. Low SES/low school achievement | 56 | 13 | 3.4 | — | — | 3.4 |
| 4. High CD/ADHD | 73 | 16 | 2.4 | — | 3.2 | 2.6 |
| 5. Frequency visiting youth center | 60 | 14 | — | 3.4 | — | 2.4 |
| 6. High CD/ADHD, frequent visiting youth center. (Low SES/school achievement) | 66 | 15 | 2.9 | 3.4 | 3.5 | 2.7 |
| Mean values | | | 2.6 | 1.8 | 2.2 | 2.3 |
| Total | 446 | 100 | | | | |

existence and magnitude of different groups of boys living under quite different socioeconomic and individual conditions in late childhood.

As a natural next step, these different patterns of conditions at age 13 were related to the frequency of advanced drinking habits at age 15 (four drunkenness occasions or more) and to the frequency of alcohol problems at age 18 to 24 (one or more registrations).

As can be seen in Table 23.7, the frequency of advanced adolescent drinking habits as well as later alcohol problems was highly different among the clusters. Although there were no differences in adolescent drinking between Cluster 1 and Cluster 2, the boys in Cluster 2, with a fairly low SES as the only difference compared to Cluster 1, ran a higher risk for alcohol problems in young adulthood. In Cluster 3, represented by boys for whom low school achievement was added to low SES, the frequency of both advanced drinking habits in adolescence and later alcohol problems increased.

Clusters 4 and 6 were both characterized by high values in CD/ADHD symptoms and in both of these clusters the frequency of advanced adolescent drinking habits were higher than in the other clusters. But, when looking at the situation in young adulthood, there is a clear difference between the two clusters of boys. In Cluster 4, where high values in CD/ADHD symptoms were the only problem, the frequency of later alcohol problems were 11%, actually a little below the average for the whole study group. In Cluster 6, where high values in CD/ADHD were combined with high values in visiting youth centers and values above average in SES and school achievement, the frequency of later alcohol problems were three times

### TABLE 23.7

Patterns of Characteristics at Age 13 and Percentages With Advanced Drinking Habits at Age 15 (at Least Four Drunkenness Occasions) and Alcohol Problems at Age 18–24 (at Least One Registration), Respectively

| Pattern | N | % | Socio-economic Standarad | Visiting Youth Center | CD/ADHD Symptom | School Achievement | Percent Advanced Drinking Age 15 | Percent Alcohol Problems age 18–24 |
|---|---|---|---|---|---|---|---|---|
| 1. A generally good situation | 126 | 28 | — | — | — | — | 12 (at) | 3 (at) |
| 2. Low socioeconomic standard | 65 | 15 | 3.3 | — | — | — | 11 (at) | 8 |
| 3. Low SES/low school achievement | 56 | 13 | 3.4 | — | — | 3.4 | 18 | 13 |
| 4. High CD/ADHD | 73 | 16 | 2.4 | — | 3.2 | 2.6 | 32 (t) | 11 |
| 5. Frequency visiting youth center | 60 | 14 | — | 3.4 | — | 2.4 | 15 | 20 |
| 6. High CD/ADHD, frequent visiting youth center. (Low SES/School achievement | 66 | 15 | 2.9 | 3.3 | 3.5 | 2.7 | 31 (t) | 34 (t) |
| Mean values | | | 2.6 | 1.8 | 2.2 | 2.3 | 19 | 13 |
| Total | 446 | 100 | | | | | | |

*Note.* at = a significant "antitype" —the frequency of advanced drinking/alcohol problems is significantly less than expected by chans (*p* < 0.05); t = a significant "type" —the frequency of advanced drinking/alcohol problems is significantly higher than expected by chans (*p* < 0.05).

higher, 34%. That is, with respect to the high and significant relationship between CD/ADHD symptoms and later alcohol problems (Table 23.2), there seems to be two groups of boys, both high in CD/ADHD symptoms and in adolescent drinking habits but with very different prognosis with respect to later alcohol problems. Another comparison that can be made is between Clusters 5 and 6. Two groups of boys, both characterized by high frequency of visiting youth centers at age 13, one (Cluster 5) with a very good socio-economic situation, no tendency to CD/ADHD symptoms and about average in school achievement, and the other (Cluster 6) with quite a problematic situation in general. The first, mainly "well-adjusted," group did not show any increase in advanced drinking habits in adolescence but a tendency (not significant) towards a higher frequency of alcohol problems in early adulthood. The second, for whom frequently visiting youth centers was just one ingredient in a generally unfavorable situation, showed a significantly increased risk for advanced adolescent drinking habits as well as for alcohol problems in young adulthood.

In a last step, the frequency of longitudinal patterns including socioeconomic and individual conditions at age 13, drinking habits at age 15, and alcohol problems at age 18 to 24 were studied. However, as a consequence of splitting up the data on an initially low-frequency phenomenon such as alcohol problems, the absolute numbers of subjects became very small in some cells and therefore the results must be interpreted very carefully. With this reservation in mind, the results show an interesting pattern. As can be seen in Table 23.8, there were 111 boys from Cluster 1 at age 13 with no advanced drinking habits at age 15, while 15 boys from this cluster reported advanced drinking habits at age 15. Whether or not these boys from Cluster 1 had advanced drinking habits at age 15, the risk for later alcohol problems was very small and advanced drinking habits in adolescence did not increase the risk for later alcohol problems among these boys with a generally good socioeconomic and individual background.

A similar pattern can also be seen among the boys in Cluster 6, boys characterized by a fairly unfavorable situation at age 13. Although the frequency of alcohol problems in young adulthood was about 10 times higher in this group in general, there were no differences between those 20 boys who were characterized by advanced drinking habits at age 15 and those 46 boys who were not.

In three of the remaining four clusters (Clusters 2–4), all characterized by a more mixed situation at age 13 with respect to socioeconomic and individual conditions, advanced drinking habits at age 15 consistently increased the risk for later alcohol problems about 2 to 3 times. The fourth cluster—the "frequently visiting youth center" boys—shows a similar developmental pattern as Cluster 6 but at a lower level.

TABLE 23.8

Patterns of Characteristics at Age 13, Frequency of Advanced Drinking Habits at Age 15 (at Least Four Times of Drunkenness) and Alcohol Problems at Age 18 to 24 (at Least One Registration)

| Pattern, Age 13 | N | % | Socio-economic Staandard | Visiting Youth Center | CD/ ADHD Symptom | School Adjustment | Advanced Drinking Habits at Age 15 | Alcohol Problems at Age 18–24 | |
|---|---|---|---|---|---|---|---|---|---|
| 1. A generally good situation | 126 | 28 | — | — | — | — | No = 111<br>Yes = 15 | 3%<br>— | (n = 3)<br>— |
| 2. Low socio-economic standard | 65 | 15 | 3.3 | — | — | — | No = 58<br>Yes = 7 | 7%<br>14% | (n = 4)<br>(n = 1) |
| 3. Low SES/low school achievement | 56 | 13 | 3.4 | — | — | 3.4 | No = 46<br>Yes = 10 | 9%<br>30% | (n = 4)<br>(n = 3) |
| 4. High CD/ADHD | 73 | 16 | 2.4 | — | 3.1 | 2.6 | No = 50<br>Yes = 23 | 8%<br>17% | (n = 4)<br>(n = 4) |
| 5. Frequent visiting youth center | 60 | 13 | — | 3.4 | — | 2.4 | No = 51<br>Yes = 9 | 20%<br>22% | (n = 10)<br>(n = 2) |
| 6. High CD/ADHD, frequent visiting youth center, low SES school achievement | 66 | 15 | 2.9 | 3.3 | 3.5 | 2.7 | No = 46<br>Yes = 20 | 33%<br>35% | (n = 15)<br>(n = 7) |

## DISCUSSION

The present study was exclusively focused on boys, and on a very limited number of individual and environmental conditions during a limited period of the boys' lifetime. Thus, although the importance of the holistic and developmental perspective discussed in the Introduction has not been more than very briefly illustrated, the results demonstrate some important issues for the understanding of developmental processes leading to early manifested alcohol problems as measured by registrations from official authorities—a criteria of alcohol problem that of course can be discussed from a construct-validity perspective, and should definitely be observed from a generalization point of view.

The results confirm earlier findings that early advanced drinking habits are statistically correlated to later alcohol problems. But, the results also show that advanced drinking habits at age 15 are by no means necessarily predictive of adult alcohol problems and are actually a less-effective predictor than, for instance, CD/ADHD symptoms at age 13. The information about drinking habits at age 15 did not increase the explained variance with respect to later alcohol problems after considering socioeconomic and individual conditions at age 13.

When focusing on the issue of early alcohol problems as a question pertaining exclusively to alcohol and alcohol consumption, the "early and advanced pattern" might be seen as a natural and important aspect to consider when trying to understand the phenomenon, as well as when formulating strategies for prevention and treatment. However, regarding early manifested alcohol problems as a result of a continuous developmental process, in which early advanced drinking habits are only one of many relevant individual and environmental components, the implications will obviously be different. Obviously, alcohol drinking is necessary to develop alcohol problems, but the "early and advanced pattern" may be an important component in only some developmental processes leading to later alcohol problems, and of negligible relevance in other developmental processes ending up in alcohol problems. Keeping the earlier-mentioned reservation in mind, the results in this study indicate that early advanced drinking habits might play a minor role given a very favorable—or a very unfavorable—psychosocial background, whereas they may have a more accentuated importance for boys characterized by other patterns of psychosocial background. The results highlight the importance of not only focusing on the drinking habits in adolescence when formulating prevention strategies, but also considering psychosocial conditions far before the youngsters begin drinking alcohol and, especially, the developmental interaction between early conditions and adolescent drinking habits.

A second reflection concerns the importance of the socioeconomic background. The results in this study indicate that the socioeconomic background was of no relevance for the development of advanced drinking habits in early adolescence but was significantly related to later alcohol problems. This could indicate that individual and personality characteristics are the main factors that influence the initial drinking habits in adolescence, whereas the socioeconomic background has an influence on the progression from adolescent to adulthood drinking habits and alcohol problems. However, the results could also to some extent be a consequence of measuring two different aspects of alcohol behavior, in two different psychosocial contexts and with two different methods. Given a very high stability in social standard from childhood to early adulthood and also in general alcohol behavior from adolescence to adulthood, the results may be somewhat overestimated due to social bias in the risk for being registered by authorities when having an alcohol problem.

Early CD/ADHD symptoms are a well-documented risk factor with respect to the development of alcohol problems. The results from the correlational analyses in this study confirm these findings, but also show that the correlation was stronger with respect to advanced drinking habits in adolescence than with respect to adulthood alcohol problems, a result easily interpreted as a consequence of, or at least influenced by, the differences in time between the first and the second measurement points in the two correlations. However, the results from the complementary cluster analyses showed two subgroups of boys high in CD/ADHD symptoms at age 13, both with advanced drinking habits at age 15 but with highly different prognoses for later alcohol problems, depending on the interaction with psychosocial background factors. These results demonstrate the importance of including different aspects of individual functioning and environment over time. The finding of the two subgroups with different prognoses makes sense with regard to the decrease in the overall correlation beyond the "difference in time" and gives additional information about developmental structures including CD/ADHD symptoms.

In contrast to the holistic approach discussed in the Introduction, this study was exclusively focused on the development of alcohol problems, with no account taken of the general pattern of functioning, of which the alcohol problems are only one component. Earlier studies of the cohort have shown that many of the subjects with alcohol problems in early adulthood were also registered by authorities for either criminality or psychiatric problems, or both (Magnusson, 1988). It is reasonable to assume that the existence and characteristics of the developmental patterns illustrated in this study could be further refined if also taking this aspect into consideration. Although traditional risk factors such as CD/ADHD, low school achievement, and early advanced drinking habits are repeatedly found to be statistically related to alcohol problems as well as to other types of psychosocial maladjustment, the amount of variance explained is normally very modest. Applying a holistic and developmental approach in which, for instance, CD/ADHD is allowed to operate differently in different constellations of psychosocial developmental patterns that in turn can be related to different patterns of adult functioning in which alcohol problems are one characteristic, can perhaps generate additional information of the complexity in the development of early alcohol problems.

The results in this study demonstrate the importance of a developmental perspective when trying to understand why some boys have alcohol problems in early adulthood but most boys do not, the importance of including both individual and social aspects in the analysis, and the advantages of combining a traditional variable approach with a person approach.

## REFERENCES

American Psychiatric Association. (1980). *Diagnostic and statistical manual of mental disorders* (3rd ed.). Washington, DC: American Psychiatric Association.

Andersson, T., & Magnusson, D. (1988). Drinking habits and alcohol abuse among young men. A prospective longitudinal study. *Journal of Studies on Alcohol, 49*, 245–252.

Bergman, L. R. (1973). Parents' education and mean change in intelligence. *Scandinavian Journal of Psychology, 14*, 273–281.

Cairns, R. B., & Cairns, B. D. (1994). *Lifelines and risks. Pathways of youth in our time.* Hemel Hempstead, UK: Harvester Wheatsheaf.

Clayton, R. (1992). Transitions in drug use: Risk and protective factors. In M. Glanz & R. Pickens (Eds.), *Vulnerability to drug abuse* (pp. 15–49). Washington, DC: American Psychological Association.

Donovan, J. E., Jessor, R., & Jessor, L. (1983). Problem drinking in adolescence and young adulthood. A follow-up study. *Journal of Studies on Alcohol, 44*, 109–137.

Fillmore, K. M., Hartka, E., Johnstone, B. M., Leino, E. M., Motoyoshi, M., & Temple, M. T. (1996). A meta analysis of life course variation in drinking. *British Journal of Addiction, 86*, 1221–1268.

Glanz, M., & Pickens, R. (1992). *Vulnerability to drug abuse.* Washington, DC: American Psychological Association.

Magnusson, D. (1988). Individual development from an interactional perspective: A longitudinal study. In D. Magnusson (Ed.), *Paths through life.* Hillsdale, NJ: Lawrence Erlbaum Associates.

Magnusson, D. (1995). Individual development: A holistic integrated model. In P. Moen, G. H. Elder, & K. Lüscher (Eds.), *Linking lifes and contexts: Perspectives on the ecology of human development* (pp. 19–60). Washington, DC: American Psychological Association.

Magnusson, D., Dunér, A., & Zetterblom, G. (1975). *Adjustment: A longitudinal study.* Stockholm: Almqvist & Wiksell.

Pape, H., & Hammer, T. (1996). How does young people's alcohol consumption change during the transition to early adulthood? A longitudinal study of changes at aggregate and individual level. *British Journal of Addiction, 91*, 1345–1357.

Schulenberg, J., O'Malley, P., Bachman, J., Wadsworth, K., & Johnston, L. (1996). Getting drunk and growing up. Trajectories of frequent drinking during the transition to young adulthood. *Journal of Studies on Alcohol, 57*, 289–304.

Stattin, H., Magnusson, D., & Reichel, H. (1989). Criminal activity at different ages. A study based on a Swedish longitudinal research population. *British Journal of Criminology, 29*, 368–385.

Wagenar, A. C., & Perry, C. L. (1994). Community strategies for the reduction of youth drinking: Theory and application. *Journal of Research on Adolescence, 4*, 319–345.

# 24

# Studying the Real Child Rather Than the Ideal Child: Bringing the Person Into Developmental Studies

Hongxin Zhao
Jeanne Brooks-Gunn
Teachers College, Columbia University

Sara McLanahan
Burton Singer
Princeton University

Throughout the history of developmental inquiry, tensions are evident between more case-based and more variable-oriented approaches to studying lives through time. Studying lives through time represents the heart of developmental inquiry. Although case-oriented and variable-oriented approaches have both been applied when studying individuals, the latter is the choice of many scholars. This is true even in the face of a common criticism when employing variable-oriented approaches: The person becomes lost quite quickly. As a result, as Mishler (1996) pointed out, the mean becomes reified, as "if it is the ideal child that would have been available for study in the best of all possible worlds—if it were not for all the messiness of inter- and intraindividual variation resulting from a host of uncontrolled and unknown sources" (p. 78). Many developmental scholars would protest, arguing that the focus on individual differences, on contextual influences, and on the interaction of the two, is proof of a move away from a focus on the "average child" (Lewin, 1935). However, even longitudinal, temporally linked, and process-oriented studies typically use variable-oriented statistical techniques to examine lives (event history analyses, growth curve analyses, path analyses; Brooks-Gunn, Phelps, & Elder, 1991; Magnusson, 1988). These techniques still have as their central concern the variable, not the person. To put it another way, the study of whole lives is often missing or is fragmented.

Magnusson and his colleagues have been major proponents of bringing individuals into the study of lives through time (Magnusson, 1988; Magnusson & Bergman, 1988, 1990; Magnusson & Törestad, 1993). This volume is testimony to the impact that Magnusson has had on developmental inquiry. It also serves as a primer on the ways in which the "ideal child" (i.e., the average child of the mean) is being replaced by "real children." Many of the approaches represented in this volume are based on looking at the patterning of lives—either in terms of constellations of behaviors that co-occur at various points during lives or in light of the reciprocal processes that occur among individuals. A superb discussion of person-centered methods and models is contained in Cairns, Bergman, and Kagan (1998). In all of this work the person is emerging, however, whole lives are often not represented.

Case-oriented approaches have been the province of clinicians and scholars studying learning, not to mention theorists such as Skinner, Piaget, Erikson, and Lewin (Hinde, 1992; Mishler, 1996). Such approaches also are paradigmatic of ethnographic work (Jessor, Colby & Shweder, 1996). However useful for generating insight or theory, a case-oriented approach is not the coin of the realm of developmental inquiry. As Mishler (1990) says, paraphrasing an anonymous colleague, "Everyone knows it's all right to study individual cases to develop theory, but that's not how we're supposed to do scientific research" (p. 75).

The purpose of this chapter is to put forth a person-centered strategy for analyzing and aggregating individual histories ascertained via longitudinal surveys. Although the focus is development histories of behaviorally resilient and vulnerable children, the methodology has broad applicability for studying and comparing multiple lives through time.

This chapter is divided into three sections. In the first, principles that have informed our approach to studying risk and resilience in young children are discussed, and exemplars of more variable-oriented approaches are offered (focusing in part on our own work). The second section contains a person-centered strategy that represents one solution to the problem confronting us: How to look at the multiple pathways that subgroups of children traverse to arrive at a given outcome or set of outcomes. We considered the life courses of individuals who are resilient in the face of adversity and those of individuals who are vulnerable. We applied this strategy to data from a national longitudinal study to identify behaviorally resilient 5- and 6-year-olds whose mothers were teenagers when they gave birth. In the conclusion we comment on the usefulness of the multiple-pathways approach in the study of vulnerability and resilience.

## RISK AND RESILIENCE: CAN MULTIPLE PATHWAYS BE IDENTIFIED IN VARIABLE-ORIENTED RESEARCH? PRINCIPLES UNDERLYING RISK AND RESILIENCE

The general problem confronting us is how to look simultaneously at multiple pathways in the study of risk and resilience. Like others, our concern is with the variations in processes leading to a particular outcome (and, if we wanted to complicate matters, to different outcomes). Variations in processes no doubt look different as a function of the outcomes of interest as well as the aspect of the life course under study. Although the existence of multiple pathways to the same outcome is accepted in developmental psychology, such pathways are infrequently studied (Cicchetti & Cohen, 1995; Haggerty, Garmezy, Rutter, & Sherrod, 1994; Luthar & Zigler, 1991; Rutter, 1989, 1990; Werner & Smith, 1992). A multiple-pathways approach allows for an examination of the multiple factors and events that converge in an individual to move that person towards an outcome, or set of outcomes.

Several general principles inform our work. First, any environmental characteristic or event probably affects development differentially based on the co-occurrence of other characteristics or events. Second, characteristics of the child not only mitigate or accentuate the effects of a particular environmental characteristic, but also may exert their influence through specific combinations of environmental characteristics. Third, environmental events or characteristics are likely to influence development in a cumulative fashion. Research does focus on these principles, which have been stated in slightly different form by others (Cairns & Cairns, 1994; Garmezy, 1985, 1991, 1993; Rutter, 1989, 1990; Singer, Ryff, Carr, & Magee, 1998). Exemplars of work on young children that capture the spirit of these three principles characterizing the study of resilience are presented. These examples are taken from variable-oriented research, and limitations of this work are highlighted. To offset criticism, illustrations from our own contribution to the understanding of the "ideal child" are also presented. The focus is on family risk factors, maternal characteristics, and parenting in the first 5 years of life, in keeping with our analyses using a person-oriented approach.

### Illustrations of the General Principles From Variable-Oriented Work

One principle is that a particular event or characteristic of the environment might influence the child differently based on the co-occurrence of other events or characteristics. Consequently, the existence or strength of a particular characteristic, by itself, may not tell us much about the ways in which that characteristic, in combination with other events, actually leads to the outcome.

Links between maternal responsiveness and warmth on the one hand and child aggressive and acting out behavior on the other are used as an illustration. Maternal responsiveness and warmth (assuming similarity across age in function if not in form) might have different effects on children who are infants versus those who are preschoolers versus those who are in elementary school (responsiveness might be more salient in the early years of life, whereas other dimensions of maternal behavior, such as quality of assistance and firm control, might gain prominence in the elementary school years; Bornstein, 1995; Bornstein & Tamis-LeMonda, 1997; Sroufe & Rutter, 1984). In addition, responsiveness, in combination with other maternal behaviors, might affect children differently. For example, punitive discipline, as measured by spanking, seems to have little negative influence on young children's aggressive behavior if it occurs in the context of a warm and responsive mother–child relationship. However, punitive discipline did have significant links to aggressive behavior in 3-year-olds when mothers were not particularly responsive (Smith & Brooks-Gunn, 1997). Maternal responsiveness may have less (or more) of an effect on children whose mothers face adverse circumstances, such as poverty, single parenthood, low social support, poor mental health, and so on. The relationships that the mother has with spouse, partners, and other adults may also interact with responsiveness vis-à-vis effects on child aggressive behavior, just as the child's relationships with these same individuals may condition the effect of maternal responsiveness. The point here is not just to document the complexity and linked nature of relationships and of child behaviors, but to highlight the difficulty of constructing the multiple pathways through which maternal responsiveness and child aggressive behavior might be linked or the pathways through which some children whose mothers are unresponsive manage to exhibit emotional regulation.

Bronfenbrenner (1986) has described such series of interactions in terms of process by context interactions. However, can multiple pathways really be constructed via the examination of many interactions? Or are we left with a catalog of characteristics that influence a particular child outcome for "the average child" (i.e., that ideal child for which all other factors and interactions are controlled via regression analyses) and the factors that moderate these effects? How do we differentiate those children for whom maternal responsiveness, if expressed in the context of little harsh discipline, good maternal mental health, and a stable home environment, leads to emotional regulation from those children for whom maternal responsiveness, if expressed in a context of harsh discipline, an unstable home environment, and high levels of social support leads to emotional regulation? How many other pathways exist in any given sample of children? And how are we to discover these pathways, given that interaction terms cannot be entered into equations ad infinitum (and even if they could, would still not represent individuals, but residual effects holding other factors constant)?

A second principle is that characteristics of the child (such as birth weight and gender) may mitigate or accentuate effects of particular events or characteristics. Continuing our example, maternal responsiveness on the part of the child may be linked to characteristics of the child. So, for example, maternal responsiveness may be less linked to child emotional dysregulation for very low birth weight children (1500 grams or less) than for heavier low birth weight children, given the level of biological insult in the former group (Brooks-Gunn, Klebanov, & Liaw, 1993; Brooks-Gunn, Liaw, & Klebanov, 1992). Maternal responsiveness, in combination with harsh discipline, might affect girls and boys differentially, if boys are more resistant (or perceived to be more resistant) to disciplinary practices (Smith & Brooks-Gunn, 1997). At the same time, some girls (and boys) will do well in spite of harsh disciplinary practices and unresponsive mothers. What are the events, conditions, and characteristics that account for this success? Variable-oriented approaches give little purchase on this question.

Some pathways to a child outcome may be more biological than others. Sroufe and Rutter (1984) have distinguished two general pathways to attention deficit and hyperactivity disorder—one that is more biological and one that is characterized by unresponsive parenting. In Bronfenbrenner's terms (1979), it is critical to consider person by process by context interactions.

A third principle is that events may not influence an individual in an additive fashion, as is implied in the preceding paragraph. That is, the accumulation of events may be more critical than the experience of any one event in and of itself. Literature on multiple risk factors is relevant here. Examples from work with young children include the work of Sameroff and colleagues (Sameroff & Feil, 1985; Sameroff, Seifer, Baldwin, & Baldwin, 1993), Brooks-Gunn and colleagues (Liaw & Brooks-Gunn, 1994; Klebanov, Brooks-Gunn, McCarton & McCormick, 1998) and Garmezy and colleagues (Garmezy, Masten, & Tellegen, 1984). Young children's cognitive test scores are associated with the number of familial risk factors that a child has experienced. Using a list of 11 risk factors, adapted from the work of Sameroff et al. (1985, 1993), we examined associations between the number of risk factors and young children's intelligence test scores, as is illustrated in Fig. 24.1, taken from the Infant Health and Development Program (1990) data set. This program was a large (985 families) multisite (8 sites) randomized trial testing the efficacy of early education and family services (provided from birth until the child's third birthday) upon the well-being of low birth weight premature children (Brooks-Gunn et al., 1992, 1993; Brooks-Gunn, Klebanov, & Liaw, 1994). We looked at 3-year-olds from poor and nonpoor families who were in the follow-up-only group (poverty being defined by annual family

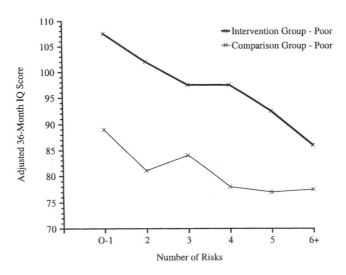

FIG. 24.1. Adjusted IQ scores by risk groups and poverty status. Redrawn from Liaw and Brooks-Gunn (1994).

income and household size, updated yearly based on the Consumer Price Index; see Duncan et al., 1994; poor is defined as an income at or below 150% of the U.S. poverty threshold in 1986, when the children in this study were 1 year of age). The accumulation of risk factors was associated with lower intelligence test scores for both poor and nonpoor children alike. Of interest is the fact that although the nonpoor children had higher scores than the poor children when few other risk factors were present in their families, as the number of risk factors increased, the differences between poor and nonpoor children decreased (a significant risk factors by poverty status interaction; Liaw & Brooks-Gunn, 1994; Brooks-Gunn, 1995). These analyses, of course, tell us nothing about the combination of risk factors (or the various combinations of risk factors) that were associated with either more positive outcomes or negative outcomes (in this case, based on IQ scores) at 3 years of age.

A related issue is whether the cumulative effects of risk factors are linear. Analyses from the Infant Health and Development Program, again, indicate that for this sample, the absence of risk factors is more salient than is the presence of many risk factors (Klebanov et al., 1998). Such analyses do not provide a clue as to whether some combinations of risk factors for those with a medium or large number of factors would be less likely to result in low IQ scores than other combinations. In typical variable-oriented approaches, it is difficult to address this issue, since risk factors tend to co-occur.

One illustration may be taken from the National Longitudinal Study of Youth-Child Supplement (Chase-Lansdale, Brooks-Gunn, Mott, & Phillips,

1991) and the Infant Health and Development Program, described earlier. In both of these data sets, children from poor families who did well, vis-à-vis verbal ability and early school achievement, came from homes that provided stimulating learning experiences (reading, learning activities, trips to museums). Indeed, about half of the variance in child outcomes ascribed to family income was accounted for by the home learning environment (Klebanov, Brooks-Gunn, Chase-Lansdale, & Gordon, 1997; Klevanov, Brooks-Gunn, & Duncan, 1994; Klebanov et al., 1998), with these effects being accounted for by the learning experiences inside the home (reading, learning activities), not outside the home (museums, cultural events). However, such a result tells us nothing about multiple pathways. What about those resilient children who did not have rich home environments?

## A PERSON-ORIENTED APPROACH TO RISK AND RESILIENCE: LIFE HISTORIES, SURVEY DATA AND MULTIPLE PATHWAYS

Our goal is to study life histories with a person-centered strategy that is not restricted to single case examples, but is appropriate for large sample survey data. We retain the person as the unit of analysis, but do so in the context of nomothetic inquiry, where the central question is how multiple lives are similar and different. We adapt a strategy of Singer and colleagues (Singer et al., 1998) to the context of child development. Our procedures utilize both numbers and narratives to assemble and interpret the early-life histories of children, thereby revealing a blend of quantitative and qualitative methods. A comprehensive understanding of multiple lives—or segments of them—requires such a synthetic approach.

### Organizing Principles and Data Structures

We employ longitudinal survey data—Child Supplement to the National Longitudinal Survey of Youth (NLSY-CS)—to assemble early-life histories of children. Such surveys, although frequently lacking the depth and detail of individual biographies and autobiographies, offer the distinct advantage of being able to compare multiple lives on the same kind of life history information. This potential has rarely been exploited, given the long-standing propensities to analyze longitudinal survey data with variable-oriented techniques.

Although analysis begins with the full set of survey responses pertaining to each individual, our strategy leads to a whittling down of theoretically relevant characteristics while retaining individual lives as the central focus. In the process, there is an inevitable tension between thinning down the descriptions of individual lives for purposes of generalization and retaining the maximal number of nuanced descriptive features. The process of thinning fine-grained descriptions into clusters of essential characteristics is, of necessity, linked to an investigator's theoretical framework.

## Sample Selection

Our data are taken from the Child Supplement to the National Longitudinal Survey of Youth (NLSY-CS), a probability sample of over 12,000 persons born between 1957 and 1964 who were teenagers at the time of the first interview (1979). These individuals have been assessed yearly through the mid-1990s (and are now being assessed every other year). African-American, Latino, and poor white youth were over-sampled. Starting in 1986, a Child Supplement was added to the NLSY, so that all women of the NLSY (half of the original 1979 sample) who were mothers had their children assessed. Data on the children were gathered every other year, and as children were born, they were added to the sample. The children of the NLSY are not a nationally representative sample because, for example, mothers who had children in the 1980s were, by definition, relatively young (Chase-Lansdale et al., 1991). However, over time, the sample becomes more representative, as more NLSY women become mothers.

For the present analyses, we selected children born between 1980 and 1984 (2,973 children). Of these, 796 were born to women who were younger than age 20 at the time of the birth. Eliminating the 48 children who were not assessed between 1986 and 1992 (for a variety of reasons), 748 children are included, all of whom were assessed when they were between 5 and 6 years of age. About one third of the 748 mothers of these children were African-American, 42% were white, and 23% were Latino. The mothers had low levels of education—69% had not completed high school or had received a General Education Diploma (GED) at the time of the child's birth. In terms of marital status, one third of the 748 mothers were married at the time of the child's birth, and an additional 13.8% were married in the first year following the child's birth. Seventy-five percent of our 748 children were first born, 50% of them were females, and 9.7% were low birth weight.

## Resilience and Vulnerability as Outcomes

To define behaviorally resilient children, we sorted the sample into quartiles based on the normed standard percentile scores on Behavioral Problems.[1] The children of teenage mothers whose BPI scores fall within the

---

[1]In the NLSY-CS, mothers were asked 28 structured questions concerning the child's problem behaviors. Three response categories ("often true," "sometimes true," and "not true") were used in the questionnaire, and were then dichotomized and summed to produce an index for each child (each item answered "often true" or "sometimes true" was given a score of one, and each item answered "not true" was given a score of zero). Thus, higher scores represent a greater level of behavior problems (Mott & Baker, 1997).

bottom quartile for BPIs at the national level were defined as behaviorally resilient (fewer problems). Seventy-eight children, or 10% of the children of teenage mothers, fit this definition. Of these children, 42% were African-American, 28% were Latino, and 30% were white.

## Analysis

Our analytical strategy involved five major steps:

1. Construct narrative histories for a subsample of cases from the behaviorally resilient and vulnerable groups.
2. Identify "commonalities" and potentially distinct pathways within each behavioral group.
3. Create response vectors that characterize the development process constrained by the organizing principles.
4. Construct thinned representations of development experiences using the tension between the idiosyncrasy of individual lives and subgroup variations.
5. Construct tests of distinguishability to assess whether the pathway features of the behaviorally resilient children are distinct from those of the behaviorally vulnerable.

Each of these steps is described in detail for the behaviorally resilient group. The same strategy, applied to the vulnerable group, yields qualitatively different pathways.

***Step1: Write Narrative Case Histories for Randomly Selected Respondents From Each Behavioral Group.*** For illustrative purposes, we present the survey-based narratives of five behaviorally resilient children taken from the NLSY surveys. At this stage, the entire-person data record was amassed with more than 250 variables. In other words, information was extracted from the mother's responses to every question asked in the annual NLSY survey starting in 1980; mother's as well as children's responses to every question asked in the child and mother supplement survey years were also extracted.

The human mind has difficulty processing this quantity of information in numerical form (Miller, 1956). However, the labor-intensive exercise of converting numerical responses into a narrative ultimately gives a representation of complex interrelationships in a form we are able to grasp: a story (Bruner, 1996; Schank, 1990).

The following narratives—in somewhat abbreviated form—are specific cases from the behaviorally resilient group:

### Child A

*Johnny was the only child. He was white. His mother married his father when she was only 18 years of age and a few months pregnant with Johnny. She managed to stay in school and obtained a high school diploma. After giving birth to Johnny, she decided to stay at home and spend more time with him, whereas his father shouldered the responsibility of being the major bread-earner for the family by working full-time and year-round most of the years. However, at the age of 3, Johnny encountered the first spell of poverty in his life when his father's earnings could not make ends meet for the family. His mother returned to the labor market and maintained a 10 hour per week job throughout Johnny's childhood. When his mother was away, his maternal grandmother who lived nearby took care of Johnny.*

*Johnny received plenty of warmth, affection, and strict discipline from both parents in his early childhood years. His father, though working full-time, always managed to have as much time with him as possible: They ate together daily and frequently went out together on weekends for various sports activities, movies, or museum exhibitions. His mother set high standards for him. She limited his TV hours to 3 each day and always tried to reason with him when he misbehaved. When he was a bit older, she would expect him to pick up after himself, to clean his own room or clean up spills. But she was also very open in showing him her love and encouragement. If Johnny made progress on something, however small that might be, she would kiss him, praise him, and make compliments to others about him. Her affection toward him was easily shown during the interview when the interviewer observed her positive feelings towards Johnny, and her patient and very constructive conversation with Johnny.*

### Child B

*Mary was the older of two girls. She was African American. Her parents got married when both were 17 years of age. At the age of 18, her mother gave birth to her and soon dropped out of school. Her mother stayed at home, while her father managed to keep a full-time moderate-wage job. The family's economic situation was not so good during these years; the family can be described as part of the working poor.*

*At age 4, her parents divorced and she and her mother and sister moved back to her maternal grandparents' household where she lived with three uncles and aunts and a few cousins. After her parents' divorce, Mary's father continued to come to visit her on a regular basis and occasionally brought checks to her mother as his child support payments. Her mother started a part-time job that allowed her to work 15 hours a week. She was strict with Mary and kept high expectations for her as well. She was described by the interviewer as being very responsive and loving. Thus, in spite of economic hardship and parental divorce, Mary was raised in an environment with continuity of emotional support.*

These narratives were written in order to provide a chronological representation of the child's first 5 or 6 years of life. They provide details about the family constellation, and changes in it over the early years, about the mother's work and marital history, about the sources of social support in the child's life, about maternal parenting behavior (warmth, provision of learning experiences, disciplinary practices), about maternal self-efficacy, and about paternal contact (with some information on whether or not the father ate meals with the child and played games or sports during the preschool years). The child's health and behavior are also available from the survey data and can be used to augment the foregoing narratives.

An intensive examination of a relatively small number of cases is necessary to complete the second step of this analytic approach. Basically, the constructed life histories are used to identify those variables that exhibit some commonalities among the behaviorally resilient children. We refer to this as a "thinning" process. This step involves decision making guided by theories and prior empirical research as well as the content of the constructed narratives. This process constitutes what may be seen as a great departure from more variable-oriented approaches. However, we would argue that decision making plays a much larger role in variable-oriented studies than is commonly recognized. That is, variable-oriented approaches often have to cull a list of variables from hundreds of events, conditions, and characteristics that might be entered into a series of regressions to represent life histories and changes. For example, in the Baltimore Study of Teenage Motherhood, decisions as to what variables to include in the 17-year follow-up of young mothers who had babies in the late 1960s were made based on prior research (i.e., welfare receipt in the family of origin and in the first years of the baby's life being likely to influence welfare receipt later on) as well as on theoretical grounds (i.e., weak labor force attachment when the mothers were still young being likely to influence later welfare receipt, educational attainment, and stability of work for both the mother and her offspring during their respective adulthoods; Baydar, Brooks-Gunn, Furstenberg, 1993; Furstenberg, Brooks-Gunn, & Morgan, 1987; Guo, Brooks-Gunn, & Harris, 1996). Additionally, bivariate associations among possible antecedent variables and outcomes were examined to augment the decision-making process.

Judgmental processes also operate in person-oriented approaches where traditional statistical techniques are utilized. For example, when cluster analyses are the method of choice, the investigator is deciding what variables are most likely to produce theoretically meaningful groupings. Our point is that individual judgment is part and parcel of any life-course study. Our person-centered multiple pathways approach may just be more explicit in the use of judgment in the "thinning" process. The decisions are based on examining individual case histories to search for commonalities.

***Step 2: Identify Common Pathways and Variation Within Each Behavioral Group.*** Comparing and contrasting the narratives suggested that a considerable number of variables in the original case listings would either not be expected to affect behavioral resilience or were not ascertained in such a way that the influence on the particular child of interest was transparent. We restricted our further considerations to roughly 80 responses per individual based on our consideration of the narratives. In addition, we randomly selected another 15 cases from the behaviorally resilient group and prepared a table based on 80-component response vectors. By looking at the 20 cases, we also identified commonalities that we expected to be theoretically prominent features of the full behaviorally resilient group. For example, a composite variable associated with social support and parenting identifies this group as satisfying the following seven conditions: (a) intact family, (b) father works full-time (if in household), (c) minimal to moderate poverty (poor 3 years or less of the first 6 years of life), (d) mother's authoritative disciplinary style, (e) mother's responsiveness to child, (f) father's high involvement, (g) child frequently taken out to visit relatives or friends, museums, and movies. Some prominent features of the full group of 20 cases are: 10 children were born of marriages where a biological father was present throughout the first 6 years of life; 6 were born outside marriage but the mother married the child's father soon after the child was born; 4 others had no father present in the household but other family members (e.g., grandparents) lived with them. Fourteen of the children were observed by the interviewer to have a very responsive mother. Mothers of half of the children did not work throughout this period and the fathers were major bread-earners. Not a single child received punitive punishment if she or he did not behave well.

Table 24.1 shows a summary of the essential elements comprising the salient experiences of behaviorally resilient children as distilled from the 5 narratives and 15 additional records based on 80 variables. This representation involves long-term protective factors that, working together, theoretically should facilitate successful child development achieved at ages 5 or 6.

To clarify how composite variables such as "persistently high on emotional support" were created, it is useful to consider a section of the data tables focused on the five variables (labeled "i" to "v") under this heading in Table 24.1. In particular, Table 24.2 shows the responses for cases focused on these variables.

Each of the cases has at least four affirmative responses. Defining a composite response that says these seven cases all have the same level of emotional support—that is, the condition that at least four out of five conditions hold—requires that we judge the individual conditions to be substitutable as sources of support. Critics may question our judgments and develop their own alternatives with accompanying substantive defense. However, what is fundamental here is that this kind of judgmental process is inescapable in any strategy of abstracting concepts—emotional or parental support, for example—beyond the idiosyncratic detail of individual cases.

TABLE 24.1

Abstracted Chronological Chart—Based on Chronological Chart of Five Behaviorally Resilient Children

| | Before Birth | After Birth | OR | |
|---|---|---|---|---|
| Health & nutrition [1] | Early prenatal care Mothers minimal negative pregnancy-related health behaviors [3] | No serious illness Immunization shots [Normal birth weight] [Normal gestation age] OR [frequent pediatrician visits first year] OR [breastfeeding] | | |
| Economic resources [2] | | [Not poor or on welfare] OR [short-term poor] At least one working adult in household Father full-time working [Mother flexible work hours] [3] OR [not working] [3] [At least one parent at least HS] OR [In school and upwardly mobile [3] | OR | Mother full-time working Child care arrangement |
| Parental resources [3] | | Father present in household Father non-teen Father's high involvement on [4]   (i) time together   (ii) outdoor activities   (iii) everyday meals (together with mother) | | [Father in households some years, other adults other years] OR [Father not in, other adults in] |
| Physical environment [4] | | At least 3 of the following in home environment (I) - (iv)   (i) safe   (ii) not dark   (iii) clean | | |

TABLE 24.1
(Continued)

| Social support & parenting [5] | Persistently high on emotional support, has at least 4 out of (i) - (v)<br>(i) frequently taken on an outing or visit friend/relatives<br>(ii) encourage hobbies<br>(iii) adequate hours of watching TV<br>(iv) parents discuss TV programs<br>(v) frequent show of affections:<br>kiss, hug, caress,<br>praise for something good,<br>compliment to another adult<br>Minimal corporal punishment when tantrum, has either of:<br>(i) talking and no spanking<br>(ii) talking and/or other forms<br>Persistently close on mother-child interaction (during interviews):<br>(i) show positive feeling toward child<br>(ii) answers child's questions verbally<br>(iii) converse a few times with child | High on either nonresidential father's involvement:<br>(i) at least monthly visit, including<br>outdoor activities<br>(ii) child support payment |
| --- | --- | --- |

TABLE 24.2
Responses on Emotional Support Variables

| | | Emotional Support Variables | | | |
| --- | --- | --- | --- | --- | --- |
| *Case* | *V1* | *V2* | *V3* | *V4* | *V5* |
| 1 | 1 | 1 | 0 | 1 | 1 |
| 2 | 0 | 1 | 1 | 1 | 1 |
| 3 | 1 | 1 | 1 | 1 | 0 |
| 4 | 1 | 1 | 0 | 1 | 1 |
| 5 | 1 | 0 | 1 | 1 | 1 |
| 6 | 1 | 1 | 1 | 0 | 1 |
| 7 | 1 | 1 | 1 | 1 | 1 |

*Note.* A response of 1 for any variaable corresponds to a positive statement. A response of 0 is negative. V1 = Outings to visit friends/relatives; V2 = Encourage hobbies; V3 = Adequate hours watching TV; V4 = Parent discussion of TV programs; V5 = Frequent demonstrations of affection

***Step 3: Response Vectors Based on "Shared" Variables Are Generated for all Persons in the Given Behavioral Group.*** The next step involves the generation of response vectors β, and the sequential examination of responses on the 80 variables mentioned previously but now using 30 cases at a time. Our objective is to refine Table 24.1 and reduce its complexity by identifying co-occurring conditions, cross-age linkages, and substitutable conditions common to many individuals. After the first 30 cases are examined, with specification of new composite variables, the result is a proposed vector of variables $\boldsymbol{\alpha} = (\alpha_1, \ldots, \alpha_n)$ that will define the ultimate class of development history representations for a given outcome group (e.g., the behaviorally resilient). The development history of a single individual is, at this point, a logical AND statement involving a response on each of the n variables in the vector, $\boldsymbol{\alpha}$. Each successive set of 30—or fewer, in smaller data sets—cases is used to assess whether the original proposed vector, $\boldsymbol{\alpha}$, should be used to represent the full outcome-group population or whether some refinements are required.

It is this step in which the maximal work of distillation or thinning occurs—in this instance going from roughly 80 variables that defined the β vectors down to 18 variables that constitute the α-vectors (See Table 24.3 for a listing of the 18 variables derived at this step.) The distillation process combines the examination of multiple sequences (looking for features of histories that are likely candidates for deletion because of low frequency of occurrence and judged inconsequential nature) and consideration of insights from prior research that might argue for substitutability of conditions and specification of composite variables. The set of realized—in the data

TABLE 24.3

Core Components Defining Behaviorally Resilient Histories of NLSY Children of Teen-age Mothers (N = 78)

| | Before/At Birth | Early Childhood | Late childhood |
|---|---|---|---|
| Parental Resources | a1. Maternal cognitive attainment<br>a2. Maternal self-esteem & attitude<br>a3. Maternal support network | a4. Nonesidential father's involvement: child support------ | |
| Economic resources | a5. Parental educational attainment------<br>a6. Parental and other household adults employment status------<br>a7. Family poverty & welfare status------ | | |
| Health & health care | a8. Parental & neonatal health risk index------ | | |
| Social support & parenting | a9. Additional adults in household------<br>a10. Birth order & sibling size------ | a11. Physical environment------ | |
| Health & health care | a12. Chronological illness status------ | | |
| Social support & parenting | | a13. Father's involvement<br>a14. Exposure to cognitive stimulation/learning<br>a15. Activities promoting emotional & cognitive support<br>a16. Types of disciplines | |

set–vectors, **α**, are referred to as admissible chronological representations (ACRs) that correspond to a prescribed outcome (e.g., behaviorally resilient).

### Step 4: Summarize and Interpret ACRs, Using the Tension Between the Idiosyncrasy of Individual Histories and Subgroup Variation.

Step 3 resulted in the identification of 18 components of ACRs that constitute the central conditions for behaviorally resilient children. Even though the life histories have been distilled into 18 components, some have multiple variables included in them, such that, of the original 80 variables, 70% are represented in the 18 components. These components represent a dramatic reduction in the number of variables with which the analysis began; however, they still are arrayed in terms of individual lives, rather than as variables. Thus, there are 78 distinct development histories that emerge from these 18 components (i.e., one for each of the 78 behaviorally resilient children). The analytic task at this point is to balance the competing aims of retaining the richness and texture of individual lives, yet at the same time reducing the variability in more nuanced summaries. Our solution is to follow procedures that reduce the complexity by focusing on subgroups of variation within the behaviorally resilient children. That is, we organize the 18 components in various combinations that illustrate diverse life-history pathways to behavioral resilience.

As a matter of principle, we a priori privilege conjunctive statements—that is, long AND statements—in any aggregation of individuals into groups defining common pathways. The point of this is that a long AND statement common to many individuals provides for a more parsimonious interpretation of the development histories. A conjunctive (i.e., AND) statement provides the most direct connection to the 18-component AND statements representing each individual. Moreover, because all such individuals share all the features specified, their development histories can be told as a single story.

Our procedure begins with a search for high frequency cells of co-occurring conditions among combinations of the 18 components. Specifically, cells of co-occurring conditions (beginning with two variables at a time of the 18 variables in Table 24.3, moving to three variables at a time, four at a time, etc.) are generated with the intent of bringing together as long a partial history of co-occurring conditions as possible, without losing a stable frequency count, set at $n > = 20$ cases. In particular, we begin with all 153 two-way tables of counts based on distinct pairs of variables in the 18-variable ACR list. In each two-way table we identify the cell with the highest frequency. We then identify the cell among all 153 two-way tables with the highest frequency. This cell corresponds to the most frequent pair of co-occurring conditions—for example, [father present in the household] AND [father worked year round].

Next, we examine all 816 three-way tables and again identify the cell among all the tables with highest frequency. This cell corresponds to the most frequent set of three co-occurring conditions—for example, [father present in household] AND [father worked year round] AND [minimal to moderate poverty]. We continue this process for k-way tables with k = 4, 5, . . . etc. until the largest value of k for which the highest frequency cell has at least 20 children. For the subgroup that we labeled "Hbr1," the process stopped at k = 7 yielding the 7-component logical AND statement defined as a representation of a subpopulation of the behaviorally resilient children with a distinctive kind of developmental experience.

The first pathway, Hbr1, consisting of 22 behaviorally resilient children, brings together as long a partial history of co-occurring conditions as possible, stopping at a partial history comprised of 7 circumstances: [Intact families] AND [Father works year-round] AND [Mother stays at home or works part-time at best] AND [Minimal to moderate poverty] AND [Father's high involvement] AND [Mother's authoritative disciplinary style: reasoning, talking, and no spanking] AND [Child receives other types of social support: frequent visits to relatives, special lessons, Head Start, etc.]. Also, a high percentage (79%) of the mothers obtained a high school diploma before the child reached age 5 or 6. Thus, these families could be classified as the "working poor" two-parent families in which at least one parent worked 50 or more weeks during any year and yet failed to accumulate a total household income above the official poverty line in some years. Nevertheless, these children were characterized by persistently high and responsive parental involvement that was evidenced by mother's warm and authoritative disciplinary style and father's frequent time spent with the child. In the case of the "working poor" families, the social support and high parental involvement children received might partially offset the income insecurity they occasionally faced.

Eliminating the 22 children in the Hbr1 pathway from further consideration, we repeated the above steps on the remaining 56 children, searching for the longest possible AND statement to characterize a second distinct pathway or subgroup. This strategy did not produce another interpretable subgroup, suggesting that the next characterization needed to include both AND and OR statements (the latter allowing for what are to be interpreted as substitutable conditions). We then privilege restricted classes of OR statements—or disjunctions. The basis for restriction is the prior theory and organizing principles of the problem at hand (i.e., characterizing behaviorally resilient children).

Examining the 18-component vectors for the remaining 56 children and specifying substitutable conditions, we defined a second pathway, "Hbr2," comprised of 35 children. They had the following characteristics: Father was present in the household most years. All children met this condition. In addition, they shared other forms of family resources that had a positive impact on the developmental environment (at least one of the following 7 conditions): [Other family adults (e.g., grandparents) in households when father was gone] OR [Father's continuous involvement in the forms of child support and/or frequent visits] OR [Close support network for mother: regular church attendance and/or relatives living nearby] OR [Minimal neonatal risks] OR [Mother's report of frequent affection towards the child: kisses, praises, compliments] OR [Child encouraged to visit relatives and keep hobbies] OR [Good provision of learning experiences (i.e., reading, books)]. In addition, a large proportion of these children's mothers (89%) were reported by the interviewers to be very responsive and warm towards the child. Although these children's families had economic hardships most of the time—close to 70 percent were poor or in poverty at least 3 years, and only half of the mothers had a high school education—these children possessed ample amounts of social support directly or indirectly. This high level of support and responsiveness may have cushioned them against the difficulties of their family economic hardships.

Repeating the above strategy after eliminating the 35 children in Hbr2, we defined a third major pathway, "Hbr3," consisting of the remaining 21 children. These children were born outside marriage and continued to live without a father throughout their early childhood years OR a father was briefly present in the household but left soon after separation or divorce from the mother. Seventy-seven percent of these children experienced sustained or persistent poverty during their first 7 years of life. However, they also shared some notable advantages by having at least one of the four following resources (representing substitutable conditions): [Informal support network available to the mother] OR [Mother had high self-esteem] OR [Mother had high expectations for the child] OR [Nonresidential father's moderate to high involvement].

***Step 5: Testing the Distinctiveness of the Behaviorally Resilient Pathways From the Behaviorally Vulnerable Pathways.*** The essential question is whether the development pathways, Hbr1, Hbr2, and Hbr3, are strongly evident in the behaviorally vulnerable group. To this end we tabulated the proportions of behaviorally resilient children who have each of these histories side by side with the proportions of behaviorally vulnerable children who have the same sets of histories (Table 24.4). We anticipated that the pathways Hbr1 to Hbr3 would be relatively rare in the vulnerable population. In particular, there should be statistically significant differences in the proportions. We assessed this by formally employing a multiple comparison strategy—Bonferroni $t$ statistics—to set two-sided simultaneous confidence intervals around the differences in proportions (Miller, 1981; Singer et al., 1998). This revealed that two of the behaviorally resilient children's path-

TABLE 24.4
Test of Distinguishability: Bonferroni *t*-test Behaviorally Resilient Against Behaviorally Vulnerable
Children

| History | Resilient | Vulnerable |
|---------|-----------|------------|
| Hbrl | .28<br>(22) | .06*<br>(11) |
| Hbr2 | .45<br>(35) | .08**<br>(16) |
| Hbr3 | .27<br>(21) | .19<br>(37) |
| Other pathway | N/A | .67<br>(128) |
| N | 78 | 192 |

*Note.* Counts for each category of history represent the number of individuals in a given behavioral group having that history. For example, 22 out of 78 resilient children have history Hbrl; 11 out of 192 vulnerable children have history Hbrl.  *$p < .05$. **$p < .01$.

ways occurred with significantly different—and higher—frequencies than the same pathways in the vulnerable population. Equally important was the fact that 67% of the vulnerable pathways did not coincide with any resilient pathway.

## Summary

It is our strong conviction that complex Boolean statements that formally represent the pathways Hbr1 to Hbr3 are difficult to understand and interpret in their raw form. This is entirely analogous to the difficulty of interpreting long strings of numerical data that represents a single (or even multiple) individual's raw survey responses. Thus, we prepared representations of Hbr1 to Hbr3 in narrative form to facilitate understanding. In this connection, the first pathway (subgroup Hbr1) comprised children whose histories of co-occurring conditions were characterized with persistently high levels of emotional support from mother and father (e.g., father's close involvement, mother's authoritative disciplinary style and activities with peers or other family members), as well as father's presence, stable paternal work, mother at home. These conditions may in part have cushioned the children against the occasional economic insecurity their families went through (Baydar, Brooks-Gunn, & Furstenberg, 1993; Furstenberg, Brooks-Gunn, & Morgan, 1987; Guo, Brooks-Gunn, & Harris, 1996).

The second pathway (subgroup Hbr2) comprised children whose fathers were present in the household during most of their early childhood. Additionally, these families were provided with different types of social support and help: Some had other adults in the household to help, some had relatives living nearby for assistance or lived in closely-knit communities (e.g., active church organizations), and others had good mother–child interaction. Analogous to Hbr1, this pathway differed significantly from the pathways that characterize vulnerable children.

The last pathway (subgroup Hbr3) consisted of the remaining behaviorally resilient children. On the negative side, these children had low but stable paternal resources (i.e., father never in the home) or experienced parents' marital dissolution. On the positive side, their parents continued to be closely involved with them in various ways: Some fathers maintained frequent contacts with the child and some mothers had high expectations for the child. Additionally, informal support network through neighbors or relatives was available to the mothers.

Our analysis shows that all three pathways include an involved father, even though the involvement differed for the three groups. The first group has an employed father present, even though income is relatively low; the second group has either a father present or has an involved nonresidential father; and the third group has no father present, but noncustodial fathers are moderately involved in their children's lives. The findings are somewhat surprising, given the relative lack of support in the variable-centered literature for effects of paternal involvement on poor children's outcomes, particularly for nonresidential fathers and primarily never married couples (Furstenberg & Harris, 1993; King, 1994; Lamb, Pleck, Charnov, & Levine, 1987; McLanahan & Sandefur, 1994; Mott, 1990). Interestingly, the more ethnographic literature suggests that paternal involvement in unwed couples is higher, and perhaps more important, than the survey data with variable-centered analyses suggest (Anderson, 1989; Burton, 1990; Edin & Lein, 1997). Using a multiple pathways approach, we find empirical support for the role of the father who is present some but not all of the time. However, the paternal involvement is important when combined with other events—in one case (pathway 2), when households had other family adults present, when the homes were characterized by reading and learning stimulation, or when the mother was very affectionate. In the other case (pathway 3), fathers were not present or left very early, in which case the following conditions seemed to be substitutable for one another: paternal involvement, maternal self-esteem or efficacy, maternal expectations for the child, or social support.

Maternal parenting emerged in all three pathways. In the first group, all mothers were authoritative (minimizing spanking, encouraging reasoning). In the second group, maternal affection and provision of reading stimulation were substitutable. In the third group, high expectations for the child were substitutable with maternal self-esteem (these two components might both reflect maternal efficacy). An intriguing question is why minimizing spanking was characteristic of all the mothers in the working-poor, father-present families but was not in the other two groups (even as a substitutable component).

A third point has to do with the components that did not characterize some of the pathways. Maternal working status was not identified in the second or third pathways, whereas working part-time or not at all was part of the first pathway's constellation. Maternal education also did not enter the pathways, even though 80% of the mothers in the first pathway had a high school education. And maternal general cognitive ability also was not part of any pathways.

## CONCLUSION

We have illustrated a person-centered multiple pathways approach for the examination of behaviorally resilient children's lives, for children born to young mothers who are relatively poor. We wish to highlight four points in our conclusion.

First, life history perspectives have always been sympathetic to using biographies in order to identify multiple pathways to a particular outcome. One particularly illuminating example comes from Brown, Bifulco, and Andrews (1990) who charted several pathways to adulthood depression in women. Constructing biographies facilitated the identification of several life strands—one was characterized by parental loss in the childhood years (death, separation, or a loss or lack of support) or the experience of other potentially highly stressful events; the other was more cognitive in nature, as these individuals perceived themselves as helpless and low in coping skills when confronted with life's challenges.

In our study, biographies were constructed from survey data in order to identify multiple pathways. This procedure has the advantage of "opening up" a number of longitudinal surveys to the person-centered multiple pathways approach (for a review of some of these studies, see Brooks-Gunn & Chase-Lansdale, 1995; Brooks-Gunn et al., 1991). Employing the same approach to a different data set, the Wisconsin Longitudinal Study, Singer et al. (1998) identified four pathways for 168 resilient women (resilience was defined as the ability to recover from early depression) by using 17 life event components, defined in terms of about 50 separate variables. The first pathway told a largely positive story in these women's lives, that is, one of the absence of adversity as well as the presence of advantage. The second pathway involved significant childhood and adult adversity, but possessed notable advantages in the interpersonal or occupational realm, along with positive comparative evaluation. The third pathway was characterized by various forms of work and family adversity occurring in adulthood, but the women began life journeys with important strengths and resources in the childhood years that likely facilitated their recovery from the adverse experiences. The fourth pathway was notable for its considerable difficulty in life. But these women's ways of framing and interpreting life difficulties may help account for their high midlife well-being. In a similar fashion, in our study of 78 behaviorally resilient children of teenage mothers, we found that 18 components of life events and person narratives could be generated, and three pathways to narratives were identified. Our point here is that detailed longitudinal survey data may be used to generate narrative snapshots of individual events. Although certainly lacking some of the texture and nuance of narratives generated from detailed interviews, these survey-generated narratives provide a representation of major events in the child's life, as well as information on parental warmth, involvement, provision of learning experience, and disciplinary practices. What is missing of course, are specific affective reactions to events (i.e., maternal reaction to a divorce or loss of job) and in many cases the ways in which individuals work with the events.

Second, the multiple pathways strategy described in this chapter focuses on lives, rather than variables. The constellation of events that make up each individual's life is preserved (or at least a large number of experiences, given that the 18 components are made up of more than 50 events). Commonalities across lives within distinct subgroups are the focus. Although 78 individual life courses are represented by the 18 components, it is possible to identify three different pathways to behavioral resilience for these children. The inclusion of OR statements allows for some variability within pathways, while still providing for commonality.

Third, the accumulation of events during a life course seems to be associated with both resilience and vulnerability. The combination of certain persistent experiences may be particularly disadvantageous (or advantageous) for subgroups of individuals. Without examining multiple pathways, it is difficult to identify the various combinations of events that lead to a particular outcome. That is, the person-centered multiple pathways approach is not limited to examining the number of negative events that occur, but focuses on the different patterns of events that lead to an outcome. In the first pathway of our behaviorally resilient children, there are very few negative events and the developmental environment is relatively stable for these children—father present, mother not working (or worked part-time at best), father working; no persistent poverty, competent parenting. Moving to the second pathway, we see more variation in the developmental environment; for example, the father is not always present and the mother is likely to be in and out of the work place. However, poverty is minimal to moderate and social support is available.

Fourth, the process by which life histories were constructed and then were examined for commonalities blends aspects of qualitative and quantitative research designs. That is, the reading of the life histories and extraction of patterning of life events is qualitative, in that individual judgment is used to construct the initial variable list and the component list. Then, more quantitative strategies are used to identify common pathways from the (still) individual life histories. The "judgment" steps are influenced by theoretical frameworks and prior empirical findings (just as more variable-oriented approaches are). These steps can be undertaken by an individual or a group of individuals reading constructed life histories. Because the life histories are constructed from publicly available longitudinal survey data, critics can utilize our analytical strategy themselves, to see whether they generate similar pathways.

## ACKNOWLEDGMENTS

This work was funded by a postdoctoral fellow grant to Hongxin Zhao from NICHD (HD08189-02), an NIA grant to Carol D. Ryff and Burton Singer (R01AG013613), and an NICHD grant for the Research Network on Child and Family Well-Being to Jeanne Brooks-Gunn. We would like to thank Carol D. Ryff for her contributions to the methodology for using a narrative approach to the study of individuals followed over time via large survey data. A version of this chapter was presented at a symposium in honor of David Magnusson's contributions to psychology, held at the Wiks Castle in Sweden in May of 1997. We also thank the members of the John D. and Catherine T. Macarthur Foundation Networks on Socioeconomic Status and Health and on Families and Work for their intellectual support.

## REFERENCES

Anderson, E. (1989). Sex codes and family life among poor inner city youths. *Annals of the American Academy of Political and Social Sciences, 501*, 59–78.

Baydar, N., Brooks-Gunn, J., & Furstenberg, F. F., Jr. (1993). Early warning signs of functional illiteracy: Predictors in childhood and adolescence. *Child Development, 64*, 815–829.

Bornstein, M. (Ed.). (1995). *Handbook of parenting: Vol. 1. Children and parenting*. Hillsdale, NJ: Lawrence Erlbaum Associates.

Bornstein, M., & Tamis-LeMonda, C. S. (1997). Maternal responsiveness and infant mental abilities: Specific predictive relations. *Infant Behavior and Development, 20*, 283–296.

Bronfenbrenner, U. (1979). *The ecology of human development: Experiments by nature and design.* Cambridge, MA: Harvard University Press.

Bronfenbrenner, U. (1986). Ecology of the family as a context for human development: Research perspectives. *Developmental Psychology, 22*, 723–742.

Brooks-Gunn, J., & Chase-Lansdale, L. (1995). Adolescent parenthood. In M. Bornstein (Ed.), *Handbook of parenting: Vol. 1. Children and parenting* (pp. 91–118). Mahwah, NJ: Lawrence Erlbaum Associates.

Brooks-Gunn, J., Klebanov, P., & Liaw, F. H. (1993). Enhancing the development of low birth weight, premature infants: Changes in cognition and behavior over the first three years. *Child Development, 64,* 736–753.

Brooks-Gunn, J., Klebanov, P., & Liaw, F. H. (1994). The learning, physical, and emotional environment of the home in the context of poverty: The Infant Health and Development Program. *Children and Youth Services Review, 17,* 251–276.

Brooks-Gunn, J., Liaw, F. H., & Klebanov, P. (1992). Effects of early intervention on low birth weight preterm infants: What aspects of cognitive functioning are enhanced? *Journal of Pediatrics, 20,* 350–359.

Brooks-Gunn, J., Phelps, E., & Elder, G., Jr. (1991). Studying lives through time: Secondary data analyses in developmental psychology. *Developmental Psychology, 27,* 899–910.

Brown, G. W., Bifulco, A., & Andrews, B. (1990). Self-esteem and depression: III. Etiological issues. *Social Psychiatry and Psychiatric Epidemiology, 25,* 235–243.

Bruner, J. (1996). *The culture of education.* Cambridge, MA: Harvard University Press.

Burton, L. (1990). Teenage childbearing as an alternative life course strategy in multigenerational black families. *Human Nature, 1,* 123–143.

Cairns, R. B., Bergman, L. R., & Kagan, J. (Eds.). (1998). *Methods and models for studying the individual.* Thousand Oaks, CA: Sage.

Cairns, R. B., & Cairns, B. (1994). *Lifelines and risks: Pathways of youth in our time.* New York: Cambridge University Press.

Chase-Lansdale, P. L., Brooks-Gunn, J., Mott, F., & Phillips, D. A. (1991). Children of the National Longitudinal Survey of Youth: A unique research opportunity. *Developmental Psychology, 27,* 918–931.

Cicchetti, D., & Cohen, D. J. (1995). Perspective on developmental psychopathology. In D. Cicchetti, & D. Cohen (Eds.), *Developmental psychopathology: Vol. 1. Theory and methods* (pp. 3–20). New York: Wiley.

Duncan, G., Brooks-Gunn, J., & Klabanov, P. K. (1994). Economic deprivation and early childhood development. *Child Development, 65,* 296–318.

Edin, K., & Lein, L. (1997). *Making ends meet: How single mothers survive welfare and low-wage work.* New York: Russell Sage Foundation.

Furstenberg, F. F., Jr., Brooks-Gunn, J., & Morgan, S. P. (1987). *Adolescent mothers in later life.* New York: Cambridge University Press.

Furstenberg, F. F., Jr., & Harris, K. M. (1993). When and why fathers matter: Impact of father involvement on children of adolescent mothers. In R. I. Lerman & T. J. Ooms (Eds.), *Young unwed fathers.* Philadelphia: Temple University Press.

Garmezy, N. (1985). Stress resistant children: The search for protective factors. In J. Stevensen (Ed.), *Recent research in developmental psychopathology.* Oxford, UK: Pergamon.

Garmezy, N. (1991). Resiliency and vulnerability to adverse developmental outcomes associated with poverty. *American Behavioral Scientist, 34,* 416–430.

Garmezy, N. (1993). Children in poverty: Resilience despite risk. *Psychiatry, 56,* 127–136.

Garmezy, N., Masten, A., & Tellegen, A. (1984). The study of stress and competence in children: A building block for developmental psychopathology. *Child Development, 55,* 97–111.

Guo, G., Brooks-Gunn, J., & Harris, K. M. (1996). Parental labor-force attachment and grade retention among urban black children. *Sociology of Education, 69,* 217–236.

Haggerty, R., Garmezy, N., Rutter, M., & Sherrod, L. (Eds.). (1994). *Stress, risk, and resilience in childhood and adolescence.* New York: Cambridge University Press.

Hinde R. A. (1992). Developmental psychology in the context of other behavioral sciences. *Developmental Psychology, 28,* 1018–1029.

The Infant Health and Development Program. (1990). Enhancing the outcomes of low birth weight, premature infants: A multisite, randomized trial. *Journal of the American Medical Association, 263,* 3035–3042.

King, V. (1994). Nonresident father involvement and child well-being: Can dads make a difference? *Journal of Family Issues, 15,* 78–96.

Klebanov, P., Brooks-Gunn, J., Chase-Lansdale, L., & Gordon, R. (1997). Are neighborhood effects on young children mediated by features of the home environment? In J. Brooks-Gunn, G. Duncan, & J. L. Aber (Eds.), *Neighborhood poverty: Context and consequences for children: Vol. 1.* (pp. 119–145). New York: Russell Sage.

Klebanov, P., Brooks-Gunn, J., & Duncan, G. (1994). Does neighborhood and family poverty affect mother's parenting, mental health, and social support? *Journal of Marriage and the Family, 56,* 441–455.

Klebanov, P., Brooks-Gunn, J., McCarton, C., & McCormick, M. M. (1998). The contribution of neighborhood and family income upon developmental test scores over the first three years of life. *Child Development, 69,* 1420–1436.

Lamb, M. E., Pleck, J., Charnov, E. L., & Levine, J. A. (1987). A biosocial perspective on paternal behavior and involvement. In J. B. Lancaster, J. Altman, A. Rossi, & L. R. Sherrod (Eds.), *Parenting across the life span: Biosocial perspective* (pp. 111–142). New York: Aldine de Gruyter.

Lewin, K. (1935). The conflict between Aristotelian and Galileian modes of thought in contemporary psychology. In K. Lewin (Ed.), *A dynamic theory of personality: Selected papers.* New York: McGraw-Hill.

Liaw, F. R., & Brooks-Gunn, J. (1994). Cumulative familial and low birth weight children's cognitive and behavioral development. *Journal of Clinical Child Psychology, 23,* 360–372.

Luthar, S., & Zigler, E. (1991). Vulnerability and competence: A review of research on resilience in childhood. *American Journal of Orthopsychiatry, 61,* 6–22.

Magnusson, D. (1988). *Paths through life: Vol. 1. Individual development from an interactional perspective: A longitudinal study.* Hillsdale, NJ: Lawrence Erlbaum Associates.

Magnusson, D., & Bergman, L. (1988). Individual and variable-based approaches to longitudinal research on early risk factors. In M. Rutter (Ed.), *Studies of psychosocial risk: The power of longitudinal data* (pp. 45–61). Cambridge, UK: Cambridge University Press.

Magnusson, D., & Bergman, L. (1990). A pattern approach to the study of pathways from childhood to adulthood. In L. N. Robins & M. Rutter (Eds.), *Straight and devious pathways from childhood to adulthood* (pp. 101–115). Cambridge, MA: Cambridge University Press.

Magnusson, D., & Törestad, B. (1993). A holistic view of personality: A model revisited. *Annual Review of Psychology, 44,* 427–452.

McLanahan, S., & Sandefur, G. (1994). *Growing up with a single parent: What helps, what hurts?* Cambridge, MA: Harvard University Press.

Miller, G. A. (1956). The magical number seven, plus or minus two: Some limits on our capacity for processing information. *Psychological Review, 62,* 81–97.

Miller, R. G. (1981). *Simultaneous statistical inference* (2nd ed.). New York: Springer-Verlag.

Mishler, E. G. (1996). Missing persons: Recovering developmental stories/histories (pp. 73–99). In R. Jessor, A. Colby, & R. A. Shweder (Eds.), *Ethnography and human development.* Chicago, IL: University of Chicago Press.

Mott, F. L. (1990). When is a father really gone? Paternal-child contact in father-absent homes. *Demography, 27,* 719–735.

Mott, F. L., & Baker, P. (1997). *1997 NLSY79 Child and Young Adult Data: Users Guide.* Columbus, OH: Center for Human Resource Research.

Rutter, M. (1989). Pathways from childhood to adult life. *Journal of Child Psychology and Psychiatry, 30,* 23–51.

Rutter, M. (1990). Psychosocial resilience and protective mechanisms. In J. Rolf, A. S. Masten, D. Cicchetti, K. H. Nuechterlein, & S. Weintraub (Eds.), *Risk and protective factors in the development of psychopathology* (pp. 181–214). New York: Cambridge University Press.

Sameroff, A. J., & Feil, L. A. (1985). Parental concepts of development. In E. Sigel (Ed.), *Parental belief systems: The psychological consequences for children* (pp. 83–105). Hillsdale, NJ: Lawrence Erlbaum Associates.

Sameroff, A. J., Seifer, R., Baldwin, A., & Baldwin., C. (1993). Stability of intelligence from preschool to adolescence: The influence of social and family risk factors. *Child Development, 64,* 80–97.

Schank, R. C. (1990). *Tell me a story.* New York: Scribner's.

Singer, B., Ryff, C., Carr, D., & Magee, W. (1998). Linking life histories and mental health: A person-centered strategy. *Sociological Methodology, 28,* 1–51.

Smith, J., & Brooks-Gunn, J. (1997). Correlates and consequences of mother's harsh discipline with young children. *Archives of Pediatric and Adolescent Medicine, 151,* 777–786.

Sroufe, L. A., & Rutter, M. (1984). The domain of developmental psychopathology. *Child Development, 55,* 17–29.

Tessor, R., Colby, A., & Shweder, R. A. (Eds.). (1996). *Ethnography and human development: Context and meaning in social inquiry.* Illinois: University of Chicago Press.

Werner, E., & Smith, R. (1992). *Overcoming the odds: High risk children from birth to adulthood.* Ithaca, NY: Cornell University Press.

# 25

# A Holistic, Integrated Model of Risk and Protection in Adolescence: A Developmental Contextual Perspective About Research, Programs, and Policies

Richard M. Lerner
Tufts University

Nicole L. Simi
Boston College

David Magnusson has provided singularly creative and historically influential scholarly and professional leadership in facilitating and integrating the research and applied activities of psychologists from across the world. Magnusson's theoretical formulations and research programs have emphasized the important role of context in human behavior and development (Magnusson, 1981, 1988, 1996a; Magnusson & Stattin, 1998). His intellectual vision includes a compelling conceptual rationale and substantive basis for internationally contextualized, comparative scholarship (Magnusson, in press-a; Magnusson & Allen, 1983; Magnusson & Stattin, 1998).

Four key elements define Magnusson's intellectual vision: Interactionism, holism, interdisciplinarity, and the longitudinal study of lives (Magnusson, 1982, 1985, 1988, 1995, 1996b; Magnusson & Stattin, 1998; Stattin & Magnusson, 1990). Within this framework, and focusing on the lives of young people—critical assets for maintaining and enhancing the social capital of all modern nations—Magnusson's scholarship has substantiated in a singular manner the importance of interactions among individuals, their social groups (e.g., peers), and their institutional settings (e.g., schools) in promoting positive psychological, health, and educational outcomes from childhood into young adulthood (Magnusson, 1982, in press-a; Magnusson &

Stattin, 1998; Stattin & Magnusson, 1990). Indeed, within the context of his extraordinarily prolific scientific career—replete with highly influential articles, chapters, and books, and involving theoretically innovative ideas and rigorous and diverse methodologies—his longitudinal study of adolescent development (which now extends into adulthood) is acknowledged to be an unparalleled masterpiece (Magnusson & Stattin, 1998; Stattin & Magnusson, 1990).

Magnusson's conceptual and empirical contributions have shaped the thinking and research of generations of social scientists, especially those concerned with using a holistic, integrated perspective involving developmental theory and research to understand problems of development and, in turn, to enhance the life chances of young people. For instance, based on the longitudinal work of Magnusson and his colleagues on person–situation relationships in regard to the development of personality, Öhman and Magnusson (1987) were able to conclude the following with regard to any problem, disorder, or disease emerging across the life course:

> [They] must be understood as resulting from a multiplicity of causal events spanning observational levels from biochemistry to sociology. Thus, any single factor, linear causal model is unrealistic for understanding disease in general, and mental disorders in particular. Instead, multiple interacting causal factors that often change in their effect over time must be postulated. (p. 18)

Magnusson's longitudinal person–situation work, embedded in his integrative, relational, and contextual and holistic model, provides a conceptually innovative and empirically compelling frame for understanding risk and resiliency in adolescence and, indeed, across the life span. We count ourselves among those developmentalists whose conceptual orientation and research agenda have been shaped by the scholarly contributions of Magnusson. Accordingly, in this chapter, we will illustrate this influence by describing how a holistic and integrative approach to the study of adolescence affords understanding of the dynamic relationships between individually distinct people and their diverse settings: The relationships constitute the basic process in developmental change and provide the basis for design of policies and programs useful in promoting positive development across the life span. Magnusson's scholarship allows us to understand that, across life, development involves change and transitions. Key bases of change, for instance, as manifested in presses on the person, are associated with the characteristics of the contexts within which the individual functions. Therefore, one must consider both the nature of the characteristics of the developing individual and of the context in trying to understand development in general, and, more specifically, individual differences in the successes or failures of the person in meeting the presses of the context and in developing in a healthy manner.

From this perspective, whether an adolescent is at risk for problems in development or has the resources available to him or her to be protected from such problems depends not just on the individual or his or her context, but on the relationship between the two. Simply, and as illustrated by the observation of Öhman and Magnusson (1987) previously quoted, Magnusson's scholarship promotes the use of models that link person and context in order to understand risk and protection in the development of health or pathology across life.

One such model, developed through the influence of the intellectual perspective championed by Magnusson, is *developmental contextualism* (cf. Lerner, 1998; Stattin & Magnusson, 1990). We review features of this model and explain how risk and protection during the adolescent period depend on the changing relationships between individuals and their specific contexts (e.g., between youth and their particular families, peers, schools, and communities). We then explain how this Magnussonian holistic developmental approach provides a vital frame for developmental description, explanation, and for interventions (policies and programs) aimed at diminishing risk, enhancing protection, and promoting positive development.

## AN OVERVIEW OF DEVELOPMENTAL CONTEXTUALISM

Over the last quarter century the study of children and their families has evolved in at least three significant directions: Changes in the conceptualization of the nature of the person, the emergence of a life-span perspective about human development, and an emphasis on the contexts of development. These trends were both products and producers of the holistic and integrated approach to developmental science advocated by Magnusson; his intellectual leadership shaped the evolution of models such as developmental contextualism (Lerner, 1998; Lerner & Kauffman, 1985; Magnusson, 1995, 1996b; Stattin & Magnusson, 1990). These holistic, integrative models provide a rationale for a synthesis of research and application, a synthesis focused on the diversity of children and on the contexts within which they develop.

Developmental contextualism is a perspective on human development that takes an integrative approach to the multiple levels of organization presumed to constitute the nature of human life; that is, "fused" (e.g., Gottlieb, 1997; Kuo, 1976; Lerner, 1986, 1991; Tobach & Greenberg, 1984) and changing relations among biological, psychological, and social contextual levels constitute the process of developmental change. Rather than approach variables from these levels of analysis in either a reductionistic or in a parallel-processing way, the developmental contextual view rests on the holistic and integrative idea that variables from these levels of analysis are dynamically interactive—they are reciprocally influential over the course of human ontogeny (Magnusson 1985, 1988, 1996a, in press-a, in press-b; Magnusson & Stattin, 1998).

If the course of human development is the product of the processes involved in the "fusions" (Tobach & Greenberg, 1984), or "dynamic interactions" (Lerner, 1978, 1984) among integrative levels, then the processes of development are more plastic than often previously believed (Brim & Kagan, 1980). Within this perspective, the context for development is not seen merely as a simple stimulus environment, but rather as Bronfenbrenner (1979) stated, an "ecological environment . . . conceived topologically as a nested arrangement of concentric structures, each contained within the next" (p. 22) and including variables from biological, psychological, physical, and sociocultural levels, all changing interdependently across history (e.g., Magnusson, in press-a, in press-b; Magnusson & Stattin 1998; Riegel, 1975; Stattin & Magnusson, 1990).

Thus, individual–context relationships involve exchanges with social networks and the larger community, societal, cultural, and historical levels of organization. Time—history—cuts through all the levels of the system. Thus, as with the people populating these systems, change is always occurring. Diversity within time is created as change across time (across history), involving both "normative" (Baltes, 1987) or, in other words, "evolutionary" (i.e., gradual) changes, and "revolutionary" (i.e., abrupt; Werner, 1957) ones, introduces variation into all the levels of organization involved in the human development system.

For instance, people develop, the family changes from one having infants and young children, to one having teenagers, to an "empty nest"; communities, societies, and cultures also vary across time (Elder, 1974; Elder, Modell, & Parke, 1993; Garbarino, 1992; Hernandez, 1993). Each of these multiple "levels" is embedded in the natural and human-designed physical ecology, a physical world that of course changes also. Changes at one or more of these levels produce changes in the other levels as well, given their bidirectional connections.

## Implications of Developmental Contextualism for Research and Application

Developmental contextualism, in emphasizing the bidirectional connections between the individual and the actual ("ecologically valid") settings within which he or she lives, brings to the fore of concern in the social and behavioral sciences both the diversity (individual differences) and the context of people and their sociocultural institutions. This emphasis has resulted in the recognition that a synthesis of perspectives from multiple collaborators—from multiple disciplines and multiple professions—is needed to understand the multilevel (e.g., person, family, and community) integrations involved in human development (Lerner, 1991; Magnusson, 1996b). Furthermore, and consistent with Magnusson's work (e.g., 1985, 1996b; Magnusson & Stattin, 1998), it is important to include the perspective of community members themselves in the set of "voices" used to shape the design and focus of research in human development; such inclusion is predicated on the vital knowledge community members have about development in their context (in their families and neighborhoods). Such inclusion builds "ownership" in the outcomes and applications of such research (Lerner, 1995).

Developmental contextualism forwards the view that, to understand the basic, relational process of human development, both descriptive and explanatory research must be conducted within the actual ecology of people's lives. Descriptive research involves the depiction, or representation, of development as it exists for a given person or group, in one or more contexts, at one or more points in time. Explanatory research involves the introduction (through manipulation or statistical modeling) of variation into such person–context relationships. These planned variations in the course of human life are predicated on: (a) theoretical ideas about the source of particular developmental phenomena (for specific combinations of people and contexts), or on (b) theoretically guided interests about the extent to which a particular developmental phenomenon (e.g., cognitive development in the aged years) may show systematic change in structure or function, that is, plasticity, across the life span (Baltes, 1987; Lerner, 1984). In the case of either (a) or (b), such researcher-introduced variation is an attempt to simulate the "natural" variation of life; if theoretical expectations are confirmed, the outcomes of such investigations provide an explanation of how developmental change occurs within a person or group.

Given the developmental contextual focus on studying person–context relationships within the ecology of human development, explanatory investigations by their very nature constitute intervention research. The goal of developmental contextual explanatory research is to understand the ways in which variations in ecologically "valid" person–context relationships account for the character of actual or potential trajectories of human development, that is, life paths enacted in the "natural laboratory" of the "real world." Therefore, to gain understanding of how theoretically relevant variations in such person–context relationships may influence actual or to-be-actualized developmental trajectories, the researcher may introduce policies and programs as "experimental manipulations" of the proximal or distal natural ecology. Evaluations of the outcomes of such interventions become a means to bring data to bear on theoretical issues pertinent to changing person–context relationships and, more specifically, to the plasticity in human development that may exist, or that may be capitalized on, to enhance human life (Lerner, 1998).

In this view, policy and program endeavors do not constitute secondary work, or derivative applications, conducted after research evidence has been compiled. Quite to the contrary, policy development and implementation, and program design and delivery, become integral components of this vision for research; the evaluation component of such policy and intervention work provides critical feedback about the adequacy of the conceptual frame from which this research agenda should derive. In summary, this conception of integrated, multidisciplinary, explanatory research focused on the diversity of individuals and contexts sees policies and programs as the "experimental" tools of such scholarship, and evaluation as a procedure for clarifying theory about basic process and for refining intervention.

The holistic conception illustrated by developmental contextualism integrates developmental scholarship simultaneously along multiple dimensions: Person–Context, Basic-Applied, Research–Policies/Programs. As such, developmental contextualism has the potential to serve as a frame not only for the advancement of understanding about human development but, as well, for enhancing the development of individuals whose quality of life is being challenged by both normative developmental problems and by risks associated with the current historical moment.

We believe that adolescence is the prototypic period within which developmental contextualism may serve an integrated agenda for the advancement of knowledge and the enhancement of life. Accordingly, we present an overview of the key issues challenging the positive development of contemporary adolescents; we will emphasize the sample case of American youth. In turn, we will indicate how the holistic and integrative ideas present in a developmental contextual perspective, ideas shaped by the contributions of Magnusson's scholarship, provide a means to envision and enact interventions promoting positive youth development.

## CONTEMPORARY ADOLESCENT RISKS AND PROTECTIVE FACTORS

The particular set of individual–context relationships that constitute a person's life span may be linked to developmental changes indicative or promotive of healthy change (and may be termed protective factors or, better, processes) or to developmental changes detrimental to healthy change (and may be termed risk factors or processes). Although in developmental contextualism there is a relativism among such factors (e.g., "difficult temperament" may be a risk or a protective factor in relation to the demands of, or fit with, the context within which it is embedded; Chess & Thomas,

1984; Lerner & Lerner, 1989), there is evidence that the set of individual–context relationships pertinent to contemporary adolescence is reflective of historically unprecedented levels of risk. Indeed, across the nations of our world adolescents are dying every day—from violence, from drug and alcohol use and abuse, from unsafe sex, from poor nutrition, and from the sequelae of persistent and pervasive poverty (e.g., Children's Defense Fund, 1996; Dryfoos, 1990; Hamburg, 1992; Huston, 1991; Lerner, 1995; Schorr, 1988; World Health Organization, 1986, 1993). And, if our youth are not dying, their life chances are being squandered—by school failure, underachievement, and dropping out; by crime; by teenage pregnancy and parenting; by lack of job preparedness; and by challenges to their health, for example, lack of immunizations, inadequate screening for disabilities, insufficient prenatal care, and lack of sufficient infant and childhood medical services (Carnegie Corporation of New York, 1995; Children's Defense Fund, 1996; di Mauro, 1995; Dryfoos, 1990; Huston, 1991; Huston, McLoyd, & Coll, 1994; Johnston, O'Malley, & Bachman, 1996; United States Department of Health and Human Services, 1996).

Although a full discussion of the nature and manifestation of risk and protection in adolescence would require consideration of individual differences linked to race or ethnicity, gender, physical ability status, sexual orientation, socioeconomic status, normative and nonnormative historical change (i.e., temporality), and indeed to the full panoply of dimensions included within a developmental contextual perspective (Lerner, 1995), it is possible to note that there are numerous manifestations of the severity and breadth of the problems besetting the youth, families, and communities of our world. Using the United States as an example, four major categories of risk behaviors in late childhood and adolescence can be considered:

1. Drug and alcohol use and abuse.
2. Unsafe sex, teenage pregnancy, and teenage parenting.
3. School underachievement, school failure, and drop out.
4. Delinquency, crime, and violence (Dryfoos, 1990).

Clearly, participation in any one of these behaviors would diminish a youth's life chances. Indeed, engagement in some of these behaviors would eliminate the young person's chances of even having a life. Such risks to the life chances of American children and adolescents are occurring, unfortunately, at historically unprecedented levels.

For instance, 1998 U.S. Bureau of the Census data indicate that there are about 38 million youths between the ages of 10 and 17 years in the U.S. Dryfoos (1990) estimates that approximately 50% of these adolescents engage in two or more of the four categories of risk behaviors, and 10% of American youth engage in all of the four categories of risk behaviors.

Within each of the several major categories of risk behavior besetting America's youth, there are burgeoning indications that problems are getting more extensive. To illustrate the breadth and depth of these problems, we will focus on each of the problems successively. However, it is important to keep in mind both the interrelation of these problems and the multiple influences that will therefore be needed to address them.

## Drug, Alcohol, and Substance Use and Abuse

Adolescents drink and use a wide variety of illegal drugs and other unhealthy substances (e.g., inhalants such as glues, aerosols, butane, and solvents). Cigarettes and other tobacco products also are used extensively. Recent trends in the United States in the use of all these substances are quite alarming. For instance, although there were declines in the use of a number of these substances throughout much of the 1980s, since 1992 an increase in the use of marijuana, cocaine, LSD, and other hallucinogens began to be apparent among eighth graders (Johnston, O'Malley, & Bachman, 1996). By 1993 and again in 1994 eighth graders continued to show increases in use of these substances and tenth and twelfth graders joined them (Johnston et al., 1996).

***Bases and Implications of Drug, Alcohol, and Substance Use and Abuse: Diversity and Context.*** The growing problems of substance use and abuse are associated with a diverse set of individual and contextual variables. In turn, the use of substances is linked to numerous negative outcomes for youth. For example, alcohol use by adolescents is associated with self-destructive thoughts and behaviors such as thinking about suicide, attempting suicide, and engaging more frequently in risky behaviors (taking someone else's medication) (Windle, Miller-Tutzauer, & Domenico, 1992). In research with both Latino and European American youth, personality problems, lack of adjustment to school, and poor parenting practices were associated with drug use (Flannery, Vazsonyi, & Rowe, 1996).

Moreover, parents' substance abuse can influence their offspring's abuse of substances (Howard, Boyd, & Zucker, 1994); and such parental behavior can also affect their adolescent children's cognitive ability. For instance, in one study the spatial and visual reasoning of 14-year-olds was related to their mother's alcohol use during pregnancy (15 years earlier): the more the mother had drunk, the poorer the adolescent's performance (Hunt, Streissguth, Kerr, & Olson, 1995).

The community context also can influence adolescent substance use. For example, in inner cities both drug use and drug trafficking (termed running, selling, or dealing) is pervasive (Feigelman, Stanton, & Ricardo, 1993). Among African American youth living in inner city areas, illicit drug use typically occurs along with cigarette and alcohol use and drug trafficking (Li, Stanton, Feigelman, & Black, 1994). However, drug trafficking is just as likely to occur with or without use of such substances.

Most youths—whether they use substances or not—see such behavior as a matter of personal discretion or personal judgment, rather than as an issue of morality or social convention (Nucci, Guerra, & Lee, 1991). Nevertheless there are personal and social factors that protect youth against their own involvement with such substances. For instance, religious commitments and beliefs are factors that protect African American adolescents against the use of alcohol (Barnes, Farrell, & Banerjee, 1994). Moreover, although peer substance use is related to substance use by an adolescent, African American youth are less susceptible to such peer influences than are European American youth (Barnes et al., 1994); in addition, African American adolescents have higher alcohol abstinence rates and lower rates of alcohol abuse than European American youth. Similarly, among Latino adolescents, both attitudes about alcohol use and positive self-concepts are associated with a decreased likelihood of alcohol use (Alva & Jones, 1994). In addition, these youths are less likely to be involved in peer groups that use alcohol. Low self-efficacy, low conventionality, and drinking simply "to get drunk" were associated with binge drinking among the male adolescents involved in the Monitoring the Future Study (Schulenberg, Wadsworth, O'Malley, Bachman, & Johnston, 1996).

Some groups of youth seem to be at particular risk for substance-abuse problems. Research with Native American adolescents (Gfellner, 1994; Mitchell, O'Nell, Beals, Dick, Keane, & Manson, 1996) suggests that this may be the case with these youths. For instance, with the exception of alcohol, Native American adolescents show higher rates and more frequent use of cigarettes, marijuana, and solvents than European American youth (Gfellner, 1994); furthermore, Native American youth have a greater involvement in problem behaviors than is the case with European American adolescents.

## Unsafe Sex, Teenage Pregnancy, and Teenage Parenting

Adolescents have always engaged in sex. Because venereal and other sexually transmitted diseases, and pregnancy and childbirth to unmarried teenagers, also have been seen across history, there is not anything new about the fact that American adolescents of today engage in sex and have such problems when they do. What is new, however, is the extent and breadth of adolescents' involvement in sex, the younger and younger ages at which this involvement occurs, and the marked increases in the depth and breadth of the problems associated with sexual behavior in adolescence.

Illustrations of the magnitude of these problems among contemporary adolescents include the fact that each year, one million American adolescents become pregnant (di Mauro, 1995); about half have babies. Indeed, about every minute, an American adolescent has a baby (Children's Defense Fund, 1996). Moreover, by age 18, 25% of American females have been pregnant at least once (Lerner, 1995).

**Bases and Implications of Unsafe Sex, Teenage Pregnancy, and Teenage Parenting: Diversity and Context.** The breadth and variation of the problems pertinent to contemporary adolescent sexual behavior is staggering. The magnitude and diversity of the manifestation of these problems is challenging the educational, health care, and social service systems of the United States. The complexity of these problems is due at least in part to their connection to the other risk behaviors of adolescence and to numerous individual and contextual influences on adolescents (Small & Luster, 1994). Indeed, the multiple influences on adolescents' problems of sexual behavior require public policies and intervention programs that are sensitive to the diverse contexts within which youths are embedded (Ensminger, 1990).

To illustrate the several individual and contextual levels playing a role in adolescent sexual problems, the biological, cognitive, and behavioral variables, and peer, family, and community ones influencing adolescent sexual problems may be considered. For example, in regard to individual influences, ambivalent attitudes toward childbearing, contraception, contraceptive efficacy, and abortions are related to adolescent childbearing (Zabin, Astone, & Emerson, 1993). Similarly, attitudes that reject societal norms, when combined with nonconforming behavior, are associated with early initiation of sexual intercourse among both African American and European American adolescents (Costa, Jessor, Donovan, & Fortenberry, 1995). In addition, among both male and female adolescents, poor psychological adjustment is linked to early initiation of sexual intercourse (Bingham & Crockett, 1996).

Among gay and bisexual male adolescents, pubertal maturation is associated with age of first orgasm and first homosexual activity and with frequency of orgasms during junior high school (Savin-Williams, 1995). It should be stressed that gay and heterosexual male adolescents did not differ in their levels of self-esteem.

However, other individual variables, if shown by gay adolescents, may not bode well for their adjustment. For instance, among African American and Latino gay and bisexual adolescent males, sexually risky attitudes, when coupled with substance abuse, conduct problems, and emotional distress, are associated with the likelihood that this set of problems will remain stable for the youth (Borus, 1995); in fact, across a 2-year period only about 20% to 30% of youths change their pattern of problem behaviors.

The peers of adolescents also influence their sexuality. For example, peer rejection in the sixth grade is associated with the number of sexual partners females will have over the next 4 years (Feldman, Rosenthal, Brown, & Canning, 1995). In turn, however, peer acceptance, when it is associated with both a lot of dating and use of alcohol with classmates, is associated as well with the number of sexual partners adolescents have by tenth grade (Feldman et al., 1995).

The number of sexually active girlfriends that an adolescent female has, as well as the number of her sexually active sisters, and whether she has an adolescent childbearing sister, are linked to her possessing permissive sexual attitudes, having positive intentions for future sex, and being more likely to be a nonvirgin (East, Felice, & Morgan, 1993). Thus, both peer and family contexts can combine to influence adolescent sexuality. This point is underscored by other research. Among African American and European American males and females, possession of a girlfriend or a boyfriend, respectively, one's educational expectations, and the educational background of one's mother were associated with being sexually active (Scott-Jones & White, 1990); although these associations did not differ across the groups of African Americans and European Americans, it was the case that the former group of youth was less likely to use contraception than the latter group.

Family and peer contexts also influence the likelihood that adolescent girls will experience an incident of unwanted sexual activity (Small & Kerns, 1993). Of the girls studied by Small and Kerns, about 20% report that unwanted sexual experiences had occurred within the past 12 month period. Approximately one third of these encounters involved forced sexual intercourse; the other two thirds of the events involved unwanted touching. Most of these experiences were initiated by boyfriends, dates, friends, or acquaintances (in this order). A girl's history of sexual abuse, a tendency to conform to peers, and having parents whose rearing style was either authoritarian or reflective of low monitoring were predictive of her being a target of an unwanted sexual advance. Similarly, in divorced families, a mother's dating behavior and her possession of sexually permissive attitudes influence both daughters' and sons' sexual activity (Whitbeck, Simons, & Kao, 1994).

The community context also influences adolescent sexuality. In poor communities, youths have higher rates of abortion and lower rates of marriage (Sullivan, 1993). Among both African American and European American female adolescents, living in a socially disorganized, low income community, one wherein family planning services are not readily available, is associated with the initiation of sexual intercourse and young women's subsequent sexual activity.

## School Underachievement, Failure, and Dropout

About 25% of the approximately 40 million children and adolescents enrolled in the United States' 82,000 public elementary and secondary schools
are at risk for school failure (Dryfoos, 1994). Each year about 700,000 youths
drop out of school, and about 25% of all 18- and 19-year-olds have not
graduated from high school (Center for the Study of Social Policy, 1993;
Dryfoos, 1990; Simons, Finlay, & Yang, 1991). The costs to society—in having
large numbers of youth ill-prepared to contribute productively to society—
and to youths themselves are enormous.

*Bases and Implications of School Problems: Diversity and Context.*
School underachievement, failure, and dropping out in adolescence are
linked to the individual and contextual variables discussed in regard to
substance abuse and sexual problems. Here the bases of the influences of
schools on a youth's development are associated with: *Individual variables*,
relating to cognitive abilities (Fuligni, Eccles, & Barber, 1995), motivation
(Wentzel, 1993), personality (Wentzel, 1991), and self (Roberts & Petersen,
1992); *Peer variables*, pertaining to peer reputation or status (Hartup, 1993),
and to the nature of the social or antisocial behaviors shown by one's peers
(Berndt & Keefe, 1995); *Family variables*, pertaining to the nature of parenting or child-rearing style (Baumrind, 1983; Lamborn, Mounts, Steinberg, &
Dornbusch, 1991), socialization practices (Chiu, Feldman, & Rosenthal, 1992;
Crystal & Stevenson, 1995; Phinney & Chavira, 1995), and types of behavioral
interactions between youth and parents (Brody, Stoneman, & Flor, 1996;
Fisher & Johnson, 1990); *community variables*, relating to poverty level (Hernandez, 1993), social support for learning (Brooks-Gunn, Gus, & Furstenberg, 1993; Levitt, Guacci-Franco, & Levitt, 1993), and programs providing
wholesome activities to youths during nonschool hours (Carnegie Corporation of New York, 1992); and school setting, pertaining to the structure and
curriculum of the school (Dryfoos, 1995), and to the sorts of peers and
teachers one encounters and to the interactions experienced with them
(Gamoran & Nystrand, 1991).

## Delinquency, Crime, and Violence

Of all the problems confronting contemporary youths, no set of issues has
attracted as much public concern and public fear as youth delinquency and
violent crimes. People point to the growth of youth gangs—groups of youth
that may, or may not (Taylor, 1990, 1993), be engaged in criminal activity
but who, nevertheless, can be found in urban centers as well as in rural
communities; in addition, people point in fear to territorial battles and drug

trafficking violence and shootings, to random street violence, and to the seemingly younger and younger ages of, often, quite violent criminals.

The breadth and depth of the problems of delinquency, crime, and violence by youths are indeed daunting to consider. For instance, youths aged 13 to 21 years accounted for 35.5% of all nontraffic related arrests in the United States during the 1980s, although this age group was only 14.3% of the population (National Research Council, 1993; Simons et al., 1991). Moreover, in the mid-1980s, 1.7 million arrests occurred among 10- to 17-year-olds. More than 500,000 of those arrested were 14 years of age or younger, and 46,000 were under 10 years (National Research Council, 1993; Simons et al., 1991). In 1991, there were 130,000 arrests made of youths aged 10 to 17 years for rape, robbery, homicide, or aggravated assault. This figure represents an increase of 48% since 1986 (Center for the Study of Social Policy, 1993).

***Bases and Implications of Delinquency, Crime, and Violence: Diversity and Context.*** As is the case with regard to other problems affecting today's adolescents, both individual and contextual variables combine to influence youth engagement in delinquency, crime, and violence. Individual influences on the adolescent involving variables related to his or her thoughts, behavior characteristics, sense of self, and biological maturation illustrate what are now familiar themes of adolescent development. In turn, peer and family influences are quite salient contextual influences.

For instance, the aggressive conduct that marks youths labeled as aggressive (Cairns & Cairns, 1995) may be associated with poor judgment (Graham, Hudley, & Williams, 1992). In situations where negative outcomes of a social interaction are unintentional, aggressive African American male adolescents make more extreme judgments of the other person and of the situation than comparable groups of nonaggressive youth (Graham & Hudley, 1994).

Biological variables, when they are expressed in a particular context, are also linked to delinquent behavior. For example, early maturing girls, when they are embedded in mixed-sex social settings, are at greater risk for delinquency (Caspi, Lynam, Moffitt, & Silva, 1993). In a longitudinal study of Swedish youth, early maturing among girls was related to norm breaking and delinquent behavior, when the girls were part of a peer group of older girls (Stattin & Magnusson, 1990). However, when early maturing girls had a same-age peer group no association was found between delinquency and maturational status.

Peer context is, then, an important influence on delinquency; however, it too acts in relation to family variables. For instance, male delinquents who have committed assaultive offenses have family relations characterized by rigidity and low cohesion; they also have peers who are highly aggressive

(Blaske, Borduin, Henggeler & Mann, 1989). In addition, these offenders and their mothers show little anxiety or interpersonal discomfort in the face of the youth's offenses. Male delinquents who have committed sexual offenses have high levels of neurotic symptoms, and their mothers show such problems as well (Blaske et al., 1989). The sexually offending youths have low-level emotional bonds with their peers, and multiple family factors (e.g., authoritarian parenting, deviant mother–child interactions, number of parent changes experienced by a child, having a single parent family, quality of family relationships, mother's reading level, and socioeconomic level) are associated with conviction by age 18 of both violent and nonviolent criminal offenses (Henry, Caspi, Moffitt, & Silva, 1996); in addition, violent offenders also show a temperamental style reflective of a lack of control.

## Conclusions

The character of and interrelation among the problems of youth development suggest that these problems should be addressed in both research and intervention programs in an integrative manner. Indeed, in regard to intervention, all the people with a stake in a youth's positive development, including the youth himself or herself, can pool their resources to protect the youth and to promote positive outcomes in his or her life.

We opt to pursue paths of application that emphasize the potential of young people for positive development and healthy lives. Current thinking about public policy and youth-serving programs supports this perspective.

## PREVENTION IN ADOLESCENCE: POLICY AND PROGRAM OPTIONS FOR PROMOTING POSITIVE YOUTH DEVELOPMENT

Across the diverse sets of individual and contextual factors that are associated with the actualization of risk behaviors in adolescence—that is, with substance use and abuse; with unsafe sex, adolescent pregnancy, and childbearing; with school failure and dropping out; and with crime and delinquency—or with the prevention of these risk behaviors, respectively, there are six common characteristics that are involved in the occurrence during adolescence of one or more of these risk behaviors (Dryfoos, 1990). Consistent with the stress on the system of relationships involving individuals and contexts as integral in human development, three individual and three contextual factors appear central in the genesis of risk behaviors or their prevention:

1. Age (earlier initiation of risk is linked to a greater likelihood of continual engagement in the behavior).

2. Expectations for education and school grades (youth who do not expect to do well in school, and who do not in fact do well, are at risk for problem behaviors).

3. General behavior (inappropriate behaviors and inadequate conduct, e.g., acting out, truancy, and conduct disorders, are related to the appearance of risk behaviors).

4. Peer influences (the nature of the peer group, having peers who engage in risk behaviors, and having a low resistance to participating with peers, are factors associated with an adolescent's showing such behaviors; Dryfoos, 1990).

5. Parental influences (authoritarian or permissive styles, as compared to an authoritative one [Baumrind, 1971, 1983] place a youth "at risk for problem behaviors"; lack of parental monitoring and of positive affective ties to parents is associated with risk).

6. Neighborhood influences (poverty, or urban, high-density living, is involved with risk actualization, as is race and minority status, since particular minority groups—African American and Latino ones—are likely to be the people living in such communities in the United States).

In short, a particular set of integrations among individual, familial, peer, and community levels is involved in the actualization of risk behaviors among adolescents (Dryfoos, 1990). Clearly, the presence of factors protective against adolescent problem behavior is quite important. Such factors do this by providing for the youth personal controls (e.g., religious beliefs, good self-concepts) or social controls (e.g., social support, authoritative parenting) against the occurrence of problem behaviors (Jessor, Van Den Boss, Vanderryn, & Costa, 1995). Indeed, as the presence of protective factors increases, there are decreases in adolescents' involvement in risk behaviors (Jessor et al., 1995). Understandably, the protective factors identified by Dryfoos (1990) and by Jessor et al. (1995) are involved in the design and delivery of successful prevention programs for "at-risk" youth.

## Features of Effective Programs for Youth

If programs are to be successful in addressing the combined individual and contextual influences on youth problems, they must engage these same levels in ways that promote the positive development of young people (Pittman, 1996). In other words, whether aimed at drug use (e.g., Rohrback et al., 1994), alcohol use (e.g., Howard et al., 1994; Wagenaar & Peery, 1994), aggression and delinquency (Guerra & Slaby, 1990), school problems (Switzer, Simmons, Dew, Regalski, & Wang, 1995), or socioeconomic disadvantage (Furstenberg & Hughes, 1995), effective programs engage the system of individual and contextual variables affecting youth development. Although there is a great deal of knowledge about the components of effective programs (Dryfoos, 1994; Hamburg, 1992; Schorr, 1988), the knowledge remains incomplete and imprecise—and thus the ability to build effective programs is imperfect. For example, there are numerous instances of exemplary programs, predicated on a theory of change consistent with the holistic and integrative ideas of Magnusson (1995) and of developmental contextualism (Lerner, 1995); these programs reflect the individual–context relationships involved in developmental systems (e.g., see the instances of full-service schools, or of community-based integrated professional service projects located in schools; Dryfoos, 1994, 1995). Nevertheless, not all instances of these particular programs, or of any others, are successful; and there are not evaluation data adequate to identify the conditions precisely linked to successful outcomes (Lerner, 1995). Thus, there is still much to learn about the conditions requisite for building invariantly effective, theory-based, youth development programs.

Data do exist that are sufficiently strong to indicate that by involving multiple characteristics of the young person—for instance, his or her developmental level, knowledge of risk taking, intrapersonal resources (e.g., self-esteem, self-competence, beliefs, and values), interpersonal management skills (e.g., being able to engage useful social support and prosocial behaviors from peers)—the probability of building a successful risk prevention program may be increased (Levitt, Selman, & Richmond, 1991). These programs do more than just focus on diminishing risk. The sort of programs that seem best emphasize the strengths and assets of young people, that is, their capacities for positive development, their possession of attributes—protective factors—that keep them moving forward in a positive developmental path. Protective factors—individual attributes, such as self-esteem, religious values, and knowledge, skills, and motivation to do well; and contextual attributes, such as the experience of having authoritative parents and a socially supportive, prosocial peer group—have been identified as integral to the healthy development of young people (e.g., Jessor et al., 1995; Stiffman, Church, & Earls, 1992).

Dryfoos (1990) notes other features of programs that enhance the probability of successfully promoting positive adolescent development. These features involve coordinated attention to the youth's characteristics of individuality and the specifics of his or her social contexts. These attributes include: intensive individualized attention; community-wide, multiagency collaboration; early identification and intervention; locus in schools; administration of school programs by agencies outside of schools; location of programs outside of schools; arrangements for staff training; youth social skills training; engagement of peers in interventions; involvement of parents; and a link to the world of work.

In essence, then, there are multiple features of person and context that may be combined to increase the chances of designing and delivering a successful program preventing the actualization of risk in adolescence. Building on the general developmental characteristics of the period—involving identity and family, peer, and institutional (e.g., school and work) contextual levels—these programs, when attuned as well to the specific characteristics and needs of the youth and his or her setting, will help the adolescent not just avoid the development of risk behaviors, but also promote positive youth development.

In summary, means may be found to design and deliver programs that help prevent, among the proportion of youth at risk for the development of major instances of problem behaviors, the development of such an undesirable status. Perhaps more significant means exist for doing more than keeping youths from following a course of negative behaviors. Knowledge of design criteria for effective youth programs serves also as a guide for devising means to capitalize on the potentials and strengths of all youths, their families, and communities and, through meeting their developmental needs, to promote their positive development.

However, if the knowledge of how to promote positive development is to reach the maximum number of youth possible, the resources of society need to be marshalled in the service of designing programs consistent with this vision for young people. To attain this end, scholars of youth development must engage public policy and policymakers in the support of effective programs for youths (Hamburg & Takanishi, 1996; Lerner, 1995; Lipsitz, 1991).

## CONCLUSIONS

The process of adolescent development, and of course of human development in general, involves systemic (that is, integrated, or fused, and holistic) relationships involving individuals and the multiple levels of their contexts. Both the risks and problem behaviors of youths and, in turn, the hope that systemic policy and programmatic actions may promote positive development, find their bases in these holistic, integrated interactions.

Accordingly, theoretical perspectives such as developmental contextualism, and indeed other models consistent with the developmental systems orientation to human development championed by Magnusson, suggest themselves as useful frames for a synthetic approach to basic and applied scholarship aimed at understanding and enhancing the lives of young people. Magnusson's scholarly vision, intellectual creativity, and professional leadership have in fact influenced a broad array of models within the developmental systems theoretical family (e.g., Baltes, Lindenberger & Staudinger, 1998; Bronfenbrenner & Morris, 1998; Cairns & Cairns, 1995; Elder, 1998; Gottlieb, Wahlsten, & Lickliter, 1998; Lerner, 1998).

As such, the contributions of David Magnusson to science and to society extend far beyond the bounds of his own prolific career. This work has influenced, and will continue to influence, generations of scientists involved in the study of human development. The intellectual frame he has given his colleagues and students enhances both scholarship about human development and, more important, the use of scholarship to further the healthy development of the youth of our world.

## ACKNOWLEDGMENT

The preparation of this chapter was supported in part by a grant to Richard M. Lerner from the W. T. Grant Foundation.

## REFERENCES

Alva, S. A., & Jones, M. (1994). Psychosocial adjustment and self-reported patterns of alcohol use among Hispanic adolescents. *Journal of Early Adolescence, 14*, 432–448.

Baltes, P. B. (1987). Theoretical propositions of life-span developmental psychology: On the dynamics between growth and decline. *Developmental Psychology, 23*, 611–626.

Baltes, P. B., Lindenberger, U., & Staudinger, U. M. (1998). Life-span theory in developmental psychology. In W. Damon (Series Ed.) & R. M. Lerner (Vol. Ed.), *Handbook of Child Psychology: Vol. 1. Theoretical models of human development* (5th ed., pp. 1029–1044). New York: Wiley.

Barnes, G. M., Farrell, M. P., & Banerjee, S. (1994). Family influences on alcohol abuse and other problem behaviors among black and white adolescents in a general population sample. *Journal of Research on Adolescence, 4*, 183–202.

Baumrind, D. (1971). Current patterns of parental authority. *Developmental Psychology Monographs, 4*, No. 1, Part 2.

Baumrind, D. (1983). Rejoinder to Lewis's reinterpretation of parental firm control effects: Are authoritative families really harmonious? *Psychological Bulletin, 94*, 132–142.

Berndt, T. J., & Keefe, K. (1995). Friends' influence on adolescents' adjustment to school. *Child Development, 66*, 1312–1329.

Bingham, C. R., & Crockett, L. J., (1996). Longitudinal adjustment patterns of boys and girls experiencing early, middle, and late sexual intercourse. *Developmental Psychology, 32*, 647–658.

Blaske, D. M., Borduin, C. M., Henggeler, S. W., & Mann, B. J. (1989). Individual, family, and peer characteristics of adolescent sex offenders and assaultive offenders. *Developmental Psychology, 25*, 846–855.

Borus, M. (1995). Prevalence, course, and predictors of multiple problem behaviors among gay and bisexual male adolescents. *Developmental Psychology, 31*(1), 75–85.

Brim, O. G., Jr., & Kagan, J. (1980). Constancy and change: A view of the issues. In O. G. Brim & J. Kagan (Eds.), *Constancy and change in human development* (pp. 1–25). Cambridge, MA: Harvard University Press.

Brody, G. H., Stoneman, Z., & Flor, D. (1996). Parental religiosity, family processes, and youth competence in rural, two-parent African American families. *Developmental Psychology, 32*(4), 696–706.

Bronfenbrenner, U. (1979). *The ecology of human development.* Cambridge, MA: Harvard University Press.

Bronfenbrenner, U., & Morris, P. (1998). The ecology of developmental processes. In R. M. Lerner (Ed.), *Handbook of Child Psychology: Vol. 1. Theoretical models of human development* (5th ed., pp. 993–1028). New York: Wiley.

Brooks-Gunn, J., Guo, G., & Furstenberg, F. F. (1993). Who drops out of and continues beyond high school? A 20-year follow-up of black urban youth. *Journal of Research on Adolescence, 3*, 271–294.

Cairns, R. & Cairns, B. (1995). Social ecology over time and space. In P. Moen, G. Elder, & K. Luscher (Eds.), *Examining lives in context.* Washington, DC: American Psychological Association.

Carnegie Corporation of New York. (1992). *A matter of time: Risk and opportunity in the nonschool hours.* Carnegie Council on Adolescent Development.

Carnegie Corporation of New York (1995). *Great transitions: Preparing adolescents for a new century.* New York: Carnegie Council on Adolescent Development.

Caspi, A., Lynam, D., Moffitt, T. E., & Silva, P. A. (1993). Unraveling girls' delinquency: Biological, dispositional, and contextual contributions to adolescent misbehavior. *Developmental Psychology, 29*, 19–30.

Center for the Study of Social Policy. (1993). *Kids Count data book.* Washington, DC: Author.

Chess, S. & Thomas, A. (1984). *The origins and evolution of behavior disorders: Infancy to early adult life.* New York: Brunner/Mazel.

Children's Defense Fund. (1996). *The state of America's children yearbook.* Washington, DC: Author.

Chiu, M. L., Feldman, S. S., & Rosenthal, D. A. (1992). The influence of immigration on parental behavior and adolescent distress in Chinese families residing in two western nations. *Journal of Research on Adolescence, 2*(3), 205–239.

Costa, F. M., Jessor, R., Donovan, J. E., & Fortenberry, J. D. (1995). Early initiation of sexual intercourse: The influence of psychosocial unconventionality. *Journal of Research on Adolescence, 5*, 93–122.

Crystal, D. S. & Stevenson, H. W. (1995). What is a bad kid? Answers of adolescents and their mothers in three cultures. *Journal of Research on Adolescence, 5*(1), 71–91.

di Mauro, D. (1995). *Sexuality research in the United States: An assessment of social and behavioral sciences.* New York: The Social Science Research Council.

Dryfoos, J. G. (1990). *Adolescents at risk: Prevalence and prevention.* New York: Oxford University Press.

Dryfoos, J. G. (1994). *Full service schools: A revolution in health and social services for children, youth and families.* San Francisco: Jossey-Bass.

Dryfoos, J. G. (1995). Full service schools: Revolution or fad? *Journal of Research on Adolescence, 5*, 149–150.

East, P. L., Felice, M. E., & Morgan, M. C. (1993). Sisters' and girlfriends' sexual and childbearing behavior: Effects on early adolescent girls' sexual outcomes. *Journal of Marriage and the Family, 55*, 953–963.

Elder, G. H., Jr. (1974). *Children of the Great Depression: Social change in life experience.* Chicago: University of Chicago Press.

Elder, G. H., Jr. (1998). The life course and human development. In W. Damon (Series Ed.) & R. M. Lerner (Vol. Ed.), *Handbook of Child Psychology: Vol. 1. Theoretical models of human development* (5th ed., pp. 939–992). New York: Wiley.

Elder, G. H., Modell, J., & Parke, R. D. (1993). Studying children in a changing world. In G. H. Elder, J. Modell, & R. D. Parke (Eds.), *Children in time and place: Developmental and historical insights* (pp. 3–21). New York: Cambridge University Press.

Ensminger, M. E. (1990). Sexual activity and problem behaviors among black, urban adolescents. *Child Development, 61*, 2032–2046.

Feigelman, S., Stanton, B. F., & Ricardo, I. (1993). Perceptions of drug selling and drug use among urban youths. *Journal of Early Adolescence, 13*, 267–284.

Feldman, S. S., Rosenthal, D. R., Brown, N. L., & Canning, R. D. (1995). Predicting sexual experience in adolescent boys from peer rejection and acceptance during childhood. *Journal of Research on Adolescence, 5*, 387–411.

Fisher, C. B. & Johnson, B. L. (1990). Getting mad at mom and dad: Children's changing views of family conflict. *International Journal of Behavioral Development, 13*(1), 31–48.

Flannery, D. J., Vazsonyi, A. T., & Rowe, D. C. (1996). Caucasian and Hispanic early adolescent substance use: Parenting, personality, and school adjustment. *Journal of Early Adolescence, 16*, 71–89.

Fuligni, A. J., Eccles, J. S., & Barber, B. L. (1995). The long-term effects of seventh-grade ability grouping in mathematics. *Journal of Early Adolescence, 15*(1), 58–89.

Furstenberg, F. F., & Hughes, M. E. (1995). Social capital and successful development among at-risk youth. *Journal of Marriage and the Family, 57*, 580–592.

Gamoran, A., & Nystrand, M. (1991). Background and instructional effects on achievement in eighth-grade English and Social Studies. *Journal of Research on Adolescence, 1*(3), 277–300.

Garbarino, J. (1992). *Children and families in the social environment* (2nd ed.). New York: Aldine de Gruyter.

Gfellner, B. B. (1994). A matched group comparison of drug use and problem behavior among Canadian Indian and white adolescents: Canadian research on early adolescence [Special issue]. *Journal of Early Adolescence, 14*, 24–48.

Gottlieb, G. (1997). *Synthesizing nature-nurture: Prenatal roots of instinctive behavior*. Mahwah, NJ: Lawrence Erlbaum Associates.

Gottlieb, G., Walhsten, D., & Lickliter, R. (1998). The significance of biology for human development: A developmental psychobiological systems view. In W. Damon (Series Ed.) & R. M. Lerner (Vol. Ed.), *Handbook of Child Psychology: Vol. 1. Theoretical models of human development* (5th ed., pp. 233–274). New York: Wiley.

Graham, S., & Hudley, C. (1994). Attributions of aggressive and nonaggressive African American male early adolescents: A study of construct accessibility. *Developmental Psychology, 30*, 365–373.

Graham, S., Hudley, C., & Williams, E. (1992). Attributional and emotional determinants of aggression among African American and Latino young adolescents. *Developmental Psychology, 28*, 731–740.

Guerra, N. G., & Slaby, R. G. (1990). Cognitive mediators of aggression in adolescent offenders: Intervention. *Developmental Psychology, 26*, 269–277.

Hamburg, D. A. (1992). *Today's children: Creating a future for a generation in crisis*. New York: Time Books.

Hamburg, D. A., & Takanishi, R. (1996). Great transitions: Preparing American youth for the 21st century—the role of research. *Journal of Research on Adolescence, 6*, 379–396.

Hartup, W. W. (1993). Adolescents and their friends. *New Directions for Child Development, 60*. San Francisco: Jossey-Bass.

Henry, B., Caspi, A., Moffitt, T. E., & Silva, P. A. (1996). Temperamental and familial predictors of violent and nonviolent criminal convictions: Age 3 to age 18. *Developmental Psychology, 32*, 614–623.

Hernandez, D. J. (1993). *America's children: Resources from family, government, and the economy*. New York: Russell Sage Foundation.

Howard, J., Boyd, G. M., & Zucker, R. A. (1994). Overview of issues. *Journal of Research on Adolescence, 4*(2), 175–182.

Hunt, E., Streissguth, A. P., Kerr, B., & Olson, H. C. (1995). Mothers' alcohol consumption during pregnancy: Effects on spatial-visual reasoning in 14-year-old children. *Psychological Science, 6*(6), 339–342.

Huston, A. C. (Ed.). (1991). *Children in poverty: Child development and public policy*. Cambridge, UK: Cambridge University Press.

Huston, A. C., McLoyd, V. C., & Coll, C. T. (1994). Children and poverty: Issues in contemporary research. *Child Development, 65*, 275–282.

Jessor, R., Van Den Boss, J., Vanderryn, J., & Costa, F. M. (1995). Protective factors in adolescent problem behavior: Moderator effects and developmental change. *Developmental Psychology, 31*, 923–933.

Johnston, L., O'Malley, P. M., & Bachman, J. G. (1996). *National survey results on drug use from the monitoring the future study, 1975–1994*: Vol. II. *College students and young adults.* Washington, DC: National Institute on Drug Abuse.

Kuo, Z.-Y. (1976). *The dynamics of behavior development: An epigenetic view*. New York: Plenum.

Lamborn, S. D., Mounts, N. S., Steinberg, L. & Dornbusch, S. M. (1991). Patterns of competence and adjustment among adolescents from authoritative, authoritarian, indulgent, and neglectful families. *Child Development, 62*, 1049–1065.

Lerner, R. M. (1978). Nature, nurture, and dynamic interactionism. *Human Development, 21*, 1–20.

Lerner, R. M. (1984). *On the nature of human plasticity*. New York: Cambridge University Press.

Lerner, R. M. (1986). *Concepts and theories of human development* (2nd ed.). New York: Random House.

Lerner, R. M. (1991). Changing organism-context relations as the basic process of development: A developmental-contextual perspective. *Developmental Psychology, 27*, 27–32.

Lerner, R. M. (1995). *America's youth in crisis: Challenges and options for programs and policies*. Thousand Oaks, CA: Sage.

Lerner, R. M. (1998). Theories of human development: Contemporary perspectives. In W. Damon (Series Ed.) & R. M. Lerner (Vol. Ed.), *Handbook of Child Psychology: Vol. 1. Theoretical models of human development* (5th ed., pp. 1–24). New York: Wiley.

Lerner, R. M., & Kauffman, M. B. (1985). The concept of development in contextualism. *Developmental Review, 5*, 309–333.

Lerner, R. M., & Lerner, J. V. (1989). Organismic and social contextual bases of development: The sample case of adolescence. In W. Damon (Ed.), *Child development today and tomorrow* (pp. 69–85). San Francisco: Jossey-Bass.

Levitt, M. J., Guacci-Franco, N., & Levitt, J. L. (1993). Social support and achievement in childhood and early adolescence: A multicultural study. *Journal of Applied Developmental Psychology, 15*, 207–222.

Levitt, M. Z., Selman, R. L., & Richmond, J. B. (1991). The psychosocial foundations of early adolescents' high-risk behavior: Implications for research and practice. *Journal of Research on Adolescence, 1*, 349–378.

Li, X., Stanton, B., Feigelman, S., & Black, M. M. (1994). Drug trafficking and drug use among urban African American early adolescents. *Journal of Early Adolescence, 14*, 491–508.

Lipsitz, J. (1991). Public policy and young adolescents: A 1990's context for researchers. *Journal of Early Adolescence, 11*, 40.

Magnusson, D. (1981). *Toward a psychology of situations: An interactional perspective*. Hillsdale, NJ: Lawrence Erlbaum Associates.

Magnusson, D. (1982). Situational determinants of stress: An interactional perspective. In L. Goldberger & S. Breznitz (Eds.), *Handbook of stress* (pp. 231–253). New York: The Free Press.

Magnusson, D. (1985). Implications of an interactional paradigm of research on human development. *International Journal of Behavior and Development, 8*, 115–137.

Magnusson, D. (1988). Individual development from an interactional perspective: A longitudinal study. In D. Magnusson (Ed.), *Paths through life* (Vol. 1, pp. 3–31). Hillsdale, NJ: Lawrence Erlbaum Associates.

Magnusson, D. (1995). Individual development: A holistic integrated model. In P. Moen, G. H. Elder, & K. Luscher (Eds.), *Linking lives and contexts: Perspective on the ecology of human development* (pp. 19–60). Washington DC: American Psychological Association.

Magnusson, D. (1996a). Interactionism in developmental research. In P. Hedström & E. Kühlhorn (Eds.), *Sociology through time and space. Essays in honor of C.G. Janson* (pp. 117–126). Stockholm: Akademitryck-Edsbruk.

Magnusson, D. (1996b). *The lifespan development of individuals: Behavioral, neurobiological, and psychosocial perspectives.* Cambridge, UK: Cambridge University Press.

Magnusson, D. (in press-a). Interactionism and the person approach in developmental psychology. *European Child and Adolescent Psychiatry.*

Magnusson, D. (in press-b). An interactionist's view on individual development. *Studia Psychologica.*

Magnusson, D., & Allen, V. (1983). *Human development: An interactional perspective.* New York: Academic Press.

Magnusson, D., & Stattin, H. (1998). Person context interaction theories. In W. Damon (Series Ed.) & R. M. Lerner (Vol. Ed.), *Handbook of Child Psychology: Vol. 1. Theoretical models of human development* (5th ed., pp. 685–760). New York: Wiley.

Mitchell, C. M., O'Nell, T. D., Beals, J., Dick, R. W., Keane, E., & Manson, S. M. (1996). Dimensionality of alcohol use among American Indian adolescents: Latent structure, construct validity, and implications for developmental research. *Journal of Research on Adolescence, 6,* 151–180.

National Research Council. (1993). *Losing generations: Adolescents in high-risk settings.* Washington, DC: National Academy Press.

Nucci, L., Guerra, N., & Lee, J. (1991). Adolescent judgment of the personal, prudential, and normative aspects of drug usage. *Developmental Psychology, 27,* 841–848.

Öhman, A., & Magnusson, D. (1987). An interactional paradigm for research on psychopathology. In D. Magnusson & A. Öhman (Eds.), *Psychopathology: An interactional perspective* (pp. 3–19). Orlando, FL: Academic Press.

Phinney, J. S. & Chavira, V. (1995). Parental ethnic socialization and adolescent coping with problems related to ethnicity. *Journal of Research on Adolescence, 5*(1), 31–53.

Pittman, K. (1996). Community, youth, development: Three goals in search of connection. *New Designs for Youth Development,* Winter, 4–8.

Riegel, K. F. (1975). Toward a dialectical theory of development. *Human Development, 18,* 50–64.

Roberts, L. R., & Petersen, A. C. (1992). The relationship between academic achievement and social self-image during early adolescence. *Journal of Early Adolescence, 12,* 197–219.

Rohrback, L. A., Hodgson, C. S., Broder, B. I., Montgomery, S. B., Flay, B. R., Hansen, W. B., & Pentz, M. A. (1994). Parental participation in drug abuse prevention: Results from the midwestern prevention project. *Journal of Research on Adolescence, 4,* 295–317.

Savin-Williams, R. C. (1995). An exploratory study of pubertal maturation timing and self-esteem among gay and bisexual male youths: Sexual orientation and human development [Special issue]. *Developmental Psychology, 31,* 56–64.

Schorr, L. B. (1988). *Within our reach: Breaking the cycle of disadvantage.* New York: Doubleday.

Schulenberg, J., Wadsworth, K. N., O'Malley, P. M., Bachman, J. G., & Johnston, L. D. (1996). Adolescent risk factors for binge drinking during the transition to young adulthood: Variable- and pattern-centered approaches to change. *Developmental Psychology, 32,* 659–674.

Scott-Jones, D., & White, A. B. (1990). Correlates of sexual activity in early adolescence. *Journal of Early Adolescence, 10,* 221–238.

Simons, J. M., Finlay, B., & Yang, A. (1991). *The adolescent and young adult fact book.* Washington, DC: Children's Defense Fund.

Small, S. A., & Kerns, D. (1993). Unwanted sexual activity among peers during early and middle adolescence: Incidence and risk factors. *Journal of Marriage and the Family, 55,* 941–952.

Small, S. A., & Luster, T. (1994). An ecological, risk-factor approach to adolescent sexual activity. *Journal of Marriage and the Family, 56,* 181–192.

Stattin, H., & Magnusson, D. M. (1990). *Pubertal maturation in female development.* Hillsdale, NJ: Lawrence Erlbaum Associates.

Stiffman, A. R., Church, H., & Earls, F. (1992). Predictive modeling of change in depressive disorder and counts of depressive symptoms in urban youths. *Journal of Research on Adolescence, 2,* 295–316.

Sullivan, M. L. (1993). Culture and class as determinants of out-of-wedlock childbearing and poverty during late adolescence. *Journal of Research on Adolescence, 3,* 295–316.

Switzer, G. E., Simmons, R. G., Dew, M. A., Regalski, J. M., & Wang, C. H. (1995). The effect of a school-based helper program on adolescent self-image, attitudes, and behavior. *Journal of Early Adolescence, 15,* 429–455.

Taylor, C. S. (1990). *Dangerous society.* East Lansing: Michigan State University Press.

Taylor, C. S. (1993). *Girls, gangs, women, and drugs.* East Lansing: Michigan State University Press.

Tobach, E., & Greenberg, G. (1984). The significance of T.C. Schneirla's contribution to the concept of integration. In G. Greenberg & E. Tobach (Eds.), *Behavioral evolution and integrative levels* (pp. 1–7). Hillsdale, NJ: Lawrence Erlbaum Associates.

United States Department of Health and Human Services. (1996). *Trends in the well-being of America's children and youth: 1996.* Washington, DC: Author.

Wagenaar A. C., & Perry, C. L. (1994). Community strategies for the reduction of youth drinking: Theory and application. *Journal of Research on Adolescence, 4,* 319–345.

Wentzel, K. R. (1991). Relations between social competence and academic achievement in early adolescence. *Child Development, 62,* 1066–1078.

Wentzel, K. R. (1993). Motivation and achievement in early adolescence: The role of multiple classroom goals. *Journal of Early Adolescence, 13*(1), 4–20.

Werner, H. (1957). The concept of development from a comparative and organismic point of view. In D. B. Harris (Ed.), *The concept of development* (pp. 125–148). Minnesota: University of Minnesota Press.

Whitbeck, L. B., Simons, R. L., & Kao, M. (1994). The effects of divorced mothers' dating behaviors and sexual attitudes on the sexual attitudes and behaviors of their adolescent children. *Journal of Marriage and the Family, 56,* 615–621.

Windle, M., Miller-Tutzauer, C., & Domenico, D. (1992). Alcohol use, suicidal behavior, and risky activities among adolescents. *Journal of Research on Adolescence, 2,* 317–330.

World Health Organization. (1986). WHO study group on young people and "Health for all by the year 2000." In *Young people's health: A challenge for society* (Technical Report Series, No. 731). Geneva: Author.

World Health Organization. (1993). *The health of young people: A challenge and a promise.* Geneva: Author.

Zabin, L. S., Astone, N. M., & Emerson, M. R. (1993). Do adolescents want babies? The relationship between attitudes and behavior. *Journal of Research on Adolescence, 3,* 67–86.

## SUMMING UP

# 26

# Epilogue and Prospects

## Lars R. Bergman
Stockholm University

## Robert B. Cairns
University of North Carolina, Chapel Hill

This volume is the outcome of a symposium at Wik's Castle, Sweden, in May 1997 where leading researchers, mostly within developmental psychology, came together to discuss in depth the implications of the emerging developmental science and the holistic approach. A wealth of material was presented, discussing various aspects of the suggested new paradigm—theoretical, methodological, as well as empirical. Rather than trying to summarize this diversified and rich tapestry of thoughts and results we want to pick up a few important ideas that have profound implications for the future direction of the study of individual development.

## THE IMPLICATIONS FOR RESEARCH METHODOLOGY OF A HOLISTIC–INTERACTIONIST VIEW OF HUMAN DEVELOPMENT

Our first theme is the implications for research methodology of a holistic–interactionist view of human development. From this perspective, one way of viewing development is through the framework provided by the study of complex dynamic models. As pointed out in various chapters in this volume, the usefulness of a standard variable-oriented approach based on a linear model can be more limited than is usually believed. We would like to see increased efforts along several methodological lines such as:

1. Latent growth curve modeling.
2. The implementation of sophisticated pattern-oriented methods.
3. The use of mathematical models taken from the study of dynamic systems.
4. Theoretical work on the "science of science" aspects of theory, mathematical and statistical modeling and estimation methods within the holistic–interactionist framework for studying development.

There is a need for new methods to complement the standard methods. At least from a holistic–interactionist standpoint, in some situations there is the feeling that it is not possible to come much further using established variable-oriented methods. The person as a functioning whole appears to be lost in a complex network of relations between variables, generating an immense complexity when interactions are examined.

## IMPLEMENTING LONGITUDINAL RESEARCH

It has been said many times that longitudinal data are the life-blood of developmental research. Using a longitudinal approach makes possible the study of the process of individual development (Bergman & Magnusson, 1990; Cairns, Elder, & Costello, 1996; Ford & Lerner, 1992; Rutter, 1981). It is therefore gratifying that some of the most comprehensive longitudinal programs have been planned and implemented with reference to a holistic view of the type presented in this book (Cairns & Cairns, 1994; Magnusson, 1988). With comprehensive longitudinal information available, it becomes feasible to implement a holistic interactionist theoretical paradigm in actual empirical research to an extent that hitherto has not been possible. The synergetic effects of applying this broad perspective within a research program should also be noted: Each of the specialized studies focusing on a particular aspect of development gain strength from the other studies and together they also form the basis for integrative studies. However, as discussed in this volume, a number of important measurement issues have to be dealt with to implement the longitudinal approach as efficiently as possible.

### The Choice of Time Points of Measurement

In practice we can collect measurements only at a limited number of time points during development, and various strategies have to be considered for obtaining maximally useful data. Obviously, the start point and end point of the age period of interest should be points of measurement, but the number and spacing of the measurement points in between must depend on the specific purpose of the study. Normally, an equal spacing of measurement points is not optimal. It is better to spread the measurements so that what are thought to be the important age periods for the phenomena under study are best covered. Some modern methods of analysis demand that information be available from many points in time (for instance, latent growth curve modeling). A practical solution is then to obtain intensive information for a subsample and use the results from the analysis of the subsample together with the less-intensive information from the rest of the sample to estimate parameters applicable to the whole sample, applying modern model-based sampling methods.

## The Reference Period of the Measurements

Usually it is desirable in a longitudinal study to obtain measurements that can be regarded as "stable" in the sense that they do not fluctuate greatly on a day-to-day or situational basis (for instance, one uses reliable test scores, teachers' ratings summarizing the child's behavior during the last term, and so on; exceptions are, of course, situations when short-time processes are at focus, like when studying social interactions; see Cairns and Green, 1979). Here the length of the reference period of the measurement must be considered carefully in relation to the specific problem under study. What constitutes the developmental change we want to measure and what constitutes only temporary fluctuations we may want to ignore? Memory errors must also be considered when retrospective questions are asked (see, for instance, Janson, 1990, for an overview).

## The Concept of Time

It has been repeatedly pointed out that chronological age in certain situations is not the most suitable indicator of age. Alternative indicators are, for instance, biological age, number of years after entering the labor market, and number of years of remaining life span. Magnusson (1993) treats this problem in a careful discussion of possible errors introduced into a developmental setting by varying biological age among children of the same chronological age.

## Scaling Properties of the Measurements

In many applications, variables are used that have some or all of the following properties:

> They were constructed separately, each to maximize the usefulness of that variable viewed as a separate entity or dimension. To provide a point of comparison between the values in different variables they have to be

transformed to relative scales in relation to inter- or intraindividual variation (for instance to percentiles or $z$ scores).

They were constructed at each time of measurement separately without consideration of how change between points in time is best measured.

Variables constructed in the above way abound and, although useful in many settings, their limitations for studying individual development within a holistic—interactional paradigm should be pointed out:

No consideration is given to the fact that for certain research problems an individual's values in the different variables at a specific point in time should constitute a whole. To give an example: Let us assume that patterns of externalizing problems are the focus of interest and that the individual measurements making up each child's profile should reflect the fact that certain problems are more common in a serious form than other problems. This information is not captured by a purely relative scaling using, for instance, $z$ scores.

No consideration is given to the fact that it may be desirable or even necessary to measure change in a variable at a more sophisticated level than just change in relative position on a scale of interindividual differences. For instance, it may be that either the strong expression of a certain characteristic becomes more or less common with age or that its psychologically meaningful variation strongly increases or decreases with age, or both. That needs to be reflected in the measurements.

Broadly speaking, the necessity for constructing variables that better measure change must be seriously considered. In fact, almost all variables used by researchers have been constructed within a conceptual framework of cross-sectional research and may not be optimal for capturing change and development. This argument has been around for a long time, being put forward by, for instance, Bereiter (1963), but has had little impact on empirical research. An exception is Kliegl and Baltes' (1987) work studying micro-genetic processes.

## STUDYING THE MOTOR OF CHANGE

By studying individual development researchers attempt to understand the complex patterning of change and stability during development both from an intra- and an interindividual perspective. At the very heart of this is the need for understanding the aspects of the complex system that generate the change and absence of change in the process under study. We want to look into the motor of change. It is then a discomforting fact that most approaches for studying development really do not answer well to this purpose. The variables tend to be measurements of a "static" world and the statistical models tend to be of relations between static variables. We need to complement the ordinary approaches that are largely static with a truly dynamic approach, looking for the motor of change. In a way, this purpose is realized in the study of processes within the framework of nonlinear dynamic systems where the set of differential or difference equations "is" the motor. Considerations like these have profound implications for the choice of quantitative approach.

Realizing the difficulty of implementing complex dynamic systems modeling in the study of individual development and realizing the danger of uncritically borrowing concepts and methods constructed for the needs of the natural sciences, we still think that such an approach (here given the acronym NOLIDS) holds a potential. If successful, NOLIDS offers the possibility of understanding the dynamics of change. Examples of such approaches are given in, for instance, Barton (1994) and Smith and Thelen (1993). A NOLIDS perspective within developmental science is discussed by Cairns, Costello, and Elder (1996), although the (partial) success of this approach within certain molecular areas in the behavioral sciences does not automatically imply that a corresponding success can be achieved for more molar areas. (See Kelso, chap. 5, this volume, for a careful discussion of these issues.) The rapprochement between NOLIDS and statistical science that has begun also holds promise that better methods will be devised for parameter estimation in NOLIDS (Berliner, 1992).

For many important developmental research areas, NOLIDS modeling will probably prove to be unfeasible, at least for the near future. The systems studied there may be too complex to be captured by dynamic models. However, in spite of this the general principles and many concepts in NOLIDS may be of great value for the whole developmental field. To give just one example: The concept of chaos has profound implications, if taken seriously. It could mean that for certain systems under study, prediction is theoretically impossible, not just practically impossible, in spite of the system being largely deterministic. The concept of chaos could also provide an alternative explanation to very complex behavior of certain systems. This complex behavior would, on the surface, seem to indicate that the system is also complex with a host of factors operating, and that there is a need to give a strong role to stochastic events. NOLIDS shows us that very complex behavior can sometimes be explained by a very simple model and that sometimes only a few parameter aspects of a system need to be taken into account in order to explain essential features of its behavior.

## A LAST WORD

In writing this volume we are in line with recently emerging trends as exemplified by Magnusson (1996), presenting the results of a Nobel symposium on the cross-disciplinary importance of the holistic–interactional paradigm; by Cairns, Bergman, and Kagan (1998), discussing the individual in developmental science; by the special issue of *Developmental Psychopathology* edited by Ciccetti (1997), in which the implications of the interactional paradigm for developmental psychopathology are discussed; and by Cairns, Elder, and Costello (1996), presenting the new developmental science. The research approaches advocated in the present volume are only part of a new zeitgeist involving numerous researchers and building on ideas of holism and dynamic interaction put forth by far-sighted scholars a long time ago (see, for instance, Allport, 1937; Lewin, 1935). The perspectives we present are becoming increasingly important in many research fields in many sciences. We regret only that within the confined space of one book it has not been possible to open up a larger window to the exciting developments that are now occurring.

Finally, we should always come back to the individual. It is his or her development that is to be explained and we should never loose him or her in our endeavors as sometimes seems to be the case. The challenge is to retain the individual focus and still be able to arrive at laws applicable for explaining differences and similarities between individuals. There is a strong need, even an urgency, for a methodology that will enable us to integrate the study of intra- and interindividual development. We must bring the single individual back into developmental research, not primarily as a case study but as the solid building block for nomothetic theories.

## REFERENCES

Allport, G. W. (1937). *Personality: A psychological interpretation*. New York: Holt, Rinehart & Winston.

Barton, S. (1994). Chaos, self-organization, and psychology. *American Psychologist, 49*, 5–15.

Bergman, L. R., & Magnusson, D. (1990). General issues about data quality in longitudinal research. In D. Magnusson & L. R. Bergman (Eds.), *Data quality in longitudinal research* (pp. 1–31). Cambridge, UK: Cambridge University Press.

Bergman, L. R., & Magnusson, D. (1991). Stability and change in patterns of extrinsic adjustment problems. In D. Magnusson, L. R. Bergman, G. Rudinger & B. Törestad (Eds.), *Problems and methods in longitudinal research: Stability and change* (pp. 323–346). Cambridge, UK: Cambridge University Press.

Bereiter, C. (1963). Some persistent dilemmas in the measurment of change. In C. Harris (Ed.), *Problems in measuring change* (pp. 3–20). Madison: University of Wisconsin Press.

Berliner, L. M. (1992). Statistics, probability and chaos. *Statistical Science, 7*, 69–90.

Cairns, R. B., Bergman, L. R., & Kagan, J. (Eds.). (1998). *Methods and models for studying the individual.* Thousand Oaks, CA: Sage.

Cairns, R. B., & Cairns, B. D. (1994). *Lifelines and risks. Pathways of youth in our time.* Hemel Hempstead, UK: Harvester Wheatsheaf.

Cairns, R. B., Elder, G. H., Jr., & Costello, E. J. (1996). *Developmental science.* Cambridge, UK: Cambridge University Press.

Cairns, R. B., & Green, J. A. (1979). How to assess personality and social patterns: Ratings or observations? In R. B. Cairns (Ed.), *The analysis of social interactions Methods, issues, and illustration* (pp. 209–226). Hillsdale, NJ: Lawrence Erlbaum Associates.

Ciccetti, D. (1997). Special Issue of *Developmental Psychopathology, 9.*

Ford, D. H., & Lerner, R. M. (1992). *Developmental systems theory. An integrative approach.* Newbury Park, CA: Sage.

Janson, C. G. (1990). Retrospective data, undesirable behaviour, and the longitudinal perspective. In D. Magnusson & L. R. Bergman (Eds.), *Data quality in longitudinal research* (pp. 100–122). Cambridge, UK: Cambridge University Press.

Kliegl, R., & Baltes, P. B. (1987). Theory-guided analysis of development and aging mechanisms through testing-the-limits and research on expertise. In C. Schooler & K. W. Schaie (Eds.), *Cognitive functioning and social structure over the life course* (pp. 95–119). Norwoord, NJ: Ablex.

Lewin, K. (1935). *A dynamic theory of personality.* New York: McGraw-Hill.

Magnusson, D. (1988). *Individual development from an interactional perspective.* Hillsdale, NJ: Lawrence Erlbaum Associates.

Magnusson, D. (1993). Human ontogeny. In D. Magnusson & P. Casaer (Eds.), *Longitudinal research on individual development. Present status and future perspectives* (pp. 1–25). Cambridge, UK: Cambridge University Press.

Magnusson, D. (Ed.). (1996). *The life-span development of individuals: Behavioral, neurobiological and psychosocial perspectives. A synthesis.* Cambridge, UK: Cambridge University Press.

Rutter, M. (1981). Longitudinal studies: A psychiatric perspective. In S. A. Mednick & A. E. Baert (Eds.), *Prospective longitudinal research: An empirical basis for the primary prevention of psychosocial disorders* (pp. 326–335). New York: Oxford University Press.

Smith, L. B., & Thelen, E. (1993). *A dynamic systems approach to development. Applications.* Cambridge, MA: MIT Press.

# Author Index

## A

Achenbach, T. M., 284, 297, 355
Acitelli, L. K., 112, 117
af Klinteberg, B., 7, 37, 210-213, 218, 219, 221, 224-227, 268, 279
Afonso, D., 204, 207
Agostinelli, G., 113, 118
Ågren, G., 324
Ahnsjö, S., 342, 346
Aikens, J. E., 127, 132
Aitken, S., 156, 236, 247
Albert, P. S., 186, 200
Alho, K., 206, 208
Alku, P., 206, 208
Allebeck, P., 324, 336
Allen, L., 344, 347
Allen, M. D., 213, 226
Allen, T., 113, 118
Allen, V. L., 44, 46, 421, 442
Allik, J., 208, 266, 267, 280
Allport, G. W., 33, 265, 266, 276, 279, 282, 284, 297, 452
Alm, M., 210, 225
Alm, P. O., 210, 213, 221, 225, 226
Alonso, S. J., 204, 207
al-Shabbout, M., 240, 246
Alva, S. A., 429, 438
Anderson, E., 413, 416
Anderson, M., 344, 346
Anderson, T. W., 130, 132
Andersson, T., 8, 218, 226, 356, 373, 379, 382, 391
Andrews, B., 414, 417
Andrews, H., 325, 336
Angleitner, A., 266, 279
Annell, A.-L., 343, 346

Arahuetes, R. M., 204, 208
Arcus, D., 94, 97, 98, 151, 153
Arevalo, R., 204, 207
Aro, S., 268, 279
Åsberg, M., 211, 213, 226, 227
Asendorpf, J. B., 7, 162, 266, 271, 273, 275, 278, 281, 282, 284, 285, 288, 295
Ashburner, M., 203, 206, 208
Askins, K., 240, 247
Assmann, A., 14, 27
Astone, N. M., 430, 443
Atkinson, S., 104, 118
Atz, J. W., 58, 61

## B

Babiak, P., 306
Bachman, J. G., 378, 379, 391, 427, 428, 441, 442
Backman, C. W., 111, 117
Bae, K., 186, 199
Baert, A. E., 344, 347
Bailey, K. D., 140, 151
Bak, P., 68, 81
Baker, E., 204, 208
Baker, P., 400, 418
Baldwin, J. M., 50, 58, 60, 61
Baldwin, A, 397, 419
Baldwin, C, 397, 419
Ballinger, S. W., 199
Baltes, P. B., 5, 13-16, 18, 20-23, 25-29, 43, 46, 121, 132, 424, 425, 438, 450, 453
Bandura, A., 101, 117
Banerjee, S., 429, 438

Bank, L., 351, 375
Barber, B. L., 432, 440
Bardgett, M. E., 240, 247
Barker, R., 172, 174, 231
Barnes, G. M., 429, 438
Barratt, E. S., 210, 225
Barrett, J., 100, 107, 108, 118
Bartko, J. J., 210, 226
Barton, S., 149, 151, 451, 452
Bartusch, D. J., 210, 228
Bates, E. A., 180, 198
Baum, K., 326, 337
Baumrind, D., 432, 435, 438
Baxter, L., 114, 117
Baydar, N., 403, 416
Beals, J., 429, 442
Beardslee, W. R., 167, 175
Begg, D., 162, 163
Belbin, L., 144, 151
Bell, D. S. H., 127, 132
Bell, R. Q., 351, 362, 363, 373, 375
Belsky, J., 89, 98
Bem, D. J., 294, 298
Bender, B. G., 241, 245
Benes, F. M., 204, 207
Bennet, E. L., 187
Berden, G. F., 355, 375
Bereiter, C., 130, 132, 450, 452
Berent, S., 240, 247
Berger, D., 306, 307, 312
Bergman, A., 326, 337
Bergman, L. R., 6, 9, 12, 25, 28, 45,
    46, 51, 53, 56, 61, 62, 87, 98, 100,
    108, 117, 131, 132, 138, 142, 143,
    145-153, 162, 166, 175, 218, 224,
    226, 266-298, 319, 334, 352, 360,
    373, 374, 380, 391, 394, 418, 448,
    452, 453
Berliner, L. M., 451, 452
Berman, C. M., 106, 117
Berndt, T. J., 432, 438
Bernstein, I. H., 123, 135
Bertalanffy, L., von, 196, 197
Biederman, J., 331, 336
Biesecker, G. E., 331, 336
Bifulco, A., 414, 417

Binder-Brynes, K., 240, 248
Bingham, C. R., 430, 438
Bird, H. R., 278, 279
Bishop, Y. M. M., 142, 152
Bittman, E. L., 186, 199
Black, J. E., 193, 197
Black, M. M., 429, 441
Blackman, M. C., 257, 263
Blanchard-Fields, F., 21, 28
Blashfield, R. K., 140, 143, 144, 152,
    153, 154
Blaske, D. M., 434, 438
Bliesner, T., 351, 374
Block, J. H., 155, 157, 160, 161, 163,
    169, 174, 284, 298
Block, J., 6, 34, 44, 60, 107, 108, 117,
    124, 132, 139, 152, 155, 156, 157,
    159-163, 169, 174, 266, 278, 282,
    284-286, 295, 297
Bock, H. H., 144, 145, 152
Bocking, A. D., 204, 207
Bodnoff, S. H., 236, 245
Bohman, M., 344, 346
Bonett, D., 204, 208
Bonneau, R. H., 193, 198
Bonner, J., 187, 201
Borden, R. J., 115, 117
Borduin, C. M., 434, 438
Borkenau, P., 290, 298
Bornstein, M., 396, 416
Borum, R., 317, 334
Borus, M., 430, 438
Bowlby, J., 113, 117
Boyd, G. M., 428, 435, 440
Brazelton, A. D., 192, 201
Breckenridge, J. N., 141, 152
Bremme, K., 331, 336
Bremner, J. C., 240, 246
Brennan, P., 322, 332, 335
Bressler, S. L., 66, 73, 82, 83
Bretherton, I., 113, 117
Brewer, M. B., 115, 117
Brim, O. G. Jr., 424, 438
Broder, B. I., 435, 442
Brody, G. H., 432, 439
Bronen, R. A., 240, 246

Bronfenbrenner, U., 13, 28, 53, 61, 197, 231, 396, 397, 416, 424, 438, 439
Brooks-Gunn, J., 8, 394, 396-400, 403, 414, 416-419, 432, 439
Brown, A.-S., 204, 208
Brown, D., 126, 135
Brown, G. W., 317, 334, 414, 417
Brown, J., 278, 280
Brown, N. L., 431, 440
Brown, R. J., 115, 117
Brownfain, J. J., 260, 262
Bruhn, P., 127, 128, 132
Bruner, J., 401, 417
Bryant, F. B., 126, 135
Bryk, A. S., 282, 298
Buchanan, J. J., 73, 81
Buchanan, S., 66, 73, 82
Budescu, D. V., 143, 152
Buka, S., 231, 246, 350, 373
Bull, J. J., 186, 197
Burton, L., 413, 417
Burton, R. V., 53, 62, 358, 375
Butler, A. C., 127, 132
Byrne, D., 115, 117


C


Cairns, B. D., 53, 61, 167, 169, 174, 356, 373, 378, 391, 395, 417, 433, 438, 439, 448, 453
Cairns, R. B., 3, 5, 9, 34, 42, 46, 49, 50-52, 55-58, 61, 62, 87, 98, 100, 108, 117, 118, 122, 132, 137, 151, 152, 166, 167, 169, 174, 175, 197, 356, 373, 378, 391, 395, 417, 433, 438, 439, 448, 449, 451-453
Caldji, C., 187, 199, 236, 247
Cameron, H. A., 204, 207
Campbell, J. D., 53, 55, 62, 358, 375
Campbell, J. H., 187, 188, 197
Cann, R. L., 189, 197
Canning, R. D., 431, 440
Cannon, T. D., 204-206, 208, 326, 335
Cantor, N., 252, 262

Cantrill, J. G., 113, 118
Capasso, L., 213, 227
Capelli, S., 240, 246
Caprara, G. V., 353, 373
Carlson, E. B., 162, 164
Carlson, G. A., 326, 335
Carlson, M., 7, 44, 46, 74, 230, 231, 237, 241, 242, 246
Carlson, R., 34, 46
Carr, D., 395, 411, 414, 419
Carroll, S., 183, 198
Case, P., 74, 81
Caspi, A., 141, 154, 162-164, 210, 227, 228, 266, 281, 284-286, 294, 298, 433, 434, 439, 440
Castellucci, V. F., 188, 198
Casti, J. L., 139, 152
Catalano, S. M., 193, 197
Catell, A. K. S., 126, 130, 132
Cattell, R. B., 126, 130-132, 140, 152, 160, 163, 284, 298
Cederblad, M., 344, 346
Cervone, D., 256, 262
Chandler, M. J., 24, 25, 28
Charney, D. S., 240, 246
Charnov, E. L., 413, 418
Chase-Lansdale, P. L., 398-400, 414, 417
Chavira, V., 432, 442
Cheever, J., 96, 98
Chen, L., 331, 336
Chen, Y., 68, 81
Cheour, M., 206, 208
Chesebro, B., 182, 197
Chess, S., 426, 439
Cheyne, D., 73, 82
Chiu, M. L., 432, 439
Christie, R., 306, 308,
Chrousos, G. P., 232, 242, 246
Church, H., 436, 443
Cialdini, R. B., 115, 117
Cicchetti, D., 349, 373, 395, 417 452, 453
Cirelli, C., 193, 198
Clark, A. G., 189, 199
Clark, L. A., 157, 164

Clarke, C., 294, 298
Clayton, D. F., 186, 199
Clayton, R., 379, 391
Cleckley, H., 301, 312
Clogg, C. C., 142, 152
Cloninger, C. R., 157, 163
Close, G. C., 235, 247
Clubb, P. A., 99, 107, 119
Clutton-Brock, T. H., 100, 117
Cohen, D. J., 395, 417
Colby, 394, 419
Cole, J. A., 127, 132
Colinvaux, P., 139, 152
Coll, C. T., 427, 441
Collins, L. F., 128, 133
Collins, L. M., 142, 152
Comery, T., 192, 201
Cooley, C. H., 111, 117
Cornblatt, B. A., 162, 163
Corner, M. A., 193, 198
Cortelli, P., 182, 200
Cosmides, L., 180, 201
Costa, F. M., 430, 435, 436, 439, 441
Costa, P. T. Jr., 124, 133, 257, 263, 266, 278, 282, 298
Costello, E. J., 42, 51, 61, 137, 152, 197, 448, 451, 452, 453
Côte, G., 322, 326, 327, 329, 335
Craft, S., 240, 247
Craik, F. I. M., 21, 28
Crano, W. D., 115, 118
Crick, F., 65, 81, 180, 181, 182, 191, 198
Crick, N. R., 55, 62
Crnic, K., 89, 98
Crockett, L. J., 430, 438
Cronbach, L. J., 4, 9, 123, 133, 143, 148, 152, 160, 163, 286, 298
Crowne, D. P., 300, 312
Crystal, D. S., 432, 439
Csernansky, J. G., 247
Cuccaro, M., 351, 373
Cullen, F. T., 325, 336
Cullinan, W. E., 235, 247
Curman, H., 344, 346

Curran, T., 188, 198, 199, 200
Czogalik, D., 126, 133

D

Dabbs, J. M., 213, 226
Dahl, R. E., 240, 246
Dahlstrom, L. E., 161, 163
Dahlstrom, W. G., 161, 163
Dalgard, O. S., 324, 336
Damasio, A. R., 99, 100, 113, 117
Datan, N., 21, 28
Davidson, E. H., 182, 184, 198
Davies, N., 100, 118
Davis, D. M., 326, 337
De Grazia, S., 306, 312
De Raad, B., 267, 279
DeArmond, S. J., 182, 200
DeGuzman, G. C., 66, 73, 81, 82
DeJesus, O., 204, 208
Delaney, R. C., 240, 246
Dennett, D. C., 112, 118
Dennis, A., 100, 108, 118, 160, 163
Depue, R., 268, 279
Dew, M. A., 436, 443
di Mauro, D., 427, 430, 439
Diamond, D. M., 236, 245
Dick, R. W., 429, 442
Dickson, N., 162, 163
DiForio, D., 326, 337
Digman, J. M., 124, 133, 266
Ding, M., 66, 68, 73, 81, 82, 83
Diorio, J., 187, 199, 236, 247
Dishion, T. J., 350, 351, 374
Dittmann-Kohli, F., 15, 18, 21, 27-29
Dixon, R. A., 15, 18, 21, 27, 128, 133
Domenico, D., 428, 443
Donovan, J. E., 378, 379, 391, 430, 439
Dorer, D. J., 167, 175
Dornbusch, S. M., 432, 441
Dragomir, C., 237, 246
Dryfoos, J. G., 427, 432, 434-436, 439
Duncan, G., 398, 399, 417, 418
Dunér, A., 45, 47, 380, 381, 391

E

Earls, F., 7, 44, 46, 74, 230-232, 237,
  241, 243, 246, 247, 350, 373, 436, 443
East, P. L., 431, 439
Eaves, D., 324, 337
Eberwine, J., 192, 201
Eccles, J. S., 432, 440
Eckes, T., 148, 153
Edelbrock, C. S., 284, 297
Edelbrock, C., 143, 146, 153
Edelman, G. M., 67-69, 74, 80-83
Edelstein, W., 162, 163, 284, 286, 298
Edery, I., 186, 199
Edin, K., 413, 417
Edman, G., 211, 213, 226, 227
Egyházi, E., 185, 186, 187, 199
Ehret, G., 186, 198
Eigen, M., 81, 82
Eiselse, S., 204, 208
Eisenberg, L., 243, 247
Eizenman, D. R., 126, 129, 133
Ekman, G., 149, 153
Elder, G. H. Jr., 13, 29, 42, 46, 51,
  61, 108, 119, 137, 152, 174, 197,
  281, 294, 298, 394, 414, 417, 424,
  438, 439, 448, 451-453
Eldredge, N., 81, 82
Eliason, S. R., 142, 152
El-Khouri, B. M., 131, 132, 146-148,
  152, 218, 226, 360, 373
Elman, J. L., 180, 198
Elmgren, J., 345, 347
Emde, R., 350, 373
Emerson, M. R., 430, 443
Emery, R. E., 167, 174
Endler, N. S., 12, 28, 108, 117
Eneroth, P., 331, 336
Engberg, M., 322, 332, 335
Engfer, A., 168, 175
Engle, M., 204, 208
Ensminger, M. E., 430, 440
Epstein, D. B., 139, 153
Ericsson, K. A., 14, 19, 28
Erlenmeyer-Kimling, L., 162, 163
Eronen, M., 325, 335

Esser, G., 355, 374
Estrada, A. U., 126, 135
Eyer, J., 233, 247
Eysenck, H. J., 126, 133, 157, 163,
  212, 226
Eysenck, S. B. G., 212, 226

F

Fairbanks, L. A., 239, 246
Faith, D. P., 144, 151
Faraone, S. V., 331, 336
Farrell, M. P., 429, 438
Farrell, M., 237, 246
Farrell, P., 204, 208
Farrington, D. P., 351, 374
Featherman, D. L., 121, 122, 126,
  129, 133, 134
Feigelman, S., 428, 429, 440, 441
Feil, L. A., 397, 418
Feinberg, S. E., 142, 152
Feldman, S. S., 431, 432, 439, 440
Felice, M. E., 431, 439
Felson, R. B., 325, 336
Fergusson, D. M., 331, 335
Festinger, L., 114, 117
Fielding, B. A., 235, 247
Filipp, S.-H., 21, 29
Fillmore, K. M., 379, 391
Finlay, B., 432, 442
Fisher, C. B., 432, 440
Fisher, C., 195, 198, 199
Fisher, R., 186, 195
Fitness, J., 113, 117
Flannery, D. J., 428, 440
Flay, B. R., 435, 442
Fletcher, G. J. O., 113, 117
Flor, D., 432, 439
Flugel, J. C., 125, 133
Flynn, H. A., 127, 132
Fogel, A., 74, 83
Fombonne, E., 326, 335
Ford, D. H., 124, 133, 448, 453
Fortenberry, J. D., 430, 439
Forth, A. E., 301, 313
Fowler, C. J., 213, 226

Fo , N. A., 89, 98, 127, 133
Francis, D., 187, 199, 236, 247
Frank, D. A., 243, 246
Frankenhaeuser, M., 37, 46, 343, 347
Freedman, A., 236, 247
Freeland, D., 210, 227
Freeman, S., 115, 117
Freud, S., 57, 58, 62
Fried, I., 341, 347
Friedrich, R., 73, 82
Friston, K., 67, 82
Fuchs, A., 66, 73, 82
Fuligni, A. J., 432, 440
Funder, D. C., 257, 262, 263
Furby, L., 123, 133
Furnham, A., 254, 263
Furstenberg, F. F. Jr, 403, 413, 416,
    417, 432, 436, 439, 440

G

Gabizon, R., 182, 200
Gabor-Miklos, G. L., 185
Gacono, C., 221, 226
Gambetti, P., 182, 200
Gamoran, A., 432, 440
Gangestad, S., 139, 153, 162, 163,
    286, 298
Garbarino, J., 424, 440
Garber, T. L., 183, 198
Garcia-Coll, C, 294, 298
Garfein, A. J., 126, 133
Gariépy, J. L., 356, 373
Garmezy, N., 395, 397, 417
Gebarski, S., 240, 247
Geis, F. L., 306, 307, 308
Gel-Mann, M., 63, 69, 73, 82
Geni, J., 240, 248
Gerbasi, K. C., 300
Gerber, D. K., 240, 248
Gergen, K. J., 122, 133
Gesell, A., 344, 345, 347
Gfellner, B. B., 429, 440
Ghisletta, P., 5, 141
Giller, E. L., 240, 248
Gillner, A., 210, 226

Ginsberg, L. H., 21, 28
Gjerde, P. F., 160, 162, 163, 164, 284,
    298
Glanz, M., 377, 391
Glaser, R., 187 193, 198
Gleser, G. C., 123, 133, 143, 152
Glover, A., 108, 119
Glueck, E., 344, 347
Glueck, S., 344, 347
Goelet, P., 188, 198
Goenjian, A. K., 238, 239, 246
Goffman, E., 109, 117
Gold, D. W., 89, 98
Gold, P. W., 232, 235, 240, 242, 243,
    246, 247
Goldberg, L. R., 124, 133, 266, 267,
    278
Golden, R. R., 162, 163
Goodwin, B., 97, 98
Gordon, A. D., 144, 153
Gorenflo, D. W., 115, 118
Gorenstein, E. E., 222, 226
Gorman, J. M., 204, 208
Gorsuch, R. L., 126, 135
Gottlieb, G., 6, 101, 119, 180, 184,
    189, 194, 195, 196, 198, 199, 423,
    438, 440
Gough, H. G., 300
Gould, E., 204, 207, 213, 226
Gould, M. S., 278, 279
Gould, S. J., 81, 82, 231, 247
Grady, D., 182, 198
Graf, P., 43, 46
Graham, P. J., 355, 375
Graham, S., 433, 440
Gray, A., 213, 226
Green, J. A., 55, 61, 449, 453
Greenberg, G., 423, 424, 443
Greenberg, M. E., 188, 200
Greenhouse, J. B., 331, 336
Greenough, W. T., 192, 193, 197, 201
Grego, J. M., 142, 152
Grekin, E. R., 331, 335
Grenier, J. K., 183, 198
Grey, S. J., 91, 98
Grotpeter, J. K., 55, 62

Grouse, L. D., 187, 198
Grove, W. M., 257, 263
Guacci-Franco, N., 432, 441
Guerra, N. G., 436, 440
Guerra, N., 429, 442
Guilford, J. P., 157, 163
Gulliksen, H., 122, 133
Gunnar, M., 235, 247
Guo, G., 403, 417, 432, 439
Gustafson, S. B., 1, 8, 299, 300, 301, 306
Guthrie, P., 162, 164
Guthrie, S., 213, 227
Gutkind, D., 204, 205, 208

H

Haapasalo, J., 351, 374
Haggerty, R., 395, 417
Haken, H., 63, 65, 66, 68, 69, 73, 82, 83
Hakola, P., 325, 335
Hakstian, A. R., 299, 301, 313
Hall, C. S., 266, 300
Hallgren, B., 342, 347
Hallman, J., 213, 227
Hämäläinen, M., 266, 267, 280
Hamburg, D. A., 427, 436, 437, 440
Hamburger, S. D., 210, 226
Hammer, T., 379, 391
Hampson, E., 128, 133
Hänninen, V., 268, 279
Hansen, W. B., 435, 442
Harding, R., 204, 207
Hare, R. D., 212, 226, 299, 300, 301
Harlow, H. F., 231, 247
Harlow, M. K., 231, 247
Harpur, T. J., 299, 300, 301, 313
Harrington, R., 326, 335
Harris, C. W., 145, 153
Harris, G. T., 162, 163
Harris, K. M., 403, 413, 417
Harris, R. S., 196, 198
Harris, S. M., 210, 227
Harris, T. O., 317, 334
Hart, D., 162, 163, 284, 286, 298

Hart, S. D., 301, 313
Harter, S., 278, 279
Hartka, E., 379, 391
Hartup, W. W., 116, 119, 432, 440
Harvey, J. H., 113, 118
Harvey, P. D., 240, 248
Hasher, L., 128, 134
Haslam, S. A., 114, 120
Heckhausen, J., 21, 28
Hegarty, C. M., 186, 199
Heilbrun, K., 324, 335
Helgason, T., 324, 336
Hellström, A., 341
Helson, R., 122, 133
Helzer, J. E., 325, 335
Henggeler, S. W., 434, 438
Henry, B., 434, 440
Herman, J. P., 235, 247
Hernandez, D. J., 424, 432, 440
Hershey, T., 240, 247
Hertsgaard, L., 235, 247
Hertzog, C., 128, 133
Hess, T. M., 21, 28
Hetherington, M., 351, 375
Hibbs, E. D., 210, 226
Higgins, E. T., 113, 118, 254, 259, 263
Hildebrand, D. K., 148, 153
Hillhouse, J., 193, 198
Hinde, R. A., 5, 100-102, 104, 106-108, 113, 115, 118, 160, 172, 175
Hirschi, T., 351, 374
Hjern, B., 343, 347
Ho, M.-W., 183, 199
Hodgins, S., 8, 320, 322, 324-329, 332, 333, 335, 336
Hodgson, C. S., 435, 442
Hoek, H. W., 204, 208
Hofman, V., 162, 163, 284, 286, 298
Hogan, R., 300, 313
Hogg, M. A., 114, 120
Hokanson, J. E., 127, 132
Holden, J., 204, 208
Holland, J. H., 69, 82
Holland, P. W., 142, 152
Holliday, R., 187, 188, 199
Holliday, S. G., 24, 25, 28

Hollister, M., 204, 205, 208
Holloway, A. E., 305, 308
Holmberg, D., 114, 118
Holmes, G. R., 351, 373
Holmes, J. G., 112, 119
Holroyd, T., 66, 73, 82
Holtzman, W. H., 130, 133
Honeycutt, J. M., 113, 118
Honzik, M. P., 344, 347
Hood, K. E., 356, 373
Höök, B., 344, 346
Hooker, K. A., 126, 134, 135
Hopper, C. H., 213, 226
Horgan, J., 66, 82
Horn, J. L., 128, 134
Horowitz, F. D., 197, 199
Horwood, L. J., 331, 335
Howard, J., 428, 435, 440
Hubel, D. H., 231, 246
Hudley, C., 433, 440
Hughes, M. E., 436, 440
Hull, C. L., 34, 46
Hultsch, D. F., 21, 28, 128, 133
Humble, K., 210, 213, 221, 225, 226
Humphrey, N., 112, 118
Humphreys, A. G., 236, 245
Hunt, E., 331, 335, 428, 440
Huotilainen, M., 206, 208
Husén, T., 345, 346, 347
Huston, A. C., 427, 441
Huttunen, M. O., 6, 204, 205, 206, 207, 208
Hydén, H., 179, 185, 186, 187, 199
Hyman, S. E., 192, 199

I-J

Iberall, A., 68, 82
Ilg, F. L., 344, 345, 347
Ilmoniemi, R. J., 206, 208
Ilvonen, A., 206, 208
Innis, R. B., 240, 246
Irwin, S. A., 192, 201
Itsukaichi, T., 186, 199
Jablonka, E., 183, 187, 188, 199
Jackson, D. N., 213, 226

Jacob, F., 43, 46
James, L. R., 300, 311, 313
Janson, C.-G., 320, 325, 326, 328, 332, 333, 335, 449, 453
Janson, H., 357, 363, 374
Jaramillo, B., 351, 375
Jenkins, T., 189, 199
Jensen, A. R., 127, 134
Jessor, L., 378, 379, 391
Jessor, R., 378, 379, 391, 394, 430, 435, 436, 439, 441
Jirsa, V. K., 73, 82
Joffe, J. M., 204, 207
Johansson, G., 37, 46
John, O. P., 141, 154, 162-164, 253, 257, 262, 263, 266, 284, 286, 298
Johnson, B. L., 432, 440
Johnson, M. H., 180, 198
Johnson, R., 186, 200
Johnson, S. M., 351, 374
Johnston, L. D., 429, 442
Johnston, L., 378, 379, 391, 427, 428, 441
Johnston, T. D., 197,199
Johnstone, B. M., 379, 391
Joireman, J., 157, 164
Jonassent, J. A., 186, 199
Jones, A. P., 300, 313
Jones, C. J., 126, 134
Jones, J., 331, 336
Jones, M., 429, 438
Jonsson, G., 342, 344, 346, 347
Jundell, I., 340, 347
Jurkovic, G. J., 213, 226

K

Kagan, J., 5, 11, 56, 61, 89, 94, 98, 100, 108, 117, 118, 127, 134, 151, 153, 256, 263, 288, 294, 298, 355, 374, 424, 438, 452, 453
Kahana, B., 240, 248
Kälvesten, A.-L., 344, 346
Kandel, D. B., 351, 374
Kandel, E. R., 188, 198
Kao, M., 431, 443

Kaprio, J., 206, 207
Karmiloff-Smith, A., 180, 198
Katila, H., 204, 205, 208
Katz, D., 35, 46
Katz, L. C., 193, 199
Kauffman, M. B., 197, 199, 423, 441
Kauffman, S. A., 81, 82
Keane, E., 429, 442
Keefe, K.,432, 438
Keefe, R. S. E., 240, 248
Keller, M. B., 167, 175
Keller, M., 162, 163, 284, 286, 298
Kelley, T. L., 156, 163
Kelso, J. A. S., 5, 63, 65-70, 73, 74-78, 81-83, 139, 451
Kemnitz, J., 204, 208
Kennedy, S., 193, 198
Kenny, D. A., 257, 258, 263
Kerns, D., 431, 442
Kerr, B., 331, 335, 428, 440
Key, E., 339, 347
Keyes, S., 161, 163
Keysor, C. S., 210, 226
Kidd, K., 167, 175
Kiecolt-Glaser, J. K., 193, 198
Kihlstrom, J. F., 252, 262
Kim, J. E., 129, 134
King, V., 413, 417
Kivilighan, D. M., 126, 135
Klackenberg, G, 344, 347
Klackenberg-Larsson, I., 351, 357, 361, 363, 375
Klass, P. E., 243, 246
Klebanov, P. K., 397, 398, 399, 417, 418
Klerman, G. R., 167, 175
Kliegl, R., 450, 453
Klintsova, A. Y., 192, 201
Kohn, M. L., 101, 118
Kolar, D. C., 257, 263
Kollar, E. J., 195, 199
Kollasch, E., 241, 245
Koot, H. M., 355, 375
Korfine, L., 162, 163
Koskenvuo, M., 206, 207
Kraft, M., 157, 164

Kratzer, L., 320, 327, 336
Krauth, J., 144, 148, 150, 153
Krebs, J., 100, 118
Kremen, A. M., 156, 161, 163
Kremen, A., 107, 117
Kruesi, M. J. P., 210, 226, 228
Kuhlman, D. M., 157, 164
Kuo, Z.-Y., 60, 196, 199, 423, 441

L

Labovitz, D., 204, 208
LaFosse, J., 206, 207
Lafuse, W. P., 193, 198
Lagerström, M., 331, 336
Lahey, B. B., 213, 225, 227
Laing, J. D., 148, 153
Lakhotia, S. C., 186, 200
Lalonde, N., 324, 335
Lamb, M. E., 413, 418
Lamb, M. J., 183, 187, 188, 199
Lamborn, S. D., 432, 441
Lamiell, J. T., 121, 129, 134
Lancaster, R., 73, 82
Langley, D., 162, 163
Langley, J., 162, 163
Lapalme, M., 324, 326, 335
LaPlante, P., 187, 199
Larsen, R. J., 129, 134
Larson, M., 235, 247
Larsson, L.-E., 343, 347
Lavori, P. W., 167, 175
Ledingham, J. E., 355, 374
Lee, C., 186, 199
Lee, J., 429, 442
Lehman, J. C., 236, 245
Lehrman, D. S., 196, 199
Lehtinen, V., 324, 336
Lehtokoski, A., 206, 208
Leiderman, P. H., 129, 134
Lein, L., 413, 417
Leino, E. M., 379, 391
Lemyre, L., 317, 334
Lennes, M., 206, 208
Lenzenweger, M. F., 162, 163
Leonard, H. L., 210, 228

Leppert, J., 210, 213, 225
Lerner, J. A., 241, 245
Lerner, J. V., 427, 441
Lerner, M.-J., 21, 29
Lerner, R. M., 9, 12, 28, 127, 135, 197, 199, 423, 424, 425, 426, 427, 430, 436, 437, 438, 441, 448, 453
Letendre, C. H., 187, 198
Léveillée, S., 326, 336
Levengood, R. A., 248, 240
Leverich, S. G., 334, 336
Levin, H., 351, 375
Lewin, K., 6, 50, 62, 150, 153, 159, 164, 166, 175, 231, 232, 247, 393, 394, 418, 452, 453
Levine, J. A., 413, 418
Lewis, M., 110, 118
Levitt, J. L., 432, 441
Levitt, M. J., 432, 441
Levitt, M. Z., 436, 441
Li, X., 429, 440
Liaw, F. H., 397, 398, 417, 418
Lickliter, R., 438, 440
Lidberg, L., 210, 213, 225, 226
Lienert, G. A., 144, 145, 147, 153
Lin, C.-S., 186, 200
Lin, S., 204, 208
Lindenberger, U., 21, 27, 28, 438
Lindqvist, P., 324, 336
Lindzey, G., 266, 279
Link, B. G., 325, 336
Linnoila, M., 212, 213, 224, 227, 228
Lipsitz, J., 436, 441
Liu, D., 236, 247
Lobitz, C. W., 351, 374
Loeber, R., 169, 175, 213, 227, 350, 374
Lohmiller, L., 204, 208
Long, C. J., 128, 133
Longerich, S., 196, 198
Lönquist, J., 206, 207
Lopez, D., 20, 21, 29
Lorenz, K., 100, 118
Lösel, F., 351, 374
Löw, H., 213, 227
Lubinski, D., 160, 164

Luborsky, L., 126, 134
Lugaresi, E., 182, 200
Luk, D., 186, 188, 198, 200
Lüscher, K., 13, 29
Lushene, R., 126, 135
Luster, T., 430, 442
Luthar, S., 395, 418
Luuk, A., 206, 208
Lynam, D., 433, 439

M

Maccoby, E. E., 351, 375
MacCorquodale, K., 113, 118
Macfarlane, J. W., 344, 345, 347
Machin, C., 204, 208
Machon, R. A., 204, 205, 207, 208
Maciel, A. G., 22, 25, 26, 29
Mack, K. J., 186, 188, 199
Mack, P. A., 186, 188, 199
MacKay, A. V. P., 213, 226
Macovei, O., 237, 246
Maercker, A., 21, 27
Magee, W., 395, 411, 414, 419
Magnusson, D., 3, 5, 9, 11-16, 25-28, 37, 40-47, 49-53, 57-64, 70, 83, 87, 88, 98-101, 107, 108, 110, 115-119, 121, 124, 125, 130, 131, 134, 137, 139, 143, 150-152, 153, 155, 162, 164, 166, 172, 175, 197, 199, 210-213, 218, 225-227, 229, 232, 247, 251, 262, 263, 265, 266, 268, 281, 282, 284, 296-298, 318, 319, 331, 334, 336, 345-347, 349, 350, 352, 355-357, 363, 373-375, 378-382, 390, 391, 394, 418, 421-425, 433, 436-438, 441, 442, 448, 449, 452, 453
Mangelsdorf, S., 235, 247
Mann, B. J., 434, 438
Männikkö, K., 7
Manson, S. M., 429, 442
Markus, H., 113, 119
Marlowe, D., 300, 312
Martin, R. P., 205, 208
Mason, J. W., 240, 248

Mason, W. A., 231, 247
Masten, A., 397, 417
Masters, R. D., 306, 313
Mastrianni, J., 182, 200
Mattson, A., 213, 227
May, C. P., 128, 134
Mayr, E., 183, 199, 230, 247
Mazure, C., 240, 246
McArdle, J. J., 131, 134, 139, 153
McBurnett, K., 210, 213, 227
McCall, G. J., 109, 112, 119
McCarthy, G., 240, 246
McCarton, C., 397, 398, 418
McClelland, D. C., 262, 263
McCord, J., 351, 374
McCord, W., 351, 374
McCormick, M. M., 397, 398, 418
McCrae, R. R., 124, 133, 257, 263,
    266, 278, 282, 298
McEwen, B. S., 204, 207, 213, 226,
    233, 235, 242, 243, 247
McEvoy, L., 326, 336
McGarty, C., 114, 120
McGee, R., 210, 227
McGuire, C. V., 112, 119
McGuire, S., 351, 375
McGuire, W. J., 112, 119
McKinlay, J. B., 213, 226
McLanahan, S., 8, 413, 418
McLoyd, V. C., 427, 441
McMillan, I. C., 204, 207
Mead, G. H., 111, 119
Meaney, M. J., 187, 199, 236, 245, 247
Mednick, B., 204, 205, 208
Mednick, S. A., 6, 204, 205, 207, 208,
    322, 326, 332, 335, 344, 347
Meehl, P. E., 113, 118, 140, 141, 145,
    148, 153, 154, 157, 160, 162, 164,
    257, 263
Meili, R., 35, 47
Mekos, D., 99, 107, 119
Mello, C. V., 186, 199
Meredith, W., 124, 134
Merriwether, D. A., 189, 199
Meyer, V. A., 240, 246
Milberger, S., 331, 336

Miller, G. A., 401, 418
Miller, L., 351, 375
Miller, R. G., 411, 418
Miller-Tutzauer, C., 428, 443
Milligan, G. W., 141, 143, 144, 151,
    153
Mills, J. W., 60, 62
Mintz, J., 126, 134
Minuchin, S., 351, 374
Mischel, W., 121, 124, 128, 134, 135,
    256, 264
Mishler, E. G., 393, 394, 418
Misiak, H., 143, 153
Mitchell, C. M., 429, 442
Miyashiro, K., 192, 201
Modell, J., 424, 439
Modin, I., 210, 226
Moen, P., 13, 29
Moffitt, T. E., 162, 164, 210, 227, 228,
    266, 284, 286, 298, 320, 327, 331,
    336, 433, 434, 439, 440
Molenaar, P. C. M., 126, 130, 131, 134
Montada, L., 21, 29
Montagna, P., 182, 200
Montagu, A., 196, 199
Montgomery, S. B., 435, 442
Moore, T., 361, 374
Morey, L. C., 144, 153
Morgan, J. I., 188, 198, 199, 200
Morgan, M. C., 431, 439
Morgan, S. P., 403, 417
Moriarty, A., 171, 175
Morris, P., 438, 439
Mortensen, E. L., 331, 336
Moskowitz, D. S., 355, 374
Moss, H. A., 355, 374
Moss, H. B., 213, 227
Motoyoshi, M., 379, 391
Mott, F. L., 398, 400, 413, 417, 418
Mounts, N. S., 432, 441
Müller, R., 343, 347
Müller-Isberner, J. R., 324, 336
Multon, K. D., 126, 135
Mumford, M. D., 145, 153
Munk-Jorgensen, P., 324, 336
Murphy, L., 171, 175

Murray, H. A., 251, 263
Murray, S. L., 112, 119
Myers, M. P., 186, 200

N

Näätänen, R., 206, 208
Najarian, L. M., 239, 246
Nanda, H., 123, 133
Navarro, E., 204, 207
Neale, J., 167, 174
Needleman, H. L., 331, 336
Needles, D. J., 210, 228
Nelson, D., 115, 117
Nelson, P. G., 187, 198
Nesselroade, J. R., 5, 121, 122, 126, 129, 131, 133-136, 141, 256, 264
Nestler, E. J., 192, 199
Netter, P., 213, 227
Neugebauer, R., 204, 208
Neumann, C. C., 326, 337
Newcomer, J. W., 240, 247
Newman, J. P., 222, 226, 301, 313
Newport, E. L., 180, 200
Nguyen, N., 240, 246
Nicolis, G., 63, 83
Nijhout, H. F., 184, 185, 200
Niskanen, P., 204, 207
Norman, W. T., 124, 134
Novacek, J., 300, 313
Novak, A., 74, 83, 149, 154
Noyes, J., 205, 208
Nucci, L., 429, 442
Nunnally, J. C., 123, 135
Nurius, P., 113, 119
Nurmi, J.-E., 7
Nycander, G., 343, 347
Nye, F. I., 351, 374
Nylander, I., 343, 344, 346, 347
Nystrand, M., 432, 440
Nystrom, P., 231, 237, 246

O

O'Malley, P. M., 378, 379, 391, 427, 428, 441, 442

O'Nell, T. D., 429, 442
Oakes, P. J., 114, 120
Oberdick, J., 186, 188, 198, 200
Ogilvie, D. M., 254, 259, 263
Öhman, A., 422, 423, 442
Olofsson, B., 351, 374
Olson, H. C., 331, 335, 428, 440
Olson, W., 345, 346, 347
Olweus, D., 169, 175, 213, 227, 351, 355, 374
Oppenheim, R. W., 193, 200
Oreland, L., 210, 211, 213, 221, 223-227
Ostendorf, F., 266, 290, 298
Otterström, E., 342, 347
Owens, W. A., 145, 153
Overton, W. F., 122, 135, 195, 200
Ozer, D. J., 160, 162-164, 284, 298

P

Pals, J. L., 162, 163
Pape, H., 379, 391
Parchi, P., 182, 200
Parikh, V., 186, 199
Parisi, D., 180, 198
Parke, R. D., 424, 439
Parke, S. Y., 89, 98
Parnas, J., 204, 205, 208, 326, 335
Parsons, O. A., 127, 128, 132
Patel, B., 192, 201
Patterson, G. R., 351, 374, 375
Patterson, G., 169, 175
Patton, J. H., 210, 225
Patton, M. J., 126, 135
Paulhus, D. L., 295, 298
Pearson, D., 236, 247
Pentz, M. A., 435, 442
Perel, J., 240, 246
Perkins, P., 187, 197
Perry, C. L., 378, 391, 435, 443
Pervin, L. A., 7, 39, 101, 119, 251-254, 258, 262, 263
Peters, L., 324, 335
Petersen, A. C., 432, 442
Peterson, E., 94, 98

Pfiffner, L. J., 210, 226
Phelps, E., 394, 414, 417
Phillips, D. A., 398, 400, 417
Phinney, J. S., 432, 442
Piaget, J., 50, 62, 394
Pickens, R., 377, 391
Pike, A., 351, 375
Pilgrim, D., 186, 200
Pincus, A. L., 266, 280
Pinero, A. W., 155, 164
Pinner, E., 351, 375
Pittman, K., 435, 442
Pittman, R., 193, 200
Platt, S. A., 194, 200
Pleck, J., 413, 418
Plemons, J. K., 21, 28
Plomin, R., 351, 375
Plotsky, P. M., 186, 199, 236, 247
Plunkett, K., 180, 198
Pompeiano, M., 193, 198
Porges, S. W., 127, 133
Port, R. F., 74, 83
Post, R. M., 240, 247, 334, 336
Prange, A. J., 213, 228
Price, D. A., 235, 247
Prigogine, I., 63, 83
Pritchard, D. J., 182, 184, 185, 188,
    194, 196, 200
Pruisner, S. B., 182, 200
Prusoff, B. A., 167, 175
Przybeck, T. R., 325, 332, 335, 336
Puig-Antich, J., 240, 246
Pulkkinen, L., 7, 162, 164, 266-268,
    278, 280, 284-286, 295, 298, 353,
    375
Pulver, A., 266, 267, 280
Putnam, F. W., 162, 164
Putnam, S., 89, 98
Pyhälä, R., 204, 205, 208
Pynoos, R. S., 239, 246


                    Q

Quinsey, V. L., 162, 163
Quinton, D., 167, 175

                    R

Rabbie, J., 114, 119
Rachman, S., 91, 98
Radke-Yarrow, M., 6, 53, 55, 60, 62,
    166, 175, 358, 375
Ragins, N., 127, 135
Rajaratnam, N., 123, 133
Ramer, T., 342, 346, 347
Rammsayer, T., 213, 227
Randall, P., 240, 246
Randolph, M. C., 231, 247
Rapoport, J. L., 210, 226, 228
Raskin, R., 300, 313
Raudenbush, S. W., 232, 247, 282,
    298
Rawson, J., 115, 119
Reese, H. W., 122, 135
Reeves, K., 115, 117
Regalski, J. M., 436, 443
Reichel, H., 380, 391
Reicher, S. D., 114, 120
Reid, J. B., 351, 374
Reinisch, J. M., 331, 336
Reiss, D., 351, 375
Ren, P., 186, 200
Reznick, J. S., 294, 298
Rhymer, R. M., 126, 130, 132
Ricardo, I., 428, 440
Rice, M. E., 162, 163
Richman, N., 355, 375
Richmond, J. B., 436, 441
Riddle, D. L., 186, 200
Riegel, K. F., 424, 442
Riess, J. A., 331, 336
Rimm-Kaufman, S., 94, 98
Ritzer, D. R., 299, 300, 301
Roberts, L. R., 432, 442
Roberts, M. L., 256, 264
Robertson, G., 325, 336
Robertson, L., 188, 198, 200
Robins, L. N., 212, 224, 227, 326,
    332, 336
Robins, R. W., 141, 154, 162, 164,
    257, 263, 266, 284, 286, 298
Rodkin, P. C., 151, 152

Rodriguez, M., 204, 207
Roecker, E., 204, 208
Rogers, C. R., 99, 110, 119
Rogoff, B., 101, 119
Rogosa, D., 282, 298
Rohrback, L. A., 435, 442
Rönkä, A., 268, 353, 375
Rose, G. M., 236, 245
Rose, S. P. R., 187, 200
Rosen, L. B., 188, 200
Rosenberg, M., 268, 280
Rosenberg, S. M., 196, 198
Rosenthal, D. A., 432, 439
Rosenthal, D. R., 431, 440
Rosenthal, H., 148, 153
Rosenzweig, M. R., 187
Rothenfluh-Hilfiker, A., 200
Rowe, D. C., 428, 440
Rowe, J. W., 126, 129, 133
Rúa, C., 204, 208
Rubin, D. B., 331, 336
Rubin, J. A., 127, 135
Rubin, K. H., 89, 98
Rubinow, D. R., 240, 247
Rudinger, G., 12, 28
Rune, V., 343, 347
Russell, D., 306, 313
Russell, R. L., 126, 133, 135
Russell, R. W., 35, 47
Rutter, M., 167, 175, 326, 335, 395, 396, 397, 417-419, 448, 453
Ryan, N. D., 240, 246
Rydelius, P.-A., 8, 340, 344, 348
Ryff, C., 395, 411, 414, 419

S

Sajaniemi, N., 204, 205, 208
Sakai, A., 204, 208
Salthouse, T. A., 21, 28, 29
Sameroff, A. J., 101, 119, 197, 200, 281, 298, 397, 418, 419
Sampson, R., 232, 247
Samuelson, W., 167, 175
Sandefur, G., 413, 418
Sanders, S. A., 331, 336

Sanford, N., 33, 34, 47
Sanislow, C. A., 194, 200
Sapolsky, R. M., 204, 208, 240, 241, 247
Sarrieau, A., 236, 247
Sartory, G., 91, 98
Satterfield, J. H., 210, 227
Saucier, G., 267, 280
Savard, R., 240, 247
Savin-Williams, R. C., 430, 442
Schacher, S., 188, 198
Schachter, J., 127, 135
Schaefer, E. S., 362, 363, 375
Schalling, D., 210-213, 221, 224, 226, 227, 268
Schank, R. C., 113, 119, 401, 419
Scheier, I. H., 131, 132
Schilling, K., 186, 188, 198, 200
Schlesinger, M. J., 203, 206, 208
Schmidt, L. A., 89, 98
Schmidt, M. H., 355, 374
Schneirla, T. C., 60, 196, 200
Scholz, J. P., 66, 82
Schore, A., 174, 175
Schorr, L. B., 427, 436, 442
Schrier, B. K., 187, 198
Schteingart, D. E., 240, 247
Schulenberg, J., 378, 379, 391, 429, 442
Schulkin, J., 89, 98, 235, 243, 247
Schulsinger, F., 204, 205, 208, 322, 332, 335
Schurr, T. G., 189, 199
Schwartzman, A. E., 355, 374
Schöner, G., 66, 75, 76, 82, 83
Scott, T. M., 240, 246
Scott-Jones, D., 341, 442
Sears, R. R., 351, 375
Seckl, J. P., 187, 199
Seiby, J. P. L., 240, 246
Seifer, R., 397, 419
Selman, R. L., 436, 441
Selten, J.-P., 204, 208
Sexton, V., 143, 153
Shanahan, M. J., 101, 108, 119
Shanahan, M., 51, 62

Shantz, C. U., 116, 119
Shapiro, D., 129, 134
Sharma, S., 187, 199, 236, 247
Shatz, C. J., 193, 197, 199
Sheline, Y. I., 247
Shelton, S., 204, 208
Sherrod, L., 395, 417
Sherry, S. T., 189, 199
Shields, J., 190, 200
Shifrin, K., 126, 135
Shoda, Y., 121, 124, 128, 135, 256, 264
Shweder, R.A., 394, 419
Siegler, R. S., 127, 135
Siever, L. J., 240, 248
Silva, P. A., 210, 227, 284-286, 298, 432, 434, 439, 440
Simi, N., 9
Simmons, R. G., 436, 443
Simon, H. A., 19, 28
Simons, J. M., 432, 433, 442
Simons, R. L., 431, 443
Singer, B., 8, 395, 399, 411, 414, 419
Singer, D. G., 126, 135
Singer, J. L., 126, 135
Singh, A. K., 186, 200
Sinkkonen, J., 206, 208
Sjöstrand, W., 345, 347
Skinner, H. A., 143, 144, 153, 154
Slaby, R. G., 436, 440
Slijper, E. J., 194, 200
Sloan, L. R., 115, 117
Small, S. A., 430, 431, 442
Smeyne, R. J., 186, 188, 198, 200
Smith, C. C., 89, 98
Smith, J., 14, 15, 18, 20-22, 24, 27, 29, 396, 397, 419
Smith, L. B., 38, 47, 74, 83, 149, 154, 197, 201, 451, 453
Smith, R., 395, 419
Smyer, M. A., 126, 133
Snidman, N., 94, 98, 151, 153, 294, 298
Snyder, M., 111, 119, 139, 153, 162, 163, 286, 298
Soodak, H., 68, 82

Soodyall, H., 189, 199
Sörensen, S., 210, 213, 225
Soubrié, P. H., 224, 228
Southwick, S. M., 240, 246, 248
Sowarka, D., 25, 26, 29
Sparling, J., 236, 237, 246
Speicher, C., 193, 198
Spelke, E. S., 180, 200
Spemann, H., 58, 62
Spencer, C. M., 192, 201
Spencer-Booth, Y., 102, 118
Spiel, C., 144, 154
Spielberger, C. D., 126, 135
Sporns, O., 67, 74, 80, 83
Sroufe, L. A., 396, 397, 419
Stachezza, B. M., 278, 279
Staib, L., 240, 246
Stanley, H. E., 68, 83
Stansbury, K., 247
Stanton, B. F., 428, 440
Stanton, B., 429, 441
Starkman, M. N., 240, 247
Stattin, H., 8, 12, 28, 41, 45, 47, 213, 218, 226, 227, 251, 318, 336, 350-352, 355, 356, 361, 363, 374, 375, 380, 391, 421, 422, 423, 424, 425, 433, 442
Staudinger, U. M., 13-16, 18, 20, 21-27, 29, 438
Steadman, H. J., 325, 336
Steinberg, A. M., 239, 246
Steinberg, D., 94, 98
Steinberg, L., 432, 441
Stellar, E., 233, 235, 242, 247
Stent, G., 184, 200
Stephenson, W., 160, 164
Sterling, P., 233, 247
Stern, D., 113, 119
Stern, W., 282-286, 298
Sternberg, E. M., 89, 98
Sternberg, R. J., 14, 23, 24, 25, 29
Stevenson, H. W., 432, 439
Stevenson, J., 355, 375
Stevenson-Hinde, J., 108, 119
Stiffman, A. R., 436, 443
Stoltzfus, E. R., 128, 134

Stoneman, Z., 432, 439
Stouthamer-Loeber, M., 210, 228, 266, 284, 286, 298
Strahan, R., 300, 313
Streissguth, A. P., 331, 335, 428, 440
Strohman, R. C., 185, 196, 200
Stroop, J. R., 160, 164
Strouse, J., 96, 98
Sullivan, H. S., 111, 119
Sullivan, M. L., 431, 443
Susser, E., 204, 208
Swann, W. B., 111, 119
Swanson, J. M., 210, 226
Svensson, J., 213, 227
Switzer, G. E., 436, 443

T

Tajfel, H., 114, 119
Takanishi, R., 436, 440
Tamis-LeMonda, C. S., 396, 416
Tamm, A., 341, 348
Tamm, L., 210, 227
Tamplin, A., 100, 107, 108, 118
Tanapat, P., 204, 207
Tang, C., 68, 81
Tannebaum, B., 236, 247
Tanner, J. M., 190, 200
Tashjian, M., 239, 246
Taylor, C. S., 432, 443
Taylor, E., 210, 228
Taylor, S. E., 278, 280
Tegelman, R., 213, 225
Tellegen A., 129, 135, 157, 160, 164, 397, 417
Telling, G. C., 182, 200
Temple, M. T., 379, 391
Tesser, A., 113, 119
Teta, P., 157, 164
Thaler, D. S., 196, 201
Thelen, E., 38, 44, 47, 74, 83, 149, 154, 197, 201, 451, 453
Thieme, C., 204, 208
Thomae, H., 137, 154
Thomas, A., 426, 439
Thomas, G., 113, 117

Thorburn, G. D., 204, 207
Thorell, L.-H., 213, 225
Thorndike, E. L., 60, 156, 164
Thorne, A., 115, 117
Thouless, R. H., 125, 135
Tien, G., 324, 337
Tiihonen, J., 325, 335
Tinbergen, N., 100, 119
Tipp, J., 332, 336
Tipton, K. F., 213, 226
Tissieres, A., 203, 206, 208
Tobach, E, 423, 424, 443
Tobin, M. J., 331, 336
Todd, R. D., 44, 46, 230, 246
Tononi, G., 67, 68, 80, 82, 83, 193, 198
Tooby, J., 180, 201
Törestad, B., 12, 28, 99, 107, 115, 116, 119, 155, 164, 251, 263, 394, 418
Toupin, J., 324, 326, 327, 329, 335
Trankell, A., 345, 347
Trapnell, P. D., 267, 280
Treffner, P. J., 68, 83
Trejo, J. L., 204, 208
Tremblay, R. E., 351, 374
Trull, T. J., 162, 164
Tuck, J. R., 210, 226
Tucker, D. M., 213, 228
Tudge, J., 51, 62
Tuller, B., 68, 74, 81, 83
Turner, J. C., 114, 119, 120
Turner, J., 114, 120
Turvey, M. T., 77, 83

U

Ucko, L. G., 361, 374
Uddenborg, G., 343, 348
Underwood, B. J., 159, 164
Uno, H., 204, 208
Uphouse, L. L., 187, 201

V

Vainio, M., 206, 208
Vallacher, R. R., 74, 83

Valsiner, J., 51, 62, 101, 119, 122, 124, 135, 150, 154, 197, 201
van Aken, M. A. G., 284, 297
Van Den Boss, J., 435, 436, 441
Van der Ende, J., 355, 375
van der Weele, C., 185, 186, 201
Van Gelder, T., 74, 83
van Marthens, E., 187, 188, 201
Van Os, J., 204, 208
Vanderryn, J., 435, 436, 441
Vannier, M. W., 247
Vazsonyi, A. T., 428, 440
Verhulst, F. C., 355, 375
Vermetten, E., 240, 246
Veroff, J., 114, 118
Viau, S., 236, 247
Vicario, D. S., 186, 199
Virkkunen, M., 212, 224, 228
Vogel, W. H., 213, 227
Voldsgaard, P., 204, 205, 208
von Eye, A., 144, 145, 148, 154
Vuchinich, S., 351, 375
Vygotsky, L. S., 50, 62

W

Wadsworth, K. N., 429, 442
Wadsworth, K., 378, 379, 391
Wagenar, A. C., 378, 391, 435, 443
Wager-Smith, K., 186, 200
Wahlsten, D., 195, 201, 438, 440
Walker, E. F., 326, 337
Wallace, D. C., 189, 199
Wallacher, R. B., 149, 154
Wallander, J. L., 127, 132
Wallenstein, G. V., 66, 83
Waller, N. G., 140, 141, 145, 148, 154, 160, 162, 164
Wang, C. H., 436, 443
Wang, P. W., 247
Wang, X., 204, 205, 208
Ward, J. H., 143, 144, 146, 154, 287
Warren, R., 183, 198
Wasserman, G., 351, 375
Watson, D., 157, 164
Watson, J. B., 204, 205, 208

Weber, A. L., 113, 118
Weiler, I. J., 192, 201
Weinberg, H., 73, 82
Weinheimer, S., 306, 307, 312
Weinstock,, M., 204, 208
Weintraub, S., 167, 174, 326, 335
Weiss, B. R. S., 334, 201, 336
Weiss, P., 196, 201
Weissman, M., 167, 175
Welsh, G. S., 161, 163
Wentzel, K. R., 432, 443
Werner, E., 395, 419
Werner, H., 424, 443
West, B., 125, 135
Westenberg, P. M., 162, 163
Westrin, C. G., 324, 336
Wethrell, M. S., 114, 120
Whitbeck, L. B., 431, 443
White, A. B., 431, 442
White, J. L., 210, 228
White, L. E., 102, 118
Whitington, P. M., 183, 198
Whybrow, P. C., 213, 228
Widdowson, J., 187, 199
Widén, L., 343, 347
Widiger, T. A., 162, 164
Widom, C. S., 351, 375
Wiederanders, M. R., 324, 337
Wiesel, T. N., 231, 246
Wiesenfeld, K., 68, 81
Wiggins, J. S., 266, 267, 280
Wigglesworth, V. B., 190, 201
Williams, E., 433, 440
Williams, G. C., 230, 247
Williams, S., 210, 227
Williamsson, P. A., 213, 227, 228
Wills, C., 185, 201
Wilpers, S., 281, 282, 285, 295, 297
Wilson, D., 324, 337
Windle M., 127, 135, 428, 443
Winterhoff, P. A., 113, 120
Wisenbaker, J., 205, 208
Wishart, D., 144, 148, 154
Wittgenstein, L., 88, 98
Woerner, W., 355, 374
Wohlwill, J. F., 137, 154

Woltereck, R., 194, 201
Wonderlic, E. F., 308, 313
Wood, P. K., 126, 135, 142, 144, 154
Woodrow, H., 125, 129, 135
Woolley, C. S., 204, 207
Wright, H., 174, 351, 373
Wright, J. C., 121, 124, 128, 135, 256, 264
Wright, S., 196, 201
Wu, P., 351, 374
Wugalter, S. E., 142, 152

X-Y

Xie, H., 55, 62
Yang, A., 432, 433, 442
Yang, R. K., 239, 246
Yehuda, R., 239, 240, 246-248, 433
Yoerger, K., 351, 375
York, K. L., 162, 164, 284, 286, 298

Youdim, M. B. H., 213, 226
Young, A. M., 112, 117
Young, M. W., 186, 200

Z

Zabin, L. S., 430, 443
Zahn, T. P., 210, 226, 228
Zamenhof, S., 187, 188, 201
Zanone, P. G., 74, 83
Zetterblom, G., 45, 47, 380, 381, 391
Zevon, M., 129, 135
Zigler, E., 395, 418
Zimbardo, P. G., 353, 373
Zimmerman, E. G., 187, 188, 197
Zoccolillo, M., 278, 280
Zucker, R. A., 428, 435, 440
Zuckerman, M., 157, 164, 212, 228
zur Oeveste, H., 145, 153

# Subject Index

## A

aberrant self-promoter (ASP), 7, 299-313
adaptation, 12, 37, 39, 53, 57, 156, 171, 184, 267, 355
adjusted personality type, 266, 273-278, 284, 290-295,
adjustment problems, 8, 278, 350, 352, 353, 355, 364-366, 368, 371-373
adrenal cortex, 231, 233, 234
adrenal medulla, 210, 232, 234
adrenaline, 7, 37, 213-216, 227, 232
adrenocorticotropic hormone (ACTH), 233, 234
affective disorder, 6, 205, 319, 326
age changes, 103-106, 111
age, biological, 41, 449
    chronological, 20, 21, 58, 237, 356, 449
agent, 55, 69, 81, 88, 96, 97, 100, 101, 172, 185, 243, 245, 251
aggressive behavior, 212, 216, 323, 326, 331, 380, 396
aggressiveness, 37, 210, 212, 216-220, 224, 268, 284, 350, 351, 364, 367, 372, 380
agreeableness, 254, 266-269, 273, 274, 278, 282, 291, 296
alcohol abuse, 8, 41, 210, 325, 327, 344, 377-391, 427-429
allostasis, 74, 233
Allport, Gordon, 33, 265-266, 276, 284
amygdala, 36, 89, 233, 235, 244
antisocial behavior, 37, 209-210, 212-213, 225, 299, 300-302, 304-306, 310, 311, 323, 326-327, 331-333, 350-351, 356, 432
antisocial development, 350-351
antitype, 144, 146, 150, 219, 220, 386
anxiety, 37, 87, 95, 108, 158, 170, 211-212, 217, 218, 224, 241, 259, 268, 271, 276, 279, 284, 434
Arcus, Doreen, 97
attention deficit and hyperactivity disorder (ADHD), 380, 382-391, 397
Attraction Sans Attractors principle (ASA), 76, 80
attractor, 66, 74, 80, 149
Aurelius, 27

## B

Baldwin, J. M., 50, 58, 60
Baltimore Study of Teenage Motherhood, 403
Barker, R. G., 231
Bayley Scales of Infant Development, 237, 238
behavior profile, 172
behavior stability, 355, 356
behavioral control, 266, 268, 310
behavioral development, 14, 166, 229, 236, 243
behavioral sciences, 65, 97, 127, 149, 185, 343, 345, 424, 451
behavioristic theory, 34
Berlin Relationship Study, 281, 282, 285, 286, 288, 295
bidirectional influences, 6, 188, 189, 196, 232
bifurcation, 66, 76, 77, 80, 81, 116, 117
Big Five, 124, 157, 254-257, 265-267, 269-271, 276, 278, 282, 285, 288, 296

Binet, Alfred, 33, 53, 60
biological maturation, 41, 433
biological science, 12, 36, 67
biological system, 36, 39, 40, 43, 67,
    100, 139
biology, behavioral, 49, 50, 57
    evolutionary, 97
    molecular, 42, 179-182, 188-189,
        193, 196
    neuro-, 50, 57, 230, 242
    racial, 342, 343
birth complications, 328, 331
bistability, 75, 79
Borne, Ludwig, 15
boundary conditions, 72, 78, 150
brain damage, 128, 343
    development, 36, 204, 205, 333
    imaging, 36
Bronfenbrenner, Urie, 13, 53, 231,
    396, 397, 424
Brunswik, Egon, 33


                          C

California Psychological Inventory
    (CPI), 300, 301
Carolina Consortium of Human
    Development, 50-51
case study, 56, 306, 452
case-oriented approach, 393-394
Caspi, A., 41
catastrophe theory, 38, 148
categorical measure, 170
categorization, 100, 365
    approach, 100, 108
category, 15, 88, 90, 92, 108, 139,
    144, 192, 299, 361
causal factors, 38, 422
causality, 65, 195
Center for Developmental Science,
    3, 42, 51
central dogma of molecular
    biology, 180-188
central nervous system (CNS), 77,
    128, 207, 210, 244

change, 54, 55, 57-59, 61, 63-66, 68-
    71, 74-79, 81, 104, 107, 116, 121-
    124, 129-131, 139, 141-142, 145-
    147, 150, 158, 318, 345, 422, 423,
    424, 425, 426, 449, 450-451
    motor of, 139, 450, 451
    qualitative, 63, 64, 66, 70, 71, 73,
        77
chaos, 5, 38, 67, 148, 149, 169
child and adolescent psychiatry, 8,
    245, 339-346
child-rearing research, 53, 63
Churchill, W., 97
classical interactionistic view, 40
classification, 90, 127, 140-151, 170,
    285, 332, 333, 349, 350, 358
cluster, 45, 131, 140, 143-147, 215-
    218, 266, 271-276, 278, 286, 287,
    288-294, 296, 384, 385, 387, 400
    analysis, 100, 130, 140, 143-146,
        148, 150, 271, 273, 285-287, 289,
        296, 300, 302, 307, 352, 384, 390,
        403,
    natural, 140, 145
coercion theory, 351
Coexisting Equally Valid
    Alternatives (CEVA) principle,
    75, 79
Coexisting Opponent Tendencies
    (COT) principle, 80
cognitive aging, 21, 128
cognitive developmental transition,
    127
cognitive research, 42
cohort effect, 330, 334
collective state variable, 71
collective variable, 65-68, 70-79
collinearity, 70
community variables, 430, 432
comparation research, 284
complex dynamic process, 38-40,
    42, 45, 148, 318
complex living system, 63, 65, 67,
    70-74, 77, 79, 80
complex system, 4, 5, 63-65, 67-72,
    81, 137, 252, 450

complexity, 12, 60, 64, 66-70, 73, 79, 80, 100-101, 109, 110, 165, 166, 173, 184, 229, 243, 396, 407, 409, 430, 448

concentration difficulties, 210, 216-220, 364, 367, 371, 372

conduct disorder (CD), 96, 213, 331, 355, 380, 382-391, 435

conduct problems, 8, 170, 328-330, 349, 350, 351, 352-353, 357, 358, 360-367, 371-373, 378-380, 430, 435

Configural frequency analysis (CFA), 144, 218, 352

configuration, 54, 108, 138, 139, 140, 144, 147, 168, 173, 300, 349, 352, 353, 355, 360, 363

conflict, 26, 55, 79-81, 114, 116, 251, 259-262, 282, 292, 294, 295, 296, 366

Confusius, 27

Conscientiousness, 254, 266, 267, 268, 270, 271, 273, 278, 282, 291, 296

consistency, 7, 107, 108, 111, 113, 124, 125, 128, 141, 206, 251, 252, 258, 261-262, 284

context, 6, 7, 13, 40, 50, 54-56, 58, 72, 96, 97, 109, 111-113, 116, 156, 167, 168, 174, 251-259, 261-262, 349, 350, 351, 353, 371, 378, 397, 421-426, 428, 430, 432-434
  social, 13, 55, 244, 323, 436

contextual factors, 36, 323, 326, 327, 329, 332, 334, 434

contextual level, 437

contextual observation, 257

contextual specificity, 252, 258

contextualism, 9, 12, 13, 18, 19, 25, 421, 423-427, 436, 437

continuity, 54, 55, 110-112, 114, 171, 212, 262, 288-289, 296, 358, 402

control parameter, 65-66, 68, 71, 72, 74, 75, 77

convergence, 16, 55, 156, 300, 301

correlated constraints, 55

correlation research, 283

correlational approach/design/ perspective, 64, 372-373, 379

cortisol, 204, 213, 214, 217, 230, 233-241, 243

creativity, 21, 22, 127, 437

crime, 8, 205, 210, 213, 219, 220, 223, 232, 304, 317-30, 332, 333, 427, 432-34
  violent, 205, 232, 320, 322, 324, 326, 432

criminality, 205, 268, 277, 319, 320-326, 329-335, 340, 341, 354, 378, 390

critical period, 57, 58, 203, 204, 206

critical point, 68, 71, 75

critical value, 66, 68, 97

culture, 15, 16, 18, 40, 41, 50, 79, 96, 101, 111, 112, 266, 318, 424

curative education, 339-342, 345

cytoplasm, 182, 183, 192, 230

## D

delinquency, 329, 331, 342, 344, 350, 427, 432-434

depression, 13, 126, 127, 167, 168, 170, 171, 192, 259, 268, 271, 276-279, 319, 334, 414

detachment, 211, 311

deterministic system, 451

development spurt, 205

developmental analysis, 54, 55

developmental path(way), 151, 161, 162, 183, 360, 371, 378, 411, 436

developmental pattern, 150, 377-379, 384, 387, 390, 391

developmental perspective, 50, 221, 230, 378, 380, 389, 391

developmental psychopathology, 349, 452

developmental science, 3-4, 5, 6, 9, 11, 42, 49-54, 56-58, 60, 137, 151, 197, 423, 447, 451, 452

developmental system, 137, 170, 183, 188, 194, 436-438

developmental theory, 12, 21, 53, 60, 171, 422
developmental trajectory, 328, 330, 425
diagnosis, 128, 168-170, 302, 325, 326, 381
dialectical process, 101, 116
dialectical relations, 101, 106, 114, 115
dialectics, 5, 99, 116
dimensional approach, 108, 210
disciplinary practice, 351, 352, 362, 363, 397, 403, 415
discordant mother-child relation-ship, 357, 361, 364, 372
disinhibitory syndrome, 210, 219-223
disorders of undercontrol, 350
diurnal regulation, 235, 237, 239
DNA, 38, 180-83, 187-92
dopamine, 213, 214, 217-19, 224
drinking habits, 8, 377-91
    early advanced, 8, 379, 383, 390
dropping out, 427, 432, 434
Drosophila Melanogaster, 6, 185
drug abuse, 325, 327, 354, 366, 427, 428
dyad, 5, 100-102, 107, 110, 114-116, 173
dynamic approach, 229, 451
dynamic interactions, 37, 39, 55, 424
dynamic relation, 101
dynamic system, 4, 5, 54, 74, 139, 147, 148, 251, 448, 451
    approach/perspective, 7, 50, 147, 197
dynamics, 15, 54, 63, 64, 67, 69, 71-74, 77-83, 110, 124, 451
dyslexia, 341, 342, 345
dysregulation, 233, 235, 238, 239, 241, 242, 397

**E**

early problem precursors, 350
early risk behavior, 209, 224
early-start offender, 320, 327, 328

ecological perspective, 230, 231
ecology, 7, 38, 50, 197
Eliot, T. S., 97
embryology, 58, 196, 197
emergence, 42, 64, 65, 66, 72, 139, 149
Emotional Stability, 267-70, 273-275, 291
empirical research, 5, 7, 8, 34, 35, 38, 42, 43, 45, 64, 122, 123, 125, 129, 131, 149, 317, 350, 403, 448, 450
empiricism, 157, 162
environment 5, 6, 7, 36, 37, 38-40, 42-44, 55, 63, 66, 68, 74, 97, 100, 101, 107, 110, 166, 179-180, 183-188, 193-197, 230, 232, 233, 251, 281, 318, 349, 377, 378, 395, 424
    home, 352, 356, 358, 396, 399
environmental stress, 184, 204, 235
environmentalism, 196
Epidemiological Catchment Area (ECA) study, 331
epidemiological studies, 70, 204, 207, 230, 320
epigenesis, 180-181, 184, 188-194, 196
equilibrium, 64, 81, 121, 131, 232
Erikson, E. H., 394
ethics, 7, 241-245, 306
etiology, 6, 8, 204, 205, 206, 317, 329, 334
eugenics, 342, 343
evolutionary perspective, 231
externalizing problems, 284, 355-356, 450
Extraversion, 157, 212, 214, 215, 220, 224, 266-268, 270-75, 282, 291, 296
extreme case, 5, 72, 96, 151, 356
extreme groups, 100, 286
extreme score, 91, 92, 170, 211, 286
Eysenck Personality Inventory, 260

**F**

factor analysis, 126, 130-132, 157, 258, 286, 300

factor analysis of persons, 300
feedback, 55, 101, 181, 232-34, 426
feed-forward, 101, 110, 181, 182
fetal development, 43, 203, 204,
  206, 207
five-factor model of personality,
  see "Big Five"
flexibility, 22, 71, 75, 108, 113, 114,
  235
fluctuation, 66, 68, 75-77, 128, 130,
  449
fragmentation, 34, 350
Freud, Sigmund, 57, 58, 60
functional categories, 88

G

gender, 87, 94, 95, 160, 161, 269,
  322, 397, 427
gender differences, 161, 278, 304
gene, 5, 6, 38, 69, 74, 180-189, 191,
  192, 194-196, 203, 206, 330
gene expression, 179, 182, 191-193,
  204, 206
General Behavior Inventory, 268
general law, 156, 158, 159, 161
General Self, 253, 256, 257, 260, 261
general systems theory, 38
genetic activity, 179, 180-182, 184,
  188, 189, 191, 193, 196
genetic vulnerability, 330, 332
genetics, 38, 50, 65, 179, 195, 342, 343
genome, 38, 182-185
genotype, 183, 189
gestalt, 16, 23, 139, 256
goal system functioning, 258, 260,
  261
group membership, 114, 115
group norms, 114, 115

H

health problems, 268, 271, 276, 277
high-reactive infant, 89, 91-93, 97
Hobbes, Thomas, 26
holism, 33, 60, 421, 452

holistic approach/model/paradigm,
  4-7, 9, 11, 33, 35-43, 45, 54, 60, 99-
  101, 108, 110, 115, 117, 123, 167,
  172, 174, 230, 265, 278, 339, 346,
  352-353, 378, 390, 422, 447
holistic developmental framework,
  49, 61
holistic interactionism, 40, 42-45, 318
holistic-interactional paradigm/
  perspective, 3, 4, 137, 138, 447
homeostasis, 232, 233
hormone, 50, 183, 192, 193, 213,
  214, 229-233, 236, 238, 239
hospitalization, 321, 324, 327
Humboldt, Alexander von, 26
hyperactivity, 8, 37, 70, 379, 380, 397
hypothalamic-pituitary-adrenal
  (HPA) axis,
  233-236, 242-244, 334
hypothalamus, 36, 186, 233, 234,
  236
hypothalamus paraventricular
  nucleus (PVN), 233, 235
hypothetical construct, 113, 137
hysteresis, 75
Häilpedagogie, 340, 341, 345

I

Ideal Self, 254, 259, 260, 262
identity, 114
idiographic approach/orientation/
  research, 7, 107, 108, 125, 129,
  161, 251, 252, 265, 278, 403
idiosyncrasy, 401, 409
idiothetic orientation, 125, 129
implicit assumption, 310, 311
impulse control, 284
impulsivity, 157, 210, 212, 213, 224,
  304, 331, 350, 364, 367, 372, 380
indeterminacy, 61
individual development, 3, 4, 6, 8,
  12, 14, 34, 35-40, 42-45, 116, 137,
  139, 141, 148, 149, 151, 173, 174,
  180, 185, 189, 349, 377-378, 380,
  447, 448, 450, 451

Individual Development and
    Adjustment (IDA) research
    program, 210, 225, 380
individual differences, 5, 18, 20, 41,
    53, 106, 122, 123, 129, 130, 139,
    158, 159, 161, 259, 372, 393, 422,
    424, 427
individual factors, 325-27, 334
individual functioning, 33-40, 42-
    45, 50, 54, 60, 63, 131, 174, 252,
    318, 350, 352, 380-82, 390, 422
individual stability, 147
individual variables, 54, 430, 432
individual-context relationship,
    424, 426, 427, 436
individual-environment transaction,
    251
Infant Health and Development
    Program, 397-99
informational coupling, 77
inhibited behavior, 5, 89, 91
inhibition, 278, 294
instability, 66-69, 75, 77, 80, 81, 232,
    282, 288, 296, 397
institutionalized children, 7, 229
integrative studies, 448
intelligence, 21-22, 26-29, 36, 128,
    160, 328, 329, 331, 340, 342, 355,
    397, 398
intention, 64, 78, 357
interaction, 39, 40, 57, 101, 108, 166,
    225, 232, 252, 281, 292, 294, 318,
    396, 397
    gene-environment, 6, 195
    mother-child, 102, 169, 357, 361,
        413, 434
    mother-infant, 102-107
    parent-child, 351, 353
    social, 23, 54, 58, 168, 433, 449
interactional paradigm, 3, 137, 138,
    147, 450, 452
interactionism, 12, 13, 25, 40, 42,
    281, 318, 421
interdisciplinarity, 13, 14, 421
interdyad differences, 102, 106-107
internalizing problems, 284

intervention, 188, 225, 237, 329, 423,
    425, 426, 434, 436, 437
intraindividual variability, 121-131,
    141, 158, 284
invariance of function, 75
i-state, 147, 149, 150

J

Jackson, Atlee, 72
James, Alice, 96-97
James, William, 96
jangle fallacy, 156
jingle fallacy, 156
Johnson, George, 66-67
Johnson, Lyndon, 97
Jung, C., 33
Jyväskylä Longitudinal Study of
    Personality and Social Develop-
    ment, 267

K

Kant, I., 44
Karolinska Scales of Personality
    (KSP), 7, 211, 212, 268
k-means relocation, 144, 146
knowledge, 18, 19, 24
    structure, 113, 114
Kracke, B., 41
Kuo, Z.-Y., 60, 196

L

late-start offender, 320, 327, 328
latent growth curve modeling, 139,
    448, 449
Latent Transition Analysis, 142, 352
law of (human) coordinated
    behavior, 64, 75
lawfulness of behavior, 160
level of organization, 184, 423, 424
Lewin, Kurt, 6, 33, 50, 150, 159, 166,
    231, 232, 394
LICUR, 144, 146-148

life course, 26, 38, 50, 57, 161, 318,
    394, 395, 415, 422
life sciences, 35, 42, 45, 330
life span, 14, 17, 36, 210, 225, 318,
    333, 422, 425, 426, 449
    perspective, 423
life transition, 281, 282
linear model, 100, 138, 139, 422, 447
linear regression, 130, 351
linear relationship, 251
linear transformation, 142
locus coeruleus (LC), 193, 232
Logical Inference Exercise (LIE), 312
loglinear modeling, 142, 145
longitudinal pattern, 145, 387
longitudinal research/prospective
    design, 12, 37, 40-42, 56, 225, 341,
    342, 343, 344-346, 448-450
long-term memory, 188
low-reactive infant, 89, 91, 93, 97

### M

Machiavelli, N., 306
Machiavellian, 8, 299, 306-309
maladaptive functioning, 251, 253
marital discord, 168
Marlowe-Crowne Social Desirability
    Scale, 300, 301
maternal depression, 168, 171
maternal responsiveness, 396-397
maternal stress, 204, 207
mathematical model, 4, 5, 139, 448
measurement, 3, 6, 8, 18, 19, 60, 94,
    121-124, 126, 127, 129, 130, 131,
    140, 142-143, 145-147, 149, 150,
    169-171, 238, 282, 285, 289, 296,
    333-334, 355, 356, 390, 448-451
medicine, 36, 343, 345
memory deficit, 239-241
mental processes, 35, 36, 40, 43
mental ability, 127, 311
mental disorder, 6, 8, 36, 205, 317-
    334, 349
mental health, 51, 155, 299, 317,
    324, 332, 344, 358, 396

messenger RNA (mRNA), 181, 186-
    188, 192, 193
metatheory, 12, 49
methodology, 4, 9, 53, 56, 130-131,
    285-287, 329, 379, 394, 447-448
Mills, J. W., 60
Moffit, T. E., 41
monitoring, 351, 429, 431, 435
monoamine oxidase (MAO), 210,
    215, 216
monotony avoidance, 211, 212, 220,
    224
Montesquieu, C.-L., 15
mother-child relationship, 168, 357,
    361-366, 371, 372
multidetermined stochastic
    processes, 38
multidisciplinary view, 339, 342-
    344, 426
multifunctionality, 74, 75
multimethod paradigm, 12
multiple pathway approach/
    strategy, 413-415
multivariate scaling, 142-143
multivariate taxometrics, 145

### N

narcissism, 310
Narcissistic Personality Inventory
    (NPI), 300
narrative, 113, 401, 412, 415
National Institute of Human
    Health and Child Development, 51
National Longitudinal Study of
    Youth-Child Supplement (NLSY-
    CS), 398
natural experiment, 241
natural science(s), 5, 34, 35, 38, 39,
    43, 148, 451
nature-nurture, 243, 244, 245
nearest centroid sorting, 271, 287,
    290, 294
NEO Personality Inventory (NEO-
    PI), 7, 260, 266, 267, 271, 272, 274,
    275, 277, 285, 300

neural imaging techniques, 239
neural pathway, 230, 236
neuroendocrine regulation, 229, 244
neuroendocrinology, 7, 242
neurophysiology, 230
neuropsychiatry, 343
neurotic overcontrollers (NOC), 161
neurotic undercontrollers (NUC), 161
Neuroticism, 254, 260, 261, 266-269,
　　270-273, 278, 282, 286
Newton, I., 71
NOLIDS, 148, 149, 451
nomothetic approach/inquiry, 102,
　　107, 161, 399
nomothetic laws, 129
nomothetic methods, 115
nomothetic theories, 452
nomothetic trait, 265
nonequilibrium phase transition,
　　66, 68
nonequilibrium steady state, 66
nonlinear mathematics, 39, 148
noradrenaline, 213, 214
norepinephrine (NE), 193, 232
norm of reaction, 194
novelty, 57-59, 60, 157, 211, 244


O

ontogenetic factors, 18
ontogeny, 12, 39, 53, 59, 231, 318, 424
open systems, 43, 64-66
Openness to Experience, 266-268,
　　270-275, 279, 290
operational definition, 18
order parameter 65, 67, 70, 71, 73
organismic approach, 230
Organizational Climate Question-
　　naire (OCQ), 300, 301
organizational destructiveness, 7,
　　299, 306
organizing principle, 33, 37, 399,
　　401, 410
Ought Self, 254, 262
outlier, 92, 143

overcontrolled personality type,
　　266, 273-278, 284, 290-296


P

Parental Attitude Research
　　Instrument, 362
parent-child relationship, 58, 107,
　　351, 353, 355, 356, 364, 371
parenting, 363, 372, 378, 379, 395,
　　397, 403, 404, 413, 415, 427, 428,
　　429, 430, 432, 434, 435
　　teenage, 427, 429, 430
paternal involvement, 413
pattern, 7, 8, 43, 44, 63-69, 73-75, 79,
　　81, 108, 121, 125, 128, 130-132, 138,
　　140-145, 148, 150, 159, 160, 168,
　　170-174, 211, 215-219, 221-224, 251,
　　256, 265, 282, 285-287, 288, 299,
　　300, 311, 349, 352, 353, 448, 450
　　analysis, 44-45, 63, 131, 140, 141,
　　145-147, 148, 265, 358
　　biochemical, 6-8, 211
　　development, 142, 150
　　formation, 63, 64-69, 71, 79, 81
　　of behavior, 58, 170, 285
　　of operating factors, 44, 171-173
　　of traits, 284, 286
　　-oriented methods, 141-148
　　selection, 69, 75, 81
pedagogy, 340, 341
pediatric psychiatry, 340
pediatrics, 339, 340, 341
peer network, 292, 296
peer rejection, 431
peer relationship, 292, 293, 295
perceptual-cognitive process, 36
person, 34, 44, 54, 55, 88, 107-109,
　　130, 138, 151, 158, 166, 174, 232,
　　251, 252, 253, 309, 311, 352, 393,
　　394, 399, 423, 425, 426, 437, 448
person(-centered/-oriented)
　　approach, 6, 8, 44, 45, 63, 99, 130,
　　131, 132, 140, 148, 162, 224, 251,
　　282-286, 295-297, 329, 334, 352,
　　391, 394, 399, 403, 414, 415

person-environment system, 42, 349-350, 352
person-oriented method, 149, 151
person-situation controversy, 252
personality coherence, 7, 251, 252, 261-262
personality development, 12, 57, 87, 281, 288, 296
personality dimension, 211, 214, 215
personality functioning, 7, 252, 258, 261-262
personality research, 6, 34, 124, 128
personality structure, 158
personality trait, 22, 124, 209, 210, 212, 213, 222, 224, 225, 266, 282, 285, 286, 297, 342
personality type, 145, 161, 266, 284-297
personality, consistency of, 124, 284
phase transition, 66-68, 77
phenocopy, 206
phenotype, 91, 97, 189, 195, 204
phenotypic variation, 189, 190
phylogenetic development, 231
physiological-psychological process, 99, 116
Piaget, J., 50, 394
Picasso, Pablo, 27
plasticity, 57, 58, 193, 425
posttraumatic stress disorder (PTSD), 238
poverty, 243, 396-98, 402, 404, 410, 411, 415, 427, 432, 435
prediction 55, 66, 75, 76, 123, 127, 151, 317-318, 334, 356, 451
analysis, 147
predictor, 21, 22, 38, 76, 89, 125-127, 129, 317, 389
prenatal viral infection, 204
prevention, 241, 342, 377, 389, 434-436
problem accumulation, 8, 355
problem spread, 364, 371-373
profile, 140, 142, 143, 146
prognostic utility, 351, 373

Project on Human Development in Chicago Neighborhoods (PHDCN), 231
protective factors, 404, 426, 435, 436
protein, 180-182, 184, 187, 188, 191-193, 195, 210
prototypic pattern, 285, 288, 296
proximal context, 352
psychiatric disorder, 192, 204, 206, 211
psychiatric team, 339
psychoanalysis, 57, 58
psychodynamics, 158, 343
psychography, 283, 284
psychological dysfunction, 229
psychological profile, 96
psychology, clinical, 156
    cognitive, 18
    comparative, 50
    developmental, 42, 44, 50, 52, 127, 197, 251, 345, 352, 395
    differential, 283
    education, 339, 346
    personality, 12, 155, 156, 282
    social, 42, 99, 156
psychopathology, 99, 167, 168, 170-172, 223, 225, 249, 339, 350
psychopathy, 7, 210, 299-302, 305, 306
psychosocial behavior, 169, 170
psychosocial disorder, 210
P-technique factor analysis, 45, 126, 130, 131

Q

Q-sort ratings, 284
qualitative differences, 94, 401
qualitative method, 56, 399
Quantitative differences, 5, 87
Quantitative method, 56, 399

R

race, 342, 427, 435
range of reaction, 194

reactivity regulation, 235, 236
reciprocal determination, 101
reciprocal process, 166, 173, 281, 394
rehabilitation, 241, 242
rejection, 56, 431
relative scales, 450
RELOCATE, 144
RESIDAN, 146
residual analysis, 145
residue, 143, 146, 148, 150
resilience, 394, 395, 399, 400, 404,
    414, 415
resilient children, 399-401, 403, 404,
    409-415
response, 34, 101, 115, 158, 232, 235
    vector, 401, 404, 407
Revised Psychopathy Checklist
    (PCL-R), 310,
risk, 6, 9, 96, 166, 167, 173, 204-207,
    209, 210, 218, 219, 223-225, 317,
    319, 320, 323, 325, 326, 327, 330-
    334, 341, 344, 350, 351, 353, 371-
    373, 379, 382, 385, 387, 390, 394,
    395, 397-399, 421-423, 426-437
RNA, 180, 182, 185-187, 191, 192,
role, 40, 109, 110, 252, 278, 352
Rosenberg's Self-Esteem Scale, 268
Russell, Bertrand, 88, 98


S


Sales, Franz von, 15
sampling, 53, 140, 170, 330, 334, 449
schizophrenia, 6, 204-207, 235, 236,
    333
Schneirla, T. C., 60, 196
school failure, 427, 432, 434
school psychiatrist, 341, 346
school psychiatry, 345
science of science, 139, 448
selection, 68, 69, 71, 74, 75, 81, 116,
    127, 185, 189, 231
Selection Via Instability principle
    (SVI), 81
self, 23, 55, 110-115, 252-261

self-concept, 7, 111, 112, 260, 262,
    429, 435
self-consciousness, 110
self-description, 7, 111, 265-78
self-discrepancy, 259, 260
self-esteem, 113, 114, 260, 266, 268,
    271, 276-278, 300-302, 307, 311,
    411, 413, 414, 430, 436
self-esteem lability (SEL), 127
self-image, 111, 115, 278
self-knowledge, 113
self-organization, 43, 44, 64-66, 69,
    71, 78, 81
self-organized criticality (SOC), 68
self-perception, 7, 41, 112
Self-Report of Psychopathy II (SRP
    II), 300, 301
self-system, 113, 114
sensation-seeking, 157, 211, 213,
    220, 310, 311
serotonergic activity, 210, 212, 221
sex differences, 108, 285
sexual abuse, 431
Shakespeare, W., 15
situation, 36, 37, 45, 79, 88, 96, 107-
    109-113, 121, 128, 158, 159, 252-
    259, 318, 422
Silbereisen, R. K., 41
Skinner, B. F., 394
SLEIPNER, 131, 147, 148
snowball model, 353, 355
sociability, 157, 212, 224
social adjustment, 8, 37, 266, 268,
    276, 278, 339, 352, 364, 371
    problems, 8, 278, 349
social behavior, 34, 37, 49, 58, 71,
    90, 91, 100, 115, 242, 358, 432
social deprivation, 236-243
social desirability, 220-223, 255,
    286, 300, 302, 305, 310
social development, 35, 50, 58, 59,
    231, 267, 356
social disadvantage, 231, 232
social ecology, 7, 50, 229, 230, 241-
    243
social maladjustment, 350

social network, 50, 55, 282, 424
social norms, 40, 111, 310
social relationship, 7, 281, 282, 285, 295
social sciences, 88, 179, 185, 213, 271, 424
social support, 396, 402, 404, 410, 411, 413, 415, 436
socialization, 94, 96, 211, 212, 217, 218, 220-222, 224, 300, 302, 432
sociocultural activity, 101, 102
sociocultural structure, 101, 115
socioeconomic status, 328, 331, 333, 379, 387, 389, 390, 427
Solna project, 356
species, 183, 189, 194, 231, 239, 266
stability, 55, 64, 66, 67, 68, 71, 74-77, 80, 81, 121, 122-124, 125, 126, 129-131, 141, 147, 252, 256, 260, 271, 285, 287, 288-289, 296, 355, 358, 450
    meta-, 67, 68, 77
    multi-, 75, 79
    orientation, 121-125
    structural, 147
state-trait distinction, 125, 126
statics, 124
Stern, Wilhelm, 33, 282-286
stimulus, 34, 101, 115, 183, 424
stimulus-response (S-R) model, 34, 35, 115
stress hormone, 229, 230-236, 239
stress regulation, 7, 229, 236
stress response, 233, 236, 240
stressor, 168, 225, 234, 235, 236, 237
structural maturation, 180
subindividual, 147
substance abuse, 325, 326, 428-430, 432, 434
suicide, 19, 310, 428
superiority, 305, 310, 311
Swedish Metropolitan Project, 8, 320-322, 324, 325, 330, 331, 332
symbolic interactionists, 109, 112
symmetry-breaking, 64
symptom profile, 206

synergetic effects, 448
synergy, 16, 74, 75
synthesis, 50, 51, 59, 64, 87, 243, 423, 424
synthetic approach, 399, 437
system dysfunction, 299
systemic model, 9
systemic relationships, 437
systemic-holistic perspective, 14

T

taxometrics, 145
taxon, 140, 160, 162
taxonic approach, 161
teenage mothers, 400, 401, 415
teenage pregnancy, 427, 429, 430
temperament, 88-92, 96, 127, 156, 173, 205, 207, 211, 426
temperamental bias, 91
teratogen, 203, 205
time, 12, 16, 36, 41, 50, 54-56, 63, 66, 67, 73, 74, 77, 78, 88, 108, 113, 116, 121, 122, 131, 132, 139, 143, 146, 147, 150, 158, 204, 229, 262, 393, 422, 424, 448, 449
time-dependent dynamics, 63, 73, 204
time-series data, 131,
timing, 50, 54, 58, 68, 168, 203-207, 333-334
touch deprivation, 231
trait self-esteem (TSE), 127
transaction, 25, 101, 230, 250, 281
transcription, 181, 187
transition, 59, 66-69, 75, 77, 78, 101, 102, 126, 127, 281, 282, 344, 422
translation, 138, 170, 171, 181, 182, 188, 192, 340
treatment service, 323, 326
type, 6, 139, 140-141, 144, 146, 149-151, 156, 159-162, 219, 224, 284, 360
    developmental, 6, 141, 145
typological approach, 149, 161
typology, 33, 140-141, 150, 151, 295

U

uncertainty, 18, 19, 24, 90, 95
undercontrolled personality type, 266, 273-279, 284, 290-296
Undesired Self, 254, 259, 260, 262
uninhibited behavior, 5, 91
United Nations Convention on the Rights of the Child (UNCRC), 241, 245

V

validation, 7, 150
value, 18, 42, 61, 63, 99, 101, 109, 111, 113, 114-116, 211, 436
relativism, 18, 19, 24
variability, 77, 81, 121-131, 155, 251, 252, 254-258, 261, 286, 409, 415
variable, composite, 328, 404, 407
variable, dependent, 38, 94
variable, hypothetical, 70, 130
variable, independent, 38, 65
variable, latent, 55, 142
variable, moderator, 160
variable, pattern, 63, 68, 71, 130, 173
variable, state, 71
variable, static, 451
variable-oriented approach/ research, 3, 4, 7, 40, 138, 140, 166, 266, 281-282, 296, 378, 393-399, 403, 416, 447,
variable-oriented method, 6, 7, 9, 138, 149, 151, 448

variation research, 283
verbal memory, 240, 241
violence, 8, 219-223, 244, 317, 321, 324-326, 329, 334, 427, 433
virtue, 17, 18, 73, 166, 170
visual deprivation, 231
vulnerability, 8, 205, 209-210, 211, 212, 219, 223, 224, 330, 333, 394, 400
vulnerable children, 243, 394, 411-413

W

whole, 3, 4, 13, 16, 42, 44, 64, 68, 71, 80, 98, 99, 116, 137, 138, 256, 278, 309, 345, 346, 351, 448, 450
whole-part relation, 64
Wisconsin Longitudinal Study, 414
wisdom, 5, 11, 14-27, 59, 79
within-subject differences, 286
within-subject mean, 286
Wonderlic Personnel Test, 308
Ward's hierarchical minimum variance method, 144
well-being, 16, 19, 37, 114, 243, 245, 259, 261, 266, 268, 271, 276, 278, 342, 345, 397, 415
white spot, 150, 151
Whitehead, Alfred North, 88, 97-98

Y

youth development programs, 436